Mathematics for the IB Diploma
Higher Level 1

Hugh Neill and Douglas Quadling

Series editor Hugh Neill

CAMBRIDGE
UNIVERSITY PRESS

CAMBRIDGE UNIVERSITY PRESS
Cambridge, New York, Melbourne, Madrid, Cape Town, Singapore, São Paulo, Delhi

Cambridge University Press
The Edinburgh Building, Cambridge CB2 8RU, UK

www.cambridge.org
Information on this title: www.cambridge.org/9780521699297

© Cambridge University Press 2007

First published 2007

Printed in the United Kingdom at the University Press, Cambridge

A catalogue record for this publication is available from the British Library

ISBN 978-0-521-69929-7 paperback

The authors and publishers are grateful to the following examination boards for permission to reproduce
questions from past examination papers, identified in the text as follows.
OCR   Oxford, Cambridge and RSA Examinations
IBO   International Baccalaureate Organization
The authors, and not the examination boards, are responsible for the method and accuracy of the answers
to examination questions given; these may not necessarily constitute the only possible solutions.

This material has been developed independently of the International Baccalaureate Organization (IBO).
The text is in no way connected with, nor endorsed by, the IBO.

Contents

Contents

Introduction

Mathematics Higher Level (two books) has been written especially for the International Baccalaureate Mathematics HL examination. This is Book 1.

The book is divided into small groups of connected chapters, each covering one part of the syllabus. There is a small amount of material which extends a topic beyond the syllabus as printed, with the aim of enhancing students' appreciation of the subject. This is indicated by an asterisk (*) at the appropriate place in the text.

Occasionally within the text paragraphs appear in a grey box. These paragraphs may help to give insight, suggest different approaches or provide background to a topic.

Students are expected to have access to graphic display calculators and the text places considerable emphasis on their potential for supporting the learning of mathematics.

Numerical work is presented in a form intended to discourage premature approximation. In ongoing calculations inexact numbers appear in decimal form like 3.456... , signifying that the number is held in a calculator to more places than are given. Numbers are not rounded at this stage; the full display could be, for example, 3.456 123 or 3.456 789. Final answers are then stated with some indication that they are approximate, for example '3.46, correct to 3 significant figures'.

There are plenty of exercises. After each group of connected chapters there is a Review exercise which includes some questions from past International Baccalaureate examinations, but on a different syllabus. At the time of writing, there are no current versions of the Higher Level examinations, so there is no backlog of examination questions on the newer parts of the syllabus.

The authors thank Steve Dobbs and Jane Miller who gave permission to use work from their statistics books. The authors also thank the International Baccalaureate Organization (IBO) and Oxford, Cambridge and RSA Examinations (OCR) for permission to reproduce IBO and OCR intellectual property and Cambridge University Press for their help in producing this book. Particular thanks are due to Sharon Dunkley, for her help and advice. However, the responsibility for the text, and for any errors, remains with the authors.

1 Numbers

One thread in the history of mathematics has been the extension of what is meant by a number. This has led to the invention of new symbols and techniques of calculation. When you have completed this chapter, you should

- be able to recognise various number systems, and know the notation for them
- understand inequality relations, and the rules for calculating with them
- know what is meant by the modulus of a number, and how it can be used
- be familiar with techniques for calculating with surds.

1.1 Different kinds of number

At first numbers were used only for counting, and 1, 2, 3, ... were all that was needed. These are called **positive integers**.

Sometimes you also need the number 0, or 'zero'. For example, suppose you are recording the number of sisters of every person in the class. Some will have one, two, three, ... sisters, but some will have none. The numbers 0, 1, 2, 3, ... are called **natural numbers**.

Then people found that numbers could also be useful for measurement and in commerce. For these purposes they also needed fractions. Integers and fractions together make up the **rational numbers**. These are numbers which can be expressed in the form $\frac{p}{q}$ where p and q are integers, and q is not 0.

One of the most remarkable discoveries of the ancient Greek mathematicians was that there are numbers which cannot be expressed like this. These are called **irrational numbers**. The first such number to be found was $\sqrt{2}$, which is the length of the diagonal of a square with side 1 unit, by Pythagoras' theorem (see Fig. 1.1).

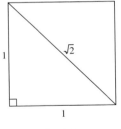

Fig. 1.1

The argument that the Greeks used to prove this can be adapted to show that the square root, cube root, ... of any positive integer is either an integer or an irrational number. For example, the square root of 8 is an irrational number, but the cube root of 8 is the integer 2. Many other numbers are now known to be irrational, of which the most famous is π.

Rational and irrational numbers together make up the **real numbers**.

When rational numbers are written as decimals, they either come to a stop after a number of places, or the sequence of decimal digits eventually starts repeating in a regular pattern. For example,

$$\tfrac{7}{10} = 0.7, \quad \tfrac{7}{11} = 0.6363..., \quad \tfrac{7}{12} = 0.5833..., \quad \tfrac{7}{13} = 0.538\,461\,538\,461\,53...,$$
$$\tfrac{7}{14} = 0.5, \quad \tfrac{7}{15} = 0.466..., \quad \tfrac{7}{16} = 0.4375, \quad \tfrac{7}{17} = 0.411\,764\,705\,882\,352\,941\,176... .$$

The reverse is also true. If a decimal number stops or repeats indefinitely then it is a rational number. So if an irrational number is written as a decimal, the pattern of the decimal digits never repeats however long you continue the calculation.

Integers, rational and irrational numbers and real numbers can all be either positive or negative.

It is helpful to have special symbols to denote the different kinds of number. The set of integers $\{..., -3, -2, -1, 0, 1, 2, 3, ...\}$ is written as $\mathbb{Z}$; the set of (positive and negative) rational numbers is $\mathbb{Q}$; and the set of real numbers is $\mathbb{R}$. If you want just the positive numbers, you use the symbols $\mathbb{Z}^+$, $\mathbb{Q}^+$, $\mathbb{R}^+$. The set of natural numbers, $\{0, 1, 2, 3, ...\}$, is written as $\mathbb{N}$; there are no negative natural numbers.

> You may wonder why these letters were chosen. The notation was first used by German mathematicians in the 19th century, and the German word for number is *Zahl*. Hence the choice of $\mathbb{Z}$ for the integers. The letter $\mathbb{Q}$ probably came from Quotient, which is the result of dividing one number by another.

You probably know the symbol $\in$, which stands for 'is an element of'. The statement '$x \in \mathbb{Z}^+$' means 'x belongs to the set of positive integers'; that is, 'x is a positive integer'. So

$$'x \in \mathbb{Z}^+' \quad \text{and} \quad 'x \text{ is a positive integer}'$$

are two ways of saying the same thing.

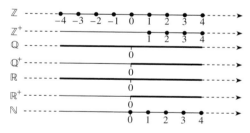

You can also draw diagrams of these sets of numbers on a **number line**, as in Fig. 1.2. The arrows at the ends of the lines indicate the positive direction; the usual convention is for this to point to the right. The larger the number, the further it is to the right on the line.

Fig. 1.2

The point which represents 0 is called the **origin** on the number line. It is usually denoted by the letter O.

But you will notice a snag. There are more real numbers than rational numbers. But in the figure $\mathbb{R}$ and $\mathbb{Q}$, and $\mathbb{R}^+$ and $\mathbb{Q}^+$, look the same. This is because there are rational numbers as close as you like to any real number. For example, $\pi \in \mathbb{R}$, but π is not a member of $\mathbb{Q}$. However, 3.141 592 65 (which is the 8 decimal place approximation to π) is a member of $\mathbb{Q}$, and you can't distinguish π from 3.141 592 65 in the figure.

The only numbers that can be shown on a calculator are rational numbers. Calculators can't handle irrational numbers. So when you key in $\sqrt{}$, 2 on your calculator, and it displays 1.414 213 562, this is only an approximation to $\sqrt{2}$. If you square the rational number 1.414 213 562, you get

$$1.414\,213\,562^2 = 1.999\,999\,998\,944\,727\,844,$$

but $\sqrt{2}^2 = 2$ exactly.

1.2 Notation for inequalities

You often want to compare one number with another and say which is the bigger. This comparison is expressed by using the inequality symbols $>$, $<$, $\leq$ and $\geq$.

The symbol $a > b$ means that a is greater than b. You can visualise this geometrically as in Fig. 1.3, which shows three number lines, with a to the right of b.

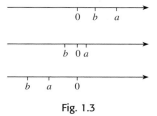

Fig. 1.3

Notice that it does not matter whether a and b are positive or negative. The position of a and b in relation to zero on the number line is irrelevant. In all three lines, $a > b$. As an example, in the bottom line, $-4 > -7$.

Similarly, the symbol $a < b$ means that a is less than b. You can visualise this geometrically on a number line, with a to the left of b.

> These expressions are equivalent.
>
> $a > b$ a is greater than b
> $b < a$ b is less than a

The symbol $a \geq b$ means 'either $a > b$ or $a = b$'; that is, a is greater than or equal to, but not less than, b. Similarly, the symbol $a \leq b$ means 'either $a < b$ or $a = b$' ; that is, a is less than or equal to, but not greater than, b.

> These expressions are equivalent.
>
> $a \geq b$ a is greater than or equal to b
> $b \leq a$ b is less than or equal to a

> Some books use the symbols $\geqslant$ and $\leqslant$ in place of $\geq$ and $\leq$.

The symbols $<$ and $>$ are called **strict** inequalities, and the symbols $\leq$ and $\geq$ are called **weak** inequalities.

Example 1.2.1
Write down the set of numbers x such that $x \in \mathbb{N}$ and $x < 6$.

> $\mathbb{N}$ is the set of natural numbers $\{0, 1, 2, 3, ...\}$. The largest number in $\mathbb{N}$ less than 6 is 5. So the set of numbers such that $x \in \mathbb{N}$ and $x < 6$ is $\{0, 1, 2, 3, 4, 5\}$.

Example 1.2.2
The points A and B on the number line represent the numbers -2 and 3. Use inequalities to describe the numbers represented by the line segment [AB] shown in Fig. 1.4.

> The notation [AB] is explained in Section 8.2.

Fig. 1.4

All the points of the line segment, except A itself, are to the right of A. So the numbers they represent satisfy the inequality $x \geq -2$. They are also, except B itself, to the left of B, so the numbers satisfy $x \leq 3$.

You could also write $x \geq -2$ as $-2 \leq x$. So $-2 \leq x$ and $x \leq 3$.

These two inequalities can be combined in a single statement as $-2 \leq x \leq 3$.

> When you write an inequality of the kind $r < x$ and $x < s$ in the form $r < x < s$, it is essential that $r < s$. It makes no sense to write $7 < x < 3$; how can x be both greater than 7 and less than 3?

An inequality of the type $r < x < s$ (or $r < x \leq s$ or $r \leq x < s$ or $r \leq x \leq s$) is called an **interval**. It consists of all the numbers between r and s (including r or s where the sign adjacent to them is $\leq$).

The word 'interval' is also used for an inequality such as $x > r$, which consists of all the numbers greater than r (and similarly for $x \geq r$, $x < s$ and $x \leq s$).

1.3   Solving linear inequalities

When you solve an equation like $3x + 7 = -5$, you use two rules:

- you can add (or subtract) the same number on both sides of the equation
- you can multiply (or divide) both sides of the equation by the same number.

In this example, subtracting 7 from both sides and then dividing by 3 leads to the solution $x = -4$.

An inequality like $3x + 7 > -5$ doesn't have a single solution for x, but it can be replaced by a simpler statement about the value of x. To find this, you need rules for working with inequalities. These are similar to those for equations, but with one very important difference.

Adding or subtracting the same number on both sides
You can add or subtract the same number on both sides of an inequality. Justifying such a step involves showing that, for any number c, 'if $a > b$ then $a + c > b + c$'.

This is saying that if a is to the right of b on the number line, then $a + c$ is to the right of $b + c$. Figure 1.5 shows that this is true whether c is positive or negative.

Since subtracting c is the same as adding $-c$, you can also subtract the same number from both sides.

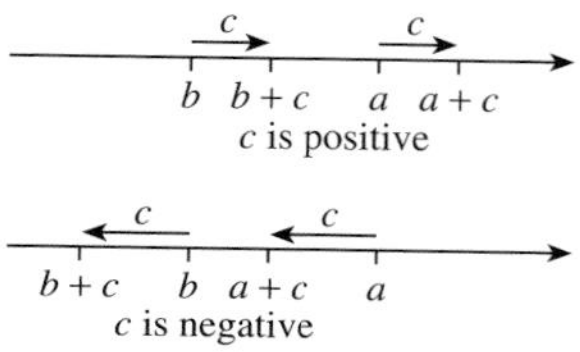

Fig. 1.5

Example 1.3.1

If $x - 3 < -4$, what can you say about the value of x?

You can add 3 on both sides of the inequality, which gives

$$x - 3 + 3 < -4 + 3,$$

that is

$$x < -1.$$

In this example, the inequality $x < -1$ is called the **solution** of the inequality $x - 3 < -4$. It is the simplest statement you can make about x which is equivalent to the given inequality.

Multiplying both sides by a positive number

You can multiply (or divide) both sides of an inequality by a positive number.

Example 1.3.2

Solve the inequality $\frac{1}{3}x \geq 2$.

Multiply both sides of the inequality by 3. This gives the equivalent inequality

$$3 \times \left(\tfrac{1}{3}x\right) \geq 3 \times 2,$$

that is

$$x \geq 6.$$

Here is a justification of the step, 'if $a > b$ and $c > 0$, then $ca > cb$'.

As $a > b$, a is to the right of b on the number line.

As $c > 0$, ca and cb are enlargements of the positions of a and b relative to the number 0.

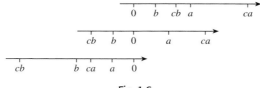

Fig. 1.6

Figure 1.6 shows that, whether a and b are positive or negative, ca is to the right of cb, so $ca > cb$.

Multiplying both sides by a negative number

If $a > b$, and you subtract $a + b$ from both sides, then you get $-b > -a$, which is the same as $-a < -b$. This shows that if you multiply both sides of an inequality by -1, then you change the direction of the inequality.

Suppose that you wish to multiply the inequality $a > b$ by -2. This is the same as multiplying $-a < -b$ by 2, so $-2a < -2b$.

You can also think of multiplying by -2 as reflecting the points corresponding to a and b in the origin, and then multiplying by 2 as an enlargement (see Fig. 1.7).

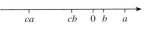

Fig. 1.7

You can summarise this by saying that if you multiply (or divide) both sides of an inequality by a negative number, you must change the direction of the inequality. Thus if $a > b$ and $c < 0$, then $ca < cb$.

Example 1.3.3
Solve the inequality $-3x < 21$.

In this example you need to divide both sides by -3. Remembering to change the direction of the inequality, $-3x < 21$ becomes $x > -7$.

> **Summary of operations on inequalities**
> - You can add or subtract a number on both sides of an inequality.
> - You can multiply or divide an inequality by a positive number.
> - You can multiply or divide an inequality by a negative number, but you must change the direction of the inequality.

Solving inequalities is simply a matter of exploiting these three rules.

> You can link the inequality operation involving multiplication with '$+ \times + = +$'. For if $a > b$ and $c > 0$, both $a - b$ and c are positive numbers, so $c(a - b)$ is also positive. So $ca - cb$ is positive, $ca - cb > 0$ and $ca > cb$.

Example 1.3.4
Solve the inequality $3 - \frac{1}{2}x \leq 5$.

Begin by subtracting 3 from both sides, to get

$$-\frac{1}{2}x \leq 2.$$

Now multiply both sides by -2, remembering to change the direction of the inequality. This gives

$$x \geq -4.$$

Example 1.3.5
Solve the inequality $4 - 2x > 3x$.

Begin by adding $2x$ on both sides, to get

$$4 > 5x.$$

Dividing both sides by 5 then gives

$$0.8 > x.$$

The answer is usually written with x on the left side, as

$$x < 0.8.$$

Exercise 1A

1 Which of the number systems $\mathbb{N}, \mathbb{Z}, \mathbb{Q}, \mathbb{R}, \mathbb{Z}^+, \mathbb{Q}^+$ and $\mathbb{R}^+$ contain the following numbers?

   (a) 6 (b) 6.6 (c) 0.666... (continued indefinitely) (d) $\sqrt[3]{125}$

   (e) $\sqrt{125}$ (f) 0 (g) $-\pi$ (h) -2

2 State in list form the sets of numbers x which satisfy the following.

   (a) $x \in \mathbb{Z}^+$ and $x \le 3$ (b) $x \in \mathbb{N}$ and $2x < 9$ (c) $x \in \mathbb{Z}$ and $-2 \le x < 2$

   (d) $x \in \mathbb{N}$ and $3 - x > 1$ (e) $x \in \mathbb{Z}^+$ and $4x - 7 < 9$ (f) $x \in \mathbb{N}$ and $10 - 3x > 1$

3 Solve the following inequalities, where $x \in \mathbb{R}$.

   (a) $x - 3 > 11$ (b) $2x + 3 \le 8$ (c) $5x + 6 \le -10$ (d) $3x - 1 \le -13$

   (e) $-5x \le 20$ (f) $-3x \ge -12$ (g) $\dfrac{x-4}{6} \le 3$ (h) $\dfrac{3x+2}{5} \le 4$

   (i) $\dfrac{5x+1}{3} > -3$ (j) $4 - 3x \le 10$ (k) $2 - 6x \le 0$ (l) $6 - 5x > 1$

   (m) $\dfrac{7-3x}{2} < -1$ (n) $x - 4 \le 5 + 2x$ (o) $2x + 5 < 4x - 7$ (p) $4x \le 3(2 - x)$

   (q) $3x \ge 5 - 2(3 - x)$

1.4 Modulus notation

Suppose that you want to find the difference between the heights of two children. With numerical information, the answer is quite straightforward: if their heights are 90 cm and 100 cm, you would answer 10 cm; and if their heights were 100 cm and 90 cm, you would still answer 10 cm.

But how would you answer the question if their heights were H cm and h cm? The answer is, it depends which is bigger: if $H > h$, you would answer $(H - h)$ cm; if $h > H$ you would answer $(h - H)$ cm; and if $h = H$ you would answer 0 cm, which is either $(H - h)$ cm or $(h - H)$ cm.

Questions like this, in which you want an answer which is always positive or zero, lead to the idea of the modulus of a number. This is a quantity which tells you the 'size' of a number regardless of its sign. For example, the modulus of 15 is 15, but the modulus of -15 is also 15.

The notation for modulus is to write the number between a pair of vertical lines. So you would write $|15| = 15$ and $|-15| = 15$.

The modulus is sometimes called the 'absolute value' of the number. Some calculators have a key marked 'abs' which produces the modulus. If yours has, try using it with a variety of inputs.

The modulus can be defined formally like this:

> The **modulus** of x, written $|x|$ and pronounced 'mod x', is defined by
>
> $|x| = x$ if $x \geq 0$,
> $|x| = -x$ if $x < 0$.

Using the modulus notation, you can now write the difference in heights as $|H - h|$ whether $H > h$, $h > H$ or $h = H$.

Another situation when the modulus is useful is when you talk about numbers which are large numerically, but which are negative, such as -1000 or $-1\,000\,000$. These are 'negative numbers with large modulus'.

For example, for large positive values of x, the value of $\dfrac{1}{x}$ is close to 0. The same is true for negative values of x with large modulus. So you can say that, when $|x|$ is large, $\left|\dfrac{1}{x}\right|$ is close to zero; or in a numerical example, when $|x| > 1000$, $\left|\dfrac{1}{x}\right| < 0.001$.

1.5 Modulus on the number line

In Fig. 1.8 A and B are points on a number line with coordinates a and b. How can you express the distance AB in terms of a and b?

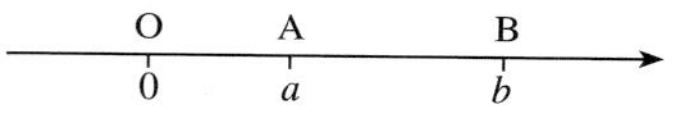

Fig. 1.8

- If B is to the right of A, then $b > a$, so $b - a > 0$ and the distance is $b - a$.
- If B is to the left of A, then $b < a$, so $b - a < 0$ and the distance is $a - b = -(b - a)$.
- If B and A coincide, then $b = a$, so $b - a = 0$ and the distance is 0.

You will recognise this as the definition of $|b - a|$.

> The distance between points on the number line representing numbers a and b is $|b - a|$.

As a special case, if a point X has coordinate x, then $|x|$ is the distance of X from the origin.

Now suppose that $|x| = 3$. What can you say about X?

There are two possibilities: since the distance $OX = 3$, either X is 3 units to the right of O so that $x = 3$, or X is 3 units to the left of O so that $x = -3$.

This is also true in reverse. If $x = 3$ or $x = -3$, then X is 3 units from O, so $|x| = 3$.

A convenient way of summarising this is to write

$|x| = 3$ means that $x = 3$ or $x = -3$.

Similarly you can write

$|x| \leq 3$ as $-3 \leq x \leq 3$,

since these are two different ways of saying that X is within 3 units of O on the number line.

In this example there is nothing special about the number 3. You could use the same argument with 3 replaced by any positive number a to show that

$|x| \le a$ means that $-a \le x \le a$.

You can get a useful generalisation by replacing x in this statement by $x - k$, where k is a constant:

If a is a positive number, $|x - k| \le a$ means that $-a \le x - k \le a$.

Now add k to each side of the inequalities $-a \le x - k$ and $x - k \le a$. You then get $k - a \le x$ and $x \le k + a$.

That is,

$k - a \le x \le k + a$.

The equivalence then becomes:

If a is a positive number,

$|x - k| \le a$ means that $k - a \le x \le k + a$.

This result is used when you give a number correct to a certain number of decimal places. For example, to say that $x = 3.87$ 'correct to 2 decimal places' is in effect saying that $|x - 3.87| \le 0.005$.

Fig. 1.9 shows that $|x - 3.87| \le 0.005$ means

$3.87 - 0.005 \le x \le 3.87 + 0.005$,

or $3.865 \le x \le 3.875$.

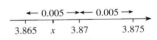

Fig. 1.9

Exercise 1B

1 Write down the values of

   (a) $|-6|$,   (b) $|13 - 15|$,   (c) $|13| + |-15|$.

2 If $|x| > 100$, what can you say about $\dfrac{1}{x^2}$? Write your answer using inequality notation.

3 The mass of a prize pumpkin is 4.76 kg correct to 2 decimal places. Denoting the mass by m kg, write this statement in mathematical form

   (a) without modulus notation,   (b) using modulus notation.

4 The length and width of a rectangle are measured as 4.8 cm and 3.6 cm, both correct to 1 decimal place. Write a statement about the perimeter, P cm, in mathematical form

   (a) without modulus notation,   (b) using modulus notation.

5 Repeat Question 4 for the area, A cm^2.

6 Write the given inequalities in an equivalent form of the type $a < x < b$ or $a \le x \le b$.

   (a) $|x - 3| < 1$ (b) $|x + 2| \le 0.1$ (c) $|2x - 3| \le 0.001$ (d) $|4x - 3| \le 8$

7 Rewrite the given inequalities using modulus notation.

(a) $1 \le x \le 2$ (b) $-1 < x < 3$ (c) $-3.8 \le x \le -3.5$ (d) $2.3 < x < 3.4$

8 What can you say about $|x|$ if $x \in \mathbb{Z}$?

1.6 Surds and their properties

When you have met expressions such as $\sqrt{2}$, $\sqrt{8}$ and $\sqrt{12}$ before, it is likely that you have used a calculator to express them in decimal form. You might have written

$$\sqrt{2} = 1.414... \quad \text{or} \quad \sqrt{2} = 1.414 \text{ correct to 3 decimal places} \quad \text{or} \quad \sqrt{2} \approx 1.414.$$

Why is the statement '$\sqrt{2} = 1.414$' incorrect?

Expressions like $\sqrt{2}$ or $\sqrt[3]{9}$ are called **surds**. However, expressions like $\sqrt{4}$ or $\sqrt[3]{27}$, which are whole numbers, are not surds.

This section is about calculating with surds. You need to remember that $\sqrt{x}$ always means the **positive** square root of x, or 0 if x is 0.

The main properties that you will use are:

If x and y are positive numbers, then

$$\sqrt{xy} = \sqrt{x} \times \sqrt{y} \quad \text{and} \quad \sqrt{\frac{x}{y}} = \frac{\sqrt{x}}{\sqrt{y}}.$$

You can use these properties to express square roots like $\sqrt{8}$ and $\sqrt{12}$ in terms of smaller surds:

$$\sqrt{8} = \sqrt{4 \times 2} = \sqrt{4} \times \sqrt{2} = 2\sqrt{2}; \qquad \sqrt{12} = \sqrt{4 \times 3} = \sqrt{4} \times \sqrt{3} = 2\sqrt{3}.$$

You can also simplify products and quotients of square roots:

$$\sqrt{18} \times \sqrt{2} = \sqrt{18 \times 2} = \sqrt{36} = 6; \qquad \frac{\sqrt{27}}{\sqrt{3}} = \sqrt{\frac{27}{3}} = \sqrt{9} = 3.$$

Use a calculator to check the results of these calculations.

To show that the statements in the blue box are true, remember that the number $\sqrt{x}$ has two properties:

$$\sqrt{x} \times \sqrt{x} = x, \quad \text{and} \quad \sqrt{x} \text{ is positive.}$$

Similarly

$$\sqrt{y} \times \sqrt{y} = y, \quad \text{and} \quad \sqrt{y} \text{ is positive.}$$

So, to prove that $\sqrt{xy} = \sqrt{x} \times \sqrt{y}$, you have to show that

$$(\sqrt{x} \times \sqrt{y}) \times (\sqrt{x} \times \sqrt{y}) = xy, \quad \text{and that} \quad \sqrt{x} \times \sqrt{y} \text{ is positive.}$$

The second of these is obvious, since the result of multiplying two positive numbers together is always a positive number. To prove the first, change the order of multiplying the numbers:

$$(\sqrt{x} \times \sqrt{y}) \times (\sqrt{x} \times \sqrt{y}) = (\sqrt{x} \times \sqrt{x}) \times (\sqrt{y} \times \sqrt{y})$$
$$= x \times y$$
$$= xy.$$

So $\sqrt{xy} = \sqrt{x} \times \sqrt{y}$.

Similarly, to prove that $\sqrt{\dfrac{x}{y}} = \dfrac{\sqrt{x}}{\sqrt{y}}$, you have to show that

$$\frac{\sqrt{x}}{\sqrt{y}} \times \frac{\sqrt{x}}{\sqrt{y}} = \frac{x}{y}, \quad \text{and that} \quad \frac{\sqrt{x}}{\sqrt{y}} \text{ is positive.}$$

The second of these is obvious, since the result of dividing one positive number by another positive number is always a positive number. To prove the first, use the rule for multiplying fractions, $\dfrac{a}{b} \times \dfrac{c}{d} = \dfrac{ac}{bd}$:

$$\frac{\sqrt{x}}{\sqrt{y}} \times \frac{\sqrt{x}}{\sqrt{y}} = \frac{\sqrt{x} \times \sqrt{x}}{\sqrt{y} \times \sqrt{y}} = \frac{x}{y}.$$

So $\sqrt{\dfrac{x}{y}} = \dfrac{\sqrt{x}}{\sqrt{y}}$.

Example 1.6.1

Simplify   (a) $\sqrt{28} + \sqrt{63}$,   (b) $\sqrt{5} \times \sqrt{10}$.

Notice that alternative methods of solution may be possible, as in part (b).

(a) $\sqrt{28} + \sqrt{63} = \sqrt{4 \times 7} + \sqrt{9 \times 7}$
$$= (\sqrt{4} \times \sqrt{7}) + (\sqrt{9} \times \sqrt{7})$$
$$= 2\sqrt{7} + 3\sqrt{7} = 5\sqrt{7}.$$

(b) **Method 1** $\sqrt{5} \times \sqrt{10} = \sqrt{5 \times 10} = \sqrt{50}$
$$= \sqrt{25 \times 2} = 5\sqrt{2}.$$

Method 2 $\sqrt{5} \times \sqrt{10} = \sqrt{5} \times \sqrt{5 \times 2} = \sqrt{5} \times (\sqrt{5} \times \sqrt{2})$
$$= (\sqrt{5} \times \sqrt{5}) \times \sqrt{2} = 5\sqrt{2}.$$

Example 1.6.2

Simplify   (a) $\dfrac{\sqrt{32}}{\sqrt{2}}$,   (b) $(\sqrt{8} - \sqrt{3})(\sqrt{8} + \sqrt{3})$.

(a) **Method 1** $\dfrac{\sqrt{32}}{\sqrt{2}} = \dfrac{\sqrt{2} \times \sqrt{16}}{\sqrt{2}}$ **Method 2** $\dfrac{\sqrt{32}}{\sqrt{2}} = \sqrt{\dfrac{32}{2}}$
$$= \frac{\sqrt{2} \times 4}{\sqrt{2}} \qquad\qquad\qquad\qquad = \sqrt{16}$$
$$= 4. \qquad\qquad\qquad\qquad\qquad\quad = 4.$$

(b) $(\sqrt{8} - \sqrt{3})(\sqrt{8} + \sqrt{3}) = (\sqrt{8})^2 - (\sqrt{3})^2$
$$= 8 - 3 = 5.$$

Example 1.6.2(b) uses the formula for the difference of two squares:

> **The difference of two squares**
>
> $p^2 - q^2 = (p - q)(p + q).$

However, it is written with $p = \sqrt{x}$ and $q = \sqrt{y}$, so it appears as

$$x - y = (\sqrt{x} - \sqrt{y})(\sqrt{x} + \sqrt{y}).$$

Similar rules to those for square roots also apply to cube roots and higher roots.

Example 1.6.3

Simplify   (a) $\sqrt[3]{16}$,   (b) $\sqrt[3]{12} \times \sqrt[3]{18}$.

$$\begin{aligned} \text{(a) } \sqrt[3]{16} &= \sqrt[3]{8 \times 2} \\ &= \sqrt[3]{8} \times \sqrt[3]{2} \\ &= 2 \times \sqrt[3]{2}. \end{aligned}$$

$$\begin{aligned} \text{(b) } \sqrt[3]{12} \times \sqrt[3]{18} &= \sqrt[3]{12 \times 18} \\ &= \sqrt[3]{216} \\ &= 6. \end{aligned}$$

Example 1.6.4

Show that if neither x nor y is equal to 0, then $\sqrt{x + y}$ is never equal to $\sqrt{x} + \sqrt{y}$.

If you square $\sqrt{x + y}$, you get $x + y$.

If you square $\sqrt{x} + \sqrt{y}$, you get

$$\begin{aligned} (\sqrt{x} + \sqrt{y})(\sqrt{x} + \sqrt{y}) &= (\sqrt{x})^2 + 2\sqrt{x}\sqrt{y} + (\sqrt{y})^2 \\ &= x + 2\sqrt{xy} + y. \end{aligned}$$

But neither x nor y is equal to 0, so xy is not equal to 0, so $\sqrt{xy}$ is not equal to 0.

Hence the square of $\sqrt{x + y}$ is less than the square of $\sqrt{x} + \sqrt{y}$.

Therefore, if neither x nor y is equal to 0, then $\sqrt{x + y}$ is never equal to $\sqrt{x} + \sqrt{y}$.

It is also true that if neither x nor y is equal to 0, then $\sqrt{x - y}$ is never equal to $\sqrt{x} - \sqrt{y}$.

So beware, and do not be tempted!

> If x and y are positive numbers, then
>
> $\sqrt{x + y} \neq \sqrt{x} + \sqrt{y}$ and $\sqrt{x - y} \neq \sqrt{x} - \sqrt{y}.$

Exercise 1C

1 Simplify the following without using a calculator.

(a) $\sqrt{3} \times \sqrt{3}$ (b) $\sqrt{10} \times \sqrt{10}$ (c) $\sqrt{8} \times \sqrt{2}$ (d) $\sqrt{32} \times \sqrt{2}$

(e) $\sqrt{3} \times \sqrt{12}$ (f) $5\sqrt{3} \times \sqrt{3}$ (g) $2\sqrt{5} \times 3\sqrt{5}$ (h) $2\sqrt{20} \times 3\sqrt{5}$

(i) $(2\sqrt{7})^2$ (j) $(3\sqrt{3})^2$ (k) $\sqrt[3]{5} \times \sqrt[3]{5} \times \sqrt[3]{5}$ (l) $(2\sqrt[4]{3})^4$

2 Write the following in the form $a\sqrt{b}$.

(a) $\sqrt{18}$ (b) $\sqrt{20}$ (c) $\sqrt{24}$ (d) $\sqrt{32}$

(e) $\sqrt{40}$ (f) $\sqrt{45}$ (g) $\sqrt{48}$ (h) $\sqrt{50}$

3 Simplify the following without using a calculator.

(a) $\sqrt{8} + \sqrt{18}$ (b) $\sqrt{3} + \sqrt{12}$ (c) $\sqrt{20} - \sqrt{5}$

(d) $\sqrt{32} - \sqrt{8}$ (e) $\sqrt{50} - \sqrt{18} - \sqrt{8}$ (f) $2\sqrt{20} + 3\sqrt{45}$

4 Simplify the following without using a calculator.

(a) $\dfrac{\sqrt{8}}{\sqrt{2}}$ (b) $\dfrac{\sqrt{27}}{\sqrt{3}}$ (c) $\dfrac{\sqrt{40}}{\sqrt{10}}$ (d) $\dfrac{\sqrt{50}}{\sqrt{2}}$

(e) $\dfrac{\sqrt{125}}{\sqrt{5}}$ (f) $\dfrac{\sqrt{54}}{\sqrt{6}}$ (g) $\dfrac{\sqrt{3}}{\sqrt{48}}$ (h) $\dfrac{\sqrt{50}}{\sqrt{200}}$

5 Simplify

(a) $(\sqrt{2} - 1)(\sqrt{2} + 1)$, (b) $(3 - \sqrt{2})(3 + \sqrt{2})$, (c) $(\sqrt{7} + \sqrt{3})(\sqrt{7} - \sqrt{3})$,

(d) $(2\sqrt{2} + 1)(2\sqrt{2} - 1)$, (e) $(4\sqrt{3} - \sqrt{2})(4\sqrt{3} + \sqrt{2})$, (f) $(\sqrt{10} + \sqrt{5})(\sqrt{10} - \sqrt{5})$,

(g) $(4\sqrt{7} - \sqrt{5})(4\sqrt{7} + \sqrt{5})$, (h) $(2\sqrt{6} - 3\sqrt{3})(2\sqrt{6} + 3\sqrt{3})$.

1.7 Rationalising denominators

If you are using a calculator, then it is easy to calculate $\dfrac{1}{\sqrt{2}}$ or $\dfrac{1}{3 + \sqrt{2}}$ directly. But without a calculator, if you know that $\sqrt{2} = 1.414\,213\,562...$, finding $\dfrac{1}{\sqrt{2}}$ or $\dfrac{1}{3 + \sqrt{2}}$ as a decimal is a very unpleasant calculation.

Denominators of the form $a\sqrt{b}$

Calculating $\dfrac{1}{\sqrt{2}}$ can be greatly simplified by multiplying top and bottom by $\sqrt{2}$, giving

$$\frac{1}{\sqrt{2}} = \frac{1}{\sqrt{2}} \times \frac{\sqrt{2}}{\sqrt{2}} = \frac{1 \times \sqrt{2}}{\sqrt{2} \times \sqrt{2}} = \frac{\sqrt{2}}{2}.$$

Using this, from $\sqrt{2} = 1.414\,213\,562...$ you can find at once that

$$\frac{1}{\sqrt{2}} = 0.707\,106\,781... .$$

You can see that the result $\dfrac{1}{\sqrt{2}} = \dfrac{\sqrt{2}}{2}$ is just another way of writing $\sqrt{2} \times \sqrt{2} = 2$.

Generalising, you can deduce the following:

> To remove the surd $\sqrt{x}$ from the denominator of a fraction, multiply
> by $\dfrac{\sqrt{x}}{\sqrt{x}}$ to get
>
> $$\frac{1}{\sqrt{x}} \times \frac{\sqrt{x}}{\sqrt{x}} = \frac{\sqrt{x}}{x}.$$

Removing the surd from the denominator is called **rationalising the denominator**.

Example 1.7.1

Rationalise the denominator in the expressions   (a) $\dfrac{6}{\sqrt{2}}$,   (b) $\dfrac{3\sqrt{2}}{\sqrt{10}}$,   (c) $\dfrac{2}{3\sqrt{2}}$.

(a) $\dfrac{6}{\sqrt{2}} = \dfrac{6}{\sqrt{2}} \times \dfrac{\sqrt{2}}{\sqrt{2}} = \dfrac{6 \times \sqrt{2}}{\sqrt{2} \times \sqrt{2}} = \dfrac{6\sqrt{2}}{2} = 3\sqrt{2}.$

(b) **Method 1** $\dfrac{3\sqrt{2}}{\sqrt{10}} = \dfrac{3\sqrt{2}}{\sqrt{5} \times \sqrt{2}} = \dfrac{3}{\sqrt{5}} = \dfrac{3}{\sqrt{5}} \times \dfrac{\sqrt{5}}{\sqrt{5}} = \dfrac{3\sqrt{5}}{5}.$

Method 2 $\dfrac{3\sqrt{2}}{\sqrt{10}} = \dfrac{3\sqrt{2}}{\sqrt{10}} \times \dfrac{\sqrt{10}}{\sqrt{10}} = \dfrac{3\sqrt{2} \times \sqrt{10}}{\sqrt{10} \times \sqrt{10}}$

$\qquad\qquad = \dfrac{3\sqrt{20}}{10} = \dfrac{3\sqrt{4} \times \sqrt{5}}{10} = \dfrac{6\sqrt{5}}{10} = \dfrac{3\sqrt{5}}{5}.$

(c) $\dfrac{2}{3\sqrt{2}} = \dfrac{2}{3\sqrt{2}} \times \dfrac{\sqrt{2}}{\sqrt{2}} = \dfrac{2\sqrt{2}}{3\sqrt{2} \times \sqrt{2}} = \dfrac{2\sqrt{2}}{3 \times 2} = \dfrac{\sqrt{2}}{3}.$

Expressions like those in parts (b) and (c) are often written in the form $\frac{3}{5}\sqrt{5}$, $\frac{1}{3}\sqrt{2}$.

Calculating with surds using these rules is often useful in geometry, especially when Pythagoras' theorem is involved.

Example 1.7.2

Figure 1.10 shows the vertical cross-section of a roof of a building as a right-angled triangle ABC, with AB = 15 m. The height of the roof, BD, is 10 m.

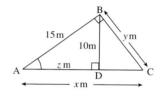

Fig. 1.10

Calculate   (a) z,   (b) cos DÂB,   (c) x,   (d) y.

(a) Use Pythagoras' theorem in triangle ADB.

$$z^2 + 10^2 = 15^2,$$
$$z^2 = 225 - 100 = 125,$$
$$z = \sqrt{125} = \sqrt{25 \times 5} = 5\sqrt{5}.$$

(b) In triangle ADB,

$$\cos D\hat{A}B = \frac{AD}{AB} = \frac{z}{15} = \frac{5\sqrt{5}}{15} = \frac{\sqrt{5}}{3}.$$

(c) Angle BAC in triangle ABC is the same as angle DAB in triangle ADB. So, in triangle ABC,

$$\frac{AB}{AC} = \cos B\hat{A}C = \cos D\hat{A}B = \frac{\sqrt{5}}{3}.$$

That is,

$$\frac{15}{x} = \frac{\sqrt{5}}{3}.$$

Multiplying both sides of the equation by $3x$,

$$45 = x \times \sqrt{5}$$
$$x = \frac{45}{\sqrt{5}} = \frac{9 \times 5}{\sqrt{5}} = 9 \times \sqrt{5} = 9\sqrt{5}.$$

(d) Use Pythagoras' theorem in triangle ABC.

$$15^2 + y^2 = (9\sqrt{5})^2,$$
$$y^2 = 81 \times 5 - 15^2 = 405 - 225 = 180.$$

So $y = \sqrt{180} = \sqrt{36 \times 5} = 6\sqrt{5}$.

Denominators of the form $a + \sqrt{b}$ or $a - \sqrt{b}$

To rationalise the denominator in an expression such as $\frac{1}{3 + \sqrt{2}}$ it is useful to look at the results of Exercise 1C Question 5. In part (b), you see that if you multiply $(3 + \sqrt{2})$ by $(3 - \sqrt{2})$ the result is an integer:

$$(3 + \sqrt{2})(3 - \sqrt{2}) = 3^2 - (\sqrt{2})^2 = 9 - 2 = 7.$$

This result suggests that to rationalise the denominator in $\frac{1}{3 + \sqrt{2}}$, you multiply by $\frac{3 - \sqrt{2}}{3 - \sqrt{2}}$, which of course is equal to 1, to get

$$\frac{1}{3 + \sqrt{2}} \times \frac{3 - \sqrt{2}}{3 - \sqrt{2}} = \frac{3 - \sqrt{2}}{(3 + \sqrt{2})(3 - \sqrt{2})} = \frac{3 - \sqrt{2}}{9 - 2} = \frac{3 - \sqrt{2}}{7}.$$

The calculation of the product $(3 + \sqrt{2})(3 - \sqrt{2})$ in the previous line uses the difference of two squares, $p^2 - q^2 = (p - q)(p + q)$, with $p = 3$ and $q = \sqrt{2}$.

| To rationalise the denominator in $\frac{1}{a + \sqrt{b}}$ multiply by $\frac{a - \sqrt{b}}{a - \sqrt{b}}$. |
| To rationalise the denominator in $\frac{1}{a - \sqrt{b}}$ multiply by $\frac{a + \sqrt{b}}{a + \sqrt{b}}$ |

Example 1.7.3

Rationalise the denominator in the expressions

(a) $\dfrac{2}{2+\sqrt{3}}$,   (b) $\dfrac{1}{3-\sqrt{5}}$,   (c) $\dfrac{2}{\sqrt{5}-2}$.

(a) Multiplying by $\dfrac{2-\sqrt{3}}{2-\sqrt{3}}$,

$$\frac{2}{2+\sqrt{3}} = \frac{2}{2+\sqrt{3}} \times \frac{2-\sqrt{3}}{2-\sqrt{3}}$$

$$= \frac{2(2-\sqrt{3})}{2^2-(\sqrt{3})^2} = \frac{4-2\sqrt{3}}{4-3} = \frac{4-2\sqrt{3}}{1} = 4-2\sqrt{3}.$$

(b) $\dfrac{1}{3-\sqrt{5}} = \dfrac{1}{3-\sqrt{5}} \times \dfrac{3+\sqrt{5}}{3+\sqrt{5}}$

$$= \frac{3+\sqrt{5}}{(3)^2-(\sqrt{5})^2}$$

$$= \frac{3+\sqrt{5}}{9-5} = \frac{3+\sqrt{5}}{4} = \tfrac{3}{4}+\tfrac{1}{4}\sqrt{5}.$$

(c) $\dfrac{2}{\sqrt{5}-2} = \dfrac{2}{\sqrt{5}-2} \times \dfrac{\sqrt{5}+2}{\sqrt{5}+2}$

$$= \frac{2(\sqrt{5}+2)}{(\sqrt{5})^2-2^2}$$

$$= \frac{2\sqrt{5}+4}{5-4} = 2\sqrt{5}+4.$$

Example 1.7.4

In Fig. 1.11 ABC is a right-angled isosceles triangle with AB = BC = 1 unit, and ACD is an isosceles triangle with AC = CD.

(a) Find the size of $A\hat{D}C$.   (b) Deduce that $\tan 22\tfrac{1}{2}° = \sqrt{2}-1$.

> The notation '$\triangle ABC$' is often used to mean 'triangle ABC'.

(a) Since $\triangle ABC$ is isosceles and $A\hat{B}C = 90°$, $A\hat{C}B = 45°$.
Also, since $A\hat{C}B$ is an exterior angle of $\triangle ACD$,
$A\hat{C}B = A\hat{D}C + D\hat{A}C$. But $A\hat{D}C = D\hat{A}C$, because $\triangle ACD$
is isosceles. Therefore $A\hat{C}B = 2 \times A\hat{D}C$. So $A\hat{D}C = 22\tfrac{1}{2}°$.

(b) By Pythagoras' theorem, $AC^2 = 1+1 = 2$, so $AC = \sqrt{2}$ units.
And since $\triangle ACD$ is isosceles, $CD = AC = \sqrt{2}$ units.
Therefore, in the right-angled triangle ABD, with $A\hat{D}B = 22\tfrac{1}{2}°$,

$$\tan 22\tfrac{1}{2}° = \frac{AB}{BD} = \frac{1}{\sqrt{2}+1}$$

$$= \frac{1}{\sqrt{2}+1} \times \frac{\sqrt{2}-1}{\sqrt{2}-1} = \frac{\sqrt{2}-1}{2-1} = \sqrt{2}-1.$$

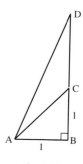

Fig. 1.11

Exercise 1D

1 Rationalise the denominator in each of the following expressions, and simplify them.

(a) $\dfrac{1}{\sqrt{3}}$ (b) $\dfrac{1}{\sqrt{5}}$ (c) $\dfrac{4}{\sqrt{2}}$ (d) $\dfrac{6}{\sqrt{6}}$

(e) $\dfrac{11}{\sqrt{11}}$ (f) $\dfrac{2}{\sqrt{8}}$ (g) $\dfrac{12}{\sqrt{3}}$ (h) $\dfrac{14}{\sqrt{7}}$

(i) $\dfrac{\sqrt{6}}{\sqrt{2}}$ (j) $\dfrac{\sqrt{2}}{\sqrt{6}}$ (k) $\dfrac{3\sqrt{5}}{\sqrt{3}}$ (l) $\dfrac{4\sqrt{6}}{\sqrt{5}}$

(m) $\dfrac{7\sqrt{2}}{2\sqrt{3}}$ (n) $\dfrac{4\sqrt{2}}{\sqrt{12}}$ (o) $\dfrac{9\sqrt{12}}{2\sqrt{18}}$ (p) $\dfrac{2\sqrt{18}}{9\sqrt{12}}$

2 Simplify the following, giving each answer in the form $k\sqrt{3}$.

(a) $\sqrt{75} + \sqrt{12}$ (b) $6 + \sqrt{3}(4 - 2\sqrt{3})$

(c) $\dfrac{12}{\sqrt{3}} - \sqrt{27}$ (d) $\dfrac{2}{\sqrt{3}} + \dfrac{\sqrt{2}}{\sqrt{6}}$

(e) $\sqrt{2} \times \sqrt{8} \times \sqrt{27}$ (f) $(3 - \sqrt{3})(2 - \sqrt{3}) - \sqrt{3} \times \sqrt{27}$

3 ABCD is a rectangle in which $AB = 4\sqrt{5}$ cm and $BC = \sqrt{10}$ cm. Giving each answer in simplified surd form, find

(a) the area of the rectangle,   (b) the length of the diagonal AC.

4 Solve the following equations, giving each answer in the form $k\sqrt{2}$.

(a) $x\sqrt{2} = 10$ (b) $2y\sqrt{2} - 3 = \dfrac{5y}{\sqrt{2}} + 1$ (c) $z\sqrt{32} - 16 = z\sqrt{8} - 4$

5 Express in the form $k\sqrt[3]{3}$

(a) $\sqrt[3]{24}$,   (b) $\sqrt[3]{81} + \sqrt[3]{3}$,   (c) $(\sqrt[3]{3})^4$,   (d) $\sqrt[3]{3000} - \sqrt[3]{375}$.

6 Find the length of the third side in each of the following right-angled triangles, giving each answer in simplified surd form.

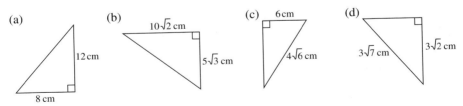

(a) 12 cm, 8 cm   (b) $10\sqrt{2}$ cm, $5\sqrt{3}$ cm   (c) 6 cm, $4\sqrt{6}$ cm   (d) $3\sqrt{7}$ cm, $3\sqrt{2}$ cm

7 You are given that, correct to 12 decimal places, $\sqrt{26} = 5.099\ 019\ 513\ 593$.

(a) Find the value of $\sqrt{104}$ correct to 10 decimal places.

(b) Find the value of $\sqrt{650}$ correct to 10 decimal places.

(c) Find the value of $\dfrac{13}{\sqrt{26}}$ correct to 10 decimal places.

8 Solve the simultaneous equations $7x - (3\sqrt{5})y = 9\sqrt{5}$ and $(2\sqrt{5})x + y = 34$.

9 Rationalise the denominators and simplify the following expressions.

(a) $\dfrac{1}{\sqrt{2}-1}$ (b) $\dfrac{2}{3-\sqrt{3}}$ (c) $\dfrac{2}{4-\sqrt{2}}$ (d) $\dfrac{2}{6-\sqrt{2}}$

(e) $\dfrac{\sqrt{2}-1}{\sqrt{2}+1}$ (f) $\dfrac{3-\sqrt{3}}{2-\sqrt{3}}$ (g) $\dfrac{2+\sqrt{2}}{4-\sqrt{2}}$ (h) $\dfrac{1+2\sqrt{2}}{4-\sqrt{2}}$

10 In triangle ABC, B is a right angle, $AB = 5 - \sqrt{2}$ and $AC = 5 + \sqrt{2}$. Calculate and simplify $\cos B\hat{A}C$.

11 Solve the simultaneous equations $x\sqrt{5} + 2y = 3$ and $x + y = 1$, giving your answers in as simple a form as possible.

12 A formula for the radius of the circle touching all three sides of a triangle is $r = \dfrac{2\Delta}{p}$, where Δ is the area of the triangle and p is the perimeter. Find, in as simple a form as possible, the radius of this circle for right-angled triangles having sides

(a) 1 cm, 1 cm, $\sqrt{2}$ cm

(b) 1 cm, $\sqrt{3}$ cm, 2 cm

(c) 1 cm, 2 cm, $\sqrt{5}$ cm

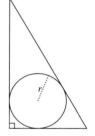

2 Sequences

This chapter is about sequences of numbers. When you have completed it, you should

- know that a sequence can be constructed from a formula or an inductive definition
- be familiar with triangle and arithmetic sequences
- know how to find the sum of an arithmetic series
- know how to use a graphic display calculator to find terms of sequences and sums of series
- be able to use sigma notation.

> From here on 'calculator' is taken to mean 'graphic display calculator'.

2.1 Constructing sequences

Here are six rows of numbers, each forming a pattern of some kind. What are the next three numbers in each row?

(a) $1, \quad 4, \quad 9, \quad 16, \quad 25, \quad \dots$
(b) $\frac{1}{2}, \quad \frac{2}{3}, \quad \frac{3}{4}, \quad \frac{4}{5}, \quad \frac{5}{6}, \quad \dots$

(c) $99, \quad 97, \quad 95, \quad 93, \quad 91, \quad \dots$
(d) $1, \quad 1.1, \quad 1.21, \quad 1.331, \quad 1.4641, \quad \dots$

(e) $2, \quad 4, \quad 8, \quad 14, \quad 22, \quad \dots$
(f) $3, \quad 1, \quad 4, \quad 1, \quad 5, \quad \dots$

Rows of this kind are called **sequences**, and the separate numbers are called **terms**.

The usual notation for the first, second, third, ... terms of a sequence is u_1, u_2, u_3, and so on. If n is a positive integer, then the nth term is written as u_n. In this notation, the letter n is called a **suffix**.

In (a) and (b) you would have no difficulty in writing a formula for the nth term of the sequence. The numbers in (a) could be rewritten as $1^2, 2^2, 3^2, 4^2, 5^2$, and the pattern could be summed up by writing

$$u_n = n^2.$$

The terms of (b) are $\dfrac{1}{1+1}, \dfrac{2}{2+1}, \dfrac{3}{3+1}, \dfrac{4}{4+1}, \dfrac{5}{5+1}$, so $u_n = \dfrac{n}{n+1}$.

In (c), (d) and (e) you probably expect that there is a formula, but it is not so easy to find it. What is more obvious is how to get each term from the one before. For example, in (c) the terms go down by 2 at each step, so that $u_2 = u_1 - 2$, $u_3 = u_2 - 2$, $u_4 = u_3 - 2$, and so on. These steps can be summarised by the single equation

$$u_n = u_{n-1} - 2.$$

The terms in (d) are multiplied by 1.1 at each step, so the rule is

$$u_n = 1.1u_{n-1}.$$

Unfortunately, there are many other sequences which satisfy the equation $u_n = u_{n-1} - 2$. Other examples are 10, 8, 6, 4, 2, ... and $-2, -4, -6, -8, -10, ...$.

The definition is not complete until you know the first term. So to complete the definitions of the sequences (c) and (d) you have to write

(c) $u_1 = 99$ and $u_n = u_{n-1} - 2$,

(d) $u_1 = 1$ and $u_n = 1.1u_{n-1}$.

Definitions like these are called **inductive definitions**, or sometimes 'recursive definitions'.

Sequence (e) comes from geometry. It gives the greatest number of regions into which a plane can be split by different numbers of circles. (Try drawing your own diagrams with 1, 2, 3, 4, ... circles.) This sequence is developed as $u_2 = u_1 + 2$, $u_3 = u_2 + 4$, $u_4 = u_3 + 6$, and so on. You will see that the increases 2, 4, 6, ... are themselves double the suffixes on the right of each equation; thus $u_2 = u_1 + 2 \times 1$, $u_3 = u_2 + 2 \times 2$, $u_4 = u_3 + 2 \times 3$, and so on. These equations can be summarised by the inductive definition

$u_1 = 2$ and $u_n = u_{n-1} + 2(n - 1)$.

For (f) you may have given the next three terms as 1, 6, 1 (expecting the even-placed terms all to be 1, and the odd-placed terms to go up by 1 at each step). In fact this sequence had a quite different origin, as the first five digits of π in decimal form! With this meaning, the next three terms would be 9, 2, 6.

This illustrates an important point, that a sequence can never be uniquely defined by giving just the first few terms. Try, for example, working out the first eight terms of the sequence defined by

$u_n = n^2 + (n - 1)(n - 2)(n - 3)(n - 4)(n - 5)$.

You will find that the first five terms are the same as those given in (a), but the next three are probably very different from your original guess.

A sequence can only be described unambiguously by giving a formula, an inductive definition in terms of a general natural number n, or some other general rule.

There is nothing special about the choice of the letter u for a sequence. Other letters such as v, x, t and I are often used instead, especially if the sequence appears in some application. The nth term is then v_n, x_n, t_n or I_n.

You will also sometimes find different letters used in place of n for the suffix. The most common alternatives are i and r, so that a term of the sequence may be written as u_i or u_r.

Sometimes it is convenient to number the terms u_0, u_1, u_2, ... , starting with $n = 0$, but you then have to be careful in referring to 'the first term': do you mean u_0 or u_1?

2.2 Sequences on a calculator

If you know the definition of a sequence, your calculator can produce a table of values of u_n for different values of n.

- If the sequence is defined by a formula, you will have to enter the formula for u_n and the first value of n for which the value is required.

- If the definition is inductive, you will also have to enter the value of the first term of the sequence.

The actual key sequence varies for different calculators, so you will need to consult the instruction manual for your particular model.

Exercise 2A

1 Write down the first five terms of the sequences with the following definitions.

(a) $u_1 = 7, \quad u_n = u_{n-1} + 7$

(b) $u_1 = 13, \quad u_n = u_{n-1} - 5$

(c) $u_1 = 4, \quad u_n = 3u_{n-1}$

(d) $u_1 = 6, \quad u_n = \frac{1}{2}u_{n-1}$

(e) $u_1 = 2, \quad u_n = 3u_{n-1} + 1$

(f) $u_1 = 1, \quad u_n = u_{n-1}^2 + 3$

Use a calculator to check your answers.

2 Suggest inductive definitions which would produce the following sequences.

(a) 2, 4, 6, 8, 10, ...

(b) 11, 9, 7, 5, 3, ...

(c) 2, 6, 10, 14, 18, ...

(d) 2, 6, 18, 54, 162, ...

(e) $\frac{1}{3}$, $\frac{1}{9}$, $\frac{1}{27}$, $\frac{1}{81}$, ...

(f) $\frac{1}{2}a$, $\frac{1}{4}a$, $\frac{1}{8}a$, $\frac{1}{16}a$, ...

(g) 1, -1, 1, -1, 1, ...

(h) 1, $1+x$, $(1+x)^2$, $(1+x)^3$, ...

Use a calculator to check your answers to parts (a) to (d).

3 Write down the first five terms of each sequence and give an inductive definition for it.

(a) $u_n = 2n + 3$

(b) $u_n = n^2$

(c) $u_n = \frac{1}{2}n(n+1)$

(d) $u_n = \frac{1}{6}n(n+1)(2n+1)$

(e) $u_n = 2 \times 3^n$

(f) $u_n = \frac{3}{5} \times 5^n$

Use a calculator to show that the given formula and your inductive definition give the same table of values.

4 For each of the following sequences give a possible formula for the nth term.

(a) 9, 8, 7, 6, ...

(b) 6, 18, 54, 162, ...

(c) 4, 7, 12, 19, ...

(d) 4, 12, 24, 40, 60, ...

(e) $\frac{1}{4}$, $\frac{3}{5}$, $\frac{5}{6}$, $\frac{7}{7}$, ...

(f) $\frac{2}{2}$, $\frac{5}{4}$, $\frac{10}{8}$, $\frac{17}{16}$, ...

2.3 The triangle number sequence

The numbers of crosses in the triangular patterns in Fig. 2.1 are called triangle numbers. If t_n denotes the nth triangle number, you can see by counting the numbers of crosses in successive rows that

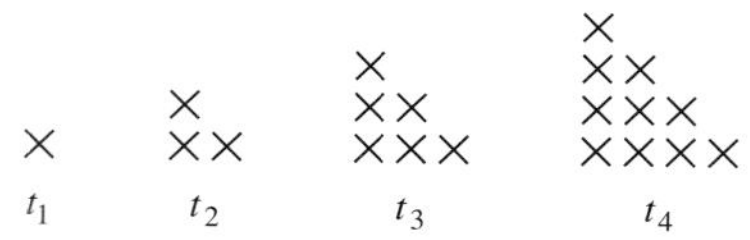

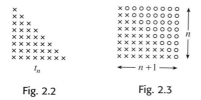

Fig. 2.1

$$t_1 = 1, \quad t_2 = 1 + 2 = 3, \quad t_3 = 1 + 2 + 3 = 6,$$

and in general $t_n = 1 + 2 + 3 + ... + n$, where the dots indicate that all the positive integers between 3 and n have to be included in the addition.

Fig. 2.2

Fig. 2.3

Figure 2.2 shows a typical pattern of crosses forming a triangle number t_n. (It is in fact drawn for $n = 8$, but any other value of n could have been chosen.) An easy way of finding a formula for t_n is to make a similar pattern of 'noughts', and then to turn it upside down and place it alongside the pattern of crosses, as in Fig. 2.3. The noughts and crosses together then make a rectangular pattern, $n + 1$ objects wide and n objects high. So the total number of objects is $n(n + 1)$, half of them crosses and half noughts. The number of crosses alone is therefore

$$t_n = \tfrac{1}{2}n(n + 1).$$

This shows that:

> The sum of all the positive integers from 1 to n is $\tfrac{1}{2}n(n + 1)$.

Example 2.3.1

Find (a) the sum of the first 50 positive integers,
(b) the sum of the positive integers from 31 to 50 inclusive,
(c) the sum of the first 30 even numbers.

(a) Using the result in the box, the sum of the first 50 positive integers is

$$1 + 2 + ... + 50 = \tfrac{1}{2} \times 50 \times (50 + 1) = 25 \times 51 = 1275.$$

(b) Using an 'add and subtract method',

$$31 + 32 + ... + 50 = (1 + 2 + ... + 50) - (1 + 2 + ... + 30)$$
$$= 1275 - \tfrac{1}{2} \times 30 \times (30 + 1)$$
$$= 1275 - 15 \times 31 = 810.$$

(c) The 30th even number is 60, so

$$2 + 4 + ... + 60 = 2(1 + 2 + ... + 30)$$
$$= 2 \times \tfrac{1}{2} \times 30 \times (30 + 1)$$
$$= 30 \times 31 = 930.$$

You can put the geometric argument which gives the result in the box into algebraic form. If you count the crosses in Fig. 2.2 from the top downwards you get

$$t_n = \quad 1 \quad + \quad 2 \quad + \quad 3 \quad + \quad ... \quad + (n-2) + (n-1) + \quad n.$$

But if you count the noughts from the top downwards you get

$$t_n = \quad n \quad + (n-1) + (n-2) + \quad ... \quad + \quad 3 \quad + \quad 2 \quad + \quad 1.$$

Counting all the objects in the rectangle is equivalent to adding these two equations:

$$2t_n = (n+1) + (n+1) + (n+1) + \quad ... \quad + (n+1) + (n+1) + (n+1),$$

with one $(n+1)$ bracket for each of the n rows. It follows that $2t_n = n(n+1)$, so that

$$t_n = \tfrac{1}{2}n(n+1).$$

It is also possible to give an inductive definition for the sequence t_n. Figure 2.1 shows that to get from any triangle number to the next you simply add an extra row of crosses underneath. Thus $t_2 = t_1 + 2, t_3 = t_2 + 3, t_4 = t_3 + 4$, and in general

$$t_n = t_{n-1} + n.$$

You can complete this definition by starting either with $t_1 = 1$ or $t_0 = 0$. If you choose $t_0 = 0$, then you can find t_1 by putting $n = 1$ in the general equation, as $t_1 = t_0 + 1 = 0 + 1 = 1$. So you may as well define the triangle number sequence by

$$t_0 = 0 \quad \text{and} \quad t_n = t_{n-1} + n, \quad \text{where } n = 1, 2, 3, ... \, .$$

Exercise 2B

1 Calculate
    (a) $1 + 2 +$ (all the integers up to) $+ 40$,
    (b) $21 + 22 +$ (all the integers up to) $+ 40$,
    (c) $2 + 4 +$ (all the even integers up to) $+ 40$,
    (d) $1 + 3 +$ (all the odd integers up to) $+ 39$.

2 Using Fig. 2.3 as an example,
    (a) draw a pattern of crosses to represent the nth triangle number t_n,
    (b) draw another pattern of noughts to represent t_{n-1},
    (c) combine these two patterns to show that $t_n + t_{n-1} = n^2$.
    (d) Use the fact that $t_n = \tfrac{1}{2}n(n+1)$ to show the result in part (c) algebraically.

3 (a) Find an expression in terms of n for $t_n - t_{n-1}$ for all $n \geq 1$.
    (b) Use this result and that in Question 2(c) to show that $t_n^2 - t_{n-1}^2 = n^3$.
    (c) Use part (b) to write expressions in terms of triangle numbers for $1^3, 2^3, 3^3, ... , n^3$.
    Hence show that $1^3 + 2^3 + 3^3 + ... + n^3 = \tfrac{1}{4}n^2(n+1)^2$.

2.4   Arithmetic sequences

An **arithmetic sequence**, or **arithmetic progression**, is a sequence whose terms go up or down by constant steps.

Here are some examples.

(a) 1,   3,   5,   7,   9,   ...
(b) 2,   5,   8,   11,   14,   ...
(c) 99, 97, 95,   93,   91,   ...
(d) 3, 1.5,   0, −1.5,   −3,   ...

It is easy to write down inductive definitions for these sequences. In sequence (a), for example, the step from each term to the next is +2. You can write this as an equation, $u_n = u_{n-1} + 2$. You also need to state that the first term, u_1, is 1. The complete definition is then

$$u_1 = 1, \quad u_n = u_{n-1} + 2.$$

Check for yourself that the other three sequences have inductive definitions

(b) $u_1 = 2, \quad u_n = u_{n-1} + 3,$
(c) $u_1 = 99, \quad u_n = u_{n-1} - 2,$
(d) $u_1 = 3, \quad u_n = u_{n-1} - 1.5.$

You will see that these definitions all have the form

$$u_1 = a, \quad u_n = u_{n-1} + d$$

for different values of a and d. The letter a is usually chosen for the first term of the sequence. The step d is called the **common difference**.

Example 2.4.1
An arithmetic sequence is defined by

$$u_1 = 5, \quad u_n = u_{n-1} + 7.$$

Find   (a) the fifth term,   (b) the fiftieth term.

(a) It is simple to count up

$$u_2 = u_1 + 7 = 5 + 7 = 12, \quad u_3 = u_2 + 7 = 12 + 7 = 19,$$
$$u_4 = u_3 + 7 = 19 + 7 = 26, \quad u_5 = u_4 + 7 = 26 + 7 = 33.$$

The fifth term of the sequence is 33.

(b) You certainly wouldn't want to carry on as in part (a) until you reach u_{50}. It is simpler to note that, in going from the first term to the fiftieth, you have to add 7 on 49 times. So

$$u_{50} = u_1 + 49 \times 7 = 5 + 343 = 348.$$

The fiftieth term of the sequence is 348.

The method used in part (b) of Example 2.4.1 can be applied to any sequence with first term a and common difference d to find a formula for u_n, the nth term. In going from the first term to the nth term you have to add the step d on $(n-1)$ times. Since the first term is a, the nth term is

$u_n = a + (n-1)d.$

> An arithmetic sequence with first term a and common difference d is defined inductively by
>
> $$u_1 = a, \quad u_n = u_{n-1} + d.$$
>
> The nth term of the sequence is given by
>
> $$u_n = a + (n-1)d.$$

Example 2.4.2

The 10th term of the sequence (b) at the beginning of this section is also a term of the sequence (c). Which term is it?

For the sequence (b), $a = 2$ and $d = 3$, so the 10th term is

$$2 + (10 - 1) \times 3 = 2 + 27 = 29.$$

For the sequence (c), $a = 99$ and $d = -2$, so the nth term is

$$99 + (n - 1) \times (-2) = 99 - 2n + 2$$
$$= 101 - 2n.$$

This has to equal 29, so

$$101 - 2n = 29,$$

giving $n = 36$.

The 10th term of sequence (b) is the 36th term of sequence (c).

Example 2.4.3

The 12th term of an arithmetic sequence is 23 and the 19th term is 65. Find the first term and the common difference.

You can either reason this out arithmetically or use algebra, whichever you prefer.

Method 1 In getting from the 12th term to the 19th you take 7 steps of the common difference. In doing this the terms increase by $65 - 23$, which is 42. So each step is of amount $42 \div 7$, which is 6.

Therefore, in getting from the first term to the 12th the terms increase by 11 steps of 6, a total increase of 66. So the first term is $23 - 66 = -43$.

Method 2   Let the first term be a and the common difference d. Then, using the formula for the nth term,

$$a + (12 - 1)d = 23 \quad \text{and} \quad a + (19 - 1)d = 65.$$

So a and d can be found from the simultaneous equations

$$a + 11d = 23,$$
$$a + 18d = 65.$$

Subtracting the first equation from the second,

$$7d = 42,$$

which gives $d = 6$. Substituting this in the first equation gives

$$a + 11 \times 6 = 23,$$

so $a = -43$.

The first term is -43 and the common difference is 6.

Example 2.4.4

A person who usually eats 600 grams of bread a day tries to lose weight by reducing his consumption by 15 grams each day. After how many days will his consumption be less than 200 grams?

After 1, 2, 3, ... days his consumption (in grams) will be 585, 570, 555, ... This is an arithmetic sequence with first term $a = 585$ and common difference $d = -15$. Using the formula, his consumption on the nth day will be

$$585 - (n - 1) \times (-15) = 585 - 15\,(n - 1)$$
$$= 600 - 15n.$$

The questions asks for the smallest value of n for which this is less than 200. This is found by solving the inequality

$$600 - 15n < 200,$$

which gives

$$-15n < 200 - 600$$
$$= -400.$$

Dividing both sides by -15, remembering to change the direction of the inequality,

$$n > \frac{-400}{-15} = 26\tfrac{2}{3}.$$

The smallest integer value for n for which this is true is 27.

He will get his consumption down below 200 grams after 27 days.

2.5 Finding the sum of arithmetic series

Example 2.5.1

Sarah would like to give a sum of money to a charity each year for 10 years. She decides to give $100 in the first year, and to increase her contribution by $20 each year. How much does she give in the last year, and how much does the charity receive from her altogether?

Although she makes 10 contributions, there are only 9 increases. So in the last year she gives $\$(100 + 9 \times 20) = \$280$.

If the total amount the charity receives is $\$S$, then

$$S = 100 + 120 + 140 + ... + 240 + 260 + 280.$$

With only 10 numbers it is easy enough to add these up, but you can also find the sum by a method similar to that used in Section 2.3 to find a formula for t_n. If you add up the numbers in reverse order, you get

$$S = 280 + 260 + 240 + ... + 140 + 120 + 100.$$

Adding the two equations then gives

$$2S = 380 + 380 + 380 + ... + 380 + 380 + 380,$$

where the number 380 occurs 10 times. So

$$2S = 380 \times 10 = 3800, \text{ giving } S = 1900.$$

Over the 10 years the charity receives $1900.

This calculation can be illustrated with diagrams similar to Figs. 2.2 and 2.3. Sarah's contributions are shown by Fig. 2.4, with the first year in the top row. (Each cross is worth $20.) In Fig. 2.5 a second copy, with noughts instead of crosses, is put alongside it, but turned upside down. There are then 10 rows, each with 19 crosses or noughts and worth $380.

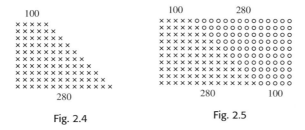

Fig. 2.4   Fig. 2.5

Two features of Example 2.5.1 are typical of arithmetic sequences.

• They usually only continue for a finite number of terms.

• It is often interesting to know the sum of all the terms. In this case, it is usual to describe the sequence as a **series**.

In Example 2.5.1, the annual contributions

$$100, 120, 140, \dots , 240, 260, 280$$

form an arithmetic sequence, but if they are added as

$$100 + 120 + 140 + \dots + 240 + 260 + 280$$

they become an **arithmetic series**.

You can use a method similar to that in Example 2.5.1 to find a formula for the sum of any arithmetic series with first term a and common difference d.

Suppose that the general arithmetic sequence

$$a, a + d, a + 2d, a + 3d, \dots$$

has n terms in all. Denote the last term, u_n, by l. Then you know that

$$l = a + (n - 1)d.$$

From this equation you can calculate any one of the four quantities a, l, n, d if you know the other three.

Let S be the sum of the arithmetic series formed by adding these terms. Then it is possible to find a formula for S in terms of a, n and either d or l.

Method 1   This generalises the argument used in Example 2.5.1.

If the last term is l, the last but one term is $l - d$, and the term before that is $l - 2d$. So the series can be written as

$$S = \quad a \quad + (a + d) + (a + 2d) + \dots + (l - 2d) + (l - d) + l.$$

Turning this back to front,

$$S = \quad l \quad + (l - d) + (l - 2d) + \dots + (a + 2d) + (a + d) + a.$$

Adding these,

$$2S = (a + l) + (a + l) + (a + l) + \dots + (a + l) + (a + l) + (a + l),$$

where the bracket $(a + l)$ occurs n times. So

$$2S = n(a + l), \text{ which gives } S = \tfrac{1}{2}n(a + l).$$

Method 2   This uses the formula for triangle numbers found in Section 2.3.

In the series

$$S = a + (a + d) + (a + 2d) + \dots + (a + (n - 1)d)$$

you can collect separately the terms involving a and those involving d:

$$S = (a + a + \dots + a) + (1 + 2 + 3 + \dots + (n - 1))d.$$

In the first bracket a occurs n times. The second bracket is the sum of the positive integers from 1 to $n - 1$, or t_{n-1}; using the formula $t_n = \frac{1}{2}n(n+1)$ with n replaced by $n - 1$ gives this sum as

$$t_{n-1} = \frac{1}{2}(n-1)\left((n-1)+1\right)$$
$$= \frac{1}{2}(n-1)n.$$

Therefore

$$S = na + \frac{1}{2}(n-1)nd$$
$$= \frac{1}{2}n(2a + (n-1)d).$$

Since $l = a + (n-1)d$, this is the same answer as that given by Method 1.

Here is a summary of the results about arithmetic series.

> An arithmetic series of n terms with first term a and common difference d has nth term
>
> $$l = a + (n-1)d$$
>
> and sum
>
> $$S = \frac{1}{2}n(a+l) = \frac{1}{2}n(2a + (n-1)d).$$

Example 2.5.2
Find a formula for the nth term and the sum of n terms for the arithmetic sequence 1, 4, 7, 10, 13, ...

In this sequence $a = 1$ and $d = 3$.

Using the formulae in the blue box,

the nth term is $1 + (n-1) \times 3 = 3n - 2$,
the sum of n terms is $\frac{1}{2}n(2 \times 1 + (n-1) \times 3) = \frac{1}{2}n(2 + 3n - 3) = \frac{1}{2}n(3n - 1)$.

> It is worth checking the sum by putting n equal to a small number, say 3. In that case you can check whether the answer gives $1 + 4 + 7 = 12$.

Example 2.5.3
The first two terms of an arithmetic sequence are 4 and 2. The nth term is -36. Find the number of terms.

For this sequence, $a = 4$ and $d = -2$.

Using the formula for the nth term, $l = a + (n-1)d$,

$$-36 = 4 + (n-1) \times (-2) = 4 - 2n + 2$$
$$-36 = 6 - 2n$$
$$n = 21.$$

The sequence has 21 terms.

Example 2.5.4

Find the sum of the first n odd positive integers.

> **Method 1**   The odd numbers 1, 3, 5, ... form an arithmetic series with first term $a = 1$ and common difference $d = 2$. So
>
> $$\begin{aligned} S &= \tfrac{1}{2}n(2a + (n-1)\,d) \\ &= \tfrac{1}{2}n(2 + (n-1) \times 2) \\ &= \tfrac{1}{2}n(2n) = n^2. \end{aligned}$$

> **Method 2**   Take the positive integers from 1 to $2n$, and remove the n even numbers 2, 4, 6, ... , $2n$. You are left with the first n odd numbers.

To find the sum of the numbers from 1 to $2n$, use the formula $t_n = \tfrac{1}{2}n(n+1)$ with n replaced by $2n$; that is,

$$\begin{aligned} t_{2n} &= \tfrac{1}{2}(2n)(2n+1) \\ &= n(2n+1). \end{aligned}$$

The sum of the n even numbers is

$$\begin{aligned} 2 + 4 + 6 + \ldots + 2n &= 2(1 + 2 + 3 + \ldots + n) \\ &= 2t_n \\ &= n(n+1). \end{aligned}$$

So the sum of the first n odd numbers is

$$\begin{aligned} n(2n+1) - n(n+1) &= n((2n+1) - (n+1)) \\ &= n(n) \\ &= n^2. \end{aligned}$$

> **Method 3**   Figure 2.6 shows a square of n rows with n crosses in each row (drawn for $n = 7$).

You can count the crosses in the square by adding the numbers in the 'channels' between the dotted L-shaped lines, which gives

$$n^2 = 1 + 3 + 5 + \ldots \text{ (to } n \text{ terms)}.$$

Fig. 2.6

Example 2.5.5

A student reading a 426-page book finds that he reads faster as he gets into the subject. He reads 19 pages on the first day, and his rate of reading then goes up by 3 pages each day. How long does he take to finish the book?

> You are given that $a = 19$ and $d = 3$. The formula $S = \tfrac{1}{2}n(2a + (n-1)d)$ gives
>
> $$\begin{aligned} S &= \tfrac{1}{2}n(38 + (n-1) \times 3) \\ &= \tfrac{1}{2}n(3n + 35). \end{aligned}$$

You may recognise that, when you put S equal to 426, you get a quadratic equation. If so, you could rearrange it in the usual form as $3n^2 + 35n - 852 = 0$ and then solve it by using the standard formula (see Section 11.4).

But if not, you can use your calculator to display a table of values of the sequence $u_n = \frac{1}{2}n(3n + 35)$ for different values of n. Scroll through the table until you reach the entries

n	u_n
...	...
10	325
11	374
12	426
13	481
...	...

You can see that $u_n = 426$ when $n = 12$.

The student takes 12 days to finish the book.

In this section the letters a, l and S have been used to keep the algebra simple. But since a is the first term and l is the last, a could have been written as u_1 and l as u_n. It is also quite common to use S_n (rather than simply S) for the sum of n terms. The formulae for an arithmetic series would then take the form:

$$u_n = u_1 + (n - 1)d,$$
$$S_n = \tfrac{1}{2}n(u_1 + u_n) = \tfrac{1}{2}n(2u_1 + (n - 1)d).$$

Your calculator also has a procedure for finding the sum of the terms of a sequence. If you key in the formula for the nth term, and the first and last values of n for which you want to add up the terms, the calculator will give the sum. You will find detailed instructions in the calculator manual.

The calculator procedure is not restricted to arithmetic sequences; it works for any sequence, provided that you know a formula for u_n. But of course you can only use it for sequences with numerical terms.

Exercise 2C

1 Which of the following sequences are the first four terms of an arithmetic sequence? For those that are, write down the value of the common difference.

(a) 7   10   13   16   ...

(b) 3   5   9   15   ...

(c) 1   0.1   0.01   0.001   ...

(d) 4   2   0 -2 ...

(e) 2 -3 4 -5 ...

(f) $p - 2q$ $p - q$ p $p + q$ ...

(g) $\frac{1}{2}a$ $\frac{1}{3}a$ $\frac{1}{4}a$ $\frac{1}{5}a$ ...

(h) x $2x$ $3x$ $4x$ ...

2 Write down the sixth term, and an expression for the nth term, of the arithmetic sequences which begin as follows.

(a) 2   4   6   ...

(b) 17   20   23   ...

(c) 5   2 -1 ...

(d) 1.3   1.7   2.1   ...

(e) 1 $1\frac{1}{2}$ 2   ...

(f) 73   67   61   ...

(g) x $x + 2$ $x + 4$ ...

(h) $1 - x$ 1 $1 + x$ ...

3 In the following arithmetic progressions, the first three terms and the last term are given. Find the number of terms.

(a) 4   5   6   ...   17

(b) 3   9   15   ...   525

(c) 8   2 -4 ... -202

(d) $2\frac{1}{8}$ $3\frac{1}{4}$ $4\frac{3}{8}$ ... $13\frac{3}{8}$

4 Find the sum of the given number of terms of the following arithmetic series.

(a) $2 + 5 + 8 + ...$ (20 terms)

(b) $4 + 11 + 18 + ...$ (15 terms)

(c) $8 + 5 + 2 + ...$ (12 terms)

(d) $\frac{1}{2} + 1 + 1\frac{1}{2} + ...$ (58 terms)

(e) $7 + 3 + (-1) + ...$ (25 terms)

(f) $1 + 3 + 5 + ...$ (999 terms)

Use your calculator to check your answers.

5 Find the number of terms and the sum of each of the following arithmetic series.

(a) $5 + 7 + 9 + ... + 111$

(b) $8 + 12 + 16 + ... + 84$

(c) $7 + 13 + 19 + ... + 277$

(d) $8 + 5 + 2 + ... + (-73)$

(e) $-14 - 10 - 6 - ... + 94$

(f) $157 + 160 + 163 + ... + 529$

(g) $10 + 20 + 30 + ... + 10\,000$

(h) $1.8 + 1.2 + 0.6 + ... + (-34.2)$

6 In each of the following arithmetic sequences you are given two terms. Find the first term and the common difference.

(a) 4th term $= 15$,   9th term $= 35$

(b) 3rd term $= 12$,   10th term $= 47$

(c) 8th term $= 3.5$,   13th term $= 5.0$

(d) 5th term $= 2$,   11th term $= -13$

(e) 12th term $= -8$,   20th term $= -32$

(f) 3rd term $= -3$,   7th term $= 5$

7 Find how many terms of the given arithmetic series must be taken to reach the given sum.

(a) $3 + 7 + 11 + ...,$ sum $= 820$

(b) $8 + 9 + 10 + ...,$ sum $= 162$

(c) $20 + 23 + 26 + ...,$ sum $= 680$

8 A squirrel is collecting nuts. It collects 5 nuts on the first day of the month, 8 nuts on the second, 11 on the third and so on in arithmetic progression.

(a) How many nuts will it collect on the 20th day?

(b) After how many days will it have collected more than 1000 nuts?

9 Kulsum is given an interest-free loan to buy a car. She repays the loan in unequal monthly instalments; these start at $30 in the first month and increase by $2 each month after that. She makes 24 payments.

(a) Find the amount of her final payment.

(b) Find the amount of her loan.

10 (a) Find the sum of the positive integers from 1 to 100 inclusive.

(b) Find the sum of the positive integers from 101 to 200 inclusive.

(c) Find and simplify an expression for the sum of the positive integers from $n + 1$ to $2n$ inclusive.

11 An employee started work on 1 January 2000 on an annual salary of $30 000. His pay scale will give him an increase of $800 per annum on the first of January until 1 January 2015 inclusive. He remains on this salary until he retires on 31 December 2040. How much will he earn during his working life?

2.6 Sigma notation

This section is about a notation for sums of sequences. You know that u_1, u_2, ... is called a sequence, and if you need to add the terms to get $u_1 + u_2 + ... + u_n$, the sequence changes its name and is called a series.

The first thing you need is a way of referring to any of the n terms of the series. So far you have used u_n to stand for a term of a sequence, where n can be any of the positive integers 1, 2, 3, ... But if you write the series as $u_1 + u_2 + ... + u_n$, n stands for the number of terms of the series, and u_n is the last term. You must therefore find some other way of referring to *any* term of the series. This can be done by using some different letter for the suffix, such as i. Then u_i is called the **general term** of the series, and i can take any of the values 1, 2, 3, ... , n.

The sum $u_1 + u_2 + ... + u_n$ is then written as

$$\sum_{i=1}^{n} u_i.$$

This means 'the sum of the terms of the sequence u_i from $i = 1$ to $i = n$'.

This is called **sigma notation**. It is illustrated in more detail in Fig. 2.7. The letter sigma, $\sum$, is the Greek capital letter S.

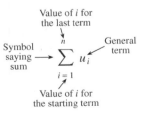

Fig. 2.7

- The symbol $\sum$ is an instruction to add.
- Following the $\sum$ symbol is an expression for the general term of a series.
- Below the $\sum$ symbol is the value of i corresponding to the starting term.
- Above the $\sum$ symbol is the value of i corresponding to the last term.

The expression $\sum_{i=1}^{n} u_i$ is read as 'sigma from 1 to n of u_i'.

Although the notation is most often used with a starting term of u_1 (or sometimes u_0), you occasionally want to use it with other starting terms. For example, $\sum_{i=3}^{6} u_i$ stands for $u_3 + u_4 + u_5 + u_6$.

Example 2.6.1

Express as addition sums (a) $\sum_{i=1}^{3} i$, (b) $\sum_{i=4}^{7} (2i - 1)$, (c) $\sum_{i=0}^{4} 1$, (d) $\sum_{i=3}^{8} i^2$.

(a) The ith term is i and, as the first term has $i = 1$, the first term is 1. For the second term, put $i = 2$, so the second term is 2. The last term is the term for which $i = 3$, so the last term is 3. The $\sum$ symbol means add, so

$$\sum_{i=1}^{3} i = 1 + 2 + 3.$$

(b) The first term is $(2 \times 4 - 1) = 7$, corresponding to $i = 4$. The second term, corresponding to $i = 5$, is $(2 \times 5 - 1) = 9$. Continuing in this way,

$$\sum_{i=4}^{7} (2i - 1) = 7 + 9 + 11 + 13.$$

(c) In this case, the ith term is 1, independent of the value of i. That is, $u_0 = u_1 = u_2 = u_3 = u_4 = 1$, so

$$\sum_{i=0}^{4} 1 = 1 + 1 + 1 + 1 + 1.$$

(d) The first term is 3^2, corresponding to $i = 3$. The second term, corresponding to $i = 4$, is 4^2. Continuing in this way,

$$\sum_{i=3}^{8} i^2 = 3^2 + 4^2 + 5^2 + 6^2 + 7^2 + 8^2.$$

Notice that, in part (c), there are 5 terms and in part (d) there are 6 terms. In general the number of terms in the series $\sum_{i=m}^{n} u_i$ is $n - m + 1$.

There is more than one way to describe a series using sigma notation. For example,

$$\sum_{i=0}^{2} (i + 1) = (0 + 1) + (1 + 1) + (2 + 1) = 1 + 2 + 3,$$

which is the same as $\sum_{i=1}^{3} i$ in Example 2.6.1(a).

Example 2.6.2

Express each of the following sums in $\sum$ notation.

(a) $2 + 4 + 6 + 8 + 10$ (b) $\dfrac{1}{2} + \dfrac{1}{3} + \dfrac{1}{4} + \dfrac{1}{5}$ (c) $6^3 + 7^3 + 8^3$

(a) The general term of this sequence is $2i$. The first term corresponds to $i = 1$, and the last to $i = 5$. So the sum can be written as $\displaystyle\sum_{i=1}^{5} 2i$.

(b) The general term of this sequence is $\dfrac{1}{i+1}$. The first term corresponds to $i = 1$, and the last to $i = 4$. So the sum can be written as $\displaystyle\sum_{i=1}^{4} \dfrac{1}{i+1}$.

(c) The general term of this sequence is i^3. The first term corresponds to $i = 6$, and the last to $i = 8$. So the sum can be written as $\displaystyle\sum_{i=6}^{8} i^3$.

These answers are not unique; they are not the only answers possible. In part (b), for example, you could easily argue that the general term is $\dfrac{1}{i}$, with the first term corresponding to $i = 2$ and the last to $i = 5$. So the sum can be written $\displaystyle\sum_{i=2}^{5} \dfrac{1}{i}$.

Sometimes you can break up a complicated series into simpler series. For example, you can write the sum $\displaystyle\sum_{i=1}^{200} (2i + 1)$ in the form

$$\sum_{i=1}^{200} (2i + 1) = (2 \times 1 + 1) + (2 \times 2 + 1) + (2 \times 3 + 1) + ... + (2 \times 200 + 1)$$

$$= (2 \times 1 + 2 \times 2 + 2 \times 3 + ... + 2 \times 200) + \overbrace{1 + 1 + 1 + ... + 1}^{200 \text{ of these}}$$

$$= 2 \times (1 + 2 + 3 + ... + 200) + \overbrace{1 + 1 + 1 + ... + 1}^{200 \text{ of these}}$$

$$= 2\sum_{i=1}^{200} i + \sum_{i=1}^{200} 1.$$

You can now go on and sum the series, using the formula for the nth triangle number in Section 2.3, since the sum $\displaystyle\sum_{i=1}^{200} i$ is the same as t_{200}. Using $t_n = \frac{1}{2}n(n+1)$,

$$t_{200} = \tfrac{1}{2} \times 200 \times 201 = 20\,100.$$

Therefore

$$\sum_{i=1}^{200} (2i + 1) = 2\sum_{i=1}^{200} i + \sum_{i=1}^{200} 1$$

$$= 2 \times 20\,100 + 200 = 40\,400.$$

In the example above, two important rules about sigma notation were used.

The first rule is called the **addition rule** for sums:

$$\sum_{i=1}^{n}(u_i + v_i) = (u_1 + v_1) + (u_2 + v_2) + ... + (u_n + v_n)$$

$$= (u_1 + u_2 + ... + u_n) + (v_1 + v_2 + ... + v_n)$$

$$= \sum_{i=1}^{n} u_i + \sum_{i=1}^{n} v_i.$$

The second rule deals with the effect of multiplying each term by a constant k. It is called the **multiple rule** for sums:

$$\sum_{i=1}^{n}(ku_i) = (ku_1 + ku_2 + ... + ku_n)$$

$$= k(u_1 + u_2 + ... + u_n)$$

$$= k\sum_{i=1}^{n} u_i.$$

Addition rule $\sum_{i=1}^{n}(u_i + v_i) = \sum_{i=1}^{n} u_i + \sum_{i=1}^{n} v_i.$

Multiple rule   For any number k, $\sum_{i=1}^{n}(ku_i) = k\sum_{i=1}^{n} u_i.$

Example 2.6.3

Find $\sum_{1=1}^{4}(2i + 2^i)$.

Using the addition rule,

$$\sum_{1=1}^{4}(2i + 2^i) = \sum_{i=1}^{4} 2i + \sum_{i=1}^{4} 2^i$$

$$= (2 + 4 + 6 + 8) + (2 + 4 + 8 + 16)$$

$$= 20 + 30 = 50.$$

Another important fact to notice about sigma notation is that the final result is nothing to do with i. For example,

$$\sum_{i=0}^{2}(3 + 2i + i^2) = 3 + (3 + 2 \times 1 + 1^2) + (3 + 2 \times 2 + 2^2)$$

$$= 3 + 6 + 11 = 20.$$

So it doesn't matter what letter you use. Thus $\sum_{i=0}^{2}(3 + 2i + i^2)$ is precisely the same sum as $\sum_{r=0}^{2}(3 + 2r + r^2)$. For this reason i is called a **dummy variable**.

When there is no possibility of confusion, the '$i =$' below the sigma symbol is sometimes omitted, especially in statistics. Thus $\sum_{i=0}^{2}(3 + 2i + i^2)$ can be written as $\sum_{0}^{2}(3 + 2i + i^2)$. However, this will not be done in this book.

2.7   Sequences with alternating signs

The general term of a sequence such as

$$-1, \quad 2, \quad -3, \quad 4, \quad \dots$$

can be awkward to write down.

It is clear that the ith term involves i, but how do you deal with the alternating sign?

The method is to multiply by $(-1)^i$ or $(-1)^{i+1}$.

The sequence $(-1)^i$ for $i = 1, 2, 3, 4, \dots$ is

$$-1, \quad 1, \quad -1, \quad 1, \quad \dots,$$

while the sequence $(-1)^{i+1}$ for $i = 1, 2, 3, 4, \dots$ is

$$1, \quad -1, \quad 1, \quad -1, \quad \dots.$$

This suggests that the general term of the sequence $-1, \quad 2, \quad -3, \quad 4, \quad \dots$ is $(-1)^i\, i$.

The general term of the sequence $1, \quad -2, \quad 3, \quad -4, \quad \dots$ is $(-1)^{i+1}\, i$.

It is important to check mentally that you have the correct alternating sign term $(-1)^i$ or $(-1)^{i+1}$.

Example 2.7.1

Write down the first four terms of the sequences with general terms

(a) $(-1)^i\, 2^i$,   (b) $(-1)^{i+1}\,(3i + 2)$.

(a) The first four terms are $(-1)^1\, 2^1 = -2$, $(-1)^2\, 2^2 = 4$, $(-1)^3\, 2^3 = -8$ and $(-1)^4\, 2^4 = 16$.

(b) The first four terms are $(-1)^{1+1}\,(3 \times 1 + 2) = 5$, $(-1)^{2+1}\,(3 \times 2 + 2) = -8$, $(-1)^{3+1}\,(3 \times 3 + 2) = 11$ and $(-1)^{4+1}\,(3 \times 4 + 2) = -14$.

Example 2.7.2

Write down the general terms of the sequences

(a) $\dfrac{1}{1}, \quad -\dfrac{1}{2}, \quad \dfrac{1}{3}, \quad -\dfrac{1}{4}, \quad \dots,$ (b) $-1, \quad 4, \quad -9, \quad 16, \quad \dots.$

(a) The fact that the first term is positive should alert you to the need to use $(-1)^{i+1}$ rather than $(-1)^i$.

The general term is $(-1)^{i+1}\, \dfrac{1}{i}$.

(b) The general term is $(-1)^i\, i^2$.

Exercise 2D

1 Express each of the following as addition sums.

(a) $\sum_{i=2}^{3} i$

(b) $\sum_{i=3}^{5} 2$

(c) $\sum_{i=1}^{4} \frac{1}{i}$

(d) $\sum_{i=1}^{4} i^2$

(e) $\sum_{i=2}^{5} (2i + 1)$

(f) $\sum_{i=0}^{2} u_i$

2 Write each of the following sums using sigma notation. (Note that your answers could differ from those given.)

(a) $2 + 3 + 4$

(b) $1 + 4 + 9 + 16$

(c) $3^3 + 4^3 + 5^3 + 6^3 + 7^3$

(d) $\frac{1}{2} + \frac{1}{4} + \frac{1}{6}$

(e) $3 + 5 + 7 + 9$

(f) $2 + 5 + 8 + 11 + 14$

3 (a) Use your calculator to check that

$$\sum_{i=1}^{20} i^2 = 2870, \qquad \sum_{i=1}^{20} i^3 = 44\,100, \qquad \sum_{i=1}^{20} i^4 = 722\,666.$$

(b) Then use the addition and multiple rules to calculate

$$\sum_{i=1}^{20} i^2 (i - 1), \qquad \sum_{i=1}^{20} i^2 (i - 1)^2, \qquad \sum_{i=1}^{20} (i^2 - 1)^2.$$

(c) Use your calculator to check your answers to part (b).

4 Say whether each of the following statements is true or false. Be prepared to justify your answer.

(a) $\sum_{i=1}^{2n} i^3 = \sum_{i=0}^{2n-1} (i + 1)^3$

(b) $\sum_{i=1}^{n} 1 = \frac{1}{2} n (n + 1)$

(c) $\sum_{i=1}^{2n} i^3 = \sum_{i=0}^{2n} i^3$

(d) $\sum_{i=1}^{n} (2 + i^2) = 2 + \sum_{i=1}^{n} i^2$

5 Calculate the value of each of the following sums.

(a) $\sum_{i=0}^{2} (-1)^i\, i$

(b) $\sum_{i=0}^{2} (-1)^{i-1}\, i$

(c) $\sum_{i=0}^{2} (-1)^{i+1}\, i$

(d) $\sum_{i=1}^{6} (-1)^i\, i^2$

(e) $\sum_{i=3}^{5} \frac{(-1)^{i+1}}{i}$

(f) $\sum_{i=3}^{5} (-1)^i$

6 Write each of the following in sigma notation.

(a) $1 - 2 + 3 - 4 + \ldots + 101$

(b) $-2^2 + 4^2 - 6^2 + \ldots - 50^2$

(c) $1 - \frac{1}{2} + \frac{1}{3} - \ldots + \frac{1}{49}$

7 It is shown in Section 2.5 that the sum of the arithmetic series

$$a + (a + d) + (a + 2d) + \ldots + (a + (n - 1)\, d) \quad \text{is} \quad \frac{1}{2} n (2a + (n - 1)\, d).$$

Use sigma notation to write this statement more concisely.

3 Permutations and combinations

This chapter is about the number of ways in which you can arrange a set of objects in order, and the number of ways in which you can make a selection from a set of objects. When you have completed it, you should

- know what a permutation is, and be able to calculate how many there are
- know the meaning and simple properties of $n!$
- know what a combination is, and be able to calculate how many there are.

3.1 The multiplication principle

Look at a street map of a town. To help you to find a street quickly, the page is probably split into rectangles by lines parallel to the sides. The strips between the vertical lines may be lettered from A on the left to H on the right, and the strips between the horizontal lines may be numbered from 1 at the bottom to 6 at the top. Each rectangle is identified by combining a letter with a number, such as C4. There are 8 possible letters and 6 possible numbers, and the total number of reference rectangles is $8 \times 6 = 48$.

This is an example of the multiplication principle. If you have a set of p elements and another set of q elements, then there are $p \times q$ ways of combining an element of the first set with an element of the second set.

3.2 Permutations

You have probably tried solving anagram puzzles. You are given a set of letters, and the problem is to arrange them to make a word.

Sometimes there is more than one solution. Suppose that you are given the letters **t**, **e** and **a**. These obviously make the word **tea**. But you might also be able to make words from other arrangements. The simplest way to find all the solutions is to make a list of all possible arrangements of the letters, and then see which you recognise as words.

You won't find it difficult to find six arrangements of these letters:

  tea **tae** **eta** **eat** **ate** **aet**

At least three of these are familiar words. (In a large dictionary you might find all six, if you count abbreviations.)

But how can you be sure that this list includes all the possible arrangements? Is there a systematic way of making the list which guarantees that you have included all the possibilities?

Imagine that you have three cards in your hand, each with one of the letters **t**, **e**, **a** written on it. You can then try to make words by laying the cards on the table side by side, one at a time.

In the first place you can put any one of the three cards. At this stage there are three possibilities:

  [t] **[e]** **[a]**

Once you have put this first card down, you have two more cards in your hand. For example, if you have put down the **t**, these are the **e** and the **a**. You can put down either of these in the second place. So there are now $3 \times 2 = 6$ possibilities:

[**t**] [**e**]   [**e**] [**t**]   [**a**] [**t**]
[**t**] [**a**]   [**e**] [**a**]   [**a**] [**e**]

Now there is only one card left in your hand, so you have no choice for the card in the third place. There are therefore $3 \times 2 \times 1 = 6$ possibilities altogether:

[**t**] [**e**] [**a**]   [**e**] [**t**] [**a**]   [**a**] [**t**] [**e**]
[**t**] [**a**] [**e**]   [**e**] [**a**] [**t**]   [**a**] [**e**] [**t**]

Now suppose that a fourth letter **m** is added. How many arrangements are there now?

If you have four cards in your hand, with **t**, **e**, **a** and **m** written on them, then you can put any of these in the first place, giving four possibilities:

[**t**]   [**e**]   [**a**]   [**m**]

Now there are three cards in your hand. For example, if you have already put down the **a**, these are **t**, **e** and **m**. You can put any of these in the second place. So there are now $4 \times 3 = 12$ possibilities:

[**t**] [**e**]   [**e**] [**t**]   [**a**] [**t**]   [**m**] [**t**]
[**t**] [**a**]   [**e**] [**a**]   [**a**] [**e**]   [**m**] [**e**]
[**t**] [**m**]   [**e**] [**m**]   [**a**] [**m**]   [**m**] [**a**]

You now have two cards left. For example, if you have already put down the **a** and the **m**, these are **t** and **e**. Either of these can go into the third place, giving $4 \times 3 \times 2 = 24$ possibilities:

[**t**] [**e**] [**a**] [**t**] [**e**] [**m**] [**e**] [**t**] [**a**] [**e**] [**t**] [**m**] [**a**] [**t**] [**e**] [**a**] [**t**] [**m**] [**m**] [**t**] [**e**] [**m**] [**t**] [**a**]
[**t**] [**a**] [**e**] [**t**] [**a**] [**m**] [**e**] [**a**] [**t**] [**e**] [**a**] [**m**] [**a**] [**e**] [**t**] [**a**] [**e**] [**m**] [**m**] [**e**] [**t**] [**m**] [**e**] [**a**]
[**t**] [**m**] [**e**] [**t**] [**m**] [**a**] [**e**] [**m**] [**t**] [**e**] [**m**] [**a**] [**a**] [**m**] [**t**] [**a**] [**m**] [**e**] [**m**] [**a**] [**t**] [**m**] [**a**] [**e**]

You are left with just one card, and one place to put it in, so you now have no choice. The total number of possibilities is therefore $4 \times 3 \times 2 \times 1 = 24$.

By reasoning in this way, you can be sure that you have included all the possible arrangements, and also that there are no repetitions. The complete list of arrangements of the letters **t**, **e**, **a** and **m** can now be written down:

team   tema   etam   etma   atem   atme   mtea   mtae
taem   tame   eatm   eamt   aetm   aemt   meta   meat
tmea   tmae   emta   emat   amte   amet   mate   maet

There is nothing special about using letters. The same argument can be used with any set of four objects.

Example 3.2.1

How many four-digit numbers can you make up using each of the digits 2, 3, 6 and 7 just once? What property do all these numbers have in common?

> Any of the four digits can be put in the 'thousands' place. Once you have done this, you have a choice of three digits to put in the 'hundreds' place. You then have a choice of two digits to put in the 'tens' place. When you have made these three choices, the remaining digit has to go in the 'units' place. So the total number of four-digit numbers you can make up is $4 \times 3 \times 2 \times 1 = 24$.
>
> The sum of the four digits is $2 + 3 + 6 + 7 = 18$, which is divisible by 9. So, whichever arrangement of the digits you choose, a number made from these digits is divisible by 9.

An arrangement in order of a set of objects – letters, digits, names, football teams, or anything you like so long as the objects can be distinguished from each other – is called a **permutation** of the set. You have seen that with three objects the number of possible permutations is $3 \times 2 \times 1 = 6$, and with four objects the number is $4 \times 3 \times 2 \times 1 = 24$.

Obviously you could use the same argument with any number of objects. If there are n objects, then you could put any of them in the first place. This leaves a choice of $n - 1$ to put in the second place, $n - 2$ in the third place, and so on. So you can summarise these calculations in a general rule:

> The number of permutations of a set of n distinct objects is
> $$n \times (n - 1) \times (n - 2) \times \ldots \times 3 \times 2 \times 1.$$

Example 3.2.2

Eight rugby teams compete in a league. In how many different orders could they finish up at the end of the season?

> The number of permutations of the eight teams is $8 \times 7 \times 6 \times 5 \times 4 \times 3 \times 2 \times 1$, which is 40 320.

Sometimes you want to find the number of arrangements which satisfy some extra condition.

Example 3.2.3

How many arrangements are there of the letters **a**, **b**, **c**, **d**, **e** in which the first place is occupied by a consonant?

> The only letters which can be put in the first place are **b**, **c** or **d**, so you have a choice of three letters for the first place.
>
> Once you have filled this place, any of the remaining four letters can be put in the second place. You will then have three letters left to put in the third place, and then two to put in the fourth place. There is just one letter left for the fifth place.
>
> So the total number of arrangements in which the first place is occupied by a consonant is $3 \times 4 \times 3 \times 2 \times 1 = 72$.

3.3   Factorial numbers

The product of the first n positive integers, $n \times (n-1) \times (n-2) \times \ldots \times 3 \times 2 \times 1$, often turns up in mathematical formulae. It is given a special name, **factorial n**, and a special symbol, $n!$.

> If n is a positive integer,
> $$n! = n \times (n-1) \times (n-2) \times \ldots \times 3 \times 2 \times 1.$$

It is easy to make a table of values of $n!$ for small values of n. A good way of doing this is to notice that $(n-1)!$, the product of the first $n-1$ positive integers, is

$$(n-1)! = (n-1) \times (n-2) \times \ldots \times 3 \times 2 \times 1.$$

If you compare this with the expression for $n!$ in the blue box, you will notice that

$$n! = n \times (n-1)!.$$

Obviously $1!$ is simply 1. (One object can be arranged in order in only one way!) You can then use this equation to calculate the values of $n!$ for $n = 2, 3, \ldots$ in turn.

$$2! = 2 \times 1! = 2$$
$$3! = 3 \times 2! = 3 \times 2 = 6$$
$$4! = 4 \times 3! = 4 \times 6 = 24$$
$$5! = 5 \times 4! = 5 \times 24 = 120$$
$$6! = 6 \times 5! = 6 \times 120 = 720$$
$$7! = 7 \times 6! = 7 \times 720 = 5040$$

This becomes laborious for large values of n, and then you will want to use a calculator. The calculator manual will explain how to do this. But you will guess from the table of values above that $n!$ will soon become too large for the calculator to display exactly. It will then only give an approximate value in standard index form. For example, a calculator will give $20!$ as

$$2.432\,902\,008 \times 10^{18}$$

rather than its exact value of

$$2\,432\,902\,008\,176\,640\,000.$$

Notice that factorial numbers are another example of a sequence, and you can use the equation $n! = n \times (n-1)!$ to give an inductive definition of $n!$.

> The factorial sequence is defined by
> $$1! = 1 \text{ and } n! = n \times (n-1)! \text{ for } n = 2, 3, 4, \ldots .$$

Example 3.3.1

Calculate   (a) $\dfrac{9!}{7!}$,   (b) $\dfrac{45!}{41!}$.

(a) Since $9! = 9 \times 8!$ and $8! = 8 \times 7!$, it follows that $9! = 9 \times 8 \times 7!$.

So $\dfrac{9!}{7!} = \dfrac{9 \times 8 \times 7!}{7!} = 9 \times 8 = 72.$

(b) Using a similar method,

$$\frac{45!}{41!} = \frac{45 \times 44 \times 43 \times 42 \times 41!}{41!} = 45 \times 44 \times 43 \times 42 = 3\,575\,880.$$

Example 3.3.2

Write the product $24 \times 23 \times 22$ in terms of factorials.

You can do this by reversing the process in Example 3.3.1. Since

$$24! = 24 \times 23 \times 22 \times 21!,$$

it follows that

$$24 \times 23 \times 22 = \frac{24!}{21!}.$$

The method used in Example 3.3.2 is important, and it can be generalised. Suppose that you have a product of r positive integers, starting with n and going down one at a time. The numbers could be written as $n - 0$, $n - 1$, $n - 2$, and so on, so the rth number will be $n - (r - 1)$, or $n - r + 1$. By using

$$n! = n \times (n - 1)!,$$
$$(n - 1)! = (n - 1) \times (n - 2)!,$$
$$(n - 2)! = (n - 2) \times (n - 3)!, \text{ and so on,}$$

finishing with

$$(n - r + 1)! = (n - r + 1) \times (n - r)!,$$

it follows that

$$n! = n \times (n - 1) \times (n - 2) \times \ldots \times (n - r + 1) \times (n - r)!.$$

You can rewrite this to give the following important result.

> If n and r are positive integers with $n > r$,
> $$n \times (n - 1) \times (n - 2) \times \ldots \times (n - r + 1) = \frac{n!}{(n - r)!}.$$

Exercise 3A

1 A child is dressing a doll. The doll has a choice of four pairs of shoes, five skirts and six tops. In how many different ways can the doll be dressed?

2 Calculate the number of arrangements of the letters in the word NUMBER.

3 Eight sprinters draw lots to decide which lanes they will run in. How many different ways are there of arranging the sprinters in lanes?

4 A team in a 5-a-side hockey tournament has its photograph taken standing in line. In how many different ways can they be arranged? How many arrangements are there with the captain standing in the middle?

5 How many 5-digit numbers can you make using each of the digits 1, 3, 5, 7, 9 once only? How many of these numbers are less than 50 000?

6 Use a calculator to find the approximate value of 50!.

7 Without using a calculator, find the values of
   (a) $\dfrac{26!}{25!}$,
   (b) $\dfrac{30!}{27!}$.

8 Write the product $20 \times 19 \times 18 \times 17$ in terms of factorials.

9 Simplify
   (a) $\dfrac{(n+1)!}{n!}$,
   (b) $\dfrac{(n+1)!}{(n-2)!}$.

3.4   Permutations with some objects left over

Suppose that in the Olympic Games eight runners compete in the final of the 5000 metre race. They might cross the finishing line in $8! = 40\,320$ different orders. But only three of the runners get medals. In how many different ways might the gold, silver and bronze medals be awarded?

The argument is like that in Section 3.2, but you only need to go as far as the third step.

Any of the eight runners could win the gold. When you know which runner this is, any of the remaining seven runners might win the silver. So the number of ways in which the gold and silver might be awarded is $8 \times 7 = 56$.

Whoever wins the gold and silver, there are then six runners, and any of these might win the bronze. So the number of ways in which all three medals might be awarded is $8 \times 7 \times 6 = 336$.

You can use a similar method whenever you have a set of objects and you want to arrange a certain number of them in order.

Example 3.4.1
A Scrabble player has seven tiles, each with a different letter on it. How many different possible arrangements are there of five of these seven letters?

> Imagine the player placing the tiles on a line of five squares on the board. Any of the seven tiles can be put on the first square. There are then six tiles left, any of which can be put on the second square. After that there are five tiles to put on the third square, four to put on the third square, and three to put on the fifth square. So the total number of possible five-letter arrangements is $7 \times 6 \times 5 \times 4 \times 3 = 2520$.

If you have n objects, and you want to make an arrangement of r of them, then you can put any of the n objects in the first place. There are then $(n-1)$ left to put in the second place, $(n-2)$ in the third, and so on. When you get to the last place, you have already used $(r-1)$ of the objects, so you have a choice of any of the remaining $(n-(r-1))$. The total number of possible arrangements is therefore

$$n \times (n-1) \times (n-2) \times \ldots \times (n-r+1).$$

You know from Section 3.3 that this product can be written as $\dfrac{n!}{(n-r)!}$.

> Given a set of n objects, the number of ways of arranging r of them in order is
>
> $$n \times (n-1) \times (n-2) \times \ldots \times (n-r+1) = \frac{n!}{(n-r)!}.$$

Example 3.4.2

In a raffle 120 people each buy one ticket. There are four prizes – a dinner for two, a bottle of wine, a box of chocolates and a cake. In how many different ways can the prizes be allocated?

> Since $n = 120$ and $r = 4$, $n - r = 116$, so the prizes can be allocated in
> $120 \times 119 \times 118 \times 117 = 197\,149\,680$ ways.

This product could also be written as $\dfrac{120!}{116!}$. But you may run into difficulty if you try to work this out with a calculator. Can you see why?

3.5   What is the value of 0!?

You may think this is a silly question. The symbol $n!$ stands for the result of multiplying together the first n positive integers. But it makes no sense to talk of 'the first 0 positive integers'.

But look back to the anagram problem in Section 3.2. With three letters there were 3! different arrangements. However, if you work this out using the formula $\dfrac{n!}{(n-r)!}$ in Section 3.4, with both $n = 3$ and $r = 3$ (since all three of the letters are being arranged in order), it gives the answer as $\dfrac{3!}{0!}$. This suggests that $3! = \dfrac{3!}{0!}$, so that $0! = 1$.

You could get round this by saying that the formula $\dfrac{n!}{(n-r)!}$ can only be used when $r < n$. But another possibility is to extend the definition of factorials to include the value $0! = 1$.

This also fits in with the rule $n! = n \times (n-1)!$ given in Section 3.3. This has so far been applied with $n = 2, 3, 4, \ldots$. But if you write it with $n = 1$, you get $1! = 1 \times 0!$. And since $1! = 1$, this suggests that $0! = 1$.

The inductive definition of $n!$ given in Section 3.3 can then be modified to read:

> The factorial sequence is defined by
>
> $0! = 1$ and $n! = n \times (n-1)!$ for $n = 1, 2, 3, 4, \ldots$.

This turns out to be a useful extension of the definition of factorial numbers.

Exercise 3B

1 Ten horses run in a race. In how many ways can the first three places be filled?

2 You have nine cards, one with each of the digits 1 to 9 printed on it. How many 4-digit numbers can you make with them? How many of them are greater than 5000?

3 Fifty books are entered for a literary prize. The judges have to produce a list of the five best books in order of merit. How many possible lists could they produce? Give your answer

(a) as an ordinary number,

(b) as an expression involving factorials.

4 Find the values of

(a) $\displaystyle\sum_{i=0}^{8} i!$,   (b) $\displaystyle\sum_{i=0}^{8} \frac{1}{i!}$.

In part (b) give your answer first as a fraction and then in decimal form correct to 4 significant figures.

3.6 Combinations

Suppose that you have five cards in your hand, each with one of the letters **t**, **e**, **a**, **m**, **y** written on it, and that you want to make all the possible 3-letter arrangements with them.

You can put any of the five cards in the first place, then there are four left for the second place, and three for the third place. So the number of possible arrangements is $5 \times 4 \times 3 = 60$, and you know that this can be written in factorials as $\dfrac{5!}{(5-3)!}$, or more simply $\dfrac{5!}{2!}$.

Here is the complete list of the 60 arrangements. You can check for yourself that none have been left out and that there are no repetitions.

tea	tem	tey	tam	tay	tmy	eam	eay	emy	amy
tae	tme	tye	tma	tya	tym	ema	eya	eym	aym
eta	etm	ety	atm	aty	mty	aem	aey	mey	may
eat	emt	eyt	amt	ayt	myt	ame	aye	mye	mya
ate	mte	yte	mta	yta	ytm	mea	yea	yem	yam
aet	met	yet	mat	yat	ymt	mae	yae	yme	yma

Notice how these arrangements have been set out in columns. In each column all the arrangements involve the same three letters. For example, the third column consists entirely of arrangements of the letters **t**, **y** and **e**. You know from Section 3.2 that the number of arrangements of three given letters is $3 \times 2 \times 1 = 6$; this is the number of rows in the array of 60 arrangements above.

This suggests a different way of making arrangements of three cards out of five. The method in Section 3.4 is to start with all five cards in your hand and to deal them into the first, second and third places in turn. But you could begin by selecting three of the cards and dumping the other two; you would then have just three cards in your hand to deal into the three vacant places.

How many ways are there of selecting the three cards? If you denote this number by s, then the total number of arrangements is $s \times 6$. But you know that the total number of arrangements is 60. So s is equal to 10. Each of the ten columns in the array corresponds to one way of selecting the three letters you are going to use.

Example 3.6.1
A club has 30 members. In how many different ways could they choose five members to form a committee?

> Suppose that the committee has to consist of a president, a secretary, a treasurer, a publicity officer and a catering officer. Then one way of making it up would be to elect the president first (out of 30), then the secretary (out of the remaining 29), then the treasurer (out of 28), and so on. The number of ways of filling the five positions would be $30 \times 29 \times 28 \times 27 \times 26$.
>
> Another way of filling the positions would be to choose the five committee members first and then to allocate the jobs. If there are s ways of choosing the five members, then the number of ways of filling the positions would be $s \times (5 \times 4 \times 3 \times 2 \times 1)$.
>
> So $\qquad s \times (5 \times 4 \times 3 \times 2 \times 1) = 30 \times 29 \times 28 \times 27 \times 26$,
>
> giving
>
> $$s = \frac{30 \times 29 \times 28 \times 27 \times 26}{5 \times 4 \times 3 \times 2 \times 1} = 142\,506.$$
>
> There are $142\,506$ ways of choosing the five members to form the committee.

If you have a set of n objects, then any selection of r objects from this set is called a **combination**. The difference between a permutation and a combination is that with a permutation you want the objects arranged in order, but with a combination the order doesn't matter.

Example 3.6.1 shows that you can find the number of combinations of r objects by calculating the number of *permutations* in two different ways. You saw in Section 3.4 that the number of permutations is $n \times (n - 1) \times (n - 2) \times \ldots \times (n - r + 1)$. But if you begin by choosing the combination of r objects and then arranging them among themselves, and if there are s possible combinations, then the number of permutations is $s \times (r \times (r - 1) \times (r - 2) \times \ldots \times 1)$. So

$$s = \frac{n \times (n - 1) \times (n - 2) \times \ldots \times (n - r + 1)}{r \times (r - 1) \times (r - 2) \times \ldots \times 1}.$$

There is a special symbol for this quantity. The number of combinations of r objects that can be made from a set of n objects is denoted by $^{n}C_{r}$. In this symbol the letter C stands for 'combinations', but some people like to read it as 'n choose r'.

Notice that in the expression for $^{n}C_{r}$ the number of factors in the top line is the same as the number in the bottom line (so long as you include the 1). This is a useful check that you have written it correctly.

Your calculator has a program to give the value of $^{n}C_{r}$ when you key in the numbers n and r. Make sure you know how to use it.

Example 3.6.2

There are 25 people waiting for a minibus. When the first one arrives it is found to have only 16 seats. In how many ways can the lucky passengers be chosen?

The number of combinations of 16 people that can be made from a set of 25 is $^{25}C_{16}$.

Using a calculator this is equal to $2\,042\,975$.

You know from Section 3.3 that both the products in the expression for ^nC_r can be written in terms of factorials. The product in the top line is $\dfrac{n!}{(n-r)!}$, and the product in the bottom line is just $r!$. It follows that

$$^nC_r = \frac{n!}{r! \times (n-r)!}$$

Notice that another way of describing a combination is as a subset of the complete set of objects. So the quantity ^nC_r could be described as 'the number of subsets of r objects contained in a set of n objects'.

> The number of combinations of r objects that can be made from a set of n objects is
> $$^nC_r = \frac{n \times (n-1) \times (n-2) \times ... \times (n-r+1)}{r \times (r-1) \times (r-2) \times ... \times 1} = \frac{n!}{r! \times (n-r)!}$$

Example 3.6.3

There are 23 men and 35 women on the town council. It is decided that the amenities committee should be made up of two men and three women. In how many ways can they be chosen?

Begin by considering the choice of the men and the women independently. The two men can be chosen in $^{23}C_2 = \dfrac{23 \times 22}{2 \times 1} = 253$ ways. The three women can be chosen in $^{35}C_3 = \dfrac{35 \times 34 \times 33}{3 \times 2 \times 1} = 6545$ ways.

Any combination of men can be paired with any combination of women, so the total number of ways of choosing the committee is $253 \times 6545 = 1\,655\,885$.

With a calculator you could just key this in as $^{23}C_2 \times {}^{35}C_3 = 1\,655\,885$.

Exercise 3C

1 Use the formula for ^nC_r to calculate

(a) $^{10}C_3$,   (b) $^{50}C_{10}$.

Check your answers by using the ^nC_r procedure on your calculator.

2 How many different 3-card hands can be dealt from a pack of 52 cards?

3 A flower arranger wants to select four varieties of rose to include in a display. She has nine varieties to choose from. How many different combinations are there?

4 The sergeant has to select five 'volunteers' for cookhouse duties from a squad of 20 recruits. In how many different ways can he pick them?

5 From a sixth form of 30 boys and 32 girls, two boys and two girls are to be chosen to represent their school. How many possible selections are there?

6 A DJ has brought 10 dance and 15 pop singles with him to a club night. He decides to use 7 of the dance and 11 of the pop records. In how many different ways could he choose them?

7 A college chess team plays 10 matches during the term. At the beginning of each match the captains toss a coin to decide which members of their teams should play with the white pieces.

    (a) Over the whole term, how many different results of the toss are possible?

    (b) For how many of these does the college captain win the toss six times and lose it four times?

8 Show that $^nC_r = {}^nC_{n-r}$

    (a) by using the formula for ^nC_r in terms of factorials,

    (b) by interpreting ^nC_r as the number of subsets of r objects in a set of n objects.

9 Calculate

    (a) $^7C_4$, $^7C_5$ and $^8C_5$,   (b) $^{10}C_3$, $^{10}C_4$ and $^{11}C_4$.

    What general rule do your answers suggest? Test the rule by trying it with some different numbers.

10 Calculate

    (a) $\displaystyle\sum_{i=0}^{4} {}^4C_i,$ (b) $\displaystyle\sum_{i=0}^{5} {}^5C_i,$ (c) $\displaystyle\sum_{i=0}^{6} {}^6C_i.$

    What general rule do your answers suggest? Give a reason for the rule by interpreting ^nC_r as the number of subsets of r objects in a set of n objects.

11 In the polygon game you have to make up words of various lengths using the letters in the cells. Every word has to include the letter in the central cell.

    (a) Suppose that you are using five letters from the polygon shown in the figure. In how many ways can the five letters be chosen if the letter in the central cell has to be one of them?

    (b) How many arrangements of five letters are there which include the letter in the central cell?

4 The binomial theorem

This chapter is about the expansion of $(a + b)^n$, where n is a positive integer. When you have completed it, you should

- be able to use Pascal's triangle to find the expansion of $(a + b)^n$ when n is small
- know how to use a calculator to find the coefficients in the expansion of $(a + b)^n$ when n is large
- be able to use the notation $\binom{n}{r}$ in the context of the binomial theorem
- know that $\binom{n}{r}$ is equal to ^nC_r.

4.1 Expanding $(a + b)^n$

The binomial theorem is a quick and easy rule for multiplying out $(a + b)^n$ where n is a positive integer. (The word 'binomial' refers to the expression $a + b$, which is the sum of two terms.)

You know that $(a + b)^2 = a^2 + 2ab + b^2$. This is proved by writing $(a + b)^2$ as $(a + b)(a + b)$. First, treating the second $(a + b)$ as a single object and using the rule $(x + y)z = xz + yz$ for multiplying out brackets,

$$(a + b)(a + b) = a(a + b) + b(a + b).$$

Then, using the rule again in the form $z(x + y) = zx + zy$,

$$a(a + b) + b(a + b) = (a^2 + ab) + (ba + b^2).$$

Since ab is the same as ba, you can set this out as

$$
\begin{aligned}
(a + b)^2 = a^2 + {} & ab \\
{} + {} & ab + b^2 \\
\hline
= a^2 + {} & 2ab + b^2.
\end{aligned}
$$

This expression is called the **expansion** of $(a + b)^2$.

You can use a similar method to find expansions of $(a + b)^3$ and $(a + b)^4$:

$$
\begin{aligned}
(a + b)^3 &= (a + b)(a + b)^2 \\
&= (a + b)(a^2 + 2ab + b^2) \\
&= a(a^2 + 2ab + b^2) + b(a^2 + 2ab + b^2) \\
&= a^3 + 2a^2b + ab^2 \\
&\quad\ + a^2b + 2ab^2 + b^3 \\
&= a^3 + 3a^2b + 3ab^2 + b^3. \\
(a + b)^4 &= (a + b)(a + b)^3 \\
&= (a + b)(a^3 + 3a^2b + 3ab^2 + b^3) \\
&= a(a^3 + 3a^2b + 3ab^2 + b^3) + b(a^3 + 3a^2b + 3ab^2 + b^3) \\
&= a^4 + 3a^3b + 3a^2b^2 + ab^3 \\
&\quad\ + a^3b + 3a^2b^2 + 3ab^3 + b^4 \\
&= a^4 + 4a^3b + 6a^2b^2 + 4ab^3 + b^4.
\end{aligned}
$$

Notice that, when you multiply out $b(...)$, the factors in each term have been written in alphabetical order. For example, $b \times (2ab)$ becomes $2ab^2$ and $b \times (3a^2b)$ becomes $3a^2b^2$.

You can summarise these results, including $(a+b)^1$, as follows. The numbers in bold type are called **binomial coefficients**.

$$(a+b)^1 = \mathbf{1}a + \mathbf{1}b$$
$$(a+b)^2 = \mathbf{1}a^2 + \mathbf{2}ab + \mathbf{1}b^2$$
$$(a+b)^3 = \mathbf{1}a^3 + \mathbf{3}a^2b + \mathbf{3}ab^2 + \mathbf{1}b^3$$
$$(a+b)^4 = \mathbf{1}a^4 + \mathbf{4}a^3b + \mathbf{6}a^2b^2 + \mathbf{4}ab^3 + \mathbf{1}b^4$$

Study these expansions carefully. You will see that there are two parts to the rule for writing out the expressions:

- The 'a and b' rule. Each row starts on the left with a^n. Moving from one term to the next, the powers of a successively go down by 1, and the powers of b go up by 1, until you reach the last term b^n.
- The coefficient rule. The coefficients form the pattern in Fig. 4.1. This is called **Pascal's triangle**. (The pattern first appeared in a Chinese manuscript by Yang Hui in the 13th century, but Blaise Pascal was one of the first Europeans to use it.)

Row 1   **1**   **1**
Row 2   **1**   **2**   **1**
Row 3   **1**   **3**   **3**   **1**
Row 4 **1**   **4**   **6**   **4**   **1**

Fig. 4.1

A simple way of building up Pascal's triangle is as follows:

- start each row with 1,
- then add pairs of numbers in the row above to get the entry positioned below and between them (the arrows in Fig. 4.1 show the number 6 in Row 4 obtained as $3 + 3$ from Row 3),
- complete the row with a 1.

This corresponds to the way in which the two rows of algebra are added to give the final result when you expand $(a+b)^2$, $(a+b)^3$ and $(a+b)^4$.

You should now be able to predict that the coefficients in the fifth row are

    1   **5**   **10**   **10**   **5**   **1**

and that

$$(a+b)^5 = a^5 + 5a^4b + 10a^3b^2 + 10a^2b^3 + 5ab^4 + b^5.$$

4.2   Substitution

You also know that $(a - b)^2 = a^2 - 2ab + b^2$.

You could prove this by a method similar to that used in Section 4.1 for $(a + b)^2$, writing

$$(a - b)^2 = (a - b)(a - b)$$
$$= a(a - b) - b(a - b)$$
$$= (a^2 - ab) - (ba - b^2)$$
$$= a^2 - \quad ab$$
$$\quad - \quad ab + b^2$$
$$= a^2 - 2ab + b^2.$$

But there is no need to do this. It is easier to write $a + b$ as $a + (-b)$, so

$$(a - b)^2 = (a + (-b))^2.$$

This is just like $(a + b)^2$ but with $(-b)$ written in place of b. So

$$(a + (-b))^2 = a^2 + 2a \times (-b) + (-b)^2.$$

Since $2a \times (-b) = -2ab$ and $(-b)^2 = b^2$,

$$(a - b)^2 = a^2 - 2ab + b^2.$$

This process is called **substitution**. You expand $(a - b)^2$ by substituting $-b$ in place of b in the expansion of $(a + b)^2$.

> In Examples 4.2.1 to 4.2.4 the coefficients from Pascal's triangle are shown in bold-faced type to help you to keep track of them.

Example 4.2.1
Write down the expansion of $(1 + b)^6$.

Use the next row of Pascal's triangle, continuing the pattern of powers and replacing a by 1:

$$(1 + b)^6 = \mathbf{1}(1)^6 + \mathbf{6}(1)^5 b + \mathbf{15}(1)^4 b^2 + \mathbf{20}(1)^3 b^3 + \mathbf{15}(1)^2 b^4 + \mathbf{6}(1) b^5 + \mathbf{1} b^6$$
$$= 1 + 6b + 15b^2 + 20b^3 + 15b^4 + 6b^5 + b^6.$$

Example 4.2.2
Multiply out the brackets in the expression $(2x + 3)^4$.

Use the expansion of $(a + b)^4$, substituting $(2x)$ for a and 3 for b:

$$(2x + 3)^4 = \mathbf{1} \times (2x)^4 + \mathbf{4} \times (2x)^3 \times 3 + \mathbf{6} \times (2x)^2 \times 3^2 + \mathbf{4} \times (2x) \times 3^3 + \mathbf{1} \times 3^4$$
$$= 16x^4 + 96x^3 + 216x^2 + 216x + 81.$$

Example 4.2.3

Expand $(x^2 + 2)^3$.

In $(a + b)^3$, substitute x^2 for a and 2 for b.

$$(x^2 + 2)^3 = \mathbf{1} \times (x^2)^3 + \mathbf{3} \times (x^2)^2 \times 2 + \mathbf{3} \times x^2 \times 2^2 + \mathbf{1} \times 2^3$$
$$= x^6 + 6x^4 + 12x^2 + 8.$$

Example 4.2.4

Expand $(2p - 3)^6$.

In $(a + b)^6$, replace a by $2p$ and b by (-3).

Don't be tempted to economise on brackets!

$$(2p - 3)^6 = \mathbf{1} \times (2p)^6 + \mathbf{6} \times (2p)^5 \times (-3) + \mathbf{15} \times (2p)^4 \times (-3)^2 + \mathbf{20} \times (2p)^3 \times (-3)^3$$
$$+ \mathbf{15} \times (2p)^2 \times (-3)^4 + \mathbf{6} \times (2p) \times (-3)^5 + \mathbf{1} \times (-3)^6$$
$$= 64p^6 + 6 \times 32p^5 \times (-3) + 15 \times 16p^4 \times 9 + 20 \times 8p^3 \times (-27)$$
$$+ 15 \times 4p^2 \times 81 + 6 \times 2p \times (-243) + 729$$
$$= 64p^6 - 576p^5 + 2160p^4 - 4320p^3 + 4860p^2 - 2916p + 729.$$

Example 4.2.5

Find the coefficient of x^3 in the expansion of $(3x - 4)^5$.

The term which involves x^3 comes third in the row with coefficients $1, 5, 10, \dots$. So this term is

$$10 \times (3x)^3 \times (-4)^2 = 10 \times 27x^3 \times 16 = 4320x^3.$$

The required coefficient is therefore 4320.

In this example notice the difference between 'the coefficient of x^3' and the 'binomial coefficient'. The first is the number which multiplies x^3 when the expansion is written out in full, but the second refers to just the number 10.

Example 4.2.6

Expand $(1 + 2x + 3x^2)^3$.

To use the binomial expansion, you need to write $1 + 2x + 3x^2$ in a form with two terms rather than three. One way to do this is to split it as $1 + (2x + 3x^2)$. Then

$$(1 + (2x + 3x^2))^3 = 1^3 + 3 \times 1^2 \times (2x + 3x^2) + 3 \times 1 \times (2x + 3x^2)^2 + (2x + 3x^2)^3$$
$$= 1 + 3(2x + 3x^2) + 3(2x + 3x^2)^2 + (2x + 3x^2)^3.$$

Now you can use the binomial theorem again to expand the bracketed terms:

$$(2x + 3x^2)^2 = (2x)^2 + 2 \times (2x) \times (3x^2) + (3x^2)^2$$
$$= 4x^2 + 12x^3 + 9x^4,$$

$$(2x + 3x^2)^3 = (2x)^3 + 3 \times (2x)^2 \times (3x^2) + 3 \times (2x) \times (3x^2)^2 + (3x^2)^3$$
$$= 8x^3 + 36x^4 + 54x^5 + 27x^6.$$

So $(1 + 2x + 3x^2)^3$

$$= 1 + 3(2x + 3x^2) + 3(4x^2 + 12x^3 + 9x^4) + (8x^3 + 36x^4 + 54x^5 + 27x^6)$$
$$= 1 + (6x + 9x^2) + (12x^2 + 36x^3 + 27x^4) + (8x^3 + 36x^4 + 54x^5 + 27x^6)$$
$$= 1 + 6x + 21x^2 + 44x^3 + 63x^4 + 54x^5 + 27x^6.$$

In this kind of detailed work, it is useful to check your answers. You could do this by expanding $(1 + 2x + 3x^2)^3$ in the form $((1 + 2x) + 3x^2)^3$ to see if you get the same answer. Rather quicker is to give x a particular value, $x = 1$ for example. Then the left side is $(1 + 2 + 3)^3 = 6^3 = 216$; the right is $1 + 6 + 21 + 44 + 63 + 54 + 27 = 216$. It is important to note that if the results are the same, it does not guarantee that the expansion is correct; but if they are different, it is certain that there is a mistake.

Exercise 4A

1 Write down the expansion of each of the following.

(a) $(x + 1)^3$ (b) $(2x + 1)^3$ (c) $(4 + p)^3$ (d) $(x - 1)^3$

(e) $(x + 2)^3$ (f) $(2p + 3q)^3$ (g) $(1 - 4x)^3$ (h) $\left(1 + \frac{1}{2}x\right)^4$

(i) $(x^2 + 2)^3$ (j) $(1 - 5x^2)^3$ (k) $(x^2 + y^3)^3$ (l) $(1 - x^3)^3$

2 Find the coefficient of x in the expansion of   (a) $(3x + 1)^4$,   (b) $(2x + 5)^3$.

3 Find the coefficient of x^2 in the expansion of   (a) $(4x + 5)^3$,   (b) $(1 - 3x)^4$.

4 Find the coefficient of x^3 in the expansion of   (a) $(1 + 3x)^5$,   (b) $(2 - 5x)^4$.

5 Write down the expansion of $(m + 4)^3$ and hence expand $(m + 1)(m + 4)^3$.

6 Expand $(3r + 2)(2r + 3)^3$.

7 In the expansion of $(1 + ax)^4$, the coefficient of x^3 is 1372. Find the constant a.

8 Expand $(a + b)^9$.

9 Find the coefficient of $x^5 y^5$ in the expansion of $(2x + y)^{10}$.

10 Expand $(1 - x + 2x^2)^3$. Check your answer by making a numerical substitution.

4.3 The binomial theorem

The treatment given in Section 4.1 is fine for calculating the coefficients in the expansion of $(a + b)^n$ where n is small, but it is hopelessly inefficient for finding the coefficient of $a^{11}b^4$ in the expansion of $(a + b)^{15}$. Just think of all the rows of Pascal's triangle which you would have to write out! What you need is a way of finding any term in the expansion of $(a + b)^n$ for any positive integer n.

Notice first how to generalise the 'a and b' rule. The first term is just a^n. For the next term, the power of a goes down by 1 and the power of b goes up by 1. It is therefore

coefficient $\times a^{n-1}b^1$.

The term after that is

coefficient $\times a^{n-2}b^2$, and so on.

You will see that the powers of a and b always add up to n. So a typical term will have the form

coefficient $\times a^{n-r}b^r$.

The coefficient depends on the values of n and r. A special symbol, $\binom{n}{r}$, is used to denote it.

All the numbers in Pascal's triangle can then be written in the form $\binom{n}{r}$. For example, Row 3 gives the coefficients in the expansion of $(a + b)^3$, so $n = 3$. The coefficient of ab^2, which is $a^{3-2}b^2$, has $r = 2$. So this coefficient is $\binom{3}{2}$.

Pascal's triangle can then be written as

Row 1 $\binom{1}{0}$ $\binom{1}{1}$

Row 2 $\binom{2}{0}$ $\binom{2}{1}$ $\binom{2}{2}$

Row 3 $\binom{3}{0}$ $\binom{3}{1}$ $\binom{3}{2}$ $\binom{3}{3}$

Row 4 $\binom{4}{0}$ $\binom{4}{1}$ $\binom{4}{2}$ $\binom{4}{3}$ $\binom{4}{4}$

and so on.

This enables you to write down a neater form of the expansion of $(a + b)^n$.

> The **binomial theorem** states that, if n is a positive integer,
> $$(a + b)^n = \binom{n}{0}a^n + \binom{n}{1}a^{n-1}b + \binom{n}{2}a^{n-2}b^2 + \ldots + \binom{n}{n}b^n.$$

So far this is just new notation. It doesn't tell you how to calculate $\binom{n}{r}$ for any given numbers n and r. To do this, you need to look at the expansion in a different way.

Think of expanding $(a + b)^2$, as

$$(a + b) \times (a + b) = aa + ab + ba + bb$$

The four slurs above and below the left side correspond to the four terms on the right. They show that each term of the expansion is got by taking either an a or a b out of each bracket and multiplying them together.

Now apply this idea to the expansion of $(a + b)^4$, which can be written as

$$(a + b) \times (a + b) \times (a + b) \times (a + b).$$

Each term of the expansion now comes by taking either an a or a b out of each of the four brackets and multiplying them together. For example, if you take the a out of each bracket you get the product $aaaa$, or a^4. There is no other way of getting a^4, so when you collect the terms together you get just $1a^4$.

But there are four ways of getting a^3b, since you can choose any one of the four brackets for the b, and then take the a from each of the others. That is, the term involving a^3b in the expansion is

$$baaa + abaa + aaba + aaab = a^3b + a^3b + a^3b + a^3b$$
$$= 4a^3b.$$

This shows that $\begin{pmatrix} 4 \\ 1 \end{pmatrix} = 4$.

This is a situation you have met before. You have four brackets, and you have to select just one 'b-bracket' out of the four. In Section 3.6 the number of ways of doing this was denoted by $^4C_1$, or '4 choose 1'. So the binomial coefficient $\begin{pmatrix} 4 \\ 1 \end{pmatrix}$ is equal to $^4C_1$.

The same argument holds for any numbers n and r, where $0 \leq r \leq n$. To expand

$$\overbrace{(a + b) \times (a + b) \times ... \times (a + b)}^{n \text{ of these}},$$

you have to add all the terms you can form by taking an a out of some brackets and a b out of the others. To get a term $a^{n-r}b^r$ you have to choose b from r of the n brackets, and a from the remaining $n - r$. And you know that the number of ways of doing this is 'n choose r', or ^nC_r.

> The binomial coefficient $\begin{pmatrix} n \\ r \end{pmatrix}$ is equal to ^nC_r.

Now you know how to find ^nC_r, either by using a calculator or from the formula

$$^nC_r = \frac{n!}{r! \times (n-r)!} = \frac{n \times (n-1) \times ... \times (n-r+1)}{r \times (r-1) \times ... \times 1}.$$

So you can calculate any binomial coefficient you need in exactly the same way.

Example 4.3.1
Calculate the coefficient of $a^{11}b^4$ in the expansion of $(a + b)^{15}$.

The coefficient is $\begin{pmatrix} 15 \\ 4 \end{pmatrix} = {}^{15}C_4$. The calculator gives $^{15}C_4 = 1365$.

Example 4.3.2
Find the coefficient of a^5 in the expansion of $(a - 2)^8$.

Substituting (-2) for b, the term you want is the one involving $a^5 b^3$. The binomial coefficient is therefore $\binom{8}{3} = 56$.

The corresponding term is
$$56 \times a^5 \times (-2)^3,$$
so the coefficient of a^5 is
$$56 \times (-8) = -448.$$

Exercise 4B

1 Use your calculator to find the value of each of the following.

(a) $\binom{7}{3}$ (b) $\binom{8}{6}$ (c) $\binom{9}{5}$ (d) $\binom{13}{4}$

(e) $\binom{6}{4}$ (f) $\binom{10}{2}$ (g) $\binom{11}{10}$ (h) $\binom{50}{2}$

2 Find the coefficient of b^3 in the expansion of each of the following.

(a) $(1 + b)^5$ (b) $(1 - b)^8$ (c) $(1 + b)^{11}$ (d) $(1 - b)^{16}$

3 Find the coefficient of x^5 in the expansion of each of the following.

(a) $(2 + x)^7$ (b) $(3 - x)^8$ (c) $(1 + 2x)^9$ (d) $\left(1 - \frac{1}{2}x\right)^{12}$

4 Find the coefficient of $x^6 y^8$ in the expansion of each of the following.

(a) $(x + y)^{14}$ (b) $(2x + y)^{14}$ (c) $(3x - 2y)^{14}$ (d) $\left(4x + \frac{1}{2}y\right)^{14}$

5 By taking particular values for a and b in the statement of the binomial theorem, prove that

(a) $\binom{n}{0} + \binom{n}{1} + \binom{n}{2} + ... + \binom{n}{n} = 2^n$,   (b) $\binom{n}{0} - \binom{n}{1} + \binom{n}{2} - ... + (-1)^n \binom{n}{n} = 0$.

4.4 Binomial coefficients as a sequence

Often you don't need a complete binomial expansion, but only the first few terms. For example, binomial expansions are sometimes used to find numerical approximations. To do this, a binomial expansion is chosen so that all the terms after the first few are very small, so that they can be neglected with only a small sacrifice of accuracy.

The next example is one in which the value of x is assumed to be small. When this is the case, say for $x = 0.01$, the successive powers of x decrease by a factor of 100 each time and become very small indeed. So, if you only need an approximate answer, higher powers can be neglected, even though for some time the binomial coefficients are still getting larger.

For this reason you are asked to put the terms of a binomial expansion in order of **ascending powers** of x. This means that you start with the term with the smallest power of x, then move to the next smallest, and so on. In this way the terms likely to have the largest absolute value are written first.

Example 4.4.1

Find the first four terms in the expansion of $(2 - 3x)^{10}$ in ascending powers of x. By putting $x = 0.01$, find an approximation to 1.97^{10} correct to the nearest whole number.

You know that $\begin{pmatrix} 10 \\ 0 \end{pmatrix} = 1$ and $\begin{pmatrix} 10 \\ 1 \end{pmatrix} = 10$. The calculator gives $\begin{pmatrix} 10 \\ 2 \end{pmatrix} = 45$ and $\begin{pmatrix} 10 \\ 3 \end{pmatrix} = 120$.

$$(2 - 3x)^{10} = \begin{pmatrix} 10 \\ 0 \end{pmatrix} \times 2^{10} + \begin{pmatrix} 10 \\ 1 \end{pmatrix} \times 2^9 \times (-3x) + \begin{pmatrix} 10 \\ 2 \end{pmatrix} \times 2^8 \times (-3x)^2$$

$$+ \begin{pmatrix} 10 \\ 3 \end{pmatrix} \times 2^7 \times (-3x)^3 + \dots$$

$$= 1024 - 10 \times 512 \times 3x + 45 \times 256 \times 9x^2 - 120 \times 128 \times 27x^3 + \dots$$

$$= 1024 - 15\,360x + 103\,680x^2 - 414\,720x^3 + \dots.$$

The first four terms are therefore $1024 - 15\,360x + 103\,680x^2 - 414\,720x^3$.

The dots at the ends of the lines indicate that the expression continues but that you are not interested in the remaining terms.

Putting $x = 0.01$ gives

$$1.97^{10} \approx 1024 - 15\,360 \times 0.01 + 103\,680 \times 0.01^2 - 414\,720 \times 0.01^3$$
$$= 880.353\,28.$$

Therefore $1.97^{10} \approx 880$.

The next term is actually $\begin{pmatrix} 10 \\ 4 \end{pmatrix} \times 2^6 \times (3x)^4 = 1\,088\,640x^4 = 0.010\,886\,4$ and the rest are very small indeed. So, by taking the first four terms of the expansion you can be sure that $1.97^{10} \approx 880$ correct to the nearest whole number. Check this directly from your calculator.

In Example 4.4.1 the binomial coefficients $\begin{pmatrix} 10 \\ 2 \end{pmatrix}$ and $\begin{pmatrix} 10 \\ 3 \end{pmatrix}$ were found with a calculator. But when you only want a few terms of an expansion it is often simpler not to use the ^nC_r program but to find the binomial coefficients directly from the formula

$$\begin{pmatrix} n \\ r \end{pmatrix} = {^nC_r} = \frac{n \times (n - 1) \times \dots \times (n - r + 1)}{r \times (r - 1) \times \dots \times 1}.$$

Before describing how to do this it is worth making a small change, by reversing the order of the factors in the bottom line to write the formula as

$$\begin{pmatrix} n \\ r \end{pmatrix} = \frac{n \times (n - 1) \times \dots \times (n - r + 1)}{1 \times 2 \times \dots \times r}.$$

The point of this is that in both lines you begin with a fixed number (n or 1) on the left. The number r which changes as the expansion proceeds appears in the factors on the right.

So, after $\binom{10}{0} = 1$, you get

$$\binom{10}{1} = \frac{10}{1}, \quad \binom{10}{2} = \frac{10 \times 9}{1 \times 2}, \quad \binom{10}{3} = \frac{10 \times 9 \times 8}{1 \times 2 \times 3},$$

and so on.

Notice that to get from $\binom{10}{0}$ to $\binom{10}{1}$ you multiply by $\frac{10}{1}$. Then to get from $\binom{10}{1}$ to $\binom{10}{2}$ you multiply by $\frac{9}{2}$; to get from $\binom{10}{2}$ to $\binom{10}{3}$ you multiply by $\frac{8}{3}$; and so on. You could generate the successive binomial coefficients by writing

$$1 \quad \overset{\times \frac{10}{1} =}{\to} \quad 10 \quad \overset{\times \frac{9}{2} =}{\to} \quad 45 \quad \overset{\times \frac{8}{3} =}{\to} \quad 120 \quad \overset{\times \frac{7}{4} =}{\to} \quad \dots \; .$$

When the numbers get large, it is very easy to do the arithmetic using the $\times$ and $\div$ keys on the calculator.

Example 4.4.2

Find the first five binomial coefficients in the expansion of $(1 + x)^{30}$.

For $n = 30$, the sequence of binomial coefficients is

$$1 \quad \overset{\times \frac{30}{1} =}{\to} \quad 30 \quad \overset{\times \frac{29}{2} =}{\to} \quad 435 \quad \overset{\times \frac{28}{3} =}{\to} \quad 4060 \quad \overset{\times \frac{27}{4} =}{\to} \quad 27405 \quad \to \quad \dots$$

The first five binomial coefficients are 1, 30, 435, 4060, 27 405.

Example 4.4.3

Expand $(1 - 2x)^{20}$ in ascending powers of x as far as the term in x^3.

The binomial coefficients are given by

$$1 \quad \overset{\times \frac{20}{1} =}{\to} \quad 20 \quad \overset{\times \frac{19}{2} =}{\to} \quad 190 \quad \overset{\times \frac{18}{3} =}{\to} \quad 1140 \quad \to \quad \dots \; .$$

So

$$(1 - 2x)^{20} = 1 + 20 \times (-2x) + 190 \times (-2x)^2 + 1140 \times (-2x)^3 + \dots$$
$$= 1 - 40x + 760x^2 - 9120x^3 + \dots \; .$$

What these examples show is that, for each value of n, the binomial coefficients form a sequence. The fraction for $\binom{n}{r}$ has r factors above the line and r factors below. So the fraction for $\binom{n}{r-1}$ has $r - 1$ factors above and $r - 1$ factors below. To get from $\binom{n}{r-1}$ to $\binom{n}{r}$ you multiply by the extra factors $(n - r + 1)$ above the line and r below the line. Since $\binom{n}{0}$ always equals 1, this gives an inductive definition for $\binom{n}{r}$.

The sequence of binomial coefficients $\binom{n}{r}$ is defined by

$$\binom{n}{0} = 1, \quad \binom{n}{r} = \frac{n-r+1}{r} \times \binom{n}{r-1} \quad \text{for } r = 1, 2, 3, \ldots, n.$$

Notice that in this definition the letter n stands for a fixed number, and the variable is represented by the letter r. In standard notation the sequence would be written as u_r, where

$$u_0 = 1 \text{ and } u_r = \frac{n-r+1}{r} \times u_{r-1} \text{ for } r = 1, 2, 3, \ldots, n.$$

That is, $u_r a^{n-r} b^r$ is the general term in the expansion of $(a+b)^n$.

Example 4.4.4

Find the first four terms in the expansion of $(1 + x + 2x^2)^{15}$ in ascending powers of x.

Start by bracketing $(1 + x + 2x^2)^{15}$ in the form $(1 + (x + 2x^2))^{15}$ and use the expansion of $(1 + y)^{15}$ with $y = x + 2x^2$.

The first four terms include the terms in x^3, so the expansion must go as far as the terms in y^3. So you will need to find the binomial coefficients

$$\binom{15}{0} = 1, \quad \binom{15}{1} = \frac{15}{1} \times 1 = 15, \quad \binom{15}{2} = \frac{14}{2} \times 15 = 105,$$

$$\binom{15}{3} = \frac{13}{3} \times 105 = 455.$$

Then

$$
\begin{aligned}
(1 + (x + 2x^2))^{15} &= (1 + y)^{15} \\
&= 1 + 15y + 105y^2 + 455y^3 + \ldots \\
&= 1 + 15(x + 2x^2) + 105(x + 2x^2)^2 + 455(x + 2x^2)^3 + \ldots \\
&= 1 + 15(x + 2x^2) + 105(x^2 + 4x^3 + \ldots) + 455(x^3 + \ldots) \\
&= 1 + 15x + 135x^2 + 875x^3 + \ldots.
\end{aligned}
$$

Note that there is no need to complete the expansions of $(x + 2x^2)^2$ and $(x + 2x^2)^3$ because the remaining terms involve x^4, x^5 and x^6, and these are not required.

The first four terms of the expansion are $1 + 15x + 135x^2 + 875x^3$.

Exercise 4C

1 Find the first four terms in the expansion in ascending powers of x of the following.

(a) $(1 + x)^{13}$ (b) $(1 - x)^{15}$ (c) $(1 + 3x)^{10}$ (d) $(2 - 5x)^7$

2 Find the first three terms in the expansion in ascending powers of x of the following.

(a) $(1 + x)^{22}$ (b) $(1 - x)^{30}$ (c) $(1 - 4x)^{18}$ (d) $(1 + 6x)^{19}$

3 Find the first three terms in the expansion, in ascending powers of x, of $(1 + 2x)^8$. By substituting $x = 0.01$, find an approximation to 1.02^8.

4 Find the first three terms in the expansion, in ascending powers of x, of $(2 + 5x)^{12}$. By substituting a suitable value for x, find an approximation to 2.005^{12} to 2 decimal places.

5 Expand $(1 + 2x)^{16}$ up to and including the term in x^3. Deduce the coefficient of x^3 in the expansion of $(1 + 3x)(1 + 2x)^{16}$.

6 Expand $(1 - 3x)^{10}$ up to and including the term in x^2. Deduce the coefficient of x^2 in the expansion of $(1 + 3x)^2 (1 - 3x)^{10}$.

7 Simplify $(1 - x)^8 + (1 + x)^8$. Substitute a suitable value of x to find the exact value of $0.99^8 + 1.01^8$.

8 Use an argument like that in Section 4.4 to show that

(a) $\dbinom{3}{2} = 3,$ (b) $\dbinom{4}{2} = 6,$ (c) $\dbinom{5}{2} = 10.$

9 Use the expression for $\dbinom{n}{r}$ in terms of factorials to show that $\dbinom{n}{r} = \dbinom{n}{n-r}$. Interpret this in terms of Pascal's triangle.

10 (a) Write down the numerical value of the fraction $\dfrac{a}{b}$ in the equation $\dbinom{6}{4} = \dfrac{a}{b} \times \dbinom{6}{3}$.

   (b) Find the numerical value of the fraction $\dfrac{c}{d}$ in the equation $\dbinom{6}{3} + \dbinom{6}{4} = \dfrac{c}{d} \times \dbinom{6}{3}$.

   (c) Deduce that $\dbinom{6}{3} + \dbinom{6}{4} = \dbinom{7}{4}$.

   (d) Write out the sixth and seventh rows of Pascal's triangle, and show how they can be used to demonstrate the result of part (c).

11* Use the property $\dbinom{n}{r} = \dfrac{n-r+1}{r} \times \dbinom{n}{r-1}$ to prove that

$\dbinom{n}{r-1} + \dbinom{n}{r} = \dfrac{n+1}{r} \times \dbinom{n}{r-1}.$

Deduce that $\dbinom{n}{r-1} + \dbinom{n}{r} = \dbinom{n+1}{r}.$

12* Prove that

(a) $x \dbinom{n}{x} = n \dbinom{n-1}{x-1}$ for $x \geq 1,$

(b) $x^2 \dbinom{n}{x} = n(n-1) \dbinom{n-2}{x-2} + n \dbinom{n-1}{x-1}$ for $x \geq 2.$

Review exercise 1

1 Simplify

  (a) $\sqrt{27} + \sqrt{12} - \sqrt{3}$,

  (b) $\sqrt{63} - \sqrt{28}$,

  (c) $\sqrt{100\,000} + \sqrt{1000} + \sqrt{10}$,

  (d) $\sqrt[3]{2} + \sqrt[3]{16}$.

2 Rationalise the denominators of the following.

  (a) $\dfrac{9}{2\sqrt{3}}$

  (b) $\dfrac{1}{5\sqrt{5}}$

  (c) $\dfrac{2\sqrt{5}}{3\sqrt{10}}$

  (d) $\dfrac{\sqrt{8}}{\sqrt{15}}$

3 In the diagram, angles $A\hat{B}C$ and $A\hat{C}D$ are right angles. Given that $AB = CD = 2\sqrt{6}$ cm and $BC = 7$ cm, show that the length of $[AD]$ is between $4\sqrt{6}$ cm and $7\sqrt{2}$ cm.

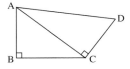

4 In the triangle PQR, $\hat{Q}$ is a right angle, $PQ = (6 - 2\sqrt{2})$ cm and $QR = (6 + 2\sqrt{2})$ cm.

  (a) Find the area of the triangle.

  (b) Show that the length of $[PR]$ is $2\sqrt{22}$ cm.

5 Simplify (a) $3\sqrt{3} + 3\sqrt{27}$, (b) $3\sqrt{2} \times 4\sqrt{8}$.

6 Solve the inequality $2(3 - x) < 4 - (2 - x)$.

7 The sequence $u_1, u_2, u_3, \ldots$ is defined by

$$u_1 = 0, \quad u_n = (2 + u_{n-1})^2.$$

Find the value of u_4.

8 Find the first four terms in the binomial expansion of $(2 - x)^7$. Use your answer to calculate 1.99^7 correct to 2 places of decimals.

9 (a) Find the sum of all the integers between 1 and 100 which are divisible by 3.

  (b) Find the sum of all the integers from 1 to 100 which are not divisible by 3.

10 Expand $\left(a^2 + \dfrac{2}{a}\right)^5$.

11 Rationalise the denominators of the following.

  (a) $\dfrac{4}{3 - \sqrt{3}}$

  (b) $\dfrac{6}{5 + \sqrt{5}}$

  (c) $\dfrac{3 - \sqrt{2}}{3 + \sqrt{2}}$

  (d) $\dfrac{2\sqrt{7} - 3}{4 + \sqrt{7}}$

12 It can be shown that $\tan 75° = \dfrac{\sqrt{3} + 1}{\sqrt{3} - 1}$. Use a calculator to check this, and write an expression for $\tan 75°$ in the form $a + b\sqrt{3}$, where a and b are rational numbers.

13 Solve the simultaneous equations $5x - 3y = 41$ and $(7\sqrt{2})x + (4\sqrt{2})y = 82$.

14 An isosceles right-angled triangle has its two shorter sides of length a. Write down an expression for its perimeter in terms of a.

A length of rope 10 metres long is to be pegged out to form an isosceles right-angled triangle. Find, in as simple a form as possible, exact expressions for the lengths of the sides.

15 You are given that y is not 0, and that x and y are not equal.
Now suppose that $\sqrt{x-y} = \sqrt{x} - \sqrt{y}$.
  (a) Show that $(\sqrt{x} - \sqrt{y})^2 = x - 2\sqrt{x}\sqrt{y} + y$.
  (b) Deduce that $y(x - y) = 0$, and hence that either $y = 0$ or $x = y$.
  (c) What can you deduce about $\sqrt{x-y}$ and $\sqrt{x} - \sqrt{y}$?

16 Find the first three terms in the expansion of $(1 + 2x)^{20}$. By substitution of a suitable value of x in each case, find approximations to
  (a) 1.002^{20},   (b) 0.996^{20}.

17 Two of the following expansions are correct and two are incorrect. Find the two expansions which are incorrect.
  A: $(3 + 4x)^5 = 243 + 1620x + 4320x^2 + 5760x^3 + 3840x^4 + 1024x^5$
  B: $(1 - 2x + 3x^2)^3 = 1 + 6x - 3x^2 + 28x^3 - 9x^4 + 54x^5 - 27x^6$
  C: $(1 - x)(1 + 4x)^4 = 1 + 15x + 80x^2 + 160x^3 - 256x^5$
  D: $(2x + y)^2 (3x + y)^3 = 108x^5 + 216x^4y + 171x^3y^2 + 67x^2y^3 + 13xy^4 + y^6$

18 (a) Expand and simplify $(\sqrt{7} + \sqrt{5})^4 + (\sqrt{7} - \sqrt{5})^4$. By using the fact that $0 < \sqrt{7} - \sqrt{5} < 1$, state the consecutive integers between which $(\sqrt{7} + \sqrt{5})^4$ lies.
  (b) Without using a calculator, find the consecutive integers between which the value of $(\sqrt{3} + \sqrt{2})^6$ lies.

19 (a) Show that
  (i) $4 \times \begin{pmatrix} 6 \\ 2 \end{pmatrix} = 3 \times \begin{pmatrix} 6 \\ 3 \end{pmatrix} = 6 \times \begin{pmatrix} 5 \\ 2 \end{pmatrix}$,
  (ii) $3 \times \begin{pmatrix} 7 \\ 4 \end{pmatrix} = 5 \times \begin{pmatrix} 7 \\ 5 \end{pmatrix} = 7 \times \begin{pmatrix} 6 \\ 4 \end{pmatrix}$.
  (b) State numbers a, b and c such that
  (i) $a \times \begin{pmatrix} 8 \\ 5 \end{pmatrix} = b \times \begin{pmatrix} 8 \\ 6 \end{pmatrix} = c \times \begin{pmatrix} 7 \\ 5 \end{pmatrix}$,
  (ii) $a \times \begin{pmatrix} 9 \\ 3 \end{pmatrix} = b \times \begin{pmatrix} 9 \\ 4 \end{pmatrix} = c \times \begin{pmatrix} 8 \\ 3 \end{pmatrix}$.
  (c) Prove that $(n - r) \times \begin{pmatrix} n \\ r \end{pmatrix} = (r + 1) \times \begin{pmatrix} n \\ r+1 \end{pmatrix} = n \times \begin{pmatrix} n-1 \\ r \end{pmatrix}$.

20 The judges in a 'Beautiful Baby' competition have to arrange 10 babies in order of merit. In how many different ways could this be done? Two babies are to be selected to be photographed. In how many ways can this selection be made?

21 In how many ways can a committee of four men and four women be seated in a row if

   (a) they can sit in any position,

   (b) no one is seated next to a person of the same sex?

22 Six people are going to travel in a six-seater minibus but only three of them can drive. In how many different ways can they seat themselves?

23 A small company producing children's toys plans an increase in output. The number of toys produced is to be increased by 8 each week until the weekly number produced reaches 1000. In week 1, the number to be produced is 280; in week 2, the number is 288; etc. Show that the weekly number produced will be 1000 in week 91.

   From week 91 onwards, the number produced each week is to remain at 1000. Find the total number of toys to be produced over the first 104 weeks of the plan.   (OCR)

24 The ith term of an arithmetic progression is $1 + 4i$. Find, in terms of n, the sum of the first n terms of the progression.   (OCR)

25 The sum of the first two terms of an arithmetic progression is 18 and the sum of the first four terms is 52. Find the sum of the first eight terms.   (OCR)

26 Find the sum of the arithmetic progression $1, 4, 7, 10, 13, 16, \dots , 1000$.

   Every third term of the above progression is removed, i.e. $7, 16$, etc. Find the sum of the remaining terms.   (OCR)

27 In 1971 a newly-built flat was sold with a 999-year lease. The terms of the sale included a requirement to pay 'ground rent' yearly. The ground rent was set at £28 per year for the first 21 years of the lease, increasing by £14 to £42 per year for the next 21 years, and then increasing again by £14 at the end of each subsequent period of 21 years.

   (a) Find how many complete 21-year periods there would be if the lease ran for the full 999 years, and how many years there would be left over.

   (b) Find the total amount of ground rent that would be paid in all of the complete 21-year periods of the lease.   (OCR)

28 The tenth term of an arithmetic progression is 125 and the sum of the first ten terms is 260.

   (a) Show that the first term in the progression is -73.

   (b) Find the common difference.   (OCR)

29 The binomial expansion of $(1 + ax)^n$, where n is a positive integer, has six terms.

   (a) Write down the value of n.

   The coefficient of the x^3 term is $\frac{5}{4}$.

   (b) Find a.   (OCR)

Examination questions

1 Find the coefficient of x in the expansion of $\left(3x - \dfrac{2}{x}\right)^5$.   (© IBO 2005)

2 Find the coefficient of x^3 in the binomial expansion of $\left(1 - \frac{1}{2}x\right)^8$.   (© IBO 2002)

3 The first four terms of an arithmetic sequence are 2, $a - b$, $2a + b + 7$ and $a - 3b$, where a and b are constants. Find a and b.   (© IBO 2003)

4 The sum of the first n terms of a series is given by $S_n = 2n^2 - n$, where $n \in \mathbb{Z}^+$.

(a) Find the first three terms of the series.

(b) Find an expression for the nth term of the series, giving your answer in terms of n.   (© IBO 2004)

5 A sequence $\{u_n\}$ is defined by $u_0 = 1$, $u_1 = 2$, $u_{n+1} = 3u_n - 2u_{n-1}$ where $n \in \mathbb{Z}^+$.

(a) Find u_2, u_3, u_4.

(b) (i) Express u_n in terms of n.

(ii) Verify that your answer to part (b)(i) satisfies the equation $u_{n+1} = 3u_n - 2u_{n-1}$.   (© IBO 2002)

5 Representation of statistical data

This chapter looks at ways of displaying numerical data using diagrams. When you have completed it, you should

- know the difference between quantitative and qualitative data
- be able to construct grouped frequency tables
- be able to draw a frequency histogram from a grouped frequency table
- be able to construct a cumulative frequency diagram from a frequency distribution table
- be able to make comparisons between sets of data by using diagrams.

5.1 Introduction

The collection, organisation and analysis of numerical information are all part of the subject called **statistics**. Pieces of numerical and other information are called **data**. A more helpful definition of 'data' is 'a series of facts from which conclusions may be drawn'.

In order to collect data you need to observe or to measure some property. This property is called a **variable**. The data which follow were taken from the internet, which has many sites containing data sources. In this example a variety of measurements was taken on brain sizes. Each column represents a variable. So, for example, 'Gender', 'FSIQ' and 'Height' are all variables.

Datafile name Brain size (Data reprinted from *Intelligence*, Vol. 15, Willerman et al, 'In vivo brain size …', 1991, with permission from Elsevier Science)

Description A team of researchers used a sample of 40 students at a university. The subjects took four subtests from the 'Wechsler (1981) Adult Intelligence Scale – Revised' test. Magnetic Resonance Imaging (MRI) was then used to measure the brain sizes of the subjects. The subjects' genders, heights and body masses are also included. The researchers withheld the masses of two subjects and the height of one subject for reasons of confidentiality.

Number of cases 40

Variable names

1 Gender: male or female

2 FSIQ: full scale IQ scores based on the four Wechsler (1981) subtests

3 VIQ: verbal IQ scores based on the four Wechsler (1981) subtests

4 PIQ: performance IQ scores based on the four Wechsler (1981) subtests

5 Mass: body mass in pounds

6 Height: height in inches (1 inch = 2.54 cm)

7 MRI_count: total pixel count from the 18 MRI scans

Brain size

Gender	FSIQ	VIQ	PIQ	Mass	Height	MRI_count
Female	133	132	124	118	64.5	816 932
Male	140	150	124	–	72.5	1 001 121
Male	139	123	150	143	73.3	1 038 437
Male	133	129	128	172	68.8	965 353
Female	137	132	134	147	65.0	951 545
Female	99	90	110	146	69.0	928 799
Female	138	136	131	138	64.5	991 305
Female	92	90	98	175	66.0	854 258
Male	89	93	84	134	66.3	904 858
Male	133	114	147	172	68.8	955 466
Female	132	129	124	118	64.5	833 868
Male	141	150	128	151	70.0	1 079 549
Male	135	129	124	155	69.0	924 059
Female	140	120	147	155	70.5	856 472
Female	96	100	90	146	66.0	878 897
Female	83	71	96	135	68.0	865 363
Female	132	132	120	127	68.5	852 244
Male	100	96	102	178	73.5	945 088
Female	101	112	84	136	66.3	808 020
Male	80	77	86	180	70.0	889 083
Male	83	83	86	–	–	892 420
Male	97	107	84	186	76.5	905 940
Female	135	129	134	122	62.0	790 619
Male	139	145	128	132	68.0	955 003
Female	91	86	102	114	63.0	831 722
Male	141	145	131	171	72.0	935 494
Female	85	90	84	140	68.0	798 612
Male	103	96	110	187	77.0	1 062 462
Female	77	83	72	106	63.0	793 549
Female	130	126	124	159	66.5	866 662
Female	133	126	132	127	62.5	857 782
Male	144	145	137	191	67.0	949 589
Male	103	96	110	192	75.5	997 925
Male	90	96	86	181	69.0	879 987
Female	83	90	81	143	66.5	834 344
Female	133	129	128	153	66.5	948 066
Male	140	150	124	144	70.5	949 395
Female	88	86	94	139	64.5	893 983
Male	81	90	74	148	74.0	930 016
Male	89	91	89	179	75.5	935 863

Table 5.1

You can see that there are different types of variable. The variable 'Gender' is non-numerical: such variables are usually called **qualitative**. The other variables are called **quantitative**, because the values they take are numerical.

Quantitative numerical data can be subdivided into two categories. For example the height of a person in inches, which can take any value in a particular range, is called a **continuous** variable. 'MRI_count', on the other hand, is a **discrete** variable: it can only take integer values because it counts pixels, and there is a clear step between each possible value. It would not be sensible, for example, to refer to an MRI_count of 1 000 000.3.

In summary:

> A variable is **qualitative** if it is not possible for it to take a numerical value.
>
> A variable is **quantitative** if it can take a numerical value.
>
> A quantitative variable which can take any value in a given range is **continuous**.
>
> A quantitative variable which has clear steps between its possible values is **discrete**.

5.2   Frequency histograms

Sometimes, for example if the data set is large, you may wish to divide the data into groups, called **class intervals**.

In the 'Brain size' data, the verbal IQ scores (VIQ) may be grouped into class intervals as in Table 5.2.

Table 5.2 is called a **grouped frequency table**. It shows how many values of the variable lie in each class interval. The pattern of a grouped frequency distribution is decided to some extent by the choice of class intervals. There would have been a different appearance to the distribution if the class intervals 71–90, 91–110, 111–130 and 131–150 had been chosen. There is no clear rule about how many class intervals should be chosen or what size they should be, but it is usual to have from 5 to 10 class intervals.

Verbal IQ	Tally	Frequency
71–80	||	2
81–90	⊮ ||||	9
91–100	⊮ ||	7
101–110	|	1
111–120	|||	3
121–130	⊮ |||	8
131–140	||||	4
141–150	⊮ |	6

Table 5.2

Grouping the data into class intervals inevitably means losing some information. For example, someone looking at the table would not know the exact values of the observations in the 71–80 category. All he or she would know for certain is that there were two such observations.

Suppose now that you were considering the mass data from the 'Brain size' data set and that you had a class interval 141–150. This refers to weights which are measured and then rounded to between 141 and 150 pounds. The class interval labelled as 141–150 actually contains values from 140.5 up to (but not including) 150.5. These real endpoints, 140.5 and 150.5, are referred to as the **interval boundaries**.

> Notice that the upper interval boundary of the class interval 141–150, which is 150.5, is the lower interval boundary of the next class interval.

Example 5.2.1
For each case below give the interval boundaries of the first class interval.

(a) The heights of 100 students were recorded to the nearest centimetre.

Height, h (cm)	160–164	165–169	170–174	...
Frequency	7	9	13	...

Table 5.3

(b) The masses in kilograms of 40 patients entering a doctor's surgery on one day were recorded to the nearest kilogram.

Mass, m (kg)	55–	60–	65–	...
Frequency	9	15	12	...

Table 5.4

(c) A group of 40 motorists was asked to state the ages at which they passed their driving tests.

Age, a (years)	17–	20–	23–	...
Frequency	6	11	7	...

Table 5.5

(a) The minimum and maximum heights for someone in the first class interval are 159.5 cm and 164.5 cm. The interval boundaries are given by $159.5 \leq h < 164.5$.

(b) The first class interval appears to go from 55 kg up to but not including 60 kg, but as the measurement has been made to the nearest kilogram the lower and upper interval boundaries are 54.5 kg and 59.5 kg. The interval boundaries are given by $54.5 \leq m < 59.5$.

(c) Age is recorded to the number of completed years, so 17– contains those who passed their tests from the day of their 17th birthday up to, but not including, the day of their 20th birthday. The interval boundaries are given by $17 \leq a < 20$.

Sometimes discrete data are grouped into class intervals. For example, the test scores of 40 students might appear as in Table 5.6.

Score	0–9	10–19	20–29	30–39	40–49	50–59
Frequency	14	9	9	3	3	2

Table 5.6

What are the interval boundaries? There is no universally accepted answer, but a common convention is to use 9.5 and 19.5 as the interval boundaries for the second class interval. Although it may appear strange, the interval boundaries for the first class interval would be −0.5 and 9.5. The **interval width** is given by

interval width = upper interval boundary − lower interval boundary.

When a grouped frequency distribution contains continuous data, one of the most common forms of graphical display is the **frequency histogram**.

> A **frequency histogram** is a bar chart with the following properties:
> - it has equal class intervals
> - there are no spaces between the bars (though there may be bars of height zero, which look like spaces)
> - the *area* of each bar is proportional to the frequency.

Since all the bars of a frequency histogram have the same width, *the height of each bar is proportional to the frequency.*

Given that the blocks have equal widths, the simplest way of making the area of a block proportional to the frequency is to make the height equal to the frequency. This means that

width of class × height is proportional to frequency.

Example 5.2.2

The grouped frequency distribution in Table 5.7 represents the heights in inches of a sample of 39 of the people from the 'Brain size' data (see Table 5.1). Represent these data in a frequency histogram.

Height (inches)	Frequency
62–63	4
64–65	5
66–67	8
68–69	9
70–71	4
72–73	3
74–75	2
76–77	4
78–79	0

Table 5.7

You need to check that all the class interval widths are equal. This is shown in Table 5.8.

Height, h (inches)	Interval boundaries	Interval width	Frequency
62–63	$61.5 \leq h < 63.5$	2	4
64–65	$63.5 \leq h < 65.5$	2	5
66–67	$65.5 \leq h < 67.5$	2	8
68–69	$67.5 \leq h < 69.5$	2	9
70–71	$69.5 \leq h < 71.5$	2	4
72–73	$71.5 \leq h < 73.5$	2	3
74–75	$73.5 \leq h < 75.5$	2	2
76–77	$75.5 \leq h < 77.5$	2	4
78–79	$77.5 \leq h < 79.5$	2	0

Table 5.8

The frequency histogram is shown in Fig. 5.9.

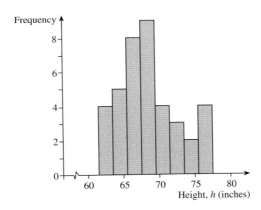

Fig. 5.9

The previous example of a frequency histogram has involved continuous data. You can also represent grouped discrete data in a frequency histogram. Table 5.10 gives the interval boundaries for the data in Table 5.6, which were the test scores of 40 students. Recall that the convention used is to take the class interval with limits 10 and 19 as having interval boundaries 9.5 and 19.5.

Score	Interval boundaries	Frequency
0–9	−0.5–9.5	14
10–19	9.5–19.5	9
20–29	19.5–29.5	9
30–39	29.5–39.5	3
40–49	39.5–49–5	3
50–59	49.5–59.5	2

Table 5.10

Fig. 5.11 shows the frequency histogram for the data. Notice that the left bar extends slightly to the left of the vertical axis, to the point −0.5. This accounts for the apparent thickness of the vertical axis.

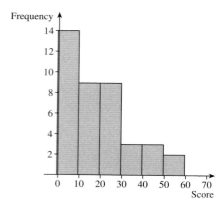

Fig. 5.11

Exercise 5A

In Question 1 below, the upper class boundary of one class is identical to the lower class boundary of the next class. If you were measuring speeds to the nearest m.p.h., then you might record a result of 40 m.p.h., and you would not know which class to put it in. This is not a problem in Question 1. You may come across data like these in examination questions, but it will be made clear what to do with them.

1 The speeds, in miles per hour, of 200 vehicles travelling on a motorway were measured by a radar device. The results are summarised in the following table.

Speed	30–40	40–50	50–60	60–70	70–80	80–90
Frequency	12	32	56	72	20	8

Draw a frequency histogram to illustrate the data.

2 The mass of each of 60 pebbles collected from a beach was measured. The results, correct to the nearest gram, are summarised in the following table.

Mass	5–9	10–14	15–19	20–24	25–29	30–34	35–39
Frequency	2	5	8	14	17	11	3

Draw a frequency histogram of the data.

3 A frequency histogram is drawn to represent a set of data.

(a) The first two class intervals have boundaries 2.0 and 2.25, and 2.25 and 2.5, with frequencies 5 and 12. The height of the first bar drawn is 2.5 cm. What is the height of the second bar?

(b) The interval boundaries of the third bar are 2.5 and 2.75. What is the corresponding frequency if the bar drawn has height 3.5 cm?

4 The following grouped frequency table shows the score received by 275 students who sat a statistics examination.

Score	0–9	10–19	20–29	30–39	40–49	50–59
Frequency	6	21	51	84	82	31

Taking the interval boundaries for 0–9 as -0.5 and 9.5, represent the data in a frequency histogram.

5 The haemoglobin levels in the blood of 45 hospital patients were measured. The results, correct to 1 decimal place, and ordered for convenience, are as follows.

9.1 10.1 10.7 10.7 10.9 11.3 11.3 11.4 11.4 11.4 11.6 11.8 12.0 12.1 12.3
12.4 12.7 12.9 13.1 13.2 13.4 13.5 13.5 13.6 13.7 13.8 13.8 14.0 14.2 14.2
14.2 14.6 14.6 14.8 14.8 15.0 15.0 15.0 15.1 15.4 15.6 15.7 16.2 16.3 16.9

(a) Form a grouped frequency table with 8 class intervals.

(b) Draw a frequency histogram of the data.

6 Each of the 34 children in a Year 3 class was given a task to perform. The times taken in minutes, correct to the nearest quarter of a minute, were as follows.

4	$3\frac{3}{4}$	5	$6\frac{1}{4}$	7	3	7	$5\frac{1}{4}$	$7\frac{1}{2}$	$8\frac{3}{4}$	$7\frac{1}{2}$	$4\frac{1}{2}$
$6\frac{1}{2}$	$4\frac{1}{4}$	8	$7\frac{1}{4}$	$6\frac{3}{4}$	$5\frac{3}{4}$	$4\frac{3}{4}$	$8\frac{1}{4}$	7	$3\frac{1}{2}$	$5\frac{1}{2}$	$7\frac{3}{4}$
$8\frac{1}{2}$	$6\frac{1}{2}$	5	$7\frac{1}{4}$	$6\frac{3}{4}$	$7\frac{3}{4}$	$5\frac{3}{4}$	6	$7\frac{3}{4}$	$6\frac{1}{2}$		

(a) Form a grouped frequency table with 6 equal class intervals beginning with $3–3\frac{3}{4}$.

(b) What are the boundaries of the first class interval?

(c) Draw a frequency histogram of the data.

7 The table shows the age distribution of the 200 members of a golf club.

Age	10–19	20–29	30–39	40–49	50–59	60–69	70–79
Number of members	12	40	44	47	32	15	10

(a) Form a table showing the interval boundaries.

(b) Draw a frequency histogram of the data.

5.3 Cumulative frequency diagrams

An alternative method of representing continuous data is a **cumulative frequency diagram**. This is a graph in which the cumulative frequencies are plotted against the upper interval boundaries of the corresponding class interval. Consider the data from Example 5.2.2. This is shown in Table 5.12 with some of the classes combined so there are now six classes instead of nine, and not all the class widths are equal.

Height, h (inches)	62–63	64–65	66–67	68–71	72–75	76–79
Frequency	4	5	8	13	5	4

Table 5.12

There are 0 observations less than 61.5.
There are 4 observations less than 63.5.
There are 4 + 5, or 9, observations less than 65.5.
There are 4 + 5 + 8, or 17, observations less than 67.5.

⋮   ⋮   ⋮

There are 39 observations less than 79.5.

This results in Table 5.13, which shows the cumulative frequency.

Height, h (inches)	<61.5	<63.5	<65.5	<67.5	<71.5	<75.5	<79.5
Cumulative frequency	0	4	9	17	30	35	39

Table 5.13

The points (61.5, 0), (63.5, 4), ... , (79.5, 39) are then plotted and are joined with a smooth curve, as shown in Fig. 5.14.

Sometimes you may see cumulative frequency graphs in which the points are joined by line segments.

You can also use the graph to read off other information. For example, you can estimate the proportion of the sample whose heights are under 69 inches. Read off the cumulative frequency corresponding to a height of 69 in Fig. 5.14. This is approximately 21.9. Therefore an estimate of the proportion of the sample whose heights were under 69 inches would be $\frac{21.9}{39} \approx 0.56$, or 56%.

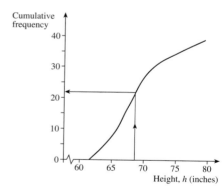

Fig. 5.14

5.4 Practical activities

In each activity collect two sets of data and then draw diagrams to make comparisons between them.

1 **One-sidedness** Investigate whether reaction times are different when you use only information from one 'side' of your body.

(a) Choose a subject and instruct them to close their left eye. Against a wall hold a ruler pointing vertically downwards with the 0 cm mark at the bottom and ask the subject to place the index finger of their right hand aligned with this 0 cm mark. Explain that you will let go of the ruler without warning, and that the subject must try to pin it against the wall using the index finger of their right hand. Measure the distance dropped.

(b) Repeat this for, say, 30 subjects.

(c) Take a further 30 subjects and carry out the experiment again for each of these subjects, but for this second set of 30 make them close their right eye and use their left hand.

(d) Draw two frequency histograms and use these to compare the distributions.

(e) Do subjects seem to react more quickly using their right side than they do using their left side? Are subjects more erratic when using their left side? How does the fact that some people are naturally left-handed affect the results? Would it be more appropriate to investigate 'dominant' side versus 'non-dominant' side rather than left versus right?

2 **High jump**   Find how high people can jump.

(a) Pick a subject and ask them to stand against a wall and stretch their arm as far up the wall as possible. Make a mark at this point. Then ask the subject to jump as high as they can and make a second mark at this highest point. Measure the distance between the two marks. This is a measure of how high they jumped.

(b) Take two samples, one of Year 11 students and another of Year 7 students, and plot a frequency histogram of the results for each group.

(c) Do Year 11 students jump higher than Year 7 students?

3 **Darts**   Compare the total scores of darts players

(a) Throw four darts at a dart-board, aiming for the treble twenty, and record the total score. Get a sample of students to repeat this. Plot the results on a frequency histogram.

(b) Take a second sample of students and ask each of them to throw four darts at the dart-board, but this time tell each student to aim for the bull. Plot these results on a second frequency histogram. Is the strategy of aiming for the treble twenty more successful than that of aiming for the bull? Does one of the strategies result in a more variable total score?

Exercise 5B

1 Draw a cumulative frequency diagram for the data in Question 1 of Exercise 5A. With the help of the diagram estimate

(a) the percentage of cars that were travelling at more than 65 m.p.h.,

(b) the speed below which 25% of the cars were travelling.

2 Draw a cumulative frequency diagram for the examination marks in Question 4 of Exercise 5A.

   (a) Candidates with at least 44 marks received Grade A. Find the percentage of the students that received Grade A.

   (b) It is known that 81.8% of these students gained Grade E or better. Find the lowest Grade E mark for these students.

3 Estimates of the age distribution of a European country for the year 2010 are given in the following table.

Age	under 16	16–39	40–64	65–79	80–99
Percentage	14.3	33.1	35.3	11.9	5.4

   (a) Draw a percentage cumulative frequency diagram.

   (b) It is expected that people who have reached the age of 60 will be drawing a state pension in 2010. If the projected population of the country is 42.5 million, estimate the number who will then be drawing this pension.

4 The records of the sales in a small grocery store for the 360 days that it opened during the year 2006 are summarised in the following table.

Sales, x (in £100s)	$x < 2$	$2 \le x < 3$	$3 \le x < 4$	$4 \le x < 5$
Number of days	15	27	64	72

Sales, x (in £100s)	$5 \le x < 6$	$6 \le x < 7$	$7 \le x < 8$	$8 \le x < 9$
Number of days	86	70	16	10

   Days for which sales fall below £325 are classified as 'poor' and those for which the sales exceed £775 are classified as 'good'. With the help of a cumulative frequency diagram estimate the number of poor days and the number of good days in 2006.

   Keep your cumulative frequency diagram for Exercise 6A Question 4.

5 A company has 132 employees who work in its city branch. The distances, x miles, measured to the nearest mile, that employees travel to work are summarised in the following grouped frequency table.

x	<5	5–9	10–14	15–19	20–24	25–29
Frequency	12	29	63	13	12	3

   Draw a cumulative frequency diagram and use it to find the number of miles below which

   (a) one-quarter   (b) three-quarters

   of the employees travel to work.

6 Measures of location

This chapter describes three different measures of location and their method of calculation. When you have completed it, you should

- know what the median is, and be able to calculate it using a calculator if necessary
- know what the mean is, and be able to calculate it using a calculator if necessary
- know what the mode and the modal class are, and be able to find them
- be able to choose which is the appropriate measure to use in a given situation.

6.1 Introduction

Suppose that you wanted to know the typical playing time for a compact disc (CD). You cannot possibly find the playing times of all CDs, that is, the **population** of CDs, but you could start by taking a few CDs (a **sample**) and finding out the playing time for each one. You might obtain a list of values such as

$$49, 56, 55, 68, 61, 57, 61, 52, 63$$

where the values have been given in minutes, to the nearest whole minute.

You can see that the values are located roughly in the region of 1 hour (rather than, say, 2 hours or 10 minutes). It would be useful to have a single value which gave some idea of this location. A single value would condense the information contained in the data set into a 'typical' value, and would allow you to compare this data set with another one. Such a value is called a **measure of location**, or a **measure of central tendency**, or, in everyday language, an **average**.

If you have chosen the sample using a method in which every CD in the population of CDs is equally likely to be picked, your sample would be a **random sample**. In this case the sample is clearly not random – almost certainly you have no CDs of, say, Japanese music and could not have picked one.

6.2 The median

You can get a clearer picture of the location of the playing times by arranging them in ascending order of size:

$$49, 52, 55, 56, 57, 61, 61, 63, 68.$$

A simple measure of location is the middle value. There are equal numbers of values above and below it. In this case there are nine values and the middle one is 57. This value is called the **median**.

If the number of values is even then there is no single 'middle' value. In the case of the six values

$$47, 49, 59, 62, 65, 68,$$

which are the playing times of another six CDs (in order), the median is taken to be halfway between the third and fourth values, which is $\frac{1}{2}(59 + 62)$, or 60.5. Again, there are equal numbers of values below and above this value: in this case, three.

> To find the **median** of a data set of n values, arrange the values in order of increasing size.
>
> If n is odd, the median is the $\frac{1}{2}(n+1)$th value. If n is even, the median is halfway between the $\frac{1}{2}n$th value and the following value.

Here is a list of the weights of the female students from the 'Brain size' datafile in Chapter 5.

118   147   146   138   175   118   155   146   135   127   136   122   114   140
106   159   127   143   153   139

First, put them in order.

106   114   118   118   122   127   127   135   136   **138**   **139**   140   143   146
146   147   153   155   159   175

There are 20 students so the median is calculated from the 10th and 11th values. These two values are shown in bold type. The median is $\frac{1}{2}(138 + 139)$, or 138.5 pounds.

Your calculator has a built-in routine for finding the median. Consult the manual to find out how to use it.

6.3   Finding the median from a frequency table

Data sets are often much larger than the ones in the previous section and the values will often have been organised in some way, maybe in a frequency table. As an example, Table 6.1 gives the number of brothers and sisters of the children in Year 8 at a school.

Number of brothers and sisters	Frequency	Cumulative frequency
0	36	36
1	94	130
2	48	178
3	15	193
4	7	200
5	3	203
6	1	204
	Total: 204	

Table 6.1

One way of finding the median is to write out a list of all the individual values, starting with 36 '0's, then 94 '1's and so on, and find the $\frac{1}{2} \times 204$, or 102nd value and the 103rd value. A much easier method is to insert a column of cumulative frequencies, as in Table 6.1. From this you can see that when you have come to the end of the '0's you have not yet reached the 102nd value but, by the end of the '1's, you have reached the 130th value. This means that the 102nd and 103rd values are both 1, so the median is also 1.

You can also use your calculator to find the median from a frequency table.

In this example the data had not been grouped, so it was possible to count to the median. Large data sets for continuous variables, however, are nearly always grouped, and the individual values are lost. This means that you cannot find the median exactly and you have to estimate it. Table 6.2 gives the frequency distribution for the playing time of a much larger selection of CDs.

Playing time, x (min)	Interval boundaries	Frequency	Cumulative frequency
40–44	$39.5 \leq x < 44.5$	1	1
45–49	$44.5 \leq x < 49.5$	7	8
50–54	$49.5 \leq x < 54.5$	12	20
55–59	$54.5 \leq x < 59.5$	24	44
60–64	$59.5 \leq x < 64.5$	29	73
65–69	$64.5 \leq x < 69.5$	14	87
70–74	$69.5 \leq x < 74.5$	5	92
75–79	$74.5 \leq x < 79.5$	3	95
		Total: 95	

Table 6.2

A column for cumulative frequency has been added to the table, and Fig. 6.3 shows a cumulative frequency graph for the data.

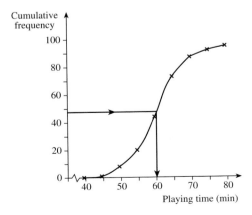

Fig. 6.3

Reminder: cumulative frequency is plotted against the upper interval boundary of each class interval.

The cumulative frequency curve allows you to find the number of CDs with a playing time less than a given value. To obtain the median playing time from the cumulative frequency graph, you read off the value corresponding to a cumulative frequency equal to half the total frequency, in this case $\frac{1}{2} \times 95$, or 47.5. This gives a playing time of 60 minutes. This value is taken as an estimate of the median, because roughly half the playing times will be below it and consequently about half will be above it.

To find the median value for grouped data from a cumulative frequency graph, read off the value of the variable corresponding to a cumulative frequency equal to half the total frequency.

Some books suggest reading off the value from the cumulative frequency graph which corresponds to a cumulative frequency of $\frac{1}{2}(n+1)$ rather than $\frac{1}{2}n$. This will give a slightly different value but the difference is not important.

Sometimes discrete data are grouped into classes so that, once again, you cannot list the individual values. An example was given in Table 5.6. To estimate the median for such data, treat the variable as though it were continuous and find the median from the cumulative frequency graph or from a calculator.

When you use your calculator to calculate the median, or any other statistical calculation, it is crucial to make sure that you enter the data correctly.

Exercise 6A

1 Find the median weight of 6.6 kg, 3.2 kg, 4.8 kg, 7.6 kg, 5.4 kg, 7.1 kg, 2.0 kg, 6.3 kg and 4.3 kg.

A weight of 6.0 kg is added to the set. What is the median of the 10 weights?

2 Obtain the medians for the following data sets.

(a) The speeds, in miles per hour, of 20 cars, measured on a city street.

41 15 4 27 21 32 43 37 18 25 29 34 28 30 25 52 12 36 6 25

(b) The times taken, in hours (to the nearest tenth), to carry out repairs to 17 pieces of machinery.

0.9 1.0 2.1 4.2 0.7 1.1 0.9 1.8 0.9 1.2 2.3 1.6 2.1 0.3 0.8 2.7 0.4

3 Obtain the median of the haemoglobin levels in Exercise 5A Question 5.

4 Using your cumulative frequency diagram from Exercise 5B Question 4, obtain an estimate of the median value of the sales.

5 The following are ignition times in seconds, correct to the nearest 0.1 s, of samples of 80 flammable materials. They are arranged in numerical order by rows.

1.2	1.4	1.4	1.5	1.5	1.6	1.7	1.8	1.8	1.9	2.1	2.2	2.3	2.5	2.5	2.5
2.5	2.6	2.7	2.8	3.1	3.2	3.5	3.6	3.7	3.8	3.8	3.9	3.9	4.0	4.1	4.2
4.3	4.5	4.5	4.6	4.7	4.7	4.8	4.9	5.1	5.1	5.1	5.2	5.2	5.3	5.4	5.5
5.6	5.8	5.9	5.9	6.0	6.3	6.4	6.4	6.4	6.4	6.7	6.8	6.8	6.9	7.3	7.4
7.4	7.6	7.9	8.0	8.6	8.8	8.8	9.2	9.4	9.6	9.7	9.8	10.6	11.2	11.8	12.8

   (a) Group the data into 8 equal classes, starting with 1.0–2.4 and 2.5–3.9, and form a grouped frequency table. Draw a frequency histogram. State what it indicates about the ignition times.

   (b) From the grouped frequency table draw a cumulative frequency diagram and use it to estimate the median ignition time.

   (c) Find the exact median from the data set, and account for any difference in your two answers.

6 The number of rejected CDs produced each day by a machine was monitored for 100 days. The results are summarised in the following table.

Number of rejects	0–9	10–19	20–29	30–39	40–49	50–59
Number of days	5	8	19	37	22	9

   Estimate the median number of rejects.

7 For the 'Brain size' data in Table 5.1, find the median heights of

   (a) the men,   (b) the women,

   and compare them.

6.4   The mean

The median does not use the actual values of the observations in a data set, apart from the middle value(s) when the data are arranged in order of increasing size. A measure of location which does make use of the actual values of all the observations is the **mean**. This is the quantity which most people are referring to when they talk about the 'average'. The mean is found by adding all the values and dividing by the number of values. For the nine CDs in Section 6.1,

$$\text{mean} = \frac{49 + 56 + 55 + 68 + 61 + 57 + 61 + 52 + 63}{9} = \frac{522}{9} = 58 \text{ minutes.}$$

> The **mean** of a data set is equal to the sum of the values in the data set divided by the number of values.

You can also use your calculator to find the mean. You may need to refer to the calculator manual.

6.5   Samples and populations

You should realise that the calculation of the mean of the nine CDs in Section 6.4 can only give you an **estimate** of the mean of the whole population of CDs. The true mean playing time of CDs can only be found by testing the playing times of the whole population of CDs. This is clearly impossible, so you have to use a sample of CDs, which gives you an approximation to the true mean.

When you are finding the mean of a population, the symbol μ is used. (The letter μ is the greek letter 'm', and is pronounced 'mu'.) If you are finding the mean of a sample to get an approximation to the mean of a population, the symbol $\bar{x}$ (pronounced 'x-bar') is used.

The fact that the sample mean is the best possible approximation to the population mean in the sense that it is an unbiased approximation is an important issue which cannot be addressed in this book.

> The word 'unbiased' is a technical word with a specific meaning, but it is being used in both in its technical and untechnical senses here.

> Note that although a population sounds as though it ought to be large, it need not be so. For example, it may be that the population you are concerned with is the total number of people in your mathematics class.

It is possible to express the definition of the mean as a mathematical formula by using the Σ-notation you met in Section 2.6. Suppose you have n data values. The symbol x_i denotes the ith value in the data set. For the playing times of the nine CDs in the previous section, $x_1 = 49$, $x_2 = 56$, $x_3 = 55$ and so on. The sum of these values is

$$x_1 + x_2 + x_3 + x_4 + x_5 + x_6 + x_7 + x_8 + x_9.$$

> The population mean, μ, of a data set of n values is given by
> $$\mu = \frac{x_1 + x_2 + \ldots + x_n}{n} = \frac{\sum_{i=1}^{n} x_i}{n}.$$
> The sample mean, $\bar{x}$, of a sample with n values is given by
> $$\bar{x} = \frac{x_1 + x_2 + \ldots + x_n}{n} = \frac{\sum_{i=1}^{n} x_i}{n}.$$

> Although the two formulae above look identical, it is important to make sure that you know when you are dealing with a population and when you are dealing with a sample, which gives an approximation to the mean of the population.

When you use your calculator to calculate the mean, you can either use the formulae above, or you can use the calculator's own built-in routine. Whichever method you use, ensure that you enter the data correctly.

6.6   Calculating the mean from a frequency table

Table 6.4 contains a copy of the data in Table 6.1, which was the frequency distribution of the number of brothers and sisters of the children in Year 8 at a school. Of the 204 values, 36 are '0's, 94 are '1's, 48 are '2's and so on. Their sum will be

$$(0 \times 36) + (1 \times 94) + (2 \times 48) + (3 \times 15) + (4 \times 7) + (5 \times 3) + (6 \times 1).$$

You can include this calculation in the table by adding a third column in which each value of the variable, x_i, is multiplied by its frequency, f_i.

Number of brothers and sisters, x_i	Frequency, f_i	$f_i x_i$
0	36	0
1	94	94
2	48	96
3	15	45
4	7	28
5	3	15
6	1	6
Totals:	$\sum_{i=1}^{n} f_i = 204$	$\sum_{i=1}^{n} f_i x_i = 284$

Table 6.4

The mean is equal to $\dfrac{284}{204} = 1.39$, correct to 3 significant figures.

Although the number of brothers and sisters of each child must be a whole number, the mean of the data values need not be a whole number.

In this example the answer is a recurring decimal, and so the answer has been rounded to 3 significant figures. This degree of accuracy is suitable for the answers to most statistical calculations. However it is important to keep more significant figures when values are carried forward for use in further calculations.

The calculation of the mean can be expressed in Σ-notation as follows:

> The population mean, μ, of a data set in which the variable takes the value x_1 with frequency f_1, x_2 with frequency f_2 and so on is given by
>
> $$\mu = \frac{f_1x_1 + f_2x_2 + ... + f_nx_n}{f_1 + f_2 + ... + f_n} = \frac{\sum\limits_{i=1}^{n} f_ix_i}{\sum\limits_{i=1}^{n} f_i}.$$
>
> The sample mean, $\bar{x}$, of a sample in which the variable takes the value x_1 with frequency f_1, x_2 with frequency f_2 and so on is given by
>
> $$\bar{x} = \frac{f_1x_1 + f_2x_2 + ... + f_nx_n}{f_1 + f_2 + ... + f_n} = \frac{\sum\limits_{i=1}^{n} f_ix_i}{\sum\limits_{i=1}^{n} f_i}.$$

If the data in a frequency table are grouped, you need a single value to represent each class before you can calculate an estimate of the mean using either of the equations in the blue box. A reasonable choice is to take the value halfway between the class boundaries. This is called the **mid-interval value**. Table 6.5 reproduces Table 6.2 for the playing times of 95 CDs. Two other columns have been included, one giving the mid-interval value for each class and the other the product of this mid-interval value and the frequency.

Playing time, x (min)	Class boundaries	Frequency, f_i	Mid-interval value, x_i	f_ix_i
40–44	$39.5 \leq x < 44.5$	1	42	42
45–49	$44.5 \leq x < 49.5$	7	47	329
50–54	$49.5 \leq x < 54.5$	12	52	624
55–59	$54.5 \leq x < 59.5$	24	57	1368
60–64	$59.5 \leq x < 64.5$	29	62	1798
65–69	$64.5 \leq x < 69.5$	14	67	938
70–74	$69.5 \leq x < 74.5$	5	72	360
75–79	$74.5 \leq x < 79.5$	3	77	231
Totals:		$\sum\limits_{i=1}^{8} f_i = 95$		$\sum\limits_{i=1}^{8} f_ix_i = 5690$

Table 6.5

Thus the estimate of the mean is $\dfrac{\sum\limits_{i=1}^{8} f_ix_i}{\sum\limits_{i=1}^{8} f_i} = \dfrac{5690}{95} = 59.9$ minutes, correct to 3 significant figures.

> This value is only an estimate of the mean playing time for the CDs, because individual values have been replaced by mid-interval values: some information has been lost by grouping the data.

6.7   Calculating the mean from a cumulative frequency graph or table

Sometimes you may need to calculate an approximation to the mean when you are given a cumulative frequency graph.

Example 6.7.1
Figure 6.6, which is a copy of Fig. 5.14, is a cumulative frequency graph representing the heights in inches of 39 people from the datafile 'Brain size'. Use the graph to calculate an approximation to the mean height.

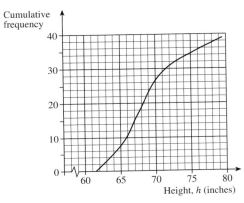

Fig. 6.6

Start by constructing a cumulative frequency table by reading from the graph. This is shown in Table 6.7. The first reading, at 61.5, was taken because there is no reading lower than 61.5. The interval width of 2 inches along the height axis was taken for convenience.

Height (inches)	Cumulative frequency
< 61.5	0
< 63.5	4
< 65.5	9
< 67.5	17
< 69.5	25
< 71.5	30
< 73.5	33
< 75.5	35
< 77.5	37
< 79.5	39

Table 6.7

Mid-interval value	Frequency
62.5	4
64.5	5
66.5	8
68.5	8
70.5	5
72.5	3
74.5	2
76.5	2
78.5	2

Table 6.8

From Table 6.7, construct Table 6.8. The value 62.5 is mid-way between 61.5 and 63.5, and the frequency 4 is the difference between 0 and 4. Similarly the next entry in the frequency column is $9 - 4 = 5$.

You can now calculate an approximation to the mean using your calculator and the method of the previous section, getting 68.75... inches.

An approximation to the mean is 68.8 inches.

Exercise 6B

1 The test marks of 8 students were 18, 2, 5, 0, 17, 15, 16 and 11. Find the mean score.

2 For the data set in Table 5.1, find the mean height of the male students.

The mean height of adult males is about 69 inches. Comment on your answer in the light of this information.

3 (a) Find $\bar{x}$ given that $\sum_{i=1}^{20} x_i = 226$.   (b) Find $\bar{y}$ given that $\sum_{i=1}^{12} (y_i - 100) = 66$.

4 The number of misprints on each page of the draft of a book containing 182 pages is summarised in the following table.

Number of misprints	0	1	2	3	4
Number of pages		144	24	10	2	2

Find the mean number of misprints on a page.

5 The following table gives the frequency distribution for the lengths of rallies (measured by the number of shots) in a tennis match.

Length of rally	1	2	3	4	5	6	7	8
Frequency		2	20	15	12	10	5	3	1

Find the mean length of a rally.

6 The table below gives the number of shoots produced by 50 plants in a botanical research laboratory.

No. of shoots	0–4	5–9	10–14	15–19	20–24	25–29	30–34	35–39	40–44
Frequency	1	1	1	6	17	16	4	2	2

Calculate the mean number of shoots per plant.

7 The speeds, in miles per hour, of 200 vehicles travelling on a motorway were measured using a radar device. The results are summarised in the following grouped frequency table.

Speed (m.p.h.)	30–40	40–50	50–60	60–70	70–80	80–90
Frequency	12	32	56	72	20	8

Estimate the mean speed.

8 Calls made by a telephone saleswoman were monitored. The lengths (in minutes, to the nearest minute) of 30 calls are summarised in the following table.

Length of call	0–2	3–5	6–8	9–11	12–14
Number of calls	17	6	4	2	1

(a) Write down the class interval boundaries.

(b) Estimate the mean length of the calls.

9 The cumulative frequency diagram below illustrates data relating the height (in cm) of 400 children at a certain school.

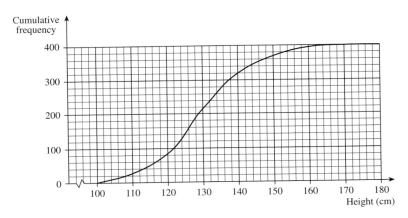

By taking intervals of width 10 cm calculate an estimate of the mean height of the children.

10 The price of a CD is denoted by £x. For 60 CDs bought in different stores it is found that $\sum_{i=1}^{60} x_i = 773.40$. Calculate the mean price of these CDs. The mean price of a further 40 CDs is found to be £11.64. Find the mean price of the 100 CDs.

11 The mean weight of eight oarsmen is 100 kg. They are joined by a cox of weight 55 kg. Calculate the mean weight of all nine people.

12 When a tug of war team of six members is joined by another member, the mean weight goes up from 110 kg to 111 kg. Find the weight of the new member.

6.8 The mode and the modal class

A third measure of location is the **mode**, sometimes called the **modal value**. This is defined to be the most frequently occurring value. You can pick it out from a frequency table (if the data have not been grouped) by looking for the value with the highest frequency. If you look back to Table 6.1 you will see that the mode for the number of brothers and sisters is 1.

If the data have been grouped then it is only possible to estimate the mode. Alternatively, you can give the **modal class interval**, which is the class interval with the highest frequency. For example, the modal class for the playing time in Table 6.2 is 60–64 minutes.

If you are given a small data set then you can find the mode just by looking at the data. For the first nine CDs in Section 6.2, with playing times

49, 52, 55, 56, 57, 61, 61, 63, 68

the mode is 61.

It is not uncommon for all the values to occur only once, so that there is no mode. For example, the next six CDs had playing times

47, 49, 59, 62, 65, 68,

and there is no modal value. Combining the two data sets gives

47, 49, 49, 52, 55, 56, 57, 59, 61, 61, 62, 63, 65, 68, 68.

Now there are three values which have a frequency of 2, giving three modes: 49, 61 and 68. One of these values is low, one high and the other is near the centre of the data set. In this case, the mode fails to provide only one measure of location to represent the data set. You can see that the mode is not a very useful measure of location for small data sets.

In contrast to the mean and median, the mode can be found for qualitative data. For example, for the datafile 'Brain size' in Table 5.1 the mode for the variable 'Gender' can be found. However, since the number of males is equal to the number of females (both 20), both 'males' and 'females' are modes.

> The **mode** of a data set is the value which occurs with the highest frequency. A data set can have more than one mode if two or more values have the same maximum frequency. A data set has no mode if all the values have the same frequency.
>
> The **modal class** for a grouped frequency table is the class with the highest frequency.

6.9 Comparison of the mean, median and mode

The examples in this chapter show that the mean, median and mode of a data set can differ from each other. For example, for the first nine CDs, the median was 57, the mean 58 and the mode 61. The question then arises as to why there are different ways of calculating the average of a data set. The answer is that an average describes a large amount of information with a single value, and there is no completely satisfactory way of doing this. Each average conveys different information and each has its advantages and disadvantages. You can see this by comparing the mean, median and mode for the following data set, which gives the monthly salaries of the thirteen employees in a small firm.

£1000 £1000 £1000 £1000 £1100 £1200 £1250
£1400 £1600 £1600 £1700 £2900 £4200

Median $= \frac{1}{2}(n + 1)$th value $= \frac{1}{2}(13 + 1)$th value $=$ 7th value $=$ £1250.

Mean $=$ sum of the values $\div n = \frac{20\,950}{13} =$ £1612, correct to the nearest pound.

Mode $=$ value with the highest frequency $=$ £1000.

A new employee who had been told that the 'average' wage was £1612 (the mean) would probably be disappointed when he learnt his own salary, because 10 out of the 13 employees earn less than £1612. In this example the median would measure the centre of the distribution better because the median is not affected by the large distance of the last two salaries from the other salaries, whereas the mean is 'pulled up' by them. Normally the median is preferable to the mean as an average when there are values which are not typical. Such values are called **outliers**. The mode is not a very useful measure of the centre in this example, because it is £1000, the lowest salary: 9 of the 13 employees earn more than this.

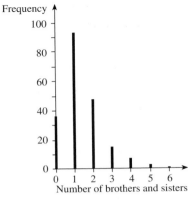

Fig. 6.9

You can see the same effect of a few high values on the mean for the data set in Table 6.4. The frequency distribution is illustrated in Fig. 6.9. The distribution is not symmetrical but is said to be **skewed**. The 'tail' of high values on the right of the distribution has the effect of making the mean (approximately 1.4) higher than the median (1).

> A distribution which has a 'tail' of low values on the left will have a mean which is less than the median.

Distributions which are roughly symmetrical will have similar values for the mean and the median. The data for the CD playing times in Table 6.2 illustrate this. The frequency histogram in Fig. 6.10, which illustrates this distribution, is approximately symmetrical; the estimates for the mean (59.9) and median (60) are nearly equal. For such a distribution the mean might be considered the 'best' average, because it uses all the information in the data set.

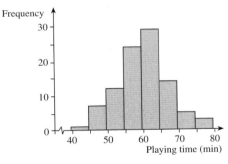

Fig. 6.10

From these examples it should be clear that the mean, median and mode often provide different information. When you are given an 'average' it is important to know whether it is the mean, the median or the mode. When you calculate an average, it is important to choose the average which is the most 'typical' value.

Example 6.9.1

A commuter who travels to work by car has a choice of two different routes, V and W. She decides to compare her journey times for each route. So she records the journey times, in minutes, for 10 consecutive working days, for each route. The results are:

Route V	53	52	48	51	49	47	42	48	57	53
Route W	43	41	39	108	52	42	38	45	39	51

Calculate the mean and median for route V, and the mean and median for route W. Which average do you think is more suitable for comparing the time taken on each route?

For route V, $\bar{v} = \dfrac{\sum\limits_{i=1}^{10} v_i}{n} = \dfrac{500}{10} = 50.$ For route W, $\bar{w} = \dfrac{\sum\limits_{i=1}^{10} w_i}{n} = \dfrac{498}{10} = 49.8.$

Arranging the values in order of increasing size gives:

Route V	42	47	48	48	49	51	52	53	53	57
Route W	38	39	39	41	42	43	45	51	52	108

For route V, median $= \frac{1}{2}$(5th + 6th) values $= \frac{1}{2}(49 + 51) = 50.$

For route W, median $= \frac{1}{2}$(5th + 6th) values $= \frac{1}{2}(42 + 43) = 42.5.$

For route V, the mean and the median are equal. For route W the mean is greater than the median, because the single high value of 108 pulls up the mean. This unusual value was probably due to bad weather or an accident and is not typical. So it is better to use the median as the average journey time, because it is not affected by such outliers. This suggests that route W, with a median of 42.5 minutes, is quicker than route V, with a median of 50 minutes.

6.10   Practical activities

1 **One-sidedness**   Calculate the mean and median for each set of data in Practical activity 1 in Section 5.4. Which average is more appropriate for comparing the reaction times? Give a reason for your choice.

2 **High jump**   Calculate the mean and median for each set of data in Practical activity 2 in Section 5.4. Which average is more appropriate for comparing the heights jumped? Give a reason for your choice.

3 **Newspapers**   Does the length of the sentences in a newspaper differ between a quality newspaper and a popular newspaper?

(a) For each type of newspaper count the number of words per sentence for at least 100 sentences. (You should ignore the headlines.)

(b) Make a frequency table of the results for each newspaper.

(c) Illustrate the results with diagrams and comment on the shape of the distributions.

(d) Calculate the mean and median for each distribution. Which would you use to compare the distributions and why?

4 **Age distribution**   The Office for National Statistics publishes many statistics relating to the United Kingdom. From the website www.statistics.gov.uk/ (click on 'Population' in the key statistics panel) or from its other publications obtain the most recent data for 'Population by gender and age.'

(a) Illustrate the data in a way which allows you to compare the age distribution for males and females, and comment on the shape of the distributions.

(b) Calculate the mean and median for the two distributions, explaining any assumptions which you may have to make.

(c) Would you use the mean or the median to compare the average age of men and women? Explain your choice.

5 **Just a minute!**   How well can people estimate time?

(a) Ask at least 100 people to estimate a time interval of one minute. You will need to decide on a standard procedure for doing this. Record the value of the estimates to the nearest second. If possible have two distinct groups of at least 50, for example children in a particular age range and adults.

(b) Calculate the mean and median for each group.

(c) Assemble the results for each group into a frequency table and illustrate the distribution for each group with a histogram.

(d) Comment on the shape of the distributions. Which would you use, mean or median, to compare the two groups? Give a reason for your choice.

Exercise 6C

1 For the following distributions state, where possible, the mode or the modal class.

(a)

x	0	1	2	3	4
f	7	4	2	5	1

(b)

x	70	75	80	85	90
f	5	5	5	5	5

(c)

x	2–3	4–5	6–7	8–9	10–11
f	7	4	4	4	1

(d)

Eye colour	Blue	Brown	Green
f	23	39	3

2 State, giving a reason, which of the mean, median or mode would be most useful in the following situations.

 (a) The manager of a shoe shop wishes to stock shoes of various sizes.

 (b) A City Council wishes to plan for a school to serve a new housing estate. In order to estimate the number of pupils, it studies family sizes on similar estates.

 (c) A person travels by car from York to Crewe regularly and has kept a record of the times taken. She wishes to make an estimate of the time that her next journey will take.

3 An estate agent makes the following statement.

 'Over 60% of houses sold this month were sold for more than the average selling price.'

 Consider the possible truth of this statement, and what is meant by 'average'.

4 State whether you would expect the following variables to have distributions which are skewed, or which are roughly symmetrical.

 (a) The heights of female students in a university.

 (b) The running times of competitors in a marathon race.

 (c) The scores obtained by candidates in an easy examination.

 (d) The numbers of pages in the books in a library.

5 A mental arithmetic test of 8 questions was given to a class of 32 pupils. The results are summarised in the following table.

Number of correct answers	0	1	2	3	4	5	6	7	8
Number of pupils	1	2	1	4	4	6	7	4	3

 (a) Find the mean, median and mode of the number of correct answers. Interpret the median and mode in the context of this maths test.

 (b) Describe the shape of the distribution.

7 Measures of spread

This chapter describes three different measures of spread and their methods of calculation. When you have completed it, you should

- know what the range is, and be able to calculate it
- know what the quartiles are and how to find the interquartile range from them
- be able to construct a box and whisker plot from a set of data
- know what the variance and standard deviation are, and be able to calculate them
- be able to select an appropriate measure of spread to use in a given situation.

7.1 Introduction

You saw in Chapter 6 how a set of data could be summarised by choosing an appropriate typical value, or 'measure of location' as it is more correctly known. Three different measures of location, the mean, the median and the mode, were introduced.

Now consider the two sets of data A and B given below.

$$A:\quad 48 \quad 52 \quad 60 \quad 60 \quad 60 \quad 68 \quad 72$$
$$B:\quad 0 \quad 10 \quad 60 \quad 60 \quad 60 \quad 110 \quad 120$$

For both data sets A and B, mean = median = mode = 60. If you were just given a measure of location for each set you might be tempted to think that the two sets of data were similar. Yet if you look in detail at the two sets of data you can see that they are quite different. The most striking difference between the two data sets is that set B is much more spread out than set A. Measures of location do not give any indication of these differences in spread, so it is necessary to devise some new measures to summarise the spread of data.

7.2 The range

The most obvious method of measuring spread is to calculate the difference between the lowest value and the highest value. This difference is called the **range**.

> The **range** of a set of data values is defined by the equation
>
> range = largest value − smallest value.

The range of data set A is $72 - 48 = 24$, whereas the range of data set B is $120 - 0 = 120$. Calculating the ranges shows clearly that data set B is more spread out than data set A.

> It is quite common for students to give the range as an interval. This would mean, for instance, that the range of data set A would be given as 48 to 72, or 48–72, or $48 \rightarrow 72$. In statistics it is usually much more helpful to give the range as a single value, so the definition above is used.

If you are going to use the range as a measure of spread it is helpful to realise its limitations. If you consider the two further data sets C and D shown below, you will see that they both have the same range, 8.

$$C: \quad 2 \quad 4 \quad 6 \quad 8 \quad 10$$
$$D: \quad 2 \quad 6 \quad 6 \quad 6 \quad 10$$

Although both data sets C and D have the same range, the patterns of their distributions are quite different from one another. Data set C is evenly spread within the interval 2 to 10 whereas data set D has more of its values 'bunched' centrally. Because the range is calculated from extreme values it ignores the pattern of spread for the rest of the values. This is a major criticism of using the range as a measure of spread. Although the range is easy to calculate, it ignores the pattern of spread and considers only the extreme values.

7.3   The interquartile range

Since the range ignores the internal spread of the values in a data set, an alternative measure is needed. One possibility is to look at the spread between two values which are at some fixed, but interior, position. A sensible choice, which is associated naturally with the median, is to choose the values that are at the positions one-quarter and three-quarters of the way through the data when the values are arranged in order. These points are known as the **lower quartile** and the **upper quartile** respectively, and they are usually denoted by the symbols Q_1 and Q_3 respectively. The difference between these values is called the **interquartile range**.

Interquartile range = upper quartile − lower quartile = $Q_3 - Q_1$.

The interquartile range is really just the range of the middle 50% of the distribution.

Notice that there is also a **middle quartile**, Q_2, which is the median.

To find the position of the quartiles for small data sets there are several possible methods that you might see in textbooks. The one suggested below is fairly easy to apply.

Finding the quartiles
- First arrange the data in ascending order.

Case 1   An even number of data values

- Split the data into their upper half and lower half.
- Then the median of the upper half is Q_3, and the median of the lower half is Q_1.

Case 2   An odd number of data values

- Find the median, Q_2, and delete it from the list.
- Split the remaining data into their upper half and lower half.
- Then the median of the upper half is Q_3, and the median of the lower half is Q_1.

Example 7.3.1
Find the quartiles and the interquartile range for each of the two sets of data below.

(a) 7 9 12 13 8 11   (b) 7 8 22 20 15 18 19 13 11

(a) First, arrange the data in numerical order.

7 8 9 11 12 13

The number of data values is even, so divide the data into its lower and upper halves:

Lower half: 7 8 9   Upper half: 11 12 13

The lower quartile Q_1 is the median of the lower half, which is 8. The upper quartile Q_3 is the median of the upper half, which is 12. So

interquartile range $= Q_3 - Q_1 = 12 - 8 = 4$.

(b) Arrange the data in numerical order.

7 8 11 13 15 18 19 20 22

Since the number of data values (9) is odd, find the median $Q_2 = 15$ and delete it.

7 8 11 13   18 19 20 22

This automatically divides the data into lower and upper halves.

The median of the lower half is the lower quartile, so $Q_1 = \frac{1}{2}(8 + 11) = 9.5$, and the median of the upper half is the upper quartile, so $Q_3 = \frac{1}{2}(19 + 20) = 19.5$.

The interquartile range is $Q_3 - Q_1 = 19.5 - 9.5 = 10$.

In Chapter 6 you saw how the median of the weights of female students taken from the 'Brain size' datafile could be found by arranging the weights in order. The list of weights is reproduced from Section 6.2.

106   114   118   118   **122**   **127**   127   135   136   **138**   **139**   140   143   146
146   **147**   153   155   159   175

Since there are 20 students, the upper and lower halves of the data set will contain 10 values each. The lower quartile is then at the position which is equivalent to the median of the lower half. This is halfway between the 5th and 6th values (in ascending order). These are shown in bold type.

Therefore $Q_1 = \frac{1}{2}(122 + 127) = 124.5$.

Similarly the upper quartile is at the position which is equivalent to the median of the upper half of the data set. This is halfway between the 15th and 16th values (in ascending order). These are also shown in bold type.

Therefore $Q_3 = \frac{1}{2}(146 + 147) = 146.5$.

The interquartile range is therefore $Q_3 - Q_1 = 146.5 - 124.5 = 22$.

It is quite likely that the size of a data set will be much larger than the ones which have so far been considered. Larger data sets are usually organised into frequency tables and it is then necessary to think carefully about how to find the position of the quartiles. In Chapter 6 you saw how to find the median of a set of data which referred to the numbers of brothers and sisters of children in a year at a school. This was given in Table 6.1. Table 7.1 below reproduces Table 6.1.

Number of brothers and sisters	Frequency	Cumulative frequency
0	36	36
1	94	130
2	48	178
3	15	193
4	7	200
5	3	203
6	1	204
	Total: 204	

Table 7.1

There were 204 observations. This means that each half will have 102 data values.

The position of the lower quartile, Q_1, will be halfway between the 51st and 52nd values (in ascending order). From the cumulative frequency column you can see that both values are 1s, so $Q_1 = 1$. The position of the upper quartile, Q_3, will be halfway between the $(102 + 51)$th and $(102 + 52)$th values (in ascending order); that is, between the 153rd and 154th values. From the cumulative frequency column you can see that both values are 2s, so $Q_3 = 2$.

For continuous variables large data sets are usually grouped and so the individual values are lost. The quartiles are estimated from a cumulative frequency graph using a method similar to that described in Chapter 6 to find the median.

Table 7.2 gives the frequency distribution for the playing times of the selection of CDs which you first met in Table 6.2.

Playing time, x (min)	Class boundaries	Frequency	Cumulative frequency
40–44	$39.5 \leq x < 44.5$	1	1
45–49	$44.5 \leq x < 49.5$	7	8
50–54	$49.5 \leq x < 54.5$	12	20
55–59	$54.5 \leq x < 59.5$	24	44
60–64	$59.5 \leq x < 64.5$	29	73
65–69	$64.5 \leq x < 69.5$	14	87
70–74	$69.5 \leq x < 74.5$	5	92
75–79	$74.5 \leq x < 79.5$	3	95
		Total: 95	

Table 7.2

To obtain an estimate of the lower quartile of the playing times you read off the value corresponding to a cumulative frequency equal to one-quarter of the total frequency, which in this case is $\frac{1}{4} \times 95 = 23.75$. From the cumulative frequency graph in Fig. 7.3 you can see that $Q_1 \approx 56$ minutes. Similarly you find an estimate of the upper quartile by reading off the value corresponding to a cumulative frequency equal to three-quarters of the total frequency, which is $\frac{3}{4} \times 95 = 71.25$. From the cumulative frequency graph in Fig. 7.3 this gives $Q_3 \approx 64$ minutes.

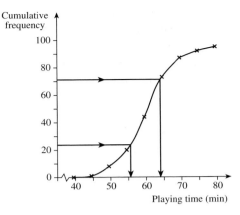

Fig. 7.3

Then the interquartile range is

$$Q_3 - Q_1 \approx 64 - 56 = 8,$$

so the interquartile range is approximately 8 minutes.

Note that you can also use your calculator to find quartiles.

Sometimes there is a need to find the data value which occupies a position other than the median or the upper and lower quartiles. For example, you might want to know the value which has 90% of the data below it. This is an example of a **percentile**; this particular percentile is called the 90th percentile. You can find its value from the cumulative frequency diagram in a similar way to that used for finding the quartiles. For example, in Fig. 7.3, the 90th percentile is found by first finding 90% of the total frequency, that is, $\frac{90}{100} \times 95 = 85.5$. From the cumulative frequency graph in Fig. 7.3, you will see that the 90th percentile is about 69 minutes. You can use a similar method to find the 95th percentile, the 40th percentile or any other percentile.

You may be wondering how to interpret the interquartile range for a set of data. For example, is the value of 8 in the example above large or small? The answer is that you cannot tell without more information. Normally you would be comparing the spread of two or more data sets. You can then make a more sensible comment on whether a particular interquartile range is large or small by comparing its size with the other interquartile ranges. The following example illustrates this idea.

Example 7.3.2
Two people did separate traffic surveys, using a radar gun, at different locations. Each person noted down the speed of 50 cars which passed their observation point. The results are given in Table 7.4.

Speed, v (km h^{-1})	A frequency	B frequency
$0 \leq v < 20$	7	1
$20 \leq v < 40$	11	3
$40 \leq v < 60$	13	5
$60 \leq v < 80$	12	20
$80 \leq v < 100$	5	18
$100 \leq v < 120$	2	3
Totals:	50	50

Table 7.4

(a) Draw a cumulative frequency diagram for each set of data and use it to estimate the median speed and the interquartile range of speeds at each observation point.

(b) Use your results to part (a) to comment on the locations.

(a) From Fig. 7.5, you can estimate the median and quartiles for the cars at location A. The median corresponds to a cumulative frequency of 25 and, from Fig. 7.5, it is approximately 51. The lower quartile corresponds to a cumulative frequency of 12.5, and it is approximately 30. The upper quartile corresponds to a cumulative frequency of 37.5, and it is approximately 69.

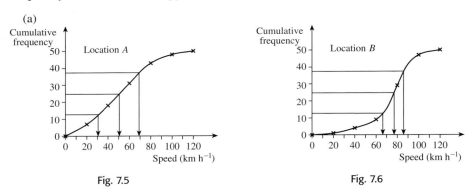

Fig. 7.5   Fig. 7.6

From Fig. 7.6, you can estimate the median and quartiles for the cars at location B. The equivalent values of the median and the quartiles are approximately 76, 66 and 86.

(b) You can now compare the medians and the interquartile ranges.

For A the median is 51 and the interquartile range is $69 - 30 = 39$.

For B the median is 76 and the interquartile range is $86 - 66 = 20$.

The median speed at A is lower than the median speed at B and the interquartile range at A is higher than the interquartile range at B. So at location A the cars generally go more slowly and there is a greater variation in their speeds. Perhaps B is on or near a motorway, and A may be in a town near some point of congestion. You cannot say for certain what types of location A and B are but the summary values do give you an idea of the type of road at each position.

7.4 The five-number summary

One helpful way of summarising data is to give values which provide essential information about the data set. One such summary is called the **five-number summary**. This summary gives the median, Q_2, the lower quartile Q_1, the upper quartile Q_3, the minimum value and the maximum value.

The five numbers of a five-number summary are usually given in numerical order.

Example 7.4.1
The data below give the number of fish caught each day over a period of 11 days by an angler. Give a five-number summary of the data.

$$0 \quad 2 \quad 5 \quad 2 \quad 0 \quad 4 \quad 4 \quad 8 \quad 9 \quad 8 \quad 8$$

Rearranging the data in order gives:

$$0 \quad 0 \quad 2 \quad 2 \quad 4 \quad 4 \quad 5 \quad 8 \quad 8 \quad 8 \quad 9$$

The median value is $Q_2 = 4$. As the number of data values is odd, deleting the middle one and finding the medians of the lower and upper halves gives

$$Q_1 = 2 \quad \text{and} \quad Q_3 = 8.$$

The five-number summary is then the minimum value, 0, the lower quartile, 2, the median, 4, the upper quartile, 8, and the maximum value, 9.

The five-number summary can also be usefully presented as a table, as in Table 7.7.

Minimum	0
Q_1	2
Q_2	4
Q_3	8
Maximum	9

Table 7.7

7.5 Box and whisker plots

You can convert this five-number summary into a useful diagram, called a **box and whisker plot**. To draw a box and whisker plot, first draw a scale, preferably using graph paper. You can draw the scale vertically or horizontally, but in this book, the scale and the diagram are always drawn

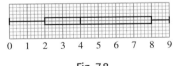

Fig. 7.8

horizontally. Above the scale draw a box (or rectangle) in which the left side is above the point corresponding to the lower quartile and the right side is above the point corresponding to the upper quartile. Then mark a third line inside the box above the point which corresponds to the median value. After this you draw the two whiskers. The left whisker extends from the lower quartile to the minimum value and the right whisker extends from the upper quartile to the maximum. Fig. 7.8 shows the box and whisker plot for the data in Example 7.4.1.

In a box and whisker plot the box itself indicates the location of the middle 50% of the data. The whiskers then show how the data is spread overall.

Another important feature of a set of data is its shape when represented as a frequency diagram. The three pictures in Fig. 7.9 show three different shapes which commonly occur when you draw frequency diagrams.

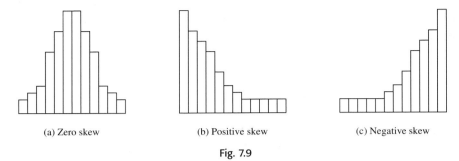

| (a) Zero skew | (b) Positive skew | (c) Negative skew |

Fig. 7.9

The distribution in Fig. 7.9a is symmetrical. If a distribution lacks symmetry it is said to be **skew**, or to have **skewness**. The distribution in Fig. 7.9a may therefore be said to have zero skewness. You were briefly introduced to the term 'skewness' in Section 6.9.

The distribution in Fig. 7.9b is certainly not symmetrical, and there is a 'tail' which stretches towards the higher values. This distribution is said to have **positive skew**, or to be **skewed positively**.

The distribution in Fig. 7.9c is also not symmetrical. There is a 'tail' which stretches towards the lower values. This distribution is said to have **negative skew**, or to be **skewed negatively**.

Another method of assessing the skewness of a distribution is to use the quartiles Q_1, Q_2 and Q_3. Remember that Q_2 denotes the median, and that Q_1 and Q_3 denote the lower and upper quartiles.

If $Q_3 - Q_2 \approx Q_2 - Q_1$ then the distribution is said to be (almost) symmetrical, and a box and whisker plot of such data, as in Fig. 7.10, would show a box in which the line corresponding to the median was in the centre of the box.

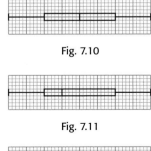

Fig. 7.10

If $Q_3 - Q_2 > Q_2 - Q_1$, as in Fig. 7.11, then the data is said to have positive skew, and the line representing the median would be nearer to the left side of the box.

Fig. 7.11

If $Q_3 - Q_2 < Q_2 - Q_1$, as in Fig. 7.12, then the data would be said to have negative skew, and the line representing the median would be nearer to the right side of the box.

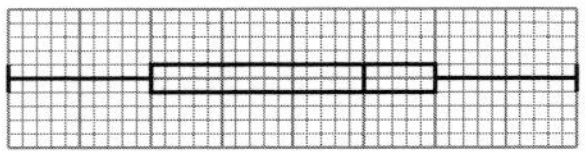

For the data in Example 7.4.1, $Q_1 = 2$, $Q_2 = 4$ and $Q_3 = 8$, so $Q_3 - Q_2 = 8 - 4 = 4$ and $Q_2 - Q_1 = 4 - 2 = 2$. The set of data in Example 7.4.1 therefore has positive skew.

Fig. 7.12

The length of the whiskers can also give some indication of skewness. If the left whisker is shorter than the right whisker then that would tend to indicate positive skew, whereas if the right whisker is shorter than the left whisker, negative skew would be implied.

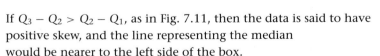

It is possible for the data to give different results for skewness depending on what measure you use. For example, it is perfectly possible for a box and whisker plot to have $Q_3 - Q_2 > Q_2 - Q_1$, indicating positive skew, but for the left whisker to be longer than the right whisker, which would tend to suggest negative skew. In such cases you must make a judgement about which method of assessing skewness you think is the more important. Fortunately data of this sort do not occur commonly.

Exercise 7A

1 Find the range and the interquartile range of each of the following data sets.

(a) 7   4   14   9   12   2   19   6   15

(b) 7.6   4.8   1.2   6.9   4.8   7.2   8.1   10.3   4.8   6.7

2 The number of times a factory machine broke down was noted over a period of 50 consecutive weeks. The results are given in the following table.

Number of breakdowns	0	1	2	3	4	5	6
Number of weeks	2	12	14	8	8	4	2

(a) Find the interquartile range of the number of breakdowns in a week.

(b) Find the 95th percentile of the number of breakdowns in a week.

3 The audience size in a theatre performing a long-running detective play was monitored over a period of 1 year. The sizes for Monday and Wednesday nights are summarised in the following table.

Audience size	50–99	100–199	200–299	300–399	400–499	500–599
Number of Mondays	12	20	12	5	3	0
Number of Wednesdays	2	3	20	18	5	4

Compare the audience sizes on Mondays and Wednesdays.

4 Draw box and whisker plots for data which have the following five-number summaries, and in each case describe the shape of the data.

(a) 6.0 kg   10.2 kg   12.7 kg   13.2 kg   15.7 kg

(b) −12 °C   −8 °C   −6 °C   3 °C   11 °C

(c) 37 m   48 m   60 m   72 m   82 m

5 The following figures are the amounts spent in a supermarket by a family for 13 weeks.

£48.25   £43.70   £52.83   £49.24   £58.28   £55.47   £47.29
£51.82   £58.42   £38.73   £42.76   £50.42   £40.85

(a) Obtain a five-number summary of the data.

(b) Construct a box and whisker plot of the data.

(c) Describe any skewness of the data.

6 State, with reasons, whether box and whisker plots or histograms are better for comparing two distributions.

7.6   Variance and standard deviation

One of the reasons for using the interquartile range in preference to the range as a measure of spread was that it took some account of how the more central values were spread rather than concentrating solely on the spread of the extreme values. The interquartile range, however, does not take account of the spread of all of the data values and so, in some sense, it is still an inadequate measure. An alternative measure of spread which does take into account the spread of all the values can be devised by finding how far each data value, x_i, is from the mean, μ, of these values. To do this you would calculate the quantities $x_i - \mu$ for each x_i.

An example in Section 6.4 used the playing times, in minutes, of nine CDs.

$$49 \quad 56 \quad 55 \quad 68 \quad 61 \quad 57 \quad 61 \quad 52 \quad 63$$

The mean of these times was found to be 58 minutes. If the mean is subtracted from each of the original values you get the following values.

$$-9 \quad -2 \quad -3 \quad 10 \quad 3 \quad -1 \quad 3 \quad -6 \quad 5$$

The negative signs cause a problem, and a simple way to remove them is to square all the numbers to get

$$81 \quad 4 \quad 9 \quad 100 \quad 9 \quad 1 \quad 9 \quad 36 \quad 25.$$

The mean of these squared distances would be a sensible measure of spread. It would represent the mean of the squared distance from the mean.

In this case the mean squared distance would be

$$\frac{81 + 4 + 9 + 100 + 9 + 1 + 9 + 36 + 25}{9} = \frac{274}{9} = 30.4\ldots.$$

Generalising, this leads to the expression $\dfrac{\sum\limits_{i=1}^{n}(x_i - \mu)^2}{n}$ as a measure of spread.

This quantity is called the **variance** of the data values. It is the mean of the squared distances from the mean. So for the data on playing times of CDs,

$$\text{variance} = \frac{\sum\limits_{i=1}^{n}(x_i - \mu)^2}{n}$$

$$= \frac{274}{9} = 30.4\ldots.$$

If the data values x_1, x_2, ... , x_n have units associated with them then the variance will be measured in units^2. In the example the data values were measured in minutes and therefore the variance would be measured in minutes^2. This is something which can be avoided by taking the positive square root of the variance. The positive square root of the variance is known as the **standard deviation**, often shortened to 'SD', and it always has the same units as the original data values. The formula for standard deviation is

$$\sqrt{\frac{\sum\limits_{i=1}^{n} (x_i - \mu)^2}{n}}.$$

So the standard deviation of the playing times of the nine CDs is $\sqrt{30.4\ldots} = 5.52$, correct to 3 significant figures.

The symbol σ^2 is used for variance and the symbol σ is used for the standard deviation. (The letter σ is the small Greek letter 'sigma'.)

The **variance** of a set of data values x_1, x_2, ... , x_n whose mean is

$$\mu = \frac{x_1 + x_2 + \ldots + x_n}{n} = \frac{\sum\limits_{i=1}^{n} x_i}{n}$$

is given by the formula

$$\sigma^2 = \frac{\sum\limits_{i=1}^{n} (x_i - \mu)^2}{n}.$$

The **standard deviation** is the positive square root of the variance.

You can use your calculator to calculate variance or standard deviation. See Section 7.9.

7.7   An alternative formula for variance

Although the formula $\sigma^2 = \dfrac{\sum\limits_{i=1}^{n} (x_i - \mu)^2}{n}$ is useful for numerical data, it is not ideal in this form for other calculations. Fortunately it can be rearranged into an alternative, more useful, form.

If you multiply out the square in the numerator, and then use the addition rule for sigma notation (see the end of Section 2.6), you get

$$\sigma^2 = \frac{\sum\limits_{i=1}^{n} (x_i - \mu)^2}{n} = \frac{\sum\limits_{i=1}^{n} (x_i^2 - 2x_i\mu + \mu^2)}{n}$$

$$= \frac{\sum\limits_{i=1}^{n} x_i^2 + \sum\limits_{i=1}^{n} (-2x_i\mu) + \sum\limits_{i=1}^{n} \mu^2}{n}.$$

Using the multiple rule for sigma notation (Section 2.6), and the definition $\mu = \dfrac{\sum\limits_{i=1}^{n} x_i}{n}$ which gives $\sum\limits_{i=1}^{n} x_i = n\mu$, the second term in the numerator simplifies to

$$\sum_{i=1}^{n} (-2x_i \mu) = -2\mu \sum_{i=1}^{n} x_i$$
$$= -2\mu (n\mu)$$
$$= -2n\mu^2.$$

The third term in the numerator is

$$\sum_{i=1}^{n} \mu^2 = \overbrace{\mu^2 + \mu^2 + \ldots + \mu^2}^{n\ of\ these} = n\mu^2.$$

So

$$\sigma^2 = \frac{\sum\limits_{i=1}^{n} x_i^2 + \sum\limits_{i=1}^{n} (-2x_i \mu) + \sum\limits_{i=1}^{n} \mu^2}{n}$$

$$= \frac{\sum\limits_{i=1}^{n} x_i^2 - 2n\mu^2 + n\mu^2}{n}$$

$$= \frac{\sum\limits_{i=1}^{n} x_i^2 - n\mu^2}{n}$$

$$= \frac{\sum\limits_{i=1}^{n} x_i^2}{n} - \mu^2.$$

This expression is easier to use in theoretical calculations than $\dfrac{\sum\limits_{i=1}^{n} (x_i - \mu)^2}{n}$.

The box in the previous section now becomes:

The **variance** of a set of data values $x_1,\ x_2, \ldots,\ x_n$ whose mean is

$$\mu = \frac{x_1 + x_2 + \ldots + x_n}{n} = \frac{\sum\limits_{i=1}^{n} x_i}{n}$$

is given by the formula

$$\sigma^2 = \frac{\sum\limits_{i=1}^{n} (x_i - \mu)^2}{n}, \quad \text{or} \quad \sigma^2 = \frac{\sum\limits_{i=1}^{n} x_i^2}{n} - \mu^2.$$

The **standard deviation** is the positive square root of the variance.

Example 7.7.1

Recalculate the variance using the alternative formula for the nine CDs with playing times 49, 56, 55, 68, 61, 57, 61, 52, 63.

The mean is 58. So

$$\sigma^2 = \frac{\sum_{i=1}^{n} x_i^2}{n} - \mu^2$$

$$= \frac{49^2 + 56^2 + 55^2 + 68^2 + 61^2 + 57^2 + 61^2 + 52^2 + 63^2}{9} - 58^2$$

$$= \frac{30\,550}{9} - 3364 = 30\tfrac{4}{9} = 30.4\ldots\,.$$

As you would expect, this gives the same result as obtained in Section 7.6.

Example 7.7.2

There are 12 boys and 13 girls, in a class of 25 students, who were given a test. The mean mark for the 12 boys was 31 and the standard deviation of the boys' marks was 6.2. The mean mark of the girls was 36 and the standard deviation of the girls' marks was 4.3. Find the mean mark and standard deviation of the marks of the whole class of 25 students.

Let x_1, x_2, ... , x_{12} be the marks of the 12 boys in the test and let y_1, y_2, ... , y_{13} be the marks of the 13 girls in the test.

Since the mean of the boys' marks is 31, $\dfrac{\sum_{i=1}^{12} x_i}{12} = 31$, so $\sum_{i=1}^{12} x_i = 12 \times 31 = 372$.

As the standard deviation of the boys' marks is 6.2, the variance is $6.2^2 = 38.44$.

Therefore, using the alternative form for variance,

$$38.44 = \frac{\sum_{i=1}^{12} x_i^2}{12} - 31^2, \text{ which gives } \sum_{i=1}^{12} x_i^2 = 12 \times (38.44 + 31^2) = 11\,993.28.$$

Similarly,

$$\sum_{i=1}^{13} y_i = 13 \times 36 = 468 \qquad \text{and} \qquad \sum_{i=1}^{13} y_i^2 = 13 \times (4.3^2 + 36^2) = 17\,088.37.$$

The overall mean is

$$\frac{\sum_{i=1}^{12} x_i + \sum_{i=1}^{13} y_i}{25} = \frac{372 + 468}{25} = 33.6.$$

The overall variance is

$$\frac{\sum_{i=1}^{12} x_i^2 + \sum_{i=1}^{13} y_i^2}{25} - 33.6^2 = \frac{11\,993.28 + 17\,088.37}{25} - 33.6^2 = 34.306.$$

The overall standard deviation is $\sqrt{34.306} = 5.86$, correct to 3 significant figures.

Example 7.7.3

Given that $n = 10$, $\sum_{i=1}^{n} x_i = 410$ and $\sigma^2 = 12$, calculate $\sum_{i=1}^{n} x_i^2$.

Using the alternative formula for variance and substituting the given values,

$$12 = \frac{\sum_{i=1}^{n} x_i^2}{10} - \left(\frac{410}{10}\right)^2,$$

so

$$\sum_{i=1}^{n} x_i^2 = 10(12 + 41^2)$$
$$= 10(12 + 1681) = 16\,930.$$

7.8   Samples and populations

In Section 6.5 your attention was drawn to the difference between finding the mean of a population and the mean of a sample which gives an estimate of the mean of a population. The same distinction needs to be made between the variance and standard deviation of a population and the variance and standard deviation of a sample.

The formulae for variance in the blue boxes in Sections 7.6 and 7.7 refer to a population. If you have a sample and you need to calculate the variance of this sample, then this variance is denoted by

$$s_n^2 = \frac{\sum_{i=1}^{n} (x_i - \bar{x})^2}{n} = \frac{\sum_{i=1}^{n} x_i^2}{n} - \bar{x}^2.$$

However, if the data from the sample are being used to estimate the variance for the whole population, it is unlikely that the data from the sample covers the full range of values in the population. In fact it usually underestimates the variance of the population. The sample variance therefore gives a *biased* estimate of the population variance. The unbiased estimate of population variance obtained from a sample of size n is $\frac{n}{n-1}s_n^2$, where s_n^2 is the variance of the n sample values. The unbiased estimate of the population variance is called s_{n-1}^2 and the corresponding standard deviation is called s_{n-1}.

The **variance** of a **sample** of size n is given by

$$s_n^2 = \frac{\sum_{i=1}^{n} (x_i - \bar{x})^2}{n} \quad \text{or} \quad s_n^2 = \frac{\sum_{i=1}^{n} x_i^2}{n} - \bar{x}^2.$$

The **standard deviation** of the **sample** is the positive square root of the variance.

An **unbiased estimate of the variance of the underlying population** is given by s_{n-1}^2, where $s_{n-1}^2 = \frac{n}{n-1}s_n^2$.

An **unbiased estimate of the standard deviation of the underlying population** is given by s_{n-1}.

Notice that in the example of the nine CDs

$$49 \quad 56 \quad 55 \quad 68 \quad 61 \quad 57 \quad 61 \quad 52 \quad 63$$

used at the beginning of Section 7.6, the standard deviation is 5.52. Taking these nine CDs as a sample of all the CDs on sale in the UK, an unbiased estimate of the standard deviation of the whole population of CDs is

$$s_{n-1} = \sqrt{\frac{n}{n-1}}\, s_n, \text{ with } n = 9,$$

that is

$$s_{n-1} = \sqrt{\frac{9}{8}} \times 5.52 = 5.85.$$

7.9 Calculating variance

Your calculator has an in-built routine for calculating the variance directly from the data, so you do not need to use the formulae of Section 7.6 and 7.7 in situations when you are given numerical data. However you will need to be sure you know how to use the routine, so you will need to consult the manual for your particular calculator.

It is imperative that you recognise, so far as variance and standard deviation are concerned, that different calculators give different quantities: some give s_n, some give s_{n-1}, and some give both. If your calculator gives two values for the variance or for the standard deviation, the higher ones give unbiased estimates for the variance and standard deviation of the population, and the lower ones give the variance or the standard deviation of the given data.

Example 7.9.1
Coins of a certain denomination were sampled randomly from a large population. Their weights in grams were

$$8.0 \quad 7.7 \quad 7.8 \quad 8.1 \quad 7.7 \quad 8.3 \quad 7.8 \quad 8.0 \quad 8.1 \quad 8.0$$

Calculate an unbiased estimate of the population mean and the population variance.

Using your calculator, the unbiased estimate of the population mean is $\bar{x} = 7.95$ g.

The unbiased estimate of the population variance is $s_{n-1}^2 = 0.0383$ g^2, correct to 3 significant figures.

Exercise 7B

1 State or find the mean of
   (a) 1, 2, 3, 4, 5, 6, 7   (b) 4, 12, −2, 7, 0, 9.
   Use your calculator to find the standard deviation of each data set.

2 Use your calculator to find the standard deviation of the following data sets.
   (a) 2, 1, 5.3, − 4.2, 6.7, 3.1   (b) 15.2, 12.3, 5.7, 4.3, 11.2, 2.5, 8.7

3 The masses, x grams, of the contents of 25 tins of Brand A anchovies are summarised by $\sum_{i=1}^{25} x_i = 1268.2$ and $\sum_{i=1}^{25} x_i^2 = 64\,585.16$. Find the mean and variance of the masses. What is the unit of measurement of the variance?

4 The runs made by two batsmen, Anwar and Brian, in 12 innings during the 2006 cricket season are shown in the following table.

Anwar	23	83	40	0	89	98	71	31	102	48	15	18
Brian	43	32	61	75	68	92	17	15	25	43	86	12

Giving your reasons, state which batsman you consider to be

(a) better,   (b) more consistent.

5 The mean and standard deviation of the heights of 12 boys in a class are 148.8 cm and 5.4 cm respectively. A boy of height 153.4 cm joins the class. Find the mean and standard deviation of the heights of the 13 boys.

6 A random sample drawn from a large population contains the following data:

13.2   5.7   8.3   6.7   9.2   11.4   9.7   8.1   6.3

Calculate unbiased estimates of the population mean and the population standard deviation, giving your answers to 3 significant figures.

7 The heights of a sample of 80 female students are summarised by the equations

$$\sum_{i=1}^{80} x_i = 13\,040 \quad \text{and} \quad \sum_{i=1}^{80} x_i^2 = 2\,133\,520.$$

Find the mean and standard deviation of the heights of the 80 female students.

7.10 Calculating variance from a frequency table

Table 7.13 reproduces Table 6.4, which gave the frequency distribution of the numbers of brothers and sisters of children in Year 8 in a school.

Number of brothers and sisters, x_i	Frequency, f_i
0	36
1	94
2	48
3	15
4	7
5	3
6	1

Table 7.13

To find the variance, use the programmed routine in your calculator. You then find that the variance is $1.218... = 1.22$ correct to 3 significant figures.

The standard deviation is then $s_n = \sqrt{1.218...} = 1.10$ correct to 3 significant figures.

If you had to calculate the variance without the built-in calculator routine, you would proceed as follows.

First calculate the mean. From Section 6.6, the mean is $\bar{x} = \dfrac{284}{204} = 1.39...$.

To calculate $\sigma^2 = \dfrac{\displaystyle\sum_{i=1}^{n}(x_i - \bar{x})^2}{n}$ for these data, you need to calculate

$$\sum_{i=1}^{n}(x_i - \bar{x})^2 = \overbrace{(0 - \bar{x})^2 + ... + (0 - \bar{x})^2}^{36 \text{ of these}} + \overbrace{(1 - \bar{x})^2 + ... + (1 - \bar{x})^2}^{94 \text{ of these}} + ...$$

$$+ \overbrace{(5 - \bar{x})^2 + ... + (5 - \bar{x})^2}^{3 \text{ of these}} + \overbrace{(1 - \bar{x})^2}^{1 \text{ of these}}$$

$$= 248.62... .$$

Then, dividing by $n = 204$, you find that the variance is $1.218... = 1.22$ correct to 3 significant figures, as before.

> You should try this calculation on your calculator. It will quickly convince you that the built-in routine is better.

Here is a summary of the method used to find the variance: the alternative version is also given, but without proof.

> The variance of data given in a frequency table in which the variable takes the value x_1 with frequency f_1, the value x_2 with frequency f_2 and so on is given by the formula
>
> $$\sigma^2 = \frac{\displaystyle\sum_{i=1}^{k} f_i (x_i - \mu)^2}{n} \quad \text{or} \quad \sigma^2 = \frac{\displaystyle\sum_{i=1}^{k} f_i x_i^2}{n} - \mu^2, \quad \text{where } n = \sum_{i=1}^{k} f_i.$$
>
> If the data in the frequency table is a sample from a population, and you need to estimate the variance of the data in the sample, as opposed to the population, the estimate is given by
>
> $$s_n^2 = \frac{\displaystyle\sum_{i=1}^{k} f_i (x_i - \bar{x})^2}{n} \quad \text{or} \quad s_n^2 = \frac{\displaystyle\sum_{i=1}^{k} f_i x_i^2}{n} - \bar{x}^2, \quad \text{where } n = \sum_{i=1}^{k} f_i.$$
>
> The unbiased estimate of the variance of the population is given by
>
> $$s_{n-1}^2 = \frac{n}{n-1} s_n^2 = \frac{\displaystyle\sum_{i=1}^{k} f_i (x_i - \bar{x})^2}{n-1}, \quad \text{where } n = \sum_{i=1}^{k} f_i.$$

If the data are grouped you need a single value to represent each class. In Section 6.6 you saw that the most reasonable choice was the mid-interval value. After you have made this simplifying assumption, use the in-built routine in your calculator.

Example 7.10.1
Calculate an estimate of the variance of the data given in Table 6.5, and give an unbiased estimate of the variance for the population of CDs from which the sample is taken.

Table 7.14 reproduces the first four columns of Table 6.5.

Playing time, x (min)	Interval boundaries	Frequency, f_i	Mid-interval value, x_i
40–44	$39.5 \leq x < 44.5$	1	42
45–49	$44.5 \leq x < 49.5$	7	47
50–54	$49.5 \leq x < 54.5$	12	52
55–59	$54.5 \leq x < 59.5$	24	57
60–64	$59.5 \leq x < 64.5$	29	62
65–69	$64.5 \leq x < 69.5$	14	67
70–74	$69.5 \leq x < 74.5$	5	72
75–79	$74.5 \leq x < 79.5$	3	77

Table 7.14

Using the in-built calculator routine, the unbiased estimate of the population variance is

$$s_{n-1}^2 = 51.9 \text{ correct to 3 significant figures.}$$

You should remember that, just as with the mean calculation in Section 6.6, this value is only an estimate, because the individual values have been replaced by mid-interval values.

There are times when you may need to calculate an estimate of the variance or the standard deviation from a cumulative frequency graph. If this is the case, you must first of all construct a frequency table, as in Example 6.7.1.

7.11   Practical activities

1 One-sidedness

(a) Calculate the variance for each set of data in Practical activity 1 in Section 5.4. Does one 'side' show more variability than the other?

(b) Find estimates for the interquartile range of each set of data by drawing two cumulative frequency diagrams. What conclusions can you draw from these two values?

2 **High jump**

(a) Calculate the variance for each set of data in Practical activity 2 in Section 5.4. Does one year group show more variability than the other?

(b) Find estimates for the interquartile range of each set of data by drawing two cumulative frequency diagrams. What conclusions can you draw from these two values?

3 **Waste paper**

(a) Select a student and ask them to try to throw a ball of paper into a waste paper bin 10 metres away with their 'natural' or stronger throwing arm. Repeat this until the student is successful and record the total number of attempts needed by the student. Repeat this experiment with about 30 students.

(b) Select a second group of students and ask them to throw the paper ball into the bin with their 'weaker' arm. Record the number of attempts needed for each student.

(c) Select an appropriate measure of spread and find it for each of the two sets of data. Does the weaker arm give more variable results than the stronger arm?

4 **Newspapers** Calculate the variance and the interquartile range for each set of data in Practical activity 3 in Section 6.10. Which paper shows greater variability in sentence length? Which measure of spread is more appropriate for these data?

5 **Just a minute!** Calculate the variance and the interquartile range for each set of data in Practical activity 5 in Section 6.10. Which group shows greater variability in estimation of time? Which measure of spread is more appropriate for these data?

Exercise 7C

1 The number of absences by employees in an office was recorded over a period of 96 days, with the following results.

Number of absences	0	1	2	3	4	5
Number of days	54	24	11	4	2	1

Use your calculator to find the mean and variance of the number of daily absences, setting out your work in a table similar to Table 7.14.

2 Plates of a certain design are painted by a particular factory employee. At the end of each day the plates are inspected and some are rejected. The table shows the number of plates rejected over a period of 30 days.

Number of rejects	0	1	2	3	4	5	6
Number of days	18	5	3	1	1	1	1

Show that the standard deviation of the daily number of rejects is approximately equal to one quarter of the range.

3 The times taken in a 20 km race were noted for 80 people. The results are summarised in the following table.

Time (minutes)	60–80	80–100	100–120	120–140	140–160	160–180	180–200
Number of people	1	4	26	24	10	7	8

Use your calculator to estimate the variance of the times of the 80 people in the race.

If the 80 people were a random sample of the 2000 people taking part in the race, calculate an approximation to the variance of the times of the 2000 runners.

4 The mass of coffee in each of 80 packets of a certain brand was measured correct to the nearest gram. The results are shown in the following table.

Mass (grams)	244–246	247–249	250–252	253–255	256–258
Number of packets	10	20	24	18	8

Use your calculator to estimate the mean and standard deviation of the masses.

State two ways in which the accuracy of these estimates could be improved.

5 The ages, in completed years, of the 104 workers in a company are summarised as follows.

Age (years)	16–20	21–25	26–30	31–35	36–40	41–50	51–60	61–70
Frequency	5	12	18	14	25	16	8	6

Estimate the mean and standard deviation of the workers' ages.

In another company, with a similar number of workers, the mean age is 28.4 years and the standard deviation is 9.9 years. Briefly compare the age distribution in the two companies.

Review exercise 2

1 Certain insects can cause small growths, called 'galls', on the leaves of trees. The numbers of galls found on 60 leaves of an oak tree are given below.

5	19	21	4	17	10	0	61	3	31	15	39	16	27	48
51	69	32	1	25	51	22	28	29	73	14	23	9	2	0
1	37	31	95	10	24	7	89	1	2	50	33	22	0	75
7	23	9	18	39	44	10	33	9	11	51	8	36	44	10

(a) Put the data into a grouped frequency table with classes 0–9, 10–19, ... , 90–99.

(b) Draw a frequency histogram of the data.

(c) Draw a cumulative frequency diagram and use it to estimate the number of leaves with fewer than 34 galls.

(d) State an assumption required for your estimate in part (c), and briefly discuss its justification in this case.

2 The following table summarises the maximum daily temperatures in two holiday resorts in July and August 2005.

Temperature (°C)	18.0–19.9	20.0–21.9	22.0–23.9	24.0–25.9	26.0–27.9	28.0–29.9
Resort 1 frequency	9	13	18	10	7	5
Resort 2 frequency	6	21	23	8	3	1

(a) State the modal classes for the two resorts.

(b) A student analysed the data and came to the conclusion that, on average, Resort 1 was hotter than Resort 2 during July and August 2005. Is this conclusion supported by your answer to part (a)? If not, then obtain some evidence that does support the conclusion.

3 The costs, $x, of 31 mobile telephone calls costing over $0.50 made during a period of one month are as follows.

1.02	0.76	0.56	0.52	0.64	0.51	0.59	0.69	0.85	0.62	0.52
0.50	0.59	0.62	0.74	0.58	0.67	0.56	0.59	0.52	0.75	0.83
0.50	1.22	1.04	0.86	0.58	0.95	1.76	0.50	0.60		

$$\sum_{i=1}^{31} x_i = 22.24$$

(a) Obtain the median, the mean and the mode for the data.

(b) Which of the median, mean and mode would be best used to give the average cost of a call costing over $0.50? Give a reason for your answer.

(c) In the same period, the number of calls which cost $0.50 or under was 125, with mean cost $0.242. Find the mean cost of all calls for the period.

4 Seven mature robins (*Erithacus rubecula*) were caught and their wingspans were measured. The results, in centimetres, were as follows.

$$23.1 \quad 22.7 \quad 22.1 \quad 24.2 \quad 23.9 \quad 20.9 \quad 25.2$$

Here are the corresponding figures for seven mature house sparrows (*Passer domesticos*).

$$22.6 \quad 24.1 \quad 23.5 \quad 21.8 \quad 21.0 \quad 24.4 \quad 22.8$$

Find the mean and standard deviation of each species' wingspan, and use these statistics to compare the two sets of figures.

5 The lengths of 120 nails of nominal length 3 cm were measured, each correct to the nearest 0.05 cm. The results are summarised in the following table.

Length (cm)	2.85	2.90	2.95	3.00	3.05	3.10	3.15
Frequency	1	11	27	41	26	12	2

(a) Draw a box and whisker plot of these results, taking the extremes as 2.825 cm and 3.175 cm.

(b) Estimate the standard deviation.

(c) It is claimed that for a roughly symmetrical distribution the statistic obtained by dividing the interquartile range by the standard deviation is approximately 1.3. Calculate the value of this statistic for these data, and comment.

6 There are 30 girls in a class. The weights of five of them, chosen at random, in kilograms are 64, 73, 57, 54 and 75. Calculate the mean and standard deviation of the sample, and hence estimate the mean and standard deviation of the 30 girls.

7 The following table gives the ages in completed years of the 141 persons convicted of shop-lifting in a large town during a particular year.

Age (years)	12–15	16–20	21–25	26–30	31–40	41–50	51–70
Frequency	15	48	28	17	14	7	12

Working in years, and giving your answers to 1 decimal place, calculate estimates of

(a) the mean and standard deviation of the ages,

(b) the median age.

Which do you consider to be the better representative average of the distribution, the mean or the median? Give a reason for your answer.

Examination questions

1 Consider the six numbers, 2, 3, 6, 9, *a* and *b*. The mean of the numbers is 6 and the variance is 10. Find the value of *a* and of *b*, if $a < b$.

(© IBO 2002)

2 The heights of 60 children entering a school were measured. The following cumulative frequency graph illustrates the data obtained.

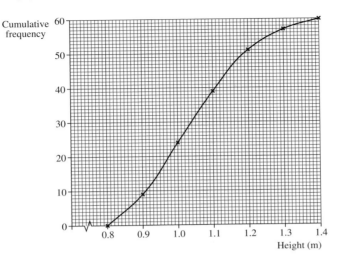

Estimate

(a) the median height,   (b) the mean height.   (© IBO 2004)

3 A teacher drives to school. She records the time taken on each of 20 randomly chosen days. She finds that $\sum_{i=1}^{20} x_i = 626$ and $\sum_{i=1}^{20} x_i^2 = 19\,780.8$, where x_i denotes the time, in minutes, taken on the ith day.

Calculate an unbiased estimate of

(a) the mean time taken to drive to school,

(b) the variance of the time taken to drive to school.   (© IBO 2003)

4 In a rental property business, the profits in euros per year for 50 properties are shown in the following cumulative table.

Profit (x)	Number of properties with profit less than x
$-10\,000$	0
$-5\,000$	3
0	7
5\,000	22
10\,000	39
15\,000	44
20\,000	50

For this population of 50 properties, calculate an estimate for the standard deviation of the profit.   (© IBO 2005)

5 The cumulative frequency curve below indicates the amount of time 250 students spend eating lunch.

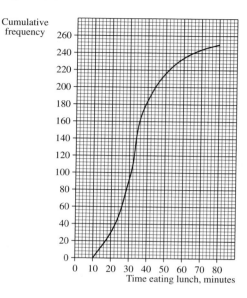

(a) Estimate the number of students who spend between 20 and 40 minutes eating lunch.

(b) If 20% of the students spend more than x minutes eating lunch, estimate the value of x.

(© IBO 2003)

6 A random sample drawn from a large population contains the following data

6.2   7.8   12.1   9.7   5.2   14.8   16.2   3.7.

Calculate an unbiased estimate of

(a) the population mean,   (b) the population variance.

(© IBO 2005)

7 Consider the 10 data items x_1, x_2, ... , x_{10}. Given that $\sum_{i=1}^{10} x_i^2 = 1341$ and the standard deviation is 6.9, find the value of μ.

(© IBO 2005)

8 Carlos drives to work every morning. He records the times taken, in minutes, to complete the journey over a 10-day period. The times are as follows:

32.8   31.3   32.7   33.2   31.9   36.3   34.3   35.8   30.9   32.6

Assuming that these times form a random sample from the population, calculate unbiased estimates of the mean and variance of this population.

(© IBO 2004)

8 Coordinates, points and lines

This chapter uses coordinates to describe points and lines in two dimensions. When you have completed it, you should be able to

- find the length, the mid-point and the gradient of a line segment, given the coordinates of its end points
- find the equation of the line through a given point with a given gradient
- recognise the equations of lines
- tell from their gradients if two lines are parallel or perpendicular.

8.1 The distance between two points

When you draw an x-axis and a y-axis intersecting at an origin O, and choose a scale for the axes, you are setting up a coordinate system. The coordinates of this system are called **Cartesian coordinates** after the French mathematician René Descartes, who lived in the 17th century.

> The reason for the word 'Cartesian' is that, at that time, Descartes would normally have been spelt as 'des Cartes'.

The axes divide the plane of the paper or screen into four quadrants, numbered as shown in Fig. 8.1.

The first quadrant is in the top right corner, where x and y are both positive. The other quadrants then follow in order going anticlockwise round the origin.

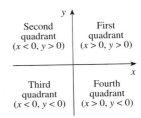

Fig. 8.1

Example 8.1.1
In which quadrants is $xy > 0$?

If the product of two numbers is positive, either both are positive or both are negative. So either $x > 0$ and $y > 0$, or $x < 0$ and $y < 0$. The point (x, y) therefore lies in either the first or the third quadrant.

Calculations with coordinates are often simplest if the points are in the first quadrant.

Example 8.1.2

The points A and B have coordinates (4, 3) and (10, 7). The point M is the mid-point of the line segment [AB].

Find   (a) the length of the line segment,   (b) the coordinates of M.

(a) Figure 8.2 shows the points A and B. A third point C has been added to form a right-angled triangle. You can see that C has the same x-coordinate as B and the same y-coordinate as A; that is, C has coordinates (10, 3).

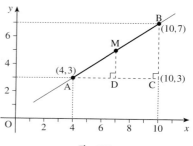

Fig. 8.2

> It is possible to use your calculator to produce a figure like Fig. 8.2, but it isn't often worth doing. If you want an accurate diagram, it is best to draw it on paper ruled in squares. But usually all you need is a sketch, with the points shown in roughly the right position.
>
> If you do use a calculator, you will only get a geometrically accurate diagram if you choose a window which gives the same scale on both axes.

It is easy to see that AC = 10 − 4 = 6, and CB = 7 − 3 = 4. Using Pythagoras' theorem in triangle ABC shows that the length of the line segment [AB] is

$$\sqrt{(10-4)^2 + (7-3)^2} = \sqrt{6^2 + 4^2} = \sqrt{36 + 16} = \sqrt{52}.$$

You can give this answer as 7.21... , if you need to, but often it is better to leave it as $\sqrt{52}$, or better still as $2\sqrt{13}$.

(b) In Fig. 8.2, M is the point of the line segment such that AM = MB, so that AM = $\frac{1}{2}$AB. The lines [MD] and [BC] have been drawn parallel to the y-axis, so they are parallel to each other. Then AD = $\frac{1}{2}$AC and DM = $\frac{1}{2}$CB. So

$$AD = \tfrac{1}{2}AC = \tfrac{1}{2}(10 - 4) = \tfrac{1}{2}(6) = 3,$$

$$DM = \tfrac{1}{2}CB = \tfrac{1}{2}(7 - 3) = \tfrac{1}{2}(4) = 2.$$

The x-coordinate of M is the same as the x-coordinate of D, which is

$$4 + AD = 4 + \tfrac{1}{2}(10 - 4) = 4 + 3 = 7.$$

The y-coordinate of M is

$$3 + DM = 3 + \tfrac{1}{2}(7 - 3) = 3 + 2 = 5.$$

So the mid-point M has coordinates (7, 5).

The idea of coordinate geometry is to use algebra so that you can do calculations like this when A and B are any points, and not just the particular points in Fig. 8.2. It often helps to use a notation which shows at a glance which point a coordinate refers to. One way of doing this is with **suffixes**, calling the coordinates of the first point (x_1, y_1), and the coordinates of the second point (x_2, y_2). So, for example, x_1 stands for 'the x-coordinate of the first point'.

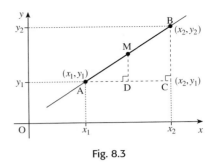

Fig. 8.3

Figure 8.3 shows these two general points, and the point C such that ACB is a right-angled triangle.

You can see that C now has coordinates (x_2, y_1), and that $AC = x_2 - x_1$ and $CB = y_2 - y_1$. Pythagoras' theorem now gives

$$AB = \sqrt{(x_2 - x_1)^2 + (y_2 - y_1)^2}.$$

The coordinates of the mid-point M can be found exactly as in Example 8.1.2. From Fig. 8.3, the x-coordinate of M is $x_1 + AD$, and the y-coordinate is $y_1 + DM$.

Then

$$
\begin{aligned}
x_1 + AD &= x_1 + \tfrac{1}{2}(x_2 - x_1) \\
&= x_1 + \tfrac{1}{2}x_2 - \tfrac{1}{2}x_1 \\
&= \tfrac{1}{2}x_1 + \tfrac{1}{2}x_2 \\
&= \tfrac{1}{2}(x_1 + x_2),
\end{aligned}
\qquad
\begin{aligned}
y_1 + DM &= y_1 + \tfrac{1}{2}(y_2 - y_1) \\
&= y_1 + \tfrac{1}{2}y_2 - \tfrac{1}{2}y_1 \\
&= \tfrac{1}{2}y_1 + \tfrac{1}{2}y_2 \\
&= \tfrac{1}{2}(y_1 + y_2).
\end{aligned}
$$

So, to find the mid-point you take the average of the x-coordinates and the average of the y-coordinates.

> The length of the line segment joining the points (x_1, y_1) and (x_2, y_2) is
>
> $$\sqrt{(x_2 - x_1)^2 + (y_2 - y_1)^2}.$$
>
> The mid-point of the line segment has coordinates
>
> $$\left(\frac{x_1 + x_2}{2}, \frac{y_1 + y_2}{2} \right).$$

An advantage of using algebra is that these formulae work whatever the shape and position of the triangle. In Fig. 8.4 the coordinates of A are negative, and in Fig. 8.5 the line slopes downhill rather than uphill as you move from left to right. Use these two figures to work out for yourself the length AB in each case. You can then use the formula to check your answers.

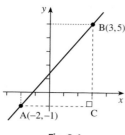

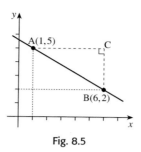

Fig. 8.4   Fig. 8.5

Also, it doesn't matter which way round you label the points A and B. If you think of B as 'the first point' (x_1, y_1) and A as 'the second point' (x_2, y_2), the formulae don't change. For example, in Fig. 8.2, they would give

$$BA = \sqrt{(4 - 10)^2 + (3 - 7)^2}$$
$$= \sqrt{(-6)^2 + (-4)^2}$$
$$= \sqrt{36 + 16} = \sqrt{52},$$

and the coordinates of M as

$$\left(\frac{10 + 4}{2}, \frac{7 + 3}{2}\right) = (7, 5), \text{ as in Example 8.1.2.}$$

There is one more point to notice. Suppose that in Fig. 8.3 the line segment [AB] slopes downhill (as in Fig. 8.5). Then $x_2 > x_1$ but $y_2 < y_1$. This means that the length CB is not $y_2 - y_1$ but $y_1 - y_2$. You could use modulus notation (see Section 1.4) to write CB = $|y_2 - y_1|$, which is true whether $y_2 > y_1$ or $y_2 < y_1$.

However, the formulae are still valid. In finding the length you have $(y_1 - y_2)^2$ instead of $(y_2 - y_1)^2$, but these are equal; the square of a negative number is the square of its modulus. And the y-coordinate of M is $y_1 - DM$ instead of $y_1 + DM$, but this is $y_1 - \frac{1}{2}(y_1 - y_2)$, which is still equal to $\frac{1}{2}(y_1 + y_2)$.

8.2   The gradient of a line

You will have noticed in Section 8.1 that the line segment joining A to B is denoted by [AB], with square brackets. If you want to refer to the whole line, of which the line segment is a part, you use the symbol (AB) with round brackets. The symbol AB without brackets is used for the length of [AB]. This is illustrated in Fig. 8.6.

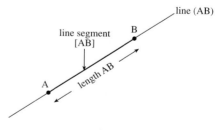

Fig. 8.6

Lines can be drawn in many different directions, and when you use coordinates you need a number to describe the direction of a line. In ordinary geometry you do this by giving the angle which the line makes with a fixed direction (such as a bearing). But this doesn't work well with coordinates, since it involves trigonometry. It is simpler to use instead the idea of 'gradient'.

The gradient of a line is a measure of its steepness. A line which goes up as you move from left to right is said to have a positive gradient. The steeper the line, the larger the gradient. A line which goes down from left to right has a negative gradient.

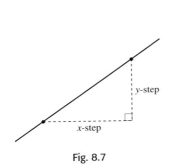

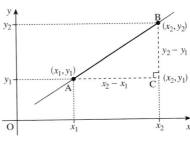

Fig. 8.8

Fig. 8.7

Unlike the distance and the mid-point, the gradient is a property of the whole line, not just of a particular line segment. If you take any two points on the line and find the increases in the x- and y-coordinates as you go from one to the other, as in Fig. 8.7, then the value of the fraction

$$\frac{y\text{-step}}{x\text{-step}}$$

is the same whichever points you choose. This is the **gradient** of the line.

In Fig. 8.8 the x-step and y-step are $x_2 - x_1$ and $y_2 - y_1$, so that:

> The gradient of the line joining (x_1, y_1) to (x_2, y_2) is $\dfrac{y_2 - y_1}{x_2 - x_1}$.

The formula in the blue box applies whether the coordinates are positive or negative. In Fig. 8.4, for example, the gradient of (AB) is $\dfrac{5 - (-1)}{3 - (-2)} = \dfrac{5 + 1}{3 + 2} = \frac{6}{5}$.

But notice that in Fig. 8.5 the gradient is $\dfrac{2 - 5}{6 - 1} = \dfrac{-3}{5} = -\frac{3}{5}$; the negative gradient tells you that the line slopes downhill as you move from left to right.

As with the other formulae, it doesn't matter which point has the suffix 1 and which has the suffix 2. In Fig. 8.2, you can calculate the gradient as either $\dfrac{7 - 3}{10 - 4} = \dfrac{4}{6} = \frac{2}{3}$, or $\dfrac{3 - 7}{4 - 10} = \dfrac{-4}{-6} = \frac{2}{3}$.

Two lines are **parallel** if they have the same gradient.

Example 8.2.1

Find the gradient of the line which passes through the points

(a) $(1, 3)$ and $(6, 2)$,   (b) $(-2, -5)$ and $(-6, -10)$.

State which of the lines slopes downwards to the right.

(a) Using the formula in the box the gradient is

$$\frac{2-3}{6-1} = \frac{-1}{5} = -\tfrac{1}{5}.$$

(b) Using the formula in the box the gradient is

$$\frac{-10-(-5)}{(-6)-(-2)} = \frac{-10+5}{-6+2} = \frac{-5}{-4} = \tfrac{5}{4}.$$

As the gradient of the first line is negative, it slopes downwards to the right.

Example 8.2.2

Show that the points $P(1, 3)$, $Q(2, 6)$, $R(4, -3)$ and $S(1, -12)$ form a trapezium but not a parallelogram.

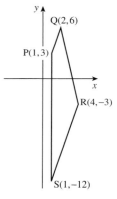

Fig. 8.9

It is a great help to draw a sketch. Figure 8.9 is an example of a sketch where the points are not accurately placed, but good enough to suggest that the parallel sides are [PQ] and [RS].

The gradient of [PQ] is $\dfrac{6-3}{2-1} = 3.$

The gradient of [QR] is $\dfrac{(-3)-6}{4-2} = \dfrac{-9}{2} = -4\tfrac{1}{2}.$

The gradient of [RS] is $\dfrac{(-12)-(-3)}{1-4} = \dfrac{-9}{-3} = 3.$

When you try to find the gradient of [SP] you get $\dfrac{(-12)-3}{1-1}$ which you cannot calculate because it involves division by 0. Figure 8.9 shows that [SP] is parallel to the y-axis.

From the gradients, [PQ] and [RS] are parallel and [QR] and [SP] are not parallel, so PQRS is a trapezium but not a parallelogram.

You should take note of the difficulty that arises with the side [PQ] in Example 8.2.2. If two points have equal x-coordinates but unequal y-coordinates, say (p, q) and (p, r) the gradient formula takes the form $\dfrac{r-q}{p-p}$, or $\dfrac{r-q}{0}$. Division by 0 is meaningless, so that the gradient is not defined.

But if two points have equal y-coordinates but unequal x-coordinates, say (r, p) and (s, p), then the gradient formula gives $\dfrac{p-p}{s-r} = \dfrac{0}{s-r}$, which is equal to 0.

> Lines parallel to the x-axis have gradient 0.
>
> The gradient is not defined for lines parallel to the y-axis.

Exercise 8A

Start each question by drawing a sketch. Do not use a calculator. Where appropriate, leave your answers in surd form.

1 Find the lengths and mid-points of the line segments joining these pairs of points.

(a) $(2, 5)$ and $(7, 17)$

(b) $(6, 5)$ and $(2, 2)$

(c) $(10, 9)$ and $(4, 1)$

(d) $(-3, 2)$ and $(1, -1)$

(e) $(4, -5)$ and $(-1, 0)$

(f) $(-3, -3)$ and $(-7, 3)$

2 Show that the points $(7, 12)$, $(-3, -12)$, $(15, 0)$, $(2, 13)$ and $(14, -5)$ lie on a circle with centre $(2, 0)$.

3 Show that the points $(3, 1)$, $(-3, -7)$ and $(11, -5)$ form an isosceles triangle. Find the mid-point of the side which is not one of the equal sides.

4 Find the gradients of the lines joining the following pairs of points.

(a) $(3, 8)$, $(5, 12)$

(b) $(1, -3)$, $(-2, 6)$

(c) $(-4, -3)$, $(0, -1)$

(d) $(-5, -3)$, $(3, -9)$

5 Find the gradients of the lines (AB) and (BC) where A is $(3, 4)$, B is $(7, 6)$ and C is $(-3, 1)$. What can you deduce about the points A, B and C?

6 The points A, B, C and D have coordinates $(2, 3)$, $(-3, 11)$, $(4, -2)$ and $(1, 8)$ respectively. Is (AB) parallel to (CD)?

7 The vertices of a quadrilateral ABCD are A$(1, 1)$, B$(7, 3)$, C$(9, -7)$ and D$(-3, -3)$. The points P, Q, R and S are the mid-points of [AB], [BC], [CD] and [DA] respectively.

(a) Find the gradient of each side of PQRS.

(b) Find the length of each side of PQRS.

(c) Find the mid-points of [PR] and [QS].

Parts (a), (b) and (c) all lead to the same conclusion about PQRS.

(d) What type of quadrilateral is PQRS?

8.3 The equation of a line

The x- and y-axes define a plane, which is the plane of the paper (or the calculator window) extended indefinitely in all directions. By giving different real number values to the coordinates x and y you can get all the points which make up the plane. The letters x and y are called **variables**.

If x and y are connected by an equation, such as $2y = 3x - 1$, then some points of the plane will have coordinates which **satisfy** the equation. For example, putting $x = 3$ and $y = 4$, the left side is $2 \times 4 = 8$ and the right side is $3 \times 3 - 1 = 8$; so the coordinates of the point $(3, 4)$ satisfy the equation. But the coordinates of the point $(4, 3)$ don't satisfy the equation, because $2 \times 3 = 6$ and $3 \times 4 - 1 = 11$, and $6 \neq 11$.

Example 8.3.1

Mark on an accurate diagram the points A(1, 1), B(−1, −4), C(0, −2), D($\frac{3}{2}$, $\frac{4}{3}$), E($\frac{2}{3}$, 0). Which three of these points have coordinates which satisfy the equation $y = 3x - 2$? Show that these three points are in a straight line.

The points are shown in Fig. 8.10.

You can easily check that

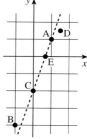

Fig. 8.10

$$\text{for A,} \quad 1 = 3 \times 1 - 2,$$
$$\text{for B,} \quad -4 \neq 3 \times (-1) - 2,$$
$$\text{for C,} \quad -2 = 3 \times 0 - 2,$$
$$\text{for D,} \quad \tfrac{4}{3} \neq 3 \times \tfrac{3}{2} - 2,$$
$$\text{for E,} \quad 0 = 3 \times \tfrac{2}{3} - 2.$$

So the coordinates of A, C and E satisfy the equation.

In Fig. 8.10 it looks as if A, E and C are in a straight line. To check this, calculate the gradients of [CE] and [EA]:

$$\text{gradient of [CE]} = \frac{0 - (-2)}{\tfrac{2}{3} - 0} = \frac{2}{\tfrac{2}{3}} = 3, \quad \text{gradient of [EA]} = \frac{1 - 0}{1 - \tfrac{2}{3}} = \frac{1}{\tfrac{1}{3}} = 3.$$

Since the line segments [CE] and [EA] have the same gradient, and both line segments share the same point E, the points A, E and C are in a straight line (drawn dotted in Fig. 8.10).

If three or more points are in a straight line, they are said to be **collinear**. In Example 8.3.1 the points A, E and C are collinear, and the equation $y = 3x - 2$ is the **equation of the line** through them.

You will notice that two of the points in Fig. 8.10, C and E, are on one or other of the axes. The y-coordinate of C, where the line cuts the y-axis, is called the **y-intercept** of the line. Similarly the x-coordinate of E, where the line cuts the x-axis, is the **x-intercept** of the line. So for the line with equation $y = 3x - 2$, the x-intercept is $\frac{2}{3}$ and the y-intercept is -2.

> To find the y-intercept of a straight line, put $x = 0$ in the equation of the line and solve for y.
>
> To find the x-intercept of a straight line, put $y = 0$ in the equation of the line and solve for x.

The question that now needs to be answered is: given a particular line, what is its equation?

Begin by asking how you might describe the line. First, you need to know its direction, and this is given by the gradient. But that isn't enough; there are many lines in any direction. To fix a particular line, you need something more. One possibility is to give the y-intercept.

Example 8.3.2
Find the equation of the line with gradient 2 and y-intercept 3.

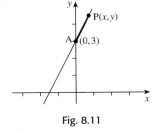

The line is drawn in Fig. 8.11, passing through A(0, 3). The figure also shows another point P on the line, with coordinates (x, y). You want to find an equation connecting x with y.

The equation has to express the fact that the line segment [AP] has gradient 2. Using the gradient formula in Section 8.2,

$$\frac{y-3}{x-0} = 2.$$

This can be written more simply as

$$y - 3 = 2x, \quad \text{or} \quad y = 2x + 3.$$

Fig. 8.11

The method used in Example 8.3.2 can be generalised to find the equation of any line with gradient m and y-intercept c. If the line segment joining $(0, c)$ to (x, y) has gradient m, then

$$\frac{y-c}{x-0} = m.$$

This can be simplified as

$$y - c = mx, \quad \text{or} \quad y = mx + c.$$

This is called the **gradient–intercept form** for the equation of a line.

> The equation of the line with gradient m through the point $(0, c)$ is
>
> $$y = mx + c.$$

Compare this with Example 8.3.1, where the gradient is 3, the y-intercept is -2, and the equation is $y = 3x - 2$.

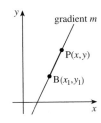

This is the simplest form for the equation of a straight line, but you can't always use it. Sometimes you don't know the y-intercept, but you know that the line passes through some other point B, with coordinates (x_1, y_1). In that case, you want an equation to express the fact that the line segment [BP] joining (x_1, y_1) to (x, y) has gradient m (see Fig. 8.12).

That is,

$$\frac{y-y_1}{x-x_1} = m,$$

or

$$y - y_1 = m(x - x_1).$$

Fig. 8.12

> The equation of the line through (x_1, y_1) with gradient m is
>
> $$y - y_1 = m(x - x_1).$$

Example 8.3.3

(a) Find the equation of the line with gradient 2 which passes through the point $(3, 1)$.

(b) Find the y-intercept of this line.

(a) Using the equation $y - y_1 = m(x - x_1)$, the equation of the line is

$$y - 1 = 2(x - 3).$$

Multiplying out the bracket and simplifying, you get $y - 1 = 2x - 6$, or

$$y = 2x - 5.$$

As a check, substitute the coordinates $(3, 1)$ into both sides of the equation, to make sure that the given point does actually lie on the line.

(b) The equation $y = 2x - 5$ is in the form $y = mx + c$ with $c = -5$.

So the y-intercept is -5.

There is one more special case to consider, when the line is parallel to one of the axes.

For a line parallel to the x-axis the gradient is 0. Putting $m = 0$ in the equation $y = mx + c$ gives $y = c$. That is, all the points on the line have coordinates of the form (something, c). Thus the points $(1, 2)$, $(-1, 2)$, $(5, 2)$, ... all lie on the straight line $y = 2$, shown in Fig. 8.13. As a special case, the x-axis has equation $y = 0$.

Similarly, a straight line parallel to the y-axis has an equation of the form $x = k$. All points on it have coordinates (k, something). Thus the points $(3, 0)$, $(3, 2)$, $(3, 4)$, ... all lie on the line $x = 3$, shown in Fig. 8.14. The y-axis itself has equation $x = 0$.

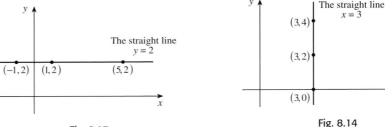

Fig. 8.13   Fig. 8.14

The line $x = k$ does not have a gradient; its gradient is undefined. Its equation cannot be written in the form $y = mx + c$.

Example 8.3.4

Find the equation of the straight line through $(3, 2)$ parallel to

(a) $y = 3x - 2$,　　(b) $x = 2$.

(a) The line $y = 3x - 2$ has gradient 3, so the equation of a line parallel to it also has gradient 3. If this line passes through $(3, 2)$, then its equation is

$$y - 2 = 3(x - 3).$$

Multiplying out the bracket,

$$y - 2 = 3x - 9,$$
$$y = 3x - 7.$$

The equation of the line is $y = 3x - 7$.

(b) The line $x = 2$ is parallel to the y-axis. The equation of any line parallel to this has the form $x = c$.

If this line passes through $(3, 2)$ then $(3, 2)$ must satisfy the equation, so

$$3 = c.$$

The equation of the line is $x = 3$.

Example 8.3.5

Find the equation of the line joining the points $(3, 4)$ and $(-1, 2)$.

First find the gradient of the line joining $(3, 4)$ to $(-1, 2)$. Then you can use the equation $y - y_1 = m(x - x_1)$.

The gradient of the line joining $(3, 4)$ to $(-1, 2)$ is $\dfrac{2 - 4}{(-1) - 3} = \dfrac{-2}{-4} = \frac{1}{2}$.

The equation of the line through $(3, 4)$ with gradient $\frac{1}{2}$ is $y - 4 = \frac{1}{2}(x - 3)$. After multiplying out you get

$$2y - 8 = x - 3,$$

which is

$$2y = x + 5.$$

Since you used the point $(3, 4)$ to find the equation, it is a good idea to check your answer by using the point $(-1, 2)$. When $x = -1$ and $y = 2$, the left side is $2 \times 2 = 4$ and the right side is $-1 + 5 = 4$.

Notice that in Example 8.3.5 the equation has been written as $2y = x + 5$ rather than in the standard gradient–intercept form $y = \frac{1}{2}x + 2\frac{1}{2}$. The advantage of this is to produce a neater equation with integer coefficients. You must of course remember to return it to the form $y = \ldots$ if you want to use the coefficients to find the gradient or the y-intercept.

Another common practice is to write the equation of a line with all the terms on one side, in the form $px + qy + r = 0$. For example, the equation $2y = x + 5$ would be written as $x - 2y + 5 = 0$, with $p = 1$, $q = -2$ and $r = 5$.

> You will often find the equation written as $ax + by + c = 0$, but the letters p, q, r are used here to avoid confusing the letter c with the y-intercept in the equation $y = mx + c$.

The advantage of using $px + qy + r = 0$ (where p and q are not both 0) is that *every* line has an equation of this form. This isn't true of $y = mx + c$, which excludes lines parallel to the y-axis for which the gradient is not defined. For example, the line $x = 3$ can be written as $px + qy + r = 0$ with $p = 1$, $q = 0$ and $r = -3$; but it can't be written as $y = mx + c$.

Example 8.3.6

For the line with equation $2x + 3y - 5 = 0$, find

(a) the gradient,   (b) the x-intercept,   (c) the y-intercept.

(a) Write the equation in the form $3y = -2x + 5$, which is

$$y = -\tfrac{2}{3}x + 1\tfrac{2}{3}.$$

This is now in gradient-intercept form, so the coefficient of x gives the gradient, which is $-\tfrac{2}{3}$.

(b) To find the x-intercept, put $y = 0$ and solve for x. This gives

$$2x - 5 = 0,$$

so the x-intercept is $\dfrac{5}{2} = 2\tfrac{1}{2}$.

(c) From the gradient–intercept form in part (a), the y-intercept is $1\tfrac{2}{3}$.
Alternatively, you could find this directly, by putting $x = 0$ and solving for y.

Exercise 8B

1 Test whether the given point lies on the straight line with the given equation.

(a) $(1, 2)$ on $y = 5x - 3$ (b) $(3, -2)$ on $3x - y - 7 = 0$

2 Find the equations of the straight lines through the given points with the gradients shown. Your final answers should not contain any fractions.

(a) $(2, 3)$, gradient 5 (b) $(1, -2)$, gradient -3

(c) $(0, 4)$, gradient $\tfrac{1}{2}$ (d) $(-2, 1)$, gradient $-\tfrac{3}{8}$

(e) $(0, 0)$, gradient -3 (f) $(3, 8)$, gradient 0

(g) $(-5, -1)$, gradient $-\tfrac{3}{4}$ (h) $(-3, 0)$, gradient $\tfrac{1}{2}$

(i) $(-3, -1)$, gradient $\tfrac{3}{8}$ (j) $(3, 4)$, gradient $-\tfrac{1}{2}$

(k) $(2, -1)$, gradient -2 (l) $(-2, -5)$, gradient 3

(m) $(0, -4)$, gradient 7 (n) $(0, 2)$, gradient -1

3 Find the equations of the lines joining the following pairs of points.

(a) $(1, 4)$ and $(3, 10)$

(b) $(4, 5)$ and $(-2, -7)$

(c) $(3, 2)$ and $(0, 4)$

(d) $(3, 7)$ and $(3, 12)$

(e) $(10, -3)$ and $(-5, -12)$

(f) $(3, -1)$ and $(-4, 20)$

(g) $(2, -3)$ and $(11, -3)$

(h) $(2, 0)$ and $(5, -1)$

(i) $(-4, 2)$ and $(-1, -3)$

(j) $(-2, -1)$ and $(5, -3)$

(k) $(-3, 4)$ and $(-3, 9)$

(l) $(-1, 0)$ and $(0, -1)$

(m) $(2, 7)$ and $(3, 10)$

(n) $(-5, 4)$ and $(-2, -1)$

(o) $(0, 0)$ and $(5, -3)$

(p) $(0, 0)$ and (p, q)

4 Find the gradients, x-intercepts and y-intercepts of the following lines.

(a) $y = -x - 3$

(b) $y = 3(x + 4)$

(c) $5x + 2y + 3 = 0$

(d) $y = 5$

(e) $3x - 2y + 4 = 0$

(f) $5x = 7$

(g) $2x + y = 7$

(h) $3x - 4y - 8 = 0$

(i) $2y = 7 - x$

5 Find the equation of the line through $(-2, 1)$ parallel to $y = \frac{1}{2}x - 3$.

6 Find the equation of the line through $(4, -2)$ parallel to $2x + y - 5 = 0$.

8.4 The gradients of perpendicular lines

In Section 8.2 it is stated that two lines are parallel if they have the same gradient. But what can you say about the gradients of two lines which are perpendicular?

First, if a line has a positive gradient, then the perpendicular line has a negative gradient, and vice versa. But you can be more exact than this.

In Fig. 8.15 if the gradient of (PB) is m, you can draw a 'gradient triangle' PAB in which PA is one unit and AB is m units.

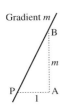

Fig. 8.15

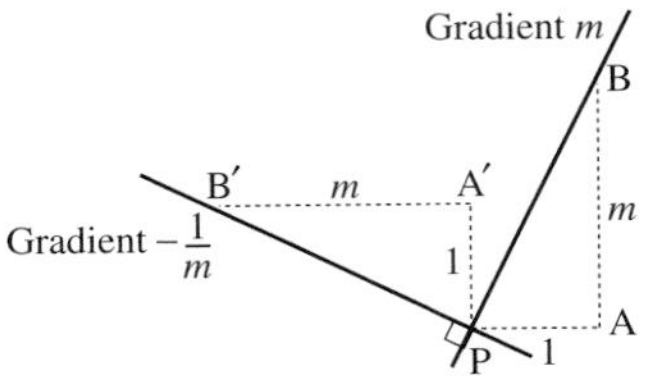

Fig. 8.16

In Fig 8.16, the gradient triangle PAB has been rotated through a right-angle to PA′B′, so that (PB′) is perpendicular to (PB). The y-step for triangle PA′B′ is 1 and the x-step is $-m$, so

$$\text{gradient of (PB′)} = \frac{y\text{-step}}{x\text{-step}} = \frac{1}{-m} = -\frac{1}{m}.$$

Therefore the gradient of the line perpendicular to (PB) is $-\dfrac{1}{m}$.

Thus if the gradients of the two perpendicular lines are m_1 and m_2, then $m_2 = -\dfrac{1}{m_1}$, so $m_1 m_2 = -1$. It is also true in reverse: if two lines have gradients m_1 and m_2, and if $m_1 m_2 = -1$, then the lines are perpendicular.

> If a line has gradient m, the gradient of the line perpendicular to it is $-\dfrac{1}{m}$.
>
> Two lines with gradients m_1 and m_2 are perpendicular if
> $$m_1 m_2 = -1.$$

Notice that the condition does not work if the lines are parallel to the axes. However, you can see that a line $x = $ constant is perpendicular to one of the form $y = $ constant.

Example 8.4.1
The gradients of four lines are 2, $\frac{2}{3}$, -3 and $-\frac{4}{3}$. Find the gradients of the four lines at right angles to them.

Using the rule $m_2 = -\dfrac{1}{m_1}$ the gradients of the perpendicular lines are, in turn, $-\frac{1}{2}$, $-\dfrac{1}{\frac{2}{3}}$, $-\dfrac{1}{-3}$ and $-\dfrac{1}{-\frac{4}{3}}$. These simplify to $-\frac{1}{2}$, $-\frac{3}{2}$, $\frac{1}{3}$ and $\frac{3}{4}$.

The gradients of the four lines are $-\frac{1}{2}$, $-\frac{3}{2}$, $\frac{1}{3}$ and $\frac{3}{4}$.

Example 8.4.2
A line is perpendicular to $3y = 2x - 4$. Find its gradient.

The line $3y = 2x - 4$ can be written as $y = \frac{2}{3}x - \frac{4}{3}$.

The gradient of this line is $\frac{2}{3}$, so the gradient of the line perpendicular to it is $-\frac{3}{2}$.

Example 8.4.3
Find the equation of the line through $(1, 6)$ which is perpendicular to $y = 2x + 3$.

The line $y = 2x + 3$ has gradient 2, so the perpendicular line has gradient $-\frac{1}{2}$.

Using $y - y_1 = m(x - x_1)$, the line through $(1, 6)$ with gradient $-\frac{1}{2}$ is

$$y - 6 = -\tfrac{1}{2}(x - 1).$$

This simplifies to $2y - 12 = -x + 1$, which is $2y = -x + 13$.

Example 8.4.4

Find the equation of the perpendicular bisector of the points A(3, 6) and B(−1, 4).

Figure 8.17 shows the situation. The perpendicular bisector of two points A and B is the line which passes through the mid-point of [AB] at right angles to [AB].

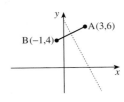

The mid-point of [AB] is $\left(\dfrac{3 + (-1)}{2}, \dfrac{6 + 4}{2} \right)$, which is (1, 5).

The gradient of [AB] is $\dfrac{4 - 6}{(-1) - 3} = \dfrac{-2}{-4} = \frac{1}{2}$.

Fig. 8.17

The gradient of the line perpendicular to [AB] is $-\dfrac{1}{\frac{1}{2}} = -2$.

The equation of the perpendicular bisector is therefore

$$y - 5 = -2(x - 1), \quad \text{or} \quad y - 5 = -2x + 2.$$

This can be simplified to $y = -2x + 7$.

Exercise 8C

1   In each part write down the gradient of a line which is perpendicular to one with the given gradient.

(a) 2

(b) −3

(c) $\frac{3}{4}$

(d) $-\frac{5}{6}$

(e) −1

(f) $1\frac{3}{4}$

(g) $-\dfrac{1}{m}$

(h) m

(i) $\dfrac{p}{q}$

(j) 0

(k) $-m$

(l) $\dfrac{a}{b - c}$

2   In each part find the equation of the line through the given point which is perpendicular to the given line. Write your final answer so that it doesn't contain fractions.

(a) (2, 3), $y = 4x + 3$

(b) (−3, 1), $y = -\frac{1}{2}x + 3$

(c) (2, −5), $y = -5x - 2$

(d) (7, −4), $y = 2\frac{1}{2}$

(e) (−1, 4), $2x + 3y = 8$

(f) (4, 3), $5y = 3x - 8$

(g) (5, −3), $2x = 3$

(h) (0, 3), $y = 2x - 1$

3   A line through a vertex of a triangle which is perpendicular to the opposite side is called an altitude. Find the equation of the altitude through the vertex A of the triangle ABC where A is the point (2, 3), B is (1, −7) and C is (4, −1).

9 Functions and graphs

This chapter introduces the idea of a function and investigates the graphs representing functions of various kinds. When you have completed it, you should

- understand function notation
- be able to use a calculator to display the shape of a graph with a given equation
- understand what is meant by an asymptote
- understand the terms 'domain' and 'range', and appreciate the importance of defining the domain of a function
- understand that a sequence is a function whose domain is the set of positive integers or natural numbers
- be able to use a calculator to display the graph of a sequence
- understand that a sequence u_n may converge to a limit as n tends to infinity.

9.1 The idea of a function

If you need to carry out a particular calculation frequently, it is useful to summarise it with a formula. For example:

the area of a circle with radius x metres is πx^2 square metres;

the volume of a cube of side x metres is x^3 cubic metres;

the time that it takes to travel k kilometres at x kilometres per hour is $\dfrac{k}{x}$ hours.

You will often have used different letters from x in these formulae, such as r for radius or s for speed, but in most of this chapter x will be used for the letter in the formula, and y for the quantity you want to calculate. Notice that some formulae also involve other letters, called **constants**; these might be either a number like π, which is irrational and cannot be written out in full, or a quantity like the distance k, which you choose for yourself depending on the distance you intend to travel.

Expressions such as πx^2, x^3 and $\dfrac{k}{x}$ are examples of **functions** of x. The essential feature of a function is that, having chosen x, you can get a *unique* value of y from it.

It is often useful to have a way of writing functions in general, rather than always having to refer to particular functions. The notation which is used for this is $f(x)$ (read 'f of x', or sometimes just 'f x'). The letter f stands for the function itself, and x for the number you choose for its evaluation.

If you want to refer to the value of the function when x has a particular value, say $x = 2$, then you write the value as $f(2)$. For example, if $f(x)$ stands for the function x^3, then $f(2) = 2^3 = 8$.

If a problem involves more than one function, you can use different letters for each function. Two functions can, for example, be written as $f(x)$ and $g(x)$.

Example 9.1.1

(a) If $f(x) = \sqrt{x}$ and $g(x) = \dfrac{1}{x}$, find $f(100)$ and $g(100)$.

(b) Are there any real numbers for which $f(x)$ or $g(x)$ cannot be calculated?

(a) Remember that $\sqrt{x}$ stands for the positive square root. So

$$f(100) = \sqrt{100} = 10, \text{ and } g(100) = \frac{1}{100} = 0.01.$$

(b) Whenever you square a number, the result is a positive number or zero. So a negative number cannot have a square root. That is, $\sqrt{x}$ can't be calculated if x is a negative real number.

By $\dfrac{1}{x}$ you mean the number y such that $x \times y = 1$. But if $x = 0$, then $x \times y = 0$ for every number y. So $\dfrac{1}{x}$ has no meaning if $x = 0$.

Investigate what happens when you try to find $\sqrt{-100}$ or $\dfrac{1}{0}$ with a calculator.

Functions are not always defined by algebraic formulae. Sometimes it is easier to describe them in words, or to define them using a flow chart or a computer program. All that matters is that each value of x chosen leads to a unique value of $y = f(x)$.

9.2 Graphs

You are familiar with drawing graphs. You set up a coordinate system for Cartesian coordinates using x- and y-axes, and choose the scales on each axis.

The graph of a function $f(x)$ is made up of all the points whose coordinates (x, y) satisfy the equation $y = f(x)$. When you draw such a graph on graph paper, you choose a few values of x and work out $y = f(x)$ for these. You then plot the points with coordinates (x, y), and join up these points by eye, usually with a smooth curve. If you have done this accurately, the coordinates of other points of the curve will also satisfy the equation $y = f(x)$. Calculators and computers make graphs in much the same way, but they can plot many more points much more quickly.

It is important to become proficient in using your calculator to display graphs. To do this you must enter the formula for the function, probably in the form '$y = \ldots$'. You also have to specify a 'window', stating intervals of values of x and y which you want to appear in the display. Obviously you can't show the whole plane in a small window, so the choice of which part of the plane to display can be very significant.

Example 9.2.1

Use your calculator to display the graph of the function $3x - \frac{1}{5}x^3$ with the following windows:

(a) $-1 \le x \le 1,\ -0.6 \le y \le 0.6,$ (b) $-5 \le x \le 5,\ -3 \le y \le 3,$ (c) $-5 \le x \le 5,\ -5 \le y \le 5.$

You should get displays like those in Fig. 9.1. In (a) the graph looks like a straight line, and there is no indication that it will go in quite different directions for larger values of $|x|$. The graph in (b) seems to be in three separate parts, which is improbable; there must be a value for $x = 2$, for example, but it doesn't show up in the display.

Reducing the y-scale as in (c) reveals all the important features of the graph. Although only a small part of the complete graph appears in the window, you will probably agree that it tells you as much as you need to know about the function.

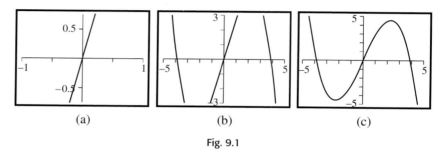

(a)   (b)   (c)

Fig. 9.1

Example 9.2.1 illustrates the importance of choosing a suitable window. You will often find that you need to experiment with several different windows before you are satisfied that the graph shows all the important features of the function.

The problem doesn't only arise when you use a calculator to draw graphs. Exactly the same considerations apply when you draw graphs by hand on graph paper.

Notice that when graphing functions it isn't usually important to use the same scale on both axes. If you can, do; but if the spread of the y-values is greater than the spread of the x-values, it is quite acceptable to squash the y-axis so as to fit the graph into the window.

> This is different from the advice in Chapter 8, where you were concerned with geometrical figures such as isosceles triangles and perpendicular lines. These will appear distorted unless you use equal scales on the two axes.

In Example 9.2.1 you will probably find that in parts (a) and (b) the scales are almost equal on the two axes, but in part (c) the y-scale is smaller than the x-scale.

Example 9.2.2

Use your calculator to display the graphs of

(a) $f(x) = 1 - \frac{1}{4}x^2,$ (b) $g(x) = \sqrt{1 - \frac{1}{4}x^2},$ with a window of $-3 \le x \le 3,\ -2 \le y \le 2.$

Describe and explain their principal features.

The two graphs are shown in Fig. 9.2.

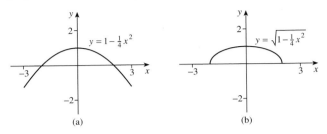

Fig. 9.2

(a) The window is large enough to show the main features. Since $x^2 \geq 0$ for all real numbers x, $1 - \frac{1}{4}x^2$ is always less than or equal to 1. But, when $|x|$ is large, $f(x)$ is a very large negative number. So the graph extends indefinitely to the left and right, and at the foot of the window. However small the scale, the window can never contain the whole graph.

Since $f(2) = f(-2) = 0$, the graph crosses the x-axis at $(2, 0)$ and $(-2, 0)$. The sign of $f(x)$ is positive if $-2 < x < 2$, and negative if $x > 2$ or $x < -2$ (that is, if $|x| > 2$).

(b) Since negative numbers don't have square roots, and $1 - \frac{1}{4}x^2 < 0$ if $|x| > 2$, the graph cannot exist outside the interval $-2 \leq x \leq 2$. In that interval $0 \leq 1 - \frac{1}{4}x^2 \leq 1$, so $0 \leq \sqrt{1 - \frac{1}{4}x^2} \leq 1$. The whole graph therefore lies in the box defined by the inequalities $-2 \leq x \leq 2$, $0 \leq y \leq 1$. It follows that, by defining a suitable window, you can display the whole graph on the calculator or on a sheet of graph paper.

Example 9.2.3

Use your calculator to display the graph of $f(x) = \dfrac{2x}{x-1}$ with a window of $-10 \leq x \leq 10$, $-10 \leq y \leq 10$. Investigate any special features of the graph.

The graph is shown in Fig. 9.3a. You can see that, even with such a small scale, the window can't contain the whole graph. The graph extends indefinitely to the left and right, and also upwards and downwards. Notice that the graph passes through the origin, because $f(0) = 0$.

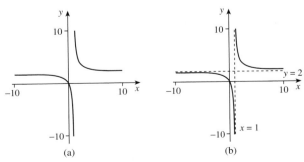

Fig. 9.3

The most obvious peculiarity of the graph occurs where $x = 1$. If you try to calculate $f(1)$ you get the form $\dfrac{2 \times 1}{1 - 1}$, or $\dfrac{2}{0}$ which has no meaning. So there is no point on the graph corresponding to $x = 1$.

To see what is happening in more detail, try evaluating $f(x)$ when x is slightly less or slightly greater than 1. For example, find $f(0.99)$, $f(0.999)$, $f(1.01)$ and $f(1.001)$. You will find that if $x - 1$ is a small positive number, $f(x)$ is a large positive number; and if $x - 1$ is a negative number with small modulus, $f(x)$ is a negative number with large modulus. Either way, if $|x - 1|$ is small, then $|f(x)|$ is large.

Another interesting feature is that the curve seems to flatten out when $|x|$ is large. To investigate this, try evaluating $f(10)$, $f(100)$, $f(-10)$ and $f(-100)$. You will find that if x is a large positive number, then $f(x)$ is slightly greater than 2; and if x is a negative number with large modulus, then $f(x)$ is slightly less than 2. But if you try to find a value of x for which $f(x) = 2$, you get the equation

$$\frac{2x}{x - 1} = 2,$$

which when simplified becomes $0 = -2$! This means that there are no values of x for which $f(x) = 2$.

You will see this clearly if you add the graph with equation $y = 2$ to your calculator display.

Figure 9.3b reproduces Fig. 9.3a with the lines $x = 1$ and $y = 2$ added. These lines are called **asymptotes** of the graph with equation $y = \dfrac{2x}{x - 1}$. They are lines which the graph approaches indefinitely closely when either $|x|$ or $|y|$ is large.

It is conventional to describe $x = 1$ as a 'vertical' asymptote and $y = 2$ as a 'horizontal' asymptote, although these terms are only really appropriate if the graph is mounted on a vertical surface.

Exercise 9A

1 Given $f(x) = 2x + 5$, find the values of
   (a) $f(3)$,   (b) $f(0)$,   (c) $f(-4)$,   (d) $f\left(-2\tfrac{1}{2}\right)$.

2 Given $f(x) = 3x^2 + 2$, find the values of
   (a) $f(4)$,   (b) $f(-1)$,   (c) $f(-3)$,   (d) $f(3)$.

3 Given $f(x) = x^2 + 4x + 3$, find the values of
   (a) $f(2)$,   (b) $f\left(\tfrac{1}{2}\right)$,   (c) $f(-1)$,   (d) $f(-3)$.

4 Given $g(x) = x^3$ and $h(x) = 4x + 1$,
   (a) find the value of $g(2) + h(2)$,   (b) find the value of $3g(-1) - 4h(-1)$,
   (c) show that $g(5) = h(31)$.

5 With a window of $-2 \le x \le 3$, $-3 \le y \le 4$, display the graph of $f(x) = x^2 - x$. Estimate from the graph the value of x for which $f(x)$ has its smallest value.

6 With a window from -2 to 4 for both x and y, display the graph of $y = f(x)$, where $f(x) = x^2(3 - x)$. Estimate from your graph the largest value taken by $f(x)$ in the interval $0 \le x \le 3$, and the value of x when $f(x)$ takes this value.

7 Use your calculator with a window of $-1 \le x \le 5$, $-1 \le y \le 3$ with equal scales on both axes to display the graphs of $y = x(3 - x)$ and $y = \sqrt{x(3 - x)}$. Suggest a name to describe the shape of the second graph.

8 With a window of $-5 \le x \le 5$, $-5 \le y \le 5$ display the graph of $y = \dfrac{x^2 + 1}{x^2 - 1}$. Suggest the equations of the three asymptotes, and check your answers with suitable calculations.

9 Choose a suitable window to show the main features of the graph of $f(x) = (x^2 - 2x)^2$.

10 Find the equations of the asymptotes of the graph of $y = \dfrac{1 - 2x}{x - 3}$.

9.3 Positive integer powers of x

This section looks at graphs of functions of the form $f(x) = x^n$, where n is a positive integer.

First look at the graphs when x is positive, using a window of $0 \le x \le 2$, $0 \le y \le 2$ with equal scales on the two axes. Then x^n is also positive, so that the graphs lie entirely in the first quadrant. Begin by showing each graph separately. Figure 9.4 shows the graphs for $n = 1, 2, 3$ and 4 for values of x from 0 to somewhere beyond 1.

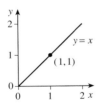 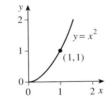 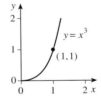 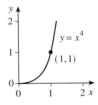

Fig. 9.4

Now put the graphs together in a single display. Points to notice are:

- $(0, 0)$ and $(1, 1)$ satisfy the equation $y = x^n$ for all these values of n, so that all the graphs include the points $(0, 0)$ and $(1, 1)$.

- $n = 1$ is a special case: it gives the straight line $y = x$ through the origin, which makes an angle of $45°$ with each axis.

- For $n > 1$ the x-axis is a tangent to the graphs at the origin. This is because, when x is small, x^n is very small. For example, $0.1^2 = 0.01$, $0.1^3 = 0.001$, $0.1^4 = 0.0001$.

- For each increase in the index n, the graph stays closer to the x-axis between $x = 0$ and $x = 1$, but then climbs more steeply beyond $x = 1$. This is because $x^{n+1} = x \times x^n$, so that $x^{n+1} < x^n$ when $0 < x < 1$ and $x^{n+1} > x^n$ when $x > 1$.

Now display the graphs again, using a window of $-2 \le x \le 2$, $-2 \le y \le 2$ with equal scales on both axes.

You will notice that what happens when x is negative depends on whether n is odd or even. To see this, suppose $x = -a$, where a is a positive number.

If n is even, $(-a)^n = a^n$. (Think of $n = 2$ or $n = 4$.)

So for the graph $y = f(x)$ where $f(x) = x^n$,

$$f(-a) = (-a)^n$$
$$= a^n \quad \text{(since } n \text{ is even).}$$
$$= f(a).$$

So the value of y on the graph is the same for $x = -a$ and $x = a$. This means that the graph is symmetrical about the y-axis. This is illustrated in Fig. 9.5 for the graphs of $y = x^2$ and $y = x^4$. Functions with the property that $f(-a) = f(a)$ for all values of a are called **even functions**.

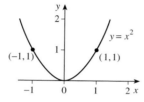 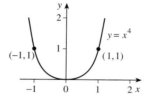

Fig. 9.5

If n is odd, $(-a)^n = -a^n$. (Think of $n = 1$ or $n = 3$.)

So for the graph $y = f(x)$ where $f(x) = x^n$,

$$f(-a) = (-a)^n$$
$$= -a^n$$
$$= -f(a).$$

The value of y for $x = -a$ is minus the value for $x = a$. Note that the points with coordinates (a, a^n) and $(-a, -a^n)$ are symmetrically placed on either side of the origin. This means that the whole graph is symmetrical about the origin. This is illustrated in Fig. 9.6 for the graphs of $y = x$ and $y = x^3$. Functions with the property that $f(-a) = -f(a)$ for all values of a are called **odd functions**.

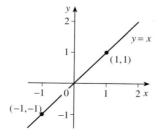 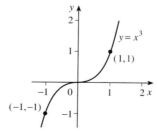

Fig. 9.6

Exercise 9B

1 Sketch the graphs of

(a) $y = x^5$,   (b) $y = x^6$,   (c) $y = x^{10}$,   (d) $y = x^{15}$.

Use your calculator to check your sketches.

2 Given $f(x) = x^n$ and $f(3) = 81$, determine the value of n.

3 Of the following functions, one is even and two are odd. Determine which is which.

(a) $f(x) = x^7$ (b) $g(x) = x^4 + 3x^2$ (c) $h(x) = x(x^2 - 1)$

9.4 The domain of a function

Example 9.1.1 gave two functions which cannot be defined for all real numbers: $\dfrac{1}{x}$, which has no meaning when x is 0, and $\sqrt{x}$, which has no meaning when x is negative.

Example 9.4.1
For what values of x does $\sqrt{x(6 - x)}$ have a meaning?

Since a negative number does not have a real square root, $\sqrt{x(6 - x)}$ exists only if $x(6 - x) \geq 0$.

For this to be true, the factors x and $6 - x$ must either be both greater than or equal to 0, or both less than or equal to 0.

If $x \geq 0$ and $6 - x \geq 0$, then $0 \leq x \leq 6$.

The alternative, that $x \leq 0$ and $6 - x \leq 0$, is impossible. The second inequality can be written as $x \geq 6$, and you can't have $x \leq 0$ and $x \geq 6$ at the same time.

So $\sqrt{x(6 - x)}$ has a meaning only if $0 \leq x \leq 6$.

There are also times when you use a function which has a meaning for all real numbers x, but you are interested in it only when x is restricted in some way. For example, the formula for the volume of a cube is $V = x^3$. Although you can calculate x^3 for any real number x, you would only use this formula for $x > 0$.

Example 9.4.2

(a) One pair of sides of a rectangle is 1 metre longer than the other pair. If the length of one of the shorter sides is x metres, find a formula for the area of the rectangle in square metres.

(b) Find a formula for the sum of the first x even numbers.

(a) The sides have lengths x metres and $(x + 1)$ metres, so the area in square metres is $x(x + 1)$.

(b) You know from Section 2.3 that the sum of all the natural numbers from 1 to n is $\frac{1}{2}n(n + 1)$. So the sum of the first x even numbers is

$$
\begin{aligned}
2 + 4 + 6 + \ldots + 2x &= 2(1 + 2 + 3 + \ldots + x) \\
&= 2 \times \tfrac{1}{2}x(x + 1) \\
&= x(x + 1).
\end{aligned}
$$

In both parts of this example the function is given by the same expression, but the variable x is understood in different ways. In part (a) the question makes sense if x is any positive real number. In part (b), x can only be a positive integer.

You could therefore distinguish three different functions:

$$f(x) = x(x + 1), \text{ where } x \text{ is a real number } (x \in \mathbb{R})$$

$$A(x) = x(x + 1), \text{ where } x \text{ is a positive real number } (x \in \mathbb{R}^+)$$

$$S(x) = x(x + 1), \text{ where } x \text{ is a positive integer } (x \in \mathbb{Z}^+).$$

Figure 9.7 shows part of the graphs of these three functions. Although they are all given by the same expression, they have different properties. For example, $f(x)$ has a minimum value when $x = -\frac{1}{2}$, but $A(x)$ and $S(x)$ are not defined for this value of x. It makes sense to write $f\left(1\frac{1}{2}\right) = 3\frac{3}{4}$ and $A\left(1\frac{1}{2}\right) = 3\frac{3}{4}$, but you can't find the sum of the first $1\frac{1}{2}$ even numbers.

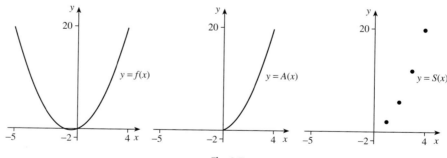

Fig. 9.7

So two possible reasons why a function $f(x)$ might not be defined for all real numbers x are

- the algebraic expression for $f(x)$ may only have meaning for some x
- only some x are relevant in the context in which the function is being used.

The set of numbers x for which a function $f(x)$ is defined is called the **domain** of the function. For example, the domain of the function in Example 9.4.1 can be taken to be the set of real numbers such that $0 \leq x \leq 6$; these are the only numbers for which $\sqrt{x(6-x)}$ exists. In Example 9.4.2 the domains can be taken to be the positive real numbers and the positive integers respectively; these are the only numbers which make sense in the contexts, even though the formula $x(x+1)$ has a meaning for any real number x.

9.5   The range of a function

Once you have decided the domain of a function $f(x)$, you can ask what values $f(x)$ can take. This is called the **range** of the function.

Example 9.5.1
Find the range of the function $x(6-x)$, and interpret this geometrically.

The expression $x(6-x)$ can be evaluated for any real number x, so the domain can be taken as the complete set of real numbers.

The simplest way to find the range is to use the graph of the function. This is shown in Fig. 9.8.

The graph looks symmetrical. If so, it will reach its highest point when $x = 3$, and y is then $3 \times (6-3) = 3 \times 3 = 9$. So the range consists of all real numbers less than or equal to 9.

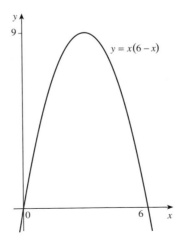

Fig. 9.8

Example 9.5.2

Find the range of the function $\sqrt{x(6-x)}$ taking its domain to be the set of numbers $0 \le x \le 6$.

You could use your calculator again to produce the graph in Fig. 9.9, but in fact all the information you need can be got from Fig. 9.8.

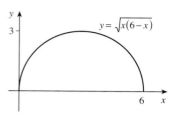

Fig. 9.9

For any value of x, the y-coordinate in Fig. 9.9 is the positive square root of the corresponding y-coordinate in Fig. 9.8. This square root only exists when $y \ge 0$ in Fig. 9.8, that is when $0 \le x \le 6$; and since the maximum value in Fig. 9.8 is 9, the maximum value in Fig. 9.9 is $\sqrt{9} = 3$. So the range of $\sqrt{x(6-x)}$ is $0 \le y \le 3$.

Example 9.5.3

A marching guardsman swings his arms so that their angle in front of the downward vertical varies from $0°$ to $80°$. When this angle is $x°$, the height of his thumbnail above the ground is y metres, where $y = 1.8 - 0.8\cos x°$. Find the range of this function as he marches.

In Fig. 9.10 the solid curve shows the graph of y in the domain $0 \le x \le 80$, and the dotted curve shows how the graph continues outside the given domain. You can see that, on the solid curve, the graph takes values between $y = 1$ (when $x = 0$) and $y = 1.661...$ (when $x = 80$).

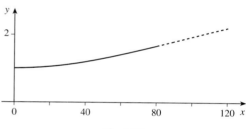

Fig. 9.10

So the range of the function is $1 \le y \le 1.66$, correct to 3 significant figures.

Exercise 9C

1 Find the set of values of x for which these algebraic expressions have a meaning.

(a) $\sqrt{x}$ (b) $\sqrt{-x}$ (c) $\sqrt{x-4}$ (d) $\sqrt{4-x}$

(e) $\sqrt{x(x-4)}$ (f) $\sqrt{2x(x-4)}$ (g) $\sqrt{x^2-9}$ (h) $\sqrt{x^3-8}$

(i) $\dfrac{1}{x-2}$ (j) $\dfrac{1}{\sqrt{x-2}}$ (k) $\dfrac{1}{1+\sqrt{x}}$ (l) $\dfrac{1}{(x-1)(x-2)}$

2 The domain of each of the following functions is the set of real numbers. Find their ranges.

(a) $f(x) = x^2 + 4$ (b) $f(x) = 2(x^2 + 5)$ (c) $f(x) = (x-1)^2 + 6$

(d) $f(x) = -(1-x)^2 + 7$ (e) $f(x) = 3(x+5)^2 + 2$ (f) $f(x) = 2(x+2)^4 - 1$

3 These functions are each defined for the given domain. Display their graphs on your calculator and find their ranges.

(a) $f(x) = 2x$ for $0 \le x \le 8$ (b) $f(x) = 3 - 2x$ for $-2 \le x \le 2$

(c) $f(x) = x^2$ for $-1 \le x \le 4$ (d) $f(x) = x^2$ for $-5 \le x \le -2$

4 The domain of each of the following functions is the set of all positive real numbers. Find the range of each function.

(a) $f(x) = 2x + 7$ (b) $f(x) = -5x$ (c) $f(x) = 3x - 1$

(d) $f(x) = x^2 - 1$ (e) $f(x) = (x + 2)(x + 1)$ (f) $f(x) = (x - 1)(x - 2)$

5 The domain of each of the following functions is the set of values of x for which the algebraic expression has a meaning. Find their ranges.

(a) $f(x) = x^8$ (b) $f(x) = x^{11}$ (c) $f(x) = \dfrac{1}{x^3}$ (d) $f(x) = \dfrac{1}{x^4}$

(e) $f(x) = x^4 + 5$ (f) $f(x) = \frac{1}{4}x + \frac{1}{8}$ (g) $f(x) = \sqrt{4 - x^2}$ (h) $f(x) = \sqrt{4 - x}$

6 A piece of wire 24 cm long has the shape of a rectangle. Given that the width is w cm, show that the area, A cm^2, of the rectangle is given by the function $A = w(12 - w)$. Suggest a suitable domain and find the corresponding range of this function in this context.

7 Use a calculator to show the graph of $y = x(8 - 2x)(22 - 2x)$. Given that y cm^3 is the volume of a cuboid with height x cm, length $(22 - 2x)$ cm and width $(8 - 2x)$ cm, state an appropriate domain for the function given above.

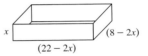

Use a graph to estimate the corresponding range.

9.6 Sequences as functions

In Section 9.4 you may have been surprised by the graph of $S(x)$ in Fig. 9.7, which is simply a set of dots. This is because the domain is the set $\mathbb{Z}^+ = \{1, 2, 3, ...\}$. The function is only defined when x is a positive integer.

In the same way, you can think of any sequence u_n as a function. To make this more obvious you could have used the notation $u(n)$ instead of the conventional notation u_n.

> If the sequence begins with u_0 rather than u_1, then the domain is the set of natural numbers $\mathbb{N} = \{0, 1, 2, ...\}$. For example, this is how the triangle numbers t_n were defined at the end of Section 2.3.

Example 9.6.1

Draw the graph of the arithmetic sequence 13, 11, 9, ... with 10 terms.

The formula for the nth term, $u_n = a + (n-1)d$
(see Section 2.4), with $a = 13$ and $d = -2$, gives

$$u_n = 13 - 2(n-1)$$
$$= 15 - 2n.$$

Notice that u_n is positive if $1 \le n \le 7$, and negative if $8 \le n \le 10$. When $n = 10$, $u_n = 15 - 2 \times 10 = -5$.

The graph is shown in Fig. 9.11. The points all lie on a straight line with gradient -2 and y-intercept 15.

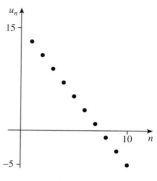

Fig. 9.11

You can produce graphs like Fig. 9.11 on your calculator. To do this, you have to put the calculator into 'sequence graphing mode'. In place of '$y = ...$' you can then enter the formula '$u_n = 15 - 2n$', and the graph will appear in the window as a line of dots.

Example 9.6.2

Sue is Don's younger sister. She was born on Don's fourth birthday; so when Sue is n years old, Don is $n + 4$. Display a graph to show the ratio of Don's age to Sue's for $1 \le n \le 50$. What happens to this ratio as they get older?

If the ratio is denoted by u_n, then $u_n = \dfrac{n+4}{n}$.

You can calculate that $u_1 = 5$, so use a window of $0 \le x \le 50$, $0 \le y \le 5$. You will then get a calculator display like Fig. 9.12.

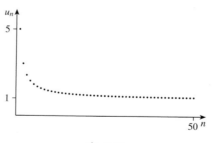

Fig. 9.12

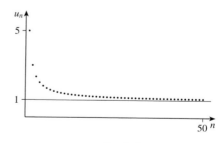

Fig. 9.13

This shows that the ratio drops very quickly to start with, but later it changes very little from year to year. However long they live, the ratio will always be greater than 1, but it will get very close to 1 as time goes on. To show this on the graph, add a horizontal line $y = 1$ to the calculator display as shown in Fig. 9.13.

In Example 9.6.2 the sequence u_n is said to **converge** (or **tend**) **to the limit 1 as n tends to infinity**. This is written

$$u_n \to 1 \text{ as } n \to \infty, \qquad \text{or} \qquad \lim_{n \to \infty} u_n = 1.$$

You read the last equation as 'the limit of u_n as n tends to infinity is equal to 1.'

Example 9.6.3

Use a calculator to show that the sum $u_n = \sum_{i=1}^{n} \frac{1}{i^2}$ converges to a limit as n tends to infinity, and estimate the value of the limit.

If you find the notation rather formidable, begin by writing the sums out in full for the first few positive integers n.

$$\sum_{i=1}^{1} \frac{1}{i^2} \text{ means simply } \frac{1}{1^2};$$

$$\sum_{i=1}^{2} \frac{1}{i^2} \text{ means } \frac{1}{1^2} + \frac{1}{2^2};$$

$$\sum_{i=1}^{3} \frac{1}{i^2} \text{ means } \frac{1}{1^2} + \frac{1}{2^2} + \frac{1}{3^2}.$$

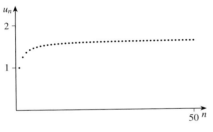

Fig. 9.14

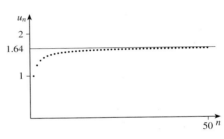

Fig. 9.15

You can see from this that

$$u_1 = 1, \quad u_2 = u_1 + \frac{1}{2^2}, \quad u_3 = u_2 + \frac{1}{3^2}, \text{ and so on.}$$

So the sequence u_n could be described by the inductive definition

$$u_1 = 1, \quad u_n = u_{n-1} + \frac{1}{n^2} \text{ for } n > 1.$$

You can now key this definition into the calculator to draw the graph of the sequence. In Fig. 9.14 it is drawn for $1 \leq n \leq 50$.

The graph shows convincingly that u_n converges to a limit as n tends to infinity, but it is not so easy to see what that limit is. The easiest way to estimate its value is to add a horizontal line to the display, and to move it gradually up the window until it seems to be above all the points of the graph, as in Fig. 9.15. It looks as if this occurs when y is about 1.64... , so that you can estimate that

$$\text{if } u_n = \sum_{i=1}^{n} \frac{1}{i^2}, \quad \text{then} \quad \lim_{n \to \infty} u_n \approx 1.64.$$

You may be surprised to know that the exact value of the limit is $\frac{1}{6}\pi^2$, which is 1.6449, correct to 4 decimal places.

Exercise 9D

1 Use your calculator to display the graphs of the arithmetic sequences with the following definitions.

(a) $u_n = 3 + 2n$ for $1 \le n \le 6$

(b) $u_n = 11 - 3n$ for $1 \le n \le 5$

(c) $a = 12, d = -1$ for $1 \le n \le 20$

(d) $a = -5, d = 1.5$ for $1 \le n \le 10$

(e) $u_1 = 10, u_n = u_{n-1} - 2$ for $1 \le n \le 10$

(f) $u_1 = -8, u_n = u_{n-1} + 6$ for $1 \le n \le 5$

2 An arithmetic sequence has first term 7 and common difference -2. Show that the sum S_n of n terms of the sequence can be defined in either of two ways:

(a) $S_n = n(8 - n)$,   or   (b) $S_1 = 7, S_n = S_{n-1} + (9 - 2n)$.

Make graphs based on each of these definitions for $1 \le n \le 10$, and check that they are the same.

3 Make graphs to show

(a) the sequence $u_n = 0.9^n$,

(b) the sequence $S_n = \sum_{i=1}^{n} u_i$,

for $1 \le n \le 25$. Investigate whether these sequences converge to a limit.

4 Use a graph to investigate whether the sequence $u_n = \sum_{i=1}^{n} \frac{1}{i}$ converges to a limit as $n \to \infty$.

5 If t_n denotes the triangle number $\frac{1}{2}n(n+1)$ (see Section 2.3), the sequence $u_n = \sum_{i=1}^{n} \frac{1}{t_i}$ tends to a limit as n tends to infinity. Use a graph to estimate the value of the limit.

10 Linear and quadratic functions

This chapter looks in more detail at two particular types of function. When you have completed it, you should

- know what is meant by a constant function, a linear function and a quadratic function
- be able to write quadratic expressions in completed square form, and to interpret this in graphical terms
- be able to apply the theory to displacement–time and velocity–time relationships for objects moving with constant velocity and constant acceleration.

10.1 Linear functions

Example 10.1.1

A function with domain the real numbers from 0 to 5 is given by $f(x) = 3$. What is its range?

The graph of the function is shown in Fig. 10.1. The set of values taken by the function consists of the single number 3. The range of the function is therefore the set $\{3\}$.

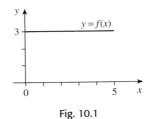

Fig. 10.1

A function whose range consists of a single number c is called a **constant function**.

You could imagine Fig. 10.1 representing something like the strength of the light from a torch which is switched on for 5 seconds. Try to think of some more examples for yourself, with a variety of domains.

If you add to a constant a second term which is a multiple of x, you get a **linear function**, with an equation of the form $f(x) = bx + c$. (But b must not be 0, or the function would just be constant.) Try showing the graphs of functions like this for different values of b and c, such as $2x + 3$, $4x - 5$, $-x + 2$, $-3x - 1$. You know from Chapter 8 that these graphs are all straight lines, which is the reason for calling the functions 'linear'.

The numbers b and c in the equation are called **coefficients**; b is the 'coefficient of x', and c is often called the **constant term**. From Section 8.3, the coefficient c is the y-intercept on the graph, and b corresponds to the gradient. But notice that, if different scales are used on the two axes, the gradient won't 'look right'. For example, a graph with $b = 1$ will not be at $45°$ to the x-axis unless the same scale is used on both axes.

If the domain of a linear function is the complete set $\mathbb{R}$ of real numbers, then the range is also $\mathbb{R}$. But in practical applications such as Example 10.1.2, the domain may be only an interval of real numbers, and then the range will also be an interval of real numbers.

Example 10.1.2

A piece of elastic 50 cm long has one end attached to a hook in the ceiling. Objects are attached to the other end and allowed to hang freely, so that the elastic stretches. For each kilogram of mass the elastic stretches by 8 cm, but if the mass exceeds 10 kg the elastic will break. Express the relation between the mass m kg and the length l cm as a function, and find the domain and range.

With an object of mass m kg attached the elastic stretches by $8m$ cm, so its total length is $(8m + 50)$ cm. The relation between mass and length is therefore expressed by the linear function equation

$$l = 8m + 50.$$

This equation only holds so long as the string doesn't break, so the domain is the interval $0 \leq m \leq 10$. In this interval the length increases from 50 cm to 130 cm, so the range is the interval $50 \leq l \leq 130$. This is illustrated by the graph in Fig. 10.2, which is the line segment joining the points with coordinates (0, 50) and (10, 130).

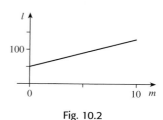

Fig. 10.2

10.2   Quadratic functions

If you add to a linear function a third term which is a multiple of x^2, you get a **quadratic function**, with an equation of the form $f(x) = ax^2 + bx + c$ (where a is not 0). The name comes from the Latin word *quadra*, meaning a square; the connection with a geometrical square is of course that a square of side x units has area x^2 units^2.

To keep things simple, most of the quadratics in this chapter have coefficients which are integers, but this is not a requirement; a, b and c can be any kind of real number.

For example, you could have $a = \frac{2}{3}$, $b = \sqrt{2}$ and $c = -\pi$, in which case the quadratic would be $f(x) = \frac{2}{3}x^2 + \sqrt{2}x - \pi$. The theory would still apply, though the arithmetic would be more complicated.

Unless stated otherwise, the domain should be assumed to be the set $\mathbb{R}$ of all real numbers.

Exercise 10A asks you to investigate the graphs of quadratic functions for various values of the coefficients, a, b and c.

Exercise 10A

1 Display, on the same set of axes, the graphs of

(a) $y = x^2 - 2x + 5$,   (b) $y = x^2 - 2x + 1$,

(c) $y = x^2 - 2x$,   (d) $y = x^2 - 2x - 6$.

2 Display, on the same set of axes, the graphs of

(a) $y = x^2 + x - 4$,   (b) $y = x^2 + x - 1$,

(c) $y = x^2 + x + 2$,   (d) $y = x^2 + x + 5$.

3 The diagram shows the graph of $y = ax^2 - bx$.
   On a copy of the diagram, sketch the graphs of

   (a) $y = ax^2 - bx + 4$,

   (b) $y = ax^2 - bx - 6$.

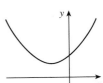

4 What is the effect on the graph of $y = ax^2 + bx + c$
   of changing the value of c?

5 Display, on the same set of axes, the graphs of

   (a) $y = x^2 - 4x + 1$,   (b) $y = x^2 - 2x + 1$,

   (c) $y = x^2 + 1$,   (d) $y = x^2 + 2x + 1$.

6 Display the graph of $y = 2x^2 + bx + 4$ for different values of b. How does changing b affect
   the curve $y = ax^2 + bx + c$?

7 Display, on the same set of axes, the graphs of

   (a) $y = x^2 + 1$,   (b) $y = 3x^2 + 1$,

   (c) $y = -3x^2 + 1$,   (d) $y = -x^2 + 1$.

8 Display, on the same set of axes, the graphs of

   (a) $y = -4x^2 + 3x + 1$,   (b) $y = -x^2 + 3x + 1$,

   (c) $y = x^2 + 3x + 1$,   (d) $y = 4x^2 + 3x + 1$.

9 Display the graph of $y = ax^2 - 2x$ for different values of a.

10 How does changing a affect the shape of the graph of $y = ax^2 + bx + c$?

11 Which of the following could be the equation of the curve
    shown in the diagram?

    (a) $y = x^2 - 2x + 5$

    (b) $y = -x^2 - 2x + 5$

    (c) $y = x^2 + 2x + 5$

    (d) $y = -x^2 + 2x + 5$

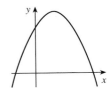

12 Which of the following could be the equation of the curve
    shown in the diagram?

    (a) $y = -x^2 + 3x + 4$

    (b) $y = x^2 - 3x + 4$

    (c) $y = x^2 + 3x + 4$

    (d) $y = -x^2 - 3x + 4$

10.3   The shapes of graphs of the form $y = ax^2 + bx + c$

In Exercise 10A, you should have found a number of results, which are summarised below.

> All the graphs have the same general shape, which is called a **parabola**. These parabolas have a vertical **axis of symmetry**. The point where a parabola meets its axis of symmetry is called the **vertex**.
>
> Changing c moves the graph up and down in the y-direction.
>
> Changing b also moves the axis of symmetry of the graph in the x-direction. If a and b have the same sign the axis of symmetry is to the left of the y-axis; if a and b have opposite signs the axis of symmetry is to the right of the y-axis.
>
> If a is positive the vertex is at the lowest point of the graph; if a is negative the vertex is at the highest point. The larger the size of $|a|$ the more the graph is elongated.

So far these are just observations based on experiments with a few particular graphs. To understand why they are true, you can use algebra to write the expression $ax^2 + bx + c$ in a different way, known as 'completed square form'. This is described in the next section.

10.4   Completed square form

Expressions like

$$f(x) = (x - 2)^2 + 3, \quad g(x) = 5 - (x - 1)^2, \quad h(x) = 2(x + 3)^2 - 7$$

and more generally

$$F(x) = a(x - r)^2 + s$$

are said to be in **completed square form**. Multiplying out the squared brackets gives

$$\begin{aligned}
f(x) &= (x^2 - 4x + 4) + 3 \\
&= x^2 - 4x + 7, \\
g(x) &= 5 - (x^2 - 2x + 1) \\
&= -x^2 + 2x + 4, \\
h(x) &= 2(x^2 + 6x + 9) - 7 \\
&= 2x^2 + 12x + 11.
\end{aligned}$$

So $f(x), g(x)$ and $h(x)$ are all quadratic functions.

You can use the completed square form of a function to write down the equation of the axis of symmetry and the coordinates of the vertex of its graph. The key point is that, whatever the value of x, the values of expressions such as $(x - 2)^2$, $(x - 1)^2$ and $(x + 3)^2$ are always greater than or equal to 0. For example, for $f(x)$,

$$(x - 2)^2 \geq 0, \quad \text{so that} \quad f(x) = (x - 2)^2 + 3 \geq 3.$$

So the smallest possible value of $f(x)$ is 3, and it has this value when $x = 2$. This means that the vertex of the graph of $y = f(x)$ is at $(2, 3)$.

You can take the argument further to show that the graph is symmetrical about the line $x = 2$. Figure 10.3 shows a pair of points on the graph whose x-coordinates are symmetrical about $x = 2$. These coordinates can be written as $x = 2 - h$ and $x = 2 + h$ for some number h. Then

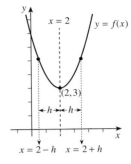

$$f(2 - h) = ((2 - h) - 2)^2 + 3$$
$$= (-h)^2 + 3$$
$$= h^2 + 3$$

and

$$f(2 + h) = ((2 + h) - 2)^2 + 3$$
$$= h^2 + 3.$$

Fig. 10.3

So $\qquad f(2 - h) = f(2 + h)$.

Since this is true whatever the value of h, this proves that the graph is symmetrical about $x = 2$.

Similar calculations can be carried out for $g(x)$ and $h(x)$.

$$(x - 1)^2 \geq 0, \quad \text{so that} \quad g(x) = 5 - (x - 1)^2 \leq 5;$$

the vertex is at $(1, 5)$ and the axis of symmetry is $x = 1$ (see Fig. 10.4).

$$(x + 3)^2 \geq 0 \quad \text{so that} \quad h(x) = 2(x + 3)^2 - 7 \geq -7;$$

the vertex is at $(-3, -7)$ and the axis of symmetry is $x = -3$ (see Fig. 10.5).

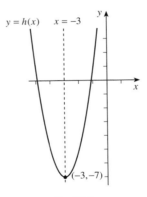

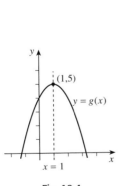

Fig. 10.4 $\qquad$ Fig. 10.5

You will notice that the values of a for $f(x)$, $g(x)$ and $h(x)$ are 1, -1 and 2 respectively. So for $f(x)$ and $h(x)$, where a is positive, the vertex is at the lowest point; but for $g(x)$, where a is negative, the vertex is at the highest point. Also $|a| = 1$ for $f(x)$ and $g(x)$, but $|a| = 2$ for $h(x)$, so the graph of $y = h(x)$ is more elongated than the graphs of $y = f(x)$ and $y = g(x)$.

Example 10.4.1

A quadratic graph has an equation of the form $y = a(x - r)^2 + s$. Its vertex is at $(1, -3)$. The graph also contains the point $(-1, 5)$.

(a) Find the values of r, s and a.

(b) For which other value of x does $y = 5$?

(c) Write the equation in the form $y = ax^2 + bx + c$.

(a) The vertex is where $(x - r)^2$ takes its least possible value, which is 0. Since $x = 1$ at the vertex, $r = 1$.

Also, when $(x - r)^2 = 0$, $y = s$. So s is the y-coordinate of the vertex, which is -3.

The equation of the graph therefore has the form

$$y = a(x - 1)^2 - 3$$

for some value of a. And since $(-1, 5)$ is on the graph,

$$5 = a(-1 - 1)^2 - 3,$$

so $8 = 4a$, which gives $a = 2$.

(b) The axis of symmetry of the graph is $x = 1$. You are given that $y = 5$ when $x = -1$, which is 2 units to the left of the axis of symmetry. So $y = 5$ also at a point 2 units to the right of the axis of symmetry, that is when $x = 3$.

(c) The equation of the graph is

$$y = 2(x - 1)^2 - 3.$$

When multiplied out, this is

$$y = 2x^2 - 4x - 1.$$

Exercise 10B

1 Find (i) the vertex and (ii) the equation of the axis of symmetry of each of the following quadratic graphs.

(a) $y = (x - 2)^2 + 3$ (b) $y = (x - 5)^2 - 4$ (c) $y = (x + 3)^2 - 7$

(d) $y = (2x - 3)^2 + 1$ (e) $y = (5x + 3)^2 + 2$ (f) $y = (3x + 7)^2 - 4$

(g) $y = (x - 3)^2 + c$ (h) $y = (x - p)^2 + q$ (i) $y = (ax + b)^2 + c$

2 Find (i) the least or the greatest value (whichever is appropriate) of each of the following quadratic expressions and (ii) the value of x for which this occurs.

(a) $(x + 2)^2 - 1$ (b) $(x - 1)^2 + 2$ (c) $5 - (x + 3)^2$

(d) $(2x + 1)^2 - 7$ (e) $3 - 2(x - 4)^2$ (f) $(x + p)^2 + q$

(g) $(x - p)^2 - q$ (h) $r - (x - t)^2$ (i) $c - (ax + b)^2$

3 For the following graphs, use the given data about a quadratic graph with equation
$y = a(x - r)^2 + s$ to find

  (i) the equation of the axis of symmetry,

  (ii) the values of r, s and a,

  (iii) the equation of the graph in the form $y = ax^2 + bx + c$.

  (a) The vertex is at $(2, 5)$ and the graph also contains the point $(0, 1)$.

  (b) The graph contains the points $(1, 2)$, $(3, 2)$ and $(2, -1)$.

10.5   Completing the square

In Section 10.4 the functions $f(x)$, $g(x)$ and $h(x)$ were first given in completed square form. Then, by multiplying out the squared brackets, it was shown that they were quadratic functions.

This section deals with the reverse problem: given a quadratic function $ax^2 + bx + c$, how can it be put into completed square form?

Begin with the simplest case in which $a = 1$.

When you try to write the quadratic expression $x^2 + bx + c$ in completed square form, the key point is to note that when you square $\left(x + \frac{1}{2}b\right)$ you get

$$\left(x + \tfrac{1}{2}b\right)^2 = x^2 + bx + \tfrac{1}{4}b^2, \text{ so } x^2 + bx = \left(x + \tfrac{1}{2}b\right)^2 - \tfrac{1}{4}b^2.$$

Now add c to both sides:

$$x^2 + bx + c = (x^2 + bx) + c = \left(x + \tfrac{1}{2}b\right)^2 - \tfrac{1}{4}b^2 + c.$$

Example 10.5.1
Write $x^2 + 10x + 32$ in completed square form.

$$\begin{aligned} x^2 + 10x + 32 &= (x^2 + 10x) + 32 \\ &= ((x + 5)^2 - 25) + 32 \\ &= (x + 5)^2 + 7. \end{aligned}$$

Don't try to learn the form $x^2 + bx + c = \left(x + \tfrac{1}{2}b\right)^2 - \tfrac{1}{4}b^2 + c$. Learn that you halve the coefficient of x, and write $x^2 + bx = \left(x + \tfrac{1}{2}b\right)^2 - \tfrac{1}{4}b^2$. Then add c to both sides.

If you need to write $ax^2 + bx + c$ in completed square form, but the coefficient a of x^2 is not 1, you can rewrite $ax^2 + bx + c$ by taking out the coefficient of x^2 as a factor from the first two terms:

$$ax^2 + bx + c = a\left(x^2 + \frac{b}{a}x\right) + c.$$

Then complete the square of the quadratic expression $x^2 + \dfrac{b}{a}x$ inside the bracket.

Example 10.5.2

Express $2x^2 + 10x + 7$ in completed square form. Use your result to find the axis of symmetry and the vertex of the graph of $y = 2x^2 + 10x + 7$.

Start by taking out the coefficient of x^2 as a factor from the first two terms:

$$2x^2 + 10x + 7 = 2(x^2 + 5x) + 7.$$

Dealing with the terms inside the bracket,

$$x^2 + 5x = \left(x + \tfrac{5}{2}\right)^2 - \tfrac{25}{4}.$$

So
$$
\begin{aligned}
2x^2 + 10x + 7 &= 2(x^2 + 5x) + 7 \\
&= 2\left(\left(x + \tfrac{5}{2}\right)^2 - \tfrac{25}{4}\right) + 7 \\
&= 2\left(x + \tfrac{5}{2}\right)^2 - \tfrac{25}{2} + 7 \\
&= 2\left(x + \tfrac{5}{2}\right)^2 - \tfrac{11}{2}.
\end{aligned}
$$

It's worth checking your result mentally at this stage.

The equation of the graph can be written as $y = 2\left(x + \tfrac{5}{2}\right)^2 - \tfrac{11}{2}$.

The smallest value of this occurs when the square $\left(x + \tfrac{5}{2}\right)^2$ is 0, which is when $x = -\tfrac{5}{2}$. The smallest value is then $y = -\tfrac{11}{2}$.

So the axis of symmetry is $x = -\tfrac{5}{2}$, and the vertex is $\left(-\tfrac{5}{2}, -\tfrac{11}{2}\right)$.

If the coefficient of x^2 is negative, the technique is similar to Example 10.5.2.

Example 10.5.3

Express $3 - 4x - 2x^2$ in completed square form. Use your result to find the axis of symmetry and the vertex of the graph of $y = 3 - 4x - 2x^2$.

Start by taking out the coefficient of x^2 as a factor from the terms which involve x:

$$3 - 4x - 2x^2 = 3 - 2(x^2 + 2x).$$

Dealing with the terms inside the bracket, $x^2 + 2x = (x + 1)^2 - 1$.

So
$$
\begin{aligned}
3 - 4x - 2x^2 &= 3 - 2(x^2 + 2x) \\
&= 3 - 2((x + 1)^2 - 1) \\
&= 3 - 2(x + 1)^2 + 2 \\
&= 5 - 2(x + 1)^2.
\end{aligned}
$$

The equation of the graph can be written as $y = 5 - 2(x + 1)^2$.

This shows that the largest value, at the vertex, is 5 when $x = -1$.

So the axis of symmetry is $x = -1$, and the vertex is $(-1, 5)$.

If you apply the procedure to the general quadratic expression $ax^2 + bx + c$, you begin by observing that $x^2 + \dfrac{b}{a}x$ are the first two terms of the expansion of $\left(x + \dfrac{b}{2a}\right)^2$, so that

$$x^2 + \frac{b}{a}x = \left(x + \frac{b}{2a}\right)^2 - \left(\frac{b}{2a}\right)^2.$$

So

$$
\begin{aligned}
ax^2 + bx + c &= a\left(x^2 + \frac{b}{a}x\right) + c \\
&= a\left(\left(x + \frac{b}{2a}\right)^2 - \frac{b^2}{4a^2}\right) + c \\
&= a\left(x + \frac{b}{2a}\right)^2 - \frac{b^2}{4a} + c.
\end{aligned}
$$

It follows that the axis of symmetry of the graph has equation $x = -\dfrac{b}{2a}$, and that the vertex is at $\left(-\dfrac{b}{2a},\ c - \dfrac{b^2}{4a}\right)$.

It isn't worth learning this as a general formula. But it is interesting to compare the algebraic results with the observations in Section 10.3. For example, the equation of the axis of symmetry depends on a and b but not on c; and if a and b have the same sign, then $-\dfrac{b}{2a}$ is negative, so that the axis of symmetry is to the left of the x-axis. So these observations are not just accidental consequences of the particular numerical examples chosen in Exercise 10A, but they are generally true for the graphs of all quadratic functions.

What this also shows is that every quadratic expression $ax^2 + bx + c$ (with $a \neq 0$), without exception, can be written in completed square form as $a(x - r)^2 + s$. The graph then has its vertex at (r, s).

Exercise 10C

1 Express the following in completed square form.

(a) $x^2 + 2x + 2$ (b) $x^2 - 8x - 3$ (c) $x^2 + 3x - 7$

(d) $5 - 6x + x^2$ (e) $x^2 + 14x + 49$ (f) $2x^2 + 12x - 5$

(g) $3x^2 - 12x + 3$ (h) $7 - 8x - 4x^2$ (i) $2x^2 + 5x - 3$

2 Use the completed square form to find as appropriate the least or greatest value of each of the following expressions, and the value of x for which this occurs.

(a) $x^2 - 4x + 7$ (b) $x^2 - 3x + 5$ (c) $4 + 6x - x^2$

(d) $2x^2 - 5x + 2$ (e) $3x^2 + 2x - 4$ (f) $3 - 7x - 3x^2$

3 By completing the square find (i) the vertex, and (ii) the equation of the axis of symmetry, of each of the following parabolas.

(a) $y = x^2 - 4x + 6$ (b) $y = x^2 + 6x - 2$ (c) $y = 7 - 10x - x^2$

(d) $y = x^2 + 3x + 1$ (e) $y = 2x^2 - 7x + 2$ (f) $y = 3x^2 - 12x + 5$

4 Find the ranges of the following quadratic functions with the given domains.

    (a) $f(x) = x^2 + 10x - 3,$ $\mathbb{R}$ (b) $f(x) = 1 + 6x - 2x^2,$ $\mathbb{R}$

    (c) $f(x) = x^2 - 4x - 5,$ $\mathbb{R}^+$ (d) $f(x) = x^2 + 4x + 5,$ $\mathbb{R}^+$

    (e) $f(x) = 3x^2 + 2x - 1,$ $-1 \le x \le 1$ (f) $f(x) = 5 + 8x - 2x^2,$ $0 \le x \le 3$

5 Express the following in completed square form.

    (a) $x^2 + 2\sqrt{2}x - 1$ (b) $2x^2 + \sqrt{3}x$ (c) $1 + 2x - \sqrt{5}x^2$

10.6 An application to kinematics

'Kinematics' is the theory of moving objects. This section and the next are about objects which move in a straight line, such as barges on a canal or balls thrown vertically upwards.

In Fig. 10.6 an observer O sees a walker and a jogger passing each other, 60 metres away, on a straight road. The walker is going away from her at a speed of 1 metre per second; the jogger is coming towards her at 2 metres per second.

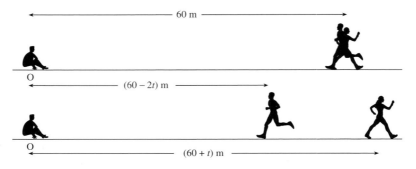

Fig. 10.6

If she looks again t seconds later, the walker will be t metres further away, and the jogger $2t$ metres closer. So the distances of the walker and the jogger from O will be $(60 + t)$ metres and $(60 - 2t)$ metres respectively.

There is one snag about this last statement. After 30 seconds the jogger will pass the observer, and the expression $(60 - 2t)$ will then become negative. So it is better not to use the word 'distance' but **displacement**, and to say that displacements are positive if made in one direction along the road, and negative in the other direction. You are already used to this when you use coordinates. The letter commonly used for displacement along a line from the origin is s. (Though x is also often used for displacement in a horizontal direction, and h, y or z for vertical displacement.) So, if s is measured in metres and t in seconds, and if displacements to the right in Fig. 10.6 are taken to be positive, you could write the equations

$$s = 60 + t$$

for the walker, and

$$s = 60 - 2t$$

for the jogger.

For a similar reason it is better to use the word **velocity**, rather than speed, and to describe velocities as positive or negative according to the direction of motion along the line. In this example the walker has velocity 1 metre per second, but the jogger's velocity is -2 metres per second. (The usual abbreviations for metres, seconds and metres per second are m, s and m s^{-1}. The reason for the superscript '-1' will become clearer when you reach Chapter 14.)

You could draw two different kinds of graph to illustrate the motion. One is a **displacement–time graph**, or (t, s) graph, shown in Fig. 10.7. The second is a **velocity–time graph**, or (t, v) graph, shown in Fig. 10.8. The graphs for the walker are shown with solid lines, and those for the jogger with dotted lines.

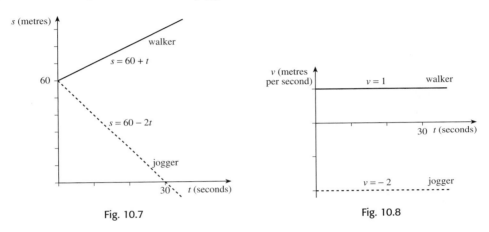

Fig. 10.7   Fig. 10.8

You can see from these graphs that:

> If the velocity is a constant function of the time, then the displacement is a linear function of the time. Also the velocity is represented by the gradient of the displacement–time graph.

(In the last statement you must, of course, take account of the fact that the graphs are drawn with unequal scales on the two axes.)

There is also a connection between the displacement and the velocity–time graph. Take a particular period of time, say 20 seconds. In that time the walker's displacement increases by 1×20 metres. The jogger's displacement decreases by 2×20 metres, which you could regard as an increase of $(-2) \times 20$ metres. How are these quantities represented on the velocity–time graph?

The answer is indicated by Fig. 10.9. Over the interval $0 \leq t \leq 20$, the space between each graph and the t-axis is a rectangle. For the walker (with the space shaded dark grey) the product 1×20 is represented by the area of the rectangle. A similar statement is true for the jogger (with light grey shading), provided that you adopt the convention that the area of a space below the t-axis is taken to be negative.

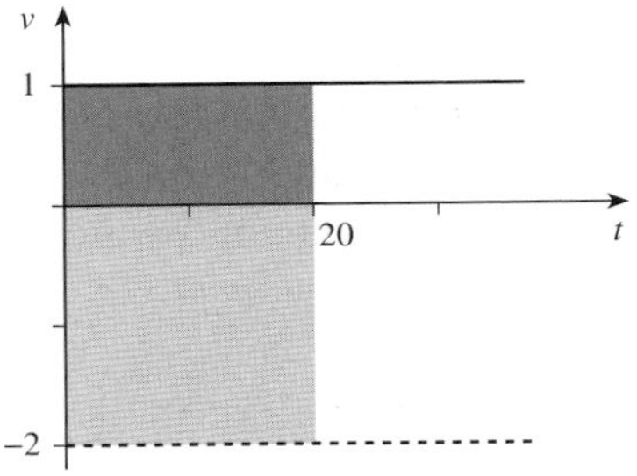

Fig. 10.9

> If the velocity is constant, the increase in the displacement over an interval of time is represented by the (signed) area of the space between the velocity–time graph and the t-axis.

The importance of the statements in the blue boxes in this section is that they are true for any motion along a straight line, not just when the velocity is constant. A particular case is discussed in the next section, but the more general application must wait until Chapters 25 and 29.

10.7   Motion with constant acceleration

In Section 10.6 the walker and the jogger both moved with constant velocity, but this is a very special type of motion. In many practical applications the velocity varies with time. For example, the driver of a sports car might increase speed from 0 to 100 km per hour in 5 seconds. You would then say that the car has average **acceleration** of 20 km per hour per second.

This is not a very sensible unit for measuring acceleration, since it involves two different measures of time, the hour and the second. It would be better to change the velocity from km per hour to metres per second ($\mathrm{m\,s^{-1}}$) and to give the acceleration in $\mathrm{m\,s^{-1}}$ per second. This is usually called 'metres per second squared', and denoted by $\mathrm{m\,s^{-2}}$.

Example 10.7.1
Express a velocity of 100 km per hour in $\mathrm{m\,s^{-1}}$.

Since 100 km = 100 000 metres, and 1 hour = 3600 seconds,

$$100 \text{ km per hour} = \frac{100\,000}{3600}\ \mathrm{m\,s^{-1}} = \frac{250}{9}\ \mathrm{m\,s^{-1}}.$$

So the velocity of the sports car increases by $\dfrac{250}{9}\ \mathrm{m\,s^{-1}}$ in 5 seconds, an average acceleration of $\dfrac{50}{9}\ \mathrm{m\,s^{-2}}$.

> You may know that the acceleration of gravity, denoted by g, is about $10\,\mathrm{m\,s^{-2}}$, so the driver experiences an average acceleration of about $\frac{5}{9}g$.

Like displacement and velocity, acceleration can be either positive or negative. Negative acceleration is called **deceleration**.

The next two examples are based on the assumption that the rule in Section 10.6 for calculating the displacement from the velocity–time graph, as an area, remains true even if the velocity is not constant.

Example 10.7.2

In taking off, an aircraft accelerates at a constant rate from 0 to 60 m s⁻¹ in 30 seconds. Use a velocity–time graph to find

(a) the acceleration,   (b) the distance the aircraft travels.

Since the acceleration is constant, the velocity–time graph is a straight line. If the time is measured from the instant when the aircraft starts to move, this line passes through the origin, as shown in Fig. 10.10.

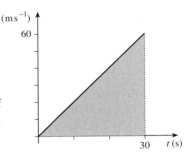

Fig. 10.10

(a) The acceleration is represented by the gradient of the line. Since the velocity is in $m\,s^{-1}$ and time is in seconds, this gives the acceleration in $m\,s^{-2}$.

So the acceleration is $\dfrac{60}{30}$ $m\,s^{-2}$, which is 2 $m\,s^{-2}$.

(b) The space between the velocity–time graph and the t-axis has the shape of a triangle, shown shaded in Fig. 10.10. The displacement of the aircraft along the runway is represented by the area of this triangle, which is $\frac{1}{2} \times 30 \times 60 = 900$.

So the aircraft travels 900 metres along the runway before leaving the ground.

Example 10.7.3

After making a catch a cricketer throws the ball up into the air with a speed of 8 m s⁻¹. The effect of gravity is to give the ball a constant acceleration towards the ground of 10 m s⁻². Use a velocity–time graph to find the velocity and height of the ball after t seconds. Hence find how high the ball rises above the cricketer's hands, and how long it is in the air before he catches it again.

Taking the upward direction to be positive, and using units of metres and seconds, the velocity–time graph is a straight line with v-intercept 8 and gradient –10, so its equation is $v = -10t + 8$. Fig. 10.11 shows that, after a time $t = 0.8$, the value of v becomes negative. This means that the ball has started to descend.

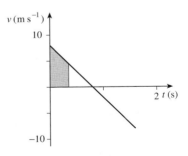

Fig. 10.11

The upward displacement of the ball, s metres after t seconds, is represented by the area of the shaded trapezium in Fig. 10.11. This trapezium is shown enlarged in Fig. 10.12. The area of this trapezium is

$$\tfrac{1}{2}(8 + (-10t + 8)) \times t = 8t - 5t^2.$$

The displacement–time equation is therefore $s = 8t - 5t^2$, which can be written in completed square form as

$$s = 3.2 - 5(t - 0.8)^2.$$

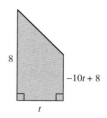

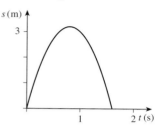

Fig. 10.12

So the ball reaches its greatest height of 3.2 metres after 0.8 seconds. Fig. 10.13 shows the displacement–time graph.

The ball is again at the level of the cricketer's hands when $8t - 5t^2 = 0$. Since

$$8t - 5t^2 = t(8 - 5t),$$

this occurs when $t = \frac{8}{5} = 1.6$. So he catches the ball after 1.6 seconds.

Fig. 10.13

Notice that the equations in Example 10.7.3 are only valid so long as the ball is in the air, that is when $0 < t < 1.6$. So although the expressions for v and s have meaning for all real values of t, the relevant domain consists only of real numbers between 0 and 1.6.

This example illustrates a general result:

> When an object moves with constant acceleration, the velocity is a linear function of time, and the displacement is a quadratic function of time.

Exercise 10D

In questions about vertical motion, take the acceleration of gravity to be 10 m s^{-2}.

1 The straightest railway line in the world runs across the Nullarbor Plain in southern Australia, a distance of 500 kilometres. A train takes $12\frac{1}{2}$ hours to cover the distance. Model the journey by drawing

   (a) a velocity–time graph,   (b) a displacement–time graph.

   Label your graphs to show the numbers 500 and $12\frac{1}{2}$ and to indicate the units used. Suggest some ways in which your models may not match the actual journey.

2 An aircraft flies due east at 800 km per hour from Kingston to Antigua, a displacement of about 1600 km. Model the flight by drawing

   (a) a displacement–time graph,   (b) a velocity–time graph.

   Label your graphs to show the numbers 800 and 1600 and to indicate the units used. Can you suggest ways in which your models could be improved to describe the actual flight more accurately?

3 A stone is dropped from rest. Taking the downwards direction to be positive, sketch the velocity–time graph. Use this to find the velocity after 3 seconds, and the distance the stone has fallen in this time.

4 A machine projects a golf ball vertically upwards with a velocity of 25 m s^{-1}. The figure shows part of the velocity–time graph while it is in the air.

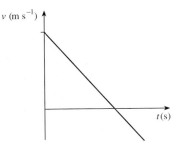

(a) Which direction has been taken to be positive?

(b) Write the equation of the velocity–time graph.

(c) When will the ball reach its highest point?

(d) What is the greatest height reached by the ball?

5 A train is travelling at 80 m s^{-1} when the driver applies the brakes. After 30 seconds the velocity has dropped to 20 m s^{-1}. The figure shows a sketch of the velocity–time graph while the train is slowing down.

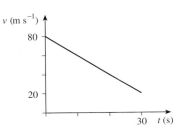

(a) Calculate the deceleration of the train.

(b) Write the equation of the velocity–time graph.

(c) How far does the train travel during this time?

6 A cyclist riding at 5 m s^{-1} accelerates at a constant rate until she reaches a speed of 7 m s^{-1}.

(a) Draw a sketch of the velocity–time graph while she is accelerating.

(b) If she covers a distance of 240 metres while accelerating, find the time she takes.

(c) Calculate her acceleration.

(d) Write the equation of the velocity–time graph.

(e) Find an expression for the distance she has cycled after t seconds. Use this to display the displacement–time graph on your calculator.

11 Equations and graphs

This chapter is about solving equations, and illustrating the solution with graphs. When you have completed it, you should

- interpret the solution of $f(x) = 0$ as the intersection of $y = f(x)$ with the x-axis
- be able to factorise quadratic expressions and use the factor form to solve quadratic equations
- know and be able to use the formula for solving quadratic equations
- understand the use of the discriminant to determine the number of roots of a quadratic equation
- recognise equations which become quadratic after a suitable substitution
- know how to find the points of intersection of two graphs
- be able to use a calculator to find the approximate solution of an equation which cannot be solved by exact methods.

11.1 Equations

If you use mathematics in designing a bridge or running a business, your decisions will often depend on finding the numerical solution to an equation (or a set of equations).

Any equation with a single unknown x can be arranged with all the terms on the left side, so that it has the form $f(x) = 0$ for some function f. So if you draw the graph of $y = f(x)$, solving the equation involves finding the x-coordinates of the points where the graph meets the x-axis. In Fig. 11.1 these points are P, Q and R, with x-coordinates p, q and r. These are called the **roots** of the equation. The set $\{p, q, r\}$ of all the roots is the **solution** of the equation.

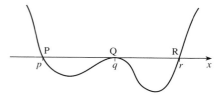

Fig. 11.1

The roots of the equation $f(x) = 0$ are sometimes called the **zeros** of the function $f(x)$.

The simplest kind of equation is when $f(x)$ is a linear function, $f(x) = bx + c$ with $b \neq 0$. The **linear equation** $f(x) = 0$ then has a single root, $-\dfrac{c}{b}$. This is the quantity called the x-intercept in Section 8.3.

11.2 Quadratic equations

Much more interesting is the **quadratic equation** $f(x) = 0$, where $f(x) = ax^2 + bx + c$ with $a \neq 0$.

Figure 11.2 shows the possible ways in which the graph of a quadratic function can be related to the x-axis.

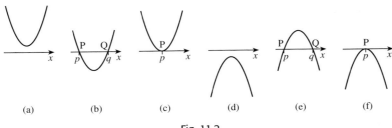

(a)   (b)   (c)   (d)   (e)   (f)

Fig. 11.2

- In (a) and (d) the graph does not meet the x-axis. The quadratic equation has no roots.
- In (b) and (e) the graph meets the x-axis at two points, P and Q, with x-coordinates p and q. The quadratic equation has two roots, p and q.
- In (c) and (f) the graph meets the x-axis at just one point P, with x-coordinate p. The quadratic equation has a single root p.

The variable x is assumed to be a real number. In more advanced mathematics a new kind of number is invented, called a complex number. If these were included, some of the statements in this chapter would have to be modified. (On some calculators it is possible for an answer to be given as a complex number.)

Example 11.2.1
Use the completed square form to show that the quadratic equation $x^2 + 6x + 10 = 0$ has no roots.

In completed square form,
$$x^2 + 6x + 10 = (x + 3)^2 + 1.$$

Since $(x + 3)^2$ can't be negative, the value of $(x + 3)^2 + 1$ is always greater than or equal to 1. Therefore $x^2 + 6x + 10$ can never equal 0.

Example 11.2.2
Verify that $(2x - 1)(x + 3) = 2x^2 + 5x - 3$. Use this to solve the quadratic equation $2x^2 + 5x - 3 = 0$.

Using the rule $(a + b)c = ac + bc$ with $(x + 3)$ for c,
$$(2x - 1)(x + 3) = 2x(x + 3) - 1(x + 3)$$
$$= 2x^2 + 6x - x - 3$$
$$= 2x^2 + 5x - 3.$$

So the quadratic equation $2x^2 + 5x - 3 = 0$ can be written as
$$(2x - 1)(x + 3) = 0.$$

The product of two numbers can only be 0 if one or the other is 0. So

either $2x - 1 = 0$ or $x + 3 = 0$;

that is,

either $x = \frac{1}{2}$ or $x = -3$.

The roots of the equation are $\frac{1}{2}$ and -3.

Example 11.2.3
Solve the equation $x^2 + 25 = 10x$.

Begin by rearranging the equation with all the terms on the left side, as

$$x^2 - 10x + 25 = 0.$$

You can recognise the expression $x^2 - 10x + 25$ as $(x - 5)^2$. So the equation is

$$(x - 5)^2 = 0.$$

This can be true only if $x - 5 = 0$, that is $x = 5$.

So the equation has just one root, 5.

These examples illustrate the possibilities suggested by Fig. 11.2, that a quadratic equation may have 0, 2 or 1 roots. They also show that, if there are any roots, a simple way of finding them is to write the quadratic expression as the product of linear factors, or as the square of a linear factor. The next section explains how to do this.

Some quadratic expressions $ax^2 + bx + c$ can be expressed in **factor form** as either

(i) $a(x - p)(x - q)$ or   (ii) $a(x - p)^2$.

In case (i), the quadratic equation $ax^2 + bx + c = 0$ has two roots, p and q.

In case (ii), the quadratic equation $ax^2 + bx + c = 0$ has just one root, p. This is sometimes called a **repeated root**, or a **double root** of the equation.

Notice that, in Example 11.2.2, $2x^2 + 5x - 3 = (2x - 1)(x + 3)$ is not strictly in factor form according to this definition. But since $2x - 1 = 2\left(x - \frac{1}{2}\right)$, the product can be written as $2\left(x - \frac{1}{2}\right)(x + 3)$, which is in factor form. The advantage of this form is that it shows the two roots, $\frac{1}{2}$ and -3, directly.

Example 11.2.4
A quadratic graph cuts the x-axis where $x = -1$ and $x = 2$, and it cuts the y-axis at $(0, 6)$. Find its equation.

Suppose that the equation of the graph in factor form is $y = a(x - p)(x - q)$. It cuts the x-axis where $y = 0$, that is when $x = p$ or $x = q$. So p and q are -1 and 2, and the equation has the form

$$y = a(x + 1)(x - 2).$$

The graph cuts the y-axis where $x = 0$, so $y = -2a$. You are given that $-2a = 6$, so $a = -3$.

The equation of the graph is therefore

$$y = -3(x + 1)(x - 2),$$

which when multiplied out gives $y = 6 + 3x - 3x^2$.

11.3 Factorising quadratics

This section is about finding factors of quadratics like $x^2 - 2x - 3$ and $3x^2 - 2x - 5$. However, the factors in this section are restricted to those cases where the coefficients of the quadratic to be factorised, and the linear factors which make it up, are all integers. In this sense, $x^2 - 3 = (x - \sqrt{3})(x + \sqrt{3})$ will be said *not* to factorise, because the terms in the linear factors contain $\sqrt{3}$.

There are three important special cases to get out of the way quickly.

No constant term
If the constant term is zero, as in $x^2 - 2x$ and $3x^2 - 2x$, the quadratic always factorises by taking out the factor x to get

$$x^2 - 2x = x(x - 2) \quad \text{and} \quad 3x^2 - 2x = x(3x - 2).$$

Difference of two squares
If the coefficient of x is zero, and the other terms have the form of the difference of two squares such as $x^2 - 9$ and $4x^2 - 25$, then using the result from Section 1.6,

$$p^2 - q^2 = (p - q)(p + q).$$

With $p = x$ and $q = 3$ this gives $x^2 - 9 = (x - 3)(x + 3)$.

And putting $p = 2x$ and $q = 5$ gives $4x^2 - 25 = (2x - 5)(2x + 5)$.

Sum of two squares
Expressions such as $x^2 + 9$ and $4x^2 + 25$ which are the *sum* of two squares *never* factorise.

It is easy to see why. Since $x^2 \geq 0$, $x^2 + 9$ is always greater than or equal to 9, so it can never be 0. But if $x^2 + 9$ had factors $(x - p)(x - q)$, it would be 0 when $x = p$ and $x = q$. Putting these two statements together, it follows that $x^2 + 9$ doesn't factorise.

The factors of $ax^2 + bx$ are given by
$$ax^2 + bx = x(ax + b).$$
The factors of $a^2x^2 - b^2$ are given by
$$(ax - b)(ax + b).$$
The sum of two squares, $a^2x^2 + b^2$, has no factors.

Example 11.3.1
Find the factors of   (a) $3x^2 + 4x$,   (b) $4x^2 - 1$.

(a) There is no constant term so
$$3x^2 + 4x = x(3x + 4).$$

(b) This has the difference of two squares form, so
$$4x^2 - 1 = (2x - 1)(2x + 1).$$

The general case
Finding the factors of other quadratics can be a hit-and-miss process. It is simple enough to factorise an expression such as $x^2 - 2x - 3$: x^2 can only split as $x \times x$, and 3 as 3×1, so if there are simple factors they must have the form $(x \dots 3)(x \dots 1)$ with $+$ or $-$ signs in place of the dots. To get a product of -3 one of these signs must be $+$ and the other $-$, and a quick check produces the answer $(x - 3)(x + 1)$.

Factorising a quadratic such as $6x^2 - 7x - 10$ is a much tougher proposition. The $6x^2$ might split either as $x \times 6x$ or as $2x \times 3x$, the 10 as 1×10 or as 2×5, and in each case there are two ways of pairing the factors. Trying all the possibilities until you get the correct coefficient of x, in this case -7, can take a long time, but if you can see the factors quickly this process is the quickest way.

Example 11.3.2
Find the factors of   (a) $x^2 - 8x + 12$,   (b) $6x^2 - x - 2$.

(a) By inspection the factors have the form $(x - \dots)(x - \dots)$.

The factors of 12 are 1×12, 2×6 and 3×4, so the possibilities are $(x - 1)(x - 12)$, $(x - 2)(x - 6)$ and $(x - 3)(x - 4)$. Multiplying each of these out gives $x^2 - 13x + 12$, $x^2 - 8x + 12$ and $x^2 - 7x + 12$ respectively, so
$$x^2 - 8x + 12 = (x - 2)(x - 6).$$

(b) The possible factors of 6 are 1×6 and 2×3, and the factors of 2 are 1×2. The sign of the constant term -2 is negative, so one factor is positive and one is negative. The possible factors of $6x^2 - x - 2$ which need to be tested are

$$(x - 1)(6x + 2), \quad (x + 1)(6x - 2), \quad (x - 2)(6x + 1), \quad (x + 2)(6x - 1),$$
$$(2x + 1)(3x - 2), \quad (2x - 1)(3x + 2), \quad (2x + 2)(3x - 1), \quad (2x - 2)(3x + 1).$$

Notice that every possible combination which gives $6x^2$ as the first term and -2 as the constant term has been taken.

When you test these, you find that the correct combination is $(2x + 1)(3x - 2)$, so

$$6x^2 - x - 2 = (2x + 1)(3x - 2).$$

There is a way of shortening the work of finding the factors of $6x^2 - x - 2$. When you write out the factors, some of them, in this case, $(x - 1)(6x + 2)$, $(x + 1)(6x - 2)$, $(2x + 2)(3x - 1)$ and $(2x - 2)(3x + 1)$, have a bracket which has a factor of 2. Each of these can be factorised further to give

$$(x - 1)(6x + 2) = 2(x - 1)(3x + 1), \qquad (x + 1)(6x - 2) = 2(x + 1)(3x - 1),$$
$$(2x + 2)(3x - 1) = 2(x + 1)(3x - 1), \quad (2x - 2)(3x + 1) = 2(x - 1)(3x + 1).$$

Each of these has a factor of 2, but 2 is not a factor of $6x^2 - x - 2$. So none of these four cases can possibly work. This leaves just

$$(x - 2)(6x + 1), \quad (x + 2)(6x - 1), \quad (2x + 1)(3x - 2), \quad (2x - 1)(3x + 2)$$

to be tested, which is much quicker than before.

Example 11.3.3
Find the factors of   (a) $6x^2 - 5x - 4$,   (b) $12x^2 - 10x - 8$.

(a) The possibilities for the factors of $6x^2 - 5x - 4$ are:

$$(x - 1)(6x + 4), \quad (x + 1)(6x - 4), \quad (x - 4)(6x + 1), \quad (x + 4)(6x - 1),$$
$$(x - 2)(6x + 2), \quad (x + 2)(6x - 2), \quad (2x + 1)(3x - 4), \quad (2x - 1)(3x + 4),$$
$$(2x + 4)(3x - 1), \quad (2x - 4)(3x + 1), \quad (2x + 2)(3x - 2), \quad (2x - 2)(3x + 2).$$

Knocking out the cases where one of the factors has a common factor leaves

$$(x - 4)(6x + 1), \quad (x + 4)(6x - 1), \quad (2x + 1)(3x - 4), \quad (2x - 1)(3x + 4),$$

to be tested.

When you test, $(2x + 1)(3x - 4)$ is the possibility that gives $-5x$ as the middle term, so

$$6x^2 - 5x - 4 = (2x + 1)(3x - 4).$$

(b) To factorise $12x^2 - 10x - 8$, first notice that you can take out the factor of 2, to get

$$12x^2 - 10x - 8 = 2(6x^2 - 5x - 4).$$

Concentrating now on $6x^2 - 5x - 4$, and using part (a),

$$12x^2 - 10x - 8 = 2(6x^2 - 5x - 4) = 2(2x + 1)(3x - 4).$$

If you count the number of possibilities for factors of $12x^2 - 10x - 8$ without first taking out the factor 2, you will quickly convince yourself of the benefit of taking out the numerical factor first.

Example 11.3.4
Solve the quadratic equations   (a) $x^2 - 8x + 12 = 0$,   (b) $6x^2 - x - 2 = 0$.

(a) From Example 11.3.2(a), $x^2 - 8x + 12 = (x - 2)(x - 6)$ in factor form.
Therefore, from Section 11.2, the roots of $x^2 - 8x + 12 = 0$ are 2 and 6.

(b) From Example 11.3.2(b), $6x^2 - x - 2 = (2x + 1)(3x - 2)$.

You can complete the solution in either of two ways.

Method 1   If $(2x + 1)(3x - 2) = 0$, then

either $2x + 1 = 0$ or $3x - 2 = 0$,

so

either $x = -\frac{1}{2}$ or $x = \frac{2}{3}$.

Method 2   Since $2x + 1 = 2(x + \frac{1}{2})$ and $3x - 2 = 3(x - \frac{2}{3})$,

$6x^2 - x - 2 = 6(x + \frac{1}{2})(x - \frac{2}{3})$

in factor form.

Therefore the roots of $6x^2 - x - 2 = 0$ are $-\frac{1}{2}$ and $\frac{2}{3}$.

Exercise 11A

1 Factorise each of the following quadratics.
(a) $x^2 + 11x + 24$ (b) $l^2 - 7l + 12$ (c) $q^2 - 12q + 35$
(d) $x^2 + x - 6$ (e) $x^2 + 5x - 24$ (f) $n^2 - 7n - 60$
(g) $r^2 - 17r + 16$ (h) $x^2 - 14x + 33$ (i) $x^2 + 4x - 21$

2 Factorise each of the following quadratics.
(a) $3x^2 - 8x + 4$ (b) $4x^2 - 12x + 5$ (c) $12x^2 + x - 1$
(d) $3x^2 - 4x - 4$ (e) $8x^2 - 15x - 2$ (f) $6x^2 + 5x - 6$
(g) $4x^2 - 8x - 5$ (h) $9x^2 - 30x + 9$ (i) $12x^2 - 10x - 8$

3 Use the 'difference of two squares' to write down the factors of the following quadratics.
(a) $x^2 - 1$ (b) $4 - 25d^2$ (c) $100 - 4z^2$
(d) $(x + 1)^2 - 4x^2$ (e) $(2x + 1)^2 - x^2$ (f) $(2x + 1)^2 - (x - 3)^2$

4 Not all quadratics have factors in which each of the coefficients is an integer. Find, where possible, factors of the following in which all the coefficients are integers.
(a) $x^2 + 2x + 2$ (b) $x^2 - 13x + 40$ (c) $x^2 + 6x - 12$
(d) $4x^2 + 16$ (e) $x^2 + 14x$ (f) $x^2 - 4x - 60$
(g) $x^2 + 16x + 12$ (h) $7 - 8x - 4x^2$ (i) $2x^2 + 5x - 3$

5 Solve the following quadratic equations.

(a) $x^2 - 2x - 35 = 0$ (b) $x^2 - 2x - 3 = 0$ (c) $x^2 + 6x - 27 = 0$

(d) $6x^2 - 5x - 6 = 0$ (e) $6 + 5x - 6x^2 = 0$ (f) $12x^2 + x - 6 = 0$

6 Find the x-coordinates of the points where the following quadratic graphs meet the x-axis.

(a) $y = x^2 + 3x - 4$ (b) $y = 2x^2 - 18$ (c) $y = 2x^2 - x - 1$

(d) $y = 2x^2 - 5x + 2$ (e) $y = x^2 - 6x + 9$ (f) $y = 1 - 9x^2$

7 A quadratic graph cuts the x-axis at $(-3, 0)$ and $(1, 0)$. It also contains the point $(2, 10)$. Find its equation in the form $y = ax^2 + bx + c$.

For what other point on the graph is the y-coordinate equal to 10?

8 A quadratic graph touches the x-axis at $(-2, 0)$. It also contains the point $(-1, 3)$. Find its equation.

11.4 The quadratic formula

All quadratic expressions can be written in completed square form, but only certain quadratics can be written in factor form. So if you have a quadratic equation to solve for which you cannot find factors, you must use another method.

Example 11.4.1
Find the roots of the quadratic equation $2x^2 + 10x + 7 = 0$.

It was shown in Example 10.5.2 that, in completed square form,

$$2x^2 + 10x + 7 = 2\left(x + \tfrac{5}{2}\right)^2 - \tfrac{11}{2}.$$

So the equation $2x^2 + 10x + 7 = 0$ can be written as

$$2\left(x + \tfrac{5}{2}\right)^2 - \tfrac{11}{2} = 0,$$

or $\left(x + \tfrac{5}{2}\right)^2 = \tfrac{11}{4}.$

Now there are two numbers whose square is $\tfrac{11}{4}$; these are $\tfrac{1}{2}\sqrt{11}$ and $-\tfrac{1}{2}\sqrt{11}$. So either

$$x + \tfrac{5}{2} = \tfrac{1}{2}\sqrt{11} \quad \text{or} \quad x + \tfrac{5}{2} = -\tfrac{1}{2}\sqrt{11}.$$

That is, either

$$x = \tfrac{1}{2}\sqrt{11} - \tfrac{5}{2} \quad \text{or} \quad x = -\tfrac{1}{2}\sqrt{11} - \tfrac{5}{2}.$$

So the exact roots of the equation are $\tfrac{1}{2}(\sqrt{11} - 5)$ and $-\tfrac{1}{2}(\sqrt{11} + 5)$. Since $\sqrt{11} = 3.3166...$, these roots are -0.842 and -4.158 correct to 3 decimal places.

The method in Example 11.4.1 can be used with any quadratic equation, whether or not it can be put into factor form. In Example 11.4.2 it is used for an equation which could also be solved using factors.

Example 11.4.2

Express $3x^2 - 8x - 3$ in completed square form, and use your result to solve the equation $3x^2 - 8x - 3 = 0$.

$$3x^2 - 8x - 3 = 3(x^2 - \tfrac{8}{3}x) - 3$$
$$= 3\left((x - \tfrac{4}{3})^2 - \tfrac{16}{9}\right) - 3$$
$$= 3\left((x - \tfrac{4}{3})^2 - \tfrac{16}{9} - 1\right)$$
$$= 3\left((x - \tfrac{4}{3})^2 - \tfrac{25}{9}\right).$$

The equation $3x^2 - 8x - 3 = 0$ is the same as $3\left((x - \tfrac{4}{3})^2 - \tfrac{25}{9}\right) = 0$.

$$3\left((x - \tfrac{4}{3})^2 - \tfrac{25}{9}\right) = 0$$
$$(x - \tfrac{4}{3})^2 - \tfrac{25}{9} = 0$$
$$(x - \tfrac{4}{3})^2 = \tfrac{25}{9}$$

giving $x - \tfrac{4}{3} = \tfrac{5}{3}$ or $x - \tfrac{4}{3} = -\tfrac{5}{3}$.

So $x = \tfrac{4}{3} + \tfrac{5}{3} = 3$ or $x = \tfrac{4}{3} - \tfrac{5}{3} = -\tfrac{1}{3}$.

Check for yourself that $3x^2 - 8x - 3$ in factor form is $3(x - 3)(x + \tfrac{1}{3})$.

These two examples show that this is a routine procedure, so you could apply it to the general quadratic equation and get a formula for the roots in terms of the coefficients a, b and c. The formula, which you should commit to memory, is:

The solution of $ax^2 + bx + c = 0$, where $a \neq 0$, is

$$x = \frac{-b \pm \sqrt{b^2 - 4ac}}{2a}.$$

For example, in Example 11.4.1, $a = 2$, $b = 10$ and $c = 7$, so the roots are

$$\frac{-10 + \sqrt{10^2 - 4 \times 2 \times 7}}{2 \times 2} = \frac{-10 + \sqrt{44}}{4} = \frac{-10 + 2\sqrt{11}}{4} = \frac{-5 + \sqrt{11}}{2}$$

and

$$\frac{-10 - \sqrt{10^2 - 4 \times 2 \times 7}}{2 \times 2} = \frac{-10 - \sqrt{44}}{4} = \frac{-10 - 2\sqrt{11}}{4} = \frac{-5 - \sqrt{11}}{2}.$$

You can get this formula from the result in Section 10.5 that

$$ax^2 + bx + c = a\left(x + \frac{b}{2a}\right)^2 - \frac{b^2}{4a} + c.$$

So, if $ax^2 + bx + c = 0$, then

$$a\left(x + \frac{b}{2a}\right)^2 = \frac{b^2}{4a} - c.$$

If you write the expression on the right as a single fraction,

$$\frac{b^2}{4a} - c = \frac{b^2}{4a} - \frac{4ac}{4a} = \frac{b^2 - 4ac}{4a},$$

and divide both sides by a, then the equation becomes

$$\left(x + \frac{b}{2a}\right)^2 = \frac{b^2 - 4ac}{4a^2}.$$

There are now two possibilities. Either

$$x + \frac{b}{2a} = +\sqrt{\frac{b^2 - 4ac}{4a^2}} = \frac{\sqrt{b^2 - 4ac}}{\sqrt{4a^2}} \quad \left(\text{using }\sqrt{\frac{p}{q}} = \frac{\sqrt{p}}{\sqrt{q}}, \text{ see Section 1.6}\right)$$

or $\qquad x + \dfrac{b}{2a} = -\sqrt{\dfrac{b^2 - 4ac}{4a^2}} = -\dfrac{\sqrt{b^2 - 4ac}}{\sqrt{4a^2}}.$

Since $4a^2 = (2a)^2$, $\sqrt{4a^2}$ is either $+2a$ (if a is positive) or $-2a$ (if a is negative). In either case

$$x + \frac{b}{2a} = \pm\frac{\sqrt{b^2 - 4ac}}{2a}.$$

So $\qquad x = -\dfrac{b}{2a} \pm \dfrac{\sqrt{b^2 - 4ac}}{2a} = \dfrac{-b \pm \sqrt{b^2 - 4ac}}{2a}.$

This shows that if $ax^2 + bx + c = 0$ and $a \neq 0$, then $x = \dfrac{-b \pm \sqrt{b^2 - 4ac}}{2a}.$

Example 11.4.3
Use the quadratic equation formula to solve the equations

(a) $2x^2 - 3x - 4 = 0,$

(b) $2x^2 - 3x + 4 = 0,$

(c) $30x^2 - 11x - 30 = 0,$

(d) $4x^2 + 4x + 1 = 0.$

(a) Comparing this with $ax^2 + bx + c = 0$, put $a = 2$, $b = -3$ and $c = -4$. Then

$$x = \frac{-(-3) \pm \sqrt{(-3)^2 - 4 \times 2 \times (-4)}}{2 \times 2} = \frac{3 \pm \sqrt{9 + 32}}{4} = \frac{3 \pm \sqrt{41}}{4}.$$

Sometimes it will be sufficient to leave the roots like this in surd form, but you may need to find the numerical values $\dfrac{3 + \sqrt{41}}{4} \approx 2.35$ and $\dfrac{3 - \sqrt{41}}{4} \approx -0.85$. Try substituting these numbers in the equation and see what happens.

(b) Putting $a = 2$, $b = -3$ and $c = 4$,

$$x = \frac{-(-3) \pm \sqrt{(-3)^2 - 4 \times 2 \times 4}}{2 \times 2} = \frac{3 \pm \sqrt{9 - 32}}{4} = \frac{3 \pm \sqrt{-23}}{4}.$$

But -23 does not have a square root. This means that the equation $2x^2 - 3x + 4 = 0$ has no roots.

Try putting $2x^2 - 3x + 4$ in completed square form; what can you deduce about the graph of $y = 2x^2 - 3x + 4$?

(c) Putting $a = 30$, $b = -11$ and $c = -30$,

$$x = \frac{-(-11) \pm \sqrt{(-11)^2 - 4 \times 30 \times (-30)}}{2 \times 30} = \frac{11 \pm \sqrt{121 + 3600}}{60}$$

$$= \frac{11 \pm \sqrt{3721}}{60} = \frac{11 \pm 61}{60}.$$

So $x = \frac{72}{60} = \frac{6}{5}$ or $x = -\frac{50}{60} = -\frac{5}{6}$.

This third example factorises, but the factors are difficult to find. But once you know the roots of the equation you can deduce that

$$30x^2 - 11x - 30 = 30\left(x + \frac{5}{6}\right)\left(x - \frac{6}{5}\right)$$
$$= (6x + 5)(5x - 6).$$

This can be a useful way of finding the factors of a complicated quadratic.

(d) Putting $a = 4$, $b = 4$ and $c = 1$,

$$x = \frac{-4 \pm \sqrt{4^2 - 4 \times 4 \times 1}}{2 \times 4} = \frac{-4 \pm \sqrt{16 - 16}}{8}$$

$$= \frac{-4 \pm \sqrt{0}}{8} = \frac{-4}{8} = -\frac{1}{2}.$$

So $x = -\frac{1}{2}$.

Exercise 11B

1 Solve the following quadratic equations. Leave any surds in your answer.

(a) $(x - 3)^2 - 3 = 0$

(b) $(x + 2)^2 - 4 = 0$

(c) $2(x + 3)^2 = 5$

(d) $(3x - 7)^2 = 8$

(e) $(x + p)^2 - q = 0$

(f) $a(x + b)^2 - c = 0$

2 Use the quadratic formula to solve the following equations. Leave irrational answers in surd form. If there is no solution, say so.

(a) $x^2 + 3x - 5 = 0$

(b) $x^2 - 4x - 7 = 0$

(c) $x^2 + 6x + 9 = 0$

(d) $x^2 + 5x + 2 = 0$

(e) $x^2 + x + 1 = 0$

(f) $3x^2 - 5x - 6 = 0$

(g) $2x^2 + 7x + 3 = 0$

(h) $8 - 3x - x^2 = 0$

(i) $5 + 4x - 6x^2 = 0$

3 Factorise the following expressions by first solving the corresponding quadratic equation.

(a) $x^2 - 2x - 35$

(b) $x^2 - 14x - 176$

(c) $x^2 + 6x - 432$

(d) $6x^2 - 5x - 6$

(e) $14 + 45x - 14x^2$

(f) $12x^2 + x - 6$

11.5 The discriminant $b^2 - 4ac$

If you look back at Example 11.4.3 you will see that in part (a) the roots of the equation involved surds, in part (b) there were no roots, in part (c) the roots were fractions and in part (d) there was only one root.

You can predict which case will arise by calculating the value of the expression under the square root sign, $b^2 - 4ac$, and thinking about the effect that this value has in the quadratic equation formula $x = \dfrac{-b \pm \sqrt{b^2 - 4ac}}{2a}$.

- If $b^2 - 4ac > 0$, the equation $ax^2 + bx + c = 0$ will have two roots.
- If $b^2 - 4ac < 0$, there will be no roots.
- If $b^2 - 4ac$ is a perfect square, the equation will have solutions which are integers or fractions.
- If $b^2 - 4ac = 0$, the root has the form $x = -\dfrac{b \pm 0}{2a} = -\dfrac{b}{2a}$, and there is one root only.

  Sometimes it is said that there are two coincident roots because the root values $-\dfrac{b+0}{2a}$ and $-\dfrac{b-0}{2a}$ are equal. But it is better to describe it as one repeated root (see Section 11.2).

The expression $b^2 - 4ac$ is called the **discriminant** of the quadratic expression $ax^2 + bx + c$ because, by its value, it discriminates between the types of solution of the equation $ax^2 + bx + c = 0$. It is sometimes denoted by the Greek letter Δ.

Example 11.5.1
What can you deduce from the values of the discriminants of these quadratic equations?

(a) $2x^2 - 3x - 4 = 0$ (b) $2x^2 - 3x - 5 = 0$ (c) $2x^2 - 4x + 5 = 0$ (d) $2x^2 - 4x + 2 = 0$

(a) As $a = 2$, $b = -3$ and $c = -4$, $b^2 - 4ac = (-3)^2 - 4 \times 2 \times (-4) = 9 + 32 = 41$.
The discriminant is positive, so the equation $2x^2 - 3x - 4 = 0$ has two roots. Also, as 41 is not a perfect square, the roots are irrational.

(b) As $a = 2$, $b = -3$, and $c = -5$, $b^2 - 4ac = (-3)^2 - 4 \times 2 \times (-5) = 9 + 40 = 49$.
The discriminant is positive, so the equation $2x^2 - 3x - 5 = 0$ has two roots. Also, as 49 is a perfect square, the roots are rational.

(c) $b^2 - 4ac = (-4)^2 - 4 \times 2 \times 5 = 16 - 40 = -24$. As the discriminant is negative, the equation $2x^2 - 4x + 5 = 0$ has no roots.

(d) $b^2 - 4ac = (-4)^2 - 4 \times 2 \times 2 = 16 - 16 = 0$. As the discriminant is zero, the equation $2x^2 - 4x + 2 = 0$ has only one (repeated) root.

Example 11.5.2
The equation $kx^2 - 2x - 7 = 0$ has two real roots. What can you deduce about the value of the constant k?

The discriminant is $(-2)^2 - 4 \times k \times (-7) = 4 + 28k$. As the equation has two real roots, the value of the discriminant is positive, so $4 + 28k > 0$, and $k > -\frac{1}{7}$.

Example 11.5.3

The equation $3x^2 + 2x + k = 0$ has a repeated root. Find the value of k.

> The equation has repeated roots if $b^2 - 4ac = 0$; that is, if $2^2 - 4 \times 3 \times k = 0$. This gives $k = \frac{1}{3}$.

> Notice how, in these examples, there is no need to solve the quadratic equation. You can find all you need to know from the discriminant.

Exercise 11C

1 Use the value of the discriminant $b^2 - 4ac$ to determine whether the following equations have two roots, one root or no roots.

(a) $x^2 - 3x - 5 = 0$ (b) $x^2 + 2x + 1 = 0$ (c) $x^2 - 3x + 4 = 0$

(d) $3x^2 - 6x + 5 = 0$ (e) $2x^2 - 7x + 3 = 0$ (f) $5x^2 + 9x + 4 = 0$

(g) $3x^2 + 42x + 147 = 0$ (h) $3 - 7x - 4x^2 = 0$

In parts (i) and (j), the values of p and q are positive.

(i) $x^2 + px - q = 0$ (j) $x^2 - px - q = 0$

2 The following equations have repeated roots. Find the value of k in each case. Leave your answers as integers, exact fractions or surds.

(a) $x^2 + 3x - k = 0$ (b) $kx^2 + 5x - 8 = 0$ (c) $x^2 - 18x + k = 0$

(d) $-3 + kx - 2x^2 = 0$ (e) $4x^2 - kx + 6 = 0$ (f) $kx^2 - px + q = 0$

3 The following equations have the number of roots shown in brackets. Deduce as much as you can about the value of k.

(a) $x^2 + 3x + k = 0$ (2)   (b) $x^2 - 7x + k = 0$ (1)   (c) $kx^2 - 3x + 5 = 0$ (0)

(d) $3x^2 + 5x - k = 0$ (2)   (e) $x^2 - 4x + 3k = 0$ (1)   (f) $kx^2 - 5x + 7 = 0$ (0)

(g) $x^2 - kx + 4 = 0$ (2)   (h) $x^2 + kx + 9 = 0$ (0)

4 Use the value of the discriminant to determine the number of points of intersection of the following graphs with the x-axis.

(a) $y = x^2 - 5x - 5$ (b) $y = x^2 + x + 1$ (c) $y = x^2 - 6x + 9$

(d) $y = x^2 + 4$ (e) $y = x^2 - 10$ (f) $y = 3 - 4x - 2x^2$

(g) $y = 3x^2 - 5x + 7$ (h) $y = x^2 + bx + b^2$ (i) $y = x^2 - 2qx + q^2$

5 If a and c are both positive, what can be said about the graph of $y = ax^2 + bx - c$?

6 If a is negative and c is positive, what can be said about the graph of $y = ax^2 + bx + c$?

11.6 Quadratic equations in disguise

Sometimes you will come across an equation which is not quadratic, but which can be changed into a quadratic equation, usually by making a suitable substitution.

Example 11.6.1
Solve the equation $t^4 - 13t^2 + 36 = 0$.

The highest power of t in this equation is 4, so it is not a quadratic equation. It is called a quartic equation, or an equation of degree 4. But since $t^4 = (t^2)^2$, if you write t^2 as x the equation becomes $x^2 - 13x + 36 = 0$, which is a quadratic equation in x. Factorising $x^2 - 13x + 36$ gives $(x - 4)(x - 9)$.

Then $(x - 4)(x - 9) = 0$, so $x = 4$ or $x = 9$.

Now recall that $x = t^2$, so $t^2 = 4$ or $t^2 = 9$, giving $t = \pm 2$ or $t = \pm 3$.

Example 11.6.2
Solve the equation $\sqrt{x} = 6 - x$

(a) by writing $\sqrt{x}$ as y,   (b) by squaring both sides of the equation.

(a) Writing $\sqrt{x} = y$, so that $x = y^2$, the equation becomes

$$y = 6 - y^2 \text{ or } y^2 + y - 6 = 0.$$

Therefore

$$(y + 3)(y - 2) = 0, \text{ so } y = 2 \text{ or } y = -3.$$

But, as $y = \sqrt{x}$, and $\sqrt{x}$ is never negative, the only solution is $y = 2$, giving $x = 4$.

(b) Squaring both sides gives

$$x = (6 - x)^2 = 36 - 12x + x^2 \text{ or } x^2 - 13x + 36 = 0.$$

Therefore $(x - 4)(x - 9) = 0$, so $x = 4$ or $x = 9$.

Checking the answers shows that when $x = 4$, the equation $\sqrt{x} = 6 - x$ is satisfied, but when $x = 9$, $\sqrt{x} = 3$ and $6 - x = -3$, so $x = 9$ is not a root.

Therefore $x = 4$ is the only root.

This is important. Squaring is not a reversible step, because it introduces the root or roots of the equation $\sqrt{x} = -(6 - x)$ as well. Notice that $x = 9$ does satisfy this last equation, but $x = 4$ doesn't! The moral is that, when you square an equation in the process of solving it, it is essential to check your answers.

Exercise 11D

1 Solve the following equations. Give irrational answers in terms of surds.

(a) $x^4 - 5x^2 + 4 = 0$ (b) $x^4 - 10x^2 + 9 = 0$ (c) $x^4 - 3x^2 - 4 = 0$

(d) $x^4 - 5x^2 - 6 = 0$ (e) $x^6 - 7x^3 - 8 = 0$ (f) $x^6 + x^3 - 12 = 0$

2 Solve the following equations.

(a) $x - 8 = 2\sqrt{x}$ (b) $x + 15 = 8\sqrt{x}$ (c) $t - 5\sqrt{t} - 14 = 0$

(d) $t = 3\sqrt{t} + 10$ (e) $t - \sqrt{t} - 6 = 0$ (f) $x - 3\sqrt{x} = 4$

3 Solve the following equations. (In most cases, multiplication by an appropriate expression will turn the equation into a form you should recognise.)

(a) $x = 3 + \dfrac{10}{x}$ (b) $x + 5 = \dfrac{6}{x}$ (c) $2t + 5 = \dfrac{3}{t}$

(d) $x = \dfrac{12}{x + 1}$ (e) $\sqrt{t} = 4 + \dfrac{12}{\sqrt{t}}$ (f) $\sqrt{t}\,(\sqrt{t} - 6) = -9$

11.7 Finding where two graphs intersect

If you draw two graphs using the same axes, it is possible that they will meet in one or more points. It is sometimes important to find the coordinates of these points.

If the graphs have equations $y = f(x)$ and $y = g(x)$, you want to find the values of x and y which satisfy both equations simultaneously. In that case you can find the values of x from the equation $f(x) = g(x)$, which can be written as $f(x) - g(x) = 0$. Having solved this equation for x, you can use either $y = f(x)$ or $y = g(x)$ to find the corresponding values of y.

Example 11.7.1

Find the point of intersection of the line $y = 2$ with the graph $y = x^2 - 3x + 4$ (see Fig. 11.3).

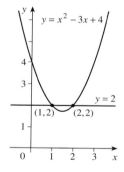

The graphs intersect where

$$x^2 - 3x + 4 = 2,$$

so

$$x^2 - 3x + 2 = 0$$
$$(x - 1)(x - 2) = 0$$

giving $x = 1$ or $x = 2$.

Substituting these values in either equation ($y = 2$ is obviously easier!) to find y, the points of intersection are (1, 2) and (2, 2).

Fig. 11.3

Example 11.7.2

Find the point of intersection of the line $y = 2x - 1$ with the graph $y = x^2$ (see Fig. 11.4).

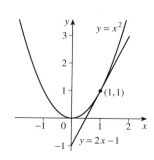

The graphs intersect where

$$2x - 1 = x^2,$$

so

$$x^2 - 2x + 1 = 0$$
$$(x - 1)(x - 1) = 0$$

giving $x = 1$.

Fig. 11.4

Substituting these values in either equation to find y gives the point of intersection as (1, 1).

The fact that there is only one point of intersection shows that this line is a tangent to the graph (see Fig. 11.4). The point (1, 1) is called the **point of contact** of the tangent and the curve.

Example 11.7.3
Find the points of intersection of the following pairs of graphs.

(a) $y = 2x + 1$ and $y = x^2 - 2x - 4$ 　　　　(b) $y = x^2 - 2x + 1$ and $y = 3 + x - x^2$

(c) $y = x^3$ and $y = 4x(x - 1)$

> Display the graphs on your calculator to illustrate the answers in this example.

(a) At the point of intersection

$$2x + 1 = x^2 - 2x - 4.$$

This can be written more simply as

$$x^2 - 4x - 5 = 0,$$

which can be put into factor form as

$$(x + 1)(x - 5) = 0.$$

So the graphs intersect where $x = -1$ and where $x = 5$.

Use the equation $y = 2x + 1$ to find the corresponding values of y. When $x = -1$, $y = 2 \times (-1) + 1 = -1$; when $x = 5$, $y = 2 \times 5 + 1 = 11$.

So the points of intersection are $(-1, -1)$ and $(5, 11)$.

> It is often a good idea to check your answer by using the other equation. Check for yourself that these points also lie on $y = x^2 - 2x - 4$.

(b) At the point of intersection,

$$x^2 - 2x + 1 = 3 + x - x^2,$$

which is $2x^2 - 3x - 2 = 0$, so

$$(2x + 1)(x - 2) = 0.$$

The graphs intersect where $x = -\frac{1}{2}$ and where $x = 2$.

Use the equation $y = x^2 - 2x + 1$, which is $y = (x - 1)^2$, to find the values of y. When $x = -\frac{1}{2}$, $y = \left(-\frac{1}{2} - 1\right)^2 = \left(-\frac{3}{2}\right)^2 = \frac{9}{4}$. When $x = 2$, $y = (2 - 1)^2 = 1$.

So the points of intersection are $\left(-\frac{1}{2}, 2\frac{1}{4}\right)$ and $(2, 1)$.

(c) At the point of intersection,

$$x^3 = 4x(x - 1),$$

so

$$x^3 - 4x^2 + 4x = 0.$$

Because the highest power of x is x^3, this is called a cubic equation. You don't have a general method for solving cubic equations, but this one is particularly simple because the terms have a common factor x. So the equation can be written as

$$x(x^2 - 4x + 4) = 0$$
$$x(x - 2)^2 = 0.$$

The product on the left is 0 if $x = 0$ or if $(x - 2)^2 = 0$, that is $x = 2$. So the graphs intersect where $x = 0$, $y = 0$ or where $x = 2$, $y = 8$.

The points of intersection are $(0, 0)$ and $(2, 8)$.

What happens at $x = 2$, where the equation has a repeated root?

11.8 Using a calculator to solve equations

However far you go in mathematics, there will always be a lot of equations that you can't solve by exact methods. But there is always the possibility of using a calculator to find approximate solutions to a high level of accuracy.

If the equation is written as $f(x) = 0$, the first step is to use the calculator to show the graph of $y = f(x)$. This will show roughly the values of x where the graph meets the x-axis.

You now need to consult your calculator manual to find how to refine these rough estimates to give solutions accurate to the required number of decimal places.

Example 11.8.1

Find the roots of the cubic equation $x^3 - 3x - 1 = 0$ correct to 4 decimal places.

Figure 11.5 shows the graph of $y = x^3 - 3x - 1$ for $-2 \leq x \leq 2$. It crosses the axis in three points, at roughly $x = -1.5$, $x = -0.4$ and $x = 1.9$.

Taking each of these in turn, they can be refined using the calculator to give the roots as $-1.532\ 089$, $-0.347\ 296\ 4$ and $1.879\ 385\ 2$.

Correct to 4 decimal places, these roots are -1.5321, -0.3473 and 1.8794.

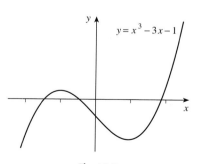

Fig. 11.5

Exercise 11E

1 Find the point or points of intersection for the following lines and curves.

(a) $x = 3$ and $y = x^2 + 4x - 7$ (b) $y = 3$ and $y = x^2 - 5x + 7$

(c) $y = 8$ and $y = x^2 + 2x$ (d) $y + 3 = 0$ and $y = 2x^2 + 5x - 6$

2 Find the points of intersection for the following lines and curves. Check your answers in each case by displaying the graphs on your calculator.

(a) $y = x + 1$ and $y = x^2 - 3x + 4$ (b) $y = 2x + 3$ and $y = x^2 + 3x - 9$

(c) $y = 3x + 11$ and $y = 2x^2 + 2x + 5$ (d) $y = 4x + 1$ and $y = 9 + 4x - 2x^2$

3 In both the following, show that the line and curve meet only once, find the point of intersection and use your calculator to check that the line touches the curve.

(a) $y = 2x + 2$ and $y = x^2 - 2x + 6$ (b) $y = -2x - 7$ and $y = x^2 + 4x + 2$

4 Find the points of intersection between the curve $y = x^2 + 5x + 18$ and the lines

(a) $y = -3x + 2$,   (b) $y = -3x + 6$.

Use your calculator to see how the lines are related to the curve.

5 Find the points of intersection between the line $y = x + 5$ and the curves

(a) $y = 2x^2 - 3x - 1$,   (b) $y = 2x^2 - 3x + 7$.

Use your calculator to see how the line and the curves are related.

6 Find the points of intersection of the following curves.

(a) $y = x^2 + 5x + 1$ and $y = x^2 + 3x + 11$ (b) $y = \frac{1}{2}x^2$ and $y = 1 - \frac{1}{2}x^2$

(c) $y = 2x^2 + 3x + 4$ and $y = x^2 + 6x + 2$ (d) $y = x^2 - 3x - 7$ and $y = x^2 + x + 1$

(e) $y = x^2 + 7x + 13$ and $y = 1 - 3x - x^2$ (f) $y = 6x^2 + 2x - 9$ and $y = x^2 + 7x + 1$

7 Use your calculator to locate roughly the roots of the following equations. Then refine the approximation to give the roots correct to 3 decimal places.

(a) $x^2 - 6x + 7 = 0$ (b) $x^3 - 9x - 2 = 0$

(c) $x^3 + 4x^2 - 4 = 0$ (d) $x^4 - 4x^3 + 10 = 0$

8 Find, correct to 2 decimal places, the points of intersection of the following pairs of graphs.

(a) $y = x^3$, $y = 12x + 20$ (b) $y = x^3$, $y = 3x^2 + 4$

(c) $y = x^2 + 1$, $y = \dfrac{10}{x + 1}$ (d) $y = 20 - x^2$, $y = \dfrac{5}{x}$

Review exercise 3

1 Show that the triangle formed by the points $(-2, 5)$, $(1, 3)$ and $(5, 9)$ is right-angled.

2 P is the point $(7, 5)$ and l_1 is the line with equation $3x + 4y = 16$.

   (a) Find the equation of the line l_2 which passes through P and is perpendicular to l_1.

   (b) Find the point of intersection of the lines l_1 and l_2.

   (c) Find the perpendicular distance of P from the line l_1.

3 Find the equation of the perpendicular bisector of the line joining $(2, -5)$ and $(-4, 3)$.

4 The diagram shows the graph of $y = x^n$, where n is an integer. Given that the curve passes between the points $(2, 200)$ and $(2, 2000)$, determine the value of n.

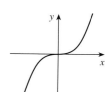

5 Find the points of intersection of the line $y = 2x + 3$ and the curve $y = 2x^2 + 3x - 7$.

6 Given that k is a positive constant, sketch the graphs of

   (a) $y = (x + k)(x - 2k)$,   (b) $y = (x + 4k)(x + 2k)$,

   (c) $y = x(x - k)(x - 5k)$,   (d) $y = (x + k)(x - 2k)^2$.

7 A curve with equation $y = ax^2 + bx + c$ crosses the x-axis at $(-4, 0)$ and $(9, 0)$ and also passes through the point $(1, 120)$. Where does the curve cross the y-axis?

8 Find, in surd form, the points of intersection of the curves $y = x^2 - 5x - 3$ and $y = 3 - 5x - x^2$.

9 Show that the line $y = 3x - 3$ and the curve $y = (3x + 1)(x + 2)$ do not meet.

10 Point O is the intersection of two roads which cross at right angles; one road runs from north to south, the other from east to west. Car A is 100 metres due west of O and travelling east at a speed of $20 \, \text{m s}^{-1}$, and Car B is 80 metres due north of O and travelling south at $20 \, \text{m s}^{-1}$.

   (a) Show that after t seconds their distance apart, d metres, is given by

$$d^2 = (100 - 20t)^2 + (80 - 20t)^2.$$

   (b) Show that this simplifies to $d^2 = 400((5 - t)^2 + (4 - t)^2)$.

   (c) Show that the minimum distance apart of the two cars is $10\sqrt{2}$ metres.

11 The following functions are defined for all real values of x. Find their ranges.

   (a) $f(x) = 9 - 2x^2$ (b) $f(x) = 5x - 7$

   (c) $f(x) = x^2 + 16x - 5$ (d) $f(x) = (2x + 5)(2x - 7)$

12 The function $f(x) = 16 - 6x - x^2$ has domain $\mathbb{R}$. Find the maximum value of $f(x)$ and state the range of $f(x)$.

13 Show that there exists a root, $x = \alpha$, of the equation $x^3 - 6x + 3 = 0$ such that $2 < \alpha < 3$. Find this root correct to 2 decimal places.

14 Let $f(x) = \dfrac{1}{(x-2)(x+2)}$. For what values of x is $f(x)$ positive? Write down the equations of the asymptotes of $y = f(x)$.

15 Find all the possible values of b for which the following quadratics can be expressed as a product of factors with integer coefficients.

(a) $2x^2 + bx - 5$ (b) $4x^2 + bx + 15$

Explain why, for these values of b, the numbers given by

(c) $b^2 + 40$,   (d) $b^2 - 240$.

are perfect squares.

16 By completing the square, express $x^2 - 2\sqrt{2}x - 1$ as the product of two linear factors.

17 The point P has coordinates $(0, 2)$. Show that the distance from P to the point on the line $3x + y = 12$ with coordinates $(x, 12 - 3x)$ is $\sqrt{10(x^2 - 6x + 10)}$. Hence find the coordinates of the point Q on the line which is closest to P.

Check your answer by showing that the line (PQ) is perpendicular to $3x + y = 12$.

18 Two lines have equations $ax + by + c = 0$ and $px + qy + r = 0$.

(a) Explain why, for the equation $ax + by + c = 0$ to represent a line, a and b cannot both be 0.

Assuming that b and q are not 0,

(b) show that the condition for the lines to be parallel (or the same line) is $aq - bp = 0$,

(c) show that the condition for the lines to be perpendicular is $ap + bq = 0$.

Show that the statements in parts (b) and (c) remain true if $b = 0$.

19 Find the equation of the straight line that passes through the points $(3, -1)$ and $(-2, 2)$. Hence find the coordinates of the point of intersection of the line and the x-axis.   (OCR)

20 (a) Solve the equation $x^2 - (6\sqrt{3})x + 24 = 0$, giving your answer in terms of surds, simplified as far as possible.

(b) Find all four solutions of the equation $x^4 - (6\sqrt{3})x^2 + 24 = 0$ giving your answers correct to 2 decimal places.   (OCR)

21 (a) Express $9x^2 + 12x + 7$ in the form $(ax + b)^2 + c$ where a, b, c are constants whose values are to be found.

(b) Find the set of values taken by $\dfrac{1}{9x^2 + 12x + 7}$ for real values of x.   (OCR)

22 (a) Express $4x^2 - 16x + 8$ in the form $a(x + b)^2 + c$.

(b) Hence find the coordinates of the vertex of the graph of $y = 4x^2 - 16x + 8$.

(c) Sketch the graph of $y = 4x^2 - 16x + 8$, giving the x-coordinates of the points where the graph meets the x-axis.   (OCR)

23 (a) Given that $\sqrt{x} = y$, show that the equation $\sqrt{x} + \dfrac{10}{\sqrt{x}} = 7$ may be written as

$y^2 - 7y + 10 = 0$.

(b) Hence solve the equation $\sqrt{x} + \dfrac{10}{\sqrt{x}} = 7$.   (OCR)

Examination questions

1 Consider the arithmetic series $2 + 5 + 8 + \dots$.

(a) Find an expression for S_n, the sum of the first n terms.

(b) Find the value of n for which $S_n = 1365$.   (© IBO 2002)

2 (a) Find the largest set S of values of x such that the function $f(x) = \dfrac{1}{\sqrt{3 - x^2}}$ takes real values.

(b) Find the range of the function f defined on the domain S.   (© IBO 2004)

3 The following diagram shows the lines $x - 2y - 4 = 0$, $x + y = 5$ and the point $P(1, 1)$. A line is drawn from P to intersect with $x - 2y - 4 = 0$ at Q, and with $x + y = 5$ at R, so that P is the mid-point of [QR].

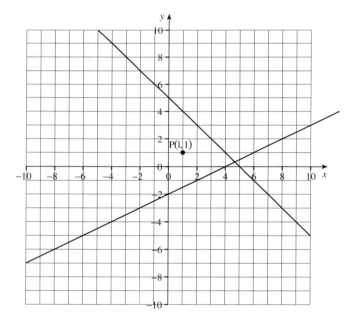

Find the exact coordinates of Q and of R.   (© IBO 2004)

4 A circle has equation $x^2 + (y - 2)^2 = 1$. The line with equation $y = kx$, where $k \in \mathbb{R}$, is a tangent to the circle. Find all possible values of k.   (© IBO 2005)

12 Differentiation

This chapter is about finding the gradient of the tangent at a point on a graph. When you have completed it, you should

- understand how the gradient of the tangent at a point can be obtained from the gradients of chords through the point
- know how to find the gradient at a point on a quadratic curve and certain other curves.

The first part of this chapter includes a number of experimental calculations from which the main results can be inferred. Proofs of some of these results are given at the end of the chapter.

12.1 The gradient of a curve

The gradient of the line $y = bx + c$ is b. It is easy to show this. Take two points on the line; the simplest are $(0, c)$ and $(1, b + c)$. The gradient of the line joining these is $\dfrac{(b + c) - c}{1 - 0}$, which is $\dfrac{b}{1}$ or just b.

You would get the same answer if you took any other two points on the line, but the algebra would be a bit more complicated.

But how could you find the gradient of a curve? Indeed, what do you mean by the gradient of a curve? A straight line has the same direction everywhere, but a curve keeps changing direction as you move along it. So you have to think about 'the gradient of a curve at a point'. The gradient will be different at different points of the curve.

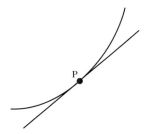

Fig. 12.1

Draw a curve and choose a particular point on it (see Fig. 12.1). Call the point P. If the curve is reasonably smooth, you can draw a **tangent** to the curve at P. This is a straight line, so you can find its gradient. The direction of the curve at P is the same as the direction of the tangent. So it seems natural to define the gradient of the curve at P as the gradient of the tangent.

> The **gradient of a curve** at any point is the gradient of the tangent to the curve at that point.

But the problem is how to calculate the gradient of the tangent. To find the gradient of a straight line you need to know the coordinates of two points on it. But, as Fig. 12.1 shows, the only point you know on the tangent is the point P. There is no obvious way of finding any other point on the tangent.

This difficulty doesn't occur for other lines through P. Fig. 12.2 shows several lines through P, including the tangent. The other lines meet the curve again, at points labelled M and N to the left of P, and R and S to the right of P. And the gradients of these lines can be calculated, as the gradients of the line segments [PM], [PN], [PR] and [PS]; these are called **chords** of the curve. (You are already familiar with chords when the curve is a circle.)

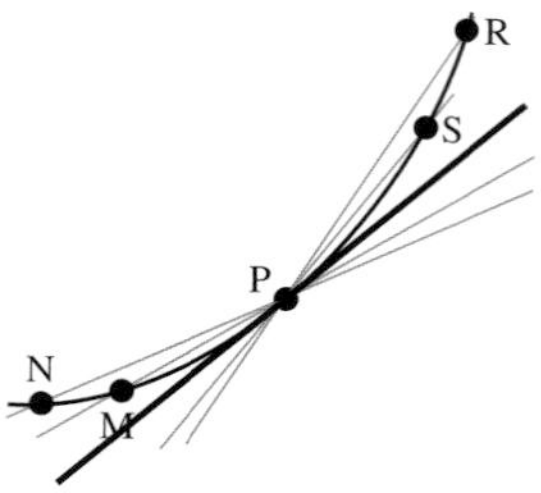

This suggests a first step to finding the gradient of the tangent. In Fig. 12.2 the gradient of the tangent is clearly less than the gradients of [PR] and [PS], and greater than the gradients of [PN] and [PM]. So although this doesn't give the gradient of the tangent exactly, it does restrict it to a small interval of possible values.

Fig. 12.2

Example 12.1.1 shows how this idea can be applied to a particular curve at a particular point.

Example 12.1.1

On the graph of $y = x^2$ take P to be the point $(0.4, 0.16)$, and let R and N be the points with x-coordinates 0.5 and 0.3 respectively. Calculate the gradients of the chords [PR] and [PN]. What can be deduced about the gradient of the tangent at P?

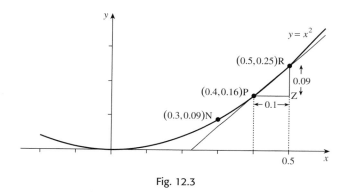

Fig. 12.3

Begin with the chord [PR], shown in Fig. 12.3. At R, with $x = 0.5$, the y-coordinate is $0.5^2 = 0.25$. To find the gradient from $P(0.4, 0.16)$ to $R(0.5, 0.25)$ calculate the x-step $0.5 - 0.4 = 0.1$ and the y-step $0.25 - 0.16 = 0.09$. These are shown in Fig. 12.3 by [PZ] and [ZR]. Then

$$\text{gradient of } [PR] = \frac{y\text{-step}}{x\text{-step}} = \frac{0.09}{0.1} = 0.9.$$

For the chord [PN] to the left of P, where N has coordinates $(0.3, 0.09)$, the x-step from P to N is $0.3 - 0.4 = -0.1$, and the y-step is $0.09 - 0.16 = -0.07$; both are negative. The gradient is then

$$\frac{-0.07}{-0.1} = 0.7.$$

You could of course take the x-step and y-step from N to P rather than from P to N in which case both would be positive. But you will see as the chapter develops why it is a good idea to take the steps from P to the point at the other end of the chord.

The gradient of the tangent at P is less than the gradient of [PR] and greater than the gradient of [PN]. So the gradient of the tangent at P is between 0.7 and 0.9.

Example 12.1.1 already gives you a useful approximation to the gradient of the curve $y = x^2$ at P, but it would be better to get a more accurate estimate. Fig. 12.2 suggests that if you take points S and M on the curve closer to P than R and N, the gradients of [PS] and [PM] will be closer to the gradient of the tangent.

Before embarking on any more calculation it is useful to introduce some new notation. The Greek letter δ (delta) is used as an abbreviation for 'the increase in'. Thus 'the increase in x' is written as δx, and 'the increase in y' as δy. These are the quantities called the 'x-step' and 'y-step' in Section 8.2. Thus in the calculations for the chord [PR] in Example 12.1.1 you can write

$$\delta x = 0.5 - 0.4 = 0.1 \quad \text{and} \quad \delta y = 0.25 - 0.16 = 0.09.$$

With this notation, you can write the gradient of the chord as $\dfrac{\delta y}{\delta x}$.

Some people use the capital letter Δ rather than δ. Either is acceptable.

Notice that, in the fraction $\dfrac{\delta y}{\delta x}$, you cannot 'cancel out' the deltas. While you are getting used to the notation it is a good idea to read δ as 'the increase in', so that you are not tempted to read it as an ordinary algebraic symbol. Remember also that δx or δy could be negative, making the x-step or y-step a decrease.

Example 12.1.2
In the context of Example 12.1.1, find a better estimate for the gradient of the tangent at P by taking points S and M on the curve with x-coordinates 0.41 and 0.39.

First you need to calculate the y-coordinates of S and M. These are $0.41^2 = 0.1681$ and $0.39^2 = 0.1521$. So S is the point $(0.41, 0.1681)$, and M is $(0.39, 0.1521)$.

For the chord [PS],

$$\delta x = 0.41 - 0.4 = 0.01 \quad \text{and} \quad \delta y = 0.1681 - 0.16 = 0.0081,$$

so the gradient is $\dfrac{\delta y}{\delta x} = \dfrac{0.0081}{0.01} = 0.81.$

Fig. 12.4 is the figure corresponding to Fig. 12.3 for the chord [PS].

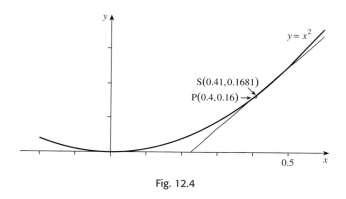

Fig. 12.4

Figure 12.4 is not very useful as an illustration, because P and S are so close together. There is a small triangle there, like the triangle in Fig. 12.3, but you could be excused for missing it. In Fig. 12.4 it has become difficult to distinguish between the chord [PS] and the tangent at P.

For the chord [PM],

$$\delta x = 0.39 - 0.4 = -0.01 \quad \text{and} \quad \delta y = 0.1521 - 0.16 = -0.0079,$$

so the gradient is $\dfrac{\delta y}{\delta x} = \dfrac{-0.0079}{-0.01} = 0.79.$

The gradient of the tangent at P is less than the gradient of [PS] and greater than the gradient of [PM]. It is therefore between 0.79 and 0.81.

By now you are probably beginning to suspect that the gradient of the tangent at P is 0.8. But if you still have doubts, try calculating the gradients of the chords [PT] and [PL], where T is $(0.4001, 0.4001^2)$ and L is $(0.3999, 0.3999^2)$. What does this tell you about the gradient of the tangent at P?

The next example uses the method for a curve with a more complicated equation.

Example 12.1.3
Make an estimate of the gradient of the curve $y = 1 + 5x - 2x^2$ at the point P with coordinates $(1, 4)$.

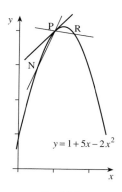

There is an important difference between this example and the previous ones. Because $1 + 5x - 2x^2$ is a quadratic with the coefficient of x^2 negative, the graph is a parabola with its vertex at the top. So if you take a point N to the left of P, the gradient of the chord PN will be greater than the gradient of the tangent at P; and if R is to the right of P, the gradient of [PR] will be less than the gradient of the tangent at P. This is illustrated in Fig. 12.5.

Fig. 12.5

Now that you know how the argument is going to proceed, you can take a short cut from the start by choosing points R and N very close to P. Suppose that the x-coordinates of R and N are taken to be 1.001 and 0.999. Then the y-coordinates are

$$1 + 5 \times 1.001 - 2 \times 1.001^2 = 4.000\,998$$

and $$1 + 5 \times 0.999 - 2 \times 0.999^2 = 3.998\,998.$$

So, for the chord [PR],

$$\delta x = 1.001 - 1 = 0.001 \quad \text{and} \quad \delta y = 4.000\,998 - 4 = 0.000\,998,$$

giving a gradient of $\dfrac{\delta y}{\delta x} = \dfrac{0.000\,998}{0.001} = 0.998.$

And for the chord [PN],

$$\delta x = 0.999 - 1 = -0.001 \quad \text{and} \quad \delta y = 3.998\,998 - 4 = -0.001\,002,$$

giving a gradient of $\dfrac{\delta y}{\delta x} = \dfrac{-0.001\,002}{-0.001} = 1.002.$

So the gradient of the curve at P is greater than 0.998 and less than 1.002. It is a reasonable guess that the gradient of the curve at P is 1.

This is still only a 'reasonable guess', not a proof. But it is best for the time being to work on the assumption that it is correct, and to defer the proof until you have seen how these calculations can be used.

Your calculator may be programmed to work out the gradient of a curve at a point. If you key in the equation of the curve and the value of x at the point you are interested in, the calculator will give the gradient of the curve at that point. The answer will not always be exact, but it will be a close approximation to the correct gradient. You could try using this to check your answers to the questions in Exercise 12A.

Exercise 12A

You should keep a record of your answers to this exercise. You will need to refer to them in the next section. If you are working with other students in a group, you can save time by splitting the work and pooling your results.

1 Carry out calculations similar to those in Examples 12.1.1 and 12.1.2 to find intervals within which the gradient of $y = x^2$ lies at the points

(a) $(2, 4)$,   (b) $(0.6, 0.36)$,   (c) $(-1, 1)$.

Use your answers to guess the gradient of the curve at these points.

2 Carry out calculations similar to those in Example 12.1.3 to find intervals within which the gradient of $y = 1 + 5x - 2x^2$ lies at the points

(a) $(0, 1)$,   (b) $(-1, -6)$,   (c) $(2, 3)$.

Use your answers to guess the gradient of the curve at these points.

3 For the given curves find intervals within which the gradient lies at the given points. Use your answers to guess the gradient of the curves at these points.

(a) $y = 10x^2$ at   (i) $(0.5, 2.5)$,   (ii) $(1.2, 14.4)$,   (iii) $(-2, 40)$.
(b) $y = x^2 + 3$ at   (i) $(0.4, 3.16)$,   (ii) $(1.5, 5.25)$,   (iii) $(-1, 4)$.
(c) $y = 3x^2 - 4x + 2$ at   (i) $(1, 1)$,   (ii) $(0, 2)$,   (iii) $(2, 6)$.

12.2 Gradient formulae

If you collect together the results of Example 12.1.2 and Exercise 12A Question 1 for the curve $y = x^2$, the gradients at various points are set out in Table 12.6.

x-coordinate of P	-1	0.4	0.6	2
Gradient at P	-2	0.8	1.2	4

Table 12.6

It is not difficult to see a pattern! At each of the four points the gradient is twice the x-coordinate. This is unlikely to be a coincidence. If you try to find the gradient at any other point on the curve you will find that the same thing happens.

You can express this algebraically by saying that the 'gradient formula' for the curve $y = x^2$ is $2x$.

Try doing the same thing for the results of Example 12.1.3 and Exercise 12A Question 2 for the curve $y = 1 + 5x - 2x^2$. You then get the values set out in Table 12.7.

x-coordinate of P	-1	0	1	2
Gradient at P	9	5	1	-3

Table 12.7

The pattern is not quite so obvious this time, but you will notice that as you move across the table the values of x go up by 1 each time, and the values of the gradient go down by 4. And since the gradient is 5 when $x = 0$, it is $5 - 4 \times 1$ when $x = 1$, $5 - 4 \times 2$ when $x = 2$, and so on. This suggests that the gradient formula for the curve $y = 1 + 5x - 2x^2$ is $5 - 4x$.

The process of finding the gradient formula for a curve is called **differentiation**. When you find the gradient formula, you are **differentiating**.

If the curve you are differentiating is written as $y = f(x)$, then the gradient formula for the curve is called the **derivative** of $f(x)$. It is denoted by $f'(x)$. This is pronounced 'f dashed x'.

So you can write

if $f(x) = x^2$, then $f'(x) = 2x$;

and   if $f(x) = 1 + 5x - 2x^2$, then $f'(x) = 5 - 4x$.

Remember that so far these formulae are just suggestions based on a few numerical experiments. They will be proved later in the chapter.

Exercise 12B

1 Use your answers to Exercise 12A Question 3 to suggest gradient formulae for the curves with equations

(a) $y = 10x^2$, (b) $y = x^2 + 3$, (c) $y = 3x^2 - 4x + 2$.

Write your conclusions using $f(x), f'(x)$ notation.

12.3 Some rules for differentiation

Now that you have several examples of gradient formulae, the next step is to look to see if you can find a pattern in the results. In Table 12.8 they are numbered according to their appearance in Exercise 12A.

	Equation of curve	Gradient formula
1	$y = x^2$	$2x$
2	$y = 1 + 5x - 2x^2$	$5 - 4x$
3(a)	$y = 10x^2$	$20x$
3(b)	$y = x^2 + 3$	$2x$
3(c)	$y = 3x^2 - 4x + 2$	$6x - 4$

Table 12.8

Remember also that, for the straight line with equation $y = bx + c$, the gradient formula is the constant b.

You will notice at once that

- if x^2 appears in the equation (as in 1, 3(b)), it becomes $2x$ in the gradient formula
- if a multiple of x^2 appears in the equation (as in 2, 3(a), 3(c)), it becomes the same multiple of $2x$ in the gradient formula
- if a multiple of x appears in the equation (as in 2, 3(c) and the straight line), the multiplier appears as a constant term in the gradient formula
- if a constant term appears in the equation (as in 2, 3(b), 3(c) and the straight line), it disappears in the gradient formula.

These rules can be summed up for any quadratic curve:

If $f(x) = ax^2 + bx + c$, then $f'(x) = 2ax + b$.

Example 12.3.1
For the curve with equation $y = 3x^2 - 8x - 2$, find the gradient at (3, 1).

Begin by finding the gradient formula from the result in the box with $a = 3$, $b = -8$ and $c = -2$. The gradient formula is then $6x - 8$.

To find the gradient at (3, 1) substitute $x = 3$ in the gradient formula to get $6 \times 3 - 8 = 10$.

You have already used the notation $f(x)$ with a particular value substituted for x (see Section 9.1). For instance, if in Example 12.3.1 $f(x)$ is used to denote $3x^2 - 8x - 2$, then $f(3)$ gives the y-coordinate of the point on the curve where $x = 3$. This idea can be extended to the expression for the derivative. When you differentiate you get $f'(x) = 6x - 8$. You can now substitute $x = 3$ and write $f'(3) = 6 \times 3 - 8 = 10$, which gives the gradient of the curve at the point where $x = 3$.

Example 12.3.2

If $f(x) = 5 - 2x - 4x^2$, find $f(-1)$ and $f'(-1)$. What do the answers tell you about the graph of $y = 5 - 2x - 4x^2$?

$$f(-1) = 5 - 2 \times (-1) - 4 \times (-1)^2$$
$$= 5 + 2 - 4 = 3.$$

Differentiating, $f'(x) = -2 - 8x$.

So $\qquad f'(-1) = -2 - 8 \times (-1)$
$$= -2 + 8 = 6.$$

Graphically, this means that the curve with equation $y = 5 - 2x - 4x^2$ contains the point $(-1, 3)$ and has gradient 6 at this point.

12.4 Extending the differentiation rule

So far differentiation has been used only for quadratic curves, but exactly the same methods can be used to find the gradients of curves whose equations contain x^3, x^4 and higher powers of x. The question is how to extend the rule for differentiating x^2 to higher powers.

Begin by noticing that the gradient formula $2x$ for the curve $y = x^2$ could be written as $2 \times x^1$.

The numerical multiplier 2 in this expression is the power of x in the equation of the curve, and the new power of x is 1 less than that power, since $2 - 1 = 1$.

Try applying the same rule to the curve $y = x^3$. The power of x is now 3, so in the gradient formula you would expect the numerical multiplier to be 3, and the new power of x to be $3 - 1$, that is 2. That is, the gradient formula would be $3x^2$.

This is a very optimistic generalisation, but there are several ways of testing it out. Look back to Chapter 9 at the graph of $y = x^3$, where it is Fig. 9.6. You will see that at the origin the x-axis is a tangent to the curve, so the gradient when $x = 0$ is 0. At every other point on the curve the gradient is positive. This is just what you would expect if the gradient formula is $3x^2$.

Another way of testing the formula would be to choose a particular point and estimate the gradient by the numerical method used in Section 12.1, as in Example 12.4.1.

Example 12.4.1

Make a numerical estimate of the gradient of $y = x^3$ at the point P with coordinates $(0.4, 0.064)$. Test whether this is the answer that you would get by using the suggested gradient formula $3x^2$.

Take points R to the right of P and N to the left of P with x-coordinates 0.401 and 0.399.

The y-coordinate of R is $0.401^3 = 0.064\,481...$, so for the chord [PR]

$$\delta x = 0.401 - 0.4 = 0.001 \quad \text{and} \quad \delta y = 0.064\,481... - 0.064 = 0.000\,481...,$$

giving

$$\frac{\delta y}{\delta x} = \frac{0.000\,481...}{0.001} = 0.481....$$

The y-coordinate of N is $0.399^3 = 0.063\,521...$, so for the chord [PN]

$$\delta x = 0.399 - 0.4 = -0.001 \quad \text{and} \quad \delta y = 0.063\,521... - 0.064 = -0.000\,478...,$$

giving

$$\frac{\delta y}{\delta x} = \frac{-0.000\,478...}{-0.001} = 0.478....$$

The gradient of the tangent at P is between $0.478...$ and $0.481...$. It is a reasonable guess that the gradient is 0.48.

Substituting $x = 0.4$ in the suggested gradient formula $3x^2$ gives

$3 \times 0.4^2 = 3 \times 0.16 = 0.48$.

With this encouragement, you could try extending the rule to $y = x^4$. The multiplier for the gradient formula would be 4, and the new power of x would be $4 - 1 = 3$. So you might expect the gradient formula to be $4x^3$. You can test this out in the same way as for $y = x^3$.

All these formulae can be summed up in a single statement by replacing the numerical powers 2, 3, 4, ... in the equations $y = x^2$, $y = x^3$, $y = x^4$, ... by the letter n:

> If $f(x) = x^n$, where n is a positive integer, then $f'(x) = nx^{n-1}$.

There is one other rule for differentiation which you have probably hardly noticed, but which needs to be stated for completeness. Look back at the rule for differentiating $ax^2 + bx + c$ in Section 12.3. This is stated for a single function with three coefficients, but it could be broken down into three separate and simpler statements:

If $f(x) = x^2$, then $f'(x) = 2x$.

If $g(x) = x$, then $g'(x) = 1$.

If $h(x) = 1$, then $h'(x) = 0$.

You could then put these together and say:

The derivative of $ax^2 + bx + c$ is $a \times (2x) + b \times 1 + c \times 0$, which is $2ax + b$.

When you do this you are using a rule for combining derivatives. It is sufficient to state it for two functions $f(x)$ and $g(x)$. If there are more than two functions, you can reach the obvious extension by using the rule more than once.

> The derivative of $af(x) + bg(x)$, where a and b are constants, is $af'(x) + bg'(x)$.

Example 12.4.2
Differentiate   (a) $x^5 - 4x^3 + 7x^2$,   (b) $(x + 2)(2x - 3)$.

(a) The derivatives of x^5, x^3 and x^2 are $5x^4$, $3x^2$ and $2x$. So the derivative of $x^5 - 4x^3 + 7x^2$ is $5x^4 - 4(3x^2) + 7(2x)$, which is $5x^4 - 12x^2 + 14x$.

(b) None of the rules for differentiation apply directly to an expression like this. But you can multiply out the brackets to get a quadratic which you can differentiate.

Since $(x + 2)(2x - 3) = 2x^2 + x - 6$, the derivative is $2(2x) + 1 = 4x + 1$.

> If you cannot immediately differentiate a given function using the rules you know, see if you can write the function in a different form which enables you to apply one of the rules.

12.5 An alternative notation

The advantage of the $f(x)$, $f'(x)$ notation is that you can use it in two ways. With x inside the bracket it refers to the function and its derivative as a whole. But if you replace x by a particular number p, then $f(p)$, $f'(p)$ stand for the value of the function and the gradient at a single point where $x = p$.

However, if you just want to use x and y and don't need $f(x)$ notation, it is useful to have a way of writing the derivative in terms of x and y.

There is already a symbol $\dfrac{\delta y}{\delta x}$ which does this for the gradient of a chord. This suggests using a similar symbol for the gradient of the tangent, writing the letter 'd' instead of the greek δ.

> If y is a function of x, $\dfrac{dy}{dx}$ denotes the derivative.

There is, though, an important difference between $\dfrac{\delta y}{\delta x}$ and $\dfrac{dy}{dx}$. The symbol $\dfrac{\delta y}{\delta x}$ stands for a genuine fraction, the result of dividing δy by δx. But $\dfrac{dy}{dx}$ is not a fraction, but a complete symbol which can't be taken apart; no meaning is given to the separate elements dy and dx. In speech it is pronounced (rather rapidly!) 'd y d x' with no hint that there is a fraction bar present.

Example 12.5.1

If $y = 4x^3 - 3x^4$, find $\dfrac{dy}{dx}$.

This is exactly the same question as 'If $f(x) = 4x^3 - 3x^4$, find $f'(x)$', or

'Differentiate $4x^3 - 3x^4$'. The answer is $\dfrac{dy}{dx} = 4(3x^2) - 3(4x^3) = 12x^2(1 - x)$.

The main advantages of $\dfrac{dy}{dx}$ notation will be seen in Chapter 25 when you come to apply differentiation to mathematical models in various real-world situations. However, there may be occasions before then when you will find it convenient, so it is worth getting used to it at this stage.

Exercise 12C

1 Write down the gradient formula for each of the following functions.

   (a) x^2 (b) $x^2 - x$ (c) $4x^2$ (d) $3x^2 - 2x$

   (e) $2 - 3x$ (f) $x - 2 - 2x^2$ (g) $2 + 4x - 3x^2$ (h) $\sqrt{2}x - \sqrt{3}x^2$

2 For each of the following functions $f(x)$, write down $f'(x)$. You may need to rearrange some of the functions before differentiating them.

   (a) $3x - 1$ (b) $2 - 3x^2$ (c) 4 (d) $1 + 2x + 3x^2$

   (e) $x^2 - 2x^2$ (f) $3(1 + 2x - x^2)$ (g) $2x(1 - x)$ (h) $x(2x + 1) - 1$

3 Find the derivative of each of the following functions $f(x)$ at $x = -3$.

   (a) $-x^2$ (b) $3x$ (c) $x^2 + 3x$ (d) $2x - x^2$

   (e) $2x^2 + 4x - 1$ (f) $-(3 - x^2)$ (g) $-x(2 + x)$ (h) $(x - 2)(2x - 1)$

4 For each of the following functions $f(x)$, find x such that $f'(x)$ has the given value.

   (a) $2x^2$ value 3   (b) $x - 2x^2$ value -1

   (c) $2 + 3x + x^2$ value 0   (d) $x^2 + 4x - 1$ value 2

   (e) $(x - 2)(x - 1)$ value 0   (f) $2x(3x + 2)$ value 10

5 Repeat the numerical test in Example 12.4.1 by estimating the gradient of $y = x^3$ at the points

   (a) $(1, 1)$,   (b) $(-0.5, -0.125)$.

6 Make numerical estimates of the gradient of $y = x^4$ at two points of your choice, and use them to check the differentiation rule $\dfrac{dy}{dx} = 4x^3$.

7 Find $\dfrac{dy}{dx}$ for each of the following equations.

   (a) $y = x^3 + 2x^2$ (b) $y = 1 - 2x^3 + 3x^2$ (c) $y = x^3 - 6x^2 + 11x - 6$

   (d) $y = 2x^3 - 3x^2 + x$ (e) $y = x(1 + x^2)$ (f) $y = (2 - x^2)(2 + x^2)$

8 Find $f'(-2)$ for each of the following functions $f(x)$.

(a) $2x - x^3$ (b) $2x - x^2$ (c) $1 - 2x - 3x^2 + 4x^3$

(d) $2 - x$ (e) $x^2(1 + x)$ (f) $(3 - x^2)^2$

9 For each of the following functions find the value(s) of x such that $f'(x)$ is equal to the given number.

(a) x^3 12   (b) $x^3 - x^2$ 8   (c) $3x - 3x^2 + x^3$ 108

(d) $x^3 - 3x^2 + 2x$ -1 (e) $x(1 + x)^2$ 0   (f) $x(1 - x)(1 + x)$ 2

12.6 Proving the gradient formulae

This section shows how some of the gradient formulae found in Sections 12.1–12.4 can be proved.

In Examples 12.1.1 and 12.1.2 the gradient of $y = x^2$ at the point P with coordinates $(0.4, 0.16)$ was guessed from the gradients of chords joining this point to points on the curve with x-coordinates 0.5, 0.3, 0.41 and 0.39. By using some simple algebra all these calculations (and many similar ones) could have been done at the same time.

The x-coordinates of the points R, S, N and M were all chosen to be close to 0.4, the x-coordinate of P. So to save time you could take a point Q with x-coordinate $0.4 + h$, work out the gradient of the chord [PQ] and then substitute various values for h such as 0.1, -0.1, 0.01 and -0.01 in this to find the gradients of the chords [PR], [PN], and so on.

Example 12.6.1

Find the gradient of the chord joining P(0.4, 0.16) to Q$(0.4 + h, (0.4 + h)^2)$

Using the delta notation,

$$\delta x = (0.4 + h) - 0.4 = h,$$

and

$$\delta y = (0.4 + h)^2 - 0.16$$
$$= (0.16 + 0.8h + h^2) - 0.16$$
$$= 0.8h + h^2,$$

so

$$\frac{\delta y}{\delta x} = \frac{0.8h + h^2}{h}$$
$$= \frac{(0.8 + h)h}{h}.$$
$$= 0.8 + h.$$

This confirms what appeared to be happening in Examples 12.1.1 and 12.1.2. For any chord to the right of P, for which $h > 0$, the gradient is greater than 0.8; and for any chord to the left, with $h < 0$, the gradient is less than 0.8.

In fact, by taking h close enough to 0, you can make the gradient of the chord as close to 0.8 as you choose. From Example 12.6.1, the gradient of the chord is $0.8 + h$. So if you want to find a chord through $(0.4, 0.16)$ with a gradient between, say, 0.799 999 and 0.800 001, you can do it by taking h somewhere between $-0.000\,001$ and $+0.000\,001$.

The only value that you cannot take for h is 0 itself. But you can say that 'in the limit, as h tends to 0, the gradient of the chord tends to 0.8'.

The conventional way of writing this is

$$\lim_{h \to 0}(\text{gradient of chord}) = \lim_{h \to 0}(0.8 + h) = 0.8.$$

The symbol $h \to 0$ is read 'as h tends to 0', or sometimes simply 'h tends to 0'.

This is fine as far as it goes, but that is not very far. Taking P to be the point with $x = 0.4$ was a special numerical example. In Exercise 12A Question 1 you then carried out similar calculations for points with $x = 2$, $x = 0.6$ and $x = -1$. All these calculations could have been done together by taking a more algebraic approach and taking P to be the point at which $x = p$.

Example 12.6.2
Find the gradient of the chord of $y = x^2$ joining $P(p, p^2)$ to $Q(p + h, (p + h)^2)$.

The argument is exactly the same as in Example 12.6.1.

$$\delta x = (p + h) - p = h,$$

and

$$\begin{aligned}\delta y &= (p + h)^2 - p^2 \\ &= (p^2 + 2ph + h^2) - p^2, \\ &= 2ph + h^2,\end{aligned}$$

so

$$\begin{aligned}\frac{\delta y}{\delta x} &= \frac{2ph + h^2}{h} \\ &= \frac{(2p + h)h}{h} \\ &= 2p + h.\end{aligned}$$

You can see that Example 12.6.1 is just a special case of this with $p = 0.4$.

Now in any particular application the value of p remains constant, but h can be varied to bring Q as close to P as you choose. Then, by the same argument as before,

$$\lim_{h \to 0}(\text{gradient of chord}) = \lim_{h \to 0}(2p + h) = 2p.$$

This shows that, as we guessed from the special cases in Section 12.2, the gradient of $y = x^2$ at any point P is double the x-coordinate of P. That is, the gradient formula for the curve $y = x^2$ is $2x$.

Example 12.6.3 uses the same method to find the derivative of the quadratic curve in Example 12.1.3.

Example 12.6.3

For the curve with equation $y = 1 + 5x - 2x^2$, prove that $\dfrac{dy}{dx} = 5 - 4x$.

Take any point P on the curve with coordinates $(p, 1 + 5p - 2p^2)$. Let Q be another point on the curve with x-coordinate $p + h$.

The y-coordinate of Q is

$$1 + 5(p + h) - 2(p + h)^2 = 1 + 5(p + h) - 2(p^2 + 2ph + h^2)$$
$$= 1 + 5p + 5h - 2p^2 - 4ph - 2h^2.$$

So, for the chord [PQ],

$$\delta x = (p + h) - p = h,$$
$$\delta y = (1 + 5p + 5h - 2p^2 - 4ph - 2h^2) - (1 + 5p - 2p^2)$$
$$= 5h - 4ph - 2h^2,$$

and

$$\frac{\delta y}{\delta x} = \frac{5h - 4ph - 2h^2}{h}$$
$$= \frac{(5 - 4p - 2h)h}{h}$$
$$= 5 - 4p - 2h.$$

Now for a fixed value of p, $\dfrac{\delta y}{\delta x}$ can be made as close to $5 - 4p$ as you like by making h small enough. That is,

$$\lim_{h \to 0} \frac{\delta y}{\delta x} = \lim_{h \to 0} (5 - 4p - 2h) = 5 - 4p.$$

This shows that the gradient of the curve at the point where $x = p$ is $5 - 4p$, for any value of p. The gradient formula for the curve is therefore

$$\frac{dy}{dx} = 5 - 4x.$$

A similar approach can be used for any curve if you know its equation.

Fig. 12.9 shows a curve which has an equation of the form $y = f(x)$. Suppose that you want the gradient of the tangent at the point P, with coordinates $(p, f(p))$. The chord joining this point to any other point Q on the curve with coordinates $(p + h, f(p + h))$ has

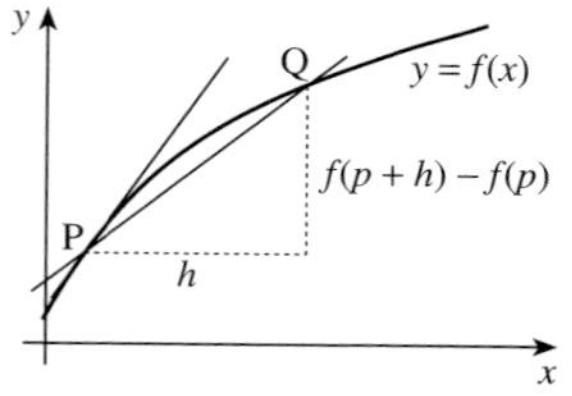

Fig. 12.9

$$\delta x = h, \quad \delta y = f(p + h) - f(p)$$

so that its gradient is

$$\frac{\delta y}{\delta x} = \frac{f(p + h) - f(p)}{h}.$$

Now let the value of h change so that the point Q takes different positions on the curve. Then, if Q is close to P, so that h is close to 0, the gradient of the chord is close to the gradient of the tangent at p. In the limit, as h tends to 0, this expression tends to $f'(p)$.

> If the curve $y = f(x)$ has a tangent at $(p, f(p))$, then its gradient is
>
> $$\lim_{h \to 0} \frac{f(p + h) - f(p)}{h}.$$
>
> This quantity is called the derivative of $f(x)$ at $x = p$; it is denoted by $f'(p)$.
> In general the derivative is $f'(x)$, where $f'(x) = \lim_{h \to 0} \dfrac{f(x + h) - f(x)}{h}$.

Example 12.6.4 uses the definition in the last line of the box to prove the result for the derivative of the general quadratic function given in Section 12.3.

Example 12.6.4
Prove that, if $f(x) = ax^2 + bx + c$, then $f'(x) = 2ax + b$.

First,

$$\begin{aligned}
f(x + h) - f(x) &= (a(x + h)^2 + b(x + h) + c) - (ax^2 + bx + c) \\
&= a((x + h)^2 - x^2) + b((x + h) - x) \\
&= a(2xh + h^2) + bh \\
&= (a(2x + h) + b)h.
\end{aligned}$$

Therefore

$$\begin{aligned}
f'(x) &= \lim_{h \to 0} \frac{(a(2x + h) + b)h}{h} \\
&= \lim_{h \to 0} (2ax + ah + b) \\
&= 2ax + b.
\end{aligned}$$

With the help of the binomial theorem, Section 4.3, you can use this method to find the derivative for higher powers of x. Example 12.6.5 shows how to do this for $f(x) = x^4$.

Example 12.6.5
Prove that, if $f(x) = x^4$, then $f'(x) = 4x^3$.

By the binomial theorem,

$$(x + h)^4 = x^4 + 4x^3h + 6x^2h^2 + 4xh^3 + h^4.$$

So

$$\begin{aligned}
f(x + h) - f(x) &= (x + h)^4 - x^4 \\
&= 4x^3h + 6x^2h^2 + 4xh^3 + h^4 \\
&= (4x^3 + 6x^2h + 4xh^2 + h^3)h
\end{aligned}$$

and

$$\frac{f(x + h) - f(x)}{h} = 4x^3 + 6x^2h + 4xh^2 + h^3.$$

The main differences between this and previous examples are that there are now three terms in this expression which involve h, and that in two of these the multiplying factor contains x. But since, as h varies, x remains constant, each of these terms separately tends to 0 as $h \to 0$. Their sum therefore also tends to 0, so that

$$\lim_{h \to 0} \frac{f(x+h) - f(x)}{h} = 4x^3.$$

That is, $f'(x) = 4x^3$.

Exercise 12D

1 Without using a general formula, prove that the gradient of $y = 3x^2 - 2x + 1$ at $x = 1$ is 4.

2 Prove that the gradient of $y = 4x - 3x^2$ at the point $(p,\ 4p - 3p^2)$ is $4 - 6p$.

3 Without using a general formula prove that, if $f(x) = 2x^2 + 3x + 2$, then $f'(x) = 4x + 3$.

4 Prove from first principles that the value of $\dfrac{dy}{dx}$ at the point $(2, 40)$ on the curve $y = 5x^3$ is 60.

5 Use the definition of $f'(x)$ to prove that, if $f(x) = x^3$, then $f'(x) = 3x^2$.

13 Tangents and normals

This chapter combines results from Chapters 8 and 12. When you have completed it, you should

- be able to find the equation of the tangent to a curve at a point
- know what is meant by a normal, and be able to find the equation of the normal to a curve at a point.

13.1 Finding equations of tangents

Now that you know how to find the gradient of the tangent at a point on a curve, it is easy to find the equation of the tangent.

Example 13.1.1
Find the equation of the tangent at the point $(2, 6)$ on the curve $y = f(x)$, where $f(x) = 2x^2 - 3x + 4$.

To find the gradient, differentiate to get $f'(x) = 4x - 3$.

The gradient of the tangent at $(2, 6)$ is $f'(2) = 4 \times 2 - 3 = 5$.

The tangent is the line through $(2, 6)$ with gradient 5. Using the equation of a line in the form $y - y_1 = m(x - x_1)$ (see Section 8.3), the equation of the tangent is

$$y - 6 = 5(x - 2), \quad \text{which is} \quad y = 5x - 4.$$

The important thing to remember is that, in the equation of a line, m has to be a number. You have to substitute the x-coordinate of the point into the gradient formula before you can find the equation of the line.

Example 13.1.2
Find the equation of the tangent to the graph of $y = x^2 - 4x + 2$ which is parallel to the x-axis.

From Section 8.2, a line parallel to the x-axis has gradient 0.

Let $f(x) = x^2 - 4x + 2$. Then $f'(x) = 2x - 4$.

To find when the gradient is 0 you need to solve $2x - 4 = 0$, giving $x = 2$.

When $x = 2$, $y = 2^2 - 4 \times 2 + 2 = -2$.

From Section 8.3, the equation of a line parallel to the x-axis has the form $y = c$. So the equation of the tangent is $y = -2$.

Example 13.1.3

Show that there are two points on the graph of $y = x^2(x - 2)$ at which the gradient is equal to 4. Find the equations of the tangents at these points.

Before you can differentiate, you must multiply out the brackets to get the equation in the form $y = x^3 - 2x^2$. The gradient formula is then $\dfrac{dy}{dx} = 3x^2 - 4x$.

This is equal to 4 if $3x^2 - 4x = 4$, that is if x is a root of the quadratic equation

$$3x^2 - 4x - 4 = 0.$$

This can be factorised as

$$(x - 2)(3x + 2) = 0,$$

so the gradient is equal to 4 if $x = 2$ or $x = -\frac{2}{3}$.

You know the gradient of the tangents, but you do not yet know the y-coordinates of the points on the curve that they have to pass through. To find these you have to substitute the values of x already found into the equation $y = x^2(x - 2)$.

When $x = 2$, $y = 2^2 \times (2 - 2) = 0$. The line through $(2, 0)$ with gradient 4 has equation

$$y - 0 = 4(x - 2), \quad \text{which is} \quad y = 4x - 8.$$

When $x = -\frac{2}{3}$, $y = \left(-\frac{2}{3}\right)^2 \times \left(-\frac{2}{3} - 2\right) = \frac{4}{9} \times \left(-\frac{8}{3}\right) = -\frac{32}{27}$. The line through $\left(-\frac{2}{3}, -\frac{32}{27}\right)$ with gradient 4 has equation

$$y - \left(-\tfrac{32}{27}\right) = 4\left(x - \left(-\tfrac{2}{3}\right)\right)$$

$$y + \tfrac{32}{27} = 4x + \tfrac{8}{3}$$

$$y = 4x + \tfrac{40}{27}.$$

The equations of the tangents with gradient 4 are $y = 4x - 8$ and $y = 4x + \frac{40}{27}$.

> Check this by displaying the curve and the two lines on your calculator.

13.2   The normal to a curve at a point

Another line which you sometimes need to find is the line through a point of a curve at right angles to the tangent at that point. This is called the **normal** to the curve at the point.

Figure 13.1 shows a curve with equation $y = f(x)$. The tangent and normal at the point A have been drawn.

If you know the gradient of the tangent at A, you can find the gradient of the normal by using the result in Section 8.4 for perpendicular lines. If the gradient of the tangent is m, the gradient of the normal is $-\dfrac{1}{m}$ provided that $m \neq 0$.

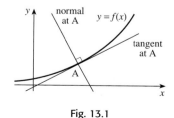

Fig. 13.1

Example 13.2.1
Find the equations of the normal to the curve at the given point in

(a) Example 13.1.1,   (b) Example 13.1.2.

   (a) For the curve with equation $y = 2x^2 - 3x + 4$ at the point $(2, 6)$, the gradient of
      the tangent is 5. The gradient of the normal is therefore $-\frac{1}{5}$.
      The equation of the normal is

$$y - 6 = -\tfrac{1}{5}(x - 2) \quad \text{which is} \quad y = -0.2x + 6.4.$$

   (b) Since the tangent at $(2, -2)$ is parallel to the x-axis, the normal is parallel to the
      y-axis. It therefore has equation $x = 2$.

For the curve in Examples 13.1.1 and 13.2.1(a), try plotting the curve $y = 2x^2 - 3x + 4$, the
tangent $y = 5x - 4$ and the normal $y = -0.2x + 6.4$ on your calculator. You may be surprised
by the results.

> If you draw a curve together with its tangent and normal at a point, the normal
> will only appear perpendicular in your diagram if the scales are the same on both
> the x- and y-axes. (Or, of course, if the tangent is horizontal and the normal is
> vertical, as in Examples 13.1.2 and 13.2.1(b).) However, no matter what the scales
> are, the tangent will always appear as a tangent.

Exercise 13

1 Find the equation of the tangent to the curve at the point with the given x-coordinate.

   (a) $y = x^2$ where $x = -1$ (b) $y = 2x^2 - x$ where $x = 0$

   (c) $y = x^2 - 2x + 3$ where $x = 2$ (d) $y = 1 - x^2$ where $x = -3$

   (e) $y = x(2 - x)$ where $x = 1$ (f) $y = (x - 1)^2$ where $x = 1$

2 Find the equation of the normal to the curve at the point with the given x-coordinate.

   (a) $y = -x^2$ where $x = 1$ (b) $y = 3x^2 - 2x - 1$ where $x = 1$

   (c) $y = 1 - 2x^2$ where $x = -2$ (d) $y = 1 - x^2$ where $x = 0$

   (e) $y = 2(2 + x + x^2)$ where $x = -1$ (f) $y = (2x - 1)^2$ where $x = \frac{1}{2}$

3 Find the equation of the tangent to the curve $y = x^2$ which is parallel to the line $y = x$.

4 Find the equation of the tangent to the curve $y = x^2$ which is parallel to the x-axis.

5 Find the equation of the tangent to the curve $y = x^2 - 2x$ which is perpendicular to the
   line $2y = x - 1$.

6 Find the equation of the normal to the curve $y = 3x^2 - 2x - 1$ which is parallel to the line
   $y = x - 3$.

7 Find the equation of the normal to the curve $y = (x - 1)^2$ which is parallel to the y-axis.

8 Find the equation of the normal to the curve $y = 2x^2 + 3x + 4$ which is perpendicular to the line $y = 7x - 5$.

9 Find the equation of the tangent to the curve $y = x^3 + x$ at the point for which $x = -1$.

10 One of the tangents to the curve with equation $y = 4x - x^3$ is the line with equation $y = x - 2$. Find the equation of the other tangent parallel to $y = x - 2$.

11 The graphs of $y = x^2 - 2x$ and $y = x^3 - 3x^2 - 2x$ both pass through the origin. Show that they share the same tangent at the origin.

12 Find the equation of the tangent to the curve with equation $y = x^3 - 3x^2 - 2x - 6$ at the point where it crosses the y-axis.

13 The line $y = x + 2$ meets the curve $y = x^2$ at A and B.

(a) Find the coordinates of A and B.

(b) Find the equations of the tangents to the curve at A and B.

(c) Find the point of intersection of the tangents at A and B.

14 Index notation

You have already used index notation in the form of squares, cubes and other integer powers. In this chapter the notation is extended to powers which are zero, negative numbers and fractions. When you have completed it, you should

- know the rules of indices
- know the meaning of negative, zero and fractional indices
- be able to simplify expressions involving indices.

14.1 Working with indices

In the 16th century, when mathematics books began to be printed, mathematicians were finding how to solve cubic and quartic equations. They found it was more economical to write and to print the products xxx and $xxxx$ as x^3 and x^4.

This is how index notation started. But it turned out to be much more than a convenient shorthand. The new notation led to important mathematical discoveries, and mathematics as it is today would be inconceivable without index notation.

You will already have used simple examples of this notation. In general, the symbol a^m stands for the result of multiplying m as together:

$$a^m = \overbrace{a \times a \times a \times ... \times a}^{m \text{ of these}}.$$

The number a is called the **base**, and the number m is the **index** (plural 'indices'). Notice that, although a can be any kind of number, m must be a positive integer. Another way of describing this is 'a raised to the mth power', or more shortly 'a to the power m'. When this notation is used, expressions can often be simplified by using a few simple rules.

One of these is the **multiplication rule**,

$$a^m \times a^n = \overbrace{a \times a \times ... \times a}^{m \text{ of these}} \times \overbrace{a \times a \times ... \times a}^{n \text{ of these}} = \overbrace{a \times a \times ... \times a}^{m+n \text{ of these}} = a^{m+n}.$$

This is used, for example, in finding the volume of a cube of side a:

$$\text{volume} = \text{base area} \times \text{height} = a^2 \times a = a^2 \times a^1 = a^{2+1} = a^3.$$

Closely linked with this is the **division rule**,

$$a^m \div a^n = \overbrace{(a \times a \times ... \times a)}^{m \text{ of these}} \div \overbrace{(a \times a \times ... \times a)}^{n \text{ of these}}$$

$$= \overbrace{a \times a \times ... \times a}^{m-n \text{ of these}} \quad (\text{since } n \text{ of the } a\text{s cancel out})$$

$$= a^{m-n}, \quad \text{provided that } m > n.$$

Example 14.1.1

Simplify   (a) $10^3 \times 10^4 \div 10^2$,   (b) $\dfrac{p^4 q^5}{p q^3}$.

(a) $10^3 \times 10^4 \div 10^2 = 10^{3+4} \div 10^2 = 10^7 \div 10^2 = 10^{7-2} = 10^5$.

(b) $\dfrac{p^4 q^5}{p q^3} = \dfrac{p^4}{p} \times \dfrac{q^5}{q^3} = (p^4 \div p) \times (q^5 \div q^3) = p^{4-1} \times q^{5-3} = p^3 q^2$.

Another rule is the **power-on-power rule**,

$$
(a^m)^n = \overbrace{\overbrace{a \times a \times \ldots \times a}^{m \text{ of these}} \times \overbrace{a \times a \times \ldots \times a}^{m \text{ of these}} \times \ldots \times \overbrace{a \times a \times \ldots \times a}^{m \text{ of these}}}^{n \text{ of these brackets}}
$$

$$
= \overbrace{a \times a \times \ldots \times a}^{m \times n \text{ of these}} = a^{m \times n}.
$$

Example 14.1.2

Express 8^4 as a power of 2.

Since $8 = 2^3$, $8^4 = (2^3)^4 = 2^{3 \times 4} = 2^{12}$.

One further rule, the **factor rule**, has two bases but just one index:

$$
(a \times b)^m = \overbrace{(a \times b) \times (a \times b) \times \ldots \times (a \times b)}^{m \text{ of these brackets}} = \overbrace{a \times a \times \ldots \times a}^{m \text{ of these}} \times \overbrace{b \times b \times \ldots \times b}^{m \text{ of these}} = a^m \times b^m.
$$

In explaining these rules multiplication signs have been used. But, as in other parts of algebra, they are usually omitted if there is no ambiguity. For completeness, here are the rules again:

The multiplication rule:	$a^m \times a^n = a^{m+n}$
The division rule:	$a^m \div a^n = a^{m-n}$, provided that $m > n$
The power-on-power rule:	$(a^m)^n = a^{m \times n}$
The factor rule:	$(a \times b)^m = a^m \times b^m$

Example 14.1.3

Given that $z x^4 = (x^3 y)^2$, express z as simply as possible in terms of x and y.

Begin by using the factor rule to separate the powers of x and y.

$$z x^4 = (x^3)^2 \times y^2.$$

Using the power-on-power rule,

$$z x^4 = x^{3 \times 2} \times y^2 = x^6 y^2.$$

Divide both sides by x^4 and rearrange the factors to get the powers of x together.

$$z = x^6 y^2 \div x^4 = (x^6 \div x^4) \times y^2.$$

Using the division rule,

$$z = x^{6-4} \times y^2 = x^2 y^2.$$

If $z x^4 = (x^3 y)^2$, then $z = x^2 y^2$.

Example 14.1.4

Simplify $(2a^2b)^3 \div (4a^4b)$.

$$
\begin{aligned}
(2a^2b)^3 \div (4a^4b) &= \left(2^3(a^2)^3 b^3\right) \div (4a^4b) && \text{factor rule}\\
&= (8a^{2\times3}b^3) \div (4a^4b) && \text{power-on-power rule}\\
&= (8 \div 4) \times (a^6 \div a^4) \times (b^3 \div b^1) && \text{rearranging}\\
&= 2a^{6-4}b^{3-1} && \text{division rule}\\
&= 2a^2b^2.
\end{aligned}
$$

Exercise 14A

1 Simplify the following expressions.

(a) $a^2 \times a^3 \times a^7$ (b) $(b^4)^2$ (c) $c^7 \div c^3$

(d) $d^5 \times d^4$ (e) $(e^5)^4$ (f) $(x^3 y^2)^2$

(g) $5g^5 \times 3g^3$ (h) $12h^{12} \div 4h^4$ (i) $(2a^2)^3 \times (3a)^2$

2 Simplify the following, giving each answer in the form 2^n.

(a) $2^{11} \times (2^5)^3$ (b) $(2^3)^2 \times (2^2)^3$ (c) 4^3

(d) 8^2 (e) $\dfrac{2^7 \times 2^8}{2^{13}}$ (f) $\dfrac{2^2 \times 2^3}{(2^2)^2}$

14.2 Zero and negative indices

The definition of a^m in Section 14.1, as the result of multiplying m as together, makes no sense if m is zero or a negative integer. You can't multiply -3 as or 0 as together. But extending the meaning of a^m when the index is zero or negative is possible, and useful, since it turns out that the rules still work with such index values.

Look at this sequence: $\quad 2^5 = 32, \quad 2^4 = 16, \quad 2^3 = 8, \quad 2^2 = 4, \dots$.

On the left sides, the base is always 2, and the indices go down by 1 at each step. On the right, the numbers are halved at each step. So you might continue the process

$$\dots, \quad 2^2 = 4, \quad 2^1 = 2, \quad 2^0 = 1, \quad 2^{-1} = \tfrac12, \quad 2^{-2} = \tfrac14, \quad 2^{-3} = \tfrac18, \dots$$

and you can go on like this indefinitely. Now compare

$$2^1 = 2 \text{ with } 2^{-1} = \tfrac12, \quad 2^2 = 4 \text{ with } 2^{-2} = \tfrac14, \quad 2^3 = 8 \text{ with } 2^{-3} = \tfrac18.$$

It looks as if 2^{-n} should be defined as $\dfrac{1}{2^n}$, with the special value in the middle $2^0 = 1$.

This can be standardised, for any base a (except 0), and any positive integer n, as the **negative power rule**:

$$a^{-n} = \frac{1}{a^n} \quad \text{and} \quad a^0 = 1.$$

Example 14.2.1

Write as a simple fraction   (a) 2^{-5},   (b) $\left(\frac{3}{5}\right)^{-2}$,   (c) $\left(1\frac{1}{2}\right)^{-1}$.

(a) $2^{-5} = \dfrac{1}{2^5} = \frac{1}{32}$.

(b) $\left(\frac{3}{5}\right)^{-2} = \dfrac{1}{\left(\frac{3}{5}\right)^2} = \dfrac{1}{\frac{9}{25}} = \frac{25}{9}$.

(c) $\left(1\frac{1}{2}\right)^{-1} = \left(\frac{3}{2}\right)^{-1} = \dfrac{1}{\frac{3}{2}} = \frac{2}{3}$.

> In hand-written work it is safer, though not strictly necessary, to insert brackets in the two-tier fraction $\dfrac{1}{\left(\frac{3}{2}\right)}$ to avoid confusing it with $\dfrac{\left(\frac{1}{3}\right)}{2}$.

Notice that in Example 14.2.1 parts (b) and (c) use the rule that $\dfrac{1}{a/b} = \dfrac{b}{a}$. This is because

$$\frac{b}{a} \times \frac{a}{b} = 1, \text{ so } \frac{b}{a} = 1 \div \frac{a}{b} = \frac{1}{a/b}.$$

Before going on to use the negative power rule, you need to be sure that the rules which were established in Section 14.1 for positive indices still work when some of the indices are negative. Here are three examples.

The multiplication rule: $a^3 \times a^{-7} = a^3 \times \dfrac{1}{a^7} = \dfrac{a^3}{a^7} = \dfrac{1}{a^7 \div a^3}$

$$= \frac{1}{a^{7-3}} \qquad \text{using the division rule for positive indices}$$

$$= \frac{1}{a^4} = a^{-4} = a^{3+(-7)}.$$

The power-on-power rule: $(a^{-2})^{-3} = \left(\dfrac{1}{a^2}\right)^{-3} = \dfrac{1}{(1/a^2)^3} = \dfrac{1}{1/(a^2)^3}$

$$= \frac{1}{1/a^6} \qquad \text{using the power-on-power rule for positive indices}$$

$$= a^6 = a^{(-2)\times(-3)}.$$

The factor rule: $(ab)^{-3} = \dfrac{1}{(ab)^3} = \dfrac{1}{a^3 b^3} \qquad \text{using the factor rule for positive indices}$

$$= \frac{1}{a^3} \times \frac{1}{b^3} = a^{-3}b^{-3}.$$

Try making up some more examples like these for yourself.

Example 14.2.2
Simplify (a) $2^{-3} \div 3^{-2}$, (b) $x^{-1} \times x^{-2}$, (c) $(x^{-1})^{-2}$, (d) $(p^3 q^{-1})^2$.

(a) $2^{-3} \div 3^{-2} = \dfrac{1}{2^3} \div \dfrac{1}{3^2} = \tfrac{1}{8} \div \tfrac{1}{9} = \tfrac{1}{8} \times 9 = \tfrac{9}{8}$.

(b) Using the multiplication rule,

$$x^{-1} \times x^{-2} = x^{(-1)+(-2)} = x^{-3} = \dfrac{1}{x^3}.$$

(c) Using the power-on-power rule,

$$(x^{-1})^{-2} = x^{(-1)\times(-2)} = x^2.$$

(d) First use the factor rule, then the power-on-power rule.

$$(p^3 q^{-1})^2 = (p^3)^2 \times (q^{-1})^2 = p^{3\times2} \times q^{(-1)\times2} = p^6 \times q^{-2} = p^6 \times \dfrac{1}{q^2} = \dfrac{p^6}{q^2}.$$

Example 14.2.3
If $a = 5$, find the value of $4a^{-2}$.

The important thing to notice is that the index -2 goes only with the a and not with the 4. So $4a^{-2}$ means $4 \times \dfrac{1}{a^2}$. When $a = 5$, $4a^{-2} = 4 \times \dfrac{1}{25} = 0.16$.

Example 14.2.4
Simplify (a) $4a^2 b \times (3ab^{-1})^{-2}$, (b) $\left(\dfrac{\text{MLT}^{-2}}{\text{L}^2}\right) \div \left(\dfrac{\text{LT}^{-1}}{\text{L}}\right)$.

(a) **Method 1** Change the expression into a form where all the indices are positive.

$$4a^2 b \times (3ab^{-1})^{-2} = 4a^2 b \times \dfrac{1}{(3a \times 1/b)^2} = 4a^2 b \times \dfrac{1}{9a^2 \times 1/b^2} = 4a^2 b \times \dfrac{b^2}{9a^2}$$

$$= \tfrac{4}{9} b^{1+2} = \tfrac{4}{9} b^3.$$

Method 2 Use the index rules directly with positive and negative indices.

$$4a^2 b \times (3ab^{-1})^{-2} = 4a^2 b \times (3^{-2} a^{-2}(b^{-1})^{-2}) \qquad \text{factor rule}$$
$$= 4a^2 b \times (3^{-2} a^{-2} b^2) \qquad \text{power-on-power rule}$$
$$= \left(4 \times \dfrac{1}{3^2}\right) \times (a^2 a^{-2}) \times (bb^2) = \tfrac{4}{9} a^0 b^3 = \tfrac{4}{9} b^3.$$

(b) This is an application in mechanics: M, L, T stand for dimensions of mass, length and time in the measurement of viscosity. Taking the brackets separately,

$$\left(\dfrac{\text{MLT}^{-2}}{\text{L}^2}\right) = \text{ML}^{1-2}\text{T}^{-2} = \text{ML}^{-1}\text{T}^{-2}$$

and $\left(\dfrac{\text{LT}^{-1}}{\text{L}}\right) = \text{L}^{1-1}\text{T}^{-1} = \text{L}^0\text{T}^{-1} = \text{T}^{-1}$,

so $\left(\dfrac{\text{MLT}^{-2}}{\text{L}^2}\right) \div \left(\dfrac{\text{LT}^{-1}}{\text{L}}\right) = (\text{ML}^{-1}\text{T}^{-2}) \div \text{T}^{-1} = \text{ML}^{-1}\text{T}^{-2-(-1)} = \text{ML}^{-1}\text{T}^{-1}.$

This may remind you of the notation m s^{-1} and m s^{-2} used in Sections 10.6 and 10.7 for the units of velocity (metres per second) and acceleration (metres per second per second).

Example 14.2.5
Find the number x such that $2^{x+1} \div 4^{x+2} = 8^{x+3}$.

Since 4 and 8 are powers of 2, the whole equation can be written in terms of powers of 2. Using the power-on-power rule followed by the division rule,

$$2^{x+1} \div (2^2)^{x+2} = (2^3)^{x+3},$$
$$2^{x+1} \div 2^{2x+4} = 2^{3x+9},$$
$$2^{(x+1)-(2x+4)} = 2^{3x+9},$$
$$2^{-x-3} = 2^{3x+9}.$$

You can now equate the indices on the two sides of the equation to get

$$-x - 3 = 3x + 9,$$

so $4x + 12 = 0$, giving $x = -3$.

Since there are several steps in the solution, it is a good idea to check the answer. If $x = -3$, $2^{x+1} = 2^{-2} = \dfrac{1}{2^2} = \frac{1}{4}$, $4^{x+2} = 4^{-1} = \frac{1}{4}$ and $8^{x+3} = 8^0 = 1$. So the left side is equal to $\frac{1}{4} \div \frac{1}{4} = 1$, which agrees with the right side.

One application of negative indices is in writing down very small numbers. You probably know how to write very large numbers in standard form, or scientific notation. For example, it is easier to write the speed of light as $3.00 \times 10^8 \text{ m s}^{-1}$ than as $300\,000\,000 \text{ m s}^{-1}$. Similarly, the wavelength of red light, about $0.000\,000\,75$ metres, is more easily appreciated written as 7.5×10^{-7} metres.

Computers and calculators often give users the option to work in scientific notation, and if numbers become too large (or too small) to be displayed in ordinary numerical form they will switch into standard form, for example 3.00E8 or 7.5E–7. The symbol E stands for **exponent**, yet another word for 'index'. You can write this in scientific notation by simply replacing the symbol E m by $\times 10^m$, for any integer m.

When you multiply or divide with numbers in standard form, the technique is to separate the powers of 10 from the rest of the expression to be evaluated, and to combine these using the rules for indices listed in Section 14.1.

At the end it may be necessary to make an adjustment to get the final answer in standard form. For example, if the calculation comes to 38.4×10^{-5}, you would write this as $(3.84 \times 10^1) \times 10^{-5}$, which is $3.84 \times (10^1 \times 10^{-5}) = 3.84 \times 10^{-4}$. If it comes to 0.093×10^{-3}, you would write it as $(9.3 \times 10^{-2}) \times 10^{-3}$, which is $9.3 \times (10^{-2} \times 10^{-3}) = 9.3 \times 10^{-5}$.

Example 14.2.6
Calculate the universal constant of gravitation, G, from $G = \dfrac{gR^2}{M}$ where, in SI units, $g \approx 9.81$, $R \approx 6.37 \times 10^6$ and $M \approx 5.97 \times 10^{24}$. ($R$ and M are the earth's radius and mass, and g is the acceleration due to gravity at the earth's surface.)

You can do this calculation directly with your calculator. If you enter the data in scientific mode, and key in the appropriate number of significant figures to retain, you will get the answer 6.67×10^{-11}.

The reasoning behind the calculation is as follows.

$$G \approx \frac{9.81 \times (6.37 \times 10^6)^2}{5.97 \times 10^{24}} = \frac{9.81 \times (6.37)^2}{5.97} \times \frac{(10^6)^2}{10^{24}}$$

$$\approx 66.7 \times \frac{10^{12}}{10^{24}} = 6.67 \times 10^1 \times 10^{-12} = 6.67 \times 10^{1-12} = 6.67 \times 10^{-11}.$$

Notice how, to get the correct power of 10, the number 66.7 has to be written as 6.67×10^1.

Exercise 14B

1 Express each of the following as an integer or a fraction.

(a) 2^{-3}
(b) 4^{-2}
(c) 5^{-1}
(d) 3^{-2}

(e) 10^{-4}
(f) 1^{-7}
(g) $\left(\frac{1}{2}\right)^{-1}$
(h) $\left(\frac{1}{3}\right)^{-3}$

(i) $\left(2\frac{1}{2}\right)^{-1}$
(j) 2^{-7}
(k) 6^{-3}
(l) $\left(1\frac{1}{3}\right)^{-3}$

2 If $x = 2$, find the value of each of the following.

(a) $4x^{-3}$
(b) $(4x)^{-3}$
(c) $\frac{1}{4}x^{-3}$

(d) $\left(\frac{1}{4}x\right)^{-3}$
(e) $(4 \div x)^{-3}$
(f) $(x \div 4)^{-3}$

3 If $y = 5$, find the value of each of the following.

(a) $(2y)^{-1}$
(b) $2y^{-1}$
(c) $\left(\frac{1}{2}y\right)^{-1}$

(d) $\frac{1}{2}y^{-1}$
(e) $\frac{1}{(2y)^{-1}}$
(f) $\frac{2}{(y^{-1})^{-1}}$

4 Express each of the following in as simple a form as possible.

(a) $a^4 \times a^{-3}$
(b) $\frac{1}{b^{-1}}$
(c) $(c^{-2})^3$

(d) $d^{-1} \times 2d$
(e) $e^{-4} \times e^{-5}$
(f) $\frac{f^{-2}}{f^3}$

(g) $12g^3 \times (2g^2)^{-2}$
(h) $(3h^2)^{-2}$
(i) $(3i^{-2})^{-2}$

(j) $\left(\frac{1}{2}j^{-2}\right)^{-3}$
(k) $(2x^3 y^{-1})^3$
(l) $(p^2 q^4 r^3)^{-4}$

(m) $(4m^2)^{-1} \times 8m^3$
(n) $(3n^{-2})^4 \times (9n)^{-1}$
(o) $(2q^{-2})^{-2} \div \left(\frac{4}{q}\right)^2$

5 Solve the following equations.

(a) $3^x = \frac{1}{9}$
(b) $5^y = 1$
(c) $2^z \times 2^{z-3} = 32$

(d) $7^{3x} \div 7^{x-2} = \frac{1}{49}$
(e) $4^y \times 2^y = 8^{120}$
(f) $3^t \times 9^{t+3} = 27^2$

6 The length of each edge of a cube is 3×10^{-2} metres.

(a) Find the volume of the cube.
(b) Find the total surface area of the cube.

7 An athlete runs 2×10^{-1} km in 7.5×10^{-3} hours. Find her average speed in km h^{-1}.

8 The volume, $V\,\text{m}^3$, of l metres of wire is given by $V = \pi r^2 l$, where r metres is the radius of the circular cross-section.

(a) Find the volume of 80 m of wire with radius of cross-section 2×10^{-3} m.

(b) Another type of wire has radius of cross-section 5×10^{-3} m. What length of this wire has a volume of $8 \times 10^{-3}\,\text{m}^3$?

(c) Another type of wire is such that a length of 61 m has a volume of $6 \times 10^{-3}\,\text{m}^3$. Find the radius of the cross-section.

9 An equation which occurs in the study of waves is $y = \dfrac{\lambda d}{a}$.

(a) Calculate y when $\lambda = 7 \times 10^{-7}$, $d = 5 \times 10^{-1}$ and $a = 8 \times 10^{-4}$.

(b) Calculate λ when $y = 10^{-3}$, $d = 0.6$ and $a = 2.7 \times 10^{-4}$.

10 Show that the binomial theorem can be written with sigma notation as

$$(a + b)^n = \sum_{i=0}^{n} \binom{n}{i} a^{n-i} b^i.$$

14.3   Fractional indices

Section 14.2 gave a meaning for the power a^m when m is any negative integer. It is possible to go further, and to find a meaning for a^m when m is any rational number.

Remember from Section 1.1 that a rational number is a number of the form $\dfrac{p}{q}$, where p and q are integers and q is not 0. For example, $\frac{3}{4}$, $\frac{8}{5}$ and $-\frac{7}{2}$ are rational numbers. The problem is to find a meaning for powers such as $a^{\frac{3}{4}}$, $a^{\frac{8}{5}}$ and $a^{-\frac{7}{2}}$.

To do this, suppose that the power-on-power rule can still be used if m is not an integer. For example, take $m = \frac{1}{2}$ and $n = 2$. Then the rule would give

$$\left(a^{\frac{1}{2}}\right)^2 = a^{\frac{1}{2} \times 2} = a^1, \quad \text{which is just } a.$$

So $a^{\frac{1}{2}}$ would be a number whose square is a.

There are only two numbers with this property, $+\sqrt{a}$ and $-\sqrt{a}$. Since in mathematics every symbol needs to have a definite meaning, a choice has to be made between these. So $a^{\frac{1}{2}}$ is defined to be the positive square root of a.

$$a^{\frac{1}{2}} = \sqrt{a}.$$

Now take $m = \frac{1}{3}$ and $n = 3$. The power-on-power rule then gives

$$\left(a^{\frac{1}{3}}\right)^3 = a^{\frac{1}{3} \times 3} = a^1 = a.$$

By the same reasoning as before, $a^{\frac{1}{3}}$ is the cube root of a. This time there is no ambiguity; each number has only one cube root.

$$a^{\frac{1}{3}} = \sqrt[3]{a}.$$

Notice that, for $a^{\frac{1}{2}} = \sqrt{a}$, the number a has to be positive or zero; $a^{\frac{1}{2}}$ has no meaning if a is negative. But for $a^{\frac{1}{3}} = \sqrt[3]{a}$, a can be positive, negative or zero; every number has a cube root.

Obviously the argument could be generalised to any rational number of the form $\dfrac{1}{q}$, using the power-on-power rule as

$$(a^{\frac{1}{q}})^q = a^{\frac{1}{q} \times q} = a^1 = a.$$

So $a^{\frac{1}{q}}$ is the qth root of a. If q is even, $a^{\frac{1}{q}}$ is defined to be the positive qth root.

$$a^{\frac{1}{q}} = \sqrt[q]{a}.$$

Example 14.3.1
Express as simply as possible   (a) $36^{\frac{1}{2}}$,   (b) $\left(\frac{1}{8}\right)^{\frac{1}{3}}$,   (c) $64^{-\frac{1}{2}}$.

(a) $36^{\frac{1}{2}} = \sqrt{36} = 6$.

(b) $\left(\frac{1}{8}\right)^{\frac{1}{3}} = \sqrt[3]{\frac{1}{8}} = \frac{1}{2}$.

(c) $64^{-\frac{1}{2}} = \dfrac{1}{64^{\frac{1}{2}}} = \frac{1}{8}$.

What about a power like $a^{\frac{2}{3}}$? You could find this by writing $\frac{2}{3}$ either as $\frac{1}{3} \times 2$ or as $2 \times \frac{1}{3}$ and using the power-on-power rule directly. This would give either

$$a^{\frac{2}{3}} = a^{\frac{1}{3} \times 2} = \left(a^{\frac{1}{3}}\right)^2 = (\sqrt[3]{a})^2, \quad \text{or} \quad a^{\frac{2}{3}} = a^{2 \times \frac{1}{3}} = (a^2)^{\frac{1}{3}} = \sqrt[3]{a^2}.$$

Both forms are equally valid. It makes no difference to the final answer whether you take the cube root first and then square, or square first and then take the cube root.

For practical calculation, the first form is the best to use if a has an exact cube root, and the second is best if it hasn't. For example, if you want to find $8^{\frac{2}{3}}$, it is slightly simpler to work out

$$8^{\frac{2}{3}} = (\sqrt[3]{8})^2 = 2^2 = 4$$

than $8^{\frac{2}{3}} = \sqrt[3]{8^2} = \sqrt[3]{64} = 4$.

But if you want $7^{\frac{2}{3}}$,

$$7^{\frac{2}{3}} = \sqrt[3]{7^2} = \sqrt[3]{49} = 3.6593...$$

has the edge over

$$7^{\frac{2}{3}} = (\sqrt[3]{7})^2 = (1.9129...)^2 = 3.6593....$$

By exactly the same reasoning, $a^{\frac{p}{q}}$ can be found either as

$$a^{\frac{p}{q}} = a^{\frac{1}{q} \times p} = \left(a^{\frac{1}{q}}\right)^p = (\sqrt[q]{a})^p, \quad \text{or as} \quad a^{\frac{p}{q}} = a^{p \times \frac{1}{q}} = (a^p)^{\frac{1}{q}} = \sqrt[q]{a^p}.$$

This is the general form of the **fractional power rule**:

$$a^{\frac{p}{q}} = (\sqrt[q]{a})^p = \sqrt[q]{a^p}.$$

Example 14.3.2

Simplify   (a) $9^{\frac{5}{2}}$,   (b) $3^{\frac{1}{2}} \times 3^{\frac{3}{2}}$,   (c) $16^{-\frac{3}{4}}$.

(a) $9^{\frac{5}{2}} = (\sqrt{9})^5 = 3^5 = 243$.

(b) $3^{\frac{1}{2}} \times 3^{\frac{3}{2}} = 3^{\frac{1}{2}+\frac{3}{2}} = 3^2 = 9$.

(c) **Method 1** $16^{-\frac{3}{4}} = (2^4)^{-\frac{3}{4}} = 2^{-3} = \frac{1}{8}$.

Method 2 $16^{-\frac{3}{4}} = \frac{1}{16^{\frac{3}{4}}} = \frac{1}{(\sqrt[4]{16})^3} = \frac{1}{2^3} = \frac{1}{8}$.

There are often good alternative ways for solving problems involving indices, and you should try experimenting with them. Many people prefer to think with positive indices rather than negative ones; if you are one of them, writing $16^{-\frac{3}{4}} = \dfrac{1}{16^{\frac{3}{4}}}$, as in Method 2 of Example 14.3.2 (c), makes good sense as a first step.

Example 14.3.3

Simplify   (a) $\left(2\frac{1}{4}\right)^{-\frac{1}{2}}$,   (b) $2x^{\frac{1}{2}} \times 3x^{-\frac{5}{2}}$,   (c) $(2x^2y^{-4})^{\frac{1}{2}}$.

(a) $\left(2\frac{1}{4}\right)^{-\frac{1}{2}} = \left(\frac{9}{4}\right)^{-\frac{1}{2}} = \dfrac{1}{\left(\frac{9}{4}\right)^{\frac{1}{2}}} = \left(\frac{4}{9}\right)^{\frac{1}{2}} = \sqrt{\frac{4}{9}} = \frac{2}{3}$.

(b) $2x^{\frac{1}{2}} \times 3x^{-\frac{5}{2}} = 6x^{\frac{1}{2}-\frac{5}{2}} = 6x^{-2} = \dfrac{6}{x^2}$.

(c) Using the factor rule and then the power-on-power rule,

$$\begin{aligned}
(2x^2y^{-4})^{\frac{1}{2}} &= 2^{\frac{1}{2}} \times (x^2)^{\frac{1}{2}} \times (y^{-4})^{\frac{1}{2}} \\
&= 2^{\frac{1}{2}} \times x^{2\times\frac{1}{2}} \times y^{-4\times\frac{1}{2}} \\
&= 2^{\frac{1}{2}} \times x^1 \times y^{-2} \\
&= \frac{x\sqrt{2}}{y^2}.
\end{aligned}$$

In Example 14.3.3, the answer given to part (c) breaks the convention of writing numbers before letters. It is sometimes safer to write $x\sqrt{2}$ rather than $\sqrt{2}x$ to avoid possible confusion with $\sqrt{2x}$.

You will quite often need to use the fractional power rule in reverse, to convert expressions involving roots into index notation. This is illustrated by the next example.

Example 14.3.4

Write in index notation   (a) $2x\sqrt{x}$,   (b) $\dfrac{6}{\sqrt[3]{x}}$,   (c) $\dfrac{1}{x^2\sqrt{x}}$.

(a) $2x\sqrt{x} = 2x^1 \times x^{\frac{1}{2}} = 2x^{1+\frac{1}{2}} = 2x^{\frac{3}{2}}$.

(b) $\dfrac{6}{\sqrt[3]{x}} = 6 \times \dfrac{1}{x^{\frac{1}{3}}} = 6x^{-\frac{1}{3}}$.

(c) $\dfrac{1}{x^2\sqrt{x}} = \dfrac{1}{x^2 \times x^{\frac{1}{2}}} = \dfrac{1}{x^{2+\frac{1}{2}}} = \dfrac{1}{x^{\frac{5}{2}}} = x^{-\frac{5}{2}}$.

14.4 Equations with rational indices

You have often solved equations such as $x^3 = 27$, $\sqrt{x} = 5$ and $\dfrac{1}{x} = 20$. But you probably have not realised that these are all equations of the same type, since they can all be written as $x^n = A$, with n equal to 3, $\tfrac{1}{2}$ and -1 respectively.

Here is a rather more complicated equation of the same type.

Example 14.4.1
Find x if $x^{\frac{3}{4}} = 27$.

If $x^{\frac{3}{4}}$ is raised to the power $\tfrac{4}{3}$, the power-on-power rule gives

$$\left(x^{\frac{3}{4}}\right)^{\frac{4}{3}} = x^{\frac{3}{4} \times \frac{4}{3}} = x^1 = x.$$

So the given equation can be solved by raising both sides to the power $\tfrac{4}{3}$. This gives

$$x = 27^{\frac{4}{3}} = (\sqrt[3]{27})^4 = 3^4 = 81.$$

As a check, if $x = 81$, then $x^{\frac{3}{4}} = 81^{\frac{3}{4}} = (\sqrt[4]{81})^3 = 3^3 = 27$.

The method used in this example can be used to solve any equation of the form $x^n = A$. Raising both sides to the power $\dfrac{1}{n}$ gives

$$(x^n)^{\frac{1}{n}} = A^{\frac{1}{n}}.$$

Since $(x^n)^{\frac{1}{n}} = x^{n \times \frac{1}{n}} = x^1 = x$, the solution of the equation is $x = A^{\frac{1}{n}}$.

Applying this to the three equations at the beginning of this section gives the solutions $27^{\frac{1}{3}} = 3$, $5^2 = 25$ and $20^{-1} = \tfrac{1}{20}$.

But you may have noticed a snag. If n is equal to 2, then $A^{\frac{1}{2}} = \sqrt{A}$ is only one of the roots of the equation $x^2 = A$; assuming that A is positive, there are two roots of the equation, $A^{\frac{1}{2}}$ and $-A^{\frac{1}{2}}$. The same happens if n is any even integer, or if it is a fraction with an even numerator such as $\tfrac{2}{3}$ or $\tfrac{4}{5}$. So to make this into a general rule it would be safer to restrict it to positive values of x and A.

> If n is a rational number and $A > 0$, the positive solution of the equation $x^n = A$ is $x = A^{\frac{1}{n}}$.

Example 14.4.2
Solve the equation $x^{\frac{3}{2}} = 10$ for $x > 0$, giving your answer correct to 3 significant figures.

If $n = \tfrac{3}{2}$, then $\dfrac{1}{n} = \tfrac{2}{3}$. The solution of the equation is therefore

$$x = 10^{\frac{2}{3}} = \sqrt[3]{10^2} = \sqrt[3]{100} = 4.64, \text{ correct to 3 significant figures.}$$

Section 11.6 introduced some equations which were not obviously quadratic, but could be converted to quadratic form by by making a suitable substitution. For example, the equation $\sqrt{x} = 6 - x$ became $y = 6 - y^2$ after writing $\sqrt{x}$ as y.

Equations like this sometimes appear in index form. For example, $\sqrt{x} = 6 - x$ might turn up as $x^{\frac{1}{2}} = 6 - x$, You would then solve it by writing $x^{\frac{1}{2}} = y$, so that $x = y^2$.

Example 14.4.3

Solve the equation $5x^{\frac{1}{3}} = x^{\frac{2}{3}} + 4$.

The key is to notice that $x^{\frac{2}{3}} = \left(x^{\frac{1}{3}}\right)^2$. So if you write $x^{\frac{1}{3}}$ as u, the equation is

$$5u = u^2 + 4,$$

a quadratic equation for u. Writing this as

$$u^2 - 5u + 4 = 0,$$
$$(u - 1)(u - 4) = 0,$$

the roots for u are 1 and 4.

Since the values of x are required, it is now necessary to solve for x the equations

$$x^{\frac{1}{3}} = 1 \quad \text{and} \quad x^{\frac{1}{3}} = 4.$$

This gives two roots for x,

$$x = 1^3 = 1 \quad \text{and} \quad x = 4^3 = 64.$$

14.5   Powers of negative bases

So far in this chapter it has been assumed that the base a is a positive number. This section investigates whether the negative and fractional power rules still apply if the base is a negative number.

You have often used positive integer powers with negative bases. For example,

$$(-5)^2 = (-5) \times (-5) = +5^2, (-5)^3 = (-5) \times (-5) \times (-5) = -5^3, \text{ and so on.}$$

There is no problem in extending this to negative integer indices. For example,

$$(-5)^{-2} = \frac{1}{(-5)^2} = \frac{1}{5^2} = +5^{-2}, (-5)^{-3} = \frac{1}{(-5)^3} = \frac{1}{-5^3} = -\frac{1}{5^3} = -5^{-3}, \text{ and so on.}$$

You can sum up these results in a single rule:

> If m is an integer (positive, negative or zero), and a is a positive number, then
>
> $$(-a)^m = \begin{cases} +a^m & \text{if } m \text{ is an even integer or zero,} \\ -a^m & \text{if } m \text{ is an odd integer.} \end{cases}$$

The situation is different when m is a fractional index. For example, taking a to be -64, you can write $(-64)^{\frac{1}{3}} = -4$. This is because $a^{\frac{1}{3}} = \sqrt[3]{a}$, and $(-4)^3 = -64$, so that $\sqrt[3]{-64} = -4$. But $(-64)^{\frac{1}{2}}$ has no meaning, because $a^{\frac{1}{2}} = \sqrt{a}$, and a negative number doesn't have a square root.

You can reason similarly for any index of the form $\frac{1}{q}$, and sum the results up in another rule:

> If q is an integer, either positive or negative but not zero, and a is a positive number, then
>
> $$(-a)^{\frac{1}{q}} = \begin{cases} \text{has no meaning if } q \text{ is even,} \\ -a^{\frac{1}{q}} \text{ if } q \text{ is odd.} \end{cases}$$

Example 14.5.1

Find, where possible, (a) $(-8)^{\frac{1}{3}}$, (b) $(-32)^{-\frac{1}{5}}$, (c) $(-81)^{\frac{1}{4}}$.

(a) $(-8)^{\frac{1}{3}} = \sqrt[3]{-8} = -2$, because $(-2)^3 = -8$.

(b) $(-32)^{-\frac{1}{5}} = \dfrac{1}{(-32)^{\frac{1}{5}}} = \dfrac{1}{-32^{\frac{1}{5}}} = -\frac{1}{2}$.

(c) $(-81)^{\frac{1}{4}}$ has no meaning; $\sqrt[4]{-81}$ doesn't exist, because there is no number x such that $x^4 = -81$.

What about other fractional powers? Here the situation is a bit more complicated, but a few numerical examples will illustrate the possibilities.

Example 14.5.2

Find, where possible,

(a) $(-27)^{\frac{2}{3}}$,   (b) $(-16)^{\frac{3}{4}}$,   (c) $(-8)^{\frac{5}{3}}$,   (d) $(-32)^{-\frac{3}{5}}$,   (e) $(-125)^{-\frac{2}{3}}$.

(a) $(-27)^{\frac{2}{3}}$ is $(\sqrt[3]{-27})^2 = (-3)^2 = 9$.

(b) $(-16)^{\frac{3}{4}}$ would be $(\sqrt[4]{-16})^3$; but since $\sqrt[4]{-16}$ does not exist, neither does $(-16)^{\frac{3}{4}}$.

(c) $(-8)^{\frac{5}{3}}$ is $(\sqrt[3]{-8})^5 = (-2)^5 = -32$.

(d) $(-32)^{-\frac{3}{5}} = \dfrac{1}{(-32)^{\frac{3}{5}}}$, which is $\dfrac{1}{(\sqrt[5]{-32})^3} = \dfrac{1}{(-2)^3} = \dfrac{1}{-8} = -\frac{1}{8}$.

(e) $(-125)^{-\frac{2}{3}} = \dfrac{1}{(-125)^{\frac{2}{3}}}$, which is $\dfrac{1}{(\sqrt[3]{-125})^2} = \dfrac{1}{(-5)^2} = \frac{1}{25}$.

You can see from this example that, when the expression has a meaning, the answer is sometimes positive and sometimes negative.

Exercise 14C

1 Evaluate the following without using a calculator.

(a) $25^{\frac{1}{2}}$ (b) $8^{\frac{1}{3}}$ (c) $36^{\frac{1}{2}}$ (d) $32^{\frac{1}{5}}$

(e) $81^{\frac{1}{4}}$ (f) $9^{-\frac{1}{2}}$ (g) $16^{-\frac{1}{4}}$ (h) $49^{-\frac{1}{2}}$

(i) $1000^{-\frac{1}{3}}$ (j) $(-27)^{\frac{1}{3}}$ (k) $64^{\frac{2}{3}}$ (l) $(-125)^{-\frac{4}{3}}$

2 Evaluate the following without using a calculator.

(a) $4^{\frac{1}{2}}$ (b) $\left(\frac{1}{4}\right)^2$ (c) $\left(\frac{1}{4}\right)^{-2}$ (d) $4^{-\frac{1}{2}}$

(e) $\left(\frac{1}{4}\right)^{-\frac{1}{2}}$ (f) $\left(\frac{1}{4}\right)^{\frac{1}{2}}$ (g) $(4^4)^{\frac{1}{2}}$ (h) $\left(\left(\frac{1}{4}\right)^{\frac{1}{4}}\right)^2$

3 Evaluate the following without using a calculator.

(a) $8^{\frac{2}{3}}$ (b) $4^{\frac{3}{2}}$ (c) $9^{-\frac{3}{2}}$ (d) $27^{\frac{4}{3}}$

(e) $32^{\frac{2}{5}}$ (f) $32^{\frac{3}{5}}$ (g) $64^{-\frac{5}{6}}$ (h) $4^{2\frac{1}{2}}$

(i) $10\,000^{-\frac{3}{4}}$ (j) $\left(\frac{1}{125}\right)^{-\frac{4}{3}}$ (k) $\left(3\frac{3}{8}\right)^{\frac{2}{3}}$ (l) $\left(2\frac{1}{4}\right)^{-\frac{1}{2}}$

4 Simplify the following expressions.

(a) $a^{\frac{1}{3}} \times a^{\frac{5}{3}}$ (b) $3b^{\frac{1}{2}} \times 4b^{-\frac{3}{2}}$ (c) $\left(6c^{\frac{1}{4}}\right) \times (4c)^{\frac{1}{2}}$

(d) $(d^2)^{\frac{1}{3}} \div \left(d^{\frac{1}{3}}\right)^2$ (e) $(24e)^{\frac{1}{3}} \div (3e)^{\frac{1}{3}}$ (f) $(25p^2q^4)^{\frac{1}{2}}$

5 Solve the following equations, given that $x > 0$.

(a) $x^{\frac{1}{2}} = 8$ (b) $x^{\frac{1}{3}} = 3$ (c) $x^{\frac{2}{3}} = 4$ (d) $x^{\frac{3}{2}} = 27$

(e) $x^{-\frac{3}{2}} = 8$ (f) $x^{-\frac{2}{3}} = 9$ (g) $x^{\frac{3}{2}} = x\sqrt{2}$ (h) $x^{\frac{3}{2}} = 2\sqrt{x}$

6 The time, T seconds, taken by a pendulum of length l metres to complete one swing is given by $T = 2\pi l^{\frac{1}{2}} g^{-\frac{1}{2}}$ where $g \approx 9.81\,\mathrm{m\,s^{-2}}$.

(a) Find the value of T for a pendulum of length 0.9 metres.

(b) Find the length of a pendulum which takes 3 seconds for a complete swing.

7 The radius, r cm, of a sphere of volume V cm^3 is given by $r = \left(\dfrac{3V}{4\pi}\right)^{\frac{1}{3}}$. Find the radius of a sphere of volume $1150\,\mathrm{cm^3}$.

8 Solve the following equations.

(a) $4^x = 32$ (b) $9^y = \frac{1}{27}$ (c) $16^z = 2$ (d) $100^x = 1000$

(e) $8^y = 16$ (f) $8^z = \frac{1}{128}$ (g) $(2^t)^3 \times 4^{t-1} = 16$

9 Solve the following equations.

(a) $x^{\frac{1}{2}} + 2x^{-\frac{1}{2}} = 3$ (b) $x + x^{\frac{1}{2}} = 12$ (c) $1 + x = 2x^{\frac{1}{2}}$

(d) $x^{\frac{2}{3}} = 2x^{\frac{1}{3}}$ (e) $x^{\frac{1}{3}} = 2x^{-\frac{1}{3}}$ (f) $2x^{\frac{1}{3}} + x^{\frac{2}{3}} = 3$

10 Rewrite the following expressions using index notation.

(a) $\dfrac{1}{\sqrt{x}}$ (b) $4\sqrt{x}$ (c) $\sqrt{4x}$

(d) $3x^2\sqrt{x}$ (e) $\dfrac{1}{\sqrt[3]{x^2}}$ (f) $\dfrac{6}{x\sqrt[3]{x}}$

11 Simplify the following by using index notation. Give your final answers in surd form.

(a) $\sqrt[3]{4} \times \sqrt[3]{6}$ (b) $\dfrac{\sqrt{50}}{\sqrt[3]{250}}$ (c) $\sqrt[6]{\frac{2}{3}} \times \sqrt[3]{18}$

12 (a) Without using a calculator, state which of these expressions has a value when $x = -64$. Find this value when it exists.

(i) $x^{\frac{2}{3}}$ (ii) $x^{\frac{3}{2}}$ (iii) $x^{-\frac{1}{3}}$ (iv) $\left(\frac{1}{2}x\right)^{\frac{4}{5}}$ (v) $x^{\frac{1}{6}}$ (vi) $(4x)^{\frac{3}{4}}$

(b) Investigate whether your calculator gives the answers you obtained in part (a).

(c) What can you say about p or q if $x^{\frac{p}{q}}$ has a value when x is negative?

15 Graphs of *n*th power functions

In this chapter the work of Chapters 9 and 12 is extended to include graphs with equations $y = x^n$ where n is any rational number. When you have completed it, you should

- be familiar with the shapes of these graphs, particularly when n is either a negative integer or $\frac{1}{2}$
- know that the rule for differentiating x^n is valid when n is any rational number.

15.1 Graphs of negative integer powers

In Section 9.3 you investigated the shapes of graphs with equations $y = x^n$ for positive integer values of n. You can now extend the investigation to negative values of n.

A negative integer n can be written as $-m$, where m is a positive integer. Then x^n becomes x^{-m}, or $\frac{1}{x^m}$.

It is simplest to begin with the part of the graph for which x is positive, then to use this to extend the graph for negative x.

Figure 9.4 showed the graphs of $y = x^n$ for $x \geq 0$ when n is 1, 2, 3 and 4. These graphs are reproduced here as Fig. 15.1.

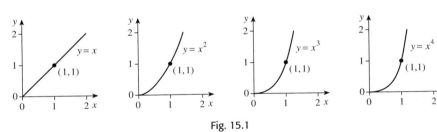

Fig. 15.1

All these graphs are in the first quadrant when $x > 0$, and they all include the origin and the point (1, 1).

When x is positive, $\frac{1}{x^m}$ is also positive, so the graphs of $y = x^{-m}$ are also in the first quadrant when $x > 0$. Also, just as when n is positive, the graphs include the point (1, 1).

But there is an important difference when $x = 0$, since then $x^m = 0$ and $\frac{1}{x^m}$ is not defined. So there is no point on these graphs for which $x = 0$.

To look at this more closely, take a value of x close to 0, say 0.01. Then for $n = -1$ the corresponding value of y is $0.01^{-1} = \frac{1}{0.01^1} = \frac{1}{0.01} = 100$; and for $n = -2$ it is $0.01^{-2} = \frac{1}{0.01^2} = \frac{1}{0.0001} = 10\,000$. Even if you use a very small scale, the graphs will disappear off the top of the page or the calculator window as x is reduced towards 0.

What happens if x is large? For example, take $x = 100$. Then for $n = -1$ the corresponding value of y is $100^{-1} = \dfrac{1}{100^1} = \frac{1}{100} = 0.01$; and for $n = -2$ it is $100^{-2} = \dfrac{1}{100^2} = \frac{1}{10\,000} = 0.0001$. So x^n becomes very small, and the graphs come very close to the x-axis.

These are the main things you need to know to draw the graphs for positive values of x. They are shown in Fig. 15.2 for $n = -1, -2, -3$ and -4.

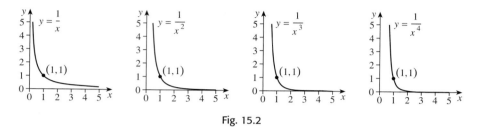

Fig. 15.2

Now consider the part of the graphs for which x is negative. You found in Chapter 9 that, for positive n, this depends on whether n is odd or even. The same is true when n is negative, and for the same reason. If n is even, x^n is an even function and its graph is symmetrical about the y-axis. If n is odd, x^n is an odd function and its graph is symmetrical about the origin.

Figure 15.3 shows the graphs of $y = x^{-1}$ and $y = x^{-2}$ extended in this way, for all values of x except 0. Notice that, for both graphs, the x- and y-axes are asymptotes.

Try sketching for yourself the corresponding graphs of $y = x^{-3}$ and $y = x^{-4}$. Then use a calculator to check your sketches.

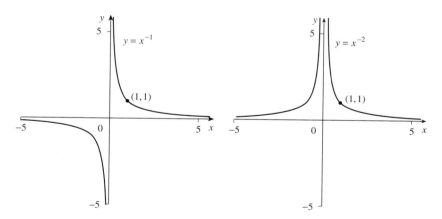

Fig. 15.3

15.2 Differentiation with negative integer indices

In Chapter 12 you found that, for positive integer powers of x, the derivative of $f(x) = x^n$ is $f'(x) = nx^{n-1}$. An obvious question to ask is whether this is still true when n is a negative integer.

You could investigate this in a number of ways:

- using the evidence of the graphs
- with a numerical check
- by algebraic proof of particular cases.

The three examples which follow illustrate each of these in turn, for the cases $n = -1$ and $n = -2$. If the rule still holds when n is negative, the derivatives would be as follows.

$$n = -1: \text{if } y = x^{-1} = \frac{1}{x}, \text{ then } \frac{dy}{dx} = -1 \times x^{-2} = -\frac{1}{x^2}.$$

$$n = -2: \text{if } y = x^{-2} = \frac{1}{x^2}, \text{ then } \frac{dy}{dx} = -2 \times x^{-3} = -\frac{2}{x^3}.$$

Example 15.2.1

Find whether the suggested differentiation rules are consistent with the graphs

(a) when $n = -1$,   (b) when $n = -2$.

Some calculators are able, once you have displayed the graph of $y = f(x)$, to show with the same axes the graph of $y = f'(x)$. So for part (a), if you key in $y_1 = \frac{1}{x}$, $y_2 = \frac{dy_1}{dx}$ (consult the manual to find how to do this) and $y_3 = -\frac{1}{x^2}$, you can see whether y_2 and y_3 are the same graph. For part (b) do the same thing with $y_1 = \frac{1}{x^2}$ and $y_3 = -\frac{2}{x^3}$.

Alternatively, you can argue less precisely as follows. Note first that, for both graphs in Fig. 15.3, the gradient is very steep when x is close to 0, and very gentle when x is a long way from 0. This is in line with the expressions suggested for $\frac{dy}{dx}$ for both $n = -1$ and $n = -2$.

(a) If $y = x^{-1}$, Fig. 15.3 shows that the gradient of the graph is negative both when x is positive and when x is negative. This is consistent with the suggested derivative $\frac{dy}{dx} = -\frac{1}{x^2}$, which is negative both when $x > 0$ and when $x < 0$.

(b) If $y = x^{-2}$, Fig. 15.3 shows that the gradient of the graph is negative when x is positive, and positive when x is negative. This is consistent with the suggested derivative $\frac{dy}{dx} = -\frac{2}{x^3}$, which is negative when $x > 0$ but positive when $x < 0$.

Example 15.2.2

Make a numerical estimate of the gradient of the tangent to $y = \dfrac{1}{x^2}$ at the point $(2, 0.25)$, and check that this agrees with the value given by the rule $\dfrac{dy}{dx} = -\dfrac{2}{x^3}$.

From Fig. 15.3, you would expect the gradient of the tangent to be less than the gradient of a chord to the right of $(2, 0.25)$, and greater than the gradient of a chord to the left. (Note that all these gradients are negative.)

Take first the chord joining $(2, 0.25)$ to $(2.01, 0.247\,51...)$. For this chord,

$$\delta x = 2.01 - 2 = 0.01, \quad \delta y = 0.247\,51... - 0.25 = -0.002\,48...,$$

and $\quad \dfrac{\delta y}{\delta x} = \dfrac{-0.002\,48...}{0.01} = -0.248...$.

Now take the chord joining $(2, 0.25)$ to $(1.99, 0.252\,51...)$. For this chord,

$$\delta x = 1.99 - 2 = -0.01, \quad \delta y = 0.252\,51... - 0.25 = 0.002\,51...,$$

and $\quad \dfrac{\delta y}{\delta x} = \dfrac{0.002\,51...}{-0.01} = -0.251...$.

So the gradient of the tangent is less than $-0.248...$ and greater than $-0.251...$. A reasonable guess is that the gradient is -0.25.

When $x = 2$, the suggested derivative $-\dfrac{2}{x^3} = -\dfrac{2}{2^3} = -0.25$. So the numerical estimate supports the value given by the differentiation rule.

You could use the derivative program on a calculator to do a numerical check for some other values of x and some other negative powers.

Using the algebraic definition of $f'(x)$ given in Section 12.6 is not so easy with negative powers. Example 15.2.3 does this for the simplest case, $n = -1$.

Example 15.2.3

Find the derivative of $f(x) = \dfrac{1}{x}$ using the definition $f'(x) = \lim\limits_{h \to 0} \dfrac{f(x+h) - f(x)}{h}$.

Begin by finding

$$f(x + h) - f(x) = \frac{1}{x+h} - \frac{1}{x}.$$

To simplify this, you must write both fractions with the same denominator.

$$\frac{1}{x+h} - \frac{1}{x} = \frac{x}{x(x+h)} - \frac{x+h}{x(x+h)}$$
$$= \frac{x - (x+h)}{x(x+h)}$$
$$= \frac{-h}{x(x+h)}.$$

So $\quad \dfrac{f(x+h) - f(x)}{h} = \dfrac{-1}{x(x+h)}.$

You now want to find the limit of this as $h \to 0$. The only place where h appears is inside the bracket, and the limit of $x + h$ is simply x. It follows that

$$f'(x) = \lim_{h \to 0} \frac{f(x+h) - f(x)}{h}$$

$$= \frac{-1}{x \times x} = \frac{-1}{x^2}.$$

The results of these examples don't add up to a proof that the differentiation rule works with all negative integer indices, but the evidence is encouraging. It is in fact correct, but it is not possible to give a proof at this stage.

If you write $n = -m$, so that $f(x) = x^{-m} = \frac{1}{x^m}$, the rule gives $f'(x) = -mx^{-m-1} = -\frac{m}{x^{m+1}}$.

If $f(x) = \frac{1}{x^m}$, where m is a positive integer, then

$$f'(x) = -\frac{m}{x^{m+1}}.$$

There is no need to learn this as a separate rule. In any particular case you can just use $f'(x) = nx^{n-1}$ with a negative value for n. But after some practice you will probably find yourself using it without thinking.

Example 15.2.4

Find $\frac{dy}{dx}$ if (a) $y = \frac{2}{x^4}$, (b) $y = \frac{1}{5x^5}$, (c) $y = \frac{x-3}{x^2}$.

(a) Write y as $2 \times \frac{1}{x^4} = 2x^{-4}$.

Then $\frac{dy}{dx} = 2 \times (-4x^{-5}) = -8x^{-5} = -\frac{8}{x^5}$.

(b) Write y as $\frac{1}{5} \times \frac{1}{x^5} = \frac{1}{5}x^{-5}$.

Then $\frac{dy}{dx} = \frac{1}{5} \times (-5x^{-6}) = -x^{-6} = -\frac{1}{x^6}$.

(c) Split the function as $y = \frac{x}{x^2} - \frac{3}{x^2} = \frac{1}{x} - \frac{3}{x^2} = x^{-1} - 3x^{-2}$.

Then $\frac{dy}{dx} = -x^{-2} + 6x^{-3} = -\frac{1}{x^2} + \frac{6}{x^3}$.

You may sometimes want to write this as a single fraction, as in the original equation.

$$\frac{dy}{dx} = -\frac{x}{x^3} + \frac{6}{x^3} = \frac{-x+6}{x^3} = \frac{6-x}{x^3}.$$

Example 15.2.5

(a) Find the equation of the normal to $y = \dfrac{1}{x}$ at the point $\left(\tfrac{1}{2}, 2\right)$.

(b) Find where this normal cuts the curve again.

(a) It helps to accompany the solution with a sketch (Fig. 15.4), and to use it to check the accuracy of the calculations as you go on.

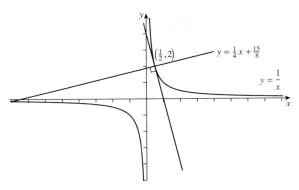

Fig. 15.4

Since $\dfrac{\mathrm{d}y}{\mathrm{d}x} = -\dfrac{1}{x^2}$, the gradient of the tangent at $\left(\tfrac{1}{2}, 2\right)$ is $-\dfrac{1}{\left(\frac{1}{2}\right)^2} = -4$. The gradient of the normal is therefore, by the rule in Section 8.4, $-\dfrac{1}{-4} = \tfrac{1}{4}$.

The equation of the normal is

$$y - 2 = \tfrac{1}{4}\left(x - \tfrac{1}{2}\right), \qquad \text{or more simply} \qquad y = \tfrac{1}{4}x + \tfrac{15}{8}.$$

(b) To find where the normal meets the curve again, equate the values of y in the two equations to get

$$\frac{1}{x} = \tfrac{1}{4}x + \tfrac{15}{8}.$$

Multiplying this by $8x$ and rearranging the terms produces the quadratic equation

$$2x^2 + 15x - 8 = 0.$$

The factors of the left side may not be immediately obvious. But remember that you already know one root, $x = \tfrac{1}{2}$, because the normal certainly cuts the curve at $\left(\tfrac{1}{2}, 2\right)$. So $2x - 1$ must be one factor. It is then easy to see that the left side factorises to give

$$(2x - 1)(x + 8) = 0.$$

The other intersection is therefore where $x = -8$. Substituting this in $y = \dfrac{1}{x}$ gives the y-coordinate of the point of intersection as $y = \dfrac{1}{-8} = -\tfrac{1}{8}$. (You could equally well substitute in $y = \tfrac{1}{4}x + \tfrac{15}{8}$, but the arithmetic is harder.)

The normal meets the curve again at $\left(-8, -\tfrac{1}{8}\right)$.

Exercise 15A

1 Find the point(s) of intersection of these pairs of graphs. Check your answers with a calculator.

(a) $y = x^2$, $y = 8x^{-1}$

(b) $y = x^{-1}$, $y = 3x^{-2}$

(c) $y = x$, $y = 4x^{-3}$

(d) $y = 8x^{-2}$, $y = 2x^{-4}$

(e) $y = 9x^{-3}$, $y = x^{-5}$

(f) $y = \frac{1}{4}x^4$, $y = 16x^{-2}$

2 For what values of x are these inequalities satisfied? Sketch graphs illustrating your answers.

(a) $0 < x^{-3} < 0.001$

(b) $x^{-2} < 0.0004$

(c) $x^{-4} \geq 100$

(d) $8x^{-4} < 0.00005$

3 Three graphs have equations   (p) $y = x^{-2}$,   (q) $y = x^{-3}$,   (r) $y = x^{-4}$.

A line $x = k$ meets the three graphs at points P, Q and R, respectively. Give the order of the points P, Q and R on the line (from the bottom up) when k takes the following values.

(a) 2

(b) $\frac{1}{2}$

(c) $-\frac{1}{2}$

(d) -2

4 Differentiate each of the following functions. For each part, give your answer in two forms: the first using a negative index, and the second with a positive index.

(a) x^{-2}

(b) x^{-5}

(c) $3x^{-3}$

(d) $-2x^{-2}$

(e) $\frac{1}{4}x^{-4}$

(f) $-\frac{1}{3}x^{-6}$

5 Differentiate each of these functions $f(x)$. Give your answers $f'(x)$ in a similar form, without negative indices.

(a) $\dfrac{5}{x}$

(b) $\dfrac{1}{4x}$

(c) $\dfrac{3}{x^2}$

(d) x^0

(e) $\dfrac{3}{x} + \dfrac{1}{3x^3}$

(f) $\dfrac{x - 2}{x^2}$

6 Find the equation of the tangent to the curve at the given point.

(a) $y = \dfrac{4}{x}$ at $(1, 4)$

(b) $y = \dfrac{1}{x^2}$ at $(1, 1)$

(c) $y = \dfrac{1}{3x^2}$ at $\left(\frac{1}{3}, 3\right)$

(d) $y = x + \dfrac{9}{x}$ at $(3, 6)$

(e) $y = \dfrac{1 - x}{x^3}$ at $(1, 0)$

(f) $y = \dfrac{x^2 - 4}{x^3}$ at $(-2, 0)$

7 Find the equation of the normal to the curve at the given point.

(a) $y = \dfrac{4}{x^2}$ at $(2, 1)$

(b) $y = \dfrac{1}{2x^4}$ at $\left(1, \frac{1}{2}\right)$

(c) $y = x^2 + \dfrac{16}{x^2}$ at $(2, 8)$

(d) $y = \dfrac{x + 2}{x^3}$ at $(-1, -1)$

15.3 Graphs of $y = x^n$ for fractional n

When fractional values of n are included, the graphs of $y = x^n$ have many different possible shapes. One new feature is that, when n is a fraction, the function x^n may or may not be defined for negative values of x. For example, $x^{\frac{1}{3}}$ (the cube root of x) and $x^{-\frac{4}{3}}$ have values when $x < 0$, but $x^{\frac{1}{2}}$ (the square root of x) and $x^{-\frac{3}{4}}$ do not. Even when x^n is defined for negative x, some calculators are not programmed to do the calculation. So it is simplest to concentrate on values of $x \geq 0$.

Much the most important of these graphs is that of $y = x^{\frac{1}{2}}$, or $y = \sqrt{x}$. The clue to finding the shape of this graph is to note that if $y = x^{\frac{1}{2}}$, then $x = y^2$. The graph can therefore be obtained from that of $y = x^2$ by swapping the x- and y-axes. This has the effect of tipping the graph on its side, so that instead of facing upwards it faces to the right.

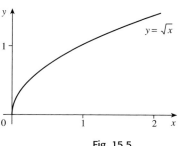

Fig. 15.5

But this is not quite the whole story. If $x = y^2$, then either $y = +\sqrt{x}$ or $y = -\sqrt{x}$. Since you want only the first of these possibilities, you must remove the part of the graph of $x = y^2$ below the x-axis, leaving only the part shown in Fig. 15.5 as the graph of $y = x^{\frac{1}{2}}$, or $y = \sqrt{x}$.

Check this with your calculator.

Notice that the graph exists only for $x \geq 0$, as you would expect. The tangent to the graph at the origin is the y-axis.

It is worth experimenting for yourself with various other fractional powers, using your calculator. You will find that:

- it is still true that the graph of $y = x^n$ contains the point $(1, 1)$;
- if n is positive it also contains the point $(0, 0)$;
- if $n > 1$ the x-axis is a tangent to the graph; if $0 < n < 1$ the y-axis is a tangent. (To show this convincingly you may need to zoom in to display an enlarged version of the graph close to the origin.)

To illustrate the variety of shapes which are possible when both positive and negative values of x are included, Fig. 15.6 shows six graphs with equation $y = x^n$ where n is a positive fraction.

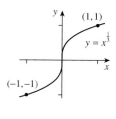
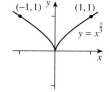
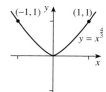

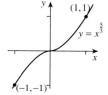
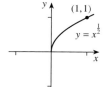
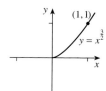

Fig. 15.6

15.4   The differentiation rule with fractional indices

You will probably not be surprised that the differentiation rule for $y = x^n$ still holds when the index n is a fraction.

Example 15.4.1

Assuming the usual differentiation rule, find $\dfrac{dy}{dx}$ when

(a) $y = \sqrt{x}$,   (b) $y = x\sqrt{x}$,   (c) $y = \dfrac{1}{\sqrt{x}}$.

(a) Since $\sqrt{x} = x^{\frac{1}{2}}$, the rule $\dfrac{dy}{dx} = nx^{n-1}$ gives $\dfrac{dy}{dx} = \frac{1}{2}x^{-\frac{1}{2}}$.

In surd notation, $x^{-\frac{1}{2}} = \dfrac{1}{x^{\frac{1}{2}}} = \dfrac{1}{\sqrt{x}}$. So $\dfrac{dy}{dx} = \frac{1}{2} \times \dfrac{1}{\sqrt{x}} = \dfrac{1}{2\sqrt{x}}$.

(b) In index notation, $x\sqrt{x} = x^1 \times x^{\frac{1}{2}} = x^{\frac{3}{2}}$.

So $\dfrac{dy}{dx} = \frac{3}{2}x^{\frac{1}{2}} = \frac{3}{2}\sqrt{x}$.

(c) In index notation, $\dfrac{1}{\sqrt{x}} = x^{-\frac{1}{2}}$.

So $\dfrac{dy}{dx} = -\frac{1}{2}x^{-\frac{3}{2}} = -\frac{1}{2} \times \dfrac{1}{x\sqrt{x}} = -\dfrac{1}{2x\sqrt{x}}$.

The proof of the differentiation rule with fractional indices is too difficult to give in full at this stage. You can, of course, check it for any particular function as in Examples 15.2.1 and 15.2.2, and it would be worth doing this using the derivative program on your calculator. You can also give a proof for a few special functions. Example 15.4.2 does this for $n = \frac{1}{2}$.

Example 15.4.2

Find the derivative of $f(x) = \sqrt{x}$ using the definition $f'(x) = \lim\limits_{h \to 0} \dfrac{f(x+h) - f(x)}{h}$.

You have to find the limit, as $h \to 0$, of

$$\dfrac{\sqrt{x+h} - \sqrt{x}}{h}.$$

The difficulty is to express the numerator $\sqrt{x+h} - \sqrt{x}$ in a form which makes it possible to cancel h from the top and bottom lines of the fraction.

The clue is to use the difference of two squares,

$$p^2 - q^2 = (p - q)(p + q),$$

with $p = \sqrt{x+h}$ and $q = \sqrt{x}$. This gives

$$(x + h) - x = (\sqrt{x+h} - \sqrt{x})(\sqrt{x+h} + \sqrt{x}),$$

so that

$$\sqrt{x+h} - \sqrt{x} = \dfrac{h}{\sqrt{x+h} + \sqrt{x}}.$$

Then

$$\frac{\sqrt{x+h}-\sqrt{x}}{h} = \frac{1}{\sqrt{x+h}+\sqrt{x}},$$

and

$$f'(x) = \lim_{h\to 0} \frac{\sqrt{x+h}-\sqrt{x}}{h}$$

$$= \lim_{h\to 0} \frac{1}{\sqrt{x+h}+\sqrt{x}}.$$

You will see that h appears only once in this last expression and, as $h \to 0$, $\sqrt{x+h} \to \sqrt{x}$. So

$$f'(x) = \frac{1}{\sqrt{x}+\sqrt{x}} = \frac{1}{2\sqrt{x}}.$$

This is the result obtained in Example 15.4.1(a) by using the usual rule for differentiating powers of x. Notice that, although the domain of $f(x)$ is $x \geq 0$, the domain of $f'(x)$ is $x > 0$; the derivative is not defined when $x = 0$. This is illustrated by Fig. 15.5, which shows that the tangent to $y = \sqrt{x}$ at the origin is the y-axis.

You could go on accumulating more evidence by using the method in Example 15.4.2 to differentiate other similar functions, but the algebra would be more complicated. You should by now have seen enough examples to justify the general rule for any rational power of x, positive or negative.

> If $f(x) = x^n$, where n is a rational number, then $f'(x) = nx^{n-1}$.

Compare this with the similar statement in the blue box in Section 12.4, which was restricted to positive integer values of n.

Example 15.4.3
Find the equation of the tangent to $y = \sqrt[3]{x}$ at the point $(8, 2)$.

In index notation $\sqrt[3]{x} = x^{\frac{1}{3}}$. So the rule gives $\dfrac{dy}{dx} = \frac{1}{3}x^{(\frac{1}{3}-1)} = \frac{1}{3}x^{-\frac{2}{3}}$.

In surd notation this is $\dfrac{1}{3(\sqrt[3]{x})^2}$.

The gradient of the tangent at $(8, 2)$ is therefore $\dfrac{1}{3(\sqrt[3]{8})^2} = \dfrac{1}{3 \times 2^2} = \frac{1}{12}$.

Thus the equation of the tangent is

$$y - 2 = \tfrac{1}{12}(x - 8), \text{ which is } 12y = x + 16.$$

Exercise 15B

1 Differentiate each of the following functions. Give your answer with a fractional index.

(a) $x^{\frac{1}{3}}$ (b) $x^{\frac{5}{2}}$ (c) $5x^{\frac{2}{5}}$

(d) $-5x^{-\frac{3}{5}}$ (e) $4x^{-\frac{1}{2}}$ (f) $-2x^{-\frac{3}{2}}$

2 Differentiate each of these functions $f(x)$. Give your answers $f'(x)$ in a similar form, without negative or fractional indices.

(a) $\sqrt[4]{x^3}$ (b) $6\sqrt[3]{x}$ (c) $\dfrac{4}{\sqrt{x}}$

(d) $\sqrt{16x^5}$ (e) $\dfrac{1}{\sqrt[3]{8x}}$ (f) $\dfrac{1+x}{\sqrt[4]{x}}$

3 On each of the graphs   (a) $y = x^{\frac{1}{3}}$,   (b) $y = x^{\frac{2}{3}}$,   (c) $y = x^{-\frac{2}{3}}$,   (d) $y = x^{-\frac{4}{3}}$,
P is the point where $x = 8$ and Q is the point where $x = 8.1$. Find

(i) the y-coordinates of P and Q,

(ii) the gradient of the chord [PQ],

(iii) the value of $\dfrac{dy}{dx}$ at P (assuming the differentiation rule),

(iv) the equation of the tangent at P.

4 Find the equation of the tangent to the curve at the given point.

(a) $y = \sqrt{x}$ at $(9, 3)$ (b) $y = \dfrac{6}{\sqrt[3]{x}}$ at $(8, 3)$

(c) $y = 2x\sqrt{x}$ at $(1, 2)$ (d) $y = 4x + \dfrac{1}{\sqrt{x}}$ at $(\frac{1}{4}, 3)$

5 Find the coordinates of the point(s) at which the curve has the given gradient.

(a) $y = \sqrt[3]{x^2}$, gradient $\frac{1}{3}$ (b) $y = \sqrt[3]{x}$, gradient $\frac{1}{3}$

(c) $y = \dfrac{3}{\sqrt[3]{x^2}}$, gradient $\frac{1}{16}$ (d) $y = \dfrac{x^2 + 3}{\sqrt{x}}$, gradient 0

6 Find the equation of the tangent to $y = \sqrt[4]{x}$ with gradient 2.

7 If $n > 0$ the graph of $y = x^n$ passes through the origin. Use the fact that $\dfrac{dy}{dx} = nx^{n-1}$ to show that the x-axis is a tangent if $n > 1$, and that the y-axis is a tangent if $0 < n < 1$. What happens if $n = 1$?

8 (a) Use the definition of the derivative to prove that, if $f(x) = \dfrac{1}{\sqrt{x}}$, then $f'(x) = -\dfrac{1}{2x\sqrt{x}}$.

(b) Use the definition of the derivative, and the factor form

$$p^3 - q^3 = (p - q)(p^2 + pq + q^2),$$

to prove that, if $f(x) = \sqrt[3]{x}$, then $f'(x) = -\dfrac{1}{3\sqrt[3]{x^2}}$.

16 Polynomials, factors and remainders

This chapter is about polynomials, which include linear and quadratic expressions. When you have completed it, you should

- be able to add, subtract and multiply polynomials
- be familiar with the shapes of the graphs of polynomial functions
- understand and be able to use the factor and remainder theorems
- be able to use the method of equating coefficients
- understand the words 'quotient' and 'remainder' applied to the division of polynomials
- be able to find the quotient and the remainder when a polynomial is divided by a linear polynomial
- use the quotient–remainder form to find horizontal and oblique asymptotes of rational functions.

16.1 Polynomials

You already know a good deal about polynomials from your work on quadratics. A quadratic is a special case of a polynomial. Here are some examples of polynomials.

$$3x^3 - 2x^2 + 1 \qquad 3 \qquad 4 - 2x \qquad x^2 \qquad 1 - 8x^3$$
$$2x^4 \qquad 1 - 2x + 3x^5 \qquad \sqrt{2}x^2 + \pi x \qquad \tfrac{1}{2}x^{17} + 3x^{20} \qquad x$$

> An expression consisting of one or more multiples of non-negative integer powers of x, combined by addition, is called a **polynomial** in x.
>
> Thus $ax + b$, $ax^2 + bx + c$, $ax^3 + bx^2 + cx + d$, $ax^4 + bx^3 + cx^2 + dx + e$, where a, b, etc. are numbers, are polynomials in x.

The highest power of x is called the **degree** of the polynomial. The expressions ax^4, bx^3, cx^2, dx and e which make up the polynomial are called **terms**. The numbers a, b, etc. are called **coefficients**; a is the **leading coefficient**. The coefficient of the term without x is the **constant term**.

Thus, in the quadratic polynomial $4x^2 - 3x + 1$, the degree is 2; the coefficients of x^2 and x are 4 and -3 respectively, and the constant term is 1.

Polynomials with low degree have special names: if the polynomial has

- degree 0 it is called a **constant polynomial**, or a **constant**
- degree 1 it is called a **linear polynomial**
- degree 2 it is called a **quadratic polynomial**, or a **quadratic**
- degree 3 it is called a **cubic polynomial**, or a **cubic**
- degree 4 it is called a **quartic polynomial**, or a **quartic**.

> There are names for some polynomials of higher degree, but it isn't worth learning them.

The general polynomial of degree 4 in the blue box, $ax^4 + bx^3 + cx^2 + dx + e$, is only a quartic if the leading coefficient, a, is not zero. If $a = 0$, the polynomial becomes $bx^3 + cx^2 + dx + e$, and is no longer a quartic. Similarly, if you say that $ax^2 + bx + c$ is a quadratic, then that carries with it the condition that $a \neq 0$.

When a polynomial such as $3x^4 + x^2 - 7x + 5$ is written with the term of highest degree first and the other terms in descending degree order finishing with the constant term, the terms are said to be in **descending order**. If the terms are written in the reverse order, that is, $5 - 7x + x^2 + 3x^4$, they are said to be in **ascending order** (or ascending powers of x). They are of course the same polynomial; it doesn't matter what order the terms are written in.

The functions $\dfrac{1}{x} = x^{-1}$ and $\sqrt{x} = x^{\frac{1}{2}}$ are not polynomials, because the powers of x are not positive integers or zero.

16.2 Graphs of polynomial functions

You know that all linear polynomial graphs are straight lines, and that the graphs of all quadratic polynomials are parabolas. As the degree of the polynomial goes up, the more different shapes are possible. However, there are some features which are common to all polynomial graphs, however high the degree.

- Every polynomial function has a value for all real values of x, so every polynomial graph consists of one continuous curve. A polynomial graph can't have any vertical asymptotes.

- When $|x|$ is very large, the size of the leading term ax^n is greater than that of all the other terms put together. Since $|ax^n|$ is large when $|x|$ is large, a polynomial graph can't have a horizontal asymptote (unless it is a constant).

The questions in Exercise 16A invite you to use a calculator to investigate the shapes of some polynomial graphs of various degrees, with the aim of finding some more general rules. You will probably need to experiment using different windows to be sure that you have a display which shows all the important features.

Exercise 16A

1 Display and sketch the graphs of the following cubic polynomial functions.

(a) $f(x) = x^3 - 4x$ (b) $f(x) = 2 - x^3$

(c) $f(x) = x^3 + 2x + 2$ (d) $f(x) = 3x^2 - x^3$

(e) $f(x) = x^3 + 6x^2 + 12x + 1$ (f) $f(x) = x^3 - 3x^2 + 5x - 4$

2 Display and sketch the graphs of the following quartic polynomial functions.

(a) $f(x) = x^4 - 4x^3 + 8x + 2$ (b) $f(x) = x^4 - 7x^2 + 6x - 5$

(c) $f(x) = 1 - 3x^2 - 2x^4$ (d) $f(x) = 3x - x^4$

3 Answer the following questions for the graphs in Questions 1 and 2.

   (a) Do the graphs have a vertical axis of symmetry?

   (b) Do the graphs have a point about which they are symmetrical?

4 Display and sketch the graphs of the following polynomial functions.

   (a) $f(x) = x^5 - 6x^3 + 2x + 3$ (b) $f(x) = 4x^2 - x^6$

   (c) $f(x) = x^7 - 3x^2 - 5$

5 What can you say about the quadrants occupied by polynomial graphs for large values of $|x|$?

16.3   Addition, subtraction and multiplication of polynomials

Polynomials have much in common with integers. You can add them, subtract them and multiply them together and the result is another polynomial.

To add or subtract two polynomials, you simply add or subtract the coefficients of corresponding powers; in other words, you collect like terms. Suppose that you want to add $2x^3 + 3x^2 - 4$ to $x^2 - x - 2$. Then you can set out the working like this:

$$
\begin{array}{r}
2x^3 + 3x^2 \phantom{{}+ x} - 4 \\
x^2 - x - 2 \\
\hline
2x^3 + 4x^2 - x - 6
\end{array}
$$

Notice that you must leave gaps in places where the coefficient is zero. You need to do addition so often that it is worth getting used to setting out the work in a line, thus:

$$(2x^3 + 3x^2 - 4) + (x^2 - x - 2) = (2+0)x^3 + (3+1)x^2 + (0+(-1))x + ((-4)+(-2))$$
$$= 2x^3 + 4x^2 - x - 6.$$

You will soon find that you can miss out the middle step and go straight to the answer.

The result of the polynomial calculation $(2x^3 + 3x^2 - 4) - (2x^3 + 3x^2 - 4)$ is 0. This is a special case, and it is called the **zero polynomial**. It has no degree.

> Look back at the definition of a polynomial, and see why the zero polynomial was not included there.

You have already multiplied linear polynomials when you have a quadratic expressed in factor form. The method is essentially the same when you multiply together polynomials of higher degree.

When you multiply out $(3x - 2)(4x + 5)$ the result is the sum of four terms:

$$(3x - 2) \times (4x + 5) = (3x) \times (4x) + (3x) \times 5 + (-2) \times 4x + (-2) \times 5$$
$$= 12x^2 + 15x - 8x - 10.$$

These are formed by taking all possible combinations of a term from the first bracket and a term from the second, as indicated by the slurs. The two terms in x, $15x$ and $-8x$, are then combined, to give

$$(3x - 2)(4x + 5) = 12x^2 + (15x - 8x) - 10$$
$$= 12x^2 + 7x - 10.$$

Similarly, if you want to multiply out $(5x + 3)(2x^2 - 5x + 1)$, you get the six terms

$$(5x + 3) \times (2x^2 - 5x + 1) = (5x) \times (2x^2) + (5x) \times (-5x) + (5x) \times 1$$
$$+ 3 \times (2x^2) + 3 \times (-5x) + 3 \times 1$$
$$= 10x^3 - 25x^2 + 5x + 6x^2 - 15x + 3.$$

The two terms in x^2, $-25x^2$ and $6x^2$, and the two terms in x, $5x$ and $-15x$, are then combined, to give

$$(5x + 3)(2x^2 - 5x + 1) = 10x^3 + (-25x^2 + 6x^2) + (5x - 15x) + 3$$
$$= 10x^3 - 19x^2 - 10x + 3.$$

Example 16.3.1
Find the coefficients of x and x^2 in the product $(x^2 + 2x + 3)(3x^2 - 2x + 4)$.

You get terms in x by multiplying the constant term in one bracket by the x term in the other bracket, as indicated by the slurs in

$$(x^2 + 2x + 3)(3x^2 - 2x + 4).$$

So the terms in x are $(2x) \times 4$ and $3 \times (-2x)$, whose sum is $8x - 6x = 2x$. The coefficient of x in the product is 2.

The terms in x^2 come either by multiplying the x terms in both brackets, or by multiplying the constant term in one bracket by the x^2 in the other, as indicated by the slurs in

$$(x^2 + 2x + 3)(3x^2 - 2x + 4).$$

This gives three terms, $x^2 \times 4$, $(2x) \times (-2x)$ and $3 \times 3x^2$, whose sum is $4x^2 - 4x^2 + 9x^2 = 9x^2$. The coefficient of x^2 in the product is 9.

If you multiply a polynomial of degree m by a polynomial of degree n, you have a calculation of the type

$$(ax^m + bx^{m-1} + \ldots)(Ax^n + Bx^{n-1} + \ldots) = aAx^{m+n} + \ldots .$$

In this calculation, the largest power of the product is $m + n$. Also the coefficient aA is not zero because neither of a and A is zero. This shows that:

> When you multiply two polynomials, the degree of the product polynomial is the sum of the degrees of the two polynomials.

Exercise 16B

1 State the degree of each of the following polynomials.

(a) $x^3 - 3x^2 + 2x - 7$ (b) $5x + 1$ (c) $8 + 5x - 3x^2 + 7x + 6x^4$

(d) 3 (e) $3 - 5x$ (f) x^0

2 In each part find $p(x) + q(x)$, and give your answer in descending order.

(a) $p(x) = 3x^2 + 4x - 1$, $q(x) = x^2 + 3x + 7$

(b) $p(x) = 4x^3 + 5x^2 - 7x + 3$, $q(x) = x^3 - 2x^2 + x - 6$

(c) $p(x) = 3x^4 - 2x^3 + 7x^2 - 1$, $q(x) = -3x - x^3 + 5x^4 + 2$

(d) $p(x) = 2 - 3x^3 + 2x^5$, $q(x) = 2x^4 + 3x^3 - 5x^2 + 1$

(e) $p(x) = 3 + 2x - 4x^2 - x^3$, $q(x) = 1 - 7x + 2x^2$

3 For each of the pairs of polynomials given in Question 2 find $p(x) - q(x)$.

4 Note that $p(x) + p(x)$ may be shortened to $2p(x)$. Let $p(x) = x^3 - 2x^2 + 5x - 3$ and $q(x) = x^2 - x + 4$. Express each of the following as a single polynomial.

(a) $2p(x) + q(x)$ (b) $3p(x) - q(x)$ (c) $p(x) - 2q(x)$ (d) $3p(x) - 2q(x)$

5 Find the following polynomial products.

(a) $(2x - 3)(3x + 1)$ (b) $(x^2 + 3x - 1)(x - 2)$

(c) $(x^2 + x - 3)(2x + 3)$ (d) $(3x - 1)(4x^2 - 3x + 2)$

(e) $(x^2 + 2x - 3)(x^2 + 1)$ (f) $(2x^2 - 3x + 1)(4x^2 + 3x - 5)$

(g) $(x^3 + 2x^2 - x + 6)(x + 3)$ (h) $(x^3 - 3x^2 + 2x - 1)(x^2 - 2x - 5)$

(i) $(2x + 1)(3x - 2)(x + 5)$ (j) $(3x + 4)(x + 1)(2x - 3)$

6 For each of the following products, state (i) the degrees of the separate factors, (ii) the degree of the product, (iii) the leading coefficient, (iv) the constant term.

(a) $(4x^3 - 2x + 5)(2x^4 + 3x^2 - 7)$ (b) $(3x^2 + 2x - 1)(2x^3 - 5x^2 + 4x - 3)$

(c) $(3 - 2x + 7x^3 + 3x^5)(4 + x - x^2)$ (d) $(7x^3 - 4x^2 + 3x)(2 - 6x^3 + 3x^4 - 5x^5)$

7 In each of the following products find the coefficient of x and the coefficient of x^2.

(a) $(x + 2)(x^2 - 3x + 6)$ (b) $(x - 3)(x^2 + 2x - 5)$

(c) $(2x + 1)(x^2 - 5x + 1)$ (d) $(3x - 2)(x^2 - 2x + 7)$

(e) $(2x - 3)(3x^2 - 6x + 1)$ (f) $(2x - 5)(3x^3 - x^2 + 4x + 2)$

(g) $(3x - 4)(2x - 5)(3x - 2)$ (h) $(3x^2 + 1)(2x^2 - 5x + 3)$

16.4 Factorising quadratics

In Section 11.3 you saw how to factorise quadratics. But when
quite a difficult and lengthy process.

Fortunately there is another method which is often quicker. It is
if a quadratic $p(x)$ factorises as $(x - t)(x - u)$, where t and u are nur.
$p(t) = (t - t)(t - u) = 0 \times (t - u) = 0$. So if $x - t$ is a factor of $p(x)$, the
instead of f is used for functions in this chapter, since they are all pol

> Similar working also shows that if $x - u$ is a factor then $p(u) = 0$.

This is also true in reverse. That is, if $p(t)$ is equal to 0, then $x - t$ is a factor
called the 'factor theorem for quadratics'.

> Similarly, if $p(u) = 0$, then $x - u$ is a factor of $p(x)$.

Look at the example $p(x) = 6x^2 - 7x - 10$. If this has a factor $x - t$, then t must divi
into 10, that is t must be one of ± 1, ± 2, ± 5 or ± 10. So try calculating

$$p(1) = 6 - 7 - 10 = -11, \quad p(-1) = 6 + 7 - 10 = 3, \quad p(2) = 24 - 14 - 10 = 0, \dots .$$

There is no need to go any further. Since $p(2) = 0$, $x - 2$ is a factor of $p(x)$.

Once you have one factor, it is easy to write down the other, since $6x^2$ must split as $x \times 6x$,
-10 as $(-2) \times 5$. So

$$p(x) = (x - 2)(6x + 5)$$

and you can easily check that the middle term is $5x - 12x = -7x$.

> **The factor theorem for quadratics**
>
> If $p(x) = ax^2 + bx + c$, and if $p(t) = 0$, then $x - t$ is a factor of $p(x)$.

In Exercise 16C Question 5 you will find an outline of a method of proving the statement in
the box.

Example 16.4.1
Find the factors of $p(x) = 5x^2 + 11x - 12$.

> The constant term -12 has a lot of factors, and you need to try in turn ± 1, ± 2, ± 3,
> ± 4, ± 6, ± 12 until a number t is reached such that $p(t) = 0$. You can check that
>
> $$p(1) = 4, \quad p(-1) = -18, \quad p(2) = 30, \quad p(-2) = -14, \quad p(3) = 66, \quad p(-3) = 0, \dots .$$
>
> The search can now stop. Since $p(-3) = 0$, $x - (-3)$ is a factor of $p(x)$; more simply,
> $x + 3$ is a factor.

To get the other factor, note that $5x^2 = x \times 5x$ and $-12 = 3 \times (-4)$. So the other factor is $5x - 4$.

Finally, check the middle term in the product $(x + 3)(5x - 4)$, which is $-4x + 15x = 11x$, as expected.

So the factors of $p(x) = 5x^2 + 11x - 12$ are $(x + 3)(5x - 4)$.

The advantage of this method is that you don't have to juggle with both factors at the same time. The process is carried out in two steps:

Factorising a quadratic

Step 1   Use the factor theorem to find one factor.

Step 2   Use the factor you have found to identify the second factor.

But all the examples used so far have been special, since they have all had one factor $x - t$ where t is an integer. What happens if none of the possible integer values of t give $p(t) = 0$?

Example 16.4.2
Factorise $6x^2 - 11x - 10$.

Let $p(x) = 6x^2 - 11x - 10$.

If you try evaluating $p(t)$ with $t = \pm 1, \pm 2, \pm 5, \pm 10$ you never get 0. This means that there cannot be factors with $6x^2$ split as $x \times 6x$. But it might split as $2x \times 3x$, so one factor might be one of $2x - 1$, $2x + 1$, $2x - 5$ or $2x + 5$. In that case you would get 0 if you put x equal to one of $\pm \frac{1}{2}$ or $\pm \frac{5}{2}$. So work out

$$p\left(\tfrac{1}{2}\right) = \tfrac{6}{4} - \tfrac{11}{2} - 10 = -14,\ p\left(-\tfrac{1}{2}\right) = \tfrac{6}{4} + \tfrac{11}{2} - 10 = -3,$$
$$p\left(\tfrac{5}{2}\right) = \tfrac{150}{4} - \tfrac{55}{2} - 10 = 0, \ldots \text{success!}$$

Since $p\left(\tfrac{5}{2}\right) = 0$, $2x - 5$ is a factor. This means that $6x^2$ splits as $2x \times 3x$, and -10 as $(-5) \times 2$, so the other factor is $3x + 2$.

As a check, multiply out $(2x - 5)(3x + 2)$, and make sure that the middle term is $4x - 15x = -11x$, as required.

Why were $2x - 2$, $2x + 2$, $2x - 10$, $2x + 10$ excluded from the list of possible factors?

The solution of this example is based on an extended version of the factor theorem:

The extended factor theorem for quadratics

If $p(x) = ax^2 + bx + c$, and if $p\left(\dfrac{t}{s}\right) = 0$, then $sx - t$ is a factor of $p(x)$.

16.4   Factorising quadratics

In Section 11.3 you saw how to factorise quadratics. But when the coefficients get big, it can be quite a difficult and lengthy process.

Fortunately there is another method which is often quicker. It is based on the idea that, if a quadratic $p(x)$ factorises as $(x-t)(x-u)$, where t and u are numbers, then $p(t) = (t-t)(t-u) = 0 \times (t-u) = 0$. So if $x - t$ is a factor of $p(x)$, then $p(t) = 0$. (The letter p instead of f is used for functions in this chapter, since they are all polynomials.)

> Similar working also shows that if $x - u$ is a factor then $p(u) = 0$.

This is also true in reverse. That is, if $p(t)$ is equal to 0, then $x - t$ is a factor of $p(x)$. This is called the 'factor theorem for quadratics'.

> Similarly, if $p(u) = 0$, then $x - u$ is a factor of $p(x)$.

Look at the example $p(x) = 6x^2 - 7x - 10$. If this has a factor $x - t$, then t must divide exactly into 10, that is t must be one of $\pm 1, \pm 2, \pm 5$ or ± 10. So try calculating

$$p(1) = 6 - 7 - 10 = -11, \ p(-1) = 6 + 7 - 10 = 3, \ p(2) = 24 - 14 - 10 = 0, \dots .$$

There is no need to go any further. Since $p(2) = 0$, $x - 2$ is a factor of $p(x)$.

Once you have one factor, it is easy to write down the other, since $6x^2$ must split as $x \times 6x$, and -10 as $(-2) \times 5$. So

$$p(x) = (x-2)(6x+5)$$

and you can easily check that the middle term is $5x - 12x = -7x$.

> **The factor theorem for quadratics**
>
> If $p(x) = ax^2 + bx + c$, and if $p(t) = 0$, then $x - t$ is a factor of $p(x)$.

In Exercise 16C Question 5 you will find an outline of a method of proving the statement in the box.

Example 16.4.1
Find the factors of $p(x) = 5x^2 + 11x - 12$.

The constant term -12 has a lot of factors, and you need to try in turn $\pm 1, \pm 2, \pm 3, \pm 4, \pm 6, \pm 12$ until a number t is reached such that $p(t) = 0$. You can check that

$$p(1) = 4, \ p(-1) = -18, \ p(2) = 30, \ p(-2) = -14, \ p(3) = 66, \ p(-3) = 0, \dots .$$

The search can now stop. Since $p(-3) = 0$, $x - (-3)$ is a factor of $p(x)$; more simply, $x + 3$ is a factor.

To get the other factor, note that $5x^2 = x \times 5x$ and $-12 = 3 \times (-4)$. So the other factor is $5x - 4$.

Finally, check the middle term in the product $(x + 3)(5x - 4)$, which is $-4x + 15x = 11x$, as expected.

So the factors of $p(x) = 5x^2 + 11x - 12$ are $(x + 3)(5x - 4)$.

The advantage of this method is that you don't have to juggle with both factors at the same time. The process is carried out in two steps:

Factorising a quadratic

Step 1   Use the factor theorem to find one factor.

Step 2   Use the factor you have found to identify the second factor.

But all the examples used so far have been special, since they have all had one factor $x - t$ where t is an integer. What happens if none of the possible integer values of t give $p(t) = 0$?

Example 16.4.2
Factorise $6x^2 - 11x - 10$.

Let $p(x) = 6x^2 - 11x - 10$.

If you try evaluating $p(t)$ with $t = \pm 1, \pm 2, \pm 5, \pm 10$ you never get 0. This means that there cannot be factors with $6x^2$ split as $x \times 6x$. But it might split as $2x \times 3x$, so one factor might be one of $2x - 1, 2x + 1, 2x - 5$ or $2x + 5$. In that case you would get 0 if you put x equal to one of $\pm \frac{1}{2}$ or $\pm \frac{5}{2}$. So work out

$$p\left(\tfrac{1}{2}\right) = \tfrac{6}{4} - \tfrac{11}{2} - 10 = -14, \; p\left(-\tfrac{1}{2}\right) = \tfrac{6}{4} + \tfrac{11}{2} - 10 = -3,$$
$$p\left(\tfrac{5}{2}\right) = \tfrac{150}{4} - \tfrac{55}{2} - 10 = 0, \ldots \text{success!}$$

Since $p\left(\tfrac{5}{2}\right) = 0$, $2x - 5$ is a factor. This means that $6x^2$ splits as $2x \times 3x$, and -10 as $(-5) \times 2$, so the other factor is $3x + 2$.

As a check, multiply out $(2x - 5)(3x + 2)$, and make sure that the middle term is $4x - 15x = -11x$, as required.

Why were $2x - 2, 2x + 2, 2x - 10, 2x + 10$ excluded from the list of possible factors?

The solution of this example is based on an extended version of the factor theorem:

The extended factor theorem for quadratics

If $p(x) = ax^2 + bx + c$, and if $p\left(\dfrac{t}{s}\right) = 0$, then $sx - t$ is a factor of $p(x)$.

Don't try to remember this as a formal statement. All you need to know is that you try possible values of s and t, where s divides exactly into a and t divides exactly into c. Then try $x = \dfrac{t}{s}$ to see if $p\left(\dfrac{t}{s}\right) = 0$. (It is easy to remember to put $x = \dfrac{t}{s}$ because this is the value of x that makes $sx - t$ equal to 0.)

16.5 Equating coefficients

There is another slightly different way of carrying out Step 2, finding the second factor. It is not quite so quick for quadratics as the one described in the last section, but it has the advantage that it can be used for factorising polynomials whose degree is higher than 2, such as cubics and quartics. It is best explained by an example.

Example 16.5.1
Verify that one factor of $p(x) = 15x^2 + x - 6$ is $3x + 2$. Find the other factor.

To show that $3x + 2$ is a factor, calculate

$$p\left(-\tfrac{2}{3}\right) = 15 \times \tfrac{4}{9} - \tfrac{2}{3} - 6 = \tfrac{20}{3} - \tfrac{2}{3} - 6 = 0.$$

So, by the extended factor theorem, $3x + 2$ is a factor of $p(x)$.

Suppose that the other factor is $Ax + B$, where A and B are numbers that have to be found. Then

$$15x^2 + x - 6 = (3x + 2)(Ax + B).$$

Multiply out the brackets on the right. This gives

$$
\begin{aligned}
(3x + 2)(Ax + B) &= 3Ax^2 + 3Bx + 2Ax + 2B \\
&= 3Ax^2 + (3B + 2A)x + 2B.
\end{aligned}
$$

You want this to be the same as $15x^2 + x - 6$. This will happen if

$$3A = 15, \quad 3B + 2A = 1 \quad \text{and} \quad 2B = -6.$$

These equations are easy to solve. The first gives $A = 5$. Substituting 5 for A in the second equation gives $3B + 10 = 1$, so $B = -3$.

This leaves the third equation spare for use as a check. Since $2 \times (-3) = -6$, these values of A and B satisfy all three equations.

The other factor is therefore $5x - 3$.

To appreciate what is going on, you need to understand that when you write a quadratic in factors, for example

$$15x^2 + x - 6 = (3x + 2)(5x - 3),$$

what you are writing is an **identity**. That is, it is a statement which is true for all values of x.

There is a distinction in algebra between an equation such as $15x^2 + x - 6 = 0$, which is true for only some values of x (in this case $-\tfrac{2}{3}$ and $\tfrac{3}{5}$), and an identity such as $15x^2 + x - 6 \equiv (3x + 2)(5x - 3)$, which is true for all values of x.

Notice the use of the symbol $\equiv$, to show that the statement is an identity rather than an equation.

The central part of the argument in Example 16.5.1 comes at the point where it is deduced from the identity

$$15x^2 + x - 6 \equiv 3Ax^2 + (3B + 2A)x + 2B$$

that the corresponding coefficients on the two sides are equal.

This is a particular example of a general result about quadratics:

If $ax^2 + bx + c \equiv lx^2 + mx + n$, then $a = l$, $b = m$ and $c = n$.

This is called **equating coefficients**.

You can prove this for yourself. It is Question 6 of Exercise 16C.

Example 16.5.2
For what value of c is $2x - 3$ a factor of $8x^2 + 2x + c$? Find the other factor in this case.

Let $p(x) = 8x^2 + 2x + c$.

By the extended factor theorem, $p\left(\frac{3}{2}\right) = 0$, so

$$8 \times \left(\tfrac{3}{2}\right)^2 + 2 \times \tfrac{3}{2} + c = 0,$$
$$c = -18 - 3 = -21.$$

To find the other factor, write

$$8x^2 + 2x - 21 \equiv (2x - 3)(Ax + B)$$
$$\equiv 2Ax^2 + (2B - 3A)x - 3B.$$

Equating coefficients,

$$2A = 8, \quad 2B - 3A = 2 \quad \text{and} \quad -3B = -21.$$

From the first two equations, $A = 4$ and $2B - 12 = 2$, so $B = 7$. As a check, this satisfies the third equation.

The other factor is therefore $4x + 7$.

Exercise 16C

1 In this question you are given a quadratic $p(x)$ and a linear expression $f(x)$. Use the factor theorem to find whether or not $f(x)$ is a factor of $p(x)$. If it is, find the other factor.

   (a) $3x^2 - 10x + 8$, $x - 2$ (b) $2x^2 - x - 45$, $x - 5$ (c) $4x^2 + 15x + 9$, $x + 3$

   (d) $3x^2 - 10x - 8$, $x + 4$ (e) $6x^2 - 5x - 6$, $2x - 3$ (f) $6x^2 - 17x + 5$, $3x - 1$

   (g) $8x^2 + 6x - 5$, $2x + 1$ (h) $15x^2 + 43x + 8$, $5x + 1$

2 In each of the following quadratic polynomials one factor is given. Use the method of equating coefficients to find the other factor.

(a) $x^2 + x - 12 \equiv (x + 4)(\quad)$

(b) $x^2 + 14x - 51 \equiv (x - 3)(\quad)$

(c) $3x^2 + 5x - 22 \equiv (x - 2)(\quad)$

(d) $35x^2 + 48x - 27 \equiv (5x + 9)(\quad)$

(e) $2x^2 - x - 15 \equiv (2x + 5)(\quad)$

(f) $14x^2 + 31x - 10 \equiv (2x + 5)(\quad)$

3 Use the factor theorem to find one factor of these quadratics. Then use the method of equating coefficients to find the other factor.

(a) $4x^2 + x - 5$

(b) $2x^2 - 5x - 3$

(c) $4x^2 + x - 3$

(d) $3x^2 + 10x + 8$

(e) $4x^2 - 8x - 5$

(f) $12x^2 - 19x + 4$

(g) $6x^2 + 13x + 6$

(h) $6x^2 + 13x - 15$

(i) $8x^2 + 2x - 3$

4 You are given a quadratic polynomial $p(x)$ whose coefficients involve an unknown number k, and a linear polynomial $f(x)$. Find the value(s) of k for which $f(x)$ is a factor of $p(x)$. Check your answer by finding the other factor.

(a) $x^2 + 5x + k, \quad x - 2$

(b) $2x^2 + kx + 9, \quad x + 3$

(c) $kx^2 + kx + 1, \quad 2x + 1$

(d) $6x^2 - x + k, \quad 3x - 2$

(e) $kx^2 + 2x + k^2, \quad x + 1$

(f) $3x^2 + kx - k, \quad x + 2$

5 Suppose that $p(x) = ax^2 + bx + c$, and that t is a number such that $p(t) = 0$. Explain why $c = -at^2 - bt$, and hence show that $p(x) = a(x^2 - t^2) + b(x - t)$.

Deduce that $x - t$ is a factor of $p(x)$.

6 If $ax^2 + bx + c \equiv lx^2 + mx + n$, the values of the two quadratics are the same for all values of x. By applying this with $x = 0$, $x = -1$ and $x = 1$, deduce that $a = l$, $b = m$ and $c = n$.

16.6 Factorising polynomials of higher degree

There is nothing special about quadratics. All the methods so far described apply equally to polynomials of any degree. In this chapter, to keep the examples simple, none of the applications go beyond cubics and quartics; but you should have no difficulty in seeing how to extend them to higher degree polynomials.

To factorise a cubic polynomial, the first step is to try to express it as a product of a linear expression and a quadratic. You can then examine the quadratic to see if that can be factorised further.

For a start, concentrate on finding the linear factor. Look at the highest degree term (for a cubic, the x^3 term) and the constant term, to decide how these might split. Then test the various possibilities, using the factor theorem just as for a quadratic.

Once you have found a linear factor, write the quadratic factor as $Ax^2 + Bx + C$ and use the method of equating coefficients to get equations for A, B and C. There will be four of these, one each for the x^3, x^2, x and constant terms. You can use the first three to find A, B and C, and the last one as a check.

> **Factorising a polynomial**
>
> **Step 1**   Use the factor theorem to find one factor.
>
> **Step 2**   Use the method of equating coefficients to find the second factor.

Example 16.6.1

Factorise $p(x) = x^3 + 7x^2 + 8x + 2$.

The x^3 term can only split as $x \times x^2$, and the constant term can split as 1×2 or 2×1, with both $+$ or both $-$ signs. So to find a linear factor $x - t$, work out p(t) with $t = \pm 1$, ± 2 in turn.

$$p(1) = 1 + 7 + 8 + 2 = 18, \ p(-1) = -1 + 7 - 8 + 2 = 0, \ \dots \text{ stop!}$$

By the factor theorem, there is a linear factor $x - (-1)$, that is $x + 1$.

Now write

$$x^3 + 7x^2 + 8x + 2 \equiv (x + 1)(Ax^2 + Bx + C)$$

and multiply out the right side as

$$Ax^3 + (B + A)x^2 + (C + B)x + C.$$

Equating coefficients,

$$A = 1, \ B + A = 7, \ C + B = 8 \text{ and } C = 2.$$

So $A = 1$, $B = 7 - A = 6$, $C = 8 - B = 2$. Notice that the value of C agrees with that given by the fourth equation.

It follows that

$$x^3 + 7x^2 + 8x + 2 \equiv (x + 1)(x^2 + 6x + 2).$$

The quadratic $x^2 + 6x + 2$ does not split any further into factors with integer coefficients.

> However $x^2 + 6x + 2$ does factorise if you allow surds. The roots of $x^2 + 6x + 2 = 0$ are $-3 - \sqrt{7}$ and $-3 + \sqrt{7}$, showing that $x^2 + 6x + 2 \equiv (x + 3 + \sqrt{7})(x + 3 - \sqrt{7})$.

Example 16.6.2
Show that $3x - 2$ is a factor of $p(x) = 12x^3 + 40x^2 + 13x - 30$, and hence factorise $p(x)$ completely.

Using the extended factor theorem, note that the value of x which makes $3x - 2$ equal to 0 is $\frac{2}{3}$. So calculate

$$p\left(\tfrac{2}{3}\right) = 12\left(\tfrac{2}{3}\right)^3 + 40\left(\tfrac{2}{3}\right)^2 + 13\left(\tfrac{2}{3}\right) - 30$$
$$= \frac{12 \times 8}{27} + \frac{40 \times 4}{9} + \frac{13 \times 2}{3} - 30$$
$$= \tfrac{192}{9} + \tfrac{26}{3} - 30$$
$$= \tfrac{64}{3} + \tfrac{26}{3} - 30 = \tfrac{90}{3} - 30 = 0.$$

This proves that $3x - 2$ is a factor of $p(x)$.

To find the quadratic factor, write

$$12x^3 + 40x^2 + 13x - 30 \equiv (3x - 2)(Ax^2 + Bx + C)$$

and multiply out the right side to get

$$3Ax^3 + (3B - 2A)x^2 + (3C - 2B)x - 2C.$$

Equating the coefficients of this expression with those of the given cubic,

$$3A = 12, \; 3B - 2A = 40, \; 3C - 2B = 13 \text{ and } -2C = -30.$$

So $A = 4$, $B = \dfrac{40 + 8}{3} = 16$, $C = \dfrac{13 + 32}{3} = 15$. As a check, the value of C satisfies the fourth equation.

The first stage of the factorisation is therefore

$$12x^3 + 40x^2 + 13x - 30 \equiv (3x - 2)(4x^2 + 16x + 15).$$

It remains to investigate whether the quadratic factor can be split into two linear factors. You can do this by the methods described in Section 11.3. It is left to you to show that this gives

$$4x^2 + 16x + 15 \equiv (2x + 3)(2x + 5).$$

The complete factorisation of the cubic is therefore

$$12x^3 + 40x^2 + 13x - 30 \equiv (3x - 2)(2x + 3)(2x + 5).$$

Example 16.6.3
A quartic polynomial $x^4 - x^3 + ax^2 + bx + 10$ has factors $x + 1$ and $x - 2$. Find a and b, and factorise the polynomial completely.

Since $x + 1$ and $x - 2$ are factors,

$$(-1)^4 - (-1)^3 + a(-1)^2 + b(-1) + 10 = 0$$

and $\quad 2^4 - 2^3 + a \times 2^2 + b \times 2 + 10 = 0.$

That is, $a - b + 12 = 0$ and $4a + 2b + 18 = 0$.
These simultaneous equations for a and b have solution $a = -7$, $b = 5$.

Since $(x + 1)(x - 2) \equiv x^2 - x - 2$, there is a quadratic $Ax^2 + Bx + C$ such that

$$x^4 - x^3 - 7x^2 + 5x + 10$$
$$\equiv (x^2 - x - 2)(Ax^2 + Bx + C)$$
$$\equiv Ax^4 + (B - A)x^3 + (C - B - 2A)x^2 + (-C - 2B)x - 2C.$$

Equating coefficients,

$$A = 1, B - A = -1, C - B - 2A = -7, -C - 2B = 5, -2C = 10.$$

From the first three equations,

$$A = 1, B = A - 1 = 0, C = B + 2A - 7 = -5.$$

As a check, these values also satisfy the last two equations. It follows that

$$x^4 - x^3 - 7x^2 + 5x + 10 \equiv (x + 1)(x - 2)(x^2 - 5)$$
$$\equiv (x + 1)(x - 2)(x - \sqrt{5})(x + \sqrt{5}).$$

To sum up, the methods described in Sections 16.4 and 16.5 for quadratics can be extended to polynomials $p(x)$ of any degree as follows.

The factor theorem
Let $p(x)$ be a polynomial.
If $p(t) = 0$, then $x - t$ is a factor of $p(x)$.

The extended factor theorem
If $p\left(\dfrac{t}{s}\right) = 0$, then $sx - t$ is a factor of $p(x)$.

Equating coefficients
If $p(x) = ax^n + bx^{n-1} + cx^{n-2} + ... + k$ and $\pi(x) = \alpha x^n + \beta x^{n-1} + \gamma x^{n-2} + ... + \kappa$ are two polynomials and if $p(x) \equiv \pi(x)$, then $a = \alpha, b = \beta, c = \gamma, ... , k = \kappa$.

Exercise 16D

1 In this question you are given a cubic polynomial $p(x)$ and a linear polynomial $f(x)$. Use the factor theorem to find whether or not $f(x)$ is a factor of $p(x)$. If it is, find the other factor; where possible, split this second factor into two linear factors.

(a) $x^3 + x + 2$, $x + 1$

(b) $4x^3 - 4x^2 - 21x - 9$, $x - 3$

(c) $2x^3 + 3x^2 - x + 6$, $x + 2$

(d) $x^3 - 5x + 2$, $x - 2$

(e) $2x^3 + 3x^2 + 3x + 1$, $2x + 1$

(f) $27x^3 + 27x^2 + 9x + 1$, $3x + 1$

(g) $9x^3 + 6x^2 - x - 6$, $3x - 2$

(h) $2x^3 - 5x^2 - 10x + 3$, $2x + 3$

2 The following polynomials are the product of linear factors. Find them.

(a) $x^3 + 2x^2 - 5x - 6$

(b) $x^3 + x^2 - 16x + 20$

(c) $12x^3 + 4x^2 - 3x - 1$

(d) $8x^3 - 12x^2 + 6x - 1$

(e) $9x^3 + 27x^2 - x - 3$

(f) $x^3 - 6x - 4$

(g) $x^4 + 7x^3 + 9x^2 - 7x - 10$

(h) $x^4 + 4x^3 - 7x^2 - 22x + 24$

(i) $x^4 + x^3 - 12x^2 + 4x + 16$

3 Use the factor theorem to factorise the following polynomials $p(x)$. In each case, write down the real roots of the equation $p(x) = 0$.

(a) $x^3 + 2x^2 - 11x - 12$ (b) $x^3 - 3x^2 - x + 3$ (c) $x^3 - 3x^2 - 13x + 15$

(d) $x^3 - 3x^2 - 9x - 5$ (e) $x^3 + 3x^2 - 4x - 12$ (f) $2x^3 + 7x^2 - 5x - 4$

(g) $3x^3 - x^2 - 12x + 4$ (h) $x^4 - x^2 + 4x - 4$ (i) $4x^4 + 4x^3 + 3x^2 - x - 1$

4 In this question you are given a cubic polynomial $p(x)$ involving an unknown constant k, and a linear polynomial $f(x)$. Find the value(s) of k for which $f(x)$ is a factor of $p(x)$. In this case, factorise $p(x)$ as completely as possible.

(a) $x^3 - 7x - k$, $x + 1$ (b) $4x^3 + kx - 6$, $x - 2$

(c) $kx^3 + x^2 + 25$, $2x + 5$ (d) $x^3 + 5x^2 + kx - k^2$, $x + 3$

5 Factorise the following.

(a) $x^3 - 8$ (b) $x^3 + 8$ (c) $x^3 - a^3$ (d) $x^3 + a^3$

16.7 Division of polynomials

What happens if $sx - t$ is not a factor of $p(x)$?

Example 16.7.1
A student trying to factorise $p(x) = x^3 - x + 6$ found that $p(2) = 12$ and $p(-2) = 0$, but mistakenly thought this meant that $x - 2$ (rather than $x + 2$) is a factor. What happened when he tried to find the other factor?

The student wrote

$$x^3 - x + 6 \equiv (x - 2)(Ax^2 + Bx + C)$$
$$\equiv Ax^3 + (B - 2A)x^2 + (C - 2B)x - 2C,$$

and proceeded to equate coefficients:

$$A = 1, B - 2A = 0, C - 2B = -1, -2C = 6.$$

He then found $A = 1$, $B = 2$, $C = 2 \times 2 - 1 = 3$, giving a quadratic $x^2 + 2x + 3$. But when he used the fourth equation as a check he found that it gave $-2 \times 3 = 6$. So he knew something was wrong!

In this example, to make the identity correct the student would have had to add 12 to the right side. That is, to make the original identity correct he needed to write

$$x^3 - x + 6 \equiv (x - 2)(Ax^2 + Bx + C) + R.$$

Then, when he equated coefficients, the last equation would have been $-2C + R = 6$; and since $C = 3$, R would be equal to $2C + 6 = 12$.

This would not, of course, put right his original mistake. But at least it would have stopped him writing the absurd equation $-2 \times 3 = 6$.

The number R in this calculation is called the **remainder**. To see why, think of a similar situation with numbers rather than polynomials.

Suppose that 44 members of a club turn up on a Sunday morning to play football. Then, since

$$44 = 11 \times 4,$$

exactly 4 teams of eleven players can be formed and everyone gets a game. This is because 11 is a factor of 44. The number 4 is called the **quotient** when 44 is divided by 11. (This word comes from the Latin word *quot*, which means 'how many?'. In this case it is the answer to the question 'how many teams of 11 can be made with 44 people?'.)

But if 49 members turn up, only 44 can get a game and the remaining 5 are left out. The mathematics is expressed by the equation

$$49 = 11 \times 4 + 5.$$

The quotient when 49 is divided by 11 is still 4, since it is still the answer to the question 'how many teams?'. But there is also a remainder of 5.

Compare this with the situation in Example 16.7.1, where the correct identity is

$$x^3 - x + 6 \equiv (x - 2)(x^2 + 2x + 3) + 12.$$

This has the same structure as the equation with numbers, and the same language is used to describe it:

The quotient when $x^3 - x + 6$ is divided by $x - 2$ is $x^2 + 2x + 3$, and there is a remainder of 12.

Example 16.7.2
(a) Use the factor theorem to show that $4x + 3$ is not a factor of $p(x) = 20x^3 - x^2 - 4x - 7$.

(b) Find the quotient and remainder when $20x^3 - x^2 - 4x - 7$ is divided by $4x + 3$.

(a) The value of x which makes $4x + 3$ equal to 0 is $-\frac{3}{4}$, so calculate

$$\begin{aligned}
p\left(-\tfrac{3}{4}\right) &= 20\left(-\tfrac{3}{4}\right)^3 - \left(-\tfrac{3}{4}\right)^2 - 4\left(-\tfrac{3}{4}\right) - 7 \\
&= -\frac{20 \times 27}{64} - \tfrac{9}{16} + \frac{4 \times 3}{4} - 7 \\
&= -\tfrac{135}{16} - \tfrac{9}{16} + 3 - 7 \\
&= -\tfrac{144}{16} + 3 - 7 \\
&= -9 + 3 - 7 = -13.
\end{aligned}$$

Since this is not zero, $4x + 3$ is not a factor of $p(x)$.

(b) Denote the quotient by $Ax^2 + Bx + C$ and the remainder by R. Then the problem is to find numbers A, B, C and R such that

$$20x^3 - x^2 - 4x - 7 \equiv (4x + 3)(Ax^2 + Bx + C) + R.$$

The right side when multiplied out is

$$4Ax^3 + (4B + 3A)x^2 + (4C + 3B)x + 3C + R.$$

Equating coefficients,

$$4A = 20, \ 4B + 3A = -1, \ 4C + 3B = -4, \ 3C + R = -7.$$

So $A = 5$, $B = \dfrac{-1 - 3 \times 5}{4} = -4$, $C = \dfrac{-4 - 3 \times (-4)}{4} = 2$, $R = -7 - 3 \times 2 = -13$.

The quotient is $5x^2 - 4x + 2$, and the remainder is -13.

The processes described in this section can be summed up in a single statement, which holds when $p(x)$ is a polynomial of any degree, not just for cubics.

> When a polynomial $p(x)$ is divided by a linear polynomial $sx - t$, there is a **quotient** $q(x)$ and a **remainder** R such that
>
> $$p(x) = (sx - t)\, q(x) + R.$$
>
> The degree of the quotient is one less than the degree of $p(x)$.

16.8 The remainder theorem

You probably noticed that in Example 16.7.2 the answer -13 found for the remainder in part (b) is the same as the value of $p\left(-\frac{3}{4}\right)$ found in part (a). The same was true in Example 16.7.1, where in the corrected calculation the remainder is 12, and $p(2) = 12$. This is no coincidence.

You are already used to calculating $p\left(\dfrac{t}{s}\right)$ when you try to find factors of $p(x)$. If its value is 0, then $sx - t$ is a factor. It now seems that $p\left(\dfrac{t}{s}\right)$ also has significance if $sx - t$ is not a factor of $p(x)$: it is the remainder when $p(x)$ is divided by $sx - t$.

> **The remainder theorem**
>
> If a polynomial $p(x)$ is divided by a linear polynomial $sx - t$, the remainder is $p\left(\dfrac{t}{s}\right)$.

This is very simple to prove. From the definition of quotient and remainder at the end of Section 16.7,

$$p(x) \equiv (sx - t)\, q(x) + R.$$

Since this is an identity, you can substitute any number you like for x. If you choose x so that $sx - t = 0$, that is $x = \dfrac{t}{s}$, you get

$$p\left(\frac{t}{s}\right) = \left(s \times \frac{t}{s} - t\right) q\left(\frac{t}{s}\right) + R$$
$$= (t - t)\, q\left(\frac{t}{s}\right) + R$$
$$= 0 \times q\left(\frac{t}{s}\right) + R.$$

Since $0 \times q\left(\dfrac{t}{s}\right) = 0$, it follows that $p\left(\dfrac{t}{s}\right) = R$.

Example 16.8.1

Find the remainders when $p(x) = 2x^3 + 3x^2 - x + 1$ is divided by

(a) $x - 3$,   (b) $2x + 1$.

(a) The value of x which makes $x - 3$ equal to 0 is 3, so the remainder is

$$p(3) = 54 + 27 - 3 + 1 = 79.$$

(b) The value of x which makes $2x + 1$ equal to 0 is $-\frac{1}{2}$, so the remainder is

$$p\left(-\tfrac{1}{2}\right) = -\tfrac{1}{4} + \tfrac{3}{4} + \tfrac{1}{2} + 1 = 2.$$

The factor theorem now appears as just a special case of the remainder theorem. For if $p\left(\dfrac{t}{s}\right) = 0$, the remainder R is 0, so the division identity reduces to

$$p(x) \equiv (sx - t)\,q(x).$$

This means that $sx - t$ is a factor of $p(x)$.

Exercise 16E

1 In each of the following identities find the values of A, B and R.

(a) $x^2 - 2x + 7 \equiv (x + 3)(Ax + B) + R$ (b) $x^2 + 9x - 3 \equiv (x + 1)(Ax + B) + R$

(c) $15x^2 - 14x - 8 \equiv (5x + 2)(Ax + B) + R$ (d) $6x^2 + x - 5 \equiv (2x + 1)(Ax + B) + R$

(e) $12x^2 - 5x + 2 \equiv (3x - 2)(Ax + B) + R$ (f) $21x^2 - 11x + 6 \equiv (3x - 2)(Ax + B) + R$

2 In each of the following identities find the values of A, B, C and R.

(a) $x^3 - x^2 - x + 12 \equiv (x + 2)(Ax^2 + Bx + C) + R$

(b) $x^3 - 5x^2 + 10x + 10 \equiv (x - 3)(Ax^2 + Bx + C) + R$

(c) $2x^3 + x^2 - 3x + 4 \equiv (2x - 1)(Ax^2 + Bx + C) + R$

(d) $12x^3 + 11x^2 - 7x + 5 \equiv (3x + 2)(Ax^2 + Bx + C) + R$

(e) $4x^3 + 4x^2 - 37x + 5 \equiv (2x - 5)(Ax^2 + Bx + C) + R$

(f) $9x^3 + 12x^2 - 15x - 10 \equiv (3x + 4)(Ax^2 + Bx + C) + R$

3 Find the quotient and the remainder when

(a) $x^2 - 5x + 2$ is divided by $x - 3$,   (b) $x^2 + 2x - 6$ is divided by $x + 1$,

(c) $2x^2 + 3x - 1$ is divided by $x - 2$,   (d) $2x^2 + 3x + 1$ is divided by $2x - 1$,

(e) $6x^2 - x - 2$ is divided by $3x + 1$.

4 Find the quotient and the remainder when the first polynomial is divided by the second.

(a) $x^3 + 2x^2 - 3x + 1,$ $x + 2$ (b) $x^3 - 3x^2 + 5x - 4,$ $x - 5$

(c) $2x^3 + 4x - 5,$ $x + 3$ (d) $5x^3 - 3x + 7,$ $x - 4$

(e) $2x^3 - x^2 - 3x - 7,$ $2x + 1$ (f) $6x^3 + 17x^2 - 17x + 5,$ $3x - 2$

5 Find the remainder when the first polynomial is divided by the second.

(a) $x^3 - 5x^2 + 2x - 3$, $x - 1$

(b) $x^3 + x^2 - 6x + 5$, $x + 2$

(c) $2x^3 - 3x + 5$, $x - 3$

(d) $4x^3 - 5x^2 + 3x - 7$, $x + 4$

(e) $x^3 + 3x^2 - 2x + 1$, $2x - 1$

(f) $2x^3 + 5x^2 - 3x + 6$, $3x + 1$

(g) $x^4 - x^3 + 2x^2 - 7x - 2$, $x - 2$

(h) $3x^4 + x^2 - 7x + 6$, $x + 3$

6 When $x^3 + 2x^2 - px + 1$ is divided by $x - 1$ the remainder is 5. Find the value of p.

7 When $2x^3 + x^2 - 3x + q$ is divided by $x - 2$ the remainder is 12. Find the value of q.

8 When $x^3 + 2x^2 + px - 3$ is divided by $x + 1$ the remainder is the same as when it is divided by $x - 2$. Find the value of p.

9 When $x^3 + px^2 - x - 4$ is divided by $x - 1$ the remainder is the same as when it is divided by $x + 3$. Find the value of p.

10 When $3x^3 + 2x^2 + ax + b$ is divided by $x - 1$ the remainder is 5. When divided by $3x - 1$ the remainder is $-\frac{1}{3}$. Find the values of a and b.

11 When $x^3 + ax^2 + bx + 5$ is divided by $x - 2$ the remainder is 23. When divided by $x + 1$ the remainder is 11. Find the values of a and b.

12 When $x^4 + ax^3 + bx^2 - 5$ is divided by $x - 1$ the remainder is -1. When divided by $x + 1$ the remainder is -5. Find the values of a and b.

13 When $2x^3 - x^2 + ax + b$ is divided by $x - 2$ the remainder is 25. When divided by $2x + 3$ the remainder is $-13\frac{1}{2}$. Find the values of a and b.

16.9 An application to asymptotes

In Chapter 9, Example 9.2.3, a calculator was used to draw the graph of $y = \dfrac{2x}{x - 1}$. It appeared that there was not only a vertical asymptote $x = 1$, where $\dfrac{2x}{x - 1}$ is not defined, but also a horizontal asymptote. Numerical calculation suggested that the equation of the horizontal asymptote is $y = 2$.

This can now be proved using the quotient and remainder property. You have seen examples of this with polynomials $p(x)$ of degree 2, 3 and 4. You can also use it with polynomials of degree 1. Since the degree of the quotient $q(x)$ is one less than the degree of $p(x)$, the degree of the quotient is then 0. That is, $q(x)$ is a constant.

So, if $p(x) = 2x$ is divided by $x - 1$, with quotient A and remainder R,

$$2x \equiv (x - 1)A + R.$$

The remainder theorem gives $R = p(1) = 2$, and equating the coefficients of x gives $A = 2$. Thus

$$2x \equiv (x - 1) \times 2 + 2.$$

This identity can be written in the form

$$\frac{2x}{x-1} \equiv 2 + \frac{2}{x-1}.$$

So the equation of the graph, $y = \dfrac{2x}{x-1}$, can be written as

$$y = 2 + \frac{2}{x-1}.$$

Now consider what happens when $|x|$ is large. If x is large and positive, then $\dfrac{2}{x-1}$ is a small positive number, so y is slightly more than 2. If x is negative with large modulus, then $\dfrac{2}{x-1}$ is a small negative number, so y is slightly less than 2. So for large $|x|$ the graph of $y = 2 + \dfrac{2}{x-1}$ has the form shown in Fig. 16.1. That is, $y = 2$ is an asymptote.

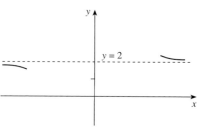

Fig. 16.1

Example 16.9.1

Find the asymptotes of the graph of $y = \dfrac{3x+1}{x+2}$, and sketch the graph.

Note first that y is undefined when $x + 2 = 0$, so there is a vertical asymptote with equation $x = -2$.

Now divide $p(x) = 3x + 1$ by $x + 2$. It is easy to show that the quotient is 3, and the remainder is $p(-2) = -5$. So

$$3x + 1 \equiv (x + 2) \times 3 - 5,$$

which can be written as

$$\frac{3x+1}{x+2} \equiv 3 - \frac{5}{x+2}.$$

This shows that, for large values of $|x|$, $y = \dfrac{3x+1}{x+2}$ is close to 3. If x is positive, y is slightly less than 3; if x is negative, y is slightly more than 3. So the horizontal asymptote has equation $y = 3$.

Before sketching the graph it is useful also to note that the y-intercept (when $x = 0$) is $\frac{1}{2}$, and the x-intercept (when $y = 0$) is $-\frac{1}{3}$. The graph is shown in Fig. 16.2.

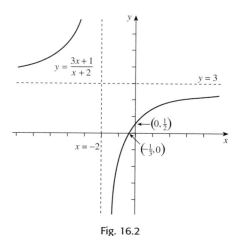

Fig. 16.2

Example 16.9.2

Sketch the graph of $y = \dfrac{x^2}{x-2}$.

Note first that y is undefined when $x - 2 = 0$, so there is a vertical asymptote with equation $x = 2$.

If you divide x^2 by $x - 2$, the quotient is a linear polynomial and the remainder is $2^2 = 4$. By equating coefficients you find that $q(x) = x + 2$. So

$$x^2 \equiv (x-2)(x+2) + 4,$$

or $\qquad \dfrac{x^2}{x-2} \equiv x + 2 + \dfrac{4}{x-2}.$

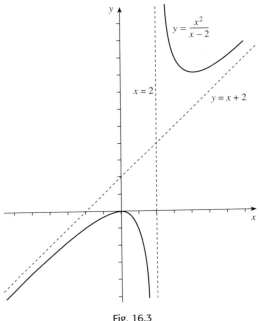

This time the graph doesn't have a horizontal asymptote. But, for large values of $|x|$, $y = x + 2 + \dfrac{4}{x-2}$ comes close to the line $y = x + 2$. If x is large and positive, $\dfrac{4}{x-2}$ is a small positive number, so y is slightly greater than $x + 2$; if x is negative with large modulus, $\dfrac{4}{x-2}$ is a small negative number, so y is slightly less than $x + 2$.

Finally, notice that the only value of x for which $y = 0$ is 0. The graph has the form shown in Fig. 16.3.

Fig. 16.3

In Example 16.9.2 the line $y = x + 2$ has the property of an asymptote, that the curve comes close to the line when x or y is large, but the line is neither vertical nor horizontal. It is called an **oblique asymptote**.

Exercise 16F

1 Without using a calculator, find the equations of the asymptotes of the following graphs. Use these, and any other relevant information, to sketch the graphs.

(a) $y = \dfrac{x+1}{x-3}$ 　　 (b) $y = \dfrac{2x-3}{x+1}$ 　　 (c) $y = \dfrac{3x}{2-x}$ 　　 (d) $y = \dfrac{x}{2x-1}$

(e) $y = \dfrac{x^2}{x+3}$ 　　 (f) $y = \dfrac{x^2+2}{x-1}$ 　　 (g) $y = \dfrac{3x^2-x+1}{x-2}$ 　　 (h) $y = \dfrac{(x+1)^2}{2x+1}$

Review exercise 4

1 Find the coordinates of the two points on the curve $y = 2x^3 - 5x^2 + 9x - 1$ at which the gradient of the tangent is 13.

2 Einstein's law $E = mc^2$ gives the energy of the radiation created by the destruction of a particle of mass m, where c is the velocity of light. The units for m, c and E are respectively kilograms, metres per second and joules. Given that the speed of light is 3.0×10^8 metres per second, find the energy created by a neutron of mass 1.7×10^{-27} kilograms.

3 The equation of a curve is $y = 2x^2 - 5x + 14$. The normal to the curve at the point $(1, 11)$ meets the curve again at the point P. Find the coordinates of P.

4 A normal to the curve $y = x^2$ has gradient 2. Find where it meets the curve.

5 Evaluate the following without using a calculator.

(a) $\left(\frac{1}{2}\right)^{-1} + \left(\frac{1}{2}\right)^{-2}$ (b) $32^{-\frac{4}{5}}$ (c) $\left(4\frac{1}{2}\right)^{-\frac{1}{3}}$ (d) $\left(1\frac{7}{9}\right)^{1\frac{1}{2}}$

6 Solve the equation $4^{2x} \times 8^{x-1} = 32$.

7 The table below shows, for three of the planets in the solar system, details of their mean distance from the sun and the time taken for one orbit round the sun.

Planet	Mean radius of orbit r metres	Period of revolution T seconds
Mercury	5.8×10^{10}	7.6×10^6
Jupiter	7.8×10^{11}	3.7×10^8
Pluto	5.9×10^{12}	7.8×10^9

(a) Show that $r^3 T^{-2}$ has approximately the same value for each planet in the table.

(b) The earth takes one year for one orbit of the sun. Find the mean radius of the earth's orbit around the sun.

8 The formulae for the volume V and the surface area S of a cube are $V = x^3$ and $S = 6x^2$, where x is the length of an edge. Find expressions for

(a) S in terms of V,   (b) V in terms of S,

giving each answer in the form $(S \text{ or } V) = 2^m \times 3^n \times (V \text{ or } S)^p$.

9 The curve $y = x^2 - 3x - 4$ crosses the x-axis at P and Q. The tangents to the curve at P and Q meet at R. The normals to the curve at P and Q meet at S. Find the distance RS.

10 For the curve $y = \dfrac{4}{x^2}$,

    (a) find the equation of the tangent at $(-2\sqrt{2}, \frac{1}{2})$,

    (b) find the equation of the normal at $(\sqrt{2}, 2)$.

    Show that the lines in parts (a) and (b) are the same. Illustrate this with a sketch.

11 The tangents at $x = \frac{1}{4}$ to $y = \sqrt{x}$ and $y = \dfrac{1}{\sqrt{x}}$ meet at P. Find the coordinates of P.

12 The normals at $x = 2$ to $y = \dfrac{1}{x^2}$ and $y = \dfrac{1}{x^3}$ meet at Q. Find the coordinates of Q.

13 (a) Draw a sketch to show the graphs of $y = \dfrac{1}{x^2}$ and $y = \sqrt{x}$ and their point of intersection at the point P$(1, 1)$. Find the gradient of each curve at P, and show that the tangent at P to each curve is the normal to the other curve.

    (b) The graphs of $y = x^m$ and $y = x^n$ intersect at the point P$(1, 1)$. Find the connection between m and n if the tangent at P to each curve is the normal to the other curve.

14 Express $(9a^4)^{-\frac{1}{2}}$ as an algebraic fraction in simplified form. (OCR)

15 By letting $y = x^{\frac{1}{3}}$, or otherwise, find the values of x for which $x^{\frac{1}{3}} - 2x^{-\frac{1}{3}} = 1$. (OCR)

16 The polynomials $f(x)$ and $g(x)$ are $2x^2 + ax - 3$ and $3x^2 - bx - 2$ respectively, where a and b are constants. In the product $f(x)g(x)$ the coefficient of x^3 is 6 and the coefficient of x is 1. Find the coefficient of x^2.

17 Let $p(x) = x^2 - 6x - 3$ and $q(x) = x^2 - 2x + 4$.

    (a) Calculate $p(x) - q(x)$ and $p(x)q(x)$.

    The polynomial $p(x) + aq(x)$, where a is a constant, is a perfect square.

    (b) Calculate the two possible values of a.

18 Find the equation of the tangent to the curve with equation $y = 2x^2 - x - 2$ which is perpendicular to the straight line with equation $2x - 3y + 4 = 0$.

19 (a) Given that $t^{\frac{1}{4}} = y$, show that the equation $t^{\frac{1}{4}} + 2t^{-\frac{1}{4}} = 3$ may be written as $y^2 - 3y + 2 = 0$.

    (b) Hence solve the equation $t^{\frac{1}{4}} + 2t^{-\frac{1}{4}} = 3$. (OCR)

20 Solve the equation $4x^3 + 8x^2 + x - 3 = 0$ given that one of the roots is an integer. (OCR)

21 On the curve with equation $y = x^2(x - 4)$ the point P has coordinates $(1, -3)$.

    (a) Find the equation of the tangent to the curve at P and the coordinates of the point where the tangent meets the curve again.

    (b) Find the equation of the normal to the curve at P and the coordinates of the points where the normal meets the curve again.

22 The diagram shows the graph of $y = x^2 - 3$ and the part of the graph of $y = \dfrac{2}{x}$ for $x > 0$. The two graphs intersect at C, and A and B are the points of intersection of $y = x^2 - 3$ with the x-axis. Write down the exact coordinates of A and B.

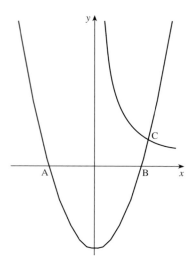

Show that the x-coordinate of C is given by the equation $x^3 - 3x - 2 = 0$.

Factorise $x^3 - 3x - 2$ completely.

Hence

(a) write down the x-coordinate of C,

(b) describe briefly the geometrical relationship between the graph of $y = x^2 - 3$ and the part of the graph of $y = \dfrac{2}{x}$ for which $x < 0$.   (OCR)

Examination questions

1 Find the equations of all the asymptotes of the graph of $y = \dfrac{x^2 - 5x - 4}{x^2 - 5x + 4}$.   (© IBO 2002)

2 Let f be a cubic polynomial function. Given that $f(0) = 2$, $f'(0) = -3$, $f(1) = f'(1)$ and $f''(1) = -6$, find $f(x)$.   (© IBO 2005)

3 When the polynomial $P(x) = 4x^3 + px^2 + qx + 1$ is divided by $(x - 1)$ the remainder is -2. When $P(x)$ is divided by $(2x - 1)$ the remainder is $\frac{13}{4}$. Find the value of p and of q.   (© IBO 2005)

4 Consider $f(x) = x^3 - 2x^2 - 5x + k$. Find the value of k if $(x + 2)$ is a factor of $f(x)$.   (© IBO 2004)

5 When the polynomial $x^4 + ax + 3$ is divided by $(x - 1)$, the remainder is 8. Find the value of a.   (© IBO 2002)

6 The polynomial $x^2 - 4x + 3$ is a factor of $x^3 + (a - 4)x^2 + (3 - 4a)x + 3$. Calculate the value of the constant a.   (© IBO 2004)

7 The polynomial $x^3 - 2x^2 + ax + b$ has a factor $(x - 1)$ and a remainder 8 when divided by $(x + 1)$. Find the value of a and of b.   (© IBO 2004)

8 The polynomial $x^3 + ax^2 - 3x + b$ is divisible by $(x - 2)$ and has a remainder 6 when divided by $(x + 1)$. Find the value of a and of b.   (© IBO 2003)

17 Trigonometry

This chapter develops work on sines, cosines and tangents. When you have completed it, you should

- know the shapes of the graphs of sine, cosine and tangent for all angles
- know, or be able to find, exact values of the sine, cosine and tangent of certain special angles.

Letters of the Greek alphabet are often used to denote angles. In this chapter, θ (theta) and ϕ (phi) will usually be used.

17.1 The graph of cos $\theta°$

You probably first used $\cos\theta°$ in calculations with right-angled triangles, so that θ lies between 0 and 90. However, if you use a calculator, you will find that it gives a value of $\cos\theta°$ for any value of θ. This section extends the definition of $\cos\theta°$ to angles of any size, positive or negative.

Figure 17.1 shows a circle of radius 1 unit with centre O; the circle meets the positive x-axis at A. Draw a line segment [OP] at an angle $\theta°$ to the x-axis, to meet the circle at P. Draw a perpendicular from P to meet the x-axis at N. Let ON $= x$ units and NP $= y$ units, so that the coordinates of P are (x, y).

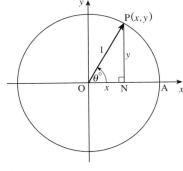

Look at triangle ONP. Using $\cos\theta° = \dfrac{\text{adjacent}}{\text{hypotenuse}} = \dfrac{\text{ON}}{\text{OP}}$,

you find that $\cos\theta° = \dfrac{x}{1} = x$.

This result, $\cos\theta° = x$, is used to define $\cos\theta°$ for all values of θ, not just acute angles.

Fig. 17.1

> Referring to Fig. 17.1,
>
> $\cos\theta° = x$, for all $\theta \in \mathbb{R}$.

Example 17.1.1 investigates the consequences of this definition whenever θ is a multiple of 90.

Example 17.1.1
Find the value of $\cos\theta°$ when   (a) $\theta = 180$,   (b) $\theta = 270$.

    (a) When $\theta = 180$, P is the point $(-1, 0)$. As the x-coordinate of P is -1,
        $\cos 180° = -1$. See Fig. 17.2.

    (b) When $\theta = 270$, P is the point $(0, -1)$, so $\cos 270° = 0$. See Fig. 17.3.

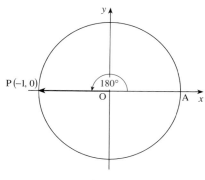

Fig. 17.2

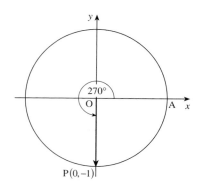

Fig. 17.3

As θ increases, the point P moves round the circle. When $\theta = 360$, P is once again at A, and as θ becomes greater than 360, the point P moves round the circle again.

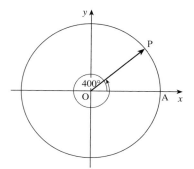

For example, when [OP] has turned through $400°$, P is in the same position as when $\theta = 40$; it follows that $\cos 400° = \cos 40°$. See Fig. 17.4.

This is a special case of a general rule that the values of $\cos \theta°$ repeat themselves every time θ increases by 360. Written as an equation,

$$\cos \theta° = \cos(\theta - 360)°.$$

Fig. 17.4

If θ is negative, P moves round the circle in the opposite (clockwise) sense, starting from A as before. Figure 17.5 shows this with $\theta = -150$, so that P is in the third quadrant. Since the x-coordinate of P is negative, this shows that $\cos(-150)°$ is negative.

In Fig. 17.5, as angle $N\hat{O}P = 30°$, ON is $1 \times \cos 30° = 0.866...$. Therefore $\cos 150° = -0.866...$.

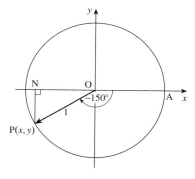

Calculators use this definition to give values of $\cos \theta°$ for all angles. Use your calculator to display the graph of $\cos \theta°$, shown in Fig. 17.6.

Fig. 17.5

You will have to input the equation of the graph of $\cos \theta°$ as $y = \cos x$ into the calculator, and make sure that it is in degree mode.

Note that the values taken by the cosine function are always between -1 and $+1$ (inclusive). The maximum value of 1 is taken at $\theta = ..., -720, -360, 0, 360, 720, ...$, and the minimum of -1 at $\theta = ..., -540, -180, 180, 540, ...$.

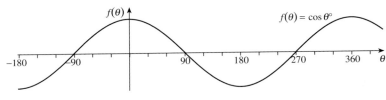

Fig. 17.6

The graph of the cosine function keeps repeating itself. Functions with this property are called **periodic**; the **period** of such a function is the smallest interval for which the function repeats itself. The period of the cosine function is therefore 360. The property that $\cos(\theta - 360)° = \cos\theta°$ is called the **periodic property**. Many natural phenomena have periodic properties, and cosines are often used in applications involving them.

Example 17.1.2
Find the greatest and least values of the following functions, and in each case give the smallest positive value of θ for which it occurs.

(a) $2 + \cos\theta°$ (b) $3\cos 2\theta°$

The greatest and least values of the cosine function are $+1$ and -1.

(a) The greatest value of $2 + \cos\theta°$ is $2 + 1 = 3$, and the least value is $2 + (-1) = 1$.

The values of θ which give the value $\cos\theta° = 1$ are $-720, -360, 0, 360, 720$, etc. The smallest positive value of these is 360.

The values of θ which give the value $\cos\theta° = -1$ are $-540, -180, 180, 540, 900$, etc. The smallest positive value of these is 180.

(b) The greatest value of $3\cos 2\theta°$ is $3 \times 1 = 3$, and the least value of $3\cos 2\theta°$ is $3 \times (-1) = -3$.

The values of 2θ which give the value 1 for $\cos 2\theta°$ are $-720, -360, 0, 360, 720$, etc. The smallest positive value of θ is when $2\theta = 360$, that is, $\theta = 180$.

The values of 2θ which give the value -1 for $\cos 2\theta°$ are $-540, -180, 180, 540, 900$, etc. The smallest positive value of θ is when $2\theta = 180$, that is, $\theta = 90$.

Example 17.1.3
The height h in metres of the water in a harbour is given approximately by the formula $h = 6 + 3\cos 30t°$ where t is the time in hours from noon. Find

(a) the height of the water at 9.45 p.m.,

(b) the highest and lowest water levels, and when they occur.

(a) At 9.45 p.m., $t = 9.75$, so

$$h = 6 + 3\cos(30 \times 9.75)°$$
$$= 6 + 3\cos 292.5°$$
$$= 7.148... .$$

The height of the water is 7.15 metres, correct to 3 significant figures.

(b) The greatest value of h occurs when the value of the cosine function is 1, and is therefore $6 + 3 \times 1 = 9$. Similarly, the least value is $6 + 3 \times (-1) = 3$. The highest and lowest water levels are 9 metres and 3 metres. The first times that they occur after noon are when $30t = 360$ and $30t = 180$; that is, at midnight and 6.00 p.m.

17.2 The graphs of $\sin \theta°$ and $\tan \theta°$

Using the same construction as for the cosine (see Fig. 17.7 which is Fig. 17.1 again), the sine function is given by

$$\sin \theta° = \frac{\text{opposite}}{\text{hypotenuse}} = \frac{NP}{OP} = \frac{y}{1} = y,$$

so $\sin \theta° = y$ is used as the definition of $\sin \theta°$ for all values of θ.

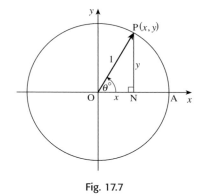

Fig. 17.7

> Referring to Fig. 17.7,
>
> $\sin \theta° = y$, for all $\theta \in \mathbb{R}$.

Like the cosine graph, the sine graph (shown in Fig. 17.8) is periodic, with period 360. It also lies between -1 and 1 inclusive.

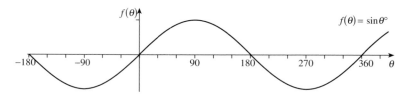

Fig. 17.8

In Fig. 17.7, you can see that $\tan \theta° = \dfrac{NP}{ON} = \dfrac{y}{x}$; this is taken as the definition of $\tan \theta°$.

> Referring to Fig. 17.7,
>
> $\tan \theta° = \dfrac{y}{x}$, for all $\theta \in \mathbb{R}$, provided $x \neq 0$.

The function $\tan \theta°$ is not defined for those angles for which x is zero, namely $\theta = \pm 90, \pm 270, \ldots$. Figure 17.9 shows the graph of $\tan \theta°$, which has asymptotes at $\theta = \pm 90, \pm 270, \ldots$.

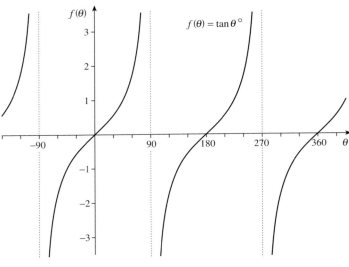

Fig. 17.9

Like the graphs of $\cos\theta°$ and $\sin\theta°$, the graph of $\tan\theta°$ is periodic, but its period is 180. Thus $\tan(\theta - 180)° = \tan\theta°$.

As $\cos\theta° = x$, $\sin\theta° = y$ and $\tan\theta° = \dfrac{y}{x}$, it follows that $\tan\theta° = \dfrac{\sin\theta°}{\cos\theta°}$. You could use this as an alternative definition of $\tan\theta°$.

Example 17.2.1
Find the greatest and least values of the following functions, and in each case give the smallest positive value of θ for which it occurs.

(a) $2\sin\theta° - 1$ (b) $\dfrac{1}{2 + \sin\theta°}$

The greatest and least values of $\sin\theta°$ are 1 and -1.

(a) The greatest value of $2\sin\theta° - 1$ is therefore $2 \times 1 - 1 = 1$, and the least value is $2 \times (-1) - 1 = -3$.

The greatest occurs when $\theta = 90$, and the least when $\theta = 270$.

(b) As $\sin\theta°$ lies between -1 and 1, $2 + \sin\theta°$ lies between 1 and 3.

The greatest value of $\dfrac{1}{2 + \sin\theta°}$ occurs when the denominator is 1, giving a greatest value of 1. This occurs when $\theta = 270$.

Similarly, the least value of $\dfrac{1}{2 + \sin\theta°}$ occurs when the denominator is 3, giving a least value of $\frac{1}{3}$. This occurs when $\theta = 90$.

You might find it interesting to display these functions on your calculator.

Example 17.2.2

Show that for values of θ between 0 and 180,
$\sin\theta° = \sin(180° - \theta°)$.

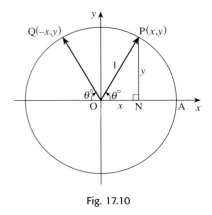

Figure 17.10 shows a modified version of Fig. 17.1 (or Fig 17.7).

You can see that for $0 < \theta < 180$, the y-coordinates of P and Q are always the same. It follows that $\sin\theta° = \sin(180° - \theta°)$.

This result will be used in the next chapter. You will see later that it is actually true for all values of θ.

Fig. 17.10

17.3   Exact values of some trigonometric functions

There are a few angles which have sines, cosines and tangents you can find exactly. The most important of these are 45°, 60° and 30°.

To find the cosine, sine and tangent of 45°, draw a right-angled isosceles triangle of side 1 unit, as in Fig. 17.11.

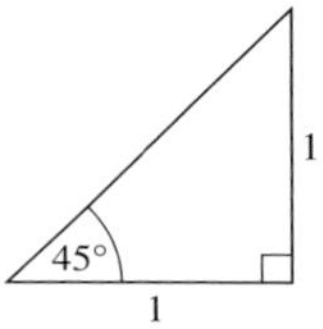

Using Pythagoras' theorem, the length of the hypotenuse is $\sqrt{2}$ units. Then

$$\cos 45° = \frac{1}{\sqrt{2}}, \quad \sin 45° = \frac{1}{\sqrt{2}}, \quad \tan 45° = 1.$$

If you rationalise the denominators you get

$$\cos 45° = \frac{\sqrt{2}}{2}, \quad \sin 45° = \frac{\sqrt{2}}{2}, \quad \tan 45° = 1.$$

Fig. 17.11

To find the cosine, sine and tangent of 60° and 30°, draw an equilateral triangle of side 2 units, as in Fig. 17.12.

Draw a perpendicular from one vertex, bisecting the opposite side. This perpendicular has length $\sqrt{3}$ units, and it makes an angle of 30° with [AC]. Then

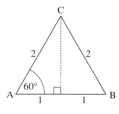

$$\cos 60° = \frac{1}{2}, \quad \sin 60° = \frac{\sqrt{3}}{2}, \quad \tan 60° = \sqrt{3};$$
$$\cos 30° = \frac{\sqrt{3}}{2}, \quad \sin 30° = \frac{1}{2}, \quad \tan 30° = \frac{1}{\sqrt{3}} = \frac{\sqrt{3}}{3}.$$

Fig. 17.12

You should be able to reproduce these results quickly.

Here is a summary of them.

θ	$\sin \theta°$	$\cos \theta°$	$\tan \theta°$
0	0	1	0
30	$\dfrac{1}{2}$	$\dfrac{\sqrt{3}}{2}$	$\dfrac{1}{\sqrt{3}} = \dfrac{\sqrt{3}}{3}$
45	$\dfrac{1}{\sqrt{2}} = \dfrac{\sqrt{2}}{2}$	$\dfrac{1}{\sqrt{2}} = \dfrac{\sqrt{2}}{2}$	1
60	$\dfrac{\sqrt{3}}{2}$	$\dfrac{1}{2}$	$\sqrt{3}$
90	1	0	undefined

Example 17.3.1

Write down the exact values of   (a) $\cos 120°$,   (b) $\sin 240°$,   (c) $\tan 495°$.

(a) **Method 1**   From the graph of $\cos \theta°$ in Fig. 17.13, the value of $\cos 120°$ is negative.

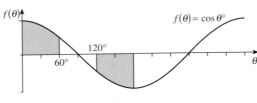

Fig. 17.13

Also from Fig. 17.13, the piece of curve between 0 and 60 is exactly the same shape as that between 120 and 180, so the numerical value (ignoring the sign) of $\cos 120°$ is the same as $\cos 60°$, which is $\frac{1}{2}$.

So $\cos 120° = -\cos 60° = -\frac{1}{2}$.

Method 2   From Fig. 17.14, $120°$ is a second quadrant angle, so the x-coordinate of P is negative and hence $\cos 120°$ is negative.

In Fig. 17.14, as angle $\text{N}\hat{\text{O}}\text{P} = 60°$,
ON is $1 \times \cos 60° = \frac{1}{2}$.

So $\cos 120° = -\cos 60° = -\frac{1}{2}$.

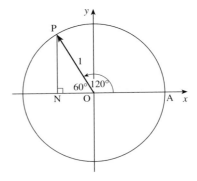

Fig. 17.14

(b) Using either Method 1 or Method 2, you first find that sin 240° is negative.

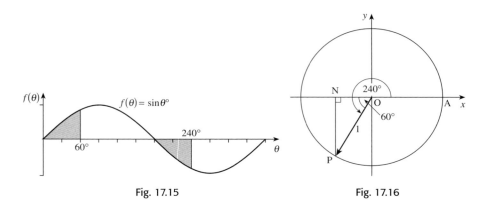

Fig. 17.15   Fig. 17.16

If you use the graph (Fig. 17.15) you see that $\sin 240° = -\sin 60°$, and as $\sin 60° = \frac{1}{2}\sqrt{3}$, $\sin 240° = -\sin 60° = -\frac{1}{2}\sqrt{3}$.

If you use Fig. 17.16, then PN is $1 \times \sin 60° = \frac{1}{2}\sqrt{3}$, so $\sin 240° = -\frac{1}{2}\sqrt{3}$.

(c) Using either Method 1 or Method 2, you first find that tan 495° is negative.

Using the graph (Fig. 17.17) you see that $\tan 495° = -\tan 45°$, and as $\tan 45° = 1$, $\tan 495° = -1$.

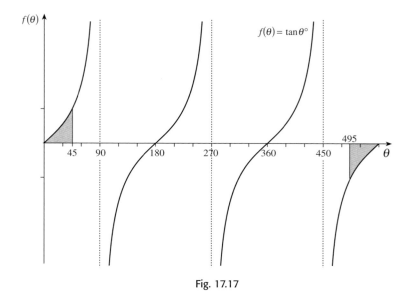

Fig. 17.17

If you use Fig. 17.18, then $\dfrac{\text{PN}}{\text{ON}} = \tan 45° = 1$. So $\tan 495° = -\tan 45° = -1$.

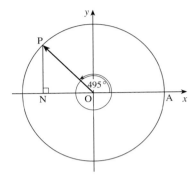

Fig. 17.18

Use either Method 1 or Method 2, whichever you prefer. But do not attempt to draw an accurate figure: a rough sketch is all that is needed.

Exercise 17

1 For each of the following values of θ find, correct to 4 decimal places, the values of
(i) $\cos \theta°$, (ii) $\sin \theta°$, (iii) $\tan \theta°$.

(a) 25   (b) 125   (c) 225   (d) 325
(e) −250   (f) 67.4   (g) 124.9   (h) 554

2 Find the greatest value and the least value of each of the following functions. In each case, give the smallest positive values of θ at which they occur.

(a) $2 + \sin \theta°$ (b) $7 - 4\cos \theta°$ (c) $5 + 8\cos 2\theta°$
(d) $\dfrac{8}{3 - \sin \theta°}$ (e) $9 + \sin(4\theta - 20)°$ (f) $\dfrac{30}{2 + \cos \theta°}$

3 (Do not use a calculator for this question.) In each part of the question a trigonometric function of a number is given. Find all the other numbers x, $0 \le x \le 360$, such that the same function of x is equal to the given trigonometric ratio. For example, if you are given $\sin 80°$, then $x = 100$, since $\sin 100° = \sin 80°$.

(a) $\sin 20°$ (b) $\cos 40°$ (c) $\tan 60°$ (d) $\sin 130°$
(e) $\cos 140°$ (f) $\tan 160°$ (g) $\sin 400°$ (h) $\cos(-30)°$
(i) $\tan 430°$ (j) $\sin(-260)°$ (k) $\cos(-200)°$ (l) $\tan 1000°$

4 Without using a calculator, write down the exact values of the following.

(a) $\sin 135°$ (b) $\cos 120°$ (c) $\sin(-30)°$ (d) $\tan 240°$
(e) $\cos 225°$ (f) $\tan(-330)°$ (g) $\cos 900°$ (h) $\tan 510°$
(i) $\sin 225°$ (j) $\cos 630°$ (k) $\tan 405°$ (l) $\sin(-315)°$
(m) $\sin 210°$ (n) $\tan 675°$ (o) $\cos(-120)°$ (p) $\sin 1260°$

5 Without using a calculator, write down the smallest positive angle which satisfies each of the following equations.

(a) $\cos\theta° = \frac{1}{2}$

(b) $\sin\phi° = -\frac{1}{2}\sqrt{3}$

(c) $\tan\theta° = -\sqrt{3}$

(d) $\cos\phi° = \frac{1}{2}\sqrt{3}$

(e) $\tan\theta° = \frac{1}{3}\sqrt{3}$

(f) $\tan\phi° = -1$

(g) $\sin\theta° = -\frac{1}{2}$

(h) $\cos\phi° = 0$

(i) $\cos\theta° = -\frac{1}{2}$

(j) $\tan\phi° = \sqrt{3}$

(k) $\sin\theta° = -1$

(l) $\cos\theta° = -1$

(m) $\sin\phi° = \frac{1}{2}\sqrt{3}$

(n) $\tan\theta° = -\frac{1}{3}\sqrt{3}$

(o) $\sin\phi° = -\frac{1}{2}\sqrt{2}$

(p) $\tan\phi° = 0$

6 Without using a calculator show that

(a) $\tan 45° + \sin 30° = 1\frac{1}{2}$,

(b) $(\sin 60°)^2 = \frac{3}{4}$,

(c) $\sin 60° \cos 30° + \cos 60° \sin 30° = 1$,

(d) $(\sin 30°)^2 + (\sin 45°)^2 = (\sin 60°)^2$,

(e) $\dfrac{\cos 30°}{\sin 30°} = \tan 60°$,

(f) $(1 + \tan 60°)^2 = 4 + 2\sqrt{3}$.

7 The water levels in a dock follow (approximately) a twelve-hour cycle, and are modelled by the equation $D = A + B\sin 30t°$, where D metres is the depth of water in the dock, A and B are positive constants, and t is the time in hours after 8 a.m.

Given that the greatest and least depths of water in the dock are 7.80 m and 2.20 m respectively, find the value of A and the value of B.

Find the depth of water in the dock at noon, giving your answer correct to the nearest cm.

18 The sine and cosine rules

This chapter shows you how to use trigonometry in triangles which are not right-angled. When you have completed it, you should

- know and be able to use the formula $\Delta = \frac{1}{2}ab\sin C$ for the area of a triangle
- know and be able to use the sine and cosine rules to find unknown sides and angles in triangles which are not right-angled.

18.1 Some notation

You have already used trigonometry to calculate lengths and angles in right-angled triangles. This chapter develops rules which you can use to calculate lengths, angles and areas in triangles which are not right-angled. To state these rules, it helps to have a standard notation.

Figure 18.1 shows a triangle ABC. In this triangle, the length of the side [BC], which is opposite the vertex A, is denoted by a units. Similarly the lengths of the sides [CA] and [AB], which are opposite B and C respectively, are denoted by b units and c units. These units could be centimetres, miles or anything else you like. However, all the sides must be measured in the same units. That is, the units must be consistent.

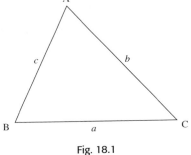

Fig. 18.1

In a practical problem, where particular units are specified, you would usually include the units when you label the sides. (See, for example, Fig. 18.4.) But where a figure might represent any triangle, such as Fig. 18.1, it is usual just to label the sides 'a, b, c' rather than 'a units, b units, c units'. You are already used to doing this when you use coordinates and write (x, y) rather than $(x$ units, y units$)$.

You are probably used to naming the angle at the vertex A as 'angle BAC', or perhaps '∠BAC' or BÂC. This gets rather clumsy, so when there is no ambiguity the letter $\hat{A}$ is used as an abbreviation for the size of this angle. Similarly, $\hat{B}$ and $\hat{C}$ stand for the size of the angles at the corresponding vertices. These angles will usually be measured in degrees. For example, you might write $\hat{A} = 60°$, $\hat{B} = 75°$ and $\hat{C} = 45°$. However, there is no reason why the angles could not be measured in some other units such as right angles if that were convenient. In that case $\hat{A} = \frac{2}{3}$ right angle, $\hat{B} = \frac{5}{6}$ right angle and $\hat{C} = \frac{1}{2}$ right angle.

Some triangles in this chapter will be labelled DEF, LMN, PQR, XYZ, etc. The same convention is used for these triangles, but with the letters changed. For example, the triangle PQR would have sides of length p units, q units and r units, and angles of size $\hat{P}$, $\hat{Q}$ and $\hat{R}$, where p is opposite the vertex P, and so on.

18.2   The area of an acute-angled triangle

You know the formula

$$\text{area of a triangle} = \tfrac{1}{2} \times \text{base} \times \text{height}$$

for the area of any triangle.

There are no units in this formula; however, the units of the lengths of the base and height must be the same and the unit of area must be consistent with these.

You can use trigonometry to write this formula in a different way.

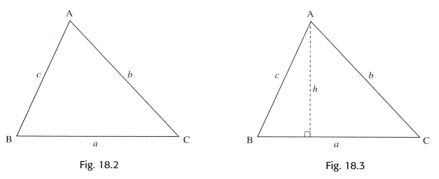

Fig. 18.2   Fig. 18.3

Suppose that you want a formula for the area of the acute-angled triangle ABC in Fig. 18.2. Then, to use the formula area $= \tfrac{1}{2} \times$ base $\times$ height, you need to find the height, which is shown as h in Fig. 18.3.

In the triangle on the right of Fig. 18.3, $\sin \hat{C} = \dfrac{h}{b}$, so $h = b \sin \hat{C}$.

The base of the triangle is a, so the area is given by

$$\text{area} = \tfrac{1}{2} \times \text{base} \times \text{height} = \tfrac{1}{2} \times a \times b \sin \hat{C} = \tfrac{1}{2}ab \sin \hat{C}.$$

The area of a triangle is denoted by $\triangle$ where $\triangle$ is the Greek capital 'd', called 'delta'. Then, for an acute-angled triangle,

$$\triangle = \tfrac{1}{2}ab \sin \hat{C}.$$

The units for $\triangle$ would correspond to the units for the sides of the triangle. So if the lengths were a cm and b cm, the area would be $\triangle$ cm^2.

> The symbol $\triangle$ is often used in two ways: when you write $\triangle$ABC it means 'triangle' and $\triangle$ABC is simply the triangle ABC; when you use $\triangle$ to mean the area of a triangle, it must have a unit. This ambiguity doesn't usually cause confusion.

Example 18.2.1
Calculate the area of triangle ABC in Fig. 18.4 in which
BC = 5 cm, AC = 6 cm and $\hat{C} = 40°$.

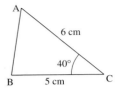

For this triangle, $a = 5$ and $b = 6$. Substituting these into
$\Delta = \frac{1}{2}ab\sin\hat{C}$ gives

$$\Delta = \frac{1}{2} \times 5 \times 6 \sin 40° = 9.641... .$$

Fig. 18.4

The area of triangle ABC is 9.64 cm², correct to 3 significant figures.

If, in Fig. 18.3, you had calculated the height h from the triangle on the left instead of the triangle on the right, you would have obtained $h = c \sin \hat{B}$ instead of $h = b \sin \hat{C}$.

Using this new expression for h gives

$$\Delta = \frac{1}{2} \times a \times c \sin \hat{B} = \frac{1}{2}ac \sin \hat{B}.$$

And, if you had drawn the perpendicular from B to the side [AC], and used [AC] as the base of the triangle you could have obtained the formula

$$\Delta = \frac{1}{2}bc \sin \hat{A}.$$

Therefore you have three ways of expressing the area of an acute-angled triangle,

$$\Delta = \frac{1}{2}bc \sin \hat{A} = \frac{1}{2}ca \sin \hat{B} = \frac{1}{2}ab \sin \hat{C}.$$

18.3 The area of an obtuse-angled triangle

Now suppose that the triangle ABC is obtuse-angled, with an obtuse angle at C, as shown in Fig. 18.5.

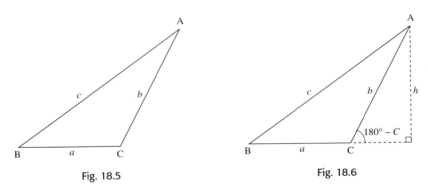

Fig. 18.5   Fig. 18.6

In Fig. 18.6, the height of the triangle ABC is shown as h; using the right-angled triangle with hypotenuse [AC] shows that $h = b\sin(180° - \hat{C})$, giving

$$\Delta = \frac{1}{2} \times a \times b\sin(180° - \hat{C})$$
$$= \frac{1}{2}ab\sin(180° - \hat{C}).$$

But from Example 17.2.2, for $0 < \theta < 180$, $\sin(180° - \theta°) = \sin\theta°$.

So in this case $\sin(180° - \hat{C}) = \sin \hat{C}$, giving

$\Delta = \frac{1}{2}ab\sin\hat{C}.$

The formula $\frac{1}{2}ab\sin\hat{C}$ can therefore be used for the area of any triangle, whether the angle at C is acute or obtuse.

> What happens if the angle at C is a right angle?

> > The area Δ of a triangle ABC is given by
> > $$\Delta = \tfrac{1}{2}bc\sin A = \tfrac{1}{2}ca\sin B = \tfrac{1}{2}ab\sin C,$$
> > where the unit of area corresponds to the units for the sides.

> Note that it is conventional to quote this formula without the circumflex over the angle. This will be the convention used in this book, but as soon as the formula is applied, the circumflex will be used.

A good way to remember the formula $\Delta = \frac{1}{2}bc\sin A = \frac{1}{2}ca\sin B = \frac{1}{2}ab\sin C$ is to think of it as

$\Delta = \frac{1}{2} \times$ one side $\times$ another side $\times$ the sine of the angle between them.

This enables you to use the formula for a triangle XYZ without having to re-label it as ABC, or do mental gymnastics with the letters concerned.

> The term 'included angle' is sometimes used for the angle between two sides.

Example 18.3.1
Find the areas of the triangles shown in Fig. 18.7.

> Note that the triangles are not drawn accurately. Only rough sketches are needed.

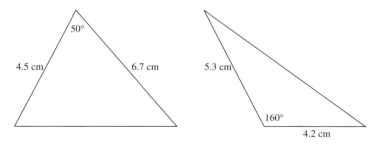

Fig. 18.7

For the left triangle, the area is given by

$$\Delta = \tfrac{1}{2} \times 4.5 \times 6.7 \times \sin 50° = 11.54... \,.$$

The area is 11.5 cm^2, correct to 3 significant figures.

For the right triangle, the area is given by

$$\Delta = \tfrac{1}{2} \times 5.3 \times 4.2 \times \sin 160° = 3.806... \,.$$

The area is 3.81 cm^2, correct to 3 significant figures.

Example 18.3.2

A triangle ABC with $BC = 3.4$ cm and $\hat{B} = 130°$ has an area of 5.72 cm^2. Find AB.

Begin by drawing a rough sketch like Fig. 18.8.

Denoting the length of side [AB] by c cm,

$$5.72 = \tfrac{1}{2} \times 3.4 \times c \times \sin 130°$$

giving

$$c = \frac{5.72}{\tfrac{1}{2} \times 3.4 \times \sin 130°} = 4.392... \,.$$

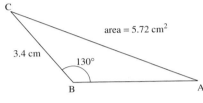

Fig. 18.8

So AB is 4.39 cm, correct to 3 significant figures.

Example 18.3.3

An obtuse-angled triangle ABC with $BC = 4.2$ m and $CA = 15$ m has an area of 7.12 m^2. Find the size of the obtuse angle at C.

Figure 18.9 shows a rough sketch of the triangle.

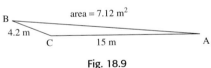

Fig. 18.9

As $7.12 = \tfrac{1}{2} \times 4.2 \times 15 \times \sin \hat{C}$,
$\sin \hat{C} = 0.2260... \,.$

The calculator gives the acute angle whose sine is 0.2260... as 13.06...°. Using the fact that for any value of θ, $\sin(180° - \theta°) = \sin \theta°$, the obtuse angle whose sine is 0.2260... is $(180 - 13.06...)\,°$.

Therefore $\hat{C} = 166.9°$, correct to 1 decimal place.

Exercise 18A

1 In each part, the lengths of two sides of a triangle and the angle between them are given. Find the area of each triangle, giving your answer in appropriate units.

(a) 3 cm, 4 cm, 90°   (b) 5 cm, 7 cm, 40°   (c) 3 m, 2 m, 140°

(d) 5 cm, 3 cm, 30°   (e) 4 cm, 3 cm, 123°   (f) 88 cm, 1 m, 45°

2 In each part, the area of a triangle, the length of one side and an angle which is not opposite to that side are given. Find the length of the other side of the triangle which is not opposite to the given angle.

(a) $5\,\text{cm}^2$, $3\,\text{cm}$, $40°$ (b) $8\,\text{cm}^2$, $4\,\text{cm}$, $90°$ (c) $3\,\text{m}^2$, $4\,\text{m}$, $110°$

(d) $23.2\,\text{cm}^2$, $7.1\,\text{cm}$, $43.3°$ (e) $15.1\,\text{cm}^2$, $1\,\text{cm}$, $136°$ (f) $1.40\,\text{m}^2$, $25\,\text{m}$, $85°$

3 In each part, the length of two sides of a triangle and its area are given. Find the angle between the two sides, given that it is acute.

(a) $3\,\text{cm}$, $6\,\text{cm}$, $5\,\text{cm}^2$,   (b) $4\,\text{cm}$, $5\,\text{cm}$, $8\,\text{cm}^2$,   (c) $5\,\text{m}$, $8\,\text{m}$, $7\,\text{m}^2$,

(d) $7.5\,\text{cm}$, $8.3\,\text{cm}$, $25.9\,\text{cm}^2$ (e) $10\,\text{cm}$, $15\,\text{cm}$, $15.1\,\text{cm}^2$,   (f) $3\,\text{m}$, $5\,\text{m}$, $1.40\,\text{m}^2$

4 With the data of Question 3, find the angle between the given sides, given that it is obtuse.

18.4 The sine rule for a triangle

In the formula $\Delta = \frac{1}{2}bc\sin \hat{A} = \frac{1}{2}ca\sin \hat{B} = \frac{1}{2}ab\sin \hat{C}$ for the area of a triangle, if you ignore the Δ and multiply all through by 2 you obtain

$$bc\sin \hat{A} = ca\sin \hat{B} = ab\sin \hat{C}$$

If you now divide each part of this equation by abc you get

$$\frac{\sin \hat{A}}{a} = \frac{\sin \hat{B}}{b} = \frac{\sin \hat{C}}{c}.$$

Just as with the formula for the area of a triangle, this formula is usually quoted without the circumflex angle signs. So

$$\frac{\sin A}{a} = \frac{\sin B}{b} = \frac{\sin C}{c}.$$

This is called the sine rule for a triangle. If you know two sides of a triangle and the angle opposite one of them, you can use it to find the angle opposite the other.

Example 18.4.1
In a triangle ABC, BC $= 11\,\text{cm}$, CA $= 15\,\text{cm}$ and angle A$\hat{B}$C $= 73°$. Find the angle B$\hat{A}$C.

Begin by drawing a rough sketch like Fig. 18.10.

You are given that $a = 11$, $b = 15$ and $\hat{B} = 73°$.

So you know $\dfrac{\sin \hat{B}}{b}$ completely, and you want to find $\hat{A}$. Neither c nor $\hat{C}$ is involved, so use $\dfrac{\sin \hat{A}}{a} = \dfrac{\sin \hat{B}}{b}$.

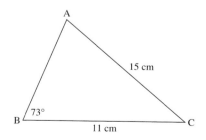

Fig. 18.10

Substituting the known values,

$$\frac{\sin \hat{A}}{11} = \frac{\sin 73°}{15},$$

so $\sin \hat{A} = \dfrac{11 \times \sin 73°}{15} = 0.701..., \quad A = 44.53...°.$

The angle BÂC is 44.5° to the nearest 0.1°.

> Notice that there is another angle, $(180 - 44.53...)°$, whose sine is also $0.701...$.
> But you can't have a triangle with one angle of 73° and another of 135.46...°,
> since their sum is greater than 180°.

You can also use the sine rule if you know two angles of a triangle and the side opposite
to one of them, and want to find the side opposite to the other. In that case the algebra is
simpler if you replace each fraction by its reciprocal (that is, turn it upside down), and give
the rule as

$$\frac{a}{\sin A} = \frac{b}{\sin B} = \frac{c}{\sin C}.$$

Example 18.4.2
In the triangle XYZ, angle $\hat{X} = 40°$, angle $\hat{Z} = 85°$ and XY = 8 cm. Calculate YZ.

The triangle is sketched in Fig. 18.11.

You know that $\hat{X} = 40°$, $\hat{Z} = 85°$ and $z = 8$, and
want to find x. So, adapting the rule with the new
letters,

$$\frac{x}{\sin 40°} = \frac{8}{\sin 85°}.$$

This gives $x = \dfrac{8 \sin 40°}{\sin 85°} = 5.161...$.

Thus YZ = 5.16 cm, correct to 3 significant figures.

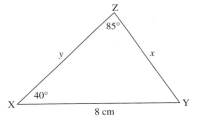

Fig. 18.11

> The **sine rule** for a triangle ABC is
>
> $$\frac{\sin A}{a} = \frac{\sin B}{b} = \frac{\sin C}{c}, \quad \text{or} \quad \frac{a}{\sin A} = \frac{b}{\sin B} = \frac{c}{\sin C}.$$
>
> Use the formula on the left to calculate the sine of an angle if you know
> the lengths of two sides and one other angle, which must not be the angle
> between the two known sides.
>
> Use the formula on the right to calculate a side if you know the length of
> another side and two of the angles of a triangle.

Example 18.4.3

In the triangle sketched in Fig. 18.12, calculate   (a) the angle $\hat{Q}$,   (b) PQ.

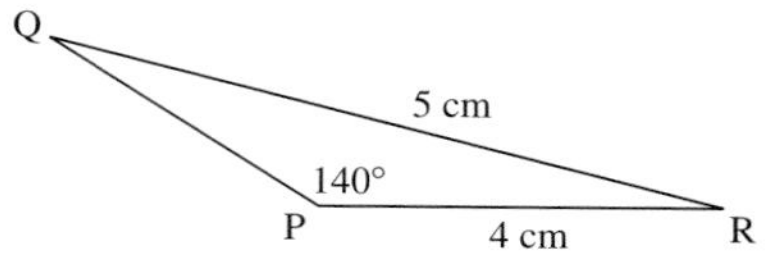

(a) You know that $p = 5$, $q = 4$ and $\hat{P} = 140°$,

so use $\dfrac{\sin \hat{P}}{p} = \dfrac{\sin \hat{Q}}{q}$.

This gives $\dfrac{\sin 140°}{5} = \dfrac{\sin \hat{Q}}{4}$, so

$$\sin \hat{Q} = \frac{4 \sin 140°}{5} = 0.5142... , \hat{Q} = 30.94...°.$$

The angle at Q is 30.9° to the nearest 0.1°.

Fig. 18.12

Another angle, $(180 - 30.9)°$, also has the property that its sine is 0.5142... , but it should be clear that this could not be an angle of a triangle in which one of the other angles is 140°.

(b) To find r you need to know the angle $\hat{R}$. This is easy, since $\hat{P} + \hat{Q} + \hat{R} = 180°$, so $\hat{R} = 180° - 140° - 30.94...° = 9.05...°$.

Now use the sine rule in the form $\dfrac{p}{\sin \hat{P}} = \dfrac{r}{\sin \hat{R}}$, to give $\dfrac{5}{\sin 140°} = \dfrac{r}{\sin 9.05...°}$,

$$r = \frac{5 \times \sin 9.05...°}{\sin 140°} = 1.224... .$$

So PQ is 1.22 cm, correct to 3 significant figures.

18.5   The longest and shortest sides of a triangle

Try drawing some sketches of triangles ABC (both acute- and obtuse-angled) with the angle at A greater than the angle at B. Is it always true that the side opposite A is longer than the side opposite B?

The answer to the question is yes:

> In any triangle ABC,
>   if $\hat{A} > \hat{B}$, then $a > b$,
> and   if $a > b$, then $\hat{A} > \hat{B}$.

You can use the sine rule to prove this, but it will not be proved in this book.

It follows from this that the longest side of a triangle is the side opposite the largest angle, and the shortest side is opposite the smallest angle; it is also true that the largest angle of a triangle is opposite the longest side and the smallest angle is opposite the shortest side.

Exercise 18B

1 In each part of this question, use the sine rule to find the length of the unknown side.

(a)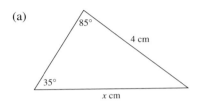

(b)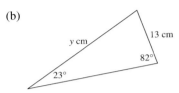

(c)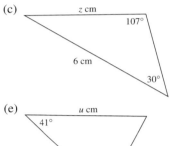

(d)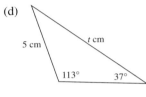

(e)

(f)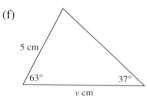

2 In each part, find the lengths of the other two sides, and the area of the triangle.

(a) In triangle ABC, $\hat{A} = 58°$, $\hat{B} = 63°$, AC = 13 cm

(b) In triangle PQR, $\hat{Q} = 118°$, $\hat{R} = 30°$, PR = 14 cm

(c) In triangle XYZ, $\hat{X} = 71°$, $\hat{Z} = 59°$, XZ = 12 cm

(d) In triangle LMN, $\hat{M} = 125°$, $\hat{N} = 15°$, LN = 13.2 cm

3 Find the remaining angles of the triangles ABC and XYZ.

(a) $\hat{B} = 91°$, BC = 11.1 cm, AC = 12.3 cm   (b) $\hat{X} = 71°$, YZ = 10.1 cm, XZ = 9.2 cm

4 The triangles LMN and DEF are both obtuse-angled. Find the remaining angles.

(a) $\hat{M} = 13°$, MN = 23.1 cm, LN = 5.2 cm   (b) $\hat{E} = 40°$, DF = 9 cm, DE = 13 cm

5 The following method is used to find the position of an object that you can see, but not get to, such as a tower across a river.

Let the tower be at T. Measure accurately the length of a base line [AB] on your side of the river, and measure the angles TÂB and TB̂A. Calculate

(a) AT,

(b) the perpendicular distance of the tower from the line segment [AB].

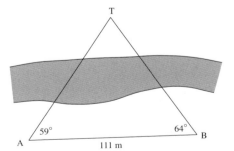

6 ABCD is a quadrilateral. The lengths of [CB] and [CD] are 4 cm and 3 cm respectively, and the diagonal CA is 5 cm. The angles at B and D are 70° and 120° respectively.

(a) Calculate angle BÂD.   (b) Calculate angle BĈD.

7 If you try to find the angle $\hat{A}$ in a triangle with $\hat{B} = 120°$, $a = 15$ cm and $b = 10$ cm you get an error message. Why?

8 ABCD is a quadrilateral. BÂC = 80°, BĈA = 30°, AĈD = 50° and AD̂C = 60°. The length of [AB] is 3 cm. Calculate

(a) AC,   (b) CD,   (c) the area of ABCD.

18.6   The cosine rule for a triangle

You have seen that, if you know one side of a triangle and the angle opposite to it, together with one other fact, you can use the sine rule to find the other sides and angles. The extra fact can either be another side (as in Example 18.4.1) or another angle (as in Example 18.4.2).

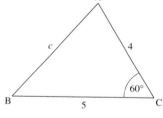

But if you know two sides and the angle between them, the sine rule is no help. For example, suppose that $a = 5$, $b = 4$ and $\hat{C} = 60°$ and you need to find c. This is shown in Fig. 18.13.

If you try to use the sine rule, you get

$$\frac{5}{\sin \hat{A}} = \frac{4}{\sin \hat{B}} = \frac{c}{\sin 60°}.$$

There is something unknown in each of the three fractions.   Fig. 18.13
To find c, you would need to know either $\sin \hat{A}$ or $\sin \hat{B}$, but you don't know either. You need another method.

In general, the problem is that you know both the lengths a units and b units and the size of the angle at C, and you need to find the length c units. The angle at C may be either acute (as in Fig. 18.14) or obtuse (as in Fig. 18.15).

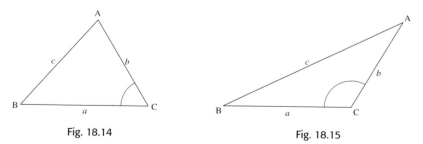

Fig. 18.14   Fig. 18.15

In Sections 17.1 and 17.2 the cosine and sine of an angle were defined using coordinates. It is convenient to go back to these definitions to derive a method for solving this problem.

In Figs. 18.16 and 18.17 the triangles in Figs. 18.14 and 18.15 have been picked up and put down on a set of coordinate axes.

The vertex C is placed on the origin, and the triangle is rotated so that the vertex A is placed on the positive x-axis. The coordinates of A are therefore $(b, 0)$.

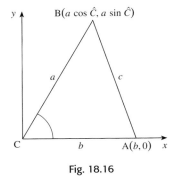
Fig. 18.16

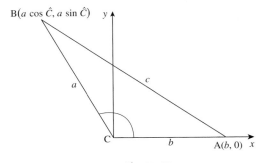
Fig. 18.17

The coordinates of the vertex B are $(a \cos \hat{C}, a \sin \hat{C})$. This is true whether the angle ACB is acute (as in Fig. 18.16) or obtuse (as in Fig. 18.17).

The formula in Section 8.1 for AB in terms of coordinates gives

$$c^2 = (a \cos \hat{C} - b)^2 + (a \sin \hat{C} - 0)^2$$
$$= (a \cos \hat{C})^2 - 2(a \cos \hat{C})b + b^2 + (a \sin \hat{C})^2$$
$$= (a \cos \hat{C})^2 + (a \sin \hat{C})^2 + b^2 - 2(a \cos \hat{C})b.$$

Using Pythagoras' theorem,

$$(a \cos \hat{C})^2 + (a \sin \hat{C})^2 = a^2.$$

Continuing with the expression for c^2

$$c^2 = (a \cos \hat{C})^2 + (a \sin \hat{C})^2 + b^2 - 2ab \cos \hat{C}$$
$$= a^2 + b^2 - 2ab \cos \hat{C}.$$

As with the previous formulae this formula, which is the cosine rule, is quoted without the circumflex sign over the angle.

So the cosine rule is

$$c^2 = a^2 + b^2 - 2ab \cos C.$$

Example 18.6.1 uses the cosine rule to solve the problem at the beginning of this section.

Example 18.6.1

In the triangle ABC, suppose that BC = 5 cm, CA = 4 cm and $\hat{C} = 60°$. Find the length of the side [AB] (see Fig. 18.18).

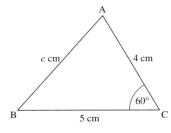

Using the cosine rule with $a = 5$, $b = 4$ and $\hat{C} = 60°$,

$$c^2 = 5^2 + 4^2 - 2 \times 5 \times 4 \times \cos 60°$$
$$= 25 + 16 - 40 \times \tfrac{1}{2}$$
$$= 21,$$

so $c = \sqrt{21} = 4.582...$.

The side [AB] has length 4.58 cm, correct to 3 significant figures.

Fig. 18.18

Of course, it may happen that you are given one of the other angles of the triangle, and the lengths of the two sides which border it. In that case you will need the rule in a different form, just as with the area formula in Section 18.3.

For a triangle ABC there are three forms of the equation:

> The **cosine rule** for a triangle ABC has one of the three forms:
>
> $$a^2 = b^2 + c^2 - 2bc \cos A,$$
> $$b^2 = c^2 + a^2 - 2ca \cos B,$$
> $$c^2 = a^2 + b^2 - 2ab \cos C.$$
>
> The cosine formula in one of these forms can be used to calculate the length of a side of a triangle when you know the lengths of the other two sides and the angle between them.

> Don't try to learn these three forms separately. Think of the formula as being like Pythagoras' theorem but with an adjustment, and remember the form of the adjustment.

Example 18.6.2

Find the length of the third side of a triangle given that two of the sides have lengths 4.58 cm and 3.51 cm, and that the angle between them is 130°.

Figure 18.19 shows a sketch which is not to scale.

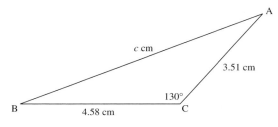

Fig. 18.19

In this case you know that $a = 4.58$, $b = 3.51$ and $\hat{C} = 130°$, so, using the cosine rule,

$$c^2 = 4.58^2 + 3.51^2 - 2 \times 4.58 \times 3.51 \times \cos 130°$$
$$= 53.963... \, ,$$

giving $c = 7.345...$.

The length of the third side is 7.35 cm, correct to 3 significant figures.

You can also use the cosine rule when you know the lengths of all three sides of a triangle and want to find one of the angles. This is illustrated in the next example.

Example 18.6.3

Nottingham is 35 km north of Leicester. Melton Mowbray is 22 km from Leicester on the east side and 27 km from Nottingham. Find the bearing of Melton Mowbray from Leicester, giving your answer to the nearest degree.

Denoting the towns by L, M and N in Fig. 18.20, you are given that $l = 27$, $m = 35$, $n = 22$ and you want to find $N\hat{L}M$.

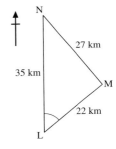

Substituting in the equation $l^2 = m^2 + n^2 - 2mn \cos L$,

$$729 = 1225 + 484 - 1540 \cos \hat{L},$$

so $1540 \cos \hat{L} = 1225 + 484 - 729 = 980,$

$$\cos \hat{L} = \tfrac{980}{1540} = 0.6363... \, .$$

This gives $L = 50.47...°$.

Fig. 18.20

The bearing of Melton Mowbray from Leicester is $050°$, to the nearest degree.

If you put the known values of a, b and c into the formulae in the blue box earlier in this section, you get equations for the unknowns $\cos \hat{A}$, $\cos \hat{B}$ and $\cos \hat{C}$. You can then solve these equations to find $\hat{A}$, $\hat{B}$ and $\hat{C}$.

For example, if you start with $c^2 = a^2 + b^2 - 2ab \cos \hat{C}$, you can rewrite it in the form

$$2ab \cos \hat{C} = a^2 + b^2 - c^2$$

which leads to

$$\cos \hat{C} = \frac{a^2 + b^2 - c^2}{2ab}.$$

You then have three equivalent formulae for finding angles:

The three forms of the cosine rule used for finding angles are

$$\cos A = \frac{b^2 + c^2 - a^2}{2bc}, \quad \cos B = \frac{c^2 + a^2 - b^2}{2ca}$$

and $\cos C = \dfrac{a^2 + b^2 - c^2}{2ab}.$

Note that the first two terms in each numerator refer to the sides which include the angle on the left side.

Example 18.6.4

Calculate the largest angle of the triangle with sides 2 cm, 3 cm and 4 cm.

The largest angle is at the vertex opposite the longest side. In Fig. 18.21, this is the angle at A.

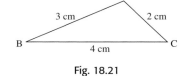

Putting the values $a = 4$, $b = 2$ and $c = 3$ into the equation $\cos \hat{A} = \dfrac{b^2 + c^2 - a^2}{2bc}$ gives

$$\cos \hat{A} = \frac{2^2 + 3^2 - 4^2}{2 \times 3 \times 2}$$

$$= \frac{4 + 9 - 16}{12}$$

$$= \frac{-3}{12} = -\tfrac{1}{4} = -0.25.$$

Thus $\hat{A} = 104.47...^\circ$.

The largest angle is 104.5°, correct to 1 decimal place.

Of course, you do not need to learn the three formulae in the box because you could go back to the earlier box and use the original form of the cosine rule. It doesn't matter which you do, as long you are confident about it and use whichever form you choose accurately.

Exercise 18C

1 In each part of this question, find the length of the remaining side.

  (a) BC = 10 cm, AC = 11 cm, $\hat{C} = 58°$

  (b) QR = 13 cm, PQ = 5 cm, $\hat{Q} = 123°$

  (c) XY = 15.1 cm, XZ = 14.2 cm, $\hat{X} = 23°$

  (d) LN = 14.8 cm, LM = 13.2 cm, $\hat{L} = 179°$

2 Find the largest angle in each of the following triangles.

  (a) $a = 10$, $b = 11$, $c = 12$ (b) $l = 8$, $m = 19$, $n = 13$

  (c) $x = 14.1$, $y = 20.0$, $z = 15.3$ (d) $d = 9$, $e = 40$, $f = 41$

3 Find the smallest angle in each of the following triangles.

  (a) $a = 10$, $b = 8$, $c = 7$ (b) $x = 9$, $y = 9$, $z = 13$

  (c) $p = 8$, $q = 4$, $r = 5$ (d) $d = 4$, $e = 3$, $f = 5$

4 Find the area of the triangle with sides 8 cm, 9 cm and 10 cm.

19 Solving triangles

This chapter shows you how to use the sine and cosine rules efficiently to find unknown sides and angles of triangles. When you have completed it, you should

- know what the ambiguous case is, and be able to deal with it
- be able to use the sine and cosine rules to find all the unknown sides and angles in triangles which are not right-angled.

19.1 The ambiguous case

Suppose that you are given the following problem.

Example 19.1.1
In a triangle ABC, AB $= 10\,$cm, $\hat{CAB} = 20°$ and BC $= 4\,$cm. Calculate $\hat{ABC}$.

As usual, start by drawing a rough sketch, shown in Fig. 19.1.

If you draw a reasonable sketch to scale, you will see a problem. When you draw an arc with centre at B, it cuts the line at 20° to (AB) twice, giving two possible values for $\hat{ABC}$.

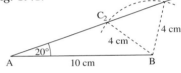

Fig. 19.1

If you use the sine formula, you find that

$$\frac{\sin \hat{ACB}}{10} = \frac{\sin 20°}{4}$$

giving

$$\sin \hat{ACB} = \frac{10 \sin 20°}{4}.$$

This shows that $\hat{ACB} = 58.76...°$.

It is clear that this corresponds to the point C_1. What has happened to the other point C_2?

You may have spotted the answer. The equation $\sin \hat{ACB} = \dfrac{10 \sin 20°}{4}$ has two solutions in the interval $0° < \hat{ACB} < 180°$. The other solution is $180° - 58.76...° = 121.23...°$.

So angle $\hat{ABC} = 58.8°$ or $121.2°$, correct to 1 decimal place.

This situation, in which the triangle is not completely specified by the information given, is called the **ambiguous case**.

It may arise when you are given two sides and one angle of a triangle, but the angle given is not the angle between the two sides.

Here is another example.

Example 19.1.2

In the triangle PQR, [PQ] has length 40 m, and $P\hat{Q}R = 40°$. The length of [PR] is 30 m. Find the possible values of the angle $R\hat{P}Q$.

Start by drawing a sketch, as in Fig. 19.2.

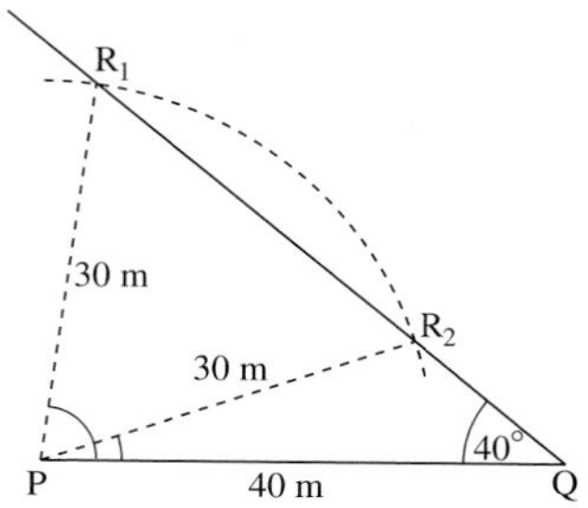

As you can see, there are two possibilities for R: call them R_1 and R_2.

You will find that you cannot use the sine formula directly to find either of the angles R_1PQ or R_2PQ, but you can find the other angle of the triangle, and then use the angle sum of the triangle to find the third angle.

Fig. 19.2

$$\frac{\sin P\hat{R}Q}{40} = \frac{\sin 40°}{30}$$

giving

$$\sin P\hat{R}Q = \frac{40 \sin 40°}{30},$$

so

$$P\hat{R}Q = 58.98...° \text{ or } 180° - 58.98...°$$
$$= 58.98...° \text{ or } 121.01...°.$$

Therefore

$$R\hat{P}Q = 180° - 40° - 58.98...° \text{ or } 180° - 40° - 121.01...°$$
$$= 81.01...° \text{ or } 18.98...°$$
$$= 81.0° \text{ or } 19.0°, \text{ correct to 1 decimal place.}$$

The next example shows another possibility when dealing with the ambiguous case.

Example 19.1.3

In the triangle XYZ, XY = 20 cm, YZ = 12 cm and angle $Z\hat{X}Y = 30°$. Calculate the possible lengths of the side [XZ].

Figure 19.3 shows the situation.

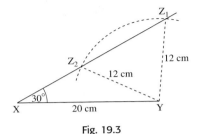

Method 1 This method uses a direct approach.

Let the length of XZ be y cm.

Then, using the cosine formula,

$$12^2 = 20^2 + y^2 - 2 \times 20 \times y \times \cos 30°$$

giving, since $\cos 30° = \frac{1}{2}\sqrt{3}$,

$$y^2 - 20\sqrt{3}y + 256 = 0.$$

Fig. 19.3

Solving this quadratic equation gives

$$y = \frac{20\sqrt{3} \pm \sqrt{(20\sqrt{3})^2 - 4 \times 1 \times 256}}{2}$$

$$= \frac{20\sqrt{3} \pm \sqrt{176}}{2}$$

$$= 10.68... \quad \text{or} \quad 23.95... .$$

So XZ is either 10.7 cm or 24.0 cm, correct to 3 significant figures.

Method 2 This method uses an indirect approach.

Use the sine formula to find the angle at Z.

$$\frac{\sin \hat{Z}}{20} = \frac{\sin 30°}{12},$$

giving $\hat{Z} = 56.44...°$ or $\hat{Z} = 180° - 56.44...° = 123.55...°$.

Referring to the diagram, $X\hat{Z}_1Y = 56.44...°$ and $X\hat{Z}_2Y = 123.55...°$.

The third angle of the triangle is then $X\hat{Y}Z_1 = 180° - 30° - 56.44...° = 93.55...°$ or $X\hat{Y}Z_2 = 180° - 30° - 123.55...° = 26.44...°$.

Now use the sine formula in each case to get

$$\frac{y}{\sin 93.55...°} = \frac{12}{\sin 30°} \quad \text{or} \quad \frac{y}{\sin 26.44...°} = \frac{12}{\sin 30°},$$

giving $y = 23.95...$ or $y = 10.68... .$

So XZ is either 10.7 cm or 24.0 cm, correct to 3 significant figures.

Exercise 19A

In this exercise, there may be more than one triangle which matches the given information.

1 Find the other angles of the triangles given.

   (a) In triangle ABC, $\hat{A} = 20°$, AB = 10 cm, BC = 4 cm.
   (b) In triangle XYZ, $\hat{Z} = 50°$, ZY = 12 cm, XY = 10 cm.
   (c) In triangle PQR, $\hat{Q} = 40°$, PQ = 12 cm, PR = 13 cm.

2 Find the length of the third side in each of the given triangles.

   (a) In triangle DEF, $\hat{D} = 25°$, DE = 13 cm, EF = 6 cm.
   (b) In triangle LMN, $\hat{L} = 45°$, MN = 11 cm, LM = 15 cm.
   (c) In triangle UVW, $\hat{U} = 80°$, VW = 19 cm, UV = 18 cm.

19.2   Calculating sides and angles

If you are given information about a triangle and are asked to find all the remaining sides and angles, you are said to be **solving the triangle**.

Precisely how you do this will depend on the information you are given.

> • If you know one side, the opposite angle and one other fact (a side or an angle) then begin by using the sine rule.
>
> • If you know two sides and the angle between them, or three sides, begin by using the cosine rule.
>
> • Once you know two angles, you can find the third by using the fact that sum of the three angles is 180°.
>
> • Once you know three sides and an angle, you can find another angle either by using the cosine rule or by using the sine rule. If you use the sine rule, it is better to use it to find the smaller angle.
>
> • If you know two sides and an angle which is not between the sides, it is possible that there may be more than one triangle. You could start either by using the sine rule or the cosine rule.
>
> • Don't approximate prematurely, or you will lose accuracy; keep the full values in your calculator memory until the end of the calculation.

Example 19.2.1

In triangle ABC, $a = 9$, $b = 10$ and $\hat{B} = 20°$. Solve the triangle.

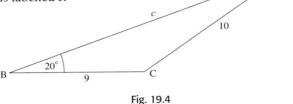

In the sketch (Fig. 19.4) side AB is labelled c.

You are given the angle $\hat{B}$ and the side b, so use the sine rule. As the other piece of information is a, use it in the form $\dfrac{\sin \hat{A}}{a} = \dfrac{\sin \hat{B}}{b}$ to get

Fig. 19.4

$$\frac{\sin \hat{A}}{9} = \frac{\sin 20°}{10}$$

giving $\sin \hat{A} = \dfrac{9 \times \sin 20°}{10} = 0.307...$,

so $\hat{A} = 17.92...°$ or $162.07...°$.

But the obtuse angle is impossible because the angle sum would be greater than $180°$, so $\hat{A} = 17.92...°$.

You can now find the third angle from $\hat{C} = 180° - 20° - 17.92...° = 142.07...°$.

To find c, use the sine formula.

$$\frac{10}{\sin 20°} = \frac{c}{\sin 142.07...°} \quad \text{gives} \quad c = \frac{10 \times \sin 142.07...°}{\sin 20°} = 17.97... \,.$$

The other two angles are $17.9°$ and $142.1°$, correct to 1 decimal place, and $c = 18.0$, correct to 3 significant figures.

Example 19.2.2

Solve the triangle shown in Fig. 19.5.

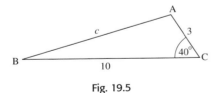

Fig. 19.5

You have no choice about how to start; use the cosine formula to find the side c.

$$c^2 = 10^2 + 3^2 - 2 \times 10 \times 3 \times \cos 40° = 63.03... \quad \text{giving} \quad c = 7.939... \,.$$

Store this number in the calculator. You are going to need it again later.

You now have a choice: you could either use the sine rule or the cosine rule.

Method 1   Using the sine rule

Find either $\hat{A}$ or $\hat{B}$; choose the smaller angle, $\hat{B}$, because the angle at $\hat{A}$ might be obtuse.

$$\frac{\sin \hat{B}}{3} = \frac{\sin 40°}{7.939...} \quad \text{giving} \quad \sin \hat{B} = \frac{3 \times \sin 40°}{7.939...} = 0.2428... \text{, and}$$

B $= 14.05...°$. This leaves angle $\hat{A}$ to be found by subtraction, giving

$$\hat{A} = 180° - 40° - 14.05...° = 125.94...°.$$

(Note that if you used $\dfrac{\sin \hat{A}}{10} = \dfrac{\sin 40°}{7.939...}$, you would get $\sin \hat{A} = 0.809...$, giving $\hat{A} = 54.05...°$, but you want $\hat{A} = 180° - 54.05...°$, *not* $54.05...°$.)

Method 2   Using the cosine rule

Find either $\hat{A}$ or $\hat{B}$ by the cosine rule.

$$\cos \hat{A} = \frac{3^2 + 7.939...^2 - 10^2}{2 \times 3 \times 7.939...} = -0.586... \text{,} \quad \text{giving} \quad \hat{A} = 125.94...°.$$

Then $\hat{B} = 180° - 40° - 125.94...° = 14.05...°$.

By either method, the angle at A is $125.9°$, the angle at B is $14.1°$, both correct to 1 decimal place, and the length of side c is 7.94 units, correct to 3 significant figures.

Exercise 19B

In each question solve the given triangle.

1 In triangle ABC, BC $= 5$ cm, $\hat{A} = 50°$ and $\hat{B} = 60°$.

2 In triangle XYZ, XY $= 6$ cm, YZ $= 7$ cm and $\hat{X} = 80°$.

3 In triangle PQR, PQ $= 3$ cm, QR $= 5$ cm and RP $= 7$ cm.

4 In triangle LMN, MN $= 10$ cm, NL $= 11$ cm and $\hat{N} = 110°$.

5 In triangle DEF, DE $= 10$ cm, EF $= 6$ cm and $\hat{D} = 30°$.

20 Radians

This chapter introduces radians, an alternative to degrees for measuring angles. When you have completed it, you should

- know how to convert from degrees to radians and vice versa
- be able to use the formula $r\theta$ for the length of a circular arc, and $\frac{1}{2}r^2\theta$ for the area of a circular sector.

20.1 Radians

Suppose that you were meeting angles for the first time, and that you were asked to suggest a unit for measuring them. It seems highly unlikely that you would suggest the degree, which was invented by the Babylonians in ancient times. The full circle, or the right angle, both seem more natural units.

However, the unit used in modern mathematics is the radian, illustrated in Fig. 20.1. This is particularly useful in differentiating trigonometric functions, as you will see when you study Chapter 21 in Higher Level 2.

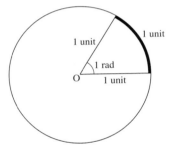

In a circle of radius 1 unit, radii joining the centre O to the ends of an arc of length 1 unit form an angle called **1 radian**. The abbreviation for radian is **rad**.

Fig. 20.1

You can see immediately from this definition that, as the circumference of the unit circle is 2π, there are 2π radians in $360°$. This leads to the following conversion rules for radians to degrees and vice versa:

> π rad $= 180°$.
>
> To convert degrees to radians, multiply by $\dfrac{\pi}{180}$.
>
> To convert radians to degrees, multiply by $\dfrac{180}{\pi}$.

You could calculate that 1 radian is equal to $57.295...°$, but no one uses this conversion. It is simplest to remember that π rad $= 180°$, and to use this to convert between radians and degrees.

> You can set your calculator to radian mode, and then work entirely in radians.
>
> You might find on your calculator another unit for angle called the 'grad'; there are 100 grads to the right angle. Grads will not be used in this course.

Example 20.1.1

Convert $40°$ to radians, leaving your answer as a multiple of π.

Using the conversion factor in the blue box,

$$40° = 40 \times \frac{\pi}{180} \text{ rad} = \tfrac{2}{9}\pi \text{ rad}.$$

It is worthwhile learning a few common conversions, so that you can think in both radians and degrees. For example, you should know and recognise the following conversions:

$$180° = \pi \text{ rad}, \qquad 90° = \tfrac{1}{2}\pi \text{ rad}, \qquad 45° = \tfrac{1}{4}\pi \text{ rad},$$
$$30° = \tfrac{1}{6}\pi \text{ rad}, \qquad 60° = \tfrac{1}{3}\pi \text{ rad}, \qquad 360° = 2\pi \text{ rad}.$$

20.2   Length of arc and area of sector

Figure 20.2 shows a circle, centre O and radius r. An arc of this circle has been drawn with a thicker line, and the two radii at the ends of the arc have been drawn. These radii have an angle θ rad between them. This is described more briefly by saying that the arc **subtends** an angle θ rad at the centre of the circle. You can calculate the length of the circular arc by noticing that the length of the arc is the fraction $\dfrac{\theta}{2\pi}$ of the length $2\pi r$ of the circumference of the circle.

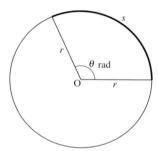

Fig. 20.2

Let s be the arc length. Then

$$s = \frac{\theta}{2\pi} \times 2\pi r = r\theta.$$

You can use a similar argument to calculate the area of a sector.

The circular sector, centre O and radius r, shown shaded in Fig. 20.3, has an angle θ rad at the centre.

The area of the circular sector is the fraction $\dfrac{\theta}{2\pi}$ of the area πr^2 of the full circle.

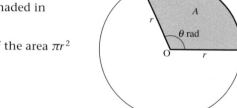

Fig. 20.3

Let A be the required area. Then

$$A = \frac{\theta}{2\pi} \times \pi r^2 = \tfrac{1}{2}r^2\theta.$$

> The length of a circular arc with radius r and angle θ rad is $s = r\theta$.
>
> The area of a circular sector with radius r and angle θ rad is $A = \tfrac{1}{2}r^2\theta$.

> No units are given in the formulae above. The units are the appropriate units associated with the length; for instance, length in m and area in m².

Example 20.2.1

In Fig. 20.4, find the length of the arc AB and the area of the sector OAB.

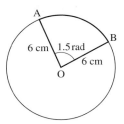

Fig. 20.4

Using the formulae in the blue box,

length of the arc AB is 6×1.5 cm $= 9$ cm,
area of sector OAB is $\frac{1}{2} \times 6^2 \times 1.5$ cm$^2 = 27$ cm^2.

Example 20.2.2

In Fig. 20.5, the area of the sector AOB is 18.4 m^2. Find AÔB.

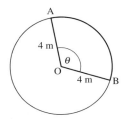

Fig. 20.5

Let AÔB $= \theta$ radians.

The area of the sector in m^2 is given by $\frac{1}{2} \times 4^2 \times \theta$, so

$$\frac{1}{2} \times 4^2 \times \theta = 18.4.$$

So $8\theta = 18.4$, giving $\theta = 2.3$.

The angle AÔB is 2.3 radians.

In degrees, this is $\left(\dfrac{180}{\pi} \times 2.3 \right)^{\circ}$, which is 132° to the nearest degree.

As the radian is a measure of angle, like the degree, you can expect to need to find the sine, cosine and tangent of an angle in radians. Fortunately, your calculator enables you to do this, usually by putting it into radian mode.

Example 20.2.3

Find the perimeter and the area of the segment cut off by a chord [PQ] of length 8 cm from a circle centre O and radius 6 cm. Give your answers correct to 3 significant figures.

> In problems of this type, it is helpful to start by thinking about the complete sector OPQ, rather than just the shaded segment of Fig. 20.6.

The perimeter of the segment consists of two parts, the straight part of length 8 cm, and the curved part; to calculate the length of the curved part you need to know the angle PÔQ.

Call this angle θ radians. As triangle POQ is isosceles, a perpendicular drawn from O to (PQ) bisects both [PQ] and angle PÔQ, shown in Fig. 20.7.

$$\sin \tfrac{1}{2}\theta = \tfrac{4}{6} = 0.666... , \text{ so } \tfrac{1}{2}\theta = 0.7297... \text{ and } \theta = 1.459... .$$

> Make sure that your calculator is in radian mode.

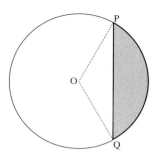

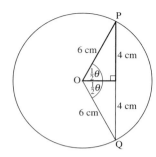

Fig. 20.6   Fig. 20.7

Then the perimeter d cm is given by $d = 8 + 6\theta = 16.756...$; the perimeter is 16.8 cm, correct to 3 significant figures.

To find the area of the segment, you need to find the area of the sector OPQ, and then subtract the area of the triangle OPQ. Using the formula $\frac{1}{2}bc \sin A$ for the area of a triangle, the area of the triangle POQ is given by $\frac{1}{2}r^2 \sin \theta$. Thus the area in cm^2 of the shaded region is

$$\tfrac{1}{2}r^2(\theta - \sin \theta) = \tfrac{1}{2} \times 6^2 \times (1.459... - \sin 1.459...)$$
$$= 8.381... .$$

The area is 8.38 cm^2, correct to 3 significant figures.

It is worthwhile using your calculator to store the value of θ to use in the calculations. If you round θ to 3 significant figures and use the rounded value, you are liable to introduce errors.

Example 20.2.4

A chord of a circle which subtends an angle of θ radians at the centre of the circle cuts off a segment equal in area to $\frac{1}{3}$ of the area of the whole circle.

(a) Show that $\theta - \sin \theta = \frac{2}{3}\pi$.

(b) Use your calculator to solve the equation $\theta - \sin \theta = \frac{2}{3}\pi$ graphically.

(a) Let r cm be the radius of the circle in Fig. 20.8. Using a method similar to the one in Example 20.2.3, the area of the segment is

$$\tfrac{1}{2}r^2(\theta - \sin \theta).$$

This is $\frac{1}{3}$ of the area of the whole circle if

$$\tfrac{1}{2}r^2(\theta - \sin \theta) = \tfrac{1}{3}\pi r^2.$$

Multiplying by 2 and dividing by r^2 you get the required result.

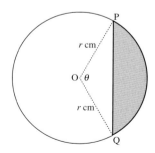

Fig. 20.8

(b) By drawing the graph of $y = \theta - \sin \theta - \frac{2}{3}\pi$ on your calculator and finding where this graph intersects the θ-axis, you find that $\theta = 2.61$ correct to 2 decimal places.

20.3 Radians or degrees?

You have probably thought up to now that degrees are the natural units for angle. However, the radian turns out to be important in differentiating and integrating trigonometric functions. For this reason, a new convention about angle will now be adopted.

In Chapter 17, when the only unit for angle that you knew was degrees, the usual way to write the cosine, sine and tangent of an angle was $\cos\theta°$, $\sin\theta°$ and $\tan\theta°$.

If the units are radians, the cosine, sine and tangent will be written without the degree sign as $\cos\theta$, $\sin\theta$ and $\tan\theta$.

If no units are given for trigonometric functions, you should assume that the units are radians, or that it doesn't matter whether the units are radians or degrees.

For example, if you see the equation $\sin\theta = 0.5$, then θ is in radians. If you are asked for the smallest positive solution of the equation, you should give $\theta = \frac{1}{6}\pi$. In this situation, where the solution is an exact multiple of π, you should express your answer as a multiple of π, but if the equation were $\sin\theta = 0.4$, you would give the answer in decimal form as 0.411... , or as 0.412, correct to 3 significant figures.

If, however, degrees are being used, then the degree sign will continue to be used. So, if you see $\sin\theta° = 0.5$, then θ is in degrees, and the smallest positive solution is $\theta = 30$.

This may seem complicated, but the context will usually make things clear.

Remember:

$$\pi\,\text{rad} = 180°.$$

Exercise 20

1 Write each of the following angles in radians, leaving your answer as a multiple of π.

(a) 90°	(b) 135°	(c) 45°	(d) 30°
(e) 72°	(f) 18°	(g) 120°	(h) $22\frac{1}{2}°$
(i) 720°	(j) 600°	(k) 270°	(l) 1°

2 Each of the following is an angle in radians. Without using a calculator change these to degrees.

(a) $\frac{1}{3}\pi$	(b) $\frac{1}{20}\pi$	(c) $\frac{1}{5}\pi$	(d) $\frac{1}{8}\pi$
(e) $\frac{1}{9}\pi$	(f) $\frac{2}{3}\pi$	(g) $\frac{5}{8}\pi$	(h) $\frac{3}{5}\pi$
(i) $\frac{1}{45}\pi$	(j) 6π	(k) $-\frac{1}{2}\pi$	(l) $\frac{5}{18}\pi$

3 The following questions refer to the diagram, where
   r = radius of circle (in cm),
   s = arc length (in cm),
   A = area of sector (in cm^2),
   θ = angle subtended at centre (in radians).

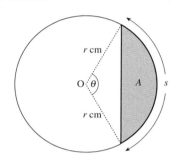

(a) $r = 7, \theta = 1.2$. Find s and A.

(b) $r = 3.5, \theta = 2.1$. Find s and A.

(c) $s = 12, r = 8$. Find θ and A.

(d) $s = 14, \theta = 0.7$. Find r and A.

(e) $A = 30, r = 5$. Find θ and s.   (f) $A = 24, r = 6$. Find s.

(g) $A = 64, s = 16$. Find r and θ.   (h) $A = 30, s = 10$. Find θ.

4 Find the area of the shaded segment in each
   of the following cases.

(a) $r = 5$ cm, $\theta = \frac{1}{3}\pi$

(b) $r = 3.1$ cm, $\theta = \frac{2}{5}\pi$

(c) $r = 28$ cm, $\theta = \frac{5}{6}\pi$

(d) $r = 6$ cm, $s = 9$ cm

(e) $r = 9.5$ cm, $s = 4$ cm

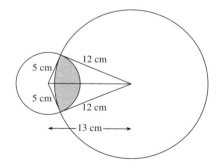

5 Find the area of the segment cut off by a chord of length 10 cm from a circle radius 13 cm.

6 Find the perimeter of the segment cut off by a chord of length 14 cm from a circle radius 25 cm.

7 Two circles of radii 5 cm and 12 cm are
   drawn, partly overlapping. Their centres
   are 13 cm apart. Find the area common
   to the two circles.

8 Two circles of radius 6 cm and 4 cm have their centres 7 cm apart. Find the perimeter and area of the region common to both circles.

9 Without the use of a calculator write down the exact values of the following.

(a) $\sin \frac{1}{3}\pi$ (b) $\cos \frac{1}{4}\pi$ (c) $\tan \frac{1}{6}\pi$ (d) $\cos \frac{3}{2}\pi$

(e) $\sin \frac{7}{4}\pi$ (f) $\cos \frac{7}{6}\pi$ (g) $\tan \frac{5}{3}\pi$ (h) $(\sin \frac{2}{3}\pi)^2$

21 Three-dimensional problems

In this chapter you will use the techniques you have developed to solve problems in three dimensions. When you have completed it, you should

*   know how to draw a suitable diagram for a three-dimensional problem
*   be able to use the right-angled triangle trigonometry to solve the problem.

21.1 A general strategy

One of the most important parts of solving problems in three dimensions is being able to visualise the situation. A good diagram is essential.

You may find it helpful to be reminded of two terms: the *angle subtended* by a line segment [AB] at a point P, is angle $A\hat{P}B$ (see Fig. 21.1); the *angle of elevation* of a point P from another point Q is the angle $Q\hat{P}H$ that the line segment [PQ] makes with the horizontal line segment [PH], where PH is horizontal, and H is vertically below P (see Fig. 21.2).

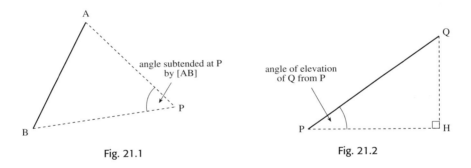

Fig. 21.1   Fig. 21.2

The problems in this chapter are of three types: pyramid, box and wedge problems.

Start by drawing a figure ensuring that no points are 'on top of each other'. It often helps to use dotted lines to indicate 'invisible' edges and to mark right angles with a 'corner' symbol (like H in Fig. 21.2).

21.2 Problems involving pyramids

Example 21.2.1
ABCD is the square base of side 6 cm of a pyramid whose vertex V is 7 cm directly above the centre O of the square. Calculate

(a) angle $A\hat{V}C$,   (b) the angle between a slanting face and the base.

Notice that in Fig. 21.3(a) there are a number of right angles which are not marked. For instance, all the corners of the square base are right angles.

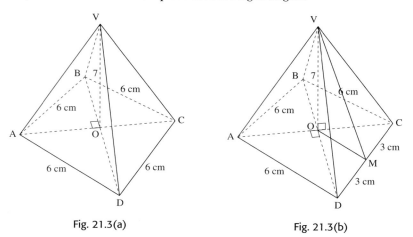

Fig. 21.3(a)   Fig. 21.3(b)

(a) AV̂C is the vertical angle of the isosceles triangle AVC, so you can calculate AV̂C by finding the angle AV̂O and doubling it.

Triangle AVO is right-angled at O, and you can find AO by using Pythagoras' theorem in the isosceles right-angled triangle AOB, in which the hypotenuse is 6 cm. Denoting AO by x cm,

$$x^2 + x^2 = 6^2,$$

giving $x = \sqrt{18}$.

Then, in triangle AVO,

$$\tan A\hat{V}O = \frac{\sqrt{18}}{7}$$

so $A\hat{V}O = 31.21...°$.
Hence

$$A\hat{V}C = 2 \times A\hat{V}O = 2 \times 31.21...° = 62.43...°.$$

$A\hat{V}C = 62.4°$, correct to 3 significant figures.

(b) The angle between a sloping face and the base is the angle OMV where M is the mid-point of [CD] in Fig. 21.3(b).

In triangle OMV, the angle at O is a right angle, OM = 3 cm and the height OV = 7 cm.

So $\tan O\hat{M}V = \frac{7}{3}$,   giving $O\hat{M}V = 66.8...°$.

The angle between the slanting face and the base is 66.8°, correct to 3 significant figures.

You can use this type of diagram to solve all pyramid problems. The shape of the base of the pyramid is only a slight complication.

21.3 Box problems

Figure 21.4 shows a typical box.

The usual way to draw the box is to draw two identical rectangles, one 'behind' the other, and then to join up the vertices appropriately. It can be useful to make some of the lines dotted to make it clear which face is in front.

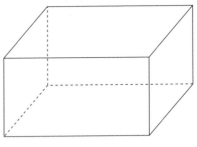

Fig. 21.4

Example 21.3.1

A rectangular room has length 5 m, width 4 m and height 2 m. Find the angle that a diagonal of the room makes with the ceiling.

Figure 21.5 shows the situation. Let the diagonal of the room be [AR], and let [CR] be the diagonal of the ceiling. Let the required angle be α.

You can use Pythagoras' theorem to find the diagonal [CR] of the ceiling and then find the angle $\alpha°$ from the triangle ACR with the right angle at C. Let CR $= x$ cm.

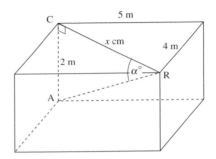

Fig. 21.5

$$x = \sqrt{4^2 + 5^2} = \sqrt{41}$$

so $$\tan \alpha° = \frac{2}{\sqrt{41}}$$

and $\alpha = 17.34\ldots$.

Therefore the diagonal makes an angle of 17.3° with the ceiling.

Sometimes a problem may not seem to be a box problem, but can be solved by using a box diagram with some edges missing.

Example 21.3.2

The top, F, of a flagpole standing on level ground subtends an angle of 10° at a point S which is 50 m due south from the bottom B of the flagpole, and 5° at a point E lying east of the flagpole. Calculate the distance SE correct to the nearest metre.

The diagram, Fig. 21.6, is part of the typical box diagram shown in Fig. 21.4.

To calculate SE, start by finding the height of the flagpole, then the length BE, and then use Pythagoras' theorem in triangle BSE to find SE.

In triangle BFS, let the height of the flagpole be h m. Then

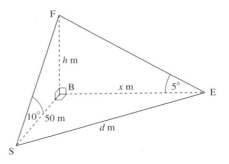

Fig. 21.6

$$\tan 10° = \frac{h}{50}$$

so $h = 50 \tan 10°$.

In triangle BFE, let BE = x m.

$$\tan 5° = \frac{h}{x} = \frac{50 \tan 10°}{x}$$

so $$x = \frac{50 \tan 10°}{\tan 5°}$$

Finally, using Pythagoras' theorem in triangle BES, and letting SE = d m,

$$d^2 = x^2 + 50^2$$
$$= \left(\frac{50 \tan 10°}{\tan 5°}\right)^2 + 50^2$$
$$= 12\ 654.86... ,$$

so   SE = 112 m, correct to the nearest metre.

You may want to calculate values for h and x as you go along, but, if you can manage it, it is better practice to do the calculation in one go at the end.

21.4   Wedge problems

The third type of problem involves drawing a wedge (see Fig. 21.7). This wedge is really only part of a box, so you could think of a wedge problem as a special case of a box problem, but it is easier to think of it in a separate category.

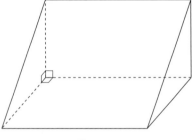

Fig. 21.7

Example 21.4.1

The line of greatest slope of a flat hillside slopes at an angle of 20° to the horizontal. To reduce the angle of climb to 15°, a walker walks on a straight path which makes an angle of α° with the line of greatest slope on the hillside. Find α.

In Fig. 21.8, let [AB] be the line of greatest slope, and [AC] be the path of the walker. The angle α° that you need to find is angle BÂC. As there are no units to the problem, let the height EB be 1 unit.

To find α you need to find some lengths in triangle BAC. You can find AB from triangle ABE, and AC from triangle ACF. Let AB = x units and AC = y units.

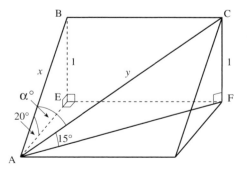

Fig. 21.8

In triangle ABE,

$$\sin 20° = \frac{1}{x}, \quad \text{so} \quad x = \frac{1}{\sin 20°}.$$

In triangle ACF,

$$\sin 15° = \frac{1}{y}, \quad \text{so} \quad y = \frac{1}{\sin 15°}.$$

Finally, in triangle BAC,

$$\cos \alpha = \frac{x}{y}$$
$$= \frac{1/\sin 20°}{1/\sin 15°}$$
$$= \frac{\sin 15°}{\sin 20°} = 0.756... .$$

Therefore $\alpha = 40.8$, correct to 3 significant figures.

Exercise 21

1 A pyramid has its vertex directly above the centre of its square base. The edges of the base are each 8 cm, and the vertical height is 10 cm. Find the angle between the slant face and the base, and the angle between a slant edge and the base.

2 A square board is suspended horizontally by four equal ropes attached to a point P directly above the centre of the board. Each rope has length 15 m and is inclined at an angle of 10° with the vertical. Calculate the length of the side of the square board.

3 A cube is standing on a horizontal base. One vertex of the base is A. Find the angle of elevation at A made by the vertex of the cube which is furthest from A.

4 A pylon is situated at a corner of a rectangular field with dimensions 120 m by 100 m. The angle subtended by the pylon at the furthest corner of the field is 5°. Find the angles subtended by the pylon at the other two corners of the field.

5 A regular tetrahedron ABCD has all its edges 8 cm in length. Find the angle which the edge [AD] makes with the line drawn from A perpendicular to BCD.

6 A vertical flagpole standing on horizontal ground has six ropes attached to it at a point 6 m from the ground. The other ends of the ropes are attached to points on the ground which lie in a regular hexagon with sides 4 m. Find the angle which a rope makes with the ground.

7 A rectangular piece of fencing ABCD of height 2 metres and width 3 metres stands vertically on horizontal ground, with [AB] on the ground. An observer notices that, at a certain time, the shadow of the point C is at the point P on the ground, where PAB is a right angle and PA = 1 metre. Find the angle of elevation of the sun at that time.

8 A triangular pyramid has a base ABC which is an isosceles triangle. AB = 3 metres, AC = 3 metres and BC = 4 metres. The vertex V is directly above the point O, which is 1 metre from A on the line joining A to the mid-point M of [BC] and OV = 4 metres. Calculate the angle between [VA] and [VB].

9 A woman is standing on level ground in front of a straight vertical wall. The perpendicular line drawn from her to the wall meets the wall at one of its ends A. The angle of elevation of the top of the wall directly above A is 10°. The base of the other end of the wall is B and the angle of elevation of the top of the wall above B is 5°. The woman walks directly towards B. When she has walked 20 metres, the angle of elevation of the top of the wall above B is 10°.

   (a) Find the height of the wall.   (b) Find the length of the wall.

   Give both answers correct to 3 significant figures.

Review exercise 5

1 Write down the period of each of the following.

    (a) $\sin x^\circ$ (b) $\tan 2x^\circ$ (OCR)

2 Draw the graph of $y = \cos \frac{1}{2}\theta^\circ$ for θ in the interval $-360 \le \theta \le 360$. Mark clearly the coordinates of the points where the graph crosses the θ- and y-axes.

3 A tuning fork is vibrating. The displacement, y centimetres, of the tip of one of the prongs from its rest position after t seconds is given by

$$y = 0.1 \sin(100\ 000t)^\circ.$$

Find

    (a) the greatest displacement and the first time at which it occurs,

    (b) the time taken for one complete oscillation of the prong,

    (c) the number of complete oscillations per second of the tip of the prong,

    (d) the total time during the first complete oscillation for which the tip of the prong is more than 0.06 centimetres from its rest position.

4 One end of a piece of elastic is attached to a point at the top of a door frame and the other end hangs freely. A small ball is attached to the free end of the elastic. When the ball is hanging freely it is pulled down a small distance and then released, so that the ball oscillates up and down on the elastic. The depth d centimetres of the ball from the top of the door frame after t seconds is given by

$$d = 100 + 10 \cos 500t^\circ.$$

Find

    (a) the greatest and least depths of the ball,

    (b) the time at which the ball first reaches its highest position,

    (c) the time taken for a complete oscillation,

    (d) the proportion of the time during a complete oscillation for which the depth of the ball is less than 99 centimetres.

5 The shortest side of a triangle is 4.3 m long. Two of the angles are 45.1° and 51.2°. Find the length of the longest side.

6 In triangle ABC the length BC = 15.1 cm, $B\hat{A}C = 56°$, $A\hat{B}C = 73°$. Calculate the lengths of the sides [AB] and [AC].

7 The length of the longest side of a triangle is 15 cm. Two of the angles are 39° and 48°. Find the length of the shortest side.

8 In a triangle XYZ find angle $\hat{Z}$ when YZ = 4.7 cm, XZ = 10.5 cm and XY = 8.9 cm.

9 The sides of a triangle are 7 cm, 9 cm and 12 cm. Find its angles and its area.

10 In triangle LMN, LN = 8.6 cm, LM = 9.9 cm, $\hat{L} = 75°$. Find the length MN, and the angles $\hat{M}$ and $\hat{N}$.

11 Two ships leave a harbour at the same time. The first steams on a bearing 045° at 16 km h⁻¹ and the second on a bearing 305° at 18 km h⁻¹. How far apart will they be after 2 hours?

12 The diagram, which is not drawn to scale, shows a triangular flower bed ABC of which the sides [BC], [CA] and [AB] have lengths 4 metres, 6 metres and 8 metres respectively.

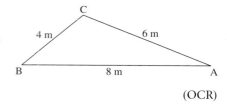

    (a) Calculate the size, in degrees, of the angle at A.

    (b) Calculate the area of the flower bed ABC.   (OCR)

13 Find the angle between two non-adjacent edges meeting at a vertex of a regular octahedron.

14 The diagram shows a sector of a circle with centre O and radius 6 cm. Angle $P\hat{O}Q = 0.6$ radians. Calculate the length of arc PQ and the area of sector POQ.   (OCR)

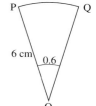

15 A sector OAB of a circle, of radius a and centre O, has $A\hat{O}B = \theta$ radians. Given that the area of the sector OAB is twice the square of the length of the arc AB, find θ.   (OCR)

16 The line of greatest slope of a hillside is $\alpha°$ with the horizontal. A walker walks at an angle $\beta°$ to the line of greatest slope on the hillside. Find an equation for the angle $\gamma°$ to the horizontal that the walker walks.

17 A walker walks on a straight horizontal path going past a tower. She finds that its angles of elevation when she is due south and due east of the tower are 15° and 18° respectively. Find the maximum angle of elevation as she walks on this path, and the bearing of the tower at this point.

18 The diagram shows a sector of a circle, with centre O and radius r. The length of the arc is equal to half the perimeter of the sector. Find the area of the sector in terms of r.   (OCR)

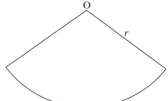

19 In the diagram, ABC is an arc of a circle with centre O and radius 5 cm. The lines [AD] and [CD] are tangents to the circle at A and C respectively. Angle $A\hat{O}C = \frac{2}{3}\pi$ radians.

    Calculate the area of the region enclosed by [AD], [DC] and the arc ABC, giving your answer correct to 2 significant figures.   (OCR)

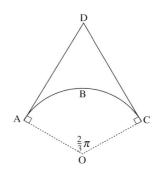

Examination questions

1 In the triangle ABC, $\hat{A} = 30°$, BC = 3 and AB = 5. Find the two possible values of $\hat{B}$.

(© IBO 2003)

2 Triangle ABC has AB = 8 cm, BC = 6 cm and $B\hat{A}C = 20°$. Find the smallest possible area of △ABC.

(© IBO 2002)

3 The diagram shows a circle centre O and radius OA = 5 cm. The angle $A\hat{O}B = 135°$.

Find the area of the shaded region.   (© IBO 2004)

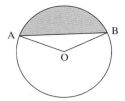

4 In triangle ABC, $A\hat{B}C = 31°$, AC = 3 cm and BC = 5 cm. Calculate the possible lengths of the side [AB].

(© IBO 2005)

5 The following diagram shows a circle centre O and radius r. The length of the arc ACB is $2r$. The area of the shaded segment may be expressed as kr^2. Find the value of k.   (© IBO 2005)

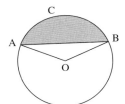

6 The following three-dimensional diagram shows the four points A, B, C and D. A, B and C are in the same horizontal plane, and AD is vertical. $A\hat{B}C = 45°$, BC = 50 m, $A\hat{B}D = 30°$, $A\hat{C}D = 20°$.

Using the cosine rule in the triangle ABC, or otherwise, find AD.   (© IBO 2004)

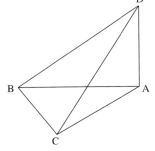

22 Inequalities

This chapter explains how to solve inequalities in a single variable. When you have completed it, you should

- be able to use graphs or algebraic methods to solve inequalities with forms like $f(x) > 0$ or $g(x) \geq f(x)$
- be familiar with the use of set notation for intervals.

22.1 Solving inequalities with graphs

Any equation $f(x) = 0$ can be solved by drawing the graph of $y = f(x)$ and finding where it meets the x-axis. Sometimes the roots can be found exactly, but if not you can use a calculator to find very close approximations.

Similarly any inequality $f(x) > 0$ can be solved by finding for what values of x the graph of $y = f(x)$ lies above the x-axis. If the inequality has the form $f(x) \geq 0$, the solution also includes the values of x where the graph lies on the x-axis.

Example 22.1.1

Solve the inequality $x^2 + 4x - 5 > 0$.

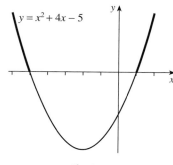

Figure 22.1 shows the graph of $y = x^2 + 4x - 5$. It cuts the x-axis at $x = -5$ and $x = 1$, and lies above the x-axis if $x < -5$ or $x > 1$. These parts of the graph are shown thicker.

So $x^2 + 4x - 5 > 0$ if $x < -5$ or $x > 1$.

Fig. 22.1

The word 'if' in the last sentence of this example should more precisely be 'if, and only if'. The argument works both ways. If $x^2 + 4x - 5 > 0$, then either $x < -5$ or $x > 1$. But also, if either $x < -5$ or $x > 1$, then $x^2 + 4x - 5 > 0$.

Example 22.1.2

Solve the inequality $\dfrac{2x + 3}{x + 1} \leq 0.$

Since the inequality sign is $\leq$, you need to find the values of x for which the graph of

$y = \dfrac{2x + 3}{x + 1}$ lies either on or below the x-axis.

The graph, which is shown in Fig. 22.2, cuts the x-axis where $x = -\frac{3}{2}$, and the vertical asymptote has equation $x = -1$. So the values of x for which the graph lies on or below the axis are given by

$-\frac{3}{2} \leq x < -1.$

Notice that, in describing this interval, the left inequality sign is $\leq$, since when $x = -\frac{3}{2}$ the graph is on the axis. But the right inequality is $<$, since $\dfrac{2x + 3}{x + 1}$ is not defined when $x = -1$.

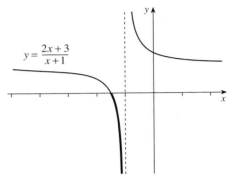

Fig. 22.2

So $\dfrac{2x + 3}{x + 1} \leq 0$ if and only if $-\frac{3}{2} \leq x < 1.$

Example 22.1.3

Solve the inequality $x^5 - 7x + 3 > 0.$

Figure 22.3 shows the graph of $y = x^5 - 7x + 3$. You can see that it crosses the x-axis three times, but you can't find exactly where since the equation $x^5 - 7x + 3 = 0$ can't be solved exactly. The graph shows that there is one root between -2 and -1, one between 0 and 1, and one between 1 and 2.

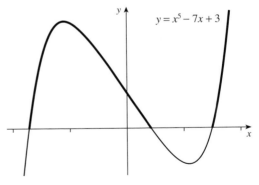

Fig. 22.3

The calculator gives the roots as $-1.719...$, $0.430...$ and $1.494...$. The graph lies above the x-axis if x is between the first and second of these, or if x is greater than the third.

So $x^5 - 7x + 3 > 0$ if and only if $-1.719... < x < 0.430...$ or $x > 1.494...$.

You have to accept a bit of fuzziness in this statement. The roots of the equation are in fact irrational, so they can't be written out in full. The dots after each number indicate that the decimal expression continues, but only the first three digits after the decimal place are stated. In fact, rounded to 3 decimal places, the roots are 1.720, 0.431 and 1.495; but it could be misleading to state the solution as '$-1.720 < x < 0.431$ or $x > 1.495$'. You will find a fuller explanation in the Introduction to this book.

22.2   Solution with a table of signs

If the expression for $f(x)$ is made up by multiplying or dividing linear polynomials, it is easy to solve an inequality such as $f(x) > 0$ by considering the signs of these polynomials separately.

An expression like $f(x) = \dfrac{(ax + b)(cx + d)}{ex + f}$ can only change sign where one of the polynomials $ax + b$, $cx + d$ or $ex + f$ changes sign. And this can only happen where one of these polynomials is zero. So you can make a table of the signs of $f(x)$ by splitting the real number line into intervals bounded by the zeros of the polynomials. These are called the **critical values** for the inequality.

Examples 22.2.1 and 22.2.2 illustrate the method by using it to solve the inequalities in Examples 22.1.1 and 22.1.2.

Example 22.2.1
Solve the inequality $x^2 + 4x - 5 > 0$.

You can write $f(x) = x^2 + 4x - 5$ in factor form as $(x + 5)(x - 1)$. Since $x + 5 = 0$ when $x = -5$, and $x - 1 = 0$ when $x = 1$, the critical values are -5 and 1. The factor $x + 5$ can only change sign where $x = -5$; it is negative for $x < -5$ and positive for $x > -5$. Similarly $x - 1$ can only change sign where $x = 1$. So the sign of $f(x)$ remains the same throughout the intervals $x < -5$, $-5 < x < 1$ and $x > 1$.

Table 22.4 shows the signs in these intervals, and the values at the points which separate them.

	$x < -5$	$x = -5$	$-5 < x < 1$	$x = 1$	$x > 1$
$x + 5$	$-$	0	$+$	$+$	$+$
$x - 1$	$-$	$-$	$-$	0	$+$
$f(x)$	$+$	0	$-$	0	$+$

Table 22.4

You can see at once that $f(x) > 0$ if and only if $x < -5$ or $x > 1$.

Example 22.2.2
Solve the inequality $\dfrac{2x + 3}{x + 1} \le 0$.

The critical values are $-\frac{3}{2}$ and -1. Table 22.5 shows the signs of the function. Note that, since $x + 1$ appears in the denominator, the function is undefined when $x = -1$.

	$x < -\frac{3}{2}$	$x = -\frac{3}{2}$	$-\frac{3}{2} < x < -1$	$x = -1$	$x > -1$
$2x + 3$	$-$	0	$+$	$+$	$+$
$x + 1$	$-$	$-$	$-$	0	$+$
$\dfrac{2x + 3}{x + 1}$	$+$	0	$-$	undefined	$+$

Table 22.5

So $\dfrac{2x + 3}{x + 1} \le 0$ if and only if $-\frac{3}{2} \le x < -1$.

Example 22.2.3

Solve the inequality $\dfrac{(4-x)^2}{4-x^2} < 0$.

The expression can be written as a combination of linear polynomials as $\dfrac{(4-x)^2}{(2-x)(2+x)}$. The critical values are -2, 2 and 4, and the signs are shown in Table 22.6.

	$x < -2$	$x = -2$	$-2 < x < 2$	$x = 2$	$2 < x < 4$	$x = 4$	$x > 4$
$(4-x)^2$	$+$	$+$	$+$	$+$	$+$	0	$+$
$2-x$	$+$	$+$	$+$	0	$-$	$-$	$-$
$2+x$	$-$	0	$+$	$+$	$+$	$+$	$+$
$\dfrac{(4-x)^2}{4-x^2}$	$-$	undefined	$+$	undefined	$-$	0	$-$

Table 22.6

$\dfrac{(4-x)^2}{4-x^2} < 0$ if and only if $x < -2$, $2 < x < 4$ or $x > 4$.

There are several points to notice about the solution to Example 22.2.3.

- Since the factors $2-x$ and $2+x$ are in the denominator of the expression, the function is undefined where these factors are zero.
- Because the coefficient of x is negative in the linear polynomial $2-x$, the signs in that row go from $+$ on the left of $x=2$ to $-$ on the right.
- The sign of the squared polynomial $(4-x)^2$ is always $+$ except at $x=4$, where its value is 0.
- You can't combine the intervals $2 < x < 4$ and $x > 4$ into a single interval $x > 2$, because the value of the function is 0 where $x=4$. But if you were asked to solve the inequality $\dfrac{(4-x)^2}{4-x^2} \leq 0$, you would find that this is satisfied for $x < 2$ and also $2 < x < 4$, $x = 4$ and $x > 4$. These last three entries could then be combined to give a single interval $x > 2$.

Example 22.2.4

Solve the inequality $x^2 + 6x - 10 \leq 0$.

The expression $x^2 + 6x - 10$ doesn't factorise in integers, but you can complete the square to obtain the factors

$$x^2 + 6x - 10 = (x+3)^2 - 9 - 10$$
$$= (x+3)^2 - 19$$
$$= (x+3-\sqrt{19})(x+3+\sqrt{19}).$$

The critical values are $-3 - \sqrt{19}$ and $-3 + \sqrt{19}$. Call these values a and b and note that $a < b$. The signs are shown in Table 22.7.

	$x < a$	$x = a$	$a < x < b$	$x = b$	$x > b$
$x - a$	$-$	0	$+$	$+$	$+$
$x - b$	$-$	$-$	$-$	0	$+$
$x^2 + 6x - 10$	$+$	0	$-$	0	$+$

Table 22.7

So $x^2 + 6x - 10 \leq 0$ if and only if $a \leq x \leq b$; that is, if and only if $-3 - \sqrt{19} \leq x \leq -3 + \sqrt{19}$.

Example 22.2.5
Solve the inequality $x^2 + 6x + 10 > 0$.

Completing the square,

$$x^2 + 6x + 10 = (x + 3)^2 - 9 + 10$$
$$= (x + 3)^2 + 1.$$

There are no critical values for this function. It is positive for all values of x, so the solution of the inequality is $x \in \mathbb{R}$.

Exercise 22A

1 Use graphs to solve the following inequalities.
   (a) $4 - x^2 > 0$
   (b) $x^2 + 2x > 0$
   (c) $x^2 + 2x - 3 \leq 0$
   (d) $4 + 3x - x^2 > 0$
   (e) $x^2 - 4x + 4 > 0$
   (f) $x^2 + x + 1 < 0$
   (g) $x^3 - 8 > 0$
   (h) $4x - x^3 \geq 0$
   (i) $x^3 - 3x^2 \geq 0$

2 Use a table of signs to solve the following inequalities.
   (a) $(x + 3)(2x - 1) \geq 0$
   (b) $(2 - x)(3 + x) > 0$
   (c) $x^2 + 5x - 6 < 0$
   (d) $x^2 - 3 \geq 0$
   (e) $\dfrac{x - 3}{x - 2} \geq 0$
   (f) $\dfrac{x}{2x + 3} \leq 0$
   (g) $\dfrac{(x + 1)(x + 3)}{x - 2} > 0$
   (h) $\dfrac{x}{x^2 - 4} \geq 0$
   (i) $x^2 + 4x + 1 < 0$

3 Use a calculator to solve the following inequalities.
   (a) $2x^3 - 4x + 1 > 0$
   (b) $3 + 5x^2 - x^3 < 0$
   (c) $x^4 - 10x^3 + 2 < 0$
   (d) $x^5 + 5x^4 - 7 > 0$

22.3   Solving $g(x) \geq f(x)$

You will sometimes come across inequalities which involve two functions $f(x)$ and $g(x)$, and you want to know the values of x for which one is greater than the other. You can do this either directly from the graphs of $y = f(x)$ and $y = g(x)$, or by writing the inequality $g(x) \geq f(x)$ as $g(x) - f(x) \geq 0$ and using one of the methods described earlier in the chapter.

Example 22.3.1
Solve the inequality $2 + x - x^2 > 2x^2 - 7x - 1$.

Method 1   Figure 22.8 shows the graphs of $y = 2x^2 - 7x - 1$ and $y = 2 + x - x^2$, intersecting at P and Q. You can see that the second graph lies above the first between P and Q.

You can find the coordinates of P and Q either by displaying the graphs with a calculator and using the 'intersection' program, or by algebra. At P and Q the y-coordinates are equal, so that

$$2 + x - x^2 = 2x^2 - 7x - 1$$
$$3x^2 - 8x - 3 = 0$$
$$(3x + 1)(x - 3) = 0.$$

So the x-coordinates of P and Q are $-\frac{1}{3}$ and 3. As a check you can calculate that the y-coordinates are $\frac{14}{9}$ and -4, though you don't need these to solve the inequality. Therefore, from Fig. 22.8, the inequality is satisfied if $-\frac{1}{3} < x < 3$.

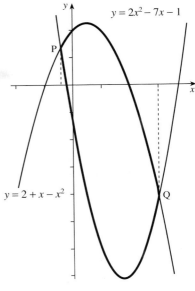

Fig. 22.8

Method 2   Subtracting $2 + x - x^2$ from both sides, the inequality can be written as

$$0 > (2x^2 - 7x - 1) - (2 + x - x^2),$$

that is

$$3x^2 - 8x - 3 < 0$$
$$(3x + 1)(x - 3) < 0$$

The signs of the expression on the left side are shown in Table 22.9.

	$x < -\frac{1}{3}$	$x = -\frac{1}{3}$	$-\frac{1}{3} < x < 3$	$x = 3$	$x > 3$
$3x + 1$	$-$	0	$+$	$+$	$+$
$x - 3$	$-$	$-$	$-$	0	$+$
$3x^2 - 8x - 3$	$+$	0	$-$	0	$+$

Table 22.9

So $2 + x - x^2 > 2x^2 - 7x - 1$ if and only if $-\frac{1}{3} < x < 3$.

You need to take special care if either of the functions has the form of a fraction. If you had an equation to solve such as

$$\frac{2x}{x - 1} = x + 2,$$

you would probably convert this, almost without thinking, to

$$2x = (x + 2)(x - 1).$$

But if you were to take the equivalent step in solving the inequality

$$\frac{2x}{x-1} \geq x+2$$

you would get the wrong answer. This is because what you are in fact doing is to multiply both sides by $x-1$. This is a perfectly acceptable step in solving the equation. But it was shown in Section 1.3 that you can only multiply both sides of an inequality by a number if that number is positive; and $x-1$ is positive for some values of x and negative for others.

To avoid this difficulty you should begin by subtracting $x+2$ from both sides of the inequality. This is a valid step whether $x+2$ is positive or negative. If you then write the expression on the left side as a single fraction, you can solve the inequality with a table of signs. The details are worked out in Example 22.3.2.

Example 22.3.2
Solve the inequality $\dfrac{2x}{x-1} \geq x+2$.

You have already seen the graph of $y = \dfrac{2x}{x-1}$ in Chapter 9 Fig. 9.3. You want to find the values of x for which this graph lies above the line $y = x+2$. These are shown by the thickened parts of the graphs in Fig. 22.10.

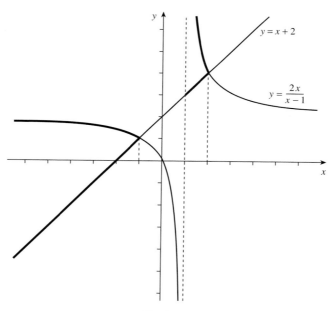

Fig. 22.10

Begin by writing the inequality as

$$\frac{2x}{x-1} - (x+2) \geq 0,$$

and express the left side as a single fraction.

$$\begin{aligned}
\frac{2x}{x-1} - (x+2) &= \frac{2x}{x-1} - \frac{(x+2)(x-1)}{x-1} \\
&= \frac{2x}{x-1} - \frac{x^2+x-2}{x-1} \\
&= \frac{2x-(x^2+x-2)}{x-1} \\
&= \frac{2+x-x^2}{x-1} \\
&= \frac{(2-x)(1+x)}{x-1}.
\end{aligned}$$

The critical values of x for this expression are -1, 1 and 2. Table 22.11 shows the signs for various intervals.

	$x < -1$	$x = -1$	$-1 < x < 1$	$x = 1$	$1 < x < 2$	$x = 2$	$x > 2$
$2-x$	$+$	$+$	$+$	$+$	$+$	0	$-$
$1+x$	$-$	0	$+$	$+$	$+$	$+$	$+$
$x-1$	$-$	$-$	$-$	0	$+$	$+$	$+$
$\frac{(2-x)(1+x)}{x-1}$	$+$	0	$-$	undefined	$+$	0	$-$

Table 22.11

So $\frac{2x}{x-1} \geq x+2$ if and only if $x \leq -1$ or $1 < x \leq 2$.

22.4 Set notation for intervals

The solutions of the inequalities in this chapter have almost all been intervals or combinations of intervals. Intervals such as $1 \leq x < 5$ or $x \geq 3$ are sets of real numbers, and it is sometimes useful to have a notation to describe them.

The set of numbers in the interval $a \leq x \leq b$ is denoted by $[a, b]$. The two statements

$$x \in \mathbb{R}, \quad a \leq x \leq b \quad \text{and} \quad x \in [a, b]$$

have exactly the same meaning. An interval which contains both its end points is called a **closed interval**.

If you want to indicate that the end points are not included in the interval, you turn the square brackets round the other way. The interval $a < x < b$ is denoted by $]a, b[$. It is called an **open interval**.

You may also have intervals which contain one end point but not the other. These are neither open nor closed. You then reverse the square bracket only at the end where the end point is not included. For example, $a \leq x < b$ is denoted by $[a, b[$.

To denote an interval that extends indefinitely in one direction, you can introduce the symbol ∞, standing for 'infinity'. This is not a number, but simply a way of indicating that there is no boundary to the interval in that direction. For example, the interval $x \geq b$ is denoted by $[b, \infty[$, and $x < a$ is written as $]-\infty, a[$.

Example 22.4.1

Use set notation to write the solutions to   (a) Example 22.3.1,   (b) Example 22.3.2.

(a) The inequality is satisfied if $-\frac{1}{3} < x < 3$, that is if $x \in]-\frac{1}{3}, 3[$.

(b) The inequality is satisfied if $x \leq -1$ or $1 < x \leq 2$. These intervals are denoted by $]-\infty, -1]$ and $]1, 2]$, and the inequality is satisfied if x belongs to either of them, and therefore to their union; that is, if $x \in]-\infty, -1] \cup]1, 2]$.

Exercise 22B

1 Use algebra to solve the following inequalities.

(a) $x^2 + 3 > 4x$

(b) $2x^2 \leq 5x + 3$

(c) $2x^2 + 3x - 5 < x^2 + 3x - 1$

(d) $3x^2 + 1 \leq 2x(x - 1)$

(e) $(x + 1)^2 > 2(1 - x^2)$

(f) $(x - 2)^2 \leq x(4 - x)$

2 Use a calculator to solve the following inequalities, and illustrate your solutions with graphs.

(a) $x^3 < 3x + 1$

(b) $x^4 > x + 3$

3 Solve the following inequalities, and illustrate your solutions with graphs.

(a) $\dfrac{2}{x} \geq 3x + 1$

(b) $\dfrac{2x + 1}{x + 2} > x$

4 Write the following sets of numbers using interval set notation.

(a) $-3 \leq x < 2$

(b) $0 < x < 3$

(c) $-2 < x \leq 3$

(d) $x \geq 0$

(e) $x < -10$

(f) $x < 2$ or $x \geq 3$

5 Write the following using inequality signs.

(a) $x \in]1, 5[$

(b) $x \in]-\infty, 2]$

(c) $x \in]-1, 4]$

(d) $x \in [-2, 2] \cup]3, \infty[$

23 Investigating shapes of graphs

This chapter explains how you can use differentiation to find the shape of a graph from its equation. When you have completed it, you should

- understand the terms 'stationary point', 'maximum point', 'minimum point' and 'turning point'
- appreciate the significance of zero, positive and negative derivatives
- be able to locate maximum and minimum points on a graph
- use this information to investigate roots of equations.

You may wonder why this chapter is necessary. With a graphic calculator you can produce the graph of any function from its equation in a few seconds. The calculator will also give the coordinates of any maximum or minimum points to a high degree of accuracy. But now that you know about differentiation, you can understand why a graph has the shape shown in the calculator display.

23.1 Stationary points

In Section 10.4 you found the coordinates of the vertex of a quadratic graph from its equation in completed square form. You used the property that the vertex of the graph is either its highest or lowest point. This is where the $(x + ...)^2$ part of the completed square expression is 0.

Another way of finding the vertex is to use differentiation. At the vertex the tangent is parallel to the x-axis, so that the gradient is 0. (See Fig. 23.1.)

Differentiation gives you the formula for the gradient. Putting this equal to 0 gives an equation for the x-coordinate of the vertex. Example 23.1.1 uses the method to find the vertex of a quadratic graph.

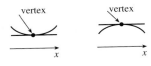

Fig. 23.1

Example 23.1.1

Locate the vertex of the parabola in Fig. 23.2 with equation $y = x^2 - 6x + 7$.

The gradient formula is $\dfrac{dy}{dx} = 2x - 6$. The gradient is zero when $2x - 6 = 0$, which gives $x = 3$. This is the x-coordinate of the vertex.

To find the y-coordinate of the vertex, substitute $x = 3$ in the equation, giving $y = 3^2 - 6 \times 3 + 7 = -2$. So the vertex has coordinates $(3, -2)$.

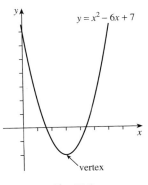

Fig. 23.2

You could of course have found the vertex in this example by writing $x^2 - 6x + 7$ as $(x - 3)^2 - 2$. But an advantage of the gradient method is that it is not restricted to quadratic graphs. Graphs with other equations do not have a 'vertex', but they may have 'peaks' or 'troughs' which occur at points where the gradient is 0.

The next two examples apply the gradient method to graphs for which $f(x)$ is a cubic and a quartic function.

Example 23.1.2

Figure 23.3 shows part of the graph with equation $y = x^3 - 6x^2 + 9x - 1$. Find the coordinates of the peak at P and the trough at T.

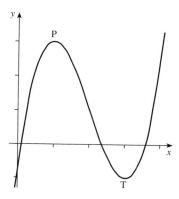

Fig. 23.3

The gradient of the curve is 0 at both P and T. Differentiating its equation gives the gradient formula

$$\frac{dy}{dx} = 3x^2 - 12x + 9.$$

So the x-coordinates of P and T satisfy the quadratic equation

$$3x^2 - 12x + 9 = 0.$$

Dividing by the common factor 3 and factorising,

$$x^2 - 4x + 3 = 0,$$
$$(x - 1)(x - 3) = 0.$$

So the x-coordinates of P and T are 1 and 3.

To find the y-coordinates of P and T, substitute 1 and 3 for x in the equation $y = x^3 - 6x^2 + 9x - 1$. This gives $y = 1 - 6 + 9 - 1 = 3$ for P, and $y = 27 - 54 + 27 - 1 = -1$ for T. So the coordinates of P are $(1, 3)$, and the coordinates of T are $(3, -1)$.

Points of a graph at which the gradient is 0 are called **stationary points**. The standard method of locating stationary points is to write down the gradient formula for the graph, and to solve the equation obtained by putting this equal to 0.

Example 23.1.3
Find the stationary points on the graph with equation $y = x^4 - 4x^3 + 4x^2$.

The gradient formula is

$$\frac{dy}{dx} = 4x^3 - 12x^2 + 8x.$$

So the x-coordinates of the stationary points satisfy the equation

$$4x^3 - 12x^2 + 8x = 0.$$

Notice that $4x$ is a factor of the left side, and you can check that the other factor $x^2 - 3x + 2$ can be split into two linear factors $(x - 1)(x - 2)$. So the equation can be written as

$$4x(x - 1)(x - 2) = 0,$$

giving $x = 0$, $x = 1$ or $x = 2$.

Substituting these values of x in the equation $y = x^4 - 4x^3 + 4x^2$ gives $y = 0$, $y = 1 - 4 + 4 = 1$ and $y = 16 - 32 + 16 = 0$ respectively. The stationary points are therefore $(0, 0)$, $(1, 1)$ and $(2, 0)$.

Finding stationary points is often an important step in finding the shape of a graph. For Example 23.1.3, Fig. 23.4 shows the three stationary points with short lines indicating the horizontal tangents at these points. From this you can be sure that between $x = 0$ and $x = 2$ the curve has the form shown by the solid line in Fig. 23.5, with a peak at $(1, 1)$. You would probably guess that there are also troughs at $(0, 0)$ and $(2, 0)$, so that the graph continues as indicated by the dotted lines. You would in fact be right, but it is not so obvious. This part of the investigation is dealt with in the next section.

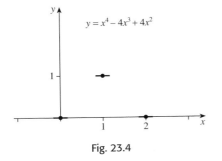

Fig. 23.4

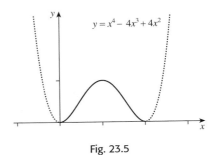

Fig. 23.5

Exercise 23A

1 Find the stationary points on the graphs with the following equations.

(a) $y = 2x^2 + 4x - 5$ (b) $y = 1 + 6x - x^2$ (c) $y = x^3 + 3x^2 - 9x$

(d) $y = x^3 - 12x$ (e) $y = x^3 - 12x^2$ (f) $y = x^5 - 5x + 4$

(g) $y = (x^2 - 4)^2$ (h) $y = x(x + 1)^2$ (i) $y = x^3 - 3x^2 + 3x$

2 Find and plot the stationary points on the graphs with the following equations. Use these, and anything else you notice about the equations, to make guesses about the shape of the graphs. Then use a calculator to check your guesses.

(a) $y = 3 + 2x - x^2$ (b) $y = x^2 + x - 8$ (c) $y = (x + 5)(1 - x)$

(d) $y = (x - 2)^2$ (e) $y = 3 + x^3$ (f) $y = x^3 + 3x^2 - 2$

(g) $y = x^2(x + 1)$ (h) $y = x^3(x + 1)$ (i) $y = x^4 - 4x^3 - 20x^2$

23.2   Maximum and minimum points

The mathematical terms for the peaks and troughs of graphs are 'maximum points' and 'minimum points'. At a maximum point the value of a function $f(x)$ is higher than anywhere else on the graph in its immediate neighbourhood; it is called a 'maximum value' of the function.

But just as you can stand on top of one hill and see higher peaks across a valley, a graph may have several maximum points, each with a different maximum value. A maximum value of a function is not necessarily the greatest value it can take, but only the greatest value amongst the points on the graph in an interval around the maximum point. For this reason it is sometimes called a 'local' maximum. This is illustrated in Fig. 23.6, in which both Q and S are maximum points.

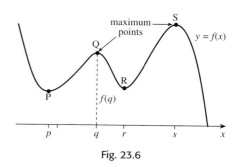

Fig. 23.6

This idea can be expressed as a precise definition:

> On the graph of $y = f(x)$ a point Q, with coordinates $(q, f(q))$, is a **(local) maximum point** if $f(q)$ is greater than the value of $f(x)$ at all the other points in an interval of values of x around q. Then $f(q)$ is called a **(local) maximum value** of $f(x)$.

The most obvious way of knowing that you have reached a peak is that you stop climbing uphill and start to walk downhill. You can use this idea to show that you are at a maximum point of a graph.

In Fig. 23.6, as you move along the curve from P to Q, the gradient $\dfrac{dy}{dx}$ is positive and you are gaining height the whole time. The mathematical term for this is that $f(x)$ is an **increasing function** between $x = p$ and $x = q$.

Once you are past Q the gradient is negative and you are losing height. Between $x = q$ and $x = r$, $f(x)$ is a **decreasing function**.

> If $f'(x)$ is positive in an interval of values of x, then $f(x)$ is an increasing function in that interval.
>
> If $f'(x)$ is negative in an interval, then $f(x)$ is a decreasing function in that interval.

> Strictly, the interval in which $f(x)$ is increasing also includes the end-points at which $f'(x) = 0$. For example, in Fig. 23.7, $f'(x) > 0$ for $p < x < q$, but $f'(x)$ is increasing for $p \le x \le q$.

You can use this idea to show that Q is a maximum point on a graph with equation $y = f(x)$. Begin by finding $\dfrac{dy}{dx} = f'(x)$. If $\dfrac{dy}{dx}$ is positive in an interval to the left of $x = q$, and negative in an interval to the right, then Q is higher than any other point on the curve in an interval around it. That is, Q is a maximum point. This is illustrated in Fig. 23.7.

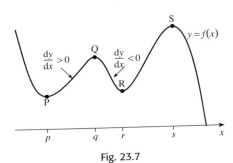

Fig. 23.7

Example 23.2.1

Find the maximum point on the graph of $y = 8 + 6x - x^2$.

The gradient formula for the graph is

$$\frac{dy}{dx} = 6 - 2x = 2(3 - x).$$

There is a stationary point where $x = 3$.

When $x < 3$, $\dfrac{dy}{dx}$ is positive; and when $x > 3$, $\dfrac{dy}{dx}$ is negative.

The stationary point at $x = 3$ is therefore a maximum point.

When $x = 3$, $y = 8 + 6 \times 3 - 3^2 = 8 + 18 - 9 = 17$.

So the maximum point has coordinates $(3, 17)$.

Example 23.2.2

For the graph of $y = x^3 - 6x^2 + 9x - 1$ in Example 23.1.2, show that $(1, 3)$ is a maximum point.

From Example 23.1.2,

$$\frac{dy}{dx} = 3x^2 - 12x + 9 = 3(x - 1)(x - 3).$$

You now want to know where $\dfrac{dy}{dx}$ is positive and where it is negative. This depends on the signs of the two factors $x - 1$ and $x - 3$; and these signs depend on whether x is greater or less than 1 and 3 respectively. These are the critical values for the expression.

If you split the domain of the function into intervals separated by the critical values, you can produce a table of signs of $\dfrac{dy}{dx}$.

	$x < 1$	$x = 1$	$1 < x < 3$	$x = 3$	$x > 3$
$x - 1$	$-$	0	$+$	$+$	$+$
$x - 3$	$-$	$-$	$-$	0	$+$
$\dfrac{dy}{dx}$	$+$	0	$-$	0	$+$

Table 23.8

The question asked is about the point with $x = 1$. Table 23.8 shows that in the interval $x < 1$ to the left of this point the gradient is positive, so that y is increasing. In the interval $1 < x < 3$ to the right the gradient is negative, so y is decreasing. This shows that $(1, 3)$ is a maximum point.

It is useful to express this method in the form of a precise rule:

On the graph of $y = f(x)$, if $\dfrac{dy}{dx} > 0$ in an interval to the left of q, and $\dfrac{dy}{dx} < 0$ in an interval to the right of q, then $(q, f(q))$ is a maximum point.

To get the corresponding conditions for a minimum point, you have to change the direction of some of the inequalities:

On the graph of $y = f(x)$ a point Q, with coordinates $(q, f(q))$, is a **(local) minimum point** if $f(q)$ is less than the value of $f(x)$ at all the other points in an interval of values of x around q. Then $f(q)$ is called a **(local) minimum value** of $f(x)$.

If $\dfrac{dy}{dx} < 0$ in an interval to the left of q, and $\dfrac{dy}{dx} > 0$ in an interval to the right of q, then $(q, f(q))$ is a minimum point.

As an example, look back to the point R in Fig. 23.6. The gradient $\dfrac{dy}{dx}$ is negative when x is between q and r, and positive between r and s. So R is a minimum point on the graph.

Example 23.2.3
Find the minimum value of $f(x) = x^2 - 8x + 12$.

Differentiating,

$$f'(x) = 2x - 8 = 2(x - 4).$$

Since $f'(x)$ is negative when $x < 4$, and positive when $x > 4$, the graph of $y = f(x)$ has a minimum point where $x = 4$.

The minimum value of $f(x)$ is

$$f(4) = 4^2 - 8 \times 4 + 12$$
$$= 16 - 32 + 12 = -4.$$

Example 23.2.4
Show that the graph of $y = x^4 - 4x^3 + 4x^2$ in Example 23.1.3 has the shape predicted in Fig. 23.5.

It was shown in Example 23.1.3 that the gradient formula is $4x(x - 1)(x - 2)$. The critical values are $x = 0$, $x = 1$ and $x = 2$, and the table of signs is shown in Table 23.9.

	$x < 0$	$x = 0$	$0 < x < 1$	$x = 1$	$1 < x < 2$	$x = 2$	$x > 2$
$4x$	$-$	0	$+$	$+$	$+$	$+$	$+$
$x - 1$	$-$	$-$	$-$	0	$+$	$+$	$+$
$x - 2$	$-$	$-$	$-$	$-$	$-$	0	$+$
$\dfrac{dy}{dx}$	$-$	0	$+$	0	$-$	0	$+$

Table 23.9

This shows that, as you pass through $x = 0$ and $x = 2$ the gradient changes from negative to positive, so $(0, 0)$ and $(2, 0)$ are minimum points. But as you pass through $x = 1$ the gradient changes from positive to negative, so $(1, 1)$ is a maximum point. These results agree with the graph in Fig. 23.5.

In all the examples so far the stationary points have been either maximum or minimum points. You may be tempted to think that this is always so, but in fact you have already met exceptions.

The simplest is the graph of $y = x^3$, shown in Fig. 23.10. Since $\dfrac{dy}{dx} = 3x^2$, the gradient is 0 when $x = 0$. That is, the origin is a stationary point. But it is neither a maximum nor a minimum point. Since $\dfrac{dy}{dx}$ is positive both to the left and to the right of $x = 0$, x^3 is an increasing function for all values of x.

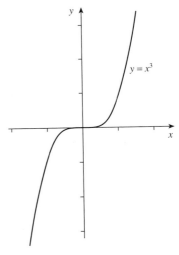

Fig. 23.10

Example 23.2.5
Find   (a) the stationary points,   (b) the maximum or minimum point
on the graph with equation $y = x^3(x - 4)$.

(a) Before differentiating you must multiply out the brackets to get $y = x^4 - 4x^3$. Then

$$\frac{dy}{dx} = 4x^3 - 12x^2 = 4x^2(x - 3).$$

It follows that $\dfrac{dy}{dx} = 0$ when $x = 0$ and when $x = 3$, where $y = 0$ and $y = 27 \times (-1) = -27$ respectively. So the stationary points are $(0, 0)$ and $(3, -27)$.

(b) The critical values of x are 0 and 3, giving the table of signs in Table 23.11.

	$x < 0$	$x = 0$	$0 < x < 3$	$x = 3$	$x > 3$
$4x^2$	$+$	0	$+$	$+$	$+$
$x - 3$	$-$	$-$	$-$	0	$+$
$\dfrac{dy}{dx}$	$-$	0	$-$	0	$+$

Table 23.11

This shows a sign change from $-$ to $+$ at $x = 3$, so $(3, -27)$ is a minimum point. But there is no sign change at $x = 0$; the gradient is negative on both sides. So this stationary point is neither a maximum nor a minimum point. This is illustrated in Fig. 23.12.

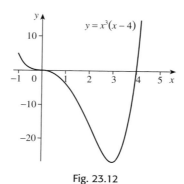

Fig. 23.12

Maximum and minimum points are sometimes also called **turning points**. A complete procedure for locating turning points, and deciding for each whether it is a maximum or a minimum, can then be summed up as follows:

> To find the minimum and maximum points on the graph of $y = f(x)$:
>
> **Step 1** Find an expression for $\dfrac{dy}{dx} = f'(x)$.
>
> **Step 2** List the values of x for which $\dfrac{dy}{dx}$ is 0.
>
> **Step 3** Taking each of these values of x in turn, find the sign of $\dfrac{dy}{dx}$ in intervals to the left and to the right of that value.
>
> **Step 4** If these signs are $-$ and $+$ respectively, the graph has a minimum point. If they are $+$ and $-$ it has a maximum point. If the signs are the same, it has neither.
>
> **Step 5** For each value of x which gives a minimum or maximum, calculate $y = f(x)$.

Example 23.2.6
Find the turning points on the graph of $y = x^2(6 - x)$, and determine whether they are maximum or minimum points.

Step 1 $y = x^2(6 - x) = 6x^2 - x^3$, which gives $\dfrac{dy}{dx} = 12x - 3x^2 = 3x(4 - x)$.

Step 2 $\dfrac{dy}{dx} = 0$ when $x = 0$ or $x = 4$.

Step 3 Using the values of x in Step 2 as critical values, the signs of $\dfrac{dy}{dx}$ are shown in Table 23.13.

	$x < 0$	$x = 0$	$0 < x < 4$	$x = 4$	$x > 4$
$3x$	$-$	0	$+$	$+$	$+$
$4 - x$	$+$	$+$	$+$	0	$-$
$\dfrac{dy}{dx}$	$-$	0	$+$	0	$-$

Table 23.13

Step 4 There is a minimum where $x = 0$ and a maximum where $x = 4$.

Step 5 When $x = 0$, $y = 0$, so $(0, 0)$ is a minimum point on the graph.

When $x = 4$, $y = 32$, so $(4, 32)$ is a maximum point on the graph.

Exercise 23B

1 For each of the following graphs in the given interval, find whether $\dfrac{dy}{dx}$ is positive or negative, and state whether y is an increasing or decreasing function of x in the interval.

(a) $y = x^2 - 4x + 7$, $x > 2$

(b) $y = 5x^2 + 7x - 3$, $x < -0.7$

(c) $y = 3 + 8x - 2x^2$, $x > 2$

(d) $y = 4 - 6x - 4x^2$, $x < -\frac{3}{4}$

(e) $y = x^3 - 3x$, $x > 1$

(f) $y = 5 - x^4$, $x < 0$

(g) $y = 3x - 4x^2 - x^3$, $x < -3$

(h) $y = x^3 - 3x^2$, $0 < x < 2$

2 For each of the following functions $f(x)$, find $f'(x)$ and the interval in which $f(x)$ is increasing.

(a) $x^2 - 5x + 6$

(b) $x^2 + 6x - 4$

(c) $7 - 3x - x^2$

(d) $3x^2 - 5x + 7$

(e) $5x^2 + 3x - 2$

(f) $7 - 4x - 3x^2$

3 For each of the following functions $f(x)$, find $f'(x)$ and the interval in which $f(x)$ is decreasing.

(a) $x^2 + 4x - 9$

(b) $x^2 - 3x - 5$

(c) $5 - 3x + x^2$

(d) $2x^2 - 8x + 7$

(e) $4 + 7x - 2x^2$

(f) $3 - 5x - 7x^2$

4 For each of the following functions $f(x)$, find $f'(x)$ and any intervals in which $f(x)$ is increasing.

(a) $x^3 - 12x$ (b) $2x^3 - 18x + 5$ (c) $2x^3 - 9x^2 - 24x + 7$

(d) $x^3 - 3x^2 + 3x + 4$ (e) $x^4 - 2x^2$ (f) $x^4 + 4x^3$

(g) $3x - x^3$ (h) $2x^5 - 5x^4 + 10$ (i) $3x + x^3$

5 For each of the following functions $f(x)$, find $f'(x)$ and any intervals in which $f(x)$ is decreasing. In part (i), n is an integer.

(a) $x^3 - 27x$ (b) $x^4 + 4x^2 - 5$ (c) $x^3 - 3x^2 + 3x - 1$

(d) $12x - 2x^3$ (e) $2x^3 + 3x^2 - 36x - 7$ (f) $3x^4 - 20x^3 + 12$

(g) $36x^2 - 2x^4$ (h) $x^5 - 5x$ (i) $x^n - nx$ $(n > 1)$

6 For the graphs of each of the following functions:

   (i) find the coordinates of the stationary point;

   (ii) say, with reasoning, whether this is a maximum or a minimum point;

   (iii) check your answer by using the method of 'completing the square' to find the vertex;

   (iv) state the range of possible values of y.

(a) $y = x^2 - 8x + 4$ (b) $y = 3x^2 + 12x + 5$ (c) $y = 5x^2 + 6x + 2$

(d) $y = 4 - 6x - x^2$ (e) $y = x^2 + 6x + 9$ (f) $y = 1 - 4x - 4x^2$

7 Find the turning points on the following graphs, and say whether they are maximum or minimum points.

(a) $y = x^3 - 12x + 5$ (b) $y = 1 - 6x^2 - x^3$ (c) $y = 2x^3 - 3x^2 - 12x$

(d) $y = x^3 - 4x^2 + 5x$ (e) $y = x^4 - 2x^2 + 3$ (f) $y = 5 + 4x - x^4$

8 Find the coordinates of the stationary points on the following graphs, and find whether these points are maxima or minima or neither. Use your answer to sketch the graphs, and then use your graphic calculator to check your sketch.

(a) $y = 2x^3 + 3x^2 - 72x + 5$ (b) $y = x^3 - 3x^2 - 45x + 7$ (c) $y = 3x^4 - 8x^3 + 6x^2$

(d) $y = 3x^5 - 20x^3 + 1$ (e) $y = 2x + x^2 - 4x^3$ (f) $y = x^3 + 3x^2 + 3x + 1$

23.3   An application to roots of equations

In Section 11.7 you saw how the points of intersection of a graph $y = f(x)$ and a line $y = k$ can be found by solving the equation $f(x) = k$.

Often you want to reverse this process. Starting with an equation $f(x) = k$, drawing the graphs of $y = f(x)$ and $y = k$ will tell you something about the roots. The x-coordinates of the points of intersection are the roots of the equation. So if you know the shape of the graph $y = f(x)$, you can find how many roots there are and their approximate values. This is illustrated in Fig. 23.14.

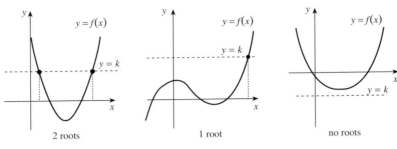

Fig. 23.14

Example 23.3.1

Show that the equation $x^3(x-4) = k$ can never have more than two roots. What can you say about the roots of the equation if k is equal to   (a) 10,   (b) −10,   (c) −30?

The shape of the graph of $y = x^3(x-4)$ was found in Example 23.2.5, and the graph is reproduced in Fig. 23.15.

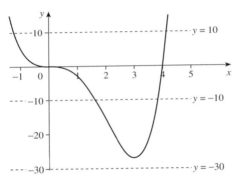

Fig. 23.15

The roots of the equation are the x-coordinates of the points of intersection of the graph with $y = k$, a line parallel to the x-axis. You can see that the largest number of points in which such a line could cut the curve is two. So the equation can never have more than two roots.

(a) If $k = 10$, the line $y = k$ is above the x-axis. One of the roots is negative and the other is greater than 4.

(b) If $k = -10$, $y = k$ is below the x-axis. Both roots are between 0 and 4.

(c) The minimum point on the graph has y-coordinate −27, so the line $y = -30$ never meets the graph. The equation with $k = -30$ has no roots.

Example 23.3.2

(a) Sketch the graph of $y = x^2(6-x)$. Verify that the point $(-2, 32)$ is on the graph.

(b) For what values of k does the equation $x^3 - 6x^2 + k = 0$ have 3 real roots? What can you then say about the values of the roots?

(c) What can you say about the roots of the equations
   (i) $6x^2 - x^3 = 0$,   (ii) $x^3 - 6x^2 + 32 = 0$?

(a) You often don't want to draw a graph accurately, but you need a rough idea of its general features: for example, maximum and minimum points, where the graph cuts the axes, and perhaps one or two other particular points. You can then put this information together to make a sketch of the graph.

For the graph of $y = x^2(6 - x)$ you already know from Example 23.2.6 that $(0, 0)$ is a minimum point and that $(4, 32)$ is a maximum point.

To find where the graph cuts the y-axis, put $x = 0$ in the equation, which gives $y = 0$. To find where it cuts the x-axis put $y = 0$, which gives $x = 0$ or $x = 6$. So the points of the graph on the axes are $(0, 0)$ and $(6, 0)$.

When $x = -2$, $y = (-2)^2 \times (6 - (-2)) = 4 \times 8 = 32$. This verifies that $(-2, 32)$ is on the graph.

Before doing any of these calculations, it is a good idea to have drawn a pair of axes on the paper. Then, as you collect each piece of information, you can add it to the diagram. Notice that in this example it would be very awkward to get the points $(4, 32)$ and $(-2, 32)$ on the graph if you use equal scales on the two axes; so this is the time to decide to have a smaller scale on the y-axis than the x-axis. You will then have drawn something like Fig. 23.16; this should be enough to be able to sketch in the graph in Fig. 23.17.

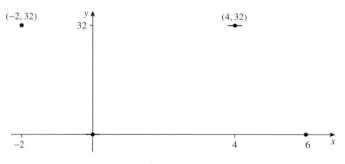

Fig. 23.16

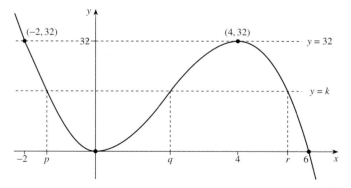

Fig. 23.17

(b) The equation $x^3 - 6x^2 + k = 0$ can be rearranged as $6x^2 - x^3 = k$, which is $x^2(6 - x) = k$. For this equation to have three real roots, the line $y = k$ must cut the graph of $y = x^2(6 - x)$ at three points. Figure 23.17 shows that for this to happen k must be between the minimum and maximum values of the function, that is between 0 and 32. So the equation has three real roots if $0 < k < 32$.

The values of these roots are the x-coordinates of the points of intersection, which are labelled p, q and r in Fig. 23.17. The graph shows that p is between -2 and 0, q is between 0 and 4, and r is between 4 and 6.

(c) (i) The equation $6x^2 - x^3 = 0$ is $x^2(6 - x) = 0$, which is satisfied by $x = 0$ and $x = 6$.

These are just the x-coordinates of the points where the graph cuts the x-axis.

The interesting thing to notice about this equation is that the root $x = 0$ comes from a factor x^2 in the equation, and this corresponds to the point where the line $y = 0$ is a tangent to the graph. The root $x = 0$ is called a repeated root. (You will remember that in Section 11.2 a quadratic equation with only one root was said to have a repeated root. This is a similar situation for a cubic equation.)

(ii) The roots of $x^3 - 6x^2 + 32 = 0$ are the x-coordinates of the points where the graph meets the line $y = 32$. Figure 23.17 shows that these roots are -2 and 4; and since the line touches the graph at $(4, 32)$, you would expect 4 to be a repeated root. And taking a hint from what happened in part (i), this suggests that the cubic equation might be written in factor form as $(x + 2)(x - 4)^2 = 0$.

You can multiply this out in the usual way.

$$(x + 2)(x - 4)^2 = (x^3 - 8x^2 + 16x) + (2x^2 - 16x + 32)$$
$$= x^3 - 6x^2 + 32,$$

which is just as expected.

Exercise 23C

1 Find the minimum point on the graph of $y = x^2 - 5x$. Use your answer to find the values of k for which the equation $x^2 - 5x = k$ has two real roots.

Check your answer using the discriminant of the quadratic $x^2 - 5x - k$.

2 Use the graph of $y = 4x - 3x^2$ to find the values of k for which the equation $3x^2 - 4x + k = 0$ has no real roots.

3 Use the graph of $y = x^4 - 4x^3 + 4x^2$ (Fig. 23.5) to find the number of roots of the equations

(a) $x^4 - 4x^3 + 4x^2 = 2$,   (b) $x^4 - 4x^3 + 4x^2 = 1$,

(c) $2x^4 - 8x^3 + 8x^2 = 1$,   (d) $x^4 - 4x^3 + 4x^2 + 1 = 0$.

4 Sketch the graph of $y = x^3 - 3x$. Use it to find the number of roots of the following equations and their approximate values.

(a) $x^3 - 3x = 1$ (b) $x^3 - 3x + 2 = 0$ (c) $x^3 = 3(x + 1)$

5 Use the graph of $y = x^3 + 4x$ to show that the equation $x^3 + 4x = k$ has exactly one root for any value of k.

6 The graph of $y = x^3 + 12x^2 + 36x$ is used to find solutions of the equation $x^3 + 12x^2 + 36x = k$ for various values of k.

(a) Find the coordinates of the maximum and minimum points, and use these to sketch the graph.

(b) Verify that the point $(-8, -32)$ is on the graph.

(c) Find the number of real roots of the equation when k is

   (i) 0,   (ii) 20,   (iii) -20,   (iv) -40.

(d) For what values of k does the equation have three real roots? What can you say about these roots?

7 The graph of $y = x^4 - 2x^3 - 2x^2$ is used to find solutions of the equation $x^4 - 2x^3 - 2x^2 = k$ for various values of k.

(a) Find the coordinates of the maximum and minimum points, and sketch the graph.

(b) Find the coordinates of the points where the graph meets the x-axis.

(c) Find the number of roots of the equation when k is   (i) 4,   (ii) -4,   (iii) -8.

(d) For what values of k does the equation have

   (i) 0,   (ii) 1,   (iii) 2,   (iv) 3,   (v) 4 real roots?

(e) In case (v) of part (d), what can you say about the values of these roots?

23.4   Graphs of other functions

So far all the functions in this chapter have been polynomials. You will recall from Section 16.1 that these are sums of terms of the form constant $\times x^r$, where r is a natural number. Although the graphs of polynomials can take many different forms, they have some features in common. For example, there are no breaks in the graphs, so that they are just a succession of peaks and troughs.

When you introduce into the equations powers of x which are not positive integers, there are some new complications. Figure 23.18 shows three graphs which you have already met in Chapter 15. None of these could possibly be graphs of polynomials.

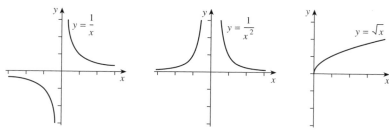

Fig. 23.18

Here are some of the new features that may appear when you draw the graph of $y = f(x)$ for functions like this.

- There may be some values of x for which $f(x)$ does not exist. For example, $\dfrac{1}{x}$ has no meaning if $x = 0$, and $\sqrt{x}$ has no meaning if $x < 0$. So the first thing to do in investigating the shape of the graph is to discard any values of x for which $f(x)$ has no meaning.

- When there is a break in the graph, the sign of the gradient may be different on either side of the break. For example, in the graph of $y = \dfrac{1}{x^2}$, $\dfrac{dy}{dx}$ is positive when $x < 0$ and negative when $x > 0$. So when you make a table of signs, it should be split into two parts, for values of x on either side of the break.

- There may be points on the graph at which the tangent is vertical. For example, the tangent to $y = \sqrt{x}$ at the origin is the y-axis. For this curve, $\dfrac{dy}{dx} = \dfrac{1}{2\sqrt{x}}$, and this has no meaning when $x = 0$.

- It is even possible for the graph to have a shape like Fig. 23.19. This is the graph of $y = \sqrt[3]{x^2} = x^{\frac{2}{3}}$, for which $\dfrac{dy}{dx} = \frac{2}{3}x^{-\frac{1}{3}} = \dfrac{2}{3\sqrt[3]{x}}$. This has the origin as a minimum point. But when $x = 0$, $\dfrac{dy}{dx}$ is not equal to 0; in fact, $\dfrac{dy}{dx}$ does not even exist for this value of x. So when you use the procedure for finding turning points, you need to consider values of x for which $f'(x)$ doesn't exist as well as those for which $f'(x)$ is equal to 0.

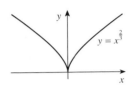

Fig. 23.19

None of these things can happen with polynomials. However, with these differences, all the results given for polynomials earlier in the chapter still apply. For example, it is still true that, if $f'(x)$ is positive in an interval of values of x, then $f(x)$ is an increasing function in that interval; you just have to be sure that the interval does not include a point where there is a break in the graph.

The similarities and differences are illustrated by the following examples.

Example 23.4.1
Find the maximum value of $f(x) = x(1 - \sqrt{x})$.

Since the function involves $\sqrt{x}$, it only exists if $x \geq 0$.

To differentiate, $f(x)$ can be expressed in terms of powers of x, as

$$f(x) = x(1 - \sqrt{x}) = x - x^{\frac{3}{2}}.$$

Then

$$f'(x) = 1 - \tfrac{3}{2}x^{\frac{1}{2}} = 1 - \tfrac{3}{2}\sqrt{x}.$$

To find where $f(x)$ takes its maximum value, put $f'(x)$ equal to 0 to get

$$\tfrac{3}{2}\sqrt{x} = 1, \quad \text{so} \quad \sqrt{x} = \tfrac{2}{3} \quad \text{and} \quad x = \tfrac{4}{9}.$$

To check that the stationary value is a maximum, note that $f'(x) > 0$ if $\frac{3}{2}\sqrt{x} < 1$, that is if $0 \le x < \frac{4}{9}$; and $f'(x) < 0$ if $\frac{3}{2}\sqrt{x} > 1$, that is if $x > \frac{4}{9}$.

The maximum value of $f(x)$ is therefore

$$f\left(\tfrac{4}{9}\right) = \tfrac{4}{9}\left(1 - \sqrt{\tfrac{4}{9}}\right)$$
$$= \tfrac{4}{9} \times \left(1 - \tfrac{2}{3}\right)$$
$$= \tfrac{4}{9} \times \tfrac{1}{3} = \tfrac{4}{27}.$$

This completes the solution, but it is interesting to check it by considering the shape of the graph of $f(x) = x(1 - \sqrt{x})$. Obviously $f(0) = f(1) = 0$, and the expression in the bracket is positive if $0 < x < 1$ and negative if $x > 1$. So the value of the function starts at 0 when $x = 0$, rises to a maximum value of $\frac{4}{27}$, when $x = \frac{4}{9}$, then falls to 0 again when $x = 1$. After that it becomes negative.

Example 23.4.2

Find the turning points on the graph of $y = x^2 + \dfrac{1}{x^2}$, and decide whether they are maximum or minimum points.

The expression has no meaning when $x = 0$, so there is a break in the graph.

Differentiating, write the equation as $y = x^2 + x^{-2}$ so that

$$\frac{dy}{dx} = 2x - 2x^{-3} = 2x - \frac{2}{x^3}.$$

There are stationary points where

$$2x - \frac{2}{x^3} = 0,$$

which is where $x = \dfrac{1}{x^3}$, that is, $x^4 = 1$, so $x = -1$ or $x = 1$.

To construct a table of signs it is best to write the expression for $\dfrac{dy}{dx}$ as a single fraction, and to factorise the numerator.

$$2x - \frac{2}{x^3} = \frac{2x^4}{x^3} - \frac{2}{x^3}$$
$$= \frac{2x^4 - 2}{x^3}$$
$$= \frac{2(x^2 - 1)(x^2 + 1)}{x^3}$$
$$= \frac{2(x - 1)(x + 1)(x^2 + 1)}{x^3}.$$

Because there is a break in the domain at $x = 0$, the table of signs should be split into two parts, for $x < 0$ and $x > 0$.

	$x < -1$	$x = -1$	$-1 < x < 0$	$0 < x < 1$	$x = 1$	$x > 1$
$x - 1$	$-$	$-$	$-$	$-$	0	$+$
$x + 1$	$-$	0	$+$	$+$	$+$	$+$
$x^2 + 1$	$+$	$+$	$+$	$+$	$+$	$+$
x^3	$-$	$-$	$-$	$+$	$+$	$+$
$\dfrac{dy}{dx}$	$-$	0	$+$	$-$	0	$+$

Table 23.20

Table 23.20 shows that, at both stationary points, the gradient changes from negative to positive, so they are both minimum points.

Display this graph on your calculator to see how this can happen. (You might have predicted it from the fact that $x^2 + \dfrac{1}{x^2}$ is an even function.)

Finally, you have to find the values of y at these points, which are $(-1)^2 + \dfrac{1}{(-1)^2} = 2$ and $1^2 + \dfrac{1}{1^2} = 2$.

The graph has two minimum points, at $(-1, 2)$ and $(1, 2)$.

The next example is of a graph which has a minimum point at which $\dfrac{dy}{dx}$ is not 0.

Example 23.4.3
Find the turning points on the graph of $y = x^{\frac{2}{3}}(1 - x)$, and determine whether they are maxima or minima.

Begin by noticing that $x^{\frac{2}{3}} = \sqrt[3]{x^2}$ has a value whether x is positive or negative, because x^2 is positive in either case. Also, this value is positive, because the cube root of a positive number is positive. So there are no values of x for which the graph doesn't exist.

The expression for y when multiplied out is $y = x^{\frac{2}{3}} - x^{\frac{5}{3}}$, which gives

$$\frac{dy}{dx} = \tfrac{2}{3}x^{-\frac{1}{3}} - \tfrac{5}{3}x^{\frac{2}{3}}.$$

This can be written as

$$\frac{dy}{dx} = \tfrac{1}{3}x^{-\frac{1}{3}}(2 - 5x).$$

The only value of x for which $\dfrac{dy}{dx} = 0$ is where $2 - 5x = 0$, that is $x = 0.4$. But you also have to consider $x = 0$, where $\dfrac{dy}{dx}$ does not exist, as a possible turning point. The table of signs is shown in Table 23.21.

Note that $x^{-\frac{1}{3}}$, that is $\dfrac{1}{\sqrt[3]{x}}$, is positive when x is positive, and negative when x is negative.

	$x < 0$	$x = 0$	$0 < x < 0.4$	$x = 0.4$	$x > 0.4$
$\frac{1}{3}x^{-\frac{1}{3}}$	$-$	no value	$+$	$+$	$+$
$2 - 5x$	$+$	$+$	$+$	0	$-$
$\dfrac{dy}{dx}$	$-$	no value	$+$	0	$-$

Table 23.21

Now notice that, although $\dfrac{dy}{dx}$ does not have a value when $x = 0$, Table 23.21 shows that $\dfrac{dy}{dx} < 0$ in an interval to the left of 0, and $\dfrac{dy}{dx} > 0$ in an interval to the right of 0.

This was the condition given in Section 23.2 for the graph to have a minimum point at $x = 0$. At $x = 0.4$ the graph has an ordinary maximum point.

The values of y at the two points are 0 and $\sqrt[3]{0.4^2} \times 0.6 = 0.3257...$.

Figure 23.22 shows the graph, with a minimum at $(0, 0)$ and a maximum at $(0.4, 0.326)$ correct to 3 decimal places.

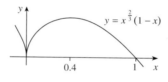

$y = x^{\frac{2}{3}}(1 - x)$

Fig. 23.22

Exercise 23D

1 Find the stationary points on the following curves and say whether they are maximum or minimum points. Check your answers with a calculator.

(a) $y = x + \dfrac{1}{x}$

(b) $y = x + \dfrac{4}{x^2}$

(c) $y = 2\sqrt{x} - x$

(d) $y = x^2 - 4\sqrt{x}$

(e) $y = \dfrac{1}{x} - \dfrac{1}{x^2}$

(f) $y = 4x^2 - \dfrac{1}{x}$

(g) $y = \sqrt{x} + \dfrac{4}{x}$

(h) $y = \dfrac{1}{x} - \dfrac{3}{x^3}$

(i) $y = x - 12\sqrt[3]{x}$

2 Find the interval(s) of values of x for which the following functions are increasing.

(a) $y = \sqrt{x} + \dfrac{2}{\sqrt{x}}$

(b) $y = x^3 + \dfrac{3}{x}$

(c) $y = x - \dfrac{1}{x}$

3 Find the turning points on the following curves and say whether they are maximum or minimum points.

(a) $y = \dfrac{2}{x^4} - \dfrac{1}{x}$

(b) $y = \dfrac{x - 3}{x^4}$

(c) $y = \dfrac{(x + 1)^2}{x}$

(d) $y = \dfrac{x^4 + 16}{x^2}$

(e) $y = x^{\frac{4}{3}}(7 - x)$

(f) $y = x^{\frac{1}{3}}(4 - x)$

24 Second derivatives

The last chapter showed the significance of the sign of the gradient in investigating the shape of a graph. This chapter carries the investigation further by considering the way in which the graph is bending. When you have completed it, you should

- know what is meant by the second derivative of a function
- know that the sign of the second derivative determines the way in which the graph is bending
- know what is meant by a point of inflexion, and be able to locate it
- be able to use second derivatives where appropriate to distinguish maximum and minimum points.

24.1 A measure of bending

You know that all quadratic graphs have one of the two shapes in Fig. 24.1. The parabola (a) on the left is said to 'bend upwards'; (b) on the right is said to 'bend downwards'.

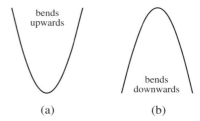

Fig. 24.1

Most of the curves in this chapter are more complicated than this. Figure 24.2, for example, can be thought of as having two parts. In the left part, as far as the point marked I, the curve bends downwards; then, after I, it bends upwards.

Some curves have three parts. For example, in Fig. 23.12 in the last chapter, if you go from left to right along the curve, it bends upwards as far as the origin; then it bends downwards as far as $x = 2$, after which it bends upwards again.

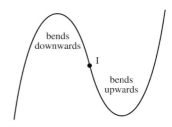

Fig. 24.2

Knowing whether a graph bends upwards or downwards is often useful in investigating its shape. The question is, how to tell from the equation which way it bends.

Figure 24.3 shows the graph of a function which is bending upwards, with the tangents at several points along the curve. The gradients of the tangents at P and Q are negative; at R the gradient is 0; then at S and T the gradient is positive. All the way, as you move from left to right, the gradient increases.

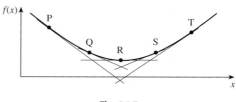

Fig. 24.3

The word 'increases' is the clue. You know that the gradient of the graph $y = f(x)$ is itself a function. It has been called the 'gradient function', and denoted by $f'(x)$. But temporarily it will help to give it a function name of its own, and to use the symbol $g(x)$ to stand for the gradient function of $f(x)$. For example, if $f(x) = x^2$, then $g(x) = 2x$.

Then Fig. 24.4 shows that $g(x)$ is an increasing function. And it was shown at the beginning of Section 23.2 that, if $g'(x) > 0$ in an interval, then $g(x)$ is an increasing function in that interval. And in that case the graph $y = f(x)$ bends upwards.

Fig. 24.4

So the way to show that the graph $y = f(x)$ bends upwards is to differentiate to get the gradient function $g(x) = f'(x)$. You then differentiate $g(x)$ to get $g'(x)$. If $g'(x)$ is positive, then the gradient function is increasing, so $y = f(x)$ bends upwards.

You will see that $g'(x)$ is what you get if you differentiate $f(x)$, and then differentiate the result a second time. This produces the 'second derivative' of $f(x)$. It is denoted by $f''(x)$. This is pronounced 'f two-dashed x', or 'f double-dashed x'.

Example 24.1.1
If $f(x) = 2x^3 + 3x^2 + 4x + 5$, find $f''(x)$.

The derivative of $f(x)$ is $f'(x) = 6x^2 + 6x + 4$.

The derivative of $f'(x)$ is $f''(x) = 12x + 6$.

Just as there are two ways of writing the derivative, either as $f'(x)$ or $\dfrac{dy}{dx}$, there are two ways of writing the second derivative. The derivative of $\dfrac{dy}{dx}$ is written as $\dfrac{d^2y}{dx^2}$. This is pronounced 'd squared y d x squared', or sometimes 'd two y d x squared'. The reason for this rather curious notation is explained in Section 25.5.

Example 24.1.2
Show that the graph of $y = 3x^2 + 7x - 2$ bends upwards for all values of x.

Two successive differentiations give $\dfrac{dy}{dx} = 6x + 7$ and $\dfrac{d^2y}{dx^2} = 6$.

Since $\dfrac{d^2y}{dx^2}$ is positive and independent of x, the graph bends upwards for all values of x.

Now draw for yourself a curve which bends downwards and draw tangents at a number of points. You will see that the gradient is decreasing as you move from left to right along the curve. If the equation is $y = f(x)$, $g(x) = f'(x)$ is a decreasing function, so that $g'(x) = f''(x)$ is negative.

A curve which bends upwards in an interval is said to be **concave up** in the interval. A curve which bends downwards is said to be **concave down**.

If $y = f(x)$, the derivative of $\dfrac{dy}{dx} = f'(x)$ is called the **second derivative** of $f(x)$ with respect to x, and is denoted by $f''(x)$ or $\dfrac{d^2y}{dx^2}$.

If $\dfrac{d^2y}{dx^2} = f''(x)$ is positive in an interval of values of x, the graph of $y = f(x)$ is concave up in that interval.

If $\dfrac{d^2y}{dx^2} = f''(x)$ is negative in an interval of values of x, the graph of $y = f(x)$ is concave down in that interval.

Example 24.1.3
For the graph of $y = x^3 - 3x^2 + 4x$,

(a) show that the gradient is always positive,

(b) find the intervals in which the graph is   (i) concave down,   (ii) concave up.

(a) $\dfrac{dy}{dx} = 3x^2 - 6x + 4$

$= 3(x-1)^2 + 1$ in completed square form.

Since $(x - 1)^2$ is never negative, the gradient of the graph is greater than or equal to 1 for all values of x.

(b) $\dfrac{d^2y}{dx^2} = 6x - 6 = 6(x - 1)$.

This is negative when $x < 1$ and positive when $x > 1$.
So the graph is

(i) concave down when $x < 1$,

(ii) concave up when $x > 1$.

These properties are illustrated in Fig. 24.5. Notice that the gradient has its smallest value of 1 at the point $(1, 2)$, which separates the part of the curve which bends downwards from the part which bends upwards.

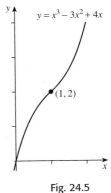

Fig. 24.5

24.2 Points of inflexion

Figure 24.2 shows a point I on a graph separating a part which is concave down from a part which is concave up. A point like this is called a **point of inflexion**.

Since the way in which a graph bends depends on the sign of the second derivative, this definition can be expressed in terms of $f''(x)$:

If, on the graph of $y = f(x)$, the sign of $f''(x)$ in an interval to the left of $x = s$ is opposite to the sign in an interval to the right of $x = s$, then the point $(s, f(s))$ is a point of inflexion.

Thus in Example 24.1.3 the point $(1, 2)$ is a point of inflexion, because $\dfrac{d^2y}{dx^2}$ changes sign from negative (for $x < 1$) to positive (for $x > 1$).

Example 24.2.1

Show that the graph of $y = \sqrt{x} + \dfrac{1}{x}$ has just one point of inflexion, and find its coordinates.

Since $\sqrt{x}$ only exists for $x \geq 0$, and $\dfrac{1}{x}$ does not exist when $x = 0$, the domain of the function is $\mathbb{R}^+$, the set of positive real numbers.

Writing $\sqrt{x}$ as $x^{\frac{1}{2}}$ and $\dfrac{1}{x}$ as x^{-1},

$$y = x^{\frac{1}{2}} + x^{-1},$$

so $\qquad \dfrac{dy}{dx} = \tfrac{1}{2}x^{-\frac{1}{2}} - x^{-2}$

and $\qquad \dfrac{d^2y}{dx^2} = -\tfrac{1}{4}x^{-\frac{3}{2}} + 2x^{-3}.$

This can be written as

$$\frac{2}{x^3} - \frac{1}{4x^{\frac{3}{2}}} = \frac{8}{4x^3} - \frac{x^{\frac{3}{2}}}{4x^3} = \frac{8 - x^{\frac{3}{2}}}{4x^3}.$$

Since $4x^3$ is always positive when $x > 0$, $\dfrac{d^2y}{dx^2}$ is positive when $x^{\frac{3}{2}} < 8$ and negative when $x^{\frac{3}{2}} > 8$.

Now $x^{\frac{3}{2}} = 8$ when $x = 8^{\frac{2}{3}} = 4$ (see Section 14.4), so $x^{\frac{3}{2}} < 8$ when $x < 4$ and $x^{\frac{3}{2}} > 8$ when $x > 4$. Therefore $\dfrac{d^2y}{dx^2}$ changes sign from positive to negative when $x = 4$, $y = \sqrt{4} + \dfrac{1}{4} = 2\tfrac{1}{4}$.

There is just one point of inflexion at $\left(4, 2\tfrac{1}{4}\right)$. This is shown in Fig. 24.6.

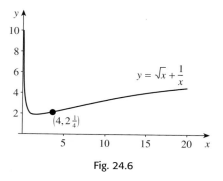

Fig. 24.6

In the solution to Example 24.2.1 you may have noticed the switch from the inequalities $x^{\frac{3}{2}} < 8$ and $x^{\frac{3}{2}} > 8$ to the equation $x^{\frac{3}{2}} = 8$. This wasn't strictly necessary, but you probably find it easier to work with the equation.

So, in the general definition, if s separates values of x for which $f''(x) < 0$ from those for which $f''(x) > 0$, what can you say about $f''(s)$?

The obvious answer to this question is that $f''(s) = 0$. However, there is another possibility (which happens much less often) that $f''(s)$ might not exist. You may not often come across a function for which this occurs, but the possibility must be included in stating a general rule:

> At a point of inflexion $(s, f(s))$ on the graph of $y = f(x)$, either $f''(s) = 0$ or $f''(s)$ does not exist.

Example 24.2.2
Find the points of inflexion on the graph of $y = x^3(4 - x)$, and show these on a sketch.

If $y = x^3(4 - x) = 4x^3 - x^4,$

then $\dfrac{dy}{dx} = 12x^2 - 4x^3$

$\qquad\qquad = 4x^2(3 - x)$

and $\dfrac{d^2y}{dx^2} = 24x - 12x^2$

$\qquad\qquad = 12x(2 - x).$

So $\dfrac{d^2y}{dx^2} = 0$ when $x = 0$ or 2. (There are no values of x for which $\dfrac{d^2y}{dx^2}$ doesn't exist.)

To check that these values of x do give points of inflexion, construct a table of signs for $\dfrac{d^2y}{dx^2}$ (Table 24.7).

	$x < 0$	$x = 0$	$0 < x < 2$	$x = 2$	$x > 2$
$12x$	$-$	0	$+$	$+$	$+$
$2 - x$	$+$	$+$	$+$	0	$-$
$\dfrac{d^2y}{dx^2}$	$-$	0	$+$	0	$-$

Table 24.7

This shows that $\dfrac{d^2y}{dx^2}$ has opposite signs on either side of $x = 0$ and also of $x = 2$.

When $x = 0$, $y = 0$ and when $x = 2$, $y = 2^3(4 - 2) = 16$.

So the points of inflexion on the graph are $(0, 0)$ and $(2, 16)$.

To sketch the graph you can make similar tables of signs for y and for $\dfrac{dy}{dx}$. Check for yourself that these can be summarised as Table 24.8 and Table 24.9 respectively.

	$x < 0$	$x = 0$	$0 < x < 4$	$x = 4$	$x > 4$
y	$-$	0	$+$	0	$-$

Table 24.8

	$x < 0$	$x = 0$	$0 < x < 3$	$x = 3$	$x > 3$
$\dfrac{\mathrm{d}y}{\mathrm{d}x}$	$+$	0	$+$	0	$-$

Table 24.9

Putting this information together produces the graph in Fig. 24.10.

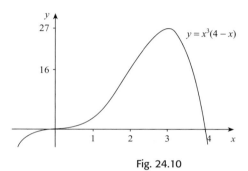

Fig. 24.10

But beware! Although points of inflexion can only occur when $f''(x)$ is 0 or undefined, it may happen that $f''(x) = 0$ where there is *not* a point of inflexion. The next example illustrates this.

Example 24.2.3
Find the points of inflexion on the graph of $y = x^4(5 - x)$.

The beginning of the solution is like that of Example 24.2.2.

If $y = x^4(5 - x) = 5x^4 - x^5$,

then $\dfrac{\mathrm{d}y}{\mathrm{d}x} = 20x^3 - 5x^4 = 5x^3(4 - x)$

and $\dfrac{\mathrm{d}^2 y}{\mathrm{d}x^2} = 60x^2 - 20x^3 = 20x^2(3 - x)$.

So $\dfrac{\mathrm{d}^2 y}{\mathrm{d}x^2} = 0$ when $x = 0$ or 3. But the table of signs now has the form of Table 24.11.

So, although $\dfrac{\mathrm{d}^2 y}{\mathrm{d}x^2} = 0$ when $x = 0$, the sign of $\dfrac{\mathrm{d}^2 y}{\mathrm{d}x^2}$ is the same in intervals on both sides of $x = 0$. This means that $(0, 0)$ is not a point of inflexion. The only point of inflexion is at $(3, 162)$.

	$x < 0$	$x = 0$	$0 < x < 3$	$x = 3$	$x > 3$
$20x^2$	$+$	0	$+$	$+$	$+$
$3 - x$	$+$	$+$	$+$	0	$-$
$\dfrac{d^2 y}{dx^2}$	$+$	0	$+$	0	$-$

Table 24.11

You can check for yourself that $(0, 0)$ is a minimum point and $(4, 256)$ is a maximum point. So the graph has the form of Fig. 24.12.

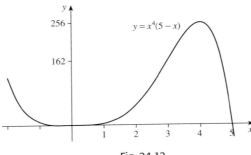

Fig. 24.12

If $f''(s) = 0$, the point $(s,\ f(s))$ is not necessarily a point of inflexion of the graph of $y = f(x)$. You have to check that $f''(x)$ has opposite signs in intervals on either side of $x = s$.

The last example is one with a point of inflexion where $f''(x)$ doesn't exist.

Example 24.2.4
Show that the graph of $y = \sqrt[3]{x}$ has a point of inflexion at the origin, but that $\dfrac{d^2 y}{dx^2}$ does not exist there.

If $y = \sqrt[3]{x}$, then $x = y^3$. So you can get the graph of $y = \sqrt[3]{x}$ from that of $y = x^3$ by interchanging the x- and y-axes. This is shown in Fig. 24.13.

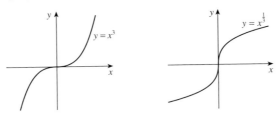

Fig. 24.13

Clearly the graph of $y = \sqrt[3]{x}$ is concave up for $x < 0$ and concave down for $x > 0$, so $(0, 0)$ is a point of inflexion.

But, if $y = \sqrt[3]{x} = x^{\frac{1}{3}}$, then

$$\frac{dy}{dx} = \frac{1}{3}x^{-\frac{2}{3}} = \frac{1}{3\sqrt[3]{x^2}} \quad \text{and} \quad \frac{d^2y}{dx^2} = -\frac{2}{9}x^{-\frac{5}{3}} = -\frac{2}{9\sqrt[3]{x^5}}.$$

So, when $x = 0$, neither $\dfrac{dy}{dx}$ nor $\dfrac{d^2y}{dx^2}$ exists.

24.3　Points of greatest or least gradient

Draw a curve with a point of inflexion, and lay a pencil along the tangent at the left end of the curve. Now move along the curve from left to right, keeping the pencil as a tangent. What happens as the point of contact passes through the point of inflexion?

You will find that the pencil has been rotating in one sense (clockwise or anticlockwise) and, at the point of inflexion, the sense of rotation changes.

What this shows is that, at the point of inflexion, the gradient of the curve has either a maximum or minimum value.

For example, in Example 24.1.3, the graph of $y = x^3 - 3x^2 + 4x$ has a point of inflexion where $x = 1$. And, because the gradient is $3(x-1)^2 + 1$, this is the value of x for which the gradient has its smallest value.

It is easy to see why. If you denote the gradient function of $y = f(x)$ by $g(x)$ (as in Section 24.1), then $g(x) = f'(x)$ and $g'(x) = f''(x)$. So if $(s, f(s))$ is a point of inflexion, so that $f''(x)$ has opposite signs on either side of $x = s$, so does $g'(x)$; and this is the condition given in Section 23.2 for $g(x)$ to have a maximum or minimum at $x = s$.

Exercise 24A

1　Compare the graphs of $y = f(x)$ and $y = f'(x)$ in each of the following cases. Show that $y = f(x)$ bends upwards when $y = f'(x)$ is decreasing, and downwards when $y = f'(x)$ is increasing.

(a)　$f(x) = x^2$ (b)　$f(x) = 5 - x^2$ (c)　$f(x) = x^2 + 4x$

(d)　$f(x) = 3x^2 - 6x$ (e)　$f(x) = (2 + x)(4 - x)$ (f)　$f(x) = (x + 3)^2$

(g)　$f(x) = x^4$ (h)　$f(x) = x^2(x - 2)$ (i)　$f(x) = 3 - 2x$

2　In each part of the question, the diagram shows the graph of $y = f(x)$. Sketch a graph of the gradient function $y = f'(x)$.

(a)

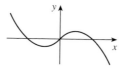

(b)

(c)

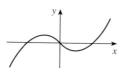

3 Write down the signs of $f'(x)$ and $f''(x)$ for the following graphs $y = f(x)$.

(a)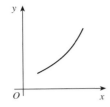

(b)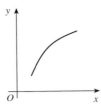

(c)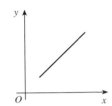

(d)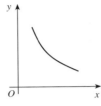

4 Find $\dfrac{d^2y}{dx^2}$ for the following equations.

(a) $y = 3x - 4$

(b) $y = 5 + 3x - 2x^2$

(c) $y = x^3 + 5x^2 - 2x + 13$

(d) $y = x^6$

5 Consider the graph of $y = f(x)$ where $f(x) = x^3 - x$.

(a) Use the fact that $f(x) = x(x^2 - 1) = x(x - 1)(x + 1)$ to find where the graph cuts the x-axis and hence sketch the graph.

(b) Find $f'(x)$ and sketch the graph of $y = f'(x)$.

(c) Find $f''(x)$ and sketch the graph of $y = f''(x)$.

(d) Check the consistency of your sketches: for example, check that the graph of $y = f(x)$ is concave up where $f''(x) > 0$.

6 For the graph of $y = f(x)$ where $f(x) = x^3 + x$

(a) use factors to show that the graph crosses the x-axis once only,

(b) find $f'(x)$ and $f''(x)$,

(c) find the interval in which the graph is bending upwards,

(d) use the information gained to sketch the graph of $y = x^3 + x$,

(e) check your work using a calculator.

7 Find the coordinates of the points of inflexion (if any) on the following graphs. Use a calculator to check your answers.

(a) $y = x^3 - 6x^2 + 7x$

(b) $y = 3x^2 - 2x^4$

(c) $y = 2x + x^4$

(d) $y = x^4 - 6x^3 + 12x^2$

(e) $y = x^6(x - 7)$

(f) $y = \sqrt{x}(x + 3)$

(g) $y = x^2 - \dfrac{1}{x}$

(h) $y = \dfrac{x - 6}{x^4}$

(i) $y = \sqrt{x} + \dfrac{1}{\sqrt{x}}$

8 Find the intervals in which the graphs of the following equations are concave up.

(a) $y = x^3 + 4x - 7$ (b) $y = 5 + 6x^2 - x^3$ (c) $y = x^2(x + 1)$

(d) $y = \dfrac{1}{x}$ (e) $y = \dfrac{1}{x^2}$ (f) $y = \dfrac{1}{x} - \dfrac{1}{x^2}$

(g) $y = \dfrac{1}{x^2} - \dfrac{1}{x^3}$ (h) $y = x^2 + \dfrac{1}{x^2}$ (i) $y = x^2 + \sqrt{x}$

9 Find the point on the graph of $y = 7 - 9x^2 - x^3$ at which the gradient is greatest, and the equation of the tangent at this point. Check that this tangent does not meet the graph at any other point.

10 Find the equation of the tangent to the graph of $y = x^5 - 5x^4 + 150x$ at which the gradient has its smallest value.

11 Find the x-coordinates of the three points where the graph of $y = x^4 - 10x^3 + 24x^2$ meets the x-axis. Show that one of these points is a point of inflexion of the graph, and find the coordinates of the other point of inflexion. Find also the equations of the tangents at the two points of inflexion, and verify that they meet the graph again at $(-2, 192)$ and $(7, 147)$ respectively. Use this information to sketch the graph as accurately as you can.

24.4 Maxima and minima revisited

One of the most important uses of the second derivative is to decide whether a stationary point on a graph is a maximum or a minimum.

Look back at Figs. 24.1 and 24.2. These show graphs with maximum or minimum points. Which is which depends on whether the graph is bending upwards or downwards. Where the graph is concave up, the stationary point is a minimum; where it is concave down, the stationary point is a maximum. So whether the graph has a maximum or minimum depends on the sign of the second derivative at the stationary point.

It is often simpler to use this instead of considering the change in sign of $f'(x)$ to decide whether a point on a graph is a minimum or a maximum. The procedure described in the blue box at the end of Section 23.2 can then be amended as follows.

To find the minimum and maximum points on the graph of $y = f(x)$:

Step 1 Find an expression for $\dfrac{dy}{dx} = f'(x)$.

Step 2 List the values of x for which $\dfrac{dy}{dx}$ is 0 (or doesn't exist).

Step 3 Find an expression for $\dfrac{d^2y}{dx^2} = f''(x)$.

Step 4 For each value of x in Step 2, find the sign of $\dfrac{d^2y}{dx^2}$. If the sign is +, the graph has a minimum point; if −, a maximum.

[If the value of $\dfrac{d^2y}{dx^2}$ is 0 (or doesn't exist), follow the old procedure (Section 23.2).]

Step 5 For each value of x giving a minimum or maximum, calculate $y = f(x)$.

Example 24.4.1
Find the turning points on the graph of $y = x^2(6 - x)$, and determine whether they are maximum or minimum points.

Step 1 $y = x^2(6 - x) = 6x^2 - x^3$, which gives $\dfrac{dy}{dx} = 12x - 3x^2 = 3x(4 - x)$.

Step 2 $\dfrac{dy}{dx} = 0$ when $x = 0$ or $x = 4$.

Step 3 $\dfrac{d^2y}{dx^2} = 12 - 6x$.

Step 4 When $x = 0$, $\dfrac{d^2y}{dx^2} = 12 - 6 \times 0 = 12$.

When $x = 4$, $\dfrac{d^2y}{dx^2} = 12 - 6 \times 4 = -12$.

So there is a minimum point where $x = 0$ and a maximum point where $x = 4$.

Step 5 When $x = 0$, $y = 0$, so $(0, 0)$ is a minimum point on the graph.

When $x = 4$, $y = 32$, so $(4, 32)$ is a maximum point on the graph.

Example 24.4.1 is the same as Example 23.2.6, but solved by the new procedure. Steps 1, 2 and 5 are the same, but there is a different way of deciding between maximum and minimum points. You can use whichever method you prefer.

The reason for having two methods is that, although the second method is often easier, it doesn't always work. This is illustrated by the next example.

Example 24.4.2
Find the nature of the stationary points on the graphs of $y = x^3$, $y = x^4$ and $y = -x^4$,

The derivatives are $\dfrac{dy}{dx} = 3x^2$, $\dfrac{dy}{dx} = 4x^3$ and $\dfrac{dy}{dx} = -4x^3$. All the graphs have stationary values where $x = 0$ and nowhere else.

The second derivatives are $\dfrac{d^2y}{dx^2} = 6x$, $\dfrac{d^2y}{dx^2} = 12x^2$ and $\dfrac{d^2y}{dx^2} = -12x^2$. For each graph the value of $\dfrac{d^2y}{dx^2}$ where $x = 0$ is 0.

The shapes of all three graphs in the neighbourhood of the origin are shown in Fig. 24.14. One has a minimum, one has a maximum and one has neither.

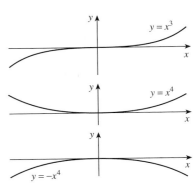

Fig. 24.14

What this example shows is that if the second derivative at a stationary point is 0, you can't use this method to decide whether it is a maximum, a minimum or neither. In that case you have to go back to the earlier method in Section 23.2.

You will also find later on that for some functions it can be very laborious to find the second derivative. In that case, it is more efficient to use the old procedure. But this will not apply to any of the functions you have met so far.

Example 24.4.3
Find the minimum and maximum points on the graph of $f(x) = x^4 + x^5$.

Step 1 $f'(x) = 4x^3 + 5x^4 = x^3(4 + 5x)$.

Step 2 $f'(x) = 0$ when $x = 0$ or $x = -0.8$.

Step 3 $f''(x) = 12x^2 + 20x^3 = 4x^2(3 + 5x)$.

Step 4 $f''(-0.8) = 4 \times (-0.8)^2 \times (3 - 4) < 0$, so $x = -0.8$ gives a maximum.

$f''(0) = 0$, so you have to use the old procedure.

	$-0.8 < x < 0$	$x = 0$	$x > 0$
x^3	$-$	0	$+$
$4 + 5x$	$+$	$+$	$+$
$f'(x)$	$-$	0	$+$

Table 24.15

Table 24.15 shows that $x = 0$ gives a minimum.

Step 5   The maximum point is $(-0.8, 0.081\,92)$; the minimum point is $(0, 0)$.

Exercise 24B

1 Use first and second derivatives to locate and describe the stationary points on the graphs of the following functions. If this method fails then you should use the change of sign of the first derivative to distinguish stationary points which are maxima, minima or neither.
   (a) $f(x) = 3x - x^3$
   (b) $f(x) = x^3 - 3x^2$
   (c) $f(x) = 3x^4 + 1$
   (d) $f(x) = 2x^3 - 3x^2 - 12x + 4$
   (e) $f(x) = 2x^3 - 12x^2 + 24x + 6$

2 Find the maximum and minimum points (if any) on the following graphs.
   (a) $y = 3x^4 - 4x^3 - 12x^2 - 3$ (b) $y = x^3 - 3x^2 + 3x + 5$ (c) $y = 16x - 3x^3$
   (d) $y = 2x^5 - 7$ (e) $y = 3x^4 - 8x^3 + 6x^2 + 1$

25 Applications of differentiation

You have now learnt what differentiation means and how to differentiate a lot of functions. This chapter shows how you can apply these ideas to real-world problems. When you have completed it, you should

- know that you can interpret a derivative as a rate of change of one variable with respect to another
- be able to apply these techniques to real-world problems
- be familiar with third and higher derivatives.

25.1 Derivatives as rates of change

The quantities x and y in a relationship $y = f(x)$ are often called variables, because x can stand for any number for which $f(x)$ has a meaning, and y for any value of the function. When you draw the graph you have a free choice of the values of x, and then work out y. So x is called the **independent variable** and y the **dependent variable**.

These variables often stand for physical or economic quantities, and then it is convenient to use other letters which suggest what these quantities are: for example t for time, V for volume, C for cost, P for population, and so on.

To illustrate this consider a situation familiar to deep sea divers, that pressure increases with depth below sea level. The independent variable is the depth, z metres, below the surface.

> It will soon be clear why the letter d was avoided for the depth. The letter z is often used for distances in the vertical direction.

The dependent variable is the pressure, p, measured in bars. At the surface the diver experiences only atmospheric pressure, about 1 bar, but the pressure increases as the diver descends. At offshore (coastal) depths the variables are connected approximately by the equation

$$p = 1 + 0.1z.$$

The (z, p) graph is a straight line, shown in Fig. 25.1.

The constant 0.1 in the equation is the amount that the pressure goes up for each extra metre of depth. This is the 'rate of change of pressure with respect to depth'.

This can be expressed algebraically using the 'delta' notation introduced in Section 12.1. If the diver descends a further distance of δz metres, the pressure goes up by δp bars; this rate of change is $\dfrac{\delta p}{\delta z}$. It is represented by the gradient of the graph.

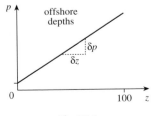

Fig. 25.1

But at ocean depths the (z, p) graph is no longer a straight line: it has the form of a curve which bends upwards, as in Fig. 25.2.

The quantity $\dfrac{\delta p}{\delta z}$ now represents the average rate of change over the extra depth δz. It is represented by the gradient of the chord in Fig. 25.2.

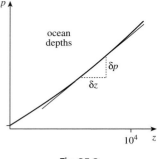

Fig. 25.2

You have already met this idea, and used this notation, in finding the gradient of the graph of $y = f(x)$. It is especially useful when you want to use different letters as variables to describe particular quantities.

In Section 12.5 the symbol $\dfrac{dy}{dx}$ was used to denote the gradient of the tangent, so that

$$\frac{dy}{dx} = \lim_{\delta x \to 0} \frac{\delta y}{\delta x}.$$

In just the same way you can use the symbol $\dfrac{dp}{dz}$, defined as

$$\frac{dp}{dz} = \lim_{\delta z \to 0} \frac{\delta p}{\delta z}.$$

It is important to understand the difference between $\dfrac{\delta p}{\delta z}$ and $\dfrac{dp}{dz}$. The symbol $\dfrac{\delta p}{\delta z}$ means the average rate of change of pressure with depth between one depth and another. For example, if the pressure is 125 bars at a depth of 1000 metres and 138 bars at a depth of 1100 metres, then $\delta p = 138 - 125 = 13$, $\delta z = 1100 - 1000 = 100$, so that $\dfrac{\delta p}{\delta z} = 0.13$. That is, the average rate of increase of pressure with depth between 1000 metres and 1100 metres is 0.13 bars per metre.

But if, for example, $\dfrac{dp}{dz} = 0.14$ when $z = 1100$, this means that at the particular depth of 1100 metres the pressure is increasing at a rate of 0.14 bars per metre. On a graph showing p against z, $\dfrac{\delta p}{\delta z}$ is the gradient of a chord and $\dfrac{dp}{dz}$ is the gradient of a tangent.

> If x and y are the independent and dependent variables respectively in a functional relationship, then
>
> $\dfrac{\delta y}{\delta x}$ represents the average rate of change of y with respect to x over an interval of values of x,
>
> $\dfrac{dy}{dx}$ represents the instantaneous rate of change of y with respect to x for a particular value of x.

This notation can be used in a wide variety of contexts. For example, if the area of burnt grass, t minutes after a fire has started, is A square metres, then $\dfrac{dA}{dt}$ measures the rate at which the fire is spreading in square metres per minute. If, at a certain point on the earth's surface, distances of x metres on the ground are represented by distances of y metres on a map, then $\dfrac{dy}{dx}$ represents the scale of the map at that point.

Example 25.1.1

Research into the growth of juvenile herrings suggests that after t years their mean length, l cm, is given approximately by the equation $l = 8t - \frac{1}{2}t^2$. According to this formula,

(a) find the rate of growth after 3 years,

(b) find how many years it will take the herrings to become fully grown.

The rate at which the herrings are growing is given by the derivative $\dfrac{\mathrm{d}l}{\mathrm{d}t} = 8 - t$.

Since the units of length and time are centimetres and years, this equation gives the rate of growth in centimetres per year.

(a) When $t = 3$, $\dfrac{\mathrm{d}l}{\mathrm{d}t} = 8 - 3 = 5$. So after 3 years the herrings are growing at a rate of 5 centimetres per year.

(b) When the herrings are fully grown the rate of growth is zero, so $\dfrac{\mathrm{d}l}{\mathrm{d}t} = 0$. This occurs when $t = 8$. So the herrings will be fully grown after 8 years.

Notice in this example that, according to the given equation, the rate of growth becomes negative when $t > 8$. This suggests that the herrings would become shorter, which is unlikely! It is far more probable that, since the research was based on measuring juvenile herrings up to 6 years old, the formula is valid only for a certain interval of values of t. This interval will certainly not extend beyond $t = 8$.

Example 25.1.2

A boy is exactly 4 years older than his sister. Write an expression for the ratio of the boy's age to his sister's age when the sister is x years old. Find the rate at which this ratio is changing when the sister is 20 years old.

Compare this with Example 9.6.2, in which the ratio was regarded as a sequence for positive integer values of n. In the present example, the ratio is considered as a function of a positive real number variable x. Which do you think is more appropriate?

When the sister's age is x, her brother's age is $x + 4$. So, denoting the ratio by R,

$R = \dfrac{x + 4}{x}$, which can be written as $R = 1 + \dfrac{4}{x} = 1 + 4x^{-1}$.

The rate at which the ratio is changing is measured by the derivative $\dfrac{\mathrm{d}R}{\mathrm{d}x}$.

Differentiating,

$$\frac{\mathrm{d}R}{\mathrm{d}x} = -4x^{-2} = -\frac{4}{x^2}.$$

When $x = 20$, $\dfrac{\mathrm{d}R}{\mathrm{d}x} = -\dfrac{4}{20^2} = -0.01$. The ratio is going down at a rate of 0.01 per year.

You can check the answer to this example by calculating the actual ratios when $x = 19$, 20 and 21; thus $\dfrac{23}{19} = 1.2105...$, $\dfrac{24}{20} = 1.2$ and $\dfrac{25}{21} = 1.1904...$.

Between $x = 20$ and $x = 21$, $\delta x = 21 - 20 = 1$ and $\delta R = 1.1904... - 1.2 = -0.0095...$, so the average rate of change is $\dfrac{\delta R}{\delta x} = -0.0095...$.

Between $x = 20$ and $x = 19$, $\delta x = 19 - 20 = -1$ and $\delta R = 1.2105... - 1.2 = 0.0105...$ so the average rate of change is $\dfrac{\delta R}{\delta x} = -0.0105...$.

These average rates are approximately equal to the rate $\dfrac{dR}{dx} = -0.01$ when $x = 20$.

> Draw a sketch of the (x, R) graph in the neighbourhood of $x = 20$ to illustrate these results.

Example 25.1.3

A sprinter in a women's 100-metre race reaches her top speed of 12 metres per second after she has run 36 metres. Up to that distance her speed is proportional to the square root of the distance she has run. Show that until she reaches full speed the rate of change of her speed with respect to distance is inversely proportional to her speed.

Suppose that after she has run x metres her speed is S metres per second. You are told that, up to $x = 36$, $S = k\sqrt{x}$, and also that $S = 12$ when $x = 36$. So

$$12 = k\sqrt{36}, \quad \text{giving} \quad k = \tfrac{12}{6} = 2.$$

The (x, S) relationship is therefore

$$S = 2\sqrt{x} \text{ for } 0 < x < 36.$$

The rate of change of speed with respect to distance is the derivative $\dfrac{dS}{dx}$. Since $S = 2x^{\frac{1}{2}}$,

$$\frac{dS}{dx} = 2 \times \tfrac{1}{2}x^{-\frac{1}{2}} = \frac{1}{\sqrt{x}}.$$

Since $\sqrt{x} = \dfrac{S}{2}$, $\dfrac{dS}{dx}$ can be written as $\dfrac{2}{S}$.

The rate of change is therefore inversely proportional to her speed.

If she maintains her top speed for the rest of the race, the rate of change of speed with respect to distance drops to 0 for $x > 36$. Fig. 25.3 shows that the gradient, which represents the rate of change, gets smaller as her speed increases, and then becomes zero once she reaches her top speed.

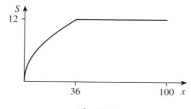

Fig. 25.3

Exercise 25A

1 In each part of this question express each derivative as 'the rate of change of ... with respect to ...', and say what it stands for in practice.

(a) $\dfrac{dh}{dx}$, where h is the height above sea level, and x is the distance travelled (measured horizontally), along a straight road

(b) $\dfrac{dN}{dt}$, where N is the number of people in a stadium at time t after the gates open

(c) $\dfrac{dM}{dr}$, where M is the magnetic force at a distance r from a magnet

(d) $\dfrac{dv}{dt}$, where v is the velocity of a train moving on a straight track at time t

(e) $\dfrac{dq}{dS}$, where q is the rate at which petrol is used in a car in litres per km, and S is the speed of the car in km per hour

2 Defining suitable notation and units, express each of the following as a derivative.

(a) the rate of change of atmospheric pressure with respect to height above sea level

(b) the rate of change of temperature with respect to the time of day

(c) the rate at which the tide is rising

(d) the rate at which a baby's weight increases in the first weeks of life

3 (a) Find $\dfrac{dz}{dt}$ where $z = 3t^2 + 7t - 5$.

   (b) Find $\dfrac{d\theta}{dx}$ where $\theta = x - \sqrt{x}$.

   (c) Find $\dfrac{dx}{dy}$ where $x = y + \dfrac{3}{y^2}$.

   (d) Find $\dfrac{dr}{dt}$ where $r = t^2 + \dfrac{1}{\sqrt{t}}$.

   (e) Find $\dfrac{dm}{dt}$ where $m = (t + 3)^2$.

   (f) Find $\dfrac{df}{ds}$ where $f = 2s^6 - 3s^2$.

   (g) Find $\dfrac{dw}{dt}$ where $w = 5t$.

   (h) Find $\dfrac{dR}{dr}$ where $R = \dfrac{1 - r^3}{r^2}$.

4 Devise suitable notation to express each of the following in mathematical form.

(a) The distance travelled along the motorway is increasing at a constant rate.

(b) The rate at which a savings bank deposit grows is proportional to the amount of money deposited.

(c) The rate at which the diameter of a tree increases is a function of the air temperature.

5 A hot air balloon is h metres above the ground t minutes after it is released. While it is ascending the equation connecting h with t is $h = 100t - 2t^2$.

(a) Find the average rate at which the balloon gains height during

   (i) the first minute,   (ii) the 20th minute.

(b) Find the rate at which the balloon is gaining height after 10 minutes.

(c) Find how long the balloon takes to reach its greatest height.

6 The index of pollution, I, at a distance of x kilometres from a city centre is given by $I = (15 - x)^2$. The formula is valid for values of x between 0 and 10.

(a) Find the average rate of decrease of the index with respect to distance in moving from the centre of the city to a point 5 kilometres from the centre.

(b) Find the average rate of decrease of the index with respect to distance in moving from a point 5 kilometres from the centre to a point 10 kilometres from the centre.

(c) Find the rate of decrease of the index with respect to distance at a point 5 kilometres from the city centre.

7 The number of people who have completed a city marathon t hours after the start is modelled by the formula $N = 19\,200 - 21\,600t + 7200t^2 - 600t^3$ for values of t between 2 and 6. The organisers use this equation to plan how many stewards they will need to have on duty at the finishing line.

(a) How many runners are expected to have completed the course after 6 hours?

(b) What is the expected average rate per minute of arrival of runners at the finish

(i) between 2 and 3 hours after the start,

(ii) between 3 and $3\frac{1}{2}$ hours after the start?

(c) At what rate per minute are runners expected to be arriving at the finish 3 hours after the start?

8 (a) A circle of radius r has area $A = \pi r^2$. Find $\dfrac{dA}{dr}$.

(b) A sphere of radius r has volume $V = \frac{4}{3}\pi r^3$. Find $\dfrac{dV}{dr}$.

What do you notice about the answers?

9 The quantity of light received by a telescope from a star x light-years away is denoted by Q. It is known that, for stars with a given luminosity, $Q = \dfrac{C}{x^2}$, where C is a constant. Find $\dfrac{dQ}{dx}$, and deduce that $\dfrac{dQ}{dx} = -\dfrac{2Q}{x}$.

10 The pressure and volume of a quantity of air are denoted by P and V. As the air expands adiabatically, the values of P and V are related by the equation $PV^{1.4} = k$, where k is constant. Find $\dfrac{dP}{dV}$ in terms of V and k. Hence show that $\dfrac{dP}{dV} = -\dfrac{1.4P}{V}$.

11 (a) A simple pendulum consists of a small metal ball attached to a fixed point by a cord of length l centimetres. It takes T seconds to make one swing, where $T = 0.2\sqrt{l}$. Find $\dfrac{dT}{dl}$.

(b) The cord originally has length 2.5 metres. If it is lengthened by 2 millimetres, calculate what effect this will have on the time of swing

(i) by using your answer to part (a),   (ii) by direct evaluation of T.

25.2 Second derivatives in practice

A local newspaper reports that 'house prices are increasing, but not as fast as they were'. This is a typical instance of a second derivative in everyday life. If p denotes the mean price of houses in the town, and t the time, then a (t, p) graph would look like Fig. 25.4.

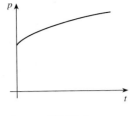

Fig. 25.4

The gradient $\dfrac{dp}{dt}$ represents the rate at which house prices are going up. The report says that this rate is going down, so the gradient is decreasing. The graph bends downwards, so the second derivative is negative. This second derivative is written as $\dfrac{d^2 p}{dt^2}$.

Second derivatives are important in many applications. For example, the number of UK households possessing a DVD player has been increasing for a long time. Manufacturers will estimate the number of such households, H, in year t, and note that the graph of H against t has a positive gradient $\dfrac{dH}{dt}$. But to plan ahead they need to know whether this rate of increase is itself increasing (so that they should increase production of models for first-time users) or decreasing (in which case they might target existing customers to update to more sophisticated equipment). So it is the value of $\dfrac{d^2 H}{dt^2}$ which affects strategic planning decisions.

Similarly, a weather forecaster observing the atmospheric pressure p at time t may not be too concerned if $\dfrac{dp}{dt}$ is negative; pressure goes up and down all the time. But if she also notices that $\dfrac{d^2 p}{dt^2}$ is negative, it may be time to issue a warning of severe weather.

Example 25.2.1

A government plans the economy on the assumption that the population, P millions, for the next 15 years can be modelled by the equation $P = 60 + 0.02t^3 - 0.001t^4$.

(a) How large is the population expected to be in 10 years time?

(b) At what annual rate is the population expected to be increasing in 10 years time?

(c) During what period does the government expect the annual rate of increase of the population to be increasing?

(a) Substituting $t = 10$ in the equation for P gives

$$P = 60 + 0.02 \times 1000 - 0.001 \times 10\,000 = 60 + 20 - 10 = 70.$$

Since P is the population in millions, the population in 10 years time is expected to be 70 million.

(b) The rate of increase of the population is given by

$$\frac{\mathrm{d}P}{\mathrm{d}t} = 0.02 \times (3t^2) - 0.001 \times (4t^3) = 0.06t^2 - 0.004t^3.$$

When $t = 10$, the value of $\dfrac{\mathrm{d}P}{\mathrm{d}t}$ is

$$0.06 \times 100 - 0.004 \times 1000 = 6 - 4 = 2.$$

In 10 years time it is expected that the population will be increasing at a rate of 2 million per year.

(c) This question asks about the rate of increase of $\dfrac{\mathrm{d}P}{\mathrm{d}t}$, which is

$$\frac{\mathrm{d}^2 P}{\mathrm{d}t^2} = 0.06 \times (2t) - 0.004 \times (3t^2) = 0.12t - 0.012t^2 = 0.012t(10 - t).$$

This is positive when $t(10 - t) > 0$, that is when $0 < t < 10$.

The rate of increase of the population is expected to increase for the next 10 years.

This is illustrated by the graph in Fig. 25.5. Between $t = 0$ and $t = 10$ the graph is concave up, which shows that the rate of increase of the population is increasing. After that, until $t = 15$, the graph is concave down; the rate of increase of the population decreases, although the population is still increasing.

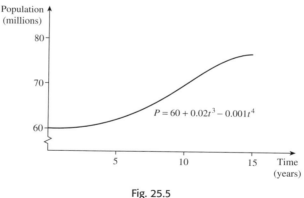

Fig. 25.5

25.3 Derivatives in kinematics

One important application of derivatives is to the motion of an object along a straight line.

In Section 10.6 it was shown that, if the velocity is constant, then the displacement is a linear function of the time, and the gradient of the displacement–time graph represents the velocity. This can now be generalised to situations in which the velocity varies with time.

Suppose that a car moving along a road has its speed checked by a radar detector at a point O (see Fig. 25.6). A pulse sent out from O locates the car at P, at a displacement s from O. A second pulse, at a time δt later, locates the car at Q, where the displacement has increased by an amount δs. Then the detector will compute the velocity of the car as $\dfrac{\delta s}{\delta t}$.

Fig. 25.6

This is not in fact the true velocity of the car, but the average velocity over the time interval δt. The advantage of using radar instead of a policeman with a stopwatch is that δt can be made much smaller. If δt is very small, the average velocity will be very close to the actual velocity at P, which is the limit of the average velocity as δt tends to 0. That is,

$$v = \lim_{\delta t \to 0} \frac{\delta s}{\delta t} = \frac{ds}{dt}.$$

There is a similar link between acceleration and velocity. It was stated in Section 10.7 that, if the acceleration is constant, then the velocity is a linear function of the time, and the gradient of the velocity–time graph represents the acceleration. This can be generalised to situations in which the acceleration is not constant.

If the velocity of the car in Fig. 25.6 is v when the car is at P, and if it increases by an amount δv by the time the car reaches Q, then $\dfrac{\delta v}{\delta t}$ measures the average acceleration of the car over the time interval δt. The actual acceleration at P is the limit of the average acceleration as δt tends to 0. That is,

$$a = \lim_{\delta t \to 0} \frac{\delta v}{\delta t} = \frac{dv}{dt}.$$

Since $v = \dfrac{ds}{dt}$, it follows that the acceleration can also be written as $\dfrac{d^2s}{dt^2}$.

> For an object moving in a straight line, if s denotes the displacement from a fixed point O of the line at time t, v denotes the velocity and a the acceleration, then
>
> $$v = \frac{ds}{dt} \quad \text{and} \quad a = \frac{dv}{dt} = \frac{d^2s}{dt^2}.$$
>
> The velocity is represented by the gradient of the (t, s) graph.
>
> The acceleration is represented by the gradient of the (t, v) graph.

Example 25.3.1

A space probe is launched by rockets. For the first stage of its ascent, which is in a vertical line and lasts for 40 seconds, the height s metres after t seconds is modelled by the equation $s = 50t^2 + \frac{1}{4}t^3$. How high is the probe at the end of the first stage, and how fast is it then moving?

To find the height, you substitute 40 for t in the equation for s, which gives

$$s = 50 \times 1600 + \tfrac{1}{4} \times 64\,000 = 96\,000.$$

To find a formula for the velocity you must differentiate, to get

$$v = \frac{ds}{dt} = 100t + \tfrac{3}{4}t^2.$$

Substituting 40 for t in this equation gives

$$v = 100 \times 40 + \tfrac{3}{4} \times 1600 = 4000 + 1200 = 5200.$$

So at the end of the first stage the probe is at a height of 96 000 m and moving at 5200 m s^{-1}. This is more conveniently expressed in kilometre units: the height is then 96 km, and the velocity is 5.2 km s^{-1}.

Example 25.3.2

A car starts to accelerate as soon as it leaves a town. After t seconds its velocity v m s^{-1} is given by the formula $v = 14 + 0.45t^2 - 0.03t^3$, until it reaches its maximum velocity. Find a formula for the acceleration. How fast is the car moving when its acceleration becomes zero?

The acceleration a is found by differentiating the formula for v, so

$$a = \frac{dv}{dt} = 0.9t - 0.09t^2.$$

This can be factorised as $a = 0.09t(10 - t)$, so the acceleration becomes zero when $t = 10$. This is when the car reaches its maximum velocity. After that the model no longer applies.

To find the maximum velocity, substitute $t = 10$ in the formula for v. This gives

$$v = 14 + 0.45 \times 100 - 0.03 \times 1000 = 14 + 45 - 30 = 29.$$

The car reaches a maximum velocity of 29 m s^{-1} after 10 seconds.

Exercise 25B

1 (a) This graph shows prices (P) plotted against time (t). The rate of inflation, measured by $\frac{dP}{dt}$, is increasing. What does $\frac{d^2P}{dt^2}$ represent and what can be said about its value?

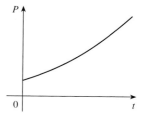

(b) Sketch a graph showing that prices are increasing but that the rate of inflation is slowing down with an overall increase tending to 20%.

2 The graph shows the price S of shares in a certain company.

(a) For each stage of the graph comment on $\frac{dS}{dt}$ and $\frac{d^2S}{dt^2}$.

(b) Describe what happened in non-technical language.

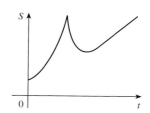

3 Colin sets off for school, which is 800 m from home. His speed is proportional to the distance he still has to go. Let x metres be the distance he has gone, and y metres be the distance that he still has to go.

(a) Sketch graphs of x against t and y against t.

(b) What are the signs of $\dfrac{dx}{dt}$, $\dfrac{d^2x}{dt^2}$, $\dfrac{dy}{dt}$ and $\dfrac{d^2y}{dt^2}$?

4 The rate of decay of a radioactive substance is proportional to the number, N, of radioactive atoms present at time t.

(a) Write an equation representing this information.

(b) Sketch a graph of N against t.

(c) What is the sign of $\dfrac{d^2N}{dt^2}$?

5 A weather forecaster predicts that, in t hours time, the pressure at a certain point, p millibars, will be given by the equation $p = 0.1t^3 - 1.5t^2 + 1000$, for $0 \le t \le 16$.

(a) Show that, according to this formula, the pressure will fall for the first few hours. When will it start to rise again?

(b) When will the rate at which the pressure is falling begin to decrease?

(c) When will the pressure get back to its original value? At what rate will it then be rising?

6 An economist predicts that, over the next few months, the price of oil, p dollars a barrel, in t weeks time will be given by the formula $p = 0.005t^3 - 0.3t^2 + 4.5t + 80$.

(a) What is the price at present, and how rapidly is it going up?

(b) How high does she expect the price to rise?

(c) She reckons that she will need to revise her prediction when the rate of price increase next begins to increase. When will this occur?

7 In this question, s metres is the displacement at time t seconds of particles moving in a straight line, v is the velocity in m s^{-1} and a is the acceleration in m s^{-2}. Only zero and positive values of t should be considered.

(a) Given that $s = t^3 + 5t$, find the displacement, velocity and acceleration when $t = 3$.

(b) Given that $s = 36 - \dfrac{4}{t}$, find the velocity and acceleration when $t = 2$.

(c) Given that $v = 3\sqrt{t}$, find the velocity and acceleration when $t = 4$.

(d) Given that $s = 120 - 15t - 6t^2 + t^3$, find the time when the velocity is zero. Find the displacement at this instant.

(e) Given that $v = t^2 - 12t + 40$, find the velocity when the acceleration is zero.

(f) Given that $s = 2t^4 + 8t$, find the displacement and the acceleration when the velocity is 35 m s^{-1}.

8 A car is accelerating from rest. At time t seconds after starting, the velocity of the car is v m s^{-1}, where $v = 6t - \frac{1}{2}t^2$, for $0 \le t \le 6$.

(a) Find the velocity of the car 6 seconds after starting.

(b) Find the acceleration of the car when its velocity is 10 m s^{-1}.

9 A train leaves a station and travels in a straight line. After t seconds the train has travelled a distance s metres, where $s = (320t^3 - 2t^4) \times 10^{-5}$. This formula is valid until the train comes to rest at the next station.

(a) Find when the train comes to rest, and hence find the distance between the two stations.

(b) Find the acceleration of the train 40 seconds after the journey begins.

(c) Find the deceleration of the train just before it stops.

(d) Find when the acceleration is zero, and hence find the maximum velocity of the train.

10 An insect flies in a straight line from one flower to another. The two flowers are 270 cm apart and the flight takes 3 seconds. At time t seconds after the flight begins, the insect is s cm from the first flower. Two alternative models are proposed:
(A) $s = 60t^2 - 10t^3$,

(B) $s = 40t^3 - 10t^4$.

For each of these models,

(a) show that the model fits the given information about the flight,

(b) find the maximum velocity of the insect,

(c) sketch the (t, v) graph.

Comment on the differences between the two models. Which do you consider to be the better model?

11 A flare is launched from a hot-air balloon and moves in a vertical line. At time t seconds, the height of the flare is x metres, where $x = 1664 - 40t - \dfrac{2560}{t}$ for $t \geq 5$.

The flare is launched when $t = 5$.

(a) Find the height and the velocity of the flare immediately after it is launched.

(b) Find the acceleration of the flare immediately after it is launched, when its velocity is zero, and when $t = 25$.

(c) Find the greatest possible downward speed of the flare.

(d) Find when the flare reaches the ground.

(e) Sketch the (t, v) graph and the (t, x) graph for the motion of the flare.

25.4   Maximum and minimum problems

In many real-world situations the aim is to find a strategy which will make some quantity as large or as small as possible. For example, a manufacturer may want to price goods so as to maximise the firm's profits, or to design a component so as to minimise the amount of raw material used. The techniques described in the last two chapters can often be useful in reaching such decisions.

The procedures are essentially similar to those for finding maximum and minimum points on graphs. But there are some differences.

One is that in practical applications you will only want to consider values of the independent variable for which the problem makes sense. For example, if the independent variable is a length x metres, you will be interested only in values of the function when $x > 0$.

Another difference is that in a practical situation it will sometimes be obvious from the nature of the problem whether the quantity has a maximum or a minimum value. Steps 3 and 4 in the procedure (in Sections 23.2 and 24.4), which are used to distinguish maximum points from minimum points, then simply serve as a check that the technique has been correctly applied.

Example 25.4.1
Figure 25.7 shows the corner of a garden, bordered by two walls at right angles. A gardener has 30 metres of rabbit fencing. What is the largest rectangular area she can fence off?

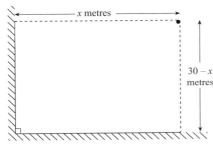

Fig. 25.7

If she makes her rectangle x metres long, she has $(30 - x)$ metres left for the other side of the rectangle. In this way she can fence off an area of A m^2, where

$$A = x(30 - x) = 30x - x^2.$$

Notice that this equation only applies if $0 < x < 30$.

The area takes its maximum value when $\dfrac{dA}{dx} = 0$, where

$$\frac{dA}{dx} = 30 - 2x.$$

So $\dfrac{dA}{dx} = 0$ when $x = 15$.

To check that this gives a maximum value of A, find

$$\frac{d^2 A}{dx^2} = -2.$$

Since this is negative, $x = 15$ gives a maximum value.

To find the maximum area, substitute $x = 15$ in $A = x(30 - x)$ to get

$$A = 15 \times (30 - 15) = 15 \times 15 = 225.$$

The largest area the gardener can fence off is 225 m^2.

Example 25.4.2

Towards the end of the day a market trader has 20 boxes of peaches left unsold. By tomorrow they will be useless. He reckons that if he offers them for sale at x cents a box, he will be able to dispose of $(20 - \frac{1}{5}x)$ boxes. At what price should he offer them to make the most money?

The trader will not sell any boxes if he sets the price at 100 cents. The only values of x which are of interest are between 0 and 100.

If he sells $(20 - \frac{1}{5}x)$ boxes at x cents a box, he will make $x(20 - \frac{1}{5}x)$ cents. He wants to maximise this function.

Let $f(x) = x(20 - \frac{1}{5}x) = 20x - \frac{1}{5}x^2$.

Then $f'(x) = 20 - \frac{2}{5}x$.

The value of x which makes $f'(x) = 0$ is given by

$$\tfrac{2}{5}x = 20, \quad \text{that is} \quad x = 50.$$

This obviously gives a maximum rather than a minimum, but you can check this by finding $f''(x) = -\frac{2}{5}$. Since this is negative, $x = 50$ gives a maximum value of the function.

He should offer the peaches at 50 cents a box.

Example 25.4.3

A pioneer wants to build a storage shed in the shape of a cuboid with a square base, with a capacity of 32 cubic metres. To conserve materials, he wants to make the total area of the roof and the four sides as small as possible. What are the best dimensions for the shed, and what is the total area with these dimensions?

The shed is illustrated in Fig. 25.8. Suppose that the base is a square of side x metres. Then, since the volume is to be 32 cubic metres, the height must be $\dfrac{32}{x^2}$ square metres.

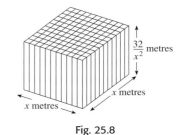

Fig. 25.8

The roof is square with area x^2 square metres. Each side is a rectangle with area $x \times \dfrac{32}{x^2}$ square metres, which is $\dfrac{32}{x}$ square metres. So, if the total area of the roof and the four sides is A square metres,

$$A = x^2 + 4 \times \frac{32}{x} = x^2 + \frac{128}{x}$$

The problem is to choose x so that A is as small as possible. To do this, follow the procedure for finding a minimum point described in Section 24.4. Note that only positive values of x are relevant in the problem.

Step 1 $\dfrac{\mathrm{d}A}{\mathrm{d}x} = 2x - \dfrac{128}{x^2}.$

Step 2 $\dfrac{\mathrm{d}A}{\mathrm{d}x} = 0$ when $2x - \dfrac{128}{x^2} = 0$, which gives $x^3 = 64$, $x = 4$.

Step 3 $\dfrac{\mathrm{d}^2 A}{\mathrm{d}x^2} = 2 + \dfrac{256}{x^3}.$

Step 4 When $x = 4$, $\dfrac{\mathrm{d}^2 A}{\mathrm{d}x^2}$ has value $2 + \dfrac{256}{4^3} = 2 + 4 = 6$, which is positive, so the stationary value is a minimum.

Step 5 When $x = 4$, $A = 4^2 + \dfrac{128}{4} = 16 + 32 = 48.$

This shows that the best dimensions for the shed are to make the base 4 metres square and the height 2 metres. This gives a total area for the roof and the sides of 48 square metres.

Notice that, in solving this problem, it was necessary to begin by choosing a suitable independent variable (in this case the length of a side of the square base). Then an equation was found for the quantity to be minimised (the total area of the sides and roof of the shed) in terms of this independent variable. Only then can you begin to use the procedure for finding the minimum point of the graph. Finally, once the procedure has been completed, the result has to be interpreted in terms of the original problem.

Example 25.4.4

A wire of length 4 metres is cut into two pieces, and each piece is bent into a square. How should this be done so that the two squares together have

(a) the smallest area,   (b) the largest area?

Let the two pieces have lengths x metres and $(4 - x)$ metres. The areas of the squares are then $\left(\tfrac{1}{4}x\right)^2$ and $\left(\tfrac{1}{4}(4 - x)\right)^2$ square metres, see Fig. 25.9. So the total area, y m^2, is given by

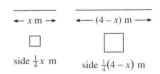

Fig. 25.9

$$y = \tfrac{1}{16}\left(x^2 + (16 - 8x + x^2)\right)$$
$$= \tfrac{1}{8}(x^2 - 4x + 8).$$

You can evaluate this expression for any real number x, but the problem only has meaning if $0 < x < 4$. Figure 25.10 shows the graph of the area function for this interval.

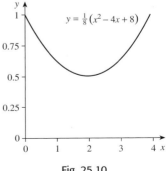

Fig. 25.10

(a) The smallest area is represented by the minimum point on the graph. Since
$\frac{dy}{dx} = \frac{1}{8}(2x - 4) = \frac{1}{4}(x - 2)$, this is where $x = 2$. Also $\frac{d^2y}{dx^2} = \frac{1}{4} > 0$, which confirms
that the stationary point is a minimum.

So the area is smallest when the wire is cut into two equal parts, each of length
2 metres. The area is then $\frac{1}{8}(2^2 - 4 \times 2 + 8)$ m^2, that is, $\frac{1}{2}$ m^2.

Since y is a quadratic function of x, this answer could also be found by writing y in
completed square form, as $y = \frac{1}{8}((x - 2)^2 + 4)$. As $(x - 2)^2 \geq 0$, y is least when
$x = 2$, and the least value of y is $\frac{1}{2}$.

(b) From the graph it looks as if the largest value of y is 1, when $x = 0$ and $x = 4$. But
these values of x are excluded, since they do not produce two pieces of wire. You
can get areas as near to 1 square metre as you like, but you cannot achieve this
target. Strictly speaking, there is no largest area.

It is important to notice in this example that the 'largest value' is not associated with a
maximum point on the graph, as defined in Section 23.2. Although largest and smallest values
can often be found by using the procedure for locating maximum and minimum points, there
are exceptional cases when this does not happen.

Example 25.4.5

It is found that the flow of traffic on congested roads can be improved by lowering the speed
at which it travels. This is because at higher speeds vehicles travel further apart. A traffic
researcher models the distance between vehicles at a speed of S metres per second as D metres,
given by the equation $D = \frac{1}{10}S^2 + \frac{1}{2}S + 10$. At this speed the time interval between successive
vehicles passing a checkpoint is T seconds, where $T = \frac{D}{S}$. Use this model to find the speed
which minimises this time, and the number of vehicles expected to pass the checkpoint in a
minute at this speed.

Note that in this situation you are only interested in positive values of S.

You want to find where $\frac{dT}{dS} = 0$, so write the equation for T in the form

$$T = \frac{D}{S} = \frac{\frac{1}{10}S^2 + \frac{1}{2}S + 10}{S} = \frac{\frac{1}{10}S^2}{S} + \frac{\frac{1}{2}S}{S} + \frac{10}{S} = \frac{1}{10}S + \frac{1}{2} + 10S^{-1}.$$

Then $\frac{dT}{dS} = \frac{1}{10} - 10S^{-2} = \frac{1}{10} - \frac{10}{S^2}.$

The minimum time interval will occur when

$$\frac{1}{10} - \frac{10}{S^2} = 0,$$

that is when $S^2 = 100$. Since only positive values of S are of interest, $S = 10$.

To check that this is a minimum, find

$$\frac{d^2T}{dS^2} = -10(-2S^{-3}) = \frac{20}{S^3},$$

which is certainly positive because S is positive. So $S = 10$ gives a minimum
value for T.

Substituting $S = 10$ in the expression for T gives the minimum value

$$T = \tfrac{1}{10} \times 10 + \tfrac{1}{2} + \frac{10}{10} = 1 + \tfrac{1}{2} + 1 = 2\tfrac{1}{2}.$$

So at 10 metres per second a vehicle passes the checkpoint every $2\tfrac{1}{2}$ seconds. The number of cars passing the checkpoint in a minute is $60 \div 2\tfrac{1}{2}$, which is 24.

In some problems of this kind the quantity you want to maximise or minimise is given by a complicated formula, perhaps including some algebraic constants, and you need to begin by disentangling the formula to simplify the mathematics.

Example 25.4.6

A hole is drilled in a metal plate, and the plate is suspended from a fixed horizontal pin which passes through the hole. If the plate is set swinging as a pendulum, the time T that it takes to make one swing is given by the formula $T = 2\pi\sqrt{\dfrac{x^2 + k^2}{gx}}$, where k and g are positive constants and x is the distance of the centre of mass of the plate from the hole, Find the value of x which makes the time for a swing as short as possible.

You don't know how to differentiate the formula for T. But notice it can be written as

$$T = \frac{2\pi}{\sqrt{g}} \times \sqrt{y}, \quad \text{where} \quad y = \frac{x^2 + k^2}{x}.$$

Since $\dfrac{2\pi}{\sqrt{g}}$ is a constant, you only need to find the value of x which makes y as small as possible. And you can put the expression for y into a form which can be differentiated by writing

$$y = \frac{x^2 + k^2}{x} = \frac{x^2}{x} + \frac{k^2}{x} = x + k^2 x^{-1}.$$

This formula still includes the letter k, but since this is a constant you can treat it just as if it was a number.

So

$$\frac{dy}{dx} = 1 + k^2 \times (-1x^{-2})$$

$$= 1 - \frac{k^2}{x^2}.$$

To find where y is least, the equation $\dfrac{dy}{dx} = 0$ gives

$$1 = \frac{k^2}{x^2}, \quad \text{that is,} \quad x^2 = k^2.$$

In this problem only positive values of x are relevant, so $x = k$.

You can check that this is in fact a minimum rather than a maximum by finding

$$\frac{d^2 y}{dx^2} = -k^2 \times (-2x^{-3}) = \frac{2k^2}{x^3}.$$

When $x = k$, this is equal to $\dfrac{2}{k}$, which is positive.

The time that the pendulum takes to swing is least when x is equal to k.

Example 25.4.7

A hollow cone with base radius a cm and height b cm is placed on a table. What is the volume of the largest cylinder that can be hidden underneath it?

The volume of a cylinder of radius r cm and height h cm is V cm^3, where,

$$V = \pi r^2 h.$$

You can obviously make this as large as you like by choosing r and h large enough. But in this problem the variables are restricted by the requirement that the cylinder has to fit under the cone. Before you can follow the procedure for finding a maximum, you need to find how this restriction affects the values of r and h.

Figure 25.11 shows the three-dimensional set-up, and Fig. 25.12 is a vertical section through the top of the cone. The similar triangles picked out with heavy lines in Figure 25.12 show that r and h are connected by the equation

$$\frac{h}{a-r} = \frac{b}{a}, \text{ so that } h = \frac{b(a-r)}{a}.$$

Fig. 25.11

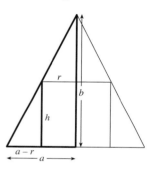

Substituting this expression for h in the formula for V then gives

$$V = \frac{\pi r^2 b(a-r)}{a} = \left(\frac{\pi b}{a}\right)(ar^2 - r^3).$$

Fig. 25.12

Notice that the original expression for V contains two independent variables r and h. The effect of the substitution is to reduce the number of independent variables to one; h has disappeared, and only r remains. This makes it possible to apply the procedure for finding a maximum.

The physical problem only has meaning if $0 < r < a$. Differentiating by the usual rule (remembering that π, a and b are constants) gives

$$\frac{dV}{dr} = \left(\frac{\pi b}{a}\right)(2ar - 3r^2) = \left(\frac{\pi b}{a}\right)r(2a - 3r).$$

The only value of r in the interval $0 < r < a$ for which $\dfrac{dV}{dr} = 0$ is $\tfrac{2}{3}a$. It is easy to check that the sign of $\dfrac{dV}{dr}$ is $+$ for $0 < r < \tfrac{2}{3}a$ and $-$ for $\tfrac{2}{3}a < r < a$.

Substituting $r = \tfrac{2}{3}a$ in the expressions for h and V gives

$$h = \frac{b\left(a - \tfrac{2}{3}a\right)}{a} = \frac{b\left(\tfrac{1}{3}a\right)}{a} = \tfrac{1}{3}b,$$

and $V = \pi r^2 h = \pi \left(\tfrac{2}{3}a\right)^2 \tfrac{1}{3}b = \tfrac{4}{27}\pi a^2 b.$

So the cylinder of maximum volume has radius $\tfrac{2}{3}a$, height $\tfrac{1}{3}b$, and volume $\tfrac{4}{27}\pi a^2 b$. Since the volume of the cone is $\tfrac{1}{3}\pi a^2 b$, the cylinder of maximum volume occupies $\tfrac{4}{9}$ of the space under the cone.

Exercise 25C

1 At a speed of S km per hour a car will travel y kilometres on each litre of petrol, where

$y = 5 + \frac{1}{5}S - \frac{1}{800}S^2.$

Calculate the speed at which the car should be driven for maximum economy.

2 A cricket ball is thrown vertically upwards. At time t seconds its height h metres is given by $h = 20t - 5t^2$. Calculate the ball's maximum height above the ground.

3 The sum of two real numbers x and y is 12. Find the maximum value of their product xy.

4 The product of two positive real numbers x and y is 20. Find the minimum possible value of their sum.

5 The volume of a cylinder is given by the formula $V = \pi r^2 h$. Find the greatest and least values of V if $r + h = 6$.

6 A loop of string of length 1 metre is formed into a rectangle with one pair of opposite sides each x cm. Calculate the value of x which will maximise the area enclosed by the string.

7 One side of a rectangular sheep pen is formed by a hedge. The other three sides are made using fencing. The length of the rectangle is x metres; 120 metres of fencing is available.
   (a) Show that the area of the rectangle is $\frac{1}{2}x(120 - x)$ m^2.
   (b) Calculate the maximum possible area of the sheep pen.

8 A rectangular sheet of metal measures 50 cm by 40 cm. Equal squares of side x cm are cut from each corner and discarded. The sheet is then folded up to make a tray of depth x cm. What are the possible values of x? Find the value of x which maximises the capacity of the tray.

9 An open rectangular box is to be made with a square base, and its capacity is to be 4000 cm^3. Find the length of the side of the base when the amount of material used to make the box is as small as possible. (Ignore 'flaps'.)

10 An open cylindrical wastepaper bin, of radius r cm and capacity V cm^3, is to have a surface area of 5000 cm^2.
   (a) Show that $V = \frac{1}{2}r(5000 - \pi r^2)$.
   (b) Calculate the maximum possible capacity of the bin.

11* A circular cylinder is cut out of a sphere of radius 10 cm. Calculate the maximum possible volume of the cylinder. (It is probably best to take as your independent variable the height, or half the height, of the cylinder.)

25.5   Extending $\dfrac{dy}{dx}$ notation

Although $\dfrac{dy}{dx}$ is a symbol which should not be split into smaller bits, it can usefully be adapted by separating off the y, as

$$\frac{d}{dx}y$$

so that if $y = f(x)$, you can write

$$f'(x) = \frac{d}{dx}f(x).$$

This can be used as a convenient shorthand. For example, instead of having to write

$$\text{if } y = x^4 \text{ then } \frac{dy}{dx} = 4x^3$$

you can abbreviate this to

$$\frac{d}{dx}x^4 = 4x^3.$$

In this equation $\dfrac{d}{dx}$ can be thought of as an instruction to differentiate whatever comes after it.

You may have seen calculators which do algebra as well as arithmetic. With these, you can input a function such as x^4, key in 'differentiate', and the output $4x^3$ appears in the display. The symbol $\dfrac{d}{dx}$, sometimes called the **differential operator**, is the equivalent of pressing the 'differentiate' key.

This explains the notation used for the second derivative, which is what you get by differentiating $\dfrac{dy}{dx}$; that is,

$$\frac{d}{dx}\frac{dy}{dx}.$$

If you collect the elements of this expression into a single symbol, the top line becomes d^2y, and the bottom line $(dx)^2$. Dropping the brackets, this takes the form

$$\frac{d^2y}{dx^2}.$$

25.6   Third and higher derivatives

Suppose you are testing a car in top gear, and you allow the speed to drop to 10 m s^{-1} (which is only 36 kilometres per hour). You put your foot down on the accelerator pedal to get back to the car's top speed of 50 m s^{-1}. At first the engine will feel very uncomfortable and the car will pick up speed quite slowly. And when it eventually reaches the top speed no further acceleration will be possible. But at speeds in the middle of the range the engine will respond vigorously and the acceleration might reach 3 or 4 m s^{-2} at best. The velocity–time graph will look something like Fig. 25.13.

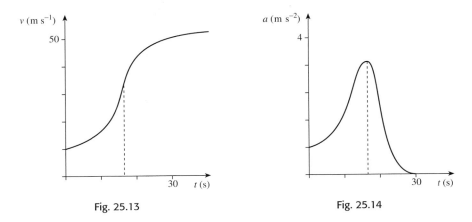

Fig. 25.13   Fig. 25.14

Figure 25.14 shows the corresponding graph for the acceleration. The time when the acceleration is greatest corresponds to the point of inflexion of the velocity–time graph. This is when $\dfrac{da}{dt} = 0$, or $\dfrac{d^2v}{dt^2} = 0$.

Now it was shown in Section 25.3 that

$$v = \frac{ds}{dt} \quad \text{and} \quad a = \frac{dv}{dt} = \frac{d}{dt}\frac{ds}{dt} = \frac{d^2s}{dt^2}.$$

So $\dfrac{da}{dt} = \dfrac{d}{dt}\dfrac{d^2s}{dt^2}$,

which is written as $\dfrac{d^3s}{dt^3}$. It is an example of a 'third derivative'.

As another example, suppose that you have a function $f(x)$ and you calculate in succession that $f(3) = 2$, $f'(3) = \tfrac{1}{2}$ and $f''(3) = 1$. As you do so, you build up what you know of the graph of $y = f(x)$ around $x = 3$. This is shown in Fig. 25.15. In graph (a), when you know only that $f(3) = 2$, all you can do is to put in the point $(3, 2)$. In graph (b) the additional fact that $f'(3) = \tfrac{1}{2}$ enables you to show the tangent at that point. This is the line shown dotted in graph (c).

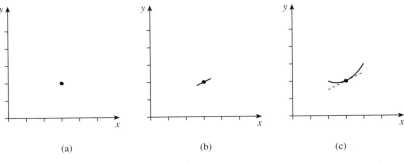

(a)   (b)   (c)

Fig. 25.15

But since $f''(3) = 1$ you know that the gradient is increasing as it passes through the point, and at what rate. So the graph is concave up. If $f''(x)$ had the constant value of 1, the gradient would be $-\frac{1}{2}$ when $x = 2$ and $1\frac{1}{2}$ when $x = 4$. The graph would then be a parabola, shown as a solid line in graph (c).

Now suppose that the true graph is produced, and that it turns out to be the solid line in Fig. 25.16, with gradients of $\frac{1}{2}$ when $x = 2$ and $2\frac{1}{2}$ when $x = 4$. (The parabola in Fig. 25.15(c) is shown dotted for comparison.) This would mean that the curve is more bendy than the parabola to the right of $(2, 3)$ and less bendy to the left. That is, the rate of bending $f''(x)$ is not in fact constant, but it increases with x. To measure how fast the rate of bending is increasing you use the third derivative, which is denoted by $f'''(x)$.

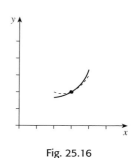

Fig. 25.16

You can obviously go on producing more and more derivatives like this, and each enables you to describe more precisely what the graph looks like around the point $(3, 2)$.

It is easy to extend $\dfrac{dy}{dx}$ notation by using the differential operator $\dfrac{d}{dx}$ to produce the derivatives $\dfrac{d^2y}{dx^2}, \dfrac{d^3y}{dx^3}, \dfrac{d^4y}{dx^4}, \dots$. The corresponding $f'(x)$ notation doesn't extend so conveniently, since you don't want to count up a lot of dashes, so after the third it is usual to write the derivatives as $f^{(4)}(x),\ f^{(5)}(x), \dots$.

Example 25.6.1

Find the first four derivatives of $f(x) = \dfrac{1}{x}$. Generalise these to find an expression for $f^{(n)}(x)$.

Starting from $f(x) = x^{-1}$, successive differentiations give

$$f'(x) = (-1)x^{-2} \qquad\qquad = -\frac{1}{x^2},$$

$$f''(x) = (-1) \times (-2)x^{-3} \qquad = \frac{2}{x^3},$$

$$f'''(x) = (-1) \times (-2) \times (-3)x^{-4} \qquad = -\frac{6}{x^4},$$

$$f^{(4)}(x) = (-1) \times (-2) \times (-3) \times (-4)x^{-5} = \frac{24}{x^5}.$$

Notice that, for each value of n, $f^{(n)}(x)$ has n minus signs, a numerical coefficient of $1 \times 2 \times 3 \times \dots \times n = n!$, and a negative exponent whose modulus is one more than n. That is,

$$f^{(n)}(x) = (-1)^n \times n! \times x^{-(n+1)} = \frac{(-1)^n n!}{x^{n+1}}.$$

Exercise 25D

1 Find the first four derivatives with respect to x of the following functions.

(a) $x^3 - 5x^2 + 2x - 3$

(b) x^8

(c) $\sqrt{x}$

2 Find expressions for $\dfrac{d^2}{dx^2}x^2$, $\dfrac{d^3}{dx^3}x^3$, $\dfrac{d^4}{dx^4}x^4$ and $\dfrac{d^5}{dx^5}x^5$. What general result is suggested by your results?

3 (a) Find the first four derivatives of $f(x) = x^4(5 - x)$, expressing your answer in factors.

(b) Prove that, if $f(x) = x^{n-1}(n - x)$, then $f'(x) = nx^{n-2}((n - 1) - x)$. Use this to write down the fifth derivative of $x^9(10 - x)$.

4 If $f(x) = \dfrac{n - x}{x^{n+1}}$, prove that $f'(x) = -n \times \dfrac{(n + 1) - x}{x^{n+2}}$. Use this to write down the fourth derivative of $\dfrac{1 - x}{x^2}$.

5 (a) Explain why, if $f''(p) = 0$ and $f'''(p) \neq 0$, then $f'(x)$ has either a maximum or a minimum where $x = p$.

(b) Explain why, if $f''(p) = 0$ and $f'''(p) \neq 0$, then the graph of $y = f(x)$ has a point of inflexion where $x = p$.

Review exercise 6

1 (a) Find the stationary points and the point of inflexion on the graph of $y = 12x + 3x^2 - 2x^3$. Sketch the graph.

(b) How does your sketch show that the equation $12x + 3x^2 - 2x^3 = 0$ has exactly three real roots?

(c) Use your graph to show that the equation $12x + 3x^2 - 2x^3 = -5$ also has exactly three real roots.

(d) For what range of values of k does the equation $12x + 3x^2 - 2x^3 = k$ have

(i) exactly three real roots,   (ii) only one real root?

2 Find the coordinates of the stationary points on the graph of $y = 3x^4 - 4x^3 - 12x^2 + 10$, and sketch the graph. For what values of k does the equation $3x^4 - 4x^3 - 12x^2 + 10 = k$ have

(a) exactly four roots,   (b) exactly two roots?

Find the coordinates of the points of inflexion, correct to 2 decimal places.

3 The rate at which Nasreen's coffee cools is proportional to the difference between its temperature, $\theta°$, and room temperature, $\alpha°$. Sketch a graph of θ against t given that $\alpha = 20$ and that $\theta = 95$ when $t = 0$. State the signs of θ, $\dfrac{d\theta}{dt}$ and $\dfrac{d^2\theta}{dt^2}$ for $t > 0$.

4 A car accelerates to overtake a truck. Its initial speed is u. The distance x that it covers in a time t after it starts to accelerate is given by $x = ut + kt^2$, where k is a constant.

Use differentiation to show that its speed is then $u + 2kt$, and show that its acceleration is constant.

5 A car is travelling at 20 m s^{-1} when the driver applies the brakes. At a time t seconds later the car has travelled a further distance s metres, where $s = 20t - 2t^2$. Use differentiation to find expressions for the speed and the acceleration of the car at this time. For how long do these formulae apply?

6 Find the least possible value of $x^2 + y^2$ given that $x + y = 10$.

7 The sum of the two shorter sides of a right-angled triangle is 18 cm. Calculate

(a) the least possible length of the hypotenuse,

(b) the greatest possible area of the triangle.

8 A curve has equation $y = 2x^3 - 9x^2 + 12x - 5$. Show that one of the stationary points lies on the x-axis, and determine whether this point is a maximum or a minimum. Find also the coordinates of the point of inflexion.

9 Find the values of k for which the following equations have two separate roots.

(a) $kx^2 + kx + 2 = 0$ (b) $kx^2 + 3x + k = 0$ (c) $x^2 - 2kx + 4 = 0$

10 Find the set of values of x for which $9x^2 + 12x + 7 > 19$.   (OCR)

11 Sketch, on the same diagram, the graphs of $y = \dfrac{1}{x}$ and $y = x - \frac{3}{2}$. Find the solution set of

the inequality $x - \frac{3}{2} > \dfrac{1}{x}$.   (OCR)

12 Find the coordinates of the stationary points on the graph of

$$y = x^3 - 12x - 12$$

and sketch the graph.

Find the set of values of k for which the equation

$$x^3 - 12x - 12 = k$$

has more than one real root.   (OCR)

13 Find the coordinates of the stationary points on the curve with equation $y = x(x - 1)^2$.
Sketch the curve.

Find the set of real values of k such that the equation $x(x - 1)^2 = k^2$ has exactly one real root.   (OCR, adapted)

14 (a) Find the coordinates of the stationary points on the curve $y = 2x^3 - 3x^2 - 12x - 7$.

(b) Determine whether each stationary point is a maximum point or a minimum point.

(c) It is given that $2x^3 - 3x^2 - 12x - 7$ can be written as $(x + 1)^2(2x - 7)$. Sketch the curve $y = (x + 1)^2(2x - 7)$.

(d) Write down the set of values of the constant k for which the equation $2x^3 - 3x^2 - 12x - 7 = k$ has exactly one real solution.   (OCR)

15 The cross-section of an object has the shape of a quarter-circle of radius r adjoining a rectangle of width x and height r, as shown in the diagram.

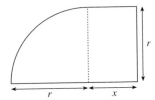

(a) The perimeter and area of the cross-section are P and A respectively. Express each of P and A in terms of r and x, and hence show that $A = \frac{1}{2}Pr - r^2$.

(b) Taking the perimeter P of the cross-section as fixed, find x in terms of r for the case when the area A of the cross-section is a maximum, and show that, for this value of x, A is a maximum and not a minimum.   (OCR)

16 The manager of a supermarket usually adds a mark-up of 20% to the wholesale prices of all the goods he sells. He reckons that he has a loyal core of F customers and that, if he lowers his mark-up to x% he will attract an extra $k(20 - x)$ customers from his rivals. Each week the average shopper buys goods whose wholesale value is $\$A$. Show that with a mark-up of x% the supermarket will have an anticipated weekly profit of

$$\$\tfrac{1}{100}Ax((F + 20k) - kx).$$

Show that the manager can increase his profit by reducing his mark-up below 20% provided that $20k > F$.   (OCR)

17 The costs of a firm which makes climbing boots are of two kinds:

Fixed costs (plant, rates, office expenses): $2000 per week;

Production costs (materials, labour): $20 for each pair of boots made.

Market research suggests that, if they price the boots at $30 a pair they will sell 500 pairs a week, but that at $55 a pair they will sell none at all; and between these values the graph of sales against price is a straight line.

If they price boots at x a pair ($30 \leq x \leq 55$) find expressions for

(a) the weekly sales,   (b) the weekly receipts,

(c) the weekly costs (assuming that just enough boots are made).

Hence show that the weekly profit, P, is given by

$$P = -20x^2 + 1500x - 24\,000.$$

Find the price at which the boots should be sold to maximise the profit.   (OCR)

Examination questions

1 A function f is defined by $f(x) = ax^3 + bx^2 + 30x + c$ where a, b and c are constants. The graph of f has a maximum at $(1, 7)$ and a point of inflexion when $x = 3$. Find the value of a, of b and of c.   (© IBO 2005)

2 The function f is given by $f(x) = \dfrac{x^5 + 2}{x}$, $x \neq 0$. There is a point of inflexion on the graph of f at the point P. Find the coordinates of P.   (© IBO 2005)

3 Solve the inequality $x^2 - 4 + \dfrac{3}{x} < 0$.   (© IBO 2002)

4 Find the range of values of m such that for all x, $m(x + 1) \leq x^2$.   (© IBO 2004)

5 The point $B(a, b)$ is on the curve $f(x) = x^2$ such that B is the point which is closest to $A(6, 0)$. Calculate the value of a.   (© IBO 2002)

6 Consider the equation $(1 + 2k)x^2 - 10x + k - 2 = 0$, $k \in \mathbb{R}$. Find the set of values of k for which the equation has real roots.   (© IBO 2003)

7 Let $f(x) = \dfrac{x + 4}{x + 1}$, $x \neq -1$, and $g(x) = \dfrac{x - 2}{x - 4}$, $x \neq 4$. Find the set of values of x such that $f(x) \leq g(x)$.   (© IBO 2003)

8 A closed cylindrical can has a volume of 500 cm^3. The height of the can is h cm and the radius of the base is r cm.

(a) Find an expression for the total surface area A of the can, in terms of r.

(b) Given that there is a minimum value of A for $r > 0$, find this value of r.   (© IBO 2004)

9 The curve $y = \frac{1}{3}x^3 - x^2 - 3x + 4$ has a local maximum point at P and a local minimum point at Q. Determine the equation of the straight line passing through P and Q, in the form $ax + by + c = 0$, where a, b, $c \in \mathbb{R}$.   (© IBO 2005)

10 Find the largest set of values of x such that the function f given by $f(x) = \sqrt{\dfrac{8x - 4}{x - 3}}$ takes real values.   (© IBO 2005)

26 Probability

This chapter is about chance, and how to develop a mathematical model of chance. When you have completed it, you should

- know what a 'sample space' is
- know the difference between an 'outcome' and an 'event' and be able to calculate the probability of an event from the probabilities of the outcomes in the sample space
- be able to use the addition law of probability
- know what is meant by mutually exclusive events.

26.1 Assigning probability

You will frequently have been unsure of the outcome of some activity or experiment, but have known what the possible outcomes were. For example, you do not know whether you will win a prize the next time you buy a raffle ticket, but you do know that you will either win or not win. You know that if you toss a coin twice, then the possible outcomes are (H, H), (H, T), (T, H) and (T, T). If you are testing a transistor to see if it is defective, then the possible outcomes are 'defective' and 'not defective'.

The list of all the possible outcomes is called the **sample space** of the experiment. The list is usually written in curly brackets { } and denoted by the symbol U.

Thus the sample space for buying a raffle ticket is $U = \{$win, not win$\}$, the sample space for tossing a coin twice is $U = \{(H, H), (H, T), (T, H), (T, T)\}$, and the sample space for testing a transistor is $U = \{$defective, not defective$\}$.

> Notice that it is conventional when writing pairs of things like H, H to put them in brackets, like coordinates.

Each of the outcomes of an experiment has a number, called its probability, assigned to it. Sometimes you can assign the probability using symmetry. For example the sample space for throwing a dice is $\{1, 2, 3, 4, 5, 6\}$, and you would assign each outcome the probability $\frac{1}{6}$, in the belief that the dice was fair, and that each outcome was equally likely. This is the usual method for calculations about games of chance.

> If the outcomes in a sample space are equally likely, then
>
> $$\text{probability of a particular outcome} = \frac{1}{\text{number of equally likely outcomes}}.$$

From the equation in the blue box you can see that the probability must be positive, and lie between 0 and 1. You can also see that if there are n equally likely outcomes, the probability of any particular outcome occurring will be $\frac{1}{n}$. The total sum of all these probabilities will be $n \times \frac{1}{n} = 1$.

Now suppose that the dice is not fair, so that you cannot use symmetry for assigning probabilities. In this case you will have to carry out an experiment and throw the dice a large number of times. Suppose that you threw the dice 1000 times and the frequencies of the six possible outcomes in the sample space were as in Table 26.1.

Outcome	1	2	3	4	5	6
Frequency	100	216	182	135	170	197

Table 26.1

The probabilities you would assign would then be $\frac{100}{1000}$, $\frac{216}{1000}$, $\frac{182}{1000}$, $\frac{135}{1000}$, $\frac{170}{1000}$ and $\frac{197}{1000}$ for the outcomes 1, 2, 3, 4, 5 and 6 respectively. These are called the **relative frequencies** of the outcomes, and you can use them as estimates of the probabilities. You should realise that if you were to roll the dice another 1000 times, the results would probably not be exactly the same, but you would hope that they would not be too different. You could roll the dice more times and hope that the relative frequency would improve as an approximation to the probability.

Sometimes you cannot assign a probability by using symmetry or by carrying out an experiment. For example, there is a probability that my house will be struck by lightning next year, and I could insure against this happening. The insurance company will have to have a probability in mind when it calculates the premium I have to pay, but it cannot calculate it by symmetry, or carry out an experiment for a few years. It will assign its probability using its experience of such matters and its records.

> When **probabilities** are assigned to the outcomes of a sample space,
>
> - each probability is a number which must lie between 0 and 1 inclusive, and
> - the sum of all the probabilities assigned must be equal to 1.

Example 26.1.1

How would you assign probabilities to the following experiments or activities?

(a) Choosing a playing card from a standard pack of cards.

(b) The combined experiment of tossing a coin and rolling a fair dice.

(c) Tossing a drawing pin on to a table to see whether it lands point down or point up.

(d) Four international football teams, Denmark, England, France and Germany, $(D, E, F$ and $G)$, play a knockout tournament. Who will be the winner?

(a) The sample space would consist of the list of the 52 playing cards $\{AC, 2C, ..., KS\}$ in some order. (Here A means ace, C means clubs, and so on.) Assuming that these cards are equally likely to be picked, the probability assigned to each of them is $\frac{1}{52}$.

(b) The sample space is $\left\{ \begin{array}{l} (H, 1), (H, 2), (H, 3), (H, 4), (H, 5), (H, 6), \\ (T, 1), (T, 2), (T, 3), (T, 4), (T, 5), (T, 6) \end{array} \right\}$, and each of the outcomes would be assigned a probability of $\frac{1}{12}$.

(c) The sample space is {point down, point up}. You would need to carry out an experiment to assign probabilities.

(d) The sample space is {D wins, E wins, F wins, G wins}. You have to assign probabilities subjectively, according to your knowledge of the game. The probabilities p_D, p_E, p_F and p_G must all be non-negative and satisfy
$$p_D + p_E + p_F + p_G = 1.$$

26.2 Probabilities of events

Sometimes you may be interested not in one particular outcome, but in two or three or more of them. For example, suppose you toss a coin twice. You might be interested in whether the result is the same both times. The list of outcomes in which you are interested is called an **event**, and is written in brackets. The event that both tosses of the coin give the same result is {$(H, H), (T, T)$}. Events are often denoted by capital letters. Thus if A denotes this event, then $A = \{(H, H), (T, T)\}$. An event can be just one outcome, or a list of outcomes or even no outcomes at all.

You can find the probability of an event by looking at the sample space and adding the probabilities of the outcomes which make up the event. For example, if you were tossing a coin twice, the sample space would be {$(H, H), (H, T), (T, H), (T, T)$}. There are four outcomes, each equally likely, so they each have probability $\frac{1}{4}$. The event A consists of the two outcomes (H, H) and (T, T), so the probability of A is $\frac{1}{4} + \frac{1}{4}$, or $\frac{1}{2}$.

This is an example of a general rule:

> The probability, P(A), of an event, A, is the sum of the probabilities of the outcomes which make up A.

If an event has no outcomes, it is denoted by the symbol $\emptyset$. In that case P($\emptyset$) = 0.

Often a list of outcomes can be constructed in such a way that all of them are equally likely. If all the outcomes are equally likely then the probability of any event A can be found by finding the number of outcomes which make up event A and dividing by the total number of outcomes. Thus:

> If $n(A)$ is the number of equally likely outcomes in an event A, and $n(U)$ is the total number of equally likely outcomes in the sample space U, then
> $$P(A) = \frac{n(A)}{n(U)}.$$

When the outcomes are not equally likely then the probability of any event has to be found by adding the individual probabilities of all the outcomes which make up event A.

You may sometimes find it helpful to draw a Venn diagram.

Example 26.2.1

In the USA, a roulette wheel consists of 38 sections of equal area: 18 are black, 18 are red and 2 are green. The wheel is spun and a ball is thrown onto the wheel. The ball will eventually land on one of the 38 sections.

(a) Find the probability of landing on a black colour.

Let A be the event that the ball does not land on a black section.

(b) Find the probability of A.

The numbers of possible outcomes for each colour are shown in Fig. 26.2.

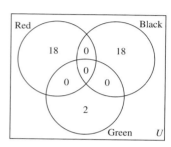

(a) Let B be the event that the ball lands on black colour.

The probabilities of each section are equally likely, so each of them has probability $\frac{1}{38}$. There are 18 black sections, see Fig. 26.2, each with probability $\frac{1}{38}$, so

$$P(B) = \frac{n(B)}{n(U)} = \frac{18}{38} = \frac{9}{19}.$$

Fig. 26.2

(b) The number of outcomes in the event A is 20, so

$$P(A) = \frac{n(A)}{n(U)} = \frac{20}{38} = \frac{10}{19}.$$

Example 26.2.2

The numbers $1, 2, \ldots, 9$ are written on separate cards. The cards are shuffled and the top one is turned over. Calculate the probability that the number on this card is prime.

The sample space for this situation is $U = \{1, 2, 3, 4, 5, 6, 7, 8, 9\}$. As each outcome is equally likely it has probability $\frac{1}{9}$.

Let B be the event that the card turned over is prime. Then $B = \{2, 3, 5, 7\}$, so

$$P(B) = \frac{n(B)}{n(U)} = \frac{4}{9}.$$

Example 26.2.3

A circular wheel is divided into three equal sectors, numbered
1, 2 and 3, as shown in Fig. 26.3. The wheel is spun twice.
Each time, the score is the number to which the black arrow
points. Calculate the probabilities of the following events:

(a) both scores are the same as each other,

(b) neither score is a 2,

(c) at least one of the scores is a 3,

(d) neither score is a 2 and both scores are the same,

(e) neither score is a 2 or both scores are the same.

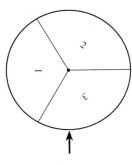

Fig. 26.3

Start by writing down the sample space, U. In this case it is helpful to write it as the
two-way table in Table 26.4.

		Second spin		
		1	2	3
	1	(1, 1)	(1, 2)	(1, 3)
First spin	2	(2, 1)	(2, 2)	(2, 3)
	3	(3, 1)	(3, 2)	(3, 3)

Table 26.4

Each cell of the table corresponds to an outcome, each outcome has equal probability,
$\frac{1}{9}$, each event corresponds to a certain number of cells and the total sample space
consists of all the cells.

(a) Let A be the event that both scores are the same. The three cells corresponding to
A lie on the main diagonal from top left to bottom right, so

$$P(A) = \frac{n(A)}{n(U)} = \frac{3}{9} = \frac{1}{3}.$$

(b) Let B be the event that neither score is a 2. The four cells corresponding to B lie
in the corners, so

$$P(B) = \frac{n(B)}{n(U)} = \frac{4}{9}.$$

(c) Let C be the event that at least one of the scores is a 3. The five cells
corresponding to C lie in the bottom row and the column on the right, so

$$P(C) = \frac{n(C)}{n(U)} = \frac{5}{9}.$$

(d) Let D be the event that neither score is a 2 *and* both scores are the same. The two
cells corresponding to D lie in the top left and bottom right corners, so

$$P(D) = \frac{2}{9}.$$

(e) Let E be the event that neither score is a 2 *or* both scores are the same. The five cells corresponding to E lie in the corners and centre of the table, so

$$P(E) = \tfrac{5}{9}.$$

The next example shows how to modify the sample space a little so the outcomes are still equally likely.

Example 26.2.4

Paul has three playing cards, two queens and a king. Anya selects one of the cards at random, and returns it to Paul, who shuffles the cards. Anya then selects a second card. Anya wins if both cards selected are kings. Find the probability that Anya wins.

Imagine that the queens are different, call them Q_1 and Q_2, and call the king K. Then the sample space is U where

$$U = \{(Q_1, Q_1), (Q_1, Q_2), (Q_1, K), (Q_2, Q_1), (Q_2, Q_2), (Q_2, K),$$
$$(K, Q_1), (K, Q_2), (K, K)\}.$$

Let A be the event that Anya wins. Then $A = \{(K, K)\}$ and

$$P(A) = \frac{n(A)}{n(U)} = \tfrac{1}{9}.$$

The probability that Anya wins is $\tfrac{1}{9}$.

> Although the event that Anya won is just a single outcome, it is still listed in curly brackets.

Sometimes it is worth using a different approach to calculating the probability of an event.

Example 26.2.5

You draw two cards from an ordinary pack. Find the probability that they are not both kings.

The problem is that the sample space has a large number of outcomes. In fact there are 52 ways of picking the first card, and then 51 ways of picking the second, so there $52 \times 51 = 2652$ possibilities. The sample space therefore consists of 2652 outcomes, each of which is assigned a probability $\frac{1}{2652}$.

To avoid counting all the outcomes which are not both kings, it is easier to look at the number of outcomes which *are* both kings.

Using an obvious notation, and writing the first card to be drawn as the first of the pair, these outcomes are $(KC, KD), (KD, KC), (KC, KH), (KH, KC), (KC, KS), (KS, KC),$ $(KD, KH), (KH, KD), (KD, KS), (KS, KD), (KH, KS)$ and (KS, KH).

There are thus 12 outcomes that are both kings. So the number which are not both kings is $2652 - 12 = 2640$. All 2640 of these outcomes have probability $\frac{1}{2652}$, so

$$P(\text{not both kings}) = \tfrac{2640}{2652} = \tfrac{220}{221}.$$

It is always worth looking out for this shortcut, and it is also useful to have some language for it. If A is an event, the event 'not A' is the event consisting of those outcomes in the sample space which are not in A. Since the sum of the probabilities assigned to outcomes in the sample space is 1,

$$P(A) + P(\text{not } A) = 1.$$

The event 'not A' is called the **complement** of the event A. The symbol A' is used to denote the complement of A.

> If A is an event, then A' is the complement of A, and
>
> $$P(A) + P(A') = 1.$$

26.3 Combining events

Suppose that you have two events, A and B, in a sample space U. Since both the events contain outcomes, so do the events $A \cup B$ and $A \cap B$. These events are illustrated in the Venn diagram in Fig. 26.5.

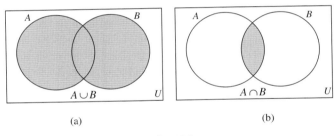

(a)   (b)

Fig. 26.5

The event $A \cup B$, called the **union** of the events A and B and illustrated in Fig. 26.5a, consists of all those outcomes which are in A or B or both, and so is the event corresponding to A **or** B. $A \cup B$ is read as 'A union B'.

Remember, A or B means either A or B or both.

The event $A \cap B$, called the **intersection** of the events A and B and illustrated in Fig. 26.5b, consists of all those outcomes which are in both A and B, and so is the event corresponding to A **and** B. $A \cap B$ is read as 'A intersection B'.

To find $P(A \cup B)$ you need to add the probabilities of the outcomes in $A \cup B$.

You can see from Fig. 26.5 that if you add the probabilities of the outcomes in A to the probabilities of those in B, that is

$$P(A) + P(B),$$

you have counted those outcomes in $A \cap B$ twice, once in the event A and once in the event B.

Hence

$$P(A \cup B) = P(A) + P(B) - P(A \cap B).$$

This formula is known as the addition law of probability.

> **The addition law of probability**
>
> If A and B are events then
>
> $$P(A \cup B) = P(A) + P(B) - P(A \cap B).$$

Example 26.3.1

Two fair cubical dice with faces numbered 1 to 6 are thrown. A prize is won if the total is 10 or if each individual score is over 4. Find the probability of winning a prize.

The sample space U of all possible outcomes is

$$U = \left\{ \begin{array}{cccccc} (1,1), & (1,2), & (1,3), & (1,4), & (1,5), & (1,6), \\ (2,1), & (2,2), & (2,3), & (2,4), & (2,5), & (2,6), \\ (3,1), & (3,2), & (3,3), & (3,4), & (3,5), & (3,6), \\ (4,1), & (4,2), & (4,3), & (4,4), & (4,5), & (4,6), \\ (5,1), & (5,2), & (5,3), & (5,4), & (5,5), & (5,6), \\ (6,1), & (6,2), & (6,3), & (6,4), & (6,5), & (6,6) \end{array} \right\}.$$

Each of the 36 outcomes is equally likely.

Let C be the event that the total score is 10, so $C = \{(5,5), (4,6), (6,4)\}$.

Let B be the event that each roll of the dice results in a score over 4 so $B = \{(5,5), (5,6), (6,5), (6,6)\}$.

The events B and C are illustrated in the Venn diagram in Fig. 26.6.

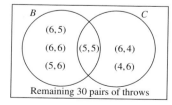

Fig. 26.6

Therefore $P(B) = \frac{4}{36} = \frac{1}{9}$, $P(C) = \frac{3}{36} = \frac{1}{12}$, $P(B \cap C) = \frac{1}{36}$.

A prize is won if B or C (or both) occur, and the possible outcomes which comprise this event are $\{(5, 5), (4, 6), (6, 4), (5, 6), (6, 5), (6, 6)\}$.

Therefore $P(B \cup C) = \frac{6}{36} = \frac{1}{6}$.

But notice that you could have used the formula in the blue box immediately, to get

$$P(B \cup C) = P(B) + P(C) - P(B \cap C)$$
$$= \tfrac{4}{36} + \tfrac{3}{36} - \tfrac{1}{36}$$
$$= \tfrac{6}{36} = \tfrac{1}{6}.$$

The probability of winning a prize is $\frac{1}{6}$.

Sometimes it will occur that the events A and B cannot both occur at the same time. The next example shows such a case.

Example 26.3.2
Consider a game in which a fair cubical dice with faces numbered 1 to 6 is rolled twice.
A prize is won if the total score on the two rolls is 4 or if both individual scores are over 4.

You can write the sample space U of all possible outcomes as 36 equally likely pairs, or as 36 equally likely cells in a two-way table (Table 26.7).

		Second roll					
		1	2	3	4	5	6
	1	(1, 1)	(1, 2)	(1, 3)	(1, 4)	(1, 5)	(1, 6)
	2	(2, 1)	(2, 2)	(2, 3)	(2, 4)	(2, 5)	(2, 6)
First	3	(3, 1)	(3, 2)	(3, 3)	(3, 4)	(3, 5)	(3, 6)
roll	4	(4, 1)	(4, 2)	(4, 3)	(4, 4)	(4, 5)	(4, 6)
	5	(5, 1)	(5, 2)	(5, 3)	(5, 4)	(5, 5)	(5, 6)
	6	(6, 1)	(6, 2)	(6, 3)	(6, 4)	(6, 5)	(6, 6)

Table 26.7

Let A be the event that the total score is 4 and let B be the event that both rolls of the dice give a score over 4.

Then $A = \{(1, 3), (2, 2), (3, 1)\}$, and $B = \{(5, 5), (5, 6), (6, 5), (6, 6)\}$, so

$$P(A) = \tfrac{3}{36}, \quad P(B) = \tfrac{4}{36}, \quad \text{and} \quad P(A \cap B) = 0.$$

A prize is won if A happens *or* if B happens, so

$$P(\text{a prize is won}) = P(A \cup B)$$
$$= P(A) + P(B) - P(A \cap B)$$
$$= \tfrac{3}{36} + \tfrac{4}{36} - 0$$
$$= \tfrac{7}{36}.$$

The probability of winning a prize is therefore $\frac{7}{36}$.

When two events A and B cannot happen together they are said to be **mutually exclusive**. If two events are mutually exclusive, then there are no outcomes in event $A \cap B$, so $P(A \cap B) = 0$.

> Two events A and B are **mutually exclusive** if $P(A \cap B) = 0$.
>
> If A and B are mutually exclusive, then the addition law of probability takes the form
>
> $$P(A \cup B) = P(A) + P(B).$$

This form of the law only applies if the events A and B are mutually exclusive.

Example 26.3.3

The events A and B are such that $P(B) = 2P(A) = \frac{1}{3}$ and $P(A \cap B) = \frac{1}{8}$. Find $P(A \cup B)$.

From the information given, $P(A) = \frac{1}{6}$, $P(B) = \frac{1}{3}$ and $P(A \cap B) = \frac{1}{8}$.

Using the addition law,

$$P(A \cup B) = P(A) + P(B) - P(A \cap B)$$
$$= \tfrac{1}{6} + \tfrac{1}{3} - \tfrac{1}{8} = \tfrac{9}{24} = \tfrac{3}{8}.$$

26.4 Practical activities

1 Cylinder   When you throw a coin it is very unlikely to land on its edge (or curved surface). However, if you were to drop a baked-beans can on the floor there is quite a good chance that it will land on its curved surface. Both the coin and the baked-beans can are (nearly) cylindrical in shape.

(a) Find several cylinders for which the ratio of the height to the radius is different, and investigate how the ratio of height to radius affects the chance of a cylinder landing on its curved surface.

(b) Throw each cylinder 50 times and work out the experimental probability that the cylinder lands on its curved surface. Plot a graph of this experimental probability against the ratio of height to radius.

(c) For what ratio of height to radius would you estimate that the cylinder was equally likely to land on its curved surface as it is to land on one of its plane faces?

2 Darts 1   Throw 100 darts at a dart-board but try not to aim for any particular section. Find the experimental probability of the dart landing in the 20 sector. Compare this with the percentage of the dart-board's area which is made up by the 20 sector.

3 Darts 2   Cut out an irregular-shaped piece of paper and stick it on the dart-board. Throw 100 darts at the dart-board again trying not to aim at any particular point and find the experimental probability of the dart landing on the piece of paper. Use this to get an estimate of the area of the piece of paper.

Exercise 26

1 A fair dice is thrown once. Find the probabilities that the score is

   (a) bigger than 3,   (b) bigger than or equal to 3,

   (c) an odd number,   (d) a prime number,

   (e) bigger than 3 and a prime number,   (f) bigger than 3 or a prime number or both,

   (g) bigger than 3 or a prime number, but not both.

2 A card is chosen at random from an ordinary pack. Find the probability that it is

   (a) red,   (b) a picture card (K, Q, J),

   (c) an honour (A, K, Q, J, 10),   (d) a red honour,

   (e) red, or an honour, or both.

3 Two fair dice are thrown simultaneously. Find the probability that

   (a) the total is 7,   (b) the total is at least 8,

   (c) the total is a prime number,   (d) neither of the scores is a 6,

   (e) at least one of the scores is a 6,   (f) exactly one of the scores is a 6,

   (g) the two scores are the same,

   (h) the difference between the scores is an odd number.

4 A fair dice is thrown twice. If the second score is the same as the first, the second throw does not count, and the dice is thrown again until a different score is obtained. The two different scores are added to give a total.

   List the possible outcomes.

   Find the probability that

   (a) the total is 7,   (b) the total is at least 8,

   (c) at least one of the two scores is a 6,   (d) the first score is higher than the last.

5 Draw a bar-chart to illustrate the probabilities of the various total scores when two fair dice are thrown simultaneously.

6 Given that $P(A) = \frac{1}{2}$, $P(A \cup B) = \frac{3}{4}$ and $P(A \cap B) = \frac{1}{8}$, find

   (a) $P(B)$,

   (b) the probability that either A occurs, or B occurs, but not both.

7 Two events A and B are mutually exclusive. $P(A) = \frac{1}{3}$ and $P(A \cup B) = \frac{1}{2}$. Calculate $P(B)$.

27 Conditional probability

This chapter is about calculating with probabilities. When you have completed it, you should

- know the multiplication law of conditional probability, and be able to use tree diagrams
- know the multiplication law for independent events
- be able to use Bayes' theorem.

27.1 Conditional probability

Consider a class of 30 pupils, of whom 17 are girls and 13 are boys. Suppose further that 5 of the girls and 6 of the boys are left-handed, and all of the remaining pupils are right-handed.

This information is shown in Fig. 27.1.

Boys	Girls	
6	5	Left-handed
7	12	Right-handed

Fig. 27.1

If a pupil is selected at random from the whole class then the chance that he or she is left-handed is $\dfrac{6+5}{30} = \dfrac{11}{30}$. However, suppose now that a pupil is selected at random from the girls in the class. The chance that this girl will be left-handed is $\frac{5}{17}$. So being told that the selected pupil is a girl alters the chance that the pupil will be left-handed. This is an example of **conditional probability**. The probability has been calculated on the basis of an extra 'condition' which you have been given.

Let L be the event that a left-handed person is chosen, and let G be the event that a girl is chosen. The symbol $P(L \mid G)$ denotes the probability that the pupil chosen is left-handed *given* that the pupil chosen is a girl. So in this case $P(L \mid G) = \frac{5}{17}$, although $P(L) = \frac{11}{30}$.

It is useful to find a connection between conditional probabilities (where some extra information is known) and probabilities where you have no extra information. Notice that the probability $P(L \mid G)$ can be written as

$$P(L \mid G) = \tfrac{5}{17} = \frac{5/30}{17/30}.$$

The fraction in the numerator, $\frac{5}{30}$, is the probability of choosing a left-handed girl if you were selecting from the whole class, and the fraction in the denominator, $\frac{17}{30}$, is the probability of choosing a girl if you were selecting from the whole class. In symbols this could be written as

$$P(L \mid G) = \frac{P(L \cap G)}{P(G)}.$$

This can be generalised to any two events A and B.

> If A and B are two events and $P(B) > 0$, then the **conditional probability** of A given B is
>
> $$P(A \mid B) = \frac{P(A \cap B)}{P(B)}$$
>
> Rewriting this equation gives
>
> $$P(A \cap B) = P(B) \times P(A \mid B)$$
>
> which is known as the **multiplication law of probability**.

As $A \cap B$ and $B \cap A$ are the same event, $P(A \cap B) = P(B \cap A)$, you can reverse the roles of A and B in the last equation to get another form of the multiplication law of probability, provided that $P(A) > 0$.

> If A and B are two events and $P(A) > 0$, then
>
> $$P(A \cap B) = P(A) \times P(B \mid A).$$
>
> This is another form of the **multiplication law of probability**.

Example 27.1.1

Suppose a jar contains 7 red discs and 4 white discs. Two discs are selected without replacement. ('Without replacement' means that the first disc is not put back in the jar before the second disc is selected.) Find

(a) the probability that both of the discs are red,

(b) the probability that both the discs are the same colour.

(a) Let R_1 be the event {the first disc is red}, R_2 be the event {the second disc is red}, W_1 be the event {the first disc is white} and W_2 be the event {the second disc is white}. To find the probability that both of the discs are red you want to find $P(R_1 \cap R_2)$.

Using the multiplication law in the second blue box to find this probability,

$$P(R_1 \cap R_2) = P(R_1) \times P(R_2 \mid R_1).$$

Now $P(R_1) = \frac{7}{11}$, since there are 7 red discs in the jar and 11 discs altogether. The probability $P(R_2 \mid R_1)$ appears more complicated, but it represents the probability that the second disc selected is red *given* that the first disc was red. To find this just imagine that one red disc has already been removed from the jar. The jar now contains 6 red discs and 4 white discs, so the probability *now* of getting a red disc is $P(R_2 \mid R_1) = \frac{6}{10}$.

Therefore, using the multiplication law,

$$P(R_1 \cap R_2) = P(R_1) \times P(R_2 \mid R_1)$$
$$= \tfrac{7}{11} \times \tfrac{6}{10} = \tfrac{42}{110} = \tfrac{21}{55}.$$

The probability that both discs are red is $\frac{21}{55}$.

(b) To find the probability that both discs are the same colour use the addition and multiplication laws together.

The event $R_1 \cap R_2$ is the event that both discs are red, and the event $W_1 \cap W_2$ is the event that both discs are white. These events cannot both be satisfied at the same time, so they are mutually exclusive. Therefore you can use the addition law, giving

$$\begin{aligned}\text{P(both discs are the same colour)} &= \text{P}((R_1 \cap R_2) \cup (W_1 \cap W_2)). \\ &= \text{P}(R_1 \cap R_2) + \text{P}(W_1 \cap W_2) \\ &= \text{P}(R_1) \times \text{P}(R_2 \mid R_1) + \text{P}(W_1) \times \text{P}(W_2 \mid W_1). \\ &= \tfrac{7}{11} \times \tfrac{6}{10} + \tfrac{4}{11} \times \tfrac{3}{10} \\ &= \tfrac{42}{110} + \tfrac{12}{110} = \tfrac{54}{110} = \tfrac{27}{55}.\end{aligned}$$

The probability that both discs are the same colour is $\frac{27}{55}$.

These calculations look rather forbidding, but they can be made much easier by using a tree diagram.

27.2 Tree diagrams

Staying with Example 27.1.1, you can represent all the possible outcomes when two discs are selected from the jar in a **tree diagram**, as in Fig. 27.2.

First disc
Second disc
$\text{P}(R_1) = \frac{7}{11}$
R_1
$\text{P}(W_1) = \frac{4}{11}$
W_1
$\text{P}(R_2 \mid R_1) = \frac{6}{10}$
$R_1 \cap R_2$
$\text{P}(W_2 \mid R_1) = \frac{4}{10}$
$R_1 \cap W_2$
$\text{P}(R_2 \mid W_1) = \frac{7}{10}$
$W_1 \cap R_2$
$\text{P}(W_2 \mid W_1) = \frac{3}{10}$
$W_1 \cap W_2$

Fig. 27.2

Notice that probabilities on the first 'layer' of branches give the chances of getting a red disc or a white disc when the first disc is selected. The probabilities on the second 'layer' are the conditional probabilities. You can use the tree diagram to calculate the probability of any of the four possibilities, $R_1 \cap R_2$, $R_1 \cap W_2$, $W_1 \cap R_2$ and $W_1 \cap W_2$.

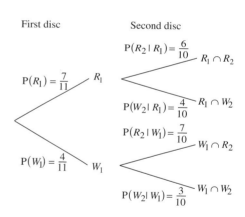

Figure 27.3 shows this calculation for the probability of getting a white disc followed by a red disc, $\text{P}(W_1 \cap R_2)$.

First disc
Second disc
$\text{P}(R_1) = \frac{7}{11}$
R_1
$\text{P}(W_1) = \frac{4}{11}$
W_1
$\text{P}(R_2 \mid R_1) = \frac{6}{10}$
$R_1 \cap R_2$
$\text{P}(W_2 \mid R_1) = \frac{4}{10}$
$R_1 \cap W_2$
$\text{P}(R_2 \mid W_1) = \frac{7}{10}$
$W_1 \cap R_2$
$\frac{4}{11} \times \frac{7}{10} = \frac{28}{110} = \frac{14}{55}$
$\text{P}(W_2 \mid W_1) = \frac{3}{10}$
$W_1 \cap W_2$

Fig. 27.3

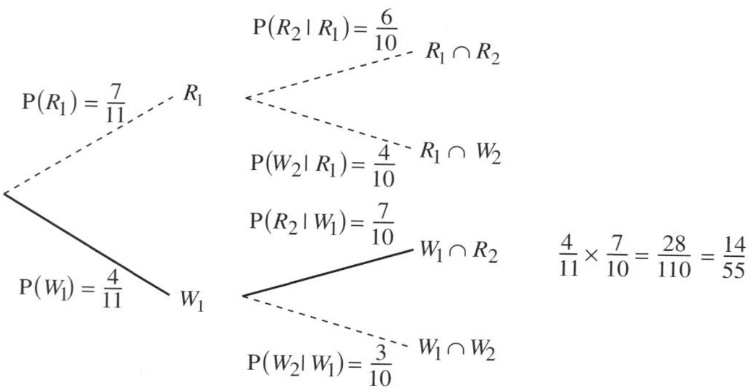

Trace the route corresponding to the event $W_1 \cap R_2$ on the tree diagram and multiply the relevant probabilities to get $P(W_1 \cap R_2) = P(W_1) \times P(R_2 \mid W_1)$.

You can also use the tree diagram for the calculation that both balls are the same colour. This time there is more than one route through the tree diagram which satisfies the event whose probability is to be found. As before, you follow the appropriate routes and multiply the probabilities. You then add all the resulting products, as in Fig. 27.4.

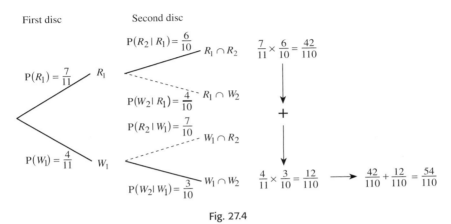

Fig. 27.4

You can use tree diagrams in any problem in which there is a clear sequence to the outcomes, including problems which are not necessarily to do with selection of objects.

Example 27.2.1
Weather records indicate that the probability that a particular day is dry is $\frac{3}{10}$. Liverton Villa is a football team whose record of success is better on dry days than on wet days. The probability that Liverton win on a dry day is $\frac{3}{8}$, whereas the probability that they win on a wet day is $\frac{3}{11}$. Liverton are due to play their next match on Saturday.

(a) What is the probability that Liverton will win?

(b) Three Saturdays ago Liverton won their match. What is the probability that it was a dry day?

Let D be the event that a day is dry, and let W be the event that Liverton win.

Here the sequence involves first the type of weather and then the result of the football match. The tree diagram in Fig. 27.5 illustrates the information.

Notice that some of the probabilities were not given in the statement of the question. The probability that it is not dry, $P(D')$, has been calculated using the equation $P(D) + P(D') = 1$. Then, given that it is dry, either Liverton win, or they don't. It follows that $P(W \mid D) + P(W' \mid D) = 1$. Similarly, $P(W \mid D') + P(W' \mid D') = 1$.

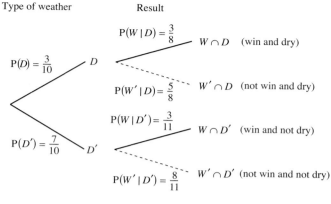

Fig. 27.5

(a) The probability that Liverton win is the sum of the probabilities at the end of the thick lines.

Using the tree diagram,

$$P(W) = P(D) \times P(W\,|D) + P(D') \times P(W\,|\,D')$$
$$= \tfrac{3}{10} \times \tfrac{3}{8} + \tfrac{7}{10} \times \tfrac{3}{11}$$
$$= \tfrac{9}{80} + \tfrac{21}{110} = \tfrac{267}{880}.$$

The probability that Liverton win is $\tfrac{267}{880}$.

(b) In this case you have been asked to calculate a conditional probability. However, here the sequence of events has been reversed and you want to find P(dry | win).

From the definition,

$$P(D\,|W) = \frac{P(D \cap W)}{P(W)}.$$

But, remembering that $P(D \cap W) = P(W \cap D)$, from the tree diagram you get

$$P(D\,|W) = \frac{P(D \cap W)}{P(W)}$$
$$= \frac{P(W \cap D)}{P(W)}$$
$$= \frac{9/80}{267/880} = \frac{99}{267}.$$

The probability that it was a dry day given that Liverton won is $\tfrac{99}{267}$.

You can think of $P(D\,|W)$ as being the proportion of times that the weather is dry out of all the times that Liverton win. You may be a bit puzzled by this, because if Liverton win, the match has already taken place and it is known whether or not it was dry that day. But suppose that you did not know, and had no meteorological information about the weather that day: then the best you can do is to calculate $P(D\,|W)$.

Example 27.2.2

The probability that a person has a disease is $\frac{1}{200}$. A company is researching a test to determine whether a person has this disease. If a person has the disease then the probability that the test indicates this is $\frac{9}{10}$. If the person doesn't have the disease, then the probability that the test indicates that the person has the disease is $\frac{1}{100}$. A person is chosen at random and given the test, which indicates that the person has the disease. What is the probability that person has the disease?

Let D be the event that the person has the disease, and let T be the event that the test is positive.

The information is shown in the tree diagram in Fig. 27.6.

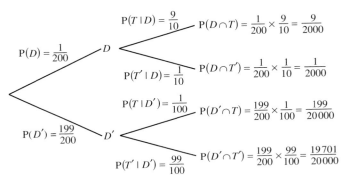

Fig. 27.6

You need to find $P(D \mid T)$. From the definition this is given by $\dfrac{P(D \cap T)}{P(T)}$.

From the tree diagram,

$$P(D \cap T) = \tfrac{1}{200} \times \tfrac{9}{10} = \tfrac{9}{2000},$$

and

$$P(T) = P(D \cap T) + P(D' \cap T)$$
$$= \tfrac{9}{2000} + \tfrac{199}{20\,000} = \tfrac{289}{20\,000}.$$

So,

$$P(D \mid T) = \frac{P(D \cap T)}{P(T)}$$
$$= \tfrac{9}{2000} \Big/ \tfrac{289}{20\,000} = \tfrac{90}{289}.$$

The probability that a person who tests positively has the disease is $\frac{90}{289}$.

You don't need to carry out all the multiplications in the tree diagram if you don't need them.

27.3   Independent events

Consider again a jar containing 7 red discs and 4 white discs. Two discs are selected, but this time with replacement. This means that the first disc is returned to the jar before the second disc is selected.

Let R_1 be the event that the first disc is red, R_2 be the event that the second disc is red, W_1 be the event that the first disc is white and W_2 be the event that the second disc is white. You can represent the selection of the two discs with Fig. 27.7, a tree diagram similar to Fig. 27.2 but with different probabilities on the second 'layer'.

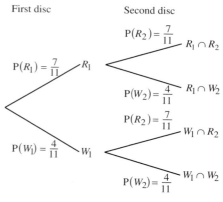

The probability $P(R_2)$ that the second disc is red can also be found using the addition and multiplication laws.

$$P(R_2) = P((R_1 \cap R_2) \cup (W_1 \cap R_2))$$
$$= P(R_1 \cap R_2) + P(W_1 \cap R_2)$$
$$= \tfrac{7}{11} \times \tfrac{7}{11} + \tfrac{4}{11} \times \tfrac{7}{11} = \tfrac{7}{11}.$$

Fig. 27.7

In this case $P(R_2) = P(R_2 \mid R_1)$, which means that the first disc's being red has no effect on the chance of the second disc being red. This is what you would expect, since the first disc was replaced before the second was removed.

Recall the definition of conditional probability, $P(A \mid B) = \dfrac{P(A \cap B)}{P(B)}$. It follows that if you have $P(A \mid B) = P(A)$, as you have with $P(R_2) = P(R_2 \mid R_1)$ above, when you equate the two expressions for $P(A \mid B)$, you get

$$\frac{P(A \cap B)}{P(B)} = P(A),$$

which when rearranged gives

$$P(A \cap B) = P(A) \times P(B).$$

The fact that you can deduce that $P(A \mid B) = P(A)$, that is, the probability of A is the same whether B happens or not, from $P(A \cap B) = P(A) \times P(B)$, suggests this definition.

> Two events A and B are **independent** if
>
> $$P(A \cap B) = P(A) \times P(B).$$
>
> This result is called the **multiplication law for independent events**.

You should not be surprised that if the events A and B are independent, then the events A and B' are also independent.

For since $P(A \cap B) + P(A \cap B') = P(A)$,

$$P(A \cap B') = P(A) - P(A \cap B).$$

And if A and B are independent, $P(A \cap B) = P(A) \times P(B)$, so it follows that

$$P(A \cap B') = P(A) - P(A) \times P(B)$$
$$= P(A)(1 - P(B)).$$

But, from the result at the end of Section 26.2, $P(B) + P(B') = 1$, so $1 - P(B) = P(B')$.

Hence, substituting for $1 - P(B)$, you get

$$P(A \cap B') = P(A) \times P(B').$$

So the events A and B' are independent.

Example 27.3.1
In a carnival game, a contestant has to first spin a fair coin and then roll a fair cubical dice whose faces are numbered 1 to 6. The contestant wins a prize if the coin shows heads and the dice score is below 3. Find the probability that a contestant wins a prize.

Let W be the event that a prize is won, H be the event that the coin shows heads and let L be the event that the score is lower than 3.

Then
$$P(W) = P(H \cap L).$$

The event that the coin shows heads and the event that the dice score is lower than 3 are independent, because the score on the dice can have no effect on the result of the spin of the coin. Therefore the multiplication law for independent events can be used, so

$$P(W) = P(H \cap L)$$
$$= P(H) \times P(L)$$
$$= \tfrac{1}{2} \times \tfrac{2}{6} = \tfrac{1}{6}.$$

The probability that the contestant wins a prize is $\tfrac{1}{6}$.

The law of multiplication for independent events can be extended to more than two events, provided they are all independent of one another.

> If $A_1, A_2, \ldots, A_n$ are n independent events then
>
> $$P(A_1 \cap A_2 \cap \ldots \cap A_n) = P(A_1) \times P(A_2) \times \ldots \times P(A_n).$$

Example 27.3.2
A fair cubical dice with faces numbered 1 to 6 is thrown four times. Find the probability that three of the four throws result in a 6.

In this case you can use the addition law of mutually exclusive events and the multiplication law of independent events to break the event that 'three of the four scores are 6' down into smaller sub-events whose probabilities you can easily determine.

Let $6_1, 6_2$, etc. be the events that a six is thrown on the first, second etc. throws, and let N_1, N_2, etc. be the events that a six is not thrown on the first, second etc. throws.

Let T be the event that three sixes are thrown. Then

$$P(T) = P\begin{pmatrix} (6_1 \cap 6_2 \cap 6_3 \cap N_4) \cup \\ (6_1 \cap 6_2 \cap N_3 \cap 6_4) \cup \\ (6_1 \cap N_2 \cap 6_3 \cap 6_4) \cup \\ (N_1 \cap 6_2 \cap 6_3 \cap 6_4) \end{pmatrix}.$$

Using the addition and multiplication laws,

$$P(T) = P\begin{pmatrix} (6_1 \cap 6_2 \cap 6_3 \cap N_4) \\ \cup (6_1 \cap 6_2 \cap N_3 \cap 6_4) \\ \cup (6_1 \cap N_2 \cap 6_3 \cap 6_4) \\ \cup (N_1 \cap 6_2 \cap 6_3 \cap 6_4) \end{pmatrix}$$

$$\begin{aligned} &= P(6_1 \cap 6_2 \cap 6_3 \cap N_4) + P(6_1 \cap 6_2 \cap N_3 \cap 6_4) \\ &\quad + P(6_1 \cap N_2 \cap 6_3 \cap 6_4) + P(N_1 \cap 6_2 \cap 6_3 \cap 6_4) \\ &= P(6_1) \times P(6_2) \times P(6_3) \times P(N_4) \\ &\quad + P(6_1) \times P(6_2) \times P(N_3) \times P(6_4) \\ &\quad + P(6_1) \times P(N_2) \times P(6_3) \times P(6_4) \\ &\quad + P(N_1) \times P(6_2) \times P(6_3) \times P(6_4) \\ &= \left(\tfrac{1}{6} \times \tfrac{1}{6} \times \tfrac{1}{6} \times \tfrac{5}{6}\right) + \left(\tfrac{1}{6} \times \tfrac{1}{6} \times \tfrac{5}{6} \times \tfrac{1}{6}\right) \\ &\quad + \left(\tfrac{1}{6} \times \tfrac{5}{6} \times \tfrac{1}{6} \times \tfrac{1}{6}\right) + \left(\tfrac{5}{6} \times \tfrac{1}{6} \times \tfrac{1}{6} \times \tfrac{1}{6}\right) \\ &= 4 \times \left(\tfrac{1}{6}\right)^3 \times \tfrac{5}{6} = \tfrac{5}{324}. \end{aligned}$$

The probability that three of the four throws result in a 6 is $\frac{5}{324}$.

27.4 Bayes' theorem

In the previous sections you have used mainly tree diagrams to solve problems on conditional probability. It is useful to derive a formula which covers this situation.

Example 27.4.1

A gambling casino has two gaming machines, X and X', which look identical. However, the probability of a win with machine X is $\frac{1}{3}$ while the probability of a win with machine X' is $\frac{1}{4}$. You choose a gaming machine at random and win. What is the probability that you chose machine X?

The situation is illustrated in Fig. 27.8. You need to find $P(X \mid W)$.

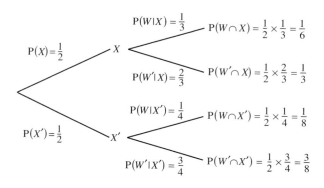

Fig. 27.8

From the definition of conditional probability,

$$P(W \cap X) = P(X) \times P(W \mid X)$$
$$= \tfrac{1}{2} \times \tfrac{1}{3} = \tfrac{1}{6}$$

and

$$P(W \cap X') = P(X') \times P(W \mid X')$$
$$= \tfrac{1}{2} \times \tfrac{1}{4} = \tfrac{1}{8}.$$

Using the tree diagram, the probability of a win is

$$P(W) = P(W \cap X) + P(W \cap X') = \tfrac{1}{6} + \tfrac{1}{8}.$$

Now, $W \cap X$ and $X \cap W$ are the same event, so $P(W \cap X) = P(X \cap W)$.

Using the definition of conditional probability again, $P(X \mid W)$, which needs to be found, is given by

$$P(X \mid W) = \frac{P(X \cap W)}{P(W)},$$

so

$$P(X \mid W) = \frac{P(X \cap W)}{P(X \cap W) + P(X' \cap W)}$$
$$= \frac{\tfrac{1}{6}}{\tfrac{1}{6} + \tfrac{1}{8}} = \tfrac{4}{7}.$$

This situation is quite typical. You carry out an experiment and get a result, and you want to know what caused the result.

However, to some extent, the tree diagram disguises the mathematics of the problem.

In the following treatment, the tree diagram will not be used, and different letters will be used, but you can, if you wish, identify A with W and B with X.

Bayes' theorem
Suppose that you have a universal set U and two events B and B', one of which must occur. Now suppose that in an experiment one of B and B' causes another event A. Then Bayes' theorem states that

$$P(B \mid A) = \frac{P(B)\,P(A \mid B)}{P(B)\,P(A \mid B) + P(B')\,P(A \mid B')}.$$

Proof   This proof will be broken down into four stages.

Stage 1   The definition of conditional probability says

$$P(B \mid A) = \frac{P(B \cap A)}{P(A)}.$$

Stage 2   Since one of B and B' must have occurred,

$$P(A) = P(A \cap B) + P(A \cap B').$$

(You may find a Venn diagram helpful here. In Fig. 27.9, the two events B and B' totally fill the universal set U. The set A consists of two parts, $A \cap B$ on the left, and $A \cap B'$ on the right. So $P(A) = P(A \cap B) + P(A \cap B')$.)

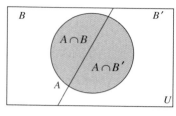

Fig. 27.9

So

$$P(B \mid A) = \frac{P(B \cap A)}{P(A \cap B) + P(A \cap B')}.$$

Stage 3   As $A \cap B$ is the same event as $B \cap A$, $P(A \cap B) = P(B \cap A)$. Substituting this in the numerator gives

$$P(B \mid A) = \frac{P(A \cap B)}{P(A \cap B) + P(A \cap B')}.$$

Stage 4   Using the definition of conditional probability again,

$$P(A \mid B) = \frac{P(A \cap B)}{P(B)} \quad \text{and} \quad P(A \mid B') = \frac{P(A \cap B')}{P(B')}.$$

Rewriting these gives $P(A \cap B) = P(B) P(A \mid B)$ and $P(A \cap B') = P(B') P(A \mid B')$. Substituting these into the numerator and denominator gives

$$P(B \mid A) = \frac{P(B) P(A \mid B)}{P(B) P(A \mid B) + P(B') P(A \mid B')}.$$

Here is an example of how you might apply this in practice. It returns to the gaming machine example, with a slight twist.

Example 27.4.2
A gambling casino has three gaming machines of two types, X and X', which look identical. The probability of choosing X is $\frac{1}{3}$, and the probability of picking X' is $\frac{2}{3}$. (There are two X' machines.) The probability of a win with machine X is $\frac{1}{3}$ while the probability of a win with machine X' is $\frac{1}{4}$. You choose a gaming machine at random and win. What is the probability that you chose machine X?

You need to find $P(X \mid W)$.

Bayes' theorem states, with X taking the place of B and W taking the place of A,

$$P(X \mid W) = \frac{P(X) P(W \mid X)}{P(X) P(W \mid X) + P(X') P(W \mid X')}.$$

From the information given, $P(X) = \frac{1}{3}$ and $P(X') = \frac{2}{3}$; $P(W \mid X) = \frac{1}{3}$ and $P(W \mid X') = \frac{1}{4}$. Putting these into the formula gives

$$P(X \mid W) = \frac{P(X)\,P(W \mid X)}{P(X)\,P(W \mid X) + P(X')\,P(W \mid X')}$$

$$= \frac{\frac{1}{3} \times \frac{1}{3}}{\frac{1}{3} \times \frac{1}{3} + \frac{2}{3} \times \frac{1}{4}} = \frac{\frac{1}{9}}{\frac{1}{9} + \frac{1}{6}} = \frac{2}{5}.$$

27.5 Practical activities

1 Cards

(a) Shuffle a pack of cards and pick a card. Record the identity of the card. Repeat this to give 50 selections in all, replacing the card and shuffling after every selection. From your data calculate the experimental probabilities of

   (i) a red card,   (ii) an even score $\{2, 4, 6, 8, 10\}$,   (iii) a picture card $\{J, Q, K\}$.

Check whether the following statements are true for your experimental probabilities:

(b) $P(\text{even or picture}) = P(\text{even}) + P(\text{picture})$,

(c) $P(\text{even or red}) = P(\text{even}) + P(\text{red})$,

(d) $P(\text{even and red}) = P(\text{even}) \times P(\text{red})$.

Compare with what you would expect theoretically.

Exercise 27

1 A bag contains six red and four green counters. Two counters are drawn, without replacement. Use a carefully labelled tree diagram to find the probabilities that

   (a) both counters are red,   (b) both counters are green,   (c) just one counter is red,

   (d) at least one counter is red, (e) the second counter is red.

2 Two cards are drawn, without replacement, from an ordinary pack. Find the probabilities that

   (a) both are picture cards (K, Q, J),   (b) neither is a picture card,

   (c) at least one is a picture card,   (d) at least one is red.

3 Events A, B and C satisfy the conditions:

   $P(A) = 0.6$, $P(B) = 0.8$, $P(B \mid A) = 0.45$, $P(B \cap C) = 0.28$.

   Calculate

   (a) $P(A \cap B)$,   (b) $P(C \mid B)$,   (c) $P(A \mid B)$.

4 A class consists of seven boys and nine girls. Two different members of the class are chosen at random. A is the event {the first person is a girl}, and B is the event {the second person is a girl}. Find the probabilities of

   (a) $B \mid A$,   (b) $B' \mid A$,   (c) $B \mid A'$,   (d) $B' \mid A'$,   (e) B.

   Is it true that

   (f) $P(B \mid A) + P(B' \mid A) = 1$,   (g) $P(B \mid A) + P(B \mid A') = 1$?

5 A weather forecaster classifies all days as wet or dry. She estimates that the probability that June 1st next year is wet is 0.4. If any particular day in June is wet, the probability that the next day is wet is 0.6; otherwise the probability that the next day is wet is 0.3. Find the probability that, next year,

(a) the first two days of June are both wet,   (b) June 2nd is wet,

(c) at least one of the first three days of June is wet.

6 A bag contains ten counters, of which six are red and four are green. A counter is chosen at random; its colour is noted and it is replaced in the bag. A second counter is then chosen at random. Find the probabilities that

(a) both counters are red,   (b) both counters are green,

(c) exactly one counter is red,   (d) at least one counter is red,

(e) the second counter is red.

7 Given that $P(A) = 0.75$, $P(B \mid A) = 0.8$ and $P(B \mid A') = 0.6$, calculate $P(B)$ and $P(A \mid B)$.

8 A class of 30 students at an international school was asked whether they supported Argentina or Brazil or neither in a cup match. They were also asked whether they were left- or right-handed.

Twelve students were left-handed, and, of these, four supported Argentina and seven said they supported Brazil.

Of the right-handed students, one supported Argentina and ten supported Brazil.

A student is picked at random from the class.

(a) Find the probability that the student is left-handed.

(b) Find the probability that the student prefers neither team.

(c) Given that the student prefers neither team, find the probability that the student is left-handed.

9 The probability that Usha wakes up early is $\frac{1}{3}$, and if she is early the probability that she is early for school is $\frac{3}{4}$. If she does not wake up early, the probability that she is early for school is $\frac{1}{5}$. On a day chosen at random she is early for school. Find the probability that she did not wake up early.

10 Three identical boxes A, B and C each have two drawers. Box A has a dollar in each drawer, Box B has 5 dollars in each drawer, and box C has one dollar in one drawer and 5 dollars in the other. A box is chosen at random and a drawer is opened, and found to contain 5 dollars. What is the probability that the other drawer also contains 5 dollars?

11 A family has two boys and two girls, one of whom is called Jane. Two of them are chosen at random.

(a) Find the probability that they are both girls, given that one of them is a girl.

(b) Find the probability that they are both girls, given that one of them is Jane.

Review exercise 7

1 Bag A contains 1 red ball and 1 black ball, and bag B contains 2 red balls; all four balls are indistinguishable apart from their colour. One ball is chosen at random from A and is transferred to B. One ball is then chosen at random from B and is transferred to A.

    (a) Draw a tree diagram to illustrate the possibilities for the colours of the balls transferred from A to B and then from B to A.

    (b) Find the probability that, after both transfers, the black ball is in bag A.   (OCR)

2 The probability that an event A occurs is $P(A) = 0.3$. The event B is independent of A and $P(B) = 0.4$.

    (a) Calculate $P(A \cup B)$.

    Event C is defined to be the event that neither A nor B occurs.

    (b) Calculate $P(C \mid A')$, where A' is the event that A does not occur.   (OCR, adapted)

3 Two cubical fair dice are thrown, one red and one blue. The scores on their faces are added together. Determine which, if either, is greater:

    (a) the probability that the total score will be 10 or more given that the red dice shows a 6,

    (b) the probability that the total score will be 10 or more given that at least one of the dice shows a 6.   (OCR)

4 Half of the A-level students in a community college study science and 30% study mathematics. Of those who study science, 40% study mathematics.

    (a) What proportion of the A-level students study both mathematics and science?

    (b) Calculate the proportion of those students who study mathematics but do not study science.   (OCR)

5 Two events A and B are such that $P(A) = \frac{3}{4}$, $P(B \mid A) = \frac{1}{5}$ and $P(B' \mid A') = \frac{4}{7}$. By use of a tree diagram, or otherwise, find

    (a) $P(A \cap B)$,   (b) $P(B)$,   (c) $P(A \mid B)$.   (OCR, adapted)

6 Students have to pass a test before they are allowed to work in a laboratory. Students do not retake the test once they have passed it. For a randomly chosen student, the probability of passing the test at the first attempt is $\frac{1}{3}$. On any subsequent attempt, the probability of failing is half the probability of failing on the previous attempt. By drawing a tree diagram, or otherwise,

    (a) show that the probability of a student passing the test in 3 attempts or fewer is $\frac{26}{27}$,

    (b) find the conditional probability that a student passed at the first attempt, given that the student passed in 3 attempts or fewer.   (OCR)

7 The probability of event A occurring is $P(A) = \frac{13}{25}$. The probability of event B occurring is $P(B) = \frac{9}{25}$. The conditional probability of A occurring given that B has occurred is $P(A \mid B) = \frac{5}{9}$.

(a) Determine the following probabilities.

(i) $P(A \cap B)$ (ii) $P(B \mid A)$ (iii) $P(A \cup B)$ (iv) $P(A' \mid B')$

(b) Determine $P(A \cup B')$ showing your working.   (OCR, adapted)

8 (a) The probability that an event A occurs is $P(A) = 0.4$. B is an event independent of A and $P(A \cup B) = 0.7$. Find $P(B)$.

(b) C and D are two events such that $P(D \mid C) = \frac{1}{5}$ and $P(C \mid D) = \frac{1}{4}$. Given that $P(C \text{ and } D \text{ occur}) = p$, express in terms of p (i) $P(C)$,   (ii) $P(D)$.

(c) Given also that $P(C \text{ or } D \text{ or both occur}) = \frac{1}{5}$, find the value of p.   (OCR, adapted)

9 A batch of forty tickets for an event at a stadium consists of ten tickets for the North stand, fourteen tickets for the East stand and sixteen tickets for the West stand. A ticket is taken from the batch at random and issued to a person, X. Write down the probability that X has a ticket for the North stand.

A second ticket is taken from the batch at random and issued to Y. Subsequently a third ticket is taken from the batch at random and issued to Z. Calculate the probability that

(a) both X and Y have tickets for the North stand,

(b) X, Y and Z all have tickets for the same stand,

(c) two of X, Y and Z have tickets for one stand and the other of X, Y and Z has a ticket for a different stand.   (OCR)

10 In a lottery there are 24 prizes allocated at random to 24 prize-winners. Ann, Ben and Cal are three of the prize-winners. Of the prizes, 4 are cars, 8 are bicycles and 12 are watches. Show that the probability that Ann gets a car and Ben gets a bicycle or a watch is $\frac{10}{69}$.

Giving each answer either as a fraction or as a decimal correct to 3 significant figures, find

(a) the probability that both Ann and Ben get cars, given that Cal gets a car,

(b) the probability that either Ann or Cal (or both) gets a car,

(c) the probability that Ann gets a car and Ben gets a car or a bicycle,

(d) the probability that Ann gets a car given that Ben gets either a car or a bicycle.   (OCR)

11 In a certain part of the world there are more wet days than dry days. If a given day is wet, the probability that the following day will also be wet is 0.8. If a given day is dry, the probability that the following day will also be dry is 0.6.

Given that Wednesday of a particular week is dry, calculate the probability that

(a) Thursday and Friday of the same week are both wet days,

(b) Friday of the same week is a wet day.

In one season there were 44 cricket matches, each played over three consecutive days, in which the first and third days were dry. For how many of these matches would you expect that the second day was wet?   (OCR)

12 A dice is known to be biased in such a way that, when it is thrown, the probability of a 6 showing is $\frac{1}{4}$. This biased dice and an ordinary fair dice are thrown. Find the probability that

(a) the fair dice shows a 6 and the biased dice does not show a 6,

(b) at least one of the two dice shows a 6,

(c) exactly one of the two dice shows a 6, given that at least one of them shows a 6. (OCR)

13 A game is played using a regular 12-faced fair dice, with faces labelled 1 to 12, a coin and a simple board with nine squares as shown in the diagram.

Initially, the coin is placed on the shaded rectangle. The game consists of rolling the dice and then moving the coin one rectangle towards **L** or **R** according to the outcome on the dice. If the outcome is a prime number (2, 3, 5, 7 or 11) the move is towards **R**, otherwise it is towards **L**. The game stops when the coin reaches either **L** or **R**. Find, giving your answers correct to 3 decimal places, the probability that the game

(a) ends on the fourth move at **R**,   (b) ends on the fourth move,

(c) ends on the fifth move,   (d) takes more than six moves.   (OCR)

14 An amateur weather forecaster has a theory about the chances of flooding affecting the region where he lives. He believes that if there are floods in one year the probability of floods again the next year is 0.7, while if there are no floods one year the probability of no floods the next year is 0.6. Last year, there were no floods in his region.

(a) Draw a tree diagram showing probabilities for floods and no floods for this year and the next two years, according to the weather forecaster's theory.

Hence find the probability that

(b) there is flooding in all of these three years,

(c) there is flooding in exactly one of these three years.

15 The probability that a football club has all their first team players fit is 70%. When the club has a fully fit team it wins 90% of its home games. When the first team is not fully fit it wins 40% of its home games.

(a) Calculate the probability that it will win its next home game.

(b) Given that it did not win its last home game, find the probability that the team was fully fit.

Examination questions

1 An integer is chosen at random from the first one thousand positive integers. Find the probability that the integer chosen is

(a) a multiple of 4,   (b) a multiple of *both* 4 and 6.   (© IBO 2002)

2 The independent events A, B are such that $P(A) = 0.4$ and $P(A \cup B) = 0.88$. Find

(a) $P(B)$,   (b) the probability that either A occurs or B occurs, but *not* both.

(© IBO 2003)

3 A desk has three drawers. Drawer 1 contains three gold coins, Drawer 2 contains two gold coins and one silver coin and Drawer 3 contains one gold coin and two silver coins. A drawer is chosen at random and from it a coin is chosen at random.

(a) Find the probability that the chosen coin is gold.

(b) Given that the chosen coin is gold, find the probability that Drawer 3 was chosen.

(© IBO 2004)

4 Robert travels to work by train every weekday from Monday to Friday. The probability that he catches the 08.00 train on Monday is 0.66. The probability that he catches the 08.00 train on any other weekday is 0.75. A weekday is chosen at random.

(a) Find the probability that he catches the train on that day.

(b) Given that he catches the 08.00 train on that day, find the probability that the chosen day is Monday.

(© IBO 2004)

5 The probability that it rains during a summer's day in a certain town is 0.2. In this town, the probability that the daily maximum temperature exceeds 25 °C is 0.3 when it rains and 0.6 when it does not rain. Given that the maximum daily temperature exceeded 25 °C on a particular summer's day, find the probability that it rained on that day.   (© IBO 2002)

6 There are 25 disks in a bag. Some of them are black and the rest are white. Two are simultaneously selected at random. Given that the probability of selecting two disks of the same colour is equal to the probability of selecting two disks of different colour, how many black disks are there in the bag?   (© IBO 2005)

7 Box A contains 6 red balls and 2 green balls. Box B contains 4 red balls and 3 green balls. A fair cubical die with faces numbered 1, 2, 3, 4, 5, 6 is thrown. If an even number is obtained, a ball is selected from box A; if an odd number is obtained, a ball is selected from box B.

(a) Calculate the probability that the ball selected was red.

(b) Given that the ball selected was red, calculate the probability that it came from box B.

(© IBO 2005)

8 Given that $(A \cup B)' = \varnothing$, $P(A'|B) = \frac{1}{3}$ and $P(A) = \frac{6}{7}$, find $P(B)$.   (© IBO 2005)

28 Integration

Integration is the reverse process of differentiation. When you have completed this chapter, you should

- understand the term 'indefinite integral' and the need to add an arbitrary constant
- be able to integrate functions which can be expressed as sums of powers of x, and be aware of any exceptions
- know how to find the equation of a graph given its derivative and a point on the graph
- be able to use integration to find displacements and velocities in kinematic problems.

28.1 Finding a function from its derivative

Example 28.1.1

Figure 28.1 shows the graph of $y = f(x)$, where $f(x) = x - \frac{1}{2}x^2 + 1$. Draw the graph of $f'(x)$, and give a geometrical description of the connection between the two graphs.

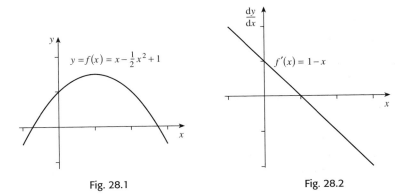

Fig. 28.1   Fig. 28.2

Since $f'(x) = 1 - \frac{1}{2}(2x) = 1 - x$, its graph is the straight line in Fig. 28.2.

For values of x to the left of 1, $f(x)$ is increasing. So the gradient $f'(x)$ is positive for $x < 1$. In Fig. 28.2, the graph of $f'(x)$ lies above the x-axis.

At $x = 1$, $f(x)$ takes its maximum value, and $f'(x) = 0$. In Fig. 28.2, the graph of $f'(x)$ crosses the x-axis.

For values of x to the right of 1, $f(x)$ is decreasing. So the gradient $f'(x)$ is negative for $x > 1$. In Fig. 28.2, the graph of $f'(x)$ lies below the x-axis.

You can add more detail to the comparison of the two graphs by noting that the graph of $f(x)$ bends downwards. That is, as you move from left to right along the curve the gradient gets smaller. This is shown in Fig. 28.2 by the fact that $f'(x)$ is a decreasing function of x.

You could make a similar comparison between the graphs of $f(x)$ and $f'(x)$ for any function you care to choose. If you know the graph of $f(x)$, then this determines the graph of $f'(x)$.

Is the reverse true? That is, if you know the graph of $f'(x)$, could you use this to draw the graph of $f(x)$?

Example 28.1.2 examines this geometrically for a graph of $f'(x)$ which is not a straight line.

Example 28.1.2
Figure 28.3 shows the graph of the derivative $f'(x)$ of some function $f(x)$. Use this to draw a sketch of the graph of $f(x)$.

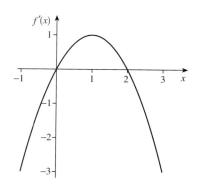

Fig. 28.3

Scanning Fig. 28.3 from left to right, you can see that:

For $x < 0$ the graph of $f'(x)$ lies below the x-axis; the gradient is negative, so $f(x)$ is decreasing.

At $x = 0$ the gradient changes from $-$ to $+$, so $f(x)$ has a minimum.

For $0 < x < 2$ the graph of $f'(x)$ lies above the x-axis; the gradient is positive, so $f(x)$ is increasing.

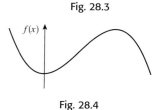

Fig. 28.4

The gradient is greatest when $x = 1$, so that is where the graph of $f(x)$ climbs most steeply. The graph of $f'(x)$ is horizontal, so the derivative of $f'(x)$ is 0 when $x = 1$; that is $f''(1) = 0$, so the graph of $f(x)$ has a point of inflexion where $x = 1$.

At $x = 2$ the gradient changes from $+$ to $-$, so $f(x)$ has a maximum.

For $x > 2$ the gradient is negative, so $f(x)$ is again decreasing.

Using this information you can make a sketch like Fig. 28.4, which gives an idea of the shape of the graph of $f(x)$. But there is no way of deciding precisely where the graph is located. You could move it up and down by any amount, and it would still have the same gradient $f'(x)$. So there is no unique answer to the problem; there are many functions $f(x)$ with the given derivative.

This suggests that the answer to the question posed above is 'yes and no'. If you know the graph of $f'(x)$, this tells you the shape of the graph of $f(x)$ but not precisely where it is.

Example 28.1.3 shows this algebraically for the graphs of $f'(x)$ in Examples 28.1.1 and 28.1.2.

Example 28.1.3
What can you say about $f(x)$ if   (a) $f'(x) = 1 - x$,   (b) $f'(x) = 2x - x^2$?

(a) In Example 28.1.1, the derivative $f'(x) = 1 - x$ was obtained from the equation $f(x) = x - \frac{1}{2}x^2 + 1$. Working backwards, the term 1 in $f'(x)$ could only have come from a term x in $f(x)$; and the term $-x$ in $f'(x)$ could only have come from a term $-\frac{1}{2}x^2$ in $f(x)$. So if $f'(x) = 1 - x$, you can be certain that

$$f(x) = x - \tfrac{1}{2}x^2 + \text{something}.$$

But there is no reason why that 'something' has to be 1, as it was in Example 28.1.1. The equation could equally well be $f(x) = x - \frac{1}{2}x^2$, or $f(x) = x - \frac{1}{2}x^2 + 5$; both these equations give $f'(x) = 1 - x$. The best that you can say about $f(x)$ is that

$$f(x) = x - \tfrac{1}{2}x^2 + k,$$

where k is some number.

Geometrically, the graph in Fig. 28.1 could be shifted up or down by any amount in the y-direction without altering the graph of the gradient function in Fig. 28.2.

(b) This is in fact the equation of the graph in Fig. 28.3, so the question is to find the equation of the graph in Fig. 28.4.

Again there are two terms in the expression for $f'(x)$. The first term, $2x$, is easy; you will recognise this at once as the derivative of x^2. The term $-x^2$ in $f'(x)$ is a bit more tricky. You would expect it to come from an expression of the form ax^3 for some number a, which has to be found. If you differentiate ax^3 the result is $3ax^2$, so you need $3a$ to equal -1; that is, $a = -\frac{1}{3}$.

So, by the same argument as in part (a), the best that you can say is that

$$f(x) = x^2 - \tfrac{1}{3}x^3 + k,$$

where k is some number.

The process of getting from $f'(x)$ to $f(x)$ is called **integration**, and the general expression for $f(x)$ is called the **indefinite integral** of $f'(x)$. Integration is the reverse process of differentiation.

The indefinite integral always includes an added constant k, which is called an **arbitrary constant**. The word 'arbitrary' means that, in any application, you can choose its value to fit some extra condition; for example, you can make the graph of $y = f(x)$ go through some given point.

It is easy to find a rule for integrating functions which are powers of x. Because differentiation reduces the index by 1, integration must increase it by 1. So the function x^n must be derived from some multiple of x^{n+1}. But the derivative of x^{n+1} is $(n+1)x^n$; so to reduce the coefficient in the derivative to 1 you have to multiply x^{n+1} by $\dfrac{1}{n+1}$.

The rule is therefore that one integral of x^n is $\dfrac{1}{n+1}x^{n+1}$.

The extension to functions which are sums of multiples of powers of x then follows from the equivalent rules for differentiation.

Example 28.1.4

Find the indefinite integral of   (a) x^4,   (b) $6x - 2x^3$,   (c) $\dfrac{4}{x^3}$.

(a) Putting $n = 4$, the indefinite integral of x^4 is $\dfrac{1}{4+1}x^{4+1} + k = \frac{1}{5}x^5 + k$, where k is an arbitrary constant.

(b) The term $6x$ is the derivative of $6\left(\frac{1}{2}x^2\right)$, and $-2x^3$ is the derivative of $-2\left(\frac{1}{4}x^4\right)$. So the indefinite integral of $6x - 2x^3$ is $3x^2 - \frac{1}{2}x^4 + k$.

(c) Write $\dfrac{4}{x^3}$ as $4x^{-3}$. If $n = -3$, $n + 1 = -3 + 1 = -2$, so the indefinite integral of $4x^{-3}$ is $4\left(\frac{1}{-2}x^{-2}\right) + k = -2x^{-2} + k = -\dfrac{2}{x^2} + k$.

But notice an important exception to this rule. The formula $\dfrac{1}{n+1}x^{n+1}$ has no meaning if $n + 1$ is 0, so it does not give the integral of x^{-1}, or $\dfrac{1}{x}$. You will find in Higher Level 2 Section 13.6 that the integral of $\dfrac{1}{x}$ is not a power of x, but a quite different kind of function.

> The indefinite integral of a function made up of the sum of multiples of x^n, where $n \neq -1$, is the corresponding sum of multiples of $\dfrac{1}{n+1}x^{n+1}$, together with an added arbitrary constant.

Example 28.1.5

The graph of $y = f(x)$ passes through $(2, 3)$, and $f'(x) = 6x^2 - 5x$. Find its equation.

The indefinite integral is $6\left(\frac{1}{3}x^3\right) - 5\left(\frac{1}{2}x^2\right) + k$, so the graph has equation

$$y = 2x^3 - \tfrac{5}{2}x^2 + k$$

for some constant k. The coordinates $x = 2$, $y = 3$ have to satisfy this equation, so

$$3 = 2 \times 8 - \tfrac{5}{2} \times 4 + k, \quad \text{giving} \quad k = 3 - 16 + 10 = -3.$$

The equation of the graph is therefore $y = 2x^3 - \frac{5}{2}x^2 - 3$.

Example 28.1.6

A gardener is weeding a plot of land. As he gets tired he works more slowly; after t minutes he is weeding at a rate of $\dfrac{2}{\sqrt{t}}$ square metres per minute. How long will it take him to weed an area of 40 square metres?

Let A square metres be the area he has weeded after t minutes. Then his rate of weeding is measured by the derivative $\dfrac{\mathrm{d}A}{\mathrm{d}t}$. So you know that $\dfrac{\mathrm{d}A}{\mathrm{d}t} = 2t^{-\frac{1}{2}}$; in this case $n = -\frac{1}{2}$, so $n + 1 = \frac{1}{2}$ and the indefinite integral is

$$A = 2\left(\tfrac{1}{1/2}t^{\frac{1}{2}}\right) + k = 4\sqrt{t} + k.$$

To find k, you need to know a pair of values of A and t. Since $A = 0$ when he starts, which is when $t = 0$, $0 = 4\sqrt{0} + k$ and so $k = 0$.

The equation connecting A with t is therefore $A = 4\sqrt{t}$.

To find how long it takes to weed 40 square metres, substitute $A = 40$:

$$40 = 4\sqrt{t}, \text{ so that } \sqrt{t} = 10, \text{ and hence } t = 100.$$

It will take him 100 minutes to weed an area of 40 square metres.

28.2 Notation for indefinite integrals

You already have a short notation for differentiation, so that instead of writing

'the derivative of $3x^2 - \frac{1}{2}x^4$ is $6x - 2x^3$'

or   'if $y = 3x^2 - \frac{1}{2}x^4$, then $\dfrac{dy}{dx} = 6x - 2x^3$'

you can simply write without any words

$$\frac{d}{dx}\left(3x^2 - \tfrac{1}{2}x^4\right) = 6x - 2x^3.$$

The symbol $\dfrac{d}{dx}$ is an instruction to differentiate whatever follows it (see Section 25.5).

There is a corresponding notation for indefinite integrals, to avoid having to write

'the indefinite integral of $6x - 2x^3$ is $3x^2 - \frac{1}{2}x^4 + k$'

or   'if $\dfrac{dy}{dx} = 6x - 2x^3$, then $y = 3x^2 - \frac{1}{2}x^4 + k$'.

The notation used to write this without words is

$$\int (6x - 2x^3)\, dx = 3x^2 - \tfrac{1}{2}x^4 + k.$$

The symbol $\displaystyle\int$ is called the 'integral sign', and 'dx' tells you the letter being used as the variable. The expression $\displaystyle\int (\ldots)\, dx$ is then an instruction to integrate the expression in the brackets; it is read

'the indefinite integral of (...) with respect to x'.

The reason for this rather odd notation will become clearer in the next chapter.

If the function you are integrating is very simple, then you can leave out the brackets. For example, it would be usual to write $\displaystyle\int x^2\, dx$ rather than $\displaystyle\int (x^2)\, dx$. But if the expression has more than one term, you should put it in brackets.

Example 28.2.1
Find $\displaystyle\int (5x^4 + 9x^2 - 2)\, dx$.

$$\int (5x^4 + 9x^2 - 2)\, dx = 5\left(\tfrac{1}{5}x^5\right) + 9\left(\tfrac{1}{3}x^3\right) - 2x + k$$
$$= x^5 + 3x^3 - 2x + k.$$

> This is all you need to write. But don't forget to put in the arbitrary constant!

The notation is often used with other letters for the variable, especially when integration is used in real-world problems. If you see $\int (...) \, dt$, for example, then t is the independent variable and you have to integrate with respect to t.

Example 28.2.2

Find   (a) $\int 8t^3 \, dt$,   (b) $\int \frac{1}{p^2} \, dp$,   (c) $\int \sqrt{u} \, du$,   (d) $\int (2x-1)(2x+1) \, dx$,   (e) $\int \frac{y^4 - 4}{y^2} \, dy$.

(a) $\int 8t^3 \, dt = 8 \left(\frac{1}{4}t^4\right) + k = 2t^4 + k.$

(b) $\int \frac{1}{p^2} \, dp = \int p^{-2} \, dp = \frac{1}{-2+1} p^{-2+1} + k = -p^{-1} + k = -\frac{1}{p} + k.$

(c) $\int \sqrt{u} \, du = \int u^{\frac{1}{2}} \, du = \frac{1}{\frac{1}{2}+1} u^{\frac{1}{2}+1} + k = \frac{1}{\frac{3}{2}} u^{\frac{3}{2}} + k = \frac{2}{3} u\sqrt{u} + k.$

(d) You must multiply out the brackets before you can integrate.

$$\int (2x-1)(2x+1) \, dx = \int (4x^2 - 1) \, dx = 4 \left(\frac{1}{3}x^3\right) - x + k = \frac{4}{3}x^3 - x + k.$$

(e) $\int \frac{y^4 - 4}{y^2} \, dy = \int \left(\frac{y^4}{y^2} - \frac{4}{y^2}\right) dy$

$\qquad = \int (y^2 - 4y^{-2}) \, dy = \frac{1}{3}y^3 - 4\left(\frac{y^{-1}}{-1}\right) + k = \frac{1}{3}y^3 + \frac{4}{y} + k.$

Exercise 28A

1 Find a general expression for the function $f(x)$ in each of the following cases.
  (a) $f'(x) = 4x^3$
  (b) $f'(x) = 6x^5$
  (c) $f'(x) = 2x$
  (d) $f'(x) = 3x^2 + 5x^4$
  (e) $f'(x) = 10x^9 - 8x^7 - 1$
  (f) $f'(x) = -7x^6 + 3x^2 + 1$

2 Find the following indefinite integrals.
  (a) $\int (9x^2 - 4x - 5) \, dx$
  (b) $\int (12x^2 + 6x + 4) \, dx$
  (c) $\int 7 dx$
  (d) $\int (16x^3 - 6x^2 + 10x - 3) \, dx$
  (e) $\int (2x^3 + 5x) \, dx$
  (f) $\int (x + 2x^2) \, dx$
  (g) $\int (2x^2 - 3x - 4) \, dx$
  (h) $\int (1 - 2x - 3x^2) \, dx$

3 Find y in terms of x in each of the following cases.
  (a) $\dfrac{dy}{dx} = x^4 + x^2 + 1$
  (b) $\dfrac{dy}{dx} = 7x - 3$
  (c) $\dfrac{dy}{dx} = 2x^2 + x - 8$
  (d) $\dfrac{dy}{dx} = 6x^3 - 5x^2 + 3x + 2$

(e) $\dfrac{dy}{dx} = \frac{2}{3}x^3 + \frac{1}{2}x^2 + \frac{1}{3}x + \frac{1}{6}$

(f) $\dfrac{dy}{dx} = \frac{1}{2}x^3 - \frac{1}{3}x^2 + x - \frac{1}{3}$

(g) $\dfrac{dy}{dx} = x - 3x^2 + 1$

(h) $\dfrac{dy}{dx} = x^3 + x^2 + x + 1$

4 The graph of $y = f(x)$ passes through the origin and $f'(x) = 8x - 5$. Find $f(x)$.

5 A curve passes through the point $(2, -5)$ and satisfies $\dfrac{dy}{dx} = 6x^2 - 1$. Find y in terms of x.

6 A curve passes through $(-4, 9)$ and is such that $\dfrac{dy}{dx} = \frac{1}{2}x^3 + \frac{1}{4}x + 1$. Find y in terms of x.

7 Given that $f'(x) = 15x^2 - 6x + 4$ and $f(1) = 0$, find $f(x)$.

8 Each of the following diagrams shows the graph of a derivative $f'(x)$. In each case, sketch the graph of a possible function $f(x)$.

State the x-coordinates and describe the shape of the graph at any stationary points. Give the x-coordinates of any points of inflexion.

(a)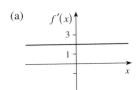

(b)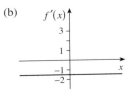

(c)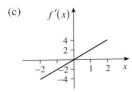

(d)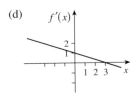

(e)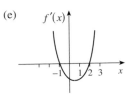

(f)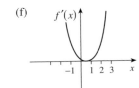

(g)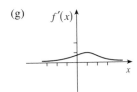

(h)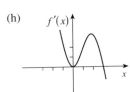

9 The graph of $y = f(x)$ passes through $(4, 25)$ and $f'(x) = 6\sqrt{x}$. Find its equation.

10 Find a general expression for the function $f(x)$ in each of the following cases.

(a) $f'(x) = x^{-2}$

(b) $f'(x) = 3x^{-4}$

(c) $f'(x) = \dfrac{6}{x^3}$

(d) $f'(x) = 4x - \dfrac{3}{x^2}$

(e) $f'(x) = \dfrac{1}{x^3} - \dfrac{1}{x^4}$

(f) $f'(x) = \dfrac{2}{x^2} - 2x^2$

11 Find y in terms of x in each of the following cases.

(a) $\dfrac{dy}{dx} = x^{\frac{1}{2}}$

(b) $\dfrac{dy}{dx} = 4x^{-\frac{2}{3}}$

(c) $\dfrac{dy}{dx} = \sqrt[3]{x}$

(d) $\dfrac{dy}{dx} = 2\sqrt{x} - \dfrac{2}{\sqrt{x}}$

(e) $\dfrac{dy}{dx} = \dfrac{5}{\sqrt[3]{x}}$

(f) $\dfrac{dy}{dx} = \dfrac{-2}{\sqrt[3]{x^2}}$

12 The graph of $y = f(x)$ passes through $(\frac{1}{2}, 5)$ and $f'(x) = \dfrac{4}{x^2}$. Find the equation of the graph.

13 A curve passes through the point $(25, 3)$ and is such that $\dfrac{dy}{dx} = \dfrac{1}{2\sqrt{x}}$. Find the equation of the curve.

14 A curve passes through the point $(1, 5)$ and is such that $\dfrac{dy}{dx} = \sqrt[3]{x} - \dfrac{6}{x^3}$. Find the equation of the curve.

15 In each of the following cases, find y in terms of x.

(a) $\dfrac{dy}{dx} = 3x(x + 2)$

(b) $\dfrac{dy}{dx} = (2x - 1)(6x + 5)$

(c) $\dfrac{dy}{dx} = \dfrac{4x^3 + 1}{x^2}$

(d) $\dfrac{dy}{dx} = \dfrac{x + 4}{\sqrt{x}}$

(e) $\dfrac{dy}{dx} = (\sqrt{x} + 5)^2$

(f) $\dfrac{dy}{dx} = \dfrac{\sqrt{x} + 5}{\sqrt{x}}$

16 Find the following indefinite integrals.

(a) $\displaystyle\int \left(u^2 + \dfrac{1}{u^2}\right) du$

(b) $\displaystyle\int t^5(3 - t)\, dt$

(c) $\displaystyle\int 4(p + 1)^3\, dp$

(d) $\displaystyle\int \dfrac{1}{y\sqrt{y}}\, dy$

(e) $\displaystyle\int \left(\sqrt[3]{z} + \dfrac{1}{\sqrt[3]{z}}\right)^2 dz$

(f) $\displaystyle\int v(1 + \sqrt{v})\, dv$

17 A tree is growing so that, after t years, its height is increasing at a rate of $\dfrac{30}{\sqrt[3]{t}}$ cm per year. Assume that, when $t = 0$, the height is 5 cm.

(a) Find the height of the tree after 4 years.

(b) After how many years will the height be 4.1 metres?

18 A pond, with surface area 48 square metres, is being invaded by a weed. At a time t months after the weed first appeared, the area of the weed on the surface is increasing at a rate of $\frac{1}{3}t$ square metres per month. How long will it be before the weed covers the whole surface of the pond?

19 The function $f(x)$ is such that $f'(x) = 9x^2 + 4x + c$, where c is a particular constant. Given that $f(2) = 14$ and $f(3) = 74$, find the value of $f(4)$.

28.3 Application to kinematics

One of the important applications of differentiation is to motion along a straight line. It was shown in Section 25.3 that the displacement, velocity and acceleration are connected by the equations

$$v = \dfrac{ds}{dt} \quad \text{and} \quad a = \dfrac{dv}{dt}.$$

But more often you want to work the other way round; that is, you know the acceleration and want to find how fast an object is moving, and how far it has travelled, after a given time.

For this you need to use integration rather than differentiation. The equations above can be turned round to find v and s as integrals.

For an object moving in a straight line, if a denotes the acceleration as a function of the time t,

$$v = \int a \, dt \quad \text{and} \quad s = \int v \, dt.$$

Remember that integration involves an arbitrary constant. You can usually find this by knowing the initial velocity and the initial displacement; these are the values of v and of s when $t = 0$.

Example 28.3.1

For the first few seconds of a race a horse's acceleration, a m s^{-2}, is modelled by the equation $a = 6 - 1.2t$, where t is the time in seconds from a standing start. Find an expression for the distance it covers in the first t seconds. Hence find the horse's acceleration 5 seconds after the start, how fast it is then moving and how far it has run.

Begin by finding an expression for the velocity,

$$v = \int a \, dt$$
$$= \int (6 - 1.2t) \, dt$$
$$= 6t - 0.6t^2 + k.$$

Since time is measured from a standing start, $v = 0$ when $t = 0$, so

$$0 = 6 \times 0 - 0.6 \times 0^2 + k,$$

which gives $k = 0$. The (t, v) function is therefore

$$v = 6t - 0.6t^2.$$

A second integration then gives

$$s = \int v \, dt$$
$$= \int (6t - 0.6t^2) \, dt$$
$$= 3t^2 - 0.2t^3 + c.$$

If s is measured from the starting gate, $s = 0$ when $t = 0$, so

$$0 = 3 \times 0^2 - 0.2 \times 0^3 + c.$$

This gives $c = 0$. The (t, s) function is therefore

$$s = 3t^2 - 0.2t^3.$$

Substituting $t = 5$ in the expressions for a, v and s gives the values $a = 0$, $v = 15$ and $s = 50$. So, according to this model, 5 seconds after the start the horse has stopped accelerating and has reached a speed of 15 metres per second. In this time it has run a distance of 50 metres.

Example 28.3.2

A train is travelling on a straight track at 48 m s^{-1} when the driver sees an amber light ahead. He applies the brakes for a period of 30 seconds, producing a deceleration of $\frac{1}{125}t(30-t)$ m s^{-2}, where t is the time in seconds after the brakes are applied. Find how fast the train is moving after 30 seconds, and how far it has travelled in that time.

The train is slowing down, so the acceleration is negative. That is,

$$a = -\frac{1}{125}t(30-t)$$
$$= \frac{1}{125}t^2 - \frac{6}{25}t.$$

Integrating to find v,

$$v = \int \left(\frac{1}{125}t^2 - \frac{6}{25}t\right)dt$$
$$= \frac{1}{375}t^3 - \frac{3}{25}t^2 + k.$$

It is given that $v = 48$ when $t = 0$. Substituting these values gives

$$48 = 0 - 0 + k, \quad \text{so} \quad k = 48.$$

The formula for v is therefore

$$v = \frac{1}{375}t^3 - \frac{3}{25}t^2 + 48.$$

Integrating a second time to find s,

$$s = \int \left(\frac{1}{375}t^3 - \frac{3}{25}t^2 + 48\right)dt$$
$$= \frac{1}{1500}t^4 - \frac{1}{25}t^3 + 48t + c.$$

If s denotes the displacement from the instant when the brakes are first applied, then $s = 0$ when $t = 0$. Substituting these values gives

$$0 = 0 - 0 + 0 + c, \quad \text{so} \quad c = 0.$$

The formula for s is therefore

$$s = \frac{1}{1500}t^4 - \frac{1}{25}t^3 + 48t.$$

To find the final speed and the distance travelled, substitute $t = 30$ in the expressions for v and s. This gives

$$v = \frac{27\,000}{375} - \frac{3\times900}{25} + 48$$
$$= 72 - 108 + 48 = 12$$

and

$$s = \frac{810\,000}{1500} - \frac{27\,000}{25} + 48 \times 30$$
$$= 540 - 1080 + 1440 = 900.$$

The train slows down to a speed of 12 m s^{-1}, and travels 900 metres during the time that the brakes are on.

Exercise 28B

1 In this question, s metres is the displacement at time t seconds of particles moving in a straight line, v is the velocity in m s^{-1} and a is the acceleration in m s^{-2}. Only zero and positive values of t should be considered.

  (a) Given that $v = 3t^2 + 8$ and that the displacement is 4 m when $t = 0$, find an expression for s in terms of t. Find the displacement and the velocity when $t = 2$.

  (b) Given that $v = 6\sqrt{t}$ and that the displacement is 30 m when $t = 4$, find the displacement, velocity and acceleration when $t = 1$.

  (c) Given that $v = 9 - t^2$ and that the displacement is 2 m when $t = 0$, find the displacement when the velocity is zero.

  (d) Given that $a = 3t - 12$, and that the velocity is 30 m s^{-1} and the displacement is 4 m when $t = 0$, find the displacement when the acceleration is zero.

  (e) Given that $a = 4 - 2t$, and that the velocity is 5 m s^{-1} when $t = 0$, find the acceleration when the velocity is zero.

  (f) Given that $v = 3t^2 + 4t + 3$, find the distance travelled between $t = 0$ and $t = 2$.

  (g) Given that $v = \dfrac{3}{t^2}$, find the distance travelled between $t = 2$ and $t = 10$.

2 A car starts from rest and for the first 4 seconds of its motion the acceleration a m s^{-2} at time t seconds after starting is given by $a = 6 - 2t$.

  (a) Find the maximum velocity of the car.

  (b) Find the velocity of the car after 4 seconds, and the distance travelled up to this time.

3 A truck, with initial velocity 6 m s^{-1}, brakes and comes to rest. At time t seconds after the brakes are applied the acceleration is a m s^{-2}, where $a = -3t$. This formula applies until the truck stops.

  (a) Find the time taken for the truck to stop.

  (b) Find the distance travelled by the truck while it is decelerating.

  (c) Find the greatest deceleration of the truck.

29 Calculating areas

An important application of integration is to calculate areas and volumes. This chapter deals only with areas. When you have completed it, you should

- know how to evaluate definite integrals
- be able to use definite integrals to find areas
- know that the area under any velocity–time graph represents displacement.

29.1 The area under a graph

The particular kind of area to be investigated is illustrated in Fig. 29.1. For any function, the problem is to calculate the area bounded by the x-axis, the graph of $y = f(x)$, and the lines $x = a$ and $x = b$. This is described as **the area under the graph** from a to b.

As a start, Example 29.1.1 finds such an area for a very special case when the graph is a straight line.

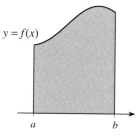

Fig. 29.1

Example 29.1.1

Find the area under the graph of $y = f(x)$, where $f(x) = 6x + 5$,

(a) from 0 to a, (b) from a to b,

where $b > a > 0$.

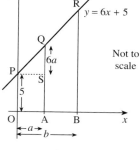

Fig. 29.2

(a) In Fig. 29.2, the area under the graph from 0 to a is the area of the trapezium OAQP. This can be split into a triangle PSQ and a rectangle OASP by a line PS parallel to the x-axis. The length of the y-intercept is 5; and, since the gradient of PQ is 6, the length SQ is $6a$. So the area of the trapezium is

$$\tfrac{1}{2} \times a \times 6a + a \times 5, \text{ or more simply } 3a^2 + 5a.$$

(b) You want the area of the trapezium ABRQ, which can be found as

area OBRP − area OAQP.

Area OAQP has already been found in part (a). The trapezium OBRP is of the same kind as OAQP, but with b in place of a, so area OBRP is $3b^2 + 5b$.

It follows that the area under the graph from a to b is

$$(3b^2 + 5b) - (3a^2 + 5a).$$

Look at the form of the answer to this example. You can think of this as the difference between the values of the function $3x^2 + 5x$ when $x = b$ and $x = a$. If $I(x)$ is used to denote this function, then the area is $I(b) - I(a)$.

What is the connection between $I(x) = 3x^2 + 5x$ and $f(x) = 6x + 5$?

Obviously, in this case, $f(x)$ is the derivative of $I(x)$. Or, put another way, $I(x)$ is an integral of $f(x)$.

It has to be 'an' integral, rather than 'the' integral, because $f(x)$ has any number of integrals, as explained in Section 28.1. But $I(x)$ is the simplest of these; that is, it is the one for which the arbitrary constant is 0.

So this example suggests a procedure for finding the area under a graph.

> To find the area under the graph $y = f(x)$ from $x = a$ to $x = b$:
>
> **Step 1** Find the 'simplest' integral of $f(x)$; call it $I(x)$.
>
> **Step 2** Work out $I(a)$ and $I(b)$.
>
> **Step 3** The area is $I(b) - I(a)$.

At present this is just a guess. You can't base a general theory on the result of just one example. But it can be proved that it is true for any function $f(x)$ with a continuous graph.

Example 29.1.2
Find the area between the graph of $y = 2x - x^2$ and the x-axis.

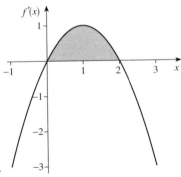

Fig. 29.3

This graph is shown in Fig. 29.3. The curve cuts the x-axis when $x = 0$ and $x = 2$, so you want the area under the graph between these values of x, shaded in the diagram.

The indefinite integral of $2x - x^2$ is $x^2 - \frac{1}{3}x^3 + k$. The simplest integral has $k = 0$, so $I(x) = x^2 - \frac{1}{3}x^3$. The area is then $I(2) - I(0)$.

So calculate

$$I(2) = 4 - \tfrac{1}{3} \times 8 = \tfrac{4}{3} \quad \text{and} \quad I(0) = 0 - 0 = 0,$$

giving an area of $\frac{4}{3} - 0 = \frac{4}{3}$.

> Although the procedure takes $I(x)$ to be the 'simplest' integral of $f(x)$, this is not essential. In Example 29.1.2, if you took $I(x)$ to be $x^2 - \frac{1}{3}x^3 + k$, you would get $I(2) = \frac{4}{3} + k$ and $I(0) = k$, giving the area as $I(2) - I(0) = (\frac{4}{3} + k) - k = \frac{4}{3}$, just as before. But there is no point in making it more complicated than necessary.

Example 29.1.3

Find the area under $y = \dfrac{1}{x^2}$ from $x = 2$ to $x = 5$.

Step 1   Let $f(x) = y$. You can write $f(x)$ as x^{-2}, so $I(x)$ is $\frac{1}{-1}x^{-1}$, or $-\dfrac{1}{x}$.

Step 2 $I(2) = -\frac{1}{2} = -0.5, \quad I(5) = -\frac{1}{5} = -0.2.$

Step 3   The area is $I(5) - I(2) = (-0.2) - (-0.5) = -0.2 + 0.5 = 0.3.$

The answers to these examples have been given without a unit, because it is not usual to attach a unit to the variables x and y when graphs are drawn. But if in a particular application x and y each denote numbers of units, then when stating the answer a corresponding unit (the x-unit $\times$ the y-unit) should be attached to it.

29.2   Definite integrals

You will carry out the procedure in Section 29.1 so often that it is worth having a special notation to describe it. This notation is an extension of that used for indefinite integrals in Section 28.2.

The 'area under $y = f(x)$ from $x = a$ to $x = b$' is denoted by

$$\int_a^b f(x)\,dx.$$

This is called a **definite integral**. Notice that a definite integral has a specific value. Unlike an indefinite integral, it is not a function of x, and it involves no arbitrary constant. For example, the result of Example 29.1.2 would be written

$$\int_0^2 (2x - x^2)\,dx = \tfrac{4}{3}.$$

The numbers a and b are often called the **limits**, or the bounds, of integration. (But notice that they are not 'limits' in the sense in which the word has been used in relation to differentiation.) The function $f(x)$ is called the **integrand**.

The symbol $\int$ was originally a letter S, standing for 'sum'. Before the link with differentiation was discovered in the 17th century, attempts were made to calculate areas as the sums of areas of rectangles of height $f(x)$ and width denoted by δx, or dx. Figure 29.4 shows such a rectangle for the area of the region in Fig. 29.1; as δx tends to 0, and the number of rectangles increases, the rectangles fill up the whole of the area under the curve.

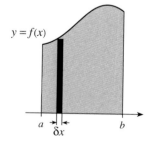

Fig. 29.4

There is also an abbreviation for $I(b) - I(a)$: it is written

$$\left[I(x) \right]_a^b.$$

So, if $I(x)$ is the simplest integral of $f(x)$, $\displaystyle\int_a^b f(x)\,dx = \big[I(x)\big]_a^b$.

Using this notation, you would write the calculation of the area in Example 29.1.3 as

$$
\begin{aligned}
\text{Area} &= \int_2^5 \frac{1}{x^2}\,dx \\
&= \left[-\frac{1}{x}\right]_2^5 \\
&= \left(-\tfrac{1}{5}\right) - \left(-\tfrac{1}{2}\right) \\
&= -0.2 + 0.5 = 0.3.
\end{aligned}
$$

Example 29.2.1

Find $\displaystyle\int_1^3 (3x-2)(4-x)\,dx$.

$$
\begin{aligned}
\int_1^3 (3x-2)(4-x)\,dx &= \int_1^3 (-3x^2 + 14x - 8)\,dx \\
&= \left[-x^3 + 7x^2 - 8x\right]_1^3 \\
&= (-27 + 63 - 24) - (-1 + 7 - 8) \\
&= 12 - (-2) = 14.
\end{aligned}
$$

Example 29.2.2

Find $\displaystyle\int_{-4}^{-1} \left(x^2 - \frac{1}{x^2}\right) dx$.

$$
\begin{aligned}
\int_{-4}^{-1} \left(x^2 - \frac{1}{x^2}\right) dx &= \int_{-4}^{-1} (x^2 - x^{-2})\,dx \\
&= \left[\tfrac{1}{3}x^3 - (-x^{-1})\right]_{-4}^{-1} \\
&= \left[\tfrac{1}{3}x^3 + \frac{1}{x}\right]_{-4}^{-1} \\
&= \tfrac{1}{3}\big((-1)^3 - (-4)^3\big) + \left(\frac{1}{-1} - \frac{1}{-4}\right) \\
&= \tfrac{1}{3}(-1 - (-64)) + (-1 + \tfrac{1}{4}) \\
&= \tfrac{1}{3} \times 63 + (-\tfrac{3}{4}) = 21 - \tfrac{3}{4} = 20\tfrac{1}{4}.
\end{aligned}
$$

Notice the different ways of completing the calculation in Examples 29.2.1 and 29.2.2. In the first case the expression in the square brackets is worked out completely for $x = 3$ and $x = 1$ before subtracting, following exactly the procedure described in the text. In the second the subtraction is carried out for the two terms separately, and the two results are then put together to get the answer. The second method often leads to simpler arithmetic when the integral contains fractions, or when one (or both) of the limits of integration is negative. You can use whichever method you prefer.

Example 29.2.3

Find the area under $y = \sqrt{x}$ from $x = 1$ to $x = 4$, shown shaded in Fig. 29.5.

$$\text{Area} = \int_1^4 \sqrt{x}\, dx$$

$$= \int_1^4 x^{\frac{1}{2}}\, dx$$

$$= \left[\tfrac{2}{3} x^{\frac{3}{2}} \right]_1^4$$

$$= \tfrac{2}{3} \times 8 - \tfrac{2}{3} \times 1 = \tfrac{14}{3}.$$

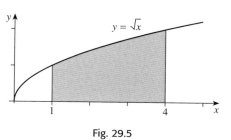

Fig. 29.5

Calculators use a version of the rectangle sum method illustrated in Fig. 29.4 to find approximate values for definite integrals of functions over a given interval, or for the areas of shaded regions under graphs. You will find details in the calculator manual. This provides a useful way of checking answers which you have found by the exact methods described in this section.

Another useful check is to find a rectangle, triangle or trapezium whose area is close to the required area. In Example 29.2.3, since $f(1) = 1$ and $f(2) = 2$, the shaded area is slightly larger than the area of the trapezium which you get by replacing the curve by the chord joining $(1, 1)$ to $(4, 2)$. The area of the trapezium is $\frac{1}{2} \times (1 + 2) \times 3 = 4\frac{1}{2}$, which can be compared with the area of $4\frac{2}{3}$ calculated in the example.

29.3 Calculating displacement from a velocity–time graph

In Section 10.6 it was shown that, for an object moving with constant velocity, the increase in the displacement over an interval of time is represented by the area under the velocity–time graph. Then in Section 10.7 it was assumed that this could be extended to situations where the velocity is not constant, but increases at a constant rate.

Now that it has been shown that integration and the calculation of area are linked, it follows that this holds for any velocity–time graph.

Example 29.3.1

An aircraft accelerates along the runway as it takes off. After t seconds it has travelled s metres and has a speed of $v\,\mathrm{m\,s^{-1}}$. For $10 < t < 20$ the motion is modelled by the equation $v = 100 - \dfrac{4000}{t^2}$. Find how far the aircraft travels in this time.

Solution using an indefinite integral   Since $v = \dfrac{ds}{dt}$ (see Section 25.3),

$$\frac{ds}{dt} = 100 - \frac{4000}{t^2}$$
$$= 100 - 4000t^{-2}.$$

Integrating,

$$s = 100t - 4000 \times (-t^{-1}) + k$$
$$= 100t + \frac{4000}{t} + k.$$

To find k you would need to know how far the aircraft has moved in the first 10 seconds, which you are not told. But you can calculate that, when $t = 10$,

$$s = 1000 + 400 + k = 1400 + k;$$

and when $t = 20$,

$$s = 2000 + 200 + k = 2200 + k.$$

So, between these times, the value of s increases by

$$(2200 + k) - (1400 + k) = 800.$$

Solution using the velocity–time graph   The area under the (t, v) graph is

$$\int_{10}^{20} \left(100 - \frac{4000}{t^2}\right) dt = \left[100t + \frac{4000}{t}\right]_{10}^{20}$$
$$= (2000 + 200) - (1000 + 400)$$
$$= 2200 - 1400 = 800.$$

The aircraft travels 800 metres in this time.

You can see from this example that the actual calculations – the integration and the numerical substitution – are the same in both forms of the solution. But the solution based on the area under the velocity–time graph is neater.

The example illustrates a general rule:

For an object moving in a straight line, with the velocity v given as a function of the time t, the displacement between times t_1 and t_2 is given by

$$\int_{t_1}^{t_2} v \, dt.$$

This displacement is represented by the area under the (t, v) graph for the interval $t_1 \le t \le t_2$.

Example 29.3.2
A car starts to accelerate as soon as it leaves a town. After t seconds its velocity v m s^{-1} is given by the formula $v = 14 + 0.45t^2 - 0.03t^3$, until it reaches its maximum velocity. Find the distance travelled while the car accelerates to its maximum velocity. (See Example 25.3.2.)

It was shown in Example 25.3.2 that the car reaches its maximum velocity of 29 m s^{-1} at time $t = 10$, so the distance travelled is

$$\int_0^{10} (14 + 0.45t^2 - 0.03t^3) \, dt = \left[14t + 0.15t^3 - 0.0075t^4\right]_0^{10}$$
$$= (140 + 150 - 75) - (0 + 0 - 0) = 215.$$

The car travels 215 metres in the 10 seconds that it takes to reach its maximum velocity.

29.4   Proof of the area procedure

So far the only justification for using integration to find areas has been that it works for the area under the straight line graph in Example 29.1.1. This section explains how it can be proved.

The problem is to show that the procedure described in Section 29.1 works for a general function $y = f(x)$, whose graph has a form like Fig. 29.1.

Since the procedure involves integration, which is the reverse of differentiation, begin by recalling how results about differentiation were proved in Section 12.6.

To find the derivative, which is the gradient of the tangent, you started by finding the gradient of a chord. This is defined by the values of x at its end-points, which can be denoted by x and $x + \delta x$. You then found the corresponding difference in y, denoted by δy, and considered the limit of $\dfrac{\delta y}{\delta x}$ as δx tends to 0.

It is not obvious how a method like this can be applied to the area in Fig. 29.1, because this involves only the fixed values of x at a and b.

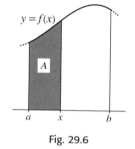

Fig. 29.6

The key is to begin by asking a more general question, which involves a variable x: what is the area, A, under the graph from $x = a$ as far as *any* value of x? This is illustrated by the region shaded in Fig. 29.6. Notice that A is also a variable; x is the independent variable, and A is the dependent variable (see Section 25.1).

The point of doing this is that x can now be varied. Suppose that x is increased by δx. Since both y and A are functions of x, you can write the corresponding increases in y and A as δy and δA. This is represented in Fig. 29.7 by the region with light shading.

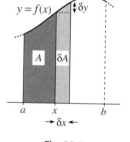

Fig. 29.7

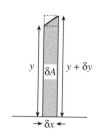

Fig. 29.8

This region is drawn by itself in Fig. 29.8. Dotted lines have been added to show that the area δA of the region is between the areas of two rectangles, each with width δx and having heights of y and $y + \delta y$. So

$$\delta A \text{ is between } y\,\delta x \text{ and } (y + \delta y)\delta x.$$

It follows from this that

$$\frac{\delta A}{\delta x} \text{ is between } y \text{ and } y + \delta y.$$

Now consider the effect of making δx tend to 0. From the definition, $\dfrac{\delta A}{\delta x}$ tends to the derivative $\dfrac{\mathrm{d}A}{\mathrm{d}x}$. Also δy tends to 0, so that $y + \delta y$ tends to y. It follows that

$$\frac{\mathrm{d}A}{\mathrm{d}x} = y.$$

And since $y = f(x)$, it follows that A is an integral of $f(x)$.

There are many such integrals, but if the 'simplest' one is denoted by $I(x)$, then you know that

$$A = I(x) + k$$

for some number k. How do you find k?

In Examples 28.1.5 and 28.1.6 the arbitrary constant could be found because you knew one pair of values taken by the variables. In this case it is clear from Fig. 29.6 that $A = 0$ when $x = a$, so

$$0 = I(a) + k, \text{ which gives } k = -I(a).$$

Therefore

$$A = I(x) - I(a).$$

You find the required area by putting $x = b$ in this expression. That is, the area from $x = a$ to $x = b$ is $I(b) - I(a)$.

This shows that the procedure described in the box in Section 29.1 works for any function, not just the special case $f(x) = 6x + 5$.

Exercise 29A

1 Evaluate the following definite integrals.

(a) $\displaystyle\int_1^2 3x^2 \, \mathrm{d}x$

(b) $\displaystyle\int_2^5 8x \, \mathrm{d}x$

(c) $\displaystyle\int_0^2 x^3 \, \mathrm{d}x$

(d) $\displaystyle\int_{-1}^1 10x^4 \, \mathrm{d}x$

(e) $\displaystyle\int_0^{\frac{1}{2}} \tfrac{1}{2}x \, \mathrm{d}x$

(f) $\displaystyle\int_0^1 2 \, \mathrm{d}x$

2 Evaluate the following definite integrals.

(a) $\displaystyle\int_0^2 (8x + 3) \, \mathrm{d}x$

(b) $\displaystyle\int_2^4 (5x - 4) \, \mathrm{d}x$

(c) $\displaystyle\int_{-2}^2 (6x^2 + 1) \, \mathrm{d}x$

(d) $\displaystyle\int_0^1 (2x + 1)(x + 3) \, \mathrm{d}x$

(e) $\displaystyle\int_{-3}^4 (6x^2 + 2x + 3) \, \mathrm{d}x$

(f) $\displaystyle\int_{-3}^3 (6x^3 + 2x) \, \mathrm{d}x$

3 Find the areas under the following curves over the stated intervals. Use a calculator to check your answers.

(a) $y = x^2$ from $x = 0$ to $x = 6$

(b) $y = 4x^3$ from $x = 1$ to $x = 2$

(c) $y = 12x^3$ from $x = 2$ to $x = 3$

(d) $y = 3x^2 + 2x$ from $x = 0$ to $x = 4$

(e) $y = 3x^2 - 2x$ from $x = -4$ to $x = 0$

(f) $y = x^4 + 5$ from $x = -1$ to $x = 1$

4 The diagram shows the region under $y = 4x + 1$ between $x = 1$ and $x = 3$. Find the area of the shaded region by

(a) using the formula for the area of a trapezium,

(b) using integration.

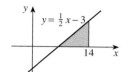

5 The diagram shows the region bounded by $y = \frac{1}{2}x - 3$, by $x = 14$ and the x-axis. Find the area of the shaded region by

(a) using the formula for the area of a triangle,

(b) using integration.

6 Find the area of the region shaded in each of the following diagrams.

(a)

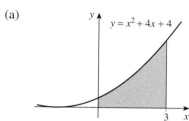

(b)

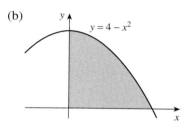

(c)

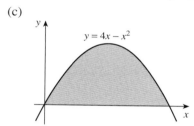

(d)

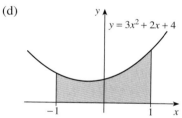

7 Evaluate the following definite integrals.

(a) $\displaystyle\int_0^8 12\sqrt[3]{x}\,dx$

(b) $\displaystyle\int_1^2 \frac{3}{x^2}\,dx$

(c) $\displaystyle\int_1^4 \frac{10}{\sqrt{x}}\,dx$

(d) $\displaystyle\int_1^2 \left(\frac{8}{x^3} + x^3\right)dx$

(e) $\displaystyle\int_4^9 \frac{2\sqrt{x} + 3}{\sqrt{x}}\,dx$

(f) $\displaystyle\int_1^8 \frac{1}{\sqrt[3]{x^2}}\,dx$

8 Find the areas under the following curves over the stated intervals.

(a) $y = \dfrac{6}{x^4}$ between $x = 1$ and $x = 2$

(b) $y = \sqrt[3]{x}$ between $x = 1$ and $x = 27$

(c) $y = \dfrac{5}{x^2}$ between $x = -3$ and $x = -1$

9 Given that $\displaystyle\int_0^a 12x^2\,dx = 1372$, find the value of the constant a.

10 Given that $\displaystyle\int_0^9 p\sqrt{x}\,dx = 90$, find the value of the constant p.

11 Find the area of the shaded region in each of the following diagrams. Use a calculator to check your answers.

(a)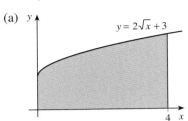

$y = 2\sqrt{x} + 3$

(b)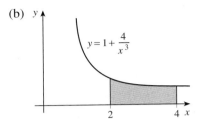

$y = 1 + \dfrac{4}{x^3}$

12 Find the area of the region between the curve $y = 9 + 15x - 6x^2$ and the x-axis.

13 An electric car accelerating from rest has a speed of $t\sqrt{t}$ m s^{-1} after t seconds. How fast is it moving after

(a) 4 seconds,   (b) 9 seconds?

Find its average speed between these times.

14 A cyclist riding at 8 m s^{-1} starts to freewheel, and her speed t seconds later is given by $\frac{1}{50}(20 - t)^2$ m s^{-1}. Find how far she will go before her speed has dropped to 2 m s^{-1}.

29.5 Some properties of definite integrals

In definite integral notation the calculation in Example 29.1.2 of the area in Fig. 29.3 would be written

$$\int_0^2 (2x - x^2)\, dx = \left[x^2 - \tfrac{1}{3}x^3\right]_0^2$$
$$= \left(\tfrac{4}{3}\right) - (0) = \tfrac{4}{3}.$$

But how should you interpret the calculation

$$\int_0^3 (2x - x^2)\, dx = \left[x^2 - \tfrac{1}{3}x^3\right]_0^3$$
$$= (0) - (0) = 0?$$

Clearly the area between the graph and the x-axis between $x = 0$ and $x = 3$ is not zero as the value of the definite integral suggests.

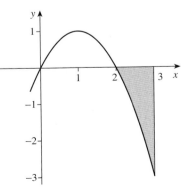

You can find the clue by calculating the integral between $x = 2$ and $x = 3$:

$$\int_2^3 (2x - x^2)\, dx = \left[x^2 - \tfrac{1}{3}x^3\right]_2^3 = (0) - \left(\tfrac{4}{3}\right) = -\tfrac{4}{3}.$$

This shows that you need to be careful in identifying the definite integral as an area. In Fig. 29.9 the area of the shaded region is $\frac{4}{3}$, and the negative sign attached to the definite integral indicates that between $x = 2$ and $x = 3$ the graph lies below the x-axis.

Fig. 29.9

410 Higher Level 1

The zero answer obtained for the integral from $x = 0$ to $x = 3$ is then explained by the fact that definite integrals are added exactly as you would expect:

$$\int_0^3 (2x - x^2)\, dx = \int_0^2 (2x - x^2)\, dx + \int_2^3 (2x - x^2)\, dx = \left(\tfrac{4}{3}\right) + \left(-\tfrac{4}{3}\right) = 0.$$

This is a special case of a general rule:

$$\int_a^b f(x)\, dx + \int_b^c f(x)\, dx = \int_a^c f(x)\, dx.$$

To prove this, let $I(x)$ denote the simplest integral of $f(x)$.

Then the sum of the integrals on the left side is equal to

$$\int_a^b f(x)\, dx + \int_b^c f(x)\, dx = \left[I(x)\right]_a^b + \left[I(x)\right]_b^c$$
$$= (I(b) - I(a)) + (I(c) - I(b)).$$
$$= I(c) - I(a),$$

and the integral on the right side is

$$\int_a^c f(x)\, dx = I(c) - I(a).$$

Example 29.5.1
Figure 29.10 shows the graph of $y = x(x - 1)(x - 3)$, which crosses the x-axis at the points $(0, 0)$, $(1, 0)$ and $(3, 0)$. Find the total area between the curve and the x-axis over the interval $0 \le x \le 3$.

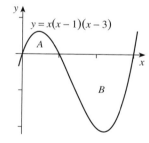

The graph shows that there is a region A above the axis for $0 \le x \le 1$, and a region B below the axis for $1 \le x \le 3$. To find the areas of these regions you have to calculate the definite integrals

$$\int_0^1 x(x - 1)(x - 3)\, dx = \int_0^1 (x^3 - 4x^2 + 3x)\, dx$$
$$= \left[\tfrac{1}{4}x^4 - \tfrac{4}{3}x^3 + \tfrac{3}{2}x^2\right]_0^1$$
$$= \tfrac{1}{4} - 1\tfrac{1}{3} + 1\tfrac{1}{2} = \tfrac{5}{12}$$

and

$$\int_1^3 x(x - 1)(x - 3)\, dx = \left[\tfrac{1}{4}x^4 - \tfrac{4}{3}x^3 + \tfrac{3}{2}x^2\right]_1^3$$
$$= (20\tfrac{1}{4} - 36 + 13\tfrac{1}{2}) - (\tfrac{1}{4} - 1\tfrac{1}{3} + 1\tfrac{1}{2})$$
$$= -2\tfrac{2}{3}.$$

The second integral is negative because the region B lies below the x-axis. In absolute value region A has area $\tfrac{5}{12}$ and region B has area $2\tfrac{2}{3}$. So the total area between the curve and the x-axis for $0 \le x \le 3$ is $\tfrac{5}{12} + 2\tfrac{2}{3}$, which is $3\tfrac{1}{12}$.

The question whether areas below the axis should be counted as negative or positive is well illustrated by applications to kinematics.

Example 29.5.2

A squirrel runs along a straight path, starting at a point O. Its velocity v m s^{-1} after t seconds is given by $v = t^2 - 3t$ for $0 \leq t \leq 5$. Find

(a) the displacement of the squirrel from O after 5 seconds,

(b) the total distance it runs in this time.

Figure 29.11 shows the velocity–time graph for the motion of the squirrel. The velocity is negative for $0 < t < 3$ and positive for $3 < t < 5$. So the squirrel runs in the negative direction along the path for 3 seconds, then turns round and runs in the positive direction.

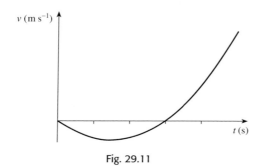

Fig. 29.11

(a) If the displacement from O after t seconds is s metres,

$$\frac{ds}{dt} = t^2 - 3t.$$

Since the displacement is zero when $t = 0$, the displacement after 5 seconds is given by

$$\int_0^5 (t^2 - 3t)\,dt = \left[\tfrac{1}{3} t^3 - \tfrac{3}{2} t^2 \right]_0^5$$
$$= \tfrac{1}{3} \times 125 - \tfrac{3}{2} \times 25 = 4\tfrac{1}{6}.$$

After 5 seconds the squirrel is $4\tfrac{1}{6}$ metres from O in the positive direction.

(b) To find the total distance it runs, you need to find the displacements of the squirrel in the two directions separately. These are given by

$$\int_0^3 (t^2 - 3t)\,dt = \left[\tfrac{1}{3} t^3 - \tfrac{3}{2} t^2 \right]_0^3$$
$$= \tfrac{1}{3} \times 27 - \tfrac{3}{2} \times 9 = -4\tfrac{1}{2}.$$

and $\displaystyle \int_3^5 (t^2 - 3t)\,dt = \left[\tfrac{1}{3} t^3 - \tfrac{3}{2} t^2 \right]_3^5$
$$= 4\tfrac{1}{6} - \left(-4\tfrac{1}{2} \right) = 8\tfrac{2}{3}.$$

So the squirrel runs $4\tfrac{1}{2}$ metres in the negative direction and then $8\tfrac{2}{3}$ metres in the positive direction. The total distance it runs is $\left(4\tfrac{1}{2} + 8\tfrac{2}{3} \right)$ metres, which is $13\tfrac{1}{6}$ metres.

> This example shows that the total distance is the sum of the areas above and below the axis, counting all areas as positive. But to find the total displacement areas below the axis must be counted as negative.

Negative definite integrals can also arise when you interchange the bounds of integration. Since

$$[I(x)]_b^a = I(a) - I(b)$$
$$= -(I(b) - I(a))$$
$$= -[I(x)]_a^b,$$

it follows that:

$$\int_b^a f(x)\,dx = -\int_a^b f(x)\,dx.$$

29.6   The area between a curve and the y-axis

When you find the area under a curve, the region whose area you are finding is bounded by parts of the x-axis and (possibly) two vertical lines with equations $x = a$ and $x = b$. The area is then given by $\int_a^b y\,dx$.

Sometimes you want to find the area of a region bounded by parts of the y-axis and (possibly) two horizontal lines with equations $y = c$ and $y = d$, as in Fig. 29.12. The method of calculating this is exactly the same, except that y and x are swapped round. The area is therefore given by $\int_c^d x\,dy$.

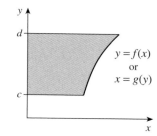

Fig. 29.12

The only new feature is that, if you are given the equation of the curve in the form $y = f(x)$, you must rearrange it in the form $x = g(y)$ before finding the integral.

Example 29.6.1
Find the area of the region bounded by parts of the y-axis, the lines $y = 1$ and $y = 8$ and the curve with equation $y = x\sqrt{x}$ (see Fig. 29.13).

The equation $y = x\sqrt{x}$ can be rewritten as $y^2 = x^3$, or as $x = y^{\frac{2}{3}}$ (for $y \geq 0$). So the area of the region is

$$\int_1^8 y^{\frac{2}{3}}\,dy = \left[\tfrac{3}{5}y^{\frac{5}{3}}\right]_1^8$$
$$= \tfrac{3}{5}(8^{\frac{5}{3}} - 1^{\frac{5}{3}})$$
$$= \tfrac{3}{5}(32 - 1) = 18.6.$$

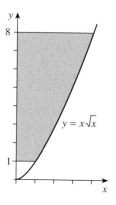

Fig. 29.13

Example 29.6.2
Figure 29.14 shows the part of the graph of $y^2 = 9 - x$ for which $x > 0$. Find the area between this curve and the y-axis.

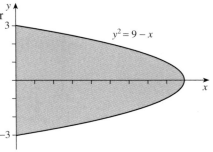

When $x = 0$, $y^2 = 9$, so $y = -3$ or $+3$.

The equation of the curve can be rearranged as $x = 9 - y^2$. So the area is

$$\int_{-3}^{3} (9 - y^2) \, dy = \left[9y - \tfrac{1}{3} y^3 \right]_{-3}^{3}$$
$$= 9(3 - (-3)) - \tfrac{1}{3}(27 - (-27))$$
$$= 9 \times 6 - \tfrac{1}{3} \times 54$$
$$= 54 - 18 = 36.$$

Fig. 29.14

29.7 Calculating other areas

You sometimes want to find the area of a region bounded by the graphs of two functions $f(x)$ and $g(x)$, and by two lines $x = a$ and $x = b$, as in Fig. 29.15.

Although you could find this as the difference of the areas of two regions of the kind illustrated in Fig. 29.1, calculated as

$$\int_{a}^{b} f(x) \, dx - \int_{a}^{b} g(x) \, dx,$$

it is often simpler to find it as a single integral

$$\int_{a}^{b} (f(x) - g(x)) \, dx.$$

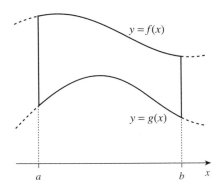

Fig. 29.15

Example 29.7.1
Figure 29.16 shows the graph of $y = x^2$ and the chord joining the points $(-1, 1)$ and $(2, 4)$ on the curve. Find the area of the shaded region between the curve and the chord.

The first step is to find the equation of the chord. Since the gradient is

$$\frac{4 - 1}{2 - (-1)} = \tfrac{3}{3} = 1,$$

its equation is

$$y - 1 = 1(x - (-1)), \quad \text{or more simply} \quad y = x + 2.$$

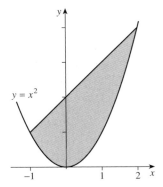

Fig. 29.16

To find the area, use the formula $\int_a^b (f(x) - g(x))\,dx$
with $f(x) = x + 2$, $g(x) = x^2$, $a = -1$ and $b = 2$.

$$\text{Area} = \int_{-1}^2 (x + 2 - x^2)\,dx$$
$$= \left[\tfrac{1}{2}x^2 + 2x - \tfrac{1}{3}x^3\right]_{-1}^2.$$

Because of the fractions, this is a calculation where it is simpler to carry out the subtractions term-by-term, as explained in Section 29.2. This gives the area as

$$\tfrac{1}{2}(2^2 - (-1)^2) + 2(2 - (-1)) - \tfrac{1}{3}(2^3 - (-1)^3)$$
$$= \tfrac{1}{2} \times 3 + 2 \times 3 - \tfrac{1}{3} \times 9$$
$$= 1\tfrac{1}{2} + 6 - 3 = 4\tfrac{1}{2}.$$

The area of the region between the curve and the chord is $4\tfrac{1}{2}$.

Notice that if you had used the formula with $f(x) = x^2$ and $g(x) = x + 2$ you would have got the answer $-4\tfrac{1}{2}$. This is because the curve lies below the chord in the interval $-1 < x < 2$. You should always try to choose the notation so that $f(x) \geq g(x)$ over the interval of values of x in which you are interested.

Example 29.7.2
Show that the graphs of $y = f(x)$ and $y = g(x)$, where $f(x) = x^3 - x^2 - 6x + 8$ and $g(x) = x^3 + 2x^2 - 1$, intersect at two points, and find the area of the region enclosed between the two curves.

The graphs intersect where the two values of y are equal, so that $f(x) = g(x)$. But before writing this as an equation for x, note that it can be written as $f(x) - g(x) = 0$.

Since you are going to need $f(x) - g(x)$ in the integral later, it will save work to begin by finding

$$f(x) - g(x) = (x^3 - x^2 - 6x + 8) - (x^3 + 2x^2 - 1)$$
$$= x^3 - x^2 - 6x + 8 - x^3 - 2x^2 + 1$$
$$= -3x^2 - 6x + 9$$
$$= -3(x^2 + 2x - 3)$$
$$= -3(x + 3)(x - 1).$$

The graphs intersect where this is 0, that is where $x = -3$ and $x = 1$. So there are two points of intersection, $(-3, -10)$ and $(1, 2)$.

Having got this far, you may find it helpful to display the two graphs on your calculator in the interval between these values of x.

You can also use this expression for $f(x) - g(x)$ in factors to check that $f(x) > g(x)$. If $-3 < x < 1$, $x + 3$ is positive and $x - 1$ is negative, so that $f(x) - g(x) > 0$ as required.

All that remains is to calculate the area between the graphs as

$$\int_{-3}^{1}(f(x)-g(x))\,dx = \int_{-3}^{1}(-3x^2-6x+9)\,dx$$
$$= \left[-x^3-3x^2+9x\right]_{-3}^{1}$$
$$= (-1-3+9)-(27-27-27)$$
$$= 5-(-27) = 32.$$

The area enclosed between the two graphs is 32.

> Notice that in this example, integrating $f(x)-g(x)$, rather than $f(x)$ and $g(x)$ separately, greatly reduces the amount of calculation.

Sometimes you need to find an area whose boundary includes part of a graph, but which is not the 'area under the graph' described in Section 29.1. Such areas can often be found by calculating the area under the graph and then adding or subtracting the area of some triangle or rectangle. Example 29.7.3 gives two typical calculations of this type.

Example 29.7.3
Figure 29.17 shows the part of the graph $y = 3 + 2x - x^2$ which lies in the first quadrant. Calculate the areas of the regions labelled A and B.

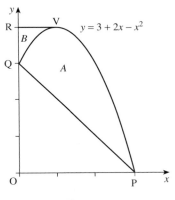

In factor form and completed square form,

$$3 + 2x - x^2 = (3-x)(1+x) = 4 - (x-1)^2.$$

Region A   Begin by finding the coordinates of P and Q, by putting $y = 0$ and $x = 0$ respectively. From the factor form, when $y = 0$, $x = 3$ (since $x > 0$). When $x = 0$, $y = 3$.

So P is $(3, 0)$ and Q is $(0, 3)$.

Fig. 29.17

If you add the triangle OPQ to the region A you get the region under the graph from $x = 0$ to $x = 3$, whose area is

$$\int_{0}^{3}(3+2x-x^2)\,dx = \left[3x+x^2-\tfrac{1}{3}x^3\right]_{0}^{3}$$
$$= (9+9-9)-(0) = 9.$$

The area of the triangle OPQ is $\tfrac{1}{2} \times 3 \times 3 = 4\tfrac{1}{2}$.

So the area of region A is $9 - 4\tfrac{1}{2} = 4\tfrac{1}{2}$.

Region B   From the completed square form, the coordinates of the vertex V
are $(1, 4)$.

Figure 29.18 shows that, if you add the region B to the
region under the graph from $x = 0$ to $x = 1$, you get the
rectangle ORVS, of width 1 and height 4.

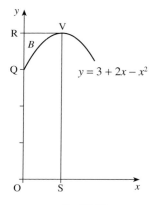

The area under the graph from $x = 0$ to $x = 1$ is

$$\int_0^1 (3 + 2x - x^2)\, dx = \left[3x + x^2 - \tfrac{1}{3}x^3 \right]_0^1$$
$$= (3 + 1 - \tfrac{1}{3}) - (0) = 3\tfrac{2}{3}.$$

The area of the rectangle is $1 \times 4 = 4$.

So the area of region B is $4 - 3\tfrac{2}{3} = \tfrac{1}{3}$.

Fig. 29.18

In Example 29.7.3 the region B is bounded on one side by part of
the y-axis, so you might expect to be able to calculate its area by
the method described in Section 29.6. But this involves rearranging the equation to give x in
terms of y. From the completed square form you can obtain

$$(x - 1)^2 = 4 - y.$$

This gives two values of x for each value of y less than 4. On the arc QV you want the smaller
of these, so

$$x = 1 - \sqrt{4 - y}.$$

The area of region B is therefore

$$\int_3^4 (1 - \sqrt{4 - y})\, dy.$$

Unfortunately you don't yet know how to integrate $\sqrt{4 - y}$. That is why it was necessary to use
a different method.

Exercise 29B

1 Evaluate $\displaystyle\int_0^2 3x(x - 2)\, dx$ and comment on your answer.

2 Find the area of the region bounded by parts of the y-axis, the curve $y = x^3$ and the lines
   $y = 1$ and $y = 27$.

3 Find the area of the region bounded by parts of the y-axis, the curve $y = \sqrt{x}$ and the lines
   $y = 1$ and $y = 4$.

4 Sketch the curve $y^2 = x + 4$, and find the area enclosed between this graph and the y-axis.
   Comment on any special features of this calculation.

5 Find the total area of the region shaded in each of the following diagrams.

(a)

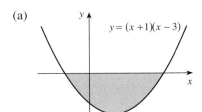

$y = (x+1)(x-3)$

(b)

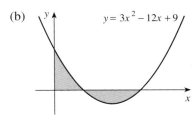

$y = 3x^2 - 12x + 9$

(c)

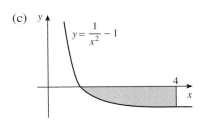

$y = \dfrac{1}{x^2} - 1$

(d)

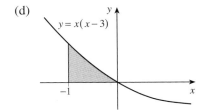

$y = x(x-3)$

6 A load is being lifted by a crane and moves in a vertical straight line. Initially the load is on the ground and after t seconds its velocity v m s^{-1} (measured upwards) is given by $v = \frac{3}{5}t(t-3)(t-4)$ for $0 \le t \le 4$.

(a) Sketch the (t, v) graph for the motion of the load.

(b) State when the magnitude of the acceleration is greatest, and calculate this greatest acceleration.

(c) State when the load is at its highest point, and find the acceleration at this instant.

(d) Find the height of the load above the ground when $t = 3$ and when $t = 4$.

(e) Sketch a graph showing the height of the load for $0 \le t \le 4$.

(f) Find the total distance moved by the load.

7 The diagram shows the graphs of
$y = 2x + 7$ and $y = 10 - x$.
Find the area of the shaded region.

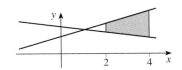

8 Find the area enclosed between the curves $y = x^2 + 7$ and $y = 2x^2 + 3$.

9 Find the area enclosed between the straight line $y = 12x + 14$ and the curve $y = 3x^2 + 6x + 5$.

10 Find the area between the curves $y = (x-4)(3x-1)$ and $y = (4-x)(1+x)$.

11 The diagram shows the graph of $y = \sqrt{x}$.
Given that the area of the shaded region is
72, find the value of the constant a.

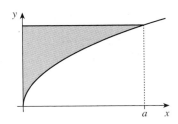

12 Parts of the graphs of $f(x) = 2x^3 + x^2 - 8x$ and $g(x) = 2x^3 - 3x - 4$ enclose a finite region. Find its area.

13 Find the area of the region shaded in each of the following diagrams.

(a)

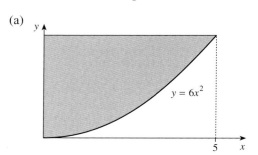

$y = 6x^2$

(b)

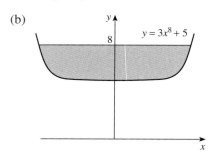

$y = 3x^8 + 5$

14 The diagram shows the graph of $y = 9x^2$. The point P has coordinates $(4, 144)$. Find the area of the shaded region.

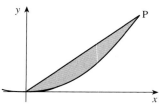

15 The diagram shows the graph of $y = \dfrac{1}{\sqrt{x}}$. Show that the area of the shaded region is $3 - \dfrac{5\sqrt{3}}{3}$.

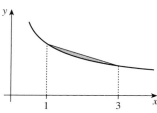

30 Geometric sequences

This chapter introduces another type of sequence, in which the ratio of successive terms is constant. When you have completed it, you should

- recognise geometric sequences and be able to do calculations on them
- know and be able to obtain the formula for the sum of a geometric series
- know the condition for a geometric series to converge, and how to find its limiting sum.

30.1 Geometric sequences

In Chapter 2 you met arithmetic sequences, in which you get from one term to the next by adding a constant. A sequence in which you get from one term to the next by multiplying by a constant is called a geometric sequence.

Example 30.1.1
Show that the numbers 4, 12, 36, 108 form a geometric sequence. If the sequence is continued, find　(a) the next two terms,　(b) the twentieth term.

Since　$12 = 4 \times 3$,　$36 = 12 \times 3$,　$108 = 36 \times 3$,

there is a constant multiplying factor of 3. So the numbers form a geometric sequence.

(a) The next term is $108 \times 3 = 324$, and the term after that is $324 \times 3 = 972$.

(b) To get from the first term to the twentieth you have to multiply by 3 nineteen times. So the twentieth term is 4×3^{19}. Correct to 4 significant figures, this is 4649 million.

Example 30.1.2
The first two terms of a geometric sequence are 4, 20 and the last term is 62 500. How many terms are there altogether?

To get from the first term to the second you must multiply by $\dfrac{20}{4} = 5$. To get from the first term to the last you must multiply by $\dfrac{62\,500}{4} = 15\,625$, which is 5^6.

So, going one step at a time, you start at the first term and then multiply by 5 six times. This means that 62 500 is the seventh term of the sequence.

A general definition for this kind of sequence is:

> A **geometric sequence**, or **geometric progression**, is a sequence defined by $u_1 = a$ and $u_n = r u_{n-1}$, where $a \neq 0, r \neq 0$ or 1, and $n = 2,3, \dots$.
>
> The constant r is called the **common ratio** of the sequence.

Notice that the ratios 0 and 1 are excluded. If you put $r = 0$ in the definition you get the sequence $a, 0, 0, 0, \ldots$; if you put $r = 1$ you get the sequence $a, a, a, a, \ldots$. Neither is very interesting, and some of the properties of geometric sequences break down if $r = 0$ or 1. However, r can be negative; in that case the terms are alternately positive and negative. For a similar reason $a = 0$ is excluded, since this would give you the sequence $0, 0, 0, 0, \ldots$.

It is easy to give a formula for the nth term. To get from u_1 to u_n you multiply by the common ratio $n - 1$ times, so $u_n = r^{n-1} \times u_1$, which gives $u_n = ar^{n-1}$.

> The nth term of a geometric sequence with first term a and common ratio r is ar^{n-1}.

Example 30.1.3
The first two terms of a geometric sequence are 10 and 11. Show that the first term greater than 1000 is the fiftieth.

The common ratio is $11 \div 10 = 1.1$. The nth term of the sequence is therefore $10 \times 1.1^{n-1}$.

Each term of the sequence is greater than the preceding term. You therefore have to show that the 49th term is less than 1000, and that the 50th term is greater than 1000.

The 49th term is $10 \times 1.1^{49-1} = 10 \times 1.1^{48} = 970.17\ldots$.

The 50th term is $10 \times 1.1^{50-1} = 10 \times 1.1^{49} = 1067.18\ldots$.

So the first term greater than 1000 is the fiftieth.

Example 30.1.4
Show that there are two geometric sequences whose first term is 5 and whose fifth term is 80. For each of these sequences, find the tenth term.

Since the first term is given, the sequence is determined by knowing the common ratio r. The fifth term is $5 \times r^{5-1} = 5 \times r^4$.

If $5 \times r^4 = 80$, $r^4 = 16$, so $r = \pm 2$.

The two sequences are $5, 10, 20, 40, 80, \ldots$ and $5, -10, 20, -40, 80, \ldots$.

The tenth term is $5 \times r^{10-1} = 5 \times r^9$.

So when $r = 2$, the tenth term is $5 \times 2^9 = 5 \times 512 = 2560$; when $r = -2$, the tenth term is $5 \times (-2)^9 = 5 \times (-512) = -2560$.

30.2 Graphs of geometric sequences

With a calculator it is easy to produce graphs of geometric sequences, using the method described in Section 9.6. To enter the sequence you can use either the inductive definition or the formula for the nth term.

For example, to get the graph of the sequence in Example 30.1.3 you could enter either

$$u_n = 10 \times 1.1^{n-1} \qquad \text{or} \qquad u_1 = 10, \quad u_n = 1.1 \times u_{n-1}.$$

You would then get a graph like Fig. 30.1. You will notice that the points soon disappear off the top of the window.

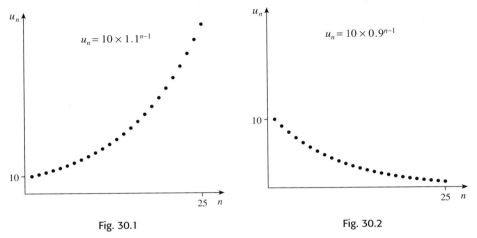

Fig. 30.1   Fig. 30.2

But this doesn't happen with all geometric sequences. If you repeat the experiment with 0.9 in place of 1.1, entering either

$$u_n = 10 \times 0.9^{n-1} \quad \text{or} \quad u_1 = 10, \quad u_n = 0.9 \times u_{n-1},$$

you will get a display like Fig. 30.2. These points will never disappear off the top of the window, however far you go. In fact, by making n large enough, points can be found as close as you like to the horizontal axis.

What happens if the common ratio r is negative? Try producing similar displays with -1.1 or -0.9 in place of 1.1. You will then get graphs like Fig. 30.3 and Fig. 30.4.

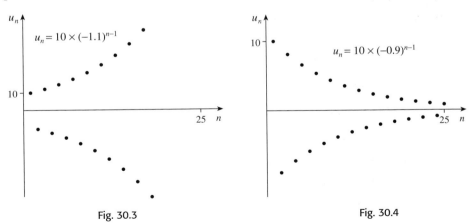

Fig. 30.3   Fig. 30.4

Comparing Fig. 30.3 with Fig. 30.1, or Fig. 30.4 with Fig. 30.2, you will see that all the points for odd values of n are the same in both graphs; but those for even values of n are reflections of each other in the horizontal axis. So the points in Fig. 30.3 soon disappear off the top or bottom of the window, but those in Fig. 30.4 approach the horizontal axis as n increases.

Try experimenting with other values of r and a for yourself. What happens if $r = -1$? Or if $r = 1$? (Look back at the definition in Section 30.1!)

The results can be summed up using the idea of convergence to a limit (see Section 9.6).

If a geometric sequence u_n has common ratio r, then

if $|r| < 1$, $\lim\limits_{n \to \infty} u_n = 0$;

if $r > 1$ or $r \le -1$, u_n does not converge to a limit as $n \to \infty$.

Exercise 30A

1 For each of the following geometric sequences find the common ratio and the next two terms.

(a) $3, 6, 12, \ldots$ (b) $2, 8, 32, \ldots$ (c) $32, 16, 8, \ldots$

(d) $2, -6, 18, -54, \ldots$ (e) $1.1, 1.21, 1.331, \ldots$ (f) $x^2, x, 1, \ldots$

2 Find an expression for the nth term of each of the following geometric sequences.

(a) $2, 6, 18, \ldots$ (b) $10, 5, 2.5, \ldots$ (c) $1, -2, 4, \ldots$

(d) $81, 27, 9, \ldots$ (e) $x, x^2, x^3, \ldots$ (f) $pq^2, q^3, p^{-1}q^4, \ldots$

Which of these sequences have terms which converge to 0 as $n \to \infty$?

3 Find the number of terms in each of these geometric progressions.

(a) $2, 4, 8, \ldots, 2048$ (b) $1, -3, 9, \ldots, 531\,441$

(c) $2, 6, 18, \ldots, 1458$ (d) $5, -10, 20, \ldots, -40\,960$

(e) $16, 12, 9, \ldots, 3.796\,875$ (f) $x^{-6}, x^{-2}, x^2, \ldots, x^{42}$

4 Find the common ratio and the first term in the geometric progressions where

(a) the 2nd term is 4 and the 5th term is 108,

(b) the 3rd term is 6 and the 7th term is 96,

(c) the 4th term is $19\,683$ and the 9th term is 81,

(d) the 3rd term is 8 and the 9th term is 64.

5 If x, y and z are the first three terms of a geometric sequence, show that x^2, y^2 and z^2 form another geometric sequence.

6 Different numbers x, y and z are the first three terms of a geometric progression with common ratio r, and also the first, second and fourth terms of an arithmetic progression.

(a) Find the value of r.

(b) Find which term of the arithmetic progression will next be equal to a term of the geometric progression.

7 Different numbers x, y and z are the first three terms of a geometric progression with common ratio r and also the first, second and fifth terms of an arithmetic progression.

(a) Find the value of r.

(b) Find which term of the arithmetic progression will next be equal to a term of the geometric progression.

30.3 Summing geometric series

Geometric sequences have many applications in finance, biology, mechanics and probability, and you often need to find the sum of all the terms. In this context it is usual to call the sequence a **geometric series**.

The method used in Chapter 2 to find the sum of an arithmetic series does not work for geometric series. You can see this by taking a simple geometric series like

$$1 + 2 + 4 + 8 + 16$$

and placing an upside-down copy next to it, as in Fig. 30.5.

When you did this with an arithmetic series the two sets of crosses and noughts made a perfect join (see Fig. 2.5), so they could easily be counted; but for the geometric series in Fig. 30.5 there is a gap in the middle.

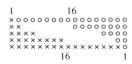

Fig. 30.5

For geometric series a different method is used to find the sum. If you multiply the equation

$$S = 1 + 2 + 4 + 8 + 16$$

by 2, then you get

$$2S = 2 + 4 + 8 + 16 + 32.$$

Notice that the right sides in these two equations have the terms $2 + 4 + 8 + 16$ in common. If you put all the other terms on the left sides, you get

$$S - 1 = 2 + 4 + 8 + 16$$

and

$$2S - 32 = 2 + 4 + 8 + 16.$$

So

$$S - 1 = 2S - 32, \quad \text{giving} \quad S = 31.$$

You can use this method to find the sum of any geometric series. Let S be the sum of the first n terms of the series. Then

$$S = a + ar + ar^2 + \ldots + ar^{n-2} + ar^{n-1}.$$

If you multiply this equation by r, you get

$$Sr = ar + ar^2 + ar^3 + \ldots + ar^{n-1} + ar^n.$$

The right sides in these two equations have the terms $ar + ar^2 + ... + ar^{n-2} + ar^{n-1}$ in common; so

$$S - a = ar + ar^2 + ... + ar^{n-2} + ar^{n-1},$$

and

$$Sr - ar^n = ar + ar^2 + ... + ar^{n-2} + ar^{n-1}.$$

Therefore

$$S - a = Sr - ar^n,$$
$$S - Sr = a - ar^n,$$
$$S(1 - r) = a(1 - r^n).$$

That is,

$$S = \frac{a(1 - r^n)}{1 - r}.$$

The **sum** S of the geometric series $a + ar + ar^2 + ... + ar^{n-1}$, with n terms, is given by

$$S = \frac{a(1 - r^n)}{1 - r}.$$

Example 30.3.1

Find the sums of the geometric series having 9 terms with

(a) first term 6561, common ratio $\frac{1}{3}$;   (b) first term 1, common ratio 3;

(c) first term 1, common ratio -3.

(a) Setting $a = 6561$, $r = \frac{1}{3}$ and $n = 9$ in the formula gives the sum

$$\frac{6561\left(1 - \left(\frac{1}{3}\right)^9\right)}{1 - \frac{1}{3}} = \frac{6561 \times \left(1 - \frac{1}{19\,683}\right)}{\frac{2}{3}} = 6561 \times \frac{19\,682}{19\,683} \times \frac{3}{2} = 9841.$$

(b) Setting $a = 1$, $r = 3$ and $n = 9$ in the formula gives the sum

$$\frac{1(1 - 3^9)}{1 - 3} = \frac{1 - 19\,683}{-2} = \frac{-19\,682}{-2} = 9841.$$

Can you see why the answers to parts (a) and (b) are the same?

(c) Setting $a = 1$, $r = -3$ and $n = 9$ in the formula gives the sum

$$\frac{1(1 - (-3)^9)}{1 - (-3)} = \frac{1 - (-19\,683)}{1 - (-3)} = \frac{1 + 19\,683}{1 + 3} = \frac{19\,684}{4} = 4921.$$

There are two points to notice in this example about the use of the formula for the sum.

- In part (c) it is used with a negative value of r. The algebraic argument used to produce the formula is equally valid whether r is positive or negative. The only value of r for which it breaks down is 1; but in the definition of a geometric sequence in Section 30.1 the value $r = 1$ is specifically excluded.

- In part (b), where r is greater than 1, both $1 - r^n$ and $1 - r$ are negative, so that when you apply the formula you get a fraction in which the top and the bottom are both negative. You could avoid the minus signs by noting that $1 - r^n = -(r^n - 1)$ and $1 - r = -(r - 1)$, so that

$$\frac{a(1 - r^n)}{1 - r} = \frac{-a(r^n - 1)}{-(r - 1)} = \frac{a(r^n - 1)}{r - 1}.$$

Some people like to use the formula in this alternative form when $r > 1$; it is one more result to remember, but you avoid the inconvenience of the minus signs. It's a matter of choice.

Example 30.3.2
A geometric series which begins $4 + 5 + \ldots$ has 15 terms. Find the sum, and compare it with the sum of the corresponding arithmetic series.

Since the first two terms are 4 and 5, the common ratio is $\frac{5}{4} = 1.25$. So the formula gives the sum of the geometric series as

$$\frac{4(1 - 1.25^{15})}{1 - 1.25} = \frac{4(1 - 28.42\ldots)}{-0.25}$$
$$= (-16) \times (-27.42\ldots)$$
$$= 438.7\ldots = 439 \text{ to the nearest integer.}$$

For the arithmetic series the common difference is 1. So the formula $S = \frac{1}{2}n(2a + (n - 1)d)$ in Section 2.5 gives

$$S = \frac{1}{2} \times 15(2 \times 4 + 14 \times 1) = 165.$$

The sum of the geometric series is between $2\frac{1}{2}$ and 3 times as large as the sum of the arithmetic series.

If you display graphs of the terms of both series on your calculator using the same axes, you will see why the sum of the geometric series is so much greater than the sum of the arithmetic series.

Example 30.3.3

(a) The first and last terms of a geometric series are a and l, and the common ratio is r. Show that the sum of the series is $\dfrac{a - lr}{1 - r}$.

(b) Given that $5 + 15 + ... + 10\,935$ is a geometric series, find what proportion of the sum is contributed by the last term.

(a) From the sum formula

$$S = \frac{a(1 - r^n)}{1 - r} = \frac{a - ar^n}{1 - r} = \frac{a - (ar^{n-1})r}{1 - r}.$$

Since the last term $l = ar^{n-1}$,

$$S = \frac{a - lr}{1 - r}.$$

(b) The series has common ratio $\frac{15}{5} = 3$. Substituting $a = 5$, $r = 3$ and $l = 10\,935$ in the formula in part (a),

$$S = \frac{5 - 3 \times 10\,935}{1 - 3} = \frac{-32\,800}{-2} = 16\,400.$$

The proportion of this sum contributed by the last term is $\dfrac{10\,935}{16\,400} = 0.667...$, which is just over $\frac{2}{3}$.

Example 30.3.4

A child lives 200 metres from school. He walks 60 metres in the first minute, and in each subsequent minute he walks 75% of the distance he walked in the previous minute. Show that he takes between 6 and 7 minutes to get to school.

The distances walked in the first, second, third, ... , nth minutes are $60\,\text{m}$, $60 \times 0.75\,\text{m}$, $60 \times 0.75^2\,\text{m}$, ... , $60 \times 0.75^{n-1}\,\text{m}$. In the first n minutes the child walks S_n metres, where

$$S_n = 60 + 60 \times 0.75^1 + 60 \times 0.75^2 + ... + 60 \times 0.75^{n-1}$$
$$= \frac{60(1 - 0.75^n)}{1 - 0.75} = \frac{60(1 - 0.75^n)}{0.25} = 240(1 - 0.75^n).$$

From this formula you can calculate that

$$S_6 = 240(1 - 0.75^6) = 240(1 - 0.177...) = 197.2...,$$

and $\quad S_7 = 240(1 - 0.75^7) = 240(1 - 0.133...) = 207.9... .$

So he has not reached school after 6 minutes, but (if he had gone on walking) he would have gone more than $200\,\text{m}$ in 7 minutes. That is, he takes between 6 and 7 minutes to walk to school.

Example 30.3.5

Show that $\sum\limits_{i=1}^{10} 2 \times 3^i$ is the sum of a geometric progression, and find its value.

Notice the use of the suffix i to describe the general term of the series. See Section 2.6.

To interpret an expression in $\sum$ notation, it is usually enough to write out the first three terms and the last term. In this case,

$$\sum_{i=1}^{10} 2 \times 3^i = 2 \times 3^1 + 2 \times 3^2 + 2 \times 3^3 + ... + 2 \times 3^{10}$$

$$= 6 + 18 + 54 + ... + 2 \times 3^{10}.$$

To get from each term to the next you multiply by 3. So this is a geometric series with $a = 6$, $r = 3$ and $n = 10$.

Notice that 2×3^i is the same as $2 \times (3 \times 3^{i-1}) = 6 \times 3^{i-1}$. You will recognise this as the standard way of writing the ith term of a geometric sequence, ar^{i-1}, with $a = 6$ and $r = 3$.

The formula for the sum of a geometric series then gives

$$\sum_{i=1}^{10} 2 \times 3^i = \frac{6(1 - 3^{10})}{1 - 3} = \frac{-6(3^{10} - 1)}{-2} = 3(3^{10} - 1) = 177\,144.$$

Example 30.3.6

Find a simple expression for the sum $p^6 - p^5q + p^4q^2 - p^3q^3 + p^2q^4 - pq^5 + q^6$.

This is a geometric series of 7 terms, with first term p^6 and common ratio $-\dfrac{q}{p}$. Its sum is therefore

$$\frac{p^6(1 - (-q/p)^7)}{1 - (-q/p)} = \frac{p^6(1 - (-q^7/p^7))}{1 + q/p} = \frac{p^7(1 + q^7/p^7)}{p(1 + q/p)} = \frac{p^7 + q^7}{p + q}.$$

Another way of writing the result of this example is

$$p^7 + q^7 = (p + q)(p^6 - p^5q + p^4q^2 - p^3q^3 + p^2q^4 - pq^5 + q^6).$$

You can use a similar method for any odd number n to express $p^n + q^n$ as the product of $p + q$ and another factor.

Exercise 30B

1 Find the sum, for the given number of terms, of each of the following geometric series. Give decimal answers correct to 4 places.

(a) $2 + 6 + 18 + ...$ 10 terms

(b) $2 - 6 + 18 - ...$ 10 terms

(c) $1 + \frac{1}{2} + \frac{1}{4} + ...$ 8 terms

(d) $1 - \frac{1}{2} + \frac{1}{4} - ...$ 8 terms

(e) $3 + 6 + 12 + ...$ 12 terms

(f) $12 - 4 + \frac{4}{3} - ...$ 10 terms

2 Find the sum of each of the following geometric series. Give numerical answers in parts (a) to (g) as rational numbers.

(a) $1 + 2 + 4 + ... + 1024$

(b) $1 - 2 + 4 - ... + 1024$

(c) $3 + 12 + 48 + ... + 196\,608$

(d) $1 + \frac{1}{2} + \frac{1}{4} + ... + \frac{1}{512}$

(e) $1 - \frac{1}{3} + \frac{1}{9} - ... - \frac{1}{19\,683}$

(f) $10 + 5 + 2.5 + ... + 0.156\,25$

(g) $\frac{1}{4} + \frac{1}{16} + \frac{1}{64} + ... + \frac{1}{1024}$

(h) $1 + \frac{1}{2} + \frac{1}{4} + ... + \frac{1}{2^n}$

3 Find the sum of each of the following geometric series. Give numerical answers as rational numbers.

(a) $\sum_{i=1}^{5} 3 \times 2^{i-1}$

(b) $\sum_{i=1}^{4} 2 \times (-2)^{i-1}$

(c) $\sum_{i=1}^{8} 16 \times \left(\frac{1}{2}\right)^{i-1}$

(d) $\sum_{i=1}^{7} 4^i$

4 A well-known story concerns the inventor of the game of chess. As a reward for inventing the game it is rumoured that he was asked to choose his own prize. He asked for 1 grain of rice to be placed on the first square of the board, 2 grains on the second square, 4 grains on the third square and so on in geometric progression until all 64 squares had been covered. Calculate the total number of grains of rice he would have received. Give your answer in standard form!

5 A problem similar to that of Question 4 is posed by the child who negotiates a pocket money deal of 1 cent on 1 February, 2 cents on 2 February, 4 cents on 3 February and so on for 28 days. How much should the child receive in total during February?

6 A firm sponsors a local orchestra for seven years. It agrees to give $2500 in the first year, and to increase its contribution by 20% each year. Show that the amounts contributed each year form a geometric sequence. How much does the firm give the orchestra altogether during the period of sponsorship?

7 An explorer sets out across the desert with 100 litres of water. He uses 6 litres on the first day. On subsequent days he rations himself to 95% of the amount he used the day before. Show that he has enough water to last for 34 days, but no more. How much will he then have left?

8 A competitor in a pie-eating contest eats one-third of his pie in the first minute. In each subsequent minute he eats three-quarters of the amount he ate in the previous minute. Find an expression for the amount of pie he has left to eat after n minutes. Show that he takes between 4 and 5 minutes to finish the pie.

9 Find expressions for the sum of n terms of the following series. Give your answer, in terms of n and x, in as simple a form as possible.

(a) $x + x^2 + x^3 + ...$ n terms

(b) $x - x^2 + x^3 - ...$ n terms

30.4   Convergent geometric series

Take any sequence, such as the sequence of triangle numbers $t_1 = 1$, $t_2 = 3$, $t_3 = 6$, ... (see Section 2.3). Form a new sequence whose terms are the sums of successive triangle numbers:

$$S_1 = t_1 = 1, \quad S_2 = t_1 + t_2 = 1 + 3 = 4, \quad S_3 = t_1 + t_2 + t_3 = 1 + 3 + 6 = 10, \text{ and so on.}$$

This is called the sum sequence of the original sequence.

Notice that $S_2 = S_1 + t_2$, $\quad S_3 = S_2 + t_3$, ...

This property can be used to give an inductive definition for the sum sequence of any sequence u_i:

> For a given sequence u_i, the **sum sequence** $S_n = u_1 + ... + u_n$ is defined by $S_1 = u_1$ and $S_n = S_{n-1} + u_n$.

If the original sequence begins with u_0 rather than u_1, the equation $S_1 = u_1$ in the definition is replaced by $S_0 = u_0$.

Example 30.4.1
A sequence is given by the formula $u_n = n^3$ for $n = 1, 2, 3, ...$. Find the first five terms of its sum sequence.

The terms of the sequence u_n are

$$u_1 = 1, \quad u_2 = 8, \quad u_3 = 27, \quad u_4 = 64, \quad u_5 = 125, \quad ... \ .$$

So the terms of the sum sequence S_n are

$$S_1 = 1, \quad S_2 = 1 + 8 = 9, \quad S_3 = 9 + 27 = 36,$$
$$S_4 = 36 + 64 = 100, \quad S_5 = 100 + 125 = 225, \quad ... \ .$$

> What general rule does this suggest?

The inductive definition for a sum sequence can be used to obtain its graph. For example, for the geometric sequence given by $u_i = 10 \times 1.1^{i-1}$, whose graph was shown in Fig. 30.1, the sum sequence is defined inductively by

$$S_1 = 10, \quad S_n = S_{n-1} + 10 \times 1.1^{n-1}.$$

Use your calculator to show the graph of the sequence S_n. You will get a display like Fig. 30.6.

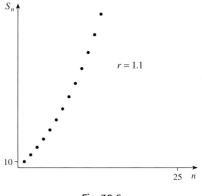

Fig. 30.6

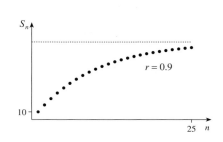

Fig. 30.7

This is not very interesting. But if you carry out the same procedure for the sequence whose graph was shown in Fig. 30.2, with 1.1 replaced by 0.9, the result is more surprising. The equations

$$S_1 = 10, \quad S_n = S_{n-1} + 10 \times 0.9^{n-1}$$

produce a display like Fig. 30.7.

This looks as if it might converge to a limit. To check this, add a horizontal line to the display, and move it up the window until it appears to lie above all the points of the graph.

This is the dotted line in Fig. 30.7. What does this suggest for the limit of S_n?

You can check this by using the formula for S_n, with $a = 10$ and $r = 0.9$. This gives

$$S_n = \frac{10(1 - 0.9^n)}{1 - 0.9}$$
$$= \frac{10(1 - 0.9^n)}{0.1}$$
$$= 100 - 100 \times 0.9^n.$$

Now when n is a large number, 0.9^n becomes very small. (Try calculating 0.9^{1000}.) In the limit, as n tends to infinity, 0.9^n tends to 0. So

$$\lim_{n \to \infty} S_n = 100.$$

Does this agree with the estimate you made from the graph of S_n?

Something similar happens with the sequence whose graph was shown in Fig. 30.4, with common ratio -0.9. The equations

$$S_1 = 10, \quad S_n = S_{n-1} + 10 \times (-0.9)^{n-1}$$

produce a display like Fig. 30.8.

This also seems to be converging to a limit; but to find this limit you have to squeeze the horizontal line between the sequence of points for odd n and the sequence for even n. It is not so easy to guess the value of this limit.

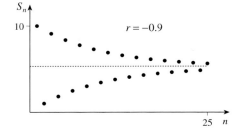

Fig. 30.8

The formula for S_n is now

$$S_n = \frac{10(1 - (-0.9)^n)}{1 - (-0.9)}$$
$$= \tfrac{100}{19} - \tfrac{100}{19} \times (-0.9)^n.$$

Now $(-0.9)^n$ is positive if n is even and negative if n is odd. So S_n is less than $\tfrac{100}{19}$ if n is even, and greater if n is odd. Also $(-0.9)^n$ tends to 0 as n tends to infinity. So

$$\lim_{n \to \infty} S_n = \tfrac{100}{19} = 5.263\ldots .$$

How close is this to your estimate from the graph?

By now you will see how the argument goes in general. The sum sequence for the general sequence $u_i = ar^{i-1}$ is given by

$$S_n = \frac{a(1 - r^n)}{1 - r}$$
$$= \frac{a}{1 - r} - \frac{a}{1 - r} \times r^n.$$

The only part of this expression which involves n is r^n. Whether or not S_n tends to a limit depends on the size of r, or more precisely on the size of $|r|$. If $|r| > 1$, then $|r^n|$ increases without limit as n increases. But if $|r| < 1$, then r^n tends to 0 as n tends to infinity. In that case,

$$\lim_{n \to \infty} S_n = \frac{a}{1 - r}.$$

> If $-1 < r < 1$, the sum of the geometric series with first term a and common ratio r tends to the limit $S_\infty = \dfrac{a}{1 - r}$ as the number of terms tends to infinity.
>
> The infinite geometric series is then said to be **convergent**.
>
> S_∞ is called the **sum to infinity** of the series.

Example 30.4.2
A geometric series begins $9 + 6 + 4 + \dots$. Find an expression for the sum of the first n terms. Show that the series is convergent, and find the sum to infinity.

The series has common ratio $\dfrac{6}{9} = \dfrac{2}{3}$. Since $a = 9$, the sum of the first n terms is

$$\frac{9\left(1 - \left(\frac{2}{3}\right)^n\right)}{1 - \frac{2}{3}} = \frac{9}{\frac{1}{3}}\left(1 - \left(\tfrac{2}{3}\right)^n\right) = 27\left(1 - \left(\tfrac{2}{3}\right)^n\right).$$

Since the common ratio is between -1 and 1, the series is convergent. The sum to infinity is $\dfrac{9}{1 - \frac{2}{3}} = \dfrac{9}{\frac{1}{3}} = 27$.

Example 30.4.3
The first term of a convergent geometric series is 20, and its sum to infinity is 15. Find the common ratio, and an expression for the sum of the first n terms.

If the common ratio is r, $\dfrac{20}{1 - r} = 15$.

So
$$20 = 15 - 15r,$$
$$15r = -5,$$
$$r = -\tfrac{1}{3}.$$

The sum of the first n terms is therefore

$$\frac{20\left(1 - \left(-\frac{1}{3}\right)^n\right)}{1 - \left(-\frac{1}{3}\right)} = \frac{20}{\frac{4}{3}}\left(1 - \left(-\tfrac{1}{3}\right)^n\right) = 15\left(1 - \left(-\tfrac{1}{3}\right)^n\right).$$

Example 30.4.4

Express the recurring decimal 0.296 296 296... as a fraction.

The decimal can be written as

$$0.296 + 0.000\ 296 + 0.000\ 000\ 296 + ...$$
$$= 0.296 + 0.296 \times 0.001 + 0.296 \times (0.001)^2 + ... ,$$

which is a geometric series with $a = 0.296$ and $r = 0.001$. Since $-1 < r < 1$, the series is convergent with limiting sum $\dfrac{0.296}{1 - 0.001} = \dfrac{296}{999}$.

Since $296 = 8 \times 37$ and $999 = 27 \times 37$, this fraction in its simplest form is $\frac{8}{27}$.

Example 30.4.5

A beetle starts at a point O on the floor. It walks 1 m east, then $\frac{1}{2}$ m west, then $\frac{1}{4}$ m east, and so on, halving the distance at each change of direction. How far from O does it end up?

The final distance from O is $1 - \frac{1}{2} + \frac{1}{4} - \frac{1}{8} + ...$, which is a geometric series with common ratio $-\frac{1}{2}$. Since $-1 < -\frac{1}{2} < 1$, the series converges to a limit

$$\frac{1}{1 - (-1/2)} = \frac{1}{3/2} = \frac{2}{3}.$$

The beetle ends up $\frac{2}{3}$ m from O.

> Notice that a point of trisection was obtained as the limit of a process of repeated halving.

Here is a summary of what you now know about a geometric sequence u_n. You may if you prefer use u_1 rather than a to denote the first term. The properties then take the form:

For $n = 1, 2, 3, ...$, the nth term is $u_n = u_1 r^{n-1}$, where $r \neq 0$ or 1.

The sum of n terms is $S_n = \dfrac{u_1(1 - r^n)}{1 - r}$.

(If $r > 1$, you may prefer to use this in the form $S_n = \dfrac{u_1(r^n - 1)}{r - 1}$.)

If $|r| < 1$, this sum converges to the limit $S_\infty = \dfrac{u_1}{1 - r}$.

30.5 Using sigma notation

Sigma notation can be used to represent a sum to infinity for a convergent series. The sum to infinity of a series with general term u_i is written as $\sum\limits_{i=1}^{\infty} u_i$. In the case of a convergent geometric series with common ratio r such that $-1 < r < 1$, the ith term is ar^{i-1}. So the sum to infinity is $\sum\limits_{i=1}^{\infty} ar^{i-1}$.

$$\text{If } -1 < r < 1, \sum_{i=1}^{\infty} ar^{i-1} = \frac{a}{1-r}.$$

Example 30.5.1

The ith term of a geometric progression is $\left(\frac{1}{4}\right)^i$. Find the first term, the common ratio and $\sum\limits_{i=1}^{\infty} \left(\frac{1}{4}\right)^i$.

The series begins

$$\left(\tfrac{1}{4}\right)^1 + \left(\tfrac{1}{4}\right)^2 + \left(\tfrac{1}{4}\right)^3 + \dots = \tfrac{1}{4} + \tfrac{1}{16} + \tfrac{1}{64} + \dots.$$

The first term is $\frac{1}{4}$, and the common ratio is $\frac{1}{16} \div \frac{1}{4} = \frac{1}{4}$.

Using the formula $\sum\limits_{i=1}^{\infty} ar^{i-1} = \dfrac{a}{1-r}$ with $a = \frac{1}{4}$ and $r = \frac{1}{4}$,

$$\sum_{i=1}^{\infty} \left(\tfrac{1}{4}\right)^i = \frac{\tfrac{1}{4}}{1-\tfrac{1}{4}} = \tfrac{1}{3}.$$

Exercise 30C

1 Find the sum to infinity of the following geometric series. Give your answers to parts (a) to (j) as whole numbers, fractions or exact decimals.

(a) $1 + \frac{1}{2} + \frac{1}{4} + \dots$

(b) $1 + \frac{1}{3} + \frac{1}{9} + \dots$

(c) $\frac{1}{5} + \frac{1}{25} + \frac{1}{125} + \dots$

(d) $0.1 + 0.01 + 0.001 + \dots$

(e) $1 - \frac{1}{3} + \frac{1}{9} - \dots$

(f) $0.2 - 0.04 + 0.008 - \dots$

(g) $\frac{3}{2} + \frac{3}{4} + \frac{3}{8} + \dots$

(h) $\frac{1}{2} - \frac{1}{4} + \frac{1}{8} - \dots$

(i) $10 - 5 + 2.5 - \dots$

(j) $50 + 10 + 2 + \dots$

(k) $x + x^2 + x^3 + \dots$, where $-1 < x < 1$

(l) $1 - x^2 + x^4 - \dots$, where $x^2 < 1$

(m) $1 + x^{-1} + x^{-2} + \dots$, where $x > 1$

(n) $x^2 - x + 1 - \dots$, where $x > 1$

2 Express each of the following recurring decimals as exact fractions.

(a) 0.363 636...

(b) 0.123 123 123...

(c) 0.555...

(d) 0.471 471 471...

(e) 0.142 857 142 857 142 857...

(f) 0.285 714 285 714 285 714...

(g) 0.714 285 714 285 714 285...

(h) 0.857 142 857 142 857 142...

3 Find the common ratio of a geometric series which has a first term of 5 and a sum to infinity of 6.

4 Find the common ratio of a geometric series which has a first term of 11 and a sum to infinity of 6.

5 Find the first term of a geometric series which has a common ratio of $\frac{3}{4}$ and a sum to infinity of 12.

6 Find the first term of a geometric series which has a common ratio of $-\frac{3}{5}$ and a sum to infinity of 12.

7 Identify the general term u_i for the following geometric progressions. Also find $\sum_{i=1}^{10} u_i$ and, if the series is convergent, $\sum_{i=1}^{\infty} u_i$.

(a) $1 + \frac{1}{5} + \frac{1}{25} + \frac{1}{125} + \dots$

(b) $2 + 4 + 8 + 16 + \dots$

(c) $4 + 2 + 1 + \frac{1}{2} + \frac{1}{4} + \dots$

(d) $1 - \frac{1}{10} + \frac{1}{100} - \frac{1}{1000} + \dots$

8 In Example 30.4.5 a beetle starts at a point O on the floor. It walks 1 m east, then $\frac{1}{2}$ m west, then $\frac{1}{4}$ m east and so on. It finishes $\frac{2}{3}$ m to the east of O. How far does it actually walk?

9 A beetle starts at a point O on the floor and walks 0.6 m east, then 0.36 m west, 0.216 m east and so on. Find its final position and how far it actually walks.

10 A 'supa-ball' is thrown upwards from ground level. It hits the ground after 2 seconds and continues to bounce. The time it is in the air for a particular bounce is always 0.8 of the time for the previous bounce. How long does it take for the ball to stop bouncing?

11 A 'supa-ball' is dropped from a height of 1 metre onto a level table. It always rises to a height equal to 0.9 of the height from which it was dropped. How far does it travel in total until it stops bouncing?

12 A frog sits at one end of a table which is 2 m long. In its first jump the frog goes a distance of 1 m along the table, with its second jump $\frac{1}{2}$ m, with its third jump $\frac{1}{4}$ m and so on.

(a) What is the frog's final position?

(b) After how many jumps will the frog be within 1 cm of the far end of the table?

31 Exponentials and logarithms

In this chapter a new type of function is introduced which has many important applications. When you have completed it, you should

- know what is meant by an exponential function, and be familiar with the shape of exponential graphs
- know what is meant by a logarithm, and be able to switch between the exponential and the logarithmic form of an equation
- know the rules for logarithms, and how they can be proved from the rules for indices
- understand the idea of a logarithmic scale
- be able to solve equations and inequalities in which the unknown appears as an index.

31.1 Exponential functions

What are the next two numbers in the sequence which begins

$$1 \qquad 1.2 \qquad 1.44 \qquad 1.728 \qquad \dots \qquad ?$$

This looks like a geometric sequence, with first term 1 and common ratio 1.2. With this interpretation, the next two numbers would be $1.728 \times 1.2 = 2.0736$ and $2.0736 \times 1.2 = 2.488\,32$.

You could also write the sequence as

$$1.2^0 \qquad 1.2^1 \qquad 1.2^2 \qquad 1.2^3 \qquad \dots \qquad .$$

This suggests thinking of the sequence as a function

$$f(x) = 1.2^x$$

which is defined for values of x which are positive integers or zero. Its graph is shown in Fig. 31.1. It consists of a lot of isolated points, one for each natural number.

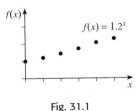

Fig. 31.1

But regarding 1.2^x as a function, there is no need to restrict x to being either an integer or positive. You know how to find 1.2^x for many other values of x. For example,

$$1.2^{\frac{1}{2}} = \sqrt{1.2} = 1.095\dots, \qquad 1.2^{-1} = \frac{1}{1.2} = 0.833\dots,$$

$$1.2^{0.8} = 1.2^{\frac{4}{5}} = \sqrt[5]{1.2^4} = 1.157\dots, \qquad 1.2^{-3.5} = \frac{1}{1.2^{3.5}} = \frac{1}{1.2^3 \times \sqrt{1.2}} = 0.528\dots, \text{ etc.}$$

In fact, the extension of index notation in Chapter 14 provides a definition of 1.2^x where x is any rational number, positive or negative. If you fill in all these additional values you get the graph in Fig. 31.2.

The only values of x for which 1.2^x doesn't yet have a meaning are the irrational numbers, like π or $\sqrt{2}$. So far you don't have a definition for powers such as 1.2^π or $1.2^{\sqrt{2}}$. This means that the graph in Fig. 31.2 has gaps in it, though you can't see them! In fact there is a way of defining expressions like b^x when x is any real number, which behave in just the same way as when x is rational. For the time being you can assume that this is true.

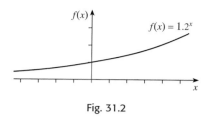

Fig. 31.2

The function 1.2^x is an example of an 'exponential function'. The reason for this name is that the variable x appears as an index, and 'exponent' is an alternative word for the index in an expression like b^x.

> An **exponential function** is a function of the form $f(x) = b^x$, where b is a positive real number and $b \neq 1$. The number b is called the **base**.

Notice the restrictions on the value of b in this definition. Negative numbers are excluded because, if $b < 0$, b^x has no meaning for some values of x; for example, $b^{\frac{1}{2}} = \sqrt{b}$ does not exist if $b < 0$. Zero is excluded for a similar reason; for example $b^{-1} = \dfrac{1}{b}$, and $\dfrac{1}{0}$ does not exist. The number 1 is also excluded, but for a different reason; since $1^x = 1$ for every value of x, the function 1^x is simply the constant number 1.

> Before reading on, use your calculator to display some exponential functions with different bases. Choose an interval with both negative and positive values of x. Use some values of b greater than 1, and some between 0 and 1.

Fig. 31.3 shows the graphs of some typical exponential functions for different values of b. From these you will notice that they have a number of properties in common.

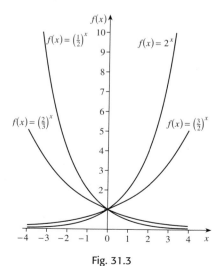

Fig. 31.3

- The point $(0, 1)$ lies on all the graphs, because $b^0 = 1$ for all positive numbers b.

- The graph of $y = b^x$ lies entirely above the x-axis, and the x-axis is an asymptote.

- If $b > 1$ the graph of $y = b^x$ has positive gradient, so the function is increasing. If $0 < b < 1$ the graph has negative gradient, so the function is decreasing.

- The graph of $y = b^x$ is concave up both for $b > 1$ and for $0 < b < 1$.

- If $b > 1$ the graph approaches the x-axis when x is negative and numerically large; if $0 < b < 1$, the graph approaches the x-axis when x is positive and numerically large.

- The graph of $y = \left(\dfrac{1}{b}\right)^x$ is the reflection in the y-axis of the graph of $y = b^x$.

To prove the last statement, use the rules of indices (Chapter 14) to show that

$$b^{-h} = \frac{1}{b^h} = \left(\frac{1}{b}\right)^h.$$

So the value of $\left(\dfrac{1}{b}\right)^x$ when $x = h$ is the same as the value of b^x when $x = -h$. Since this is true for any number h, the reflection in the y-axis of $y = b^x$ is $y = \left(\dfrac{1}{b}\right)^x$.

Exercise 31A

1 If $2^{-x} < 10^{-3}$, what can you say about 2^x?

Find the smallest integer x such that 2^{-x} is less than

(a) 10^{-3},   (b) 10^{-6},   (c) 10^{-12}.

2 If $3^x < 0.0005$, what can you say about 3^{-x}?

Find the largest integer x such that 3^x is less than

(a) 0.0005,   (b) 2.5×10^{-7},   (c) 10^{-7}.

3 (a) Use your calculator to display, with the same axes, the graphs of $y = 1.1^x$ and $y = 1.21^x$.

(b) Show that $1.1^h = 1.21^{\frac{1}{2}h}$. Draw a diagram to illustrate this property.

4 (a) Use your calculator to display, with the same axes, the graphs of $y = 1.25^x$ and $y = 0.8^x$.

(b) Show that $1.25^x = 0.8^{-x}$. What does this tell you about the graphs in part (a)?

31.2 Logarithms

You have seen that, if $b > 1$, then $y = b^x$ increases over all values of x; if $0 < b < 1$ it decreases. This means that in either case, if y is any positive number, there can only be one number x such that $b^x = y$. This number is called the **logarithm to base b** of y. It is written $x = \log_b y$.

> If x is a real number and y is a positive real number, the statements
>
> $$b^x = y \quad \text{and} \quad x = \log_b y$$
>
> are equivalent.

In words, you can say that

$\log_b y$ is the power to which b must be raised to give y.

Example 31.2.1
Find   (a) $\log_3 81$,   (b) $\log_{81} 3$,   (c) $\log_3 \left(\frac{1}{81}\right)$,   (d) $\log_{\frac{1}{3}} 81$.

(a) Since $81 = 3^4$, $\log_3 81 = 4$. The power to which 3 must be raised to give 81 is 4.

(b) $3 = 81^{\frac{1}{4}}$, so $\log_{81} 3 = \frac{1}{4}$.

(c) $\frac{1}{81} = 3^{-4}$, so $\log_3 \left(\frac{1}{81}\right) = -4$.

(d) $81 = \frac{1}{\left(\frac{1}{3}\right)^4} = \left(\frac{1}{3}\right)^{-4}$, so $\log_{\frac{1}{3}} 81 = -4$.

It is important to notice that the logarithm exists only if y is positive, because (for any base b) the graph of $y = b^x$ lies entirely above the x-axis.

Some important results about logarithms follow from what you already know about indices. Here are some examples.

Putting $x = 0$, since $b^0 = 1$, it follows that $0 = \log_b 1$.

Putting $x = 1$ gives $b^1 = b$, so that $1 = \log_b b$.

Putting $x = 2$ gives $b^2 = y$, so that $2 = \log_b b^2$.

More generally,

putting $x = n$ gives $b^n = y$, so that $n = \log_b b^n$.

> For any base b,
>
> $\log_b 1 = 0$, $\log_b b = 1$ and $\log_b b^n = n$.

The result $\log_b b^n = n$ is not restricted to integer values of n; it is true when n is any real number. If in the box at the beginning of this section you substitute b^x for y in the second statement you get

$x = \log_b b^x$.

And if you substitute $\log_b y$ for x in the first statement you get

$b^{\log_b y} = y$.

These statements are true for any number x and for any positive number. What they say, in effect, is that the processes of 'raising to a power' and 'taking logarithms' cancel each other out. If you carry out one after the other, in either order, you get back to where you started.

> For any base b,
>
> $\log_b b^x = x$ and $b^{\log_b y} = y$.

Try this with a calculator. The key labelled [log] calculates the logarithm to base 10. Choose a number, x, calculate 10^x, then calculate log(answer). Or choose a number, y, calculate log(y), then calculate 10^{answer}.

Exercise 31B

1 Write each of the following in the form $y = b^x$.

    (a) $\log_2 8 = 3$ (b) $\log_3 81 = 4$ (c) $\log_5 0.04 = -2$

    (d) $\log_7 x = 4$ (e) $\log_x 5 = t$ (f) $\log_p q = r$

2 Write each of the following in the form $x = \log_b y$.

    (a) $2^3 = 8$ (b) $3^6 = 729$ (c) $4^{-3} = \frac{1}{64}$

    (d) $a^8 = 20$ (e) $h^9 = g$ (f) $m^n = p$

3 Evaluate the following.

    (a) $\log_2 16$ (b) $\log_4 16$ (c) $\log_7 \frac{1}{49}$

    (d) $\log_4 1$ (e) $\log_5 5$ (f) $\log_{27} \frac{1}{3}$

    (g) $\log_{16} 8$ (h) $\log_2 2\sqrt{2}$ (i) $\log_{\sqrt{2}} 8\sqrt{2}$

4 Find the value of y in each of the following.

    (a) $\log_y 49 = 2$ (b) $\log_4 y = -3$ (c) $\log_3 243 = y$

    (d) $\log_{10} y = -1$ (e) $\log_2 y = 2.5$ (f) $\log_y 1296 = 4$

    (g) $\log_{\frac{1}{2}} y = 8$ (h) $\log_{\frac{1}{2}} 1024 = y$ (i) $\log_y 27 = -6$

31.3 Properties of logarithms

It was shown in Section 14.1 that expressions involving indices can be simplified by applying a number of rules, such as the multiplication and division rules and the power-on-power rule. There are corresponding rules for logarithms.

The multiplication rule for indices states that $b^r \times b^s = b^{r+s}$. Using $f(x)$ to denote the function b^x, this could be written as

$$f(r) \times f(s) = f(r + s).$$

So this rule equates the *product* of values of the function for two values of x to the value of the function for their *sum*.

Logarithms do the opposite. The rule for logarithms equates the *sum* of values of the function $\log_b x$ for two values of x to the value of the function for their *product*. That is,

$$\log_b p + \log_b q = \log_b(p \times q).$$

This is the multiplication rule for logarithms. There is also a division rule and a power rule.

For any positive real numbers p and q, any real number x, and logarithms to any base:

The multiplication rule	$\log_b(pq) = \log_b p + \log_b q$
The division rule	$\log_b\left(\dfrac{p}{q}\right) = \log_b p - \log_b q$
The power rule	$\log_b(p^x) = x \log_b p$

Example 31.3.1

If $\log_b 2 = r$ and $\log_b 3 = s$, express in terms of r and s

(a) $\log_b 16$,　　　(b) $\log_b 18$,　　　(c) $\log_b 13.5$.

(a) $\log_b 16 = \log_b 2^4 = 4 \log_b 2 = 4r$.

(b) $\log_b 18 = \log_b(2 \times 3^2) = \log_b 2 + \log_b 3^2 = \log_b 2 + 2 \log_b 3 = r + 2s$.

(c) $\log_b 13.5 = \log_b \dfrac{3^3}{2} = \log_b 3^3 - \log_b 2 = 3 \log_b 3 - \log_b 2 = 3s - r$.

Example 31.3.2

Find $\log_{10} 50 + \log_{10} 8000 - 2 \log_{10} 20$.

Use the power rule, then the multiplication and division rules.

$$2 \log_{10} 20 = \log_{10} 20^2 = \log_{10} 400,$$

so

$$\log_{10} 50 + \log_{10} 8000 - 2 \log_{10} 20 = \log_{10} 50 + \log_{10} 8000 - \log_{10} 400$$
$$= \log_{10}\left(\frac{50 \times 8000}{400}\right)$$
$$= \log_{10} 1000$$
$$= 3,$$

since $10^3 = 1000$.

Example 31.3.3

Express $\log_b\left(\dfrac{p^3 q}{r^2}\right)$ in terms of $\log_b p$, $\log_b q$ and $\log_b r$.

$$\log_b\left(\frac{p^3 q}{r^2}\right) = \log_b(p^3) + \log_b q - \log_b(r^2)$$
$$= 3 \log_b p + \log_b q - 2 \log_b r.$$

Example 31.3.4

Express as a single logarithm　　(a) $2 \log_b x - 3 \log_b y$,　　(b) $\frac{1}{3} \log_b 64$.

(a) $2 \log_b x - 3 \log_b y = \log_b(x^2) - \log_b(y^3) = \log_b\left(\dfrac{x^2}{y^3}\right)$.

(b) $\frac{1}{3} \log_b 64 = \log_b 64^{\frac{1}{3}} = \log_b \sqrt[3]{64} = \log_b 4$.

A useful special case of the power rule is when x is a fraction $\dfrac{1}{n}$ where n is a positive integer.

Then $p^x = p^{\frac{1}{n}} = \sqrt[n]{p}$, so you get:

> **The nth root rule** $\log_b \sqrt[n]{p} = \dfrac{\log_b p}{n}$

Historically logarithms were important because for many years, before calculators and computers were available, they provided the most useful form of calculating aid. With a table of logarithms (to base 10) students would, for example, find the cube root of 100 by looking up the value of log 100 and dividing it by 3. By the nth root rule, this gave log $\sqrt[3]{100}$, and the cube root could then be obtained by using the logarithm table in reverse or from a table of the function 10^x.

The rules for logarithms can be proved directly from the definition of a logarithm and the rules for indices.

Proof of the multiplication and division rules
Denote $\log_b p$ by r and $\log_b q$ by s. Then, in exponential form, $p = b^r$ and $q = b^s$. So, using the multiplication and division rules for indices,

$$pq = b^r \times b^s = b^{r+s} \quad \text{and} \quad \frac{p}{q} = \frac{b^r}{b^s} = b^{r-s}.$$

Putting these back into logarithmic form gives

$$\log_b(pq) = r + s, \quad \text{which is} \quad \log_b p + \log_b q,$$

$$\text{and} \quad \log_b\left(\frac{p}{q}\right) = r - s, \quad \text{which is} \quad \log_b p - \log_b q.$$

Proof of the power rule
Denote $\log_b p$ by r. Then $p = b^r$. So, using the power-on-power rule for indices,

$$p^x = (b^r)^x = b^{rx} = b^{xr}.$$

Putting this back into logarithmic form gives

$$\log_b(p^x) = xr, \quad \text{which is} \quad x \log_b p.$$

31.4 Special bases

Although the base of a logarithm can be any real positive number except 1, only two bases are in common use. One is a number denoted by e, for which the logarithm has a number of special properties; these are explored in Higher Level 2 Chapter 13. Logarithms to base e are denoted by 'ln', and can be found using the [ln] key on your calculator.

The other base is 10, which is important because our system of writing numbers is based on powers of 10. On your calculator the key labelled [log] gives logarithms to base 10.

From now on, when you see the symbol log by itself without a base, it will mean $\log_{10}$.

When logarithms were used to do calculations, students used tables which gave $\log_{10} x$ only for values of x between 1 and 10. So to find $\log 3456$, they would use the rules in Section 31.3 to write

$$\log 3456 = \log(3.456 \times 10^3) = \log 3.456 + \log 10^3 = \log 3.456 + 3.$$

The tables gave $\log 3.456$ as 0.5386 (correct to 4 decimal places), so $\log 3456$ is 3.5386. Notice that the number 3 before the decimal point is the same as the index when 3456 is written in standard form.

Logarithms to base 10 are sometimes useful in constructing logarithmic scales. As an example, suppose that you want to make a diagram to show the populations of countries which belong to the United Nations. In 1999 the largest of these was China, with about 1.2 billion people, and the smallest was San Marino, with 25 000. If you represented the population of China by a line of length 12 cm, then Nigeria would have length 1.1 cm, Malaysia just over 2 mm, and the line for San Marino would be only 0.0025 mm long!

Fig. 31.4 is an alternative way of showing the data.

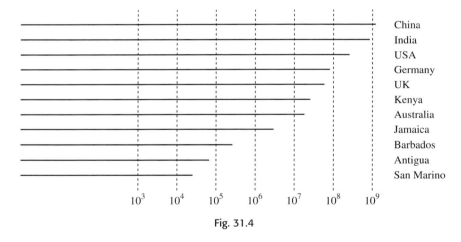

Fig. 31.4

Figure 31.4 uses a logarithmic scale, in which a country with population P is shown by a line of length $\log_{10} P$ cm. China now has a length of just over 9 cm, and San Marino a length of between 4 and 5 cm. You have to understand the diagram in a different way; an extra centimetre in length implies a population 10 times as large, rather than 100 million larger. But the countries are still placed in the correct order, and the population of any country can be found as 10^x where x is the length of its line in centimetres.

Exercise 31C

1 Write each of the following in terms of $\log_b p$, $\log_b q$ and $\log_b r$. In parts (c), (h) and (i) the logarithms are to base 10; p, q and r are positive numbers.

(a) $\log_b pqr$

(b) $\log_b pq^2r^3$

(c) $\log 100\,pr^5$

(d) $\log_b \sqrt{\dfrac{p}{q^2r}}$

(e) $\log_b \dfrac{pq}{r^2}$

(f) $\log_b \dfrac{1}{pqr}$

(g) $\log_b \dfrac{p}{\sqrt{r}}$

(h) $\log \dfrac{qr^7p}{10}$

(i) $\log \sqrt{\dfrac{10p^{10}r}{q}}$

2 Express as a single logarithm, simplifying where possible. (All the logarithms have base 10, so, for example, an answer of log 100 simplifies to 2.)

(a) $2\log 5 + \log 4$

(b) $2\log 2 + \log 150 - \log 6000$

(c) $3\log 5 + 5\log 3$

(d) $2\log 4 - 4\log 2$

(e) $\log 24 - \frac{1}{2}\log 9 + \log 125$

(f) $3\log 2 + 3\log 5 - \log 10^6$

(g) $\frac{1}{2}\log 16 + \frac{1}{3}\log 8$

(h) $\log 64 - 2\log 4 + 5\log 2 - \log 2^7$

3 If $\log_b 3 = p$, $\log_b 5 = q$ and $\log_b 10 = r$, express the following in terms of p, q and r.

(a) $\log_b 2$

(b) $\log_b 45$

(c) $\log_b \sqrt{90}$

(d) $\log_b 0.2$

(e) $\log_b 750$

(f) $\log_b 60$

(g) $\log_b \frac{1}{6}$

(h) $\log_b 4.05$

(i) $\log_b 0.15$

4 Show that the rule $\log_b b^x = x$ in Section 31.2 is a special case of the power rule $\log_b(p^x) = x\log_b p$.

5 Suppose that $\log_b c = r$ and $\log_c b = s$. Write these equations in their equivalent exponential forms, and use the rules for indices to show that $rs = 1$. Write this result as an identity connecting $\log_b c$ and $\log_c b$.

6* The acidity of a substance is measured by a quantity called pH. This is defined as the value of $-\log_{10} a_{H+}$, where a_{H+} is the hydrogen ion activity in the substance. The values of pH for a cola drink and for beer are approximately 2 and 5 respectively. What does this mean in terms of the relative levels of hydrogen ion activity in the two drinks?

7* The intensity of sound in decibels is equal to $10\log_{10}\dfrac{P^2}{P_R^2}$, where P is the amplitude of the sound pressure wave and P_R is a reference pressure of 0.0002 microbars, which is chosen as the pressure of an undetectable sound. Write this formula in a simpler form.

(a) An airport imposes a restriction of 110 decibels on aircraft taking off. To what pressure does this correspond?

(b) A man and a woman are talking on the radio. The pressure on the listener's ear of the man's voice is double that of the woman's. What is the relationship between the sound intensity of their voices?

(c) A new design of silencer reduces the noise of an engine by 10 decibels. What effect does this have on the amplitude of the sound pressure waves?

8* Earthquakes are recorded on a seismograph, which records surface waves whose amplitudes depend on the strength of the earthquake. The magnitude of an earthquake on the Richter scale is given by the formula $\log_{10}(k \times \text{amplitude of the surface wave})$, where k is a constant.

(a) Two earthquakes produce surface waves whose amplitudes are in the ratio $3 : 1$. How do their magnitudes on the Richter scale compare?

(b) Two earthquakes have magnitudes 6.9 and 7.5 on the Richter scale. How do the amplitudes of the recorded surface waves compare?

31.5 Equations and inequalities

You know that $\log_2 2 = 1$ and $\log_2 4 = 2$, but how can you find $\log_2 3$?

Suppose that $\log_2 3 = x$. Then from the definition,

$$2^x = 3.$$

So the problem is to solve an equation where the unknown appears in the index.

The trick is to use logarithms and to write the equation as

$$\log_b 2^x = \log_b 3.$$

This is often described as 'taking logarithms of both sides of the equation'. You can now use the power rule to write this as

$$x \log_b 2 = \log_b 3.$$

In this equation you can use logarithms to any base you like. In this section base 10 will be used. The log key on the calculator gives $\log 2 = 0.301\ldots$ and $\log 3 = 0.477\ldots$. So

$$x \times 0.301\ldots = 0.477\ldots,$$

which gives $x = \log_2 3 = \dfrac{0.477\ldots}{0.301\ldots} = 1.58$, correct to 3 significant figures.

This type of equation arises in various applications.

Example 31.5.1

In an area of heathland the number of rabbits increases by a factor of 2.5 every year. How many years will it take for the number of rabbits to be multiplied by 100?

After t years the number of rabbits will have been multiplied by 2.5^t. So the solution to the problem is given by the equation

$$2.5^t = 100.$$

Taking logarithms to base 10 of both sides of the equation,

$$\log 2.5^t = \log 100,$$

so $t \log 2.5 = \log 100,$

$$t = \frac{\log 100}{\log 2.5} = \frac{2}{0.397\ldots} = 5.025\ldots .$$

Assuming that the population increases continuously throughout the year, the number of rabbits will have multiplied by 100 after just over 5 years.

Example 31.5.2
Solve the equation $5^{3x-1} = 8$.

There is a choice of method. You can either take logarithms straight away, or begin by using the laws of indices to put the equation into the form $b^x = c$, which you know how to solve.

Method 1   Taking logarithms (to base 10) of both sides of the equation,

$$\log(5^{3x-1}) = \log 8.$$

Applying the power rule to the left side,

$$(3x - 1)\log 5 = \log 8,$$

so

$$3x - 1 = \frac{\log 8}{\log 5} = \frac{0.903\ldots}{0.698\ldots} = 1.292\ldots$$
$$3x = 1 + 1.292\ldots = 2.292\ldots,$$
$$x = 2.292\ldots \div 3 = 0.764, \text{ correct to 3 significant figures.}$$

If you use this method, you should keep as many figures at each stage as the calculator allows, only approximating to 3 significant figures at the end. In fact, you could if you prefer set out the solution as

$$3x = 1 + \frac{\log 8}{\log 5},$$
$$x = \left(1 + \frac{\log 8}{\log 5}\right) \div 3,$$

and save all the calculation until the end.

Method 2   Begin by using the division and power-on-power laws for indices to give

$$5^{3x-1} = 5^{3x} \div 5^1 = (5^3)^x \div 5 = 125^x \div 5.$$

The equation can then be written as

$$125^x \div 5 = 8,$$
$$125^x = 5 \times 8 = 40.$$

You have already met equations of this type. Taking logarithms (to base 10) of both sides and using the power law for logarithms,

$$x \log 125 = \log 40,$$

so

$$x = \frac{\log 40}{\log 125} = \frac{1.602\ldots}{2.096\ldots} = 0.764, \text{ correct to 3 significant figures.}$$

Some applications lead to the expression of the problem as an inequality rather than an equation. So instead of an argument of the form

$$p^x = c, \quad \text{so} \quad \log_b p^x = \log_b c,$$

you have

$$p^x > c, \quad \text{so} \quad \log_b p^x > \log_b c \quad \text{(or similarly with } < \text{ in place of } >\text{).}$$

For this to be valid it is necessary for the logarithm to be an increasing function: that is, for larger numbers to have larger logarithms. Is this true?

To answer this question, go back to the definition of a logarithm at the beginning of Section 31.2. This began with a positive number y, and it was stated that there is just one number x such that $b^x = y$. That number is called $\log_b y$. This is illustrated using the graph of $y = b^x$ in Fig. 31.5; the x-coordinate corresponding to each value of y is $\log_b y$. You can see that, as y gets larger the point P on the graph moves upwards and to the right, so $\log_b y$ also gets larger.

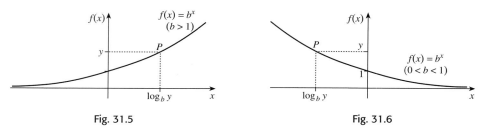

Fig. 31.5   Fig. 31.6

But this happens only because b is greater than 1. If $0 < b < 1$, you get a graph like Fig. 31.6. Now, as y gets larger, the point P moves upwards and to the left, so $\log_b y$ gets smaller.

What this implies for solving inequalities is that, if you take logarithms of both sides, then the inequality sign keeps the same direction provided that $b > 1$; but if $0 < b < 1$ you must reverse the direction of the inequality sign.

In practice, of course, nobody ever takes logarithms to a base less than 1. Both e and 10 are greater than 1. But it is still important to understand the theory on which the process is based.

> For logarithms to base $b > 1$, if $p > q$, then $\log_b p > \log_b q$.

Example 31.5.3
Iodine-131 is a radioactive isotope used in treatment of the thyroid gland. It decays so that, after t days, 1 unit of the isotope is reduced to 0.9174^t units. How many days does it take for the amount to fall to less than 0.1 units?

This requires solution of the inequality $0.9174^t < 0.1$. Since log is an increasing function, taking logarithms to base 10 gives

$$\log 0.9174^t < \log 0.1,$$

so $t \log 0.9174 < \log 0.1.$

Now beware! The value of $\log 0.9174$ is negative, so when you divide both sides by $\log 0.9174$ you must change the direction of the inequality:

$$t > \frac{\log 0.1}{\log 0.9174} = \frac{-1}{-0.0374...} = 26.708... \; .$$

The amount of iodine-131 will fall to less than 0.1 units after about 26.7 days.

Example 31.5.4

How many terms of the geometric series $1 + 1.01 + 1.01^2 + 1.01^3 + ...$ must be taken to give a sum greater than 1 million?

The sum of n terms of the series is given by the formula (see Section 30.3)

$$\frac{1 - 1.01^n}{1 - 1.01} = \frac{1 - 1.01^n}{-0.01} = 100(1.01^n - 1).$$

The problem is to find the smallest value of n for which

$$100(1.01^n - 1) > 1\,000\,000,$$

which gives $1.01^n > 10\,001$.

Taking logarithms to base 10 of both sides,

$$\log 1.01^n > \log 10\,001,$$

so

$$n \log 1.01 > \log 10\,001.$$

Since $\log 1.01$ is positive,

$$n > \frac{\log 10\,001}{\log 1.01} = \frac{4.000...}{0.004\,32...} = 925.6... \,.$$

The smallest integer n satisfying this inequality is 926.

31.6   Calculating logarithms to any base

The method used in the last section to find $\log_2 3$ can be generalised to find the logarithm of any positive number a to any positive base b (where $b \neq 1$).

Denote $\log_b a$ by x. Then the equation $x = \log_b a$ can be written in exponential form as

$$b^x = a.$$

Suppose that you know the logarithms of a and b to some base c. (In practice c will almost always be either 10 or e, but you don't have to assume this.) Taking logarithms of both sides to base c,

$$\log_c b^x = \log_c a.$$

Since by the power rule $\log_c b^x = x \times \log_c b$,

$$x \times \log_c b = \log_c a.$$

Therefore, dividing both sides by $\log_c b$,

$$x = \frac{\log_c a}{\log_c b}.$$

This gives the **change of base rule**, which you should either remember or be able to obtain quickly for yourself:

If a, b and c are positive numbers (with b and $c \neq 1$),

$$\log_b a = \frac{\log_c a}{\log_c b}.$$

Example 31.6.1
Calculate $\log_{27} 9$.

With $c = 3$, $\log_{27} 9 = \dfrac{\log_3 9}{\log_3 27} = \dfrac{2}{3}$.

You could of course get this directly, since $9 = 3^2 = (\sqrt[3]{27})^2 = 27^{\frac{2}{3}}$.

Example 31.6.2
Calculate $\log_6 5$.

With $c = 10$, $\log_6 5 = \dfrac{\log_{10} 5}{\log_{10} 6} = \dfrac{0.698...}{0.778...} = 0.898$, correct to 3 significant figures.

Exercise 31D

1 Solve the following equations, giving those answers which are inexact correct to 3 significant figures.

(a) $3^x = 5$ (b) $7^x = 21$ (c) $6^{2x} = 60$

(d) $5^{2x-1} = 10$ (e) $4^{\frac{1}{2}x} = 12$ (f) $2^{x+1} = 3^x$

(g) $\left(\frac{1}{2}\right)^{3x+2} = 25$ (h) $2^x \times 2^{x+1} = 128$ (i) $\left(\frac{1}{4}\right)^{2x-1} = 7$

2 Solve the following inequalities, giving your answers correct to 3 significant figures.

(a) $3^x > 8$ (b) $5^x < 10$ (c) $7^{2x+5} \leq 24$

(d) $0.5^x < 0.001$ (e) $0.4^x < 0.0004$ (f) $0.2^x > 25$

(g) $4^x \times 4^{3-2x} \leq 1024$ (h) $0.8^{2x+5} \geq 4$ (i) $0.8^{1-3x} \geq 10$

3 Find the number of terms in the following geometric series. In parts (c) to (f) the last terms are not exact, but are correct to the number of significant figures given.

(a) $1 + 2 + 4 + ... + 67\,108\,864$ (b) $4 + 12 + 36 + ... + 57\,395\,628$

(c) $2 + 3 + 4.5 + ... + 383\,502$ (d) $1 + 0.8 + 0.64 + ... + 0.035\,18$

(e) $4 + 3 + 2.25 + ... + 0.022\,55$ (f) $100 + 99 + 98.01 + ... + 36.97$

4 Find which term in the following geometric sequences is the first one greater than the number stated. Calculate the value of this term, in standard form correct to 4 significant figures.

(a) 1, 1.1, 1.21, ... ; greater than 1000 (b) 2, 2.4, 2.88, ... ; greater than 10^{12}

(c) 4, 5, 6.25, ... ; greater than 5000 (d) 5, 7, 9.8, ... ; greater than 10^7

5 Find which term in the following geometric sequences is the first one less than the number stated. Calculate the value of this term, in standard form correct to 4 significant figures.

    (a) 1, 0.9, 0.81, ... ; less than 10^{-3} (b) 5, 4, 3.2, ... ; less than 10^{-6}

    (c) 0.4, 0.3, 0.225, ... ; less than 10^{-4}

6 How many terms of the geometric series $1 + 2 + 4 + 8 + ...$ must be taken for the sum to exceed 10^{11}?

7 How many terms of the geometric series $2 + 6 + 18 + 54 + ...$ must be taken for the sum to exceed 3 million?

8 How many terms of the geometric series $1 + \frac{1}{2} + \frac{1}{4} + \frac{1}{8} + ...$ must be taken for its sum to differ from 2 by less than 10^{-8}?

9 How many terms of the geometric series $2 + \frac{1}{3} + \frac{1}{18} + \frac{1}{108} + ...$ must be taken for its sum to differ from its sum to infinity by less than 10^{-5}?

10 A radioactive isotope decays so that after t days an amount 0.82^t units remains. How many days does it take for the amount to fall to less than 0.15 units?

11 To say that a radioactive isotope has a half-life of 6 days means that 1 unit of isotope is reduced to $\frac{1}{2}$ unit in 6 days. So if the daily decay rate is given by r, then $r^6 = 0.5$.

    (a) For this isotope, find r.

    (b) How long will it take for the amount to fall to 0.25 units?

    (c) How long will it take for the amount to fall to 0.1 units?

12 Find the following logarithms correct to 3 significant figures.

    (a) $\log_4 12$ (b) $\log_7 100$ (c) $\log_8 2.75$

    (d) $\log_{\frac{1}{2}} 250$ (e) $\log_3 \pi$ (f) $\log_{\frac{1}{4}} 0.04$

13* If $\log_{0.1} 2 = x$, show that $10^x = \frac{1}{2}$. Hence evaluate $\log_{0.1} 2$. Use a similar method to find $\log_{0.1} 3$, and verify that $\log_{0.1} 3 < \log_{0.1} 2$.

32 Exponential growth and decay

In this chapter geometric sequences and exponential functions are shown to have applications as mathematical models in everyday situations and in physical, biological and social sciences. When you have completed it, you should

- understand what is meant by exponential growth and exponential decay in both discrete and continuous models
- be able to distinguish exponential models from other models of growth and decay, and be able to calculate the constants in exponential models.

32.1 Discrete exponential growth

Geometric sequences arise in many everyday contexts. Here are two examples. The first has a common ratio greater than 1, the second has a common ratio between 0 and 1.

Example 32.1.1
A person invests $1000 in a savings bank account which pays interest of 6% annually. Calculate the amount in the account over the next 8 years.

The interest in any year is 0.06 times the amount in the account at the beginning of the year. This is added on to the sum of money already in the account. The amount at the end of each year, after interest has been added, is 1.06 times the amount at the beginning of the year. So

Amount after 1 year = $1000 × 1.06 = $1060
Amount after 2 years = $1060 × 1.06 = $1124
Amount after 3 years = $1124 × 1.06 = $1191, and so on.

Continuing in this way, you get the amounts shown in Table 32.1, to the nearest whole number of dollars.

Number of years	0	1	2	3	4	5	6	7	8
Amount ($)	1000	1060	1124	1191	1262	1338	1419	1504	1594

Table 32.1

You can see a graph of these values in Fig. 32.2.

Notice that in the first year the interest is $60, but in the eighth year it is $90. This is because the amount on which the 6% is calculated has gone up from $1000 to $1504. This is characteristic of 'exponential growth', in which the increase is proportional to the current amount. As the amount goes up, the increase goes up.

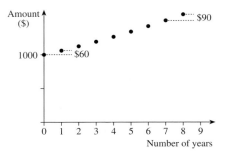

Fig. 32.2

Example 32.1.2

A car cost $30 000 when new, and each year its value decreases by 20%. Find its value on the first five anniversaries of its purchase.

The value at the end of each year is 0.8 times its value a year earlier. The results of this calculation are given in Table 32.3.

Number of years	0	1	2	3	4	5
Value ($)	30 000	24 000	19 200	15 360	12 288	9830

Table 32.3

These values are shown in the graph in Fig. 32.4.

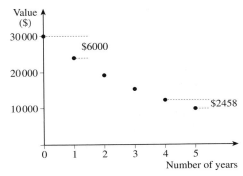

The value goes down by $6000 in the first year, but by only $2458 in the fifth year, because by then the 20% is calculated on only $12 288 rather than on $30 000. This is characteristic of 'exponential decay', in which the decrease is proportional to the current value. Notice that, if the 20% rule continues, the value never becomes zero however long you keep the car.

Fig. 32.4

In both these examples it is more natural to think of the first term of the sequence as u_0 rather than u_1.

Also, since the values are given at regular intervals of time, it is helpful to use the letter t for the 'counting variable'. That is, $\$u_t$ stands for the amount in the account, or the value of the car, after t years.

The sequence in Example 32.1.1 then has

$$u_0 = 1000 \quad \text{and} \quad u_t = 1.06u_{t-1} \quad \text{for } 1 \le t \le 8.$$

From this you can deduce that $u_1 = 1000 \times 1.06$, $u_2 = 1000 \times 1.06^2$, and more generally $u_t = 1000 \times 1.06^t$.

The sequence in Example 32.1.2 has

$$u_0 = 30\,000 \quad \text{and} \quad u_t = 0.8u_{t-1} \quad \text{for } 1 \le t \le 5.$$

In this case $u_1 = 30\,000 \times 0.8$, $u_2 = 30\,000 \times 0.8^2$ and $u_t = 30\,000 \times 0.8^t$.

These are both examples of exponential sequences. (The reason for the name is that the variable t appears in the exponent of the formula for u_t.) An exponential sequence is a special kind of geometric sequence, in which a and r are both positive. If the first term is denoted by u_0, the sequence can be defined inductively by

$$u_0 = a \quad \text{and} \quad u_t = ru_{t-1},$$

or by the formula

$$u_t = ar^t.$$

If $r > 1$ the sequence represents exponential growth; if $0 < r < 1$ it represents exponential decay.

You saw in both examples that between any term and the next the increase or decrease is proportional to the current value. This is characteristic of any exponential sequence. Thus, for any value of t,

$$u_t - u_{t-1} = ru_{t-1} - u_{t-1},$$

which is $(r - 1)$ times u_{t-1}.

> **Exponential sequences**
> In a discrete situation, a sequence u_t represents the value of a quantity after t units of time, where t is an integer and $t \geq 0$. If
>
> $$u_0 = a \text{ (where } a > 0\text{)} \quad \text{and} \quad u_t = ru_{t-1} \quad \text{for } t = 1, 2, 3, ...,$$
>
> the sequence represents
>
> > **exponential growth** if $r > 1$
>
> or   **exponential decay** if $0 < r < 1$.
>
> The sequence can be described by the formula
>
> $$u_t = ar^t \quad \text{for } t = 0, 1, 2, 3, ...$$
>
> The increase or decrease in the value of the quantity between times $t - 1$ and t is $r - 1$ times the value at time $t - 1$: that is,
>
> $$u_t - u_{t-1} = (r - 1)u_{t-1}.$$

Example 32.1.3

The cost of building a conservatory is made up of the cost of labour and the cost of materials. The price quoted in a firm's 2007 catalogue is based on labour costs of $20 000 and material costs of $16 000. In succeeding years the labour costs increase exponentially by 10% a year, and the material costs decrease exponentially by 5% a year. Find how the total costs change over the next three years, and investigate whether they change exponentially.

If the labour costs after t years are $\$L_t$, the material costs are $\$M_t$, and the total costs are $\$C_t$, then

$$L_0 = 20\,000 \quad \text{and} \quad L_t = 1.1L_{t-1};$$
$$M_0 = 16\,000 \quad \text{and} \quad M_t = 0.95M_{t-1};$$

and $C_t = L_t + M_t.$

These equations can be used, for $t = 1, 2, 3$ in turn, to calculate the labour and material costs in Table 32.5. These are then added to give the total costs.

Year	2007	2008	2009	2010
Labour costs	$20 000	$22 000	$24 200	$26 620
Material costs	$16 000	$15 200	$14 440	$13 718
Total costs	$36 000	$37 200	$38 640	$40 338

Table 32.5

A graph of the total costs is shown in Fig. 32.6.

You can see from the graph that the total costs increase each year, and also that the amount by which they increase goes up each year. But this is not in itself enough to show that they are growing exponentially. For this to be true, the ratio of the total costs in successive years should be constant. So calculate

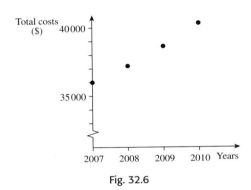

Fig. 32.6

$$\frac{C_1}{C_0} = \frac{37\,200}{36\,000} = 1.033\ldots\,, \quad \frac{C_2}{C_1} = \frac{38\,640}{37\,200} = 1.038\ldots\,, \quad \frac{C_3}{C_2} = \frac{40\,338}{38\,640} = 1.043\ldots\,.$$

Since these ratios are not the same, the growth in total costs is not exponential.

Although the independent variable in exponential growth and decay is usually time, this is not always the case. For example, you could construct a staircase in which the rise grows exponentially from each step to the next. In an example like this, you might choose to use a different letter for the variable instead of t.

Exercise 32A

1 There are at present 4000 houses in Growtown, and this number is growing exponentially by 10% every year. How many houses will there be in three years time?

Calculate the number of new houses which will be completed in each of the next three years. Show that this number is also growing exponentially by 10% every year.

2 The attendances at the last four matches played by Dudtown United were 4000, 3600, 3240 and 2916. Show that these are decreasing exponentially, and predict the attendances at the next two matches if this trend continues.

3 Each New Year's Eve Scrooge works out the value of his possessions. In 2004 it was $50 000, and he expects it to grow exponentially by 20% a year. Find the value in each year up to 2009 on this assumption.

Find how much richer he becomes in each year, and show that these amounts also increase exponentially.

4 It is estimated that the population of sparrows on an island is decaying exponentially by 20% each decade, and that the population of sparrow hawks is growing by 20%. If there were 100 000 sparrows and 1000 sparrow hawks when recording began, calculate how many of each there will be after 1, 2 and 3 decades.

Calculate how many sparrows there will be to each sparrow hawk after 1, 2 and 3 decades. How is this ratio changing?

5 A girl fills a jug with one-quarter lemon squash and three-quarters water. She fills a glass with one-tenth of the contents, drinks it and then tops up the jug with water.

(a) What proportion of the contents of the refilled jug is lemon squash?

(b) If she repeats this again and again, what proportion of the contents of the jug will be lemon squash after she has refilled it 2, 3 and 4 times?

(c) Write a formula for the proportion of lemon squash in the jug after she has refilled it t times.

6 In Example 32.1.1 find an expression for the amount of interest received in the ith year. Does the amount of interest grow exponentially?

7 In Example 32.1.2 find an expression for the reduction in the value of the car in the ith year after it was purchased. Does this reduction decay exponentially?

8 The population of Blighton is decreasing steadily at a rate of 4% each year. The population in 2006 was 21 000. Estimate the population in

(a) 2010,   (b) 1998.

9 A (rather stupid) man of mass 90 kg plans to diet and to reduce his mass to 72 kg in four weeks by a constant percentage reduction each week.

(a) What should his mass be 1 week after starting his diet?

(b) He forgets to stop after 4 weeks. Estimate his mass 1 week later.

10 The table gives the retail price index (to the nearest whole number) on 1 April for several consecutive years in a number of countries. In which countries could you say that the index is increasing or decreasing exponentially?

Country	Year 2000	2001	2002	2003	2004
Armensia	185	200	216	233	252
Bonvivia	135	150	165	180	195
Canadia	100	120	144	173	207
Declinia	180	169	159	150	141
Erewhon	80	69	59	50	41

11 In 1838 the Rev. H Moseley presented a paper to the Royal Society on his measurements of shells. One cone-shaped shell called *Turritella duplicata* grew in a series of whorls, whose successive widths, in inches, were 0.41, 0.48, 0.57, 0.67, 0.80, 0.94. Show that these measurements fit a model of exponential growth, and predict the width of the next two whorls.

12 Show that, if a sequence of data grows or decays exponentially, then the logarithms form an arithmetic sequence. Verify this from the data in Question 11, and estimate the common difference. What does this represent?

32.2   Continuous exponential growth

Exponential growth doesn't only occur in situations which increase by discrete steps. Rampant inflation, a nuclear chain reaction, the spread of an epidemic or the growth of cells are processes which take place in continuous time, and they need to be described by functions having the positive real numbers rather than the natural numbers for their domain.

For continuous exponential growth, the equation $u_t = ar^t$, where $t = 0, 1, 2, \dots$, is replaced by

$$f(t) = ab^t, \quad \text{where } t \text{ is a real number and } t \geq 0.$$

In this equation a stands for the initial value when $t = 0$, and b is a positive constant which indicates how fast the quantity is growing. (The idea of a 'common ratio' no longer applies in the continuous case, so a different letter is used.) The graph of $f(t)$ is shown in Fig. 32.7.

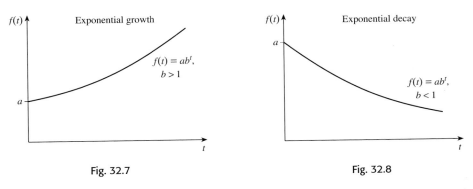

Fig. 32.7   Fig. 32.8

For exponential growth b has to be greater than 1. If $0 < b < 1$ the graph takes the form of Fig. 32.8; for large values of t the graph gets closer to the t-axis but never reaches it. This then represents exponential decay. Examples of this are the amount of radioactive uranium in a lump of ore, and the concentration of an antibiotic in the bloodstream.

The letter t has again been used for the variable, since in most examples of exponential growth and decay the quantity you are measuring is a function of the time. If this is not the case (for example, the air pressure decays exponentially with the height above the earth's surface) you might use a different letter for the variable.

> **Exponential variation**
> In a continuous situation, a function $f(t)$ represents the value of a quantity after t units of time, where t is a real number and $t \geq 0$. If
>
> $$f(t) = ab^t \quad (\text{where } a > 0),$$
>
> the function represents
>
> **exponential growth** if $b > 1$
>
> or   **exponential decay** if $0 < b < 1$.

Example 32.2.1

The population of the USA grew exponentially from the end of the War of Independence until the Civil War. It increased from 3.9 million at the 1790 census to 31.4 million in 1860. What would the population have been in 1990 if it had continued to grow at this rate?

If the population t years after 1790 is P million, and if the growth were exactly exponential, then P and t would be related by an equation of the form

$$P = 3.9b^t,$$

where $P = 31.4$ when $t = 70$. The constant b therefore satisfies the equation

$$31.4 = 3.9b^{70},$$

so
$$b^{70} = \frac{31.4}{3.9},$$
$$b = \left(\frac{31.4}{3.9}\right)^{\frac{1}{70}} = 1.030\ldots .$$

At this rate the population in 1990 would have grown to about $3.9 \times 1.030\ldots^{200}$ million, which is between 1.5 and 1.6 billion.

You can shorten this calculation as follows. In 70 years, the population multiplied by $\frac{31.4}{3.9}$. In 200 years, it therefore multiplied by $\left(\frac{31.4}{3.9}\right)^{\frac{200}{70}}$. The 1990 population can then be calculated as $3.9 \times \left(\frac{31.4}{3.9}\right)^{\frac{200}{70}}$ million, without working out b as an intermediate step.

Example 32.2.2

Carbon dating in archaeology is based on the decay of the isotope carbon-14, which has a half-life of 5715 years. By what percentage does carbon-14 decay in 100 years?

The half-life of a radioactive isotope is the time it would take half of any sample of the isotope to decay. After t years one unit of carbon-14 is reduced to b^t units, where

$$b^{5715} = 0.5 \qquad (\text{since 0.5 units are left after 5715 years})$$
so
$$b = 0.5^{\frac{1}{5715}} = 0.999\,878\ldots .$$

When $t = 100$ the quantity left is $b^{100} \approx 0.988$ units, a reduction of 0.012 units, or 1.2%.

Again, you could shorten the calculation by expressing the multiplying factor as $0.5^{\frac{100}{5715}}$. The fraction $\frac{100}{5715}$ expresses the ratio of 100 years to the half-life of 5715 years. So the multiplying factor is $\frac{1}{2}$ raised to the power of the number of half-lives.

32.3   Graphs of exponential growth

In Section 31.5 equations of the form $p^x = c$, where the unknown appears in the index, were solved by taking logarithms of both sides. This technique can be extended to deal with economic, social or scientific data which you think might exhibit exponential growth or decay.

Suppose that a quantity y is growing exponentially, so that its value at time t is given by

$$y = ab^t,$$

where a and b are constants. Taking logarithms of both sides of this equation, to any base,

$$\log y = \log(ab^t) = \log a + \log b^t = \log a + t \log b.$$

The expression on the right increases linearly with t. So if $\log y$ is plotted against t, the graph would be a straight line with gradient $\log b$ and intercept $\log a$.

Example 32.3.1
If $\log y = 0.322 - 0.531t$, where $\log y$ denotes $\log_{10} y$, express y in terms of t.

Equating the right side to $\log a + t \log b$, $\log a = 0.322$ and $\log b = -0.531$. So, since the logarithms are to base 10, $a = 10^{0.322} = 2.10$ and $b = 10^{-0.531} = 0.294$ (both correct to 3 significant figures). In exponential form the equation for y is therefore

$$y = 2.10 \times 0.294^t.$$

If you prefer you can write this calculation in a different way, using the property that if $\log y = x$ then $y = 10^x$, so $y = 10^{\log y}$. Therefore

$$y = 10^{\log y} = 10^{0.322 - 0.531t} = 10^{0.322} \times (10^{-0.531})^t = 2.10 \times 0.294^t.$$

Example 32.3.2
An investment company claims that the price of its shares has grown exponentially over the past six years, and supports its claim with Fig. 32.9. Is this claim justified?

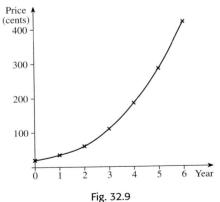

Fig. 32.9

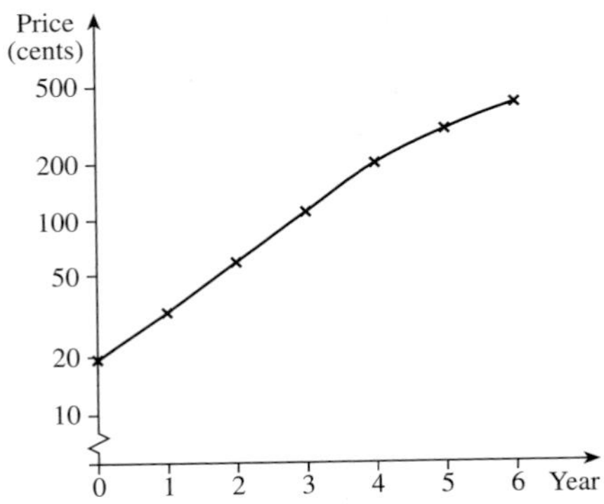

Fig. 32.10

Figure 32.10 shows this information with the price presented on a logarithmic scale (see Section 31.4). A price of y cents is represented by a length proportional to $\log y$. You can recognise this by noticing that, for example, the distance on the scale from 50 cents to 100 cents is the same as the distance from 100 cents to 200 cents; this is because $\log 100 - \log 50 = \log \frac{100}{50} = \log 2$, and $\log 200 - \log 100 = \log \frac{200}{100} = \log 2$.

If the claim were true, the graph in Fig. 32.10 would be a straight line. This seems approximately true for the first three years, but in later years the graph begins to bend downwards, suggesting that the early promise of exponential growth has not been sustained.

The ideas of the last two examples can be combined, not just to investigate whether there is an exponential relationship, but also to find the numerical constants in the equation.

Example 32.3.3

Use the census data in Table 32.11 for the USA to justify the statement in Example 32.2.1, that the population grew exponentially from 1790 to 1860.

Year	1790	1800	1810	1820	1830	1840	1850	1860
Population (millions)	3.9	5.3	7.2	9.6	12.9	17.0	23.2	31.4

Table 32.11

If you plot these figures on a graph, as in Fig. 32.12, it is clear that the points lie on a smooth curve with a steadily increasing gradient, but this doesn't by itself show that the growth is exponential.

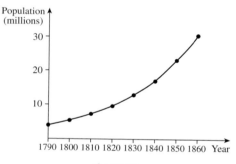

Fig. 32.12

To approach the question scientifically, the first step is to choose appropriate notation. For the population, you may as well work in millions of people, as in the table; there is no point in cluttering the data with lots of zeros, which would in any case give a false illusion of accuracy. So let P stand for the number of millions of people in the population. As for the date, since you are only interested in the period from 1790 to 1860, it is better to choose a variable t to stand for the number of years after 1790 rather than the actual year number. The theory then being investigated is that P and t are related by an equation of the form

$$P = ab^t \qquad \text{for } 0 \le t \le 70.$$

To convert this into a linear equation, take logarithms of both sides of the equation. You can use logarithms to any base you like; if you choose 10, the equation becomes

$$\log_{10} P = \log_{10} a + t \log_{10} b,$$

in which the independent variable is t and the dependent variable is $\log_{10} P$. So Table 32.13 contains values in terms of these variables.

t	0	10	20	30	40	50	60	70
$\log_{10} P$	0.59	0.72	0.86	0.98	1.11	1.23	1.37	1.50

Table 32.13

These values are used to plot the graph in Fig. 32.14. You can see that the points very nearly lie on a straight line, though not exactly so; you wouldn't expect a population to follow a precise mathematical relationship. However, it is quite close enough to justify the claim that the growth of the population was exponential.

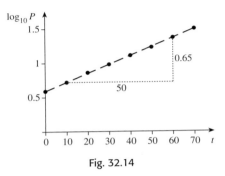

Fig. 32.14

The dashed line in Fig. 32.14 is an attempt to draw by eye a line that best fits the plotted points. By measurement, it seems that the intercept on the vertical axis is about 0.59; and, by using a suitable gradient triangle (shown with dotted lines), you can find that the gradient is about $\dfrac{0.65}{50} = 0.013$.

So the line has equation

$$\log_{10} P = 0.59 + 0.013t,$$

which is of the desired form $\log_{10} P = \log_{10} a + t \log_{10} b$ with $\log_{10} a \approx 0.59$ and $\log_{10} b \approx 0.013$.

So $\qquad a \approx 10^{0.59} \approx 3.9 \quad$ and $\quad b = 10^{0.013} \approx 1.03.$

It follows that, over the period from 1790 to 1860, the growth of the population could be described to a good degree of accuracy by the law

$$P = 3.9 \times 1.03^{t}.$$

An equation like $P = 3.9 \times 1.03^{t}$ is called a **mathematical model**. It is not an exact equation giving the precise size of the population, but it is an equation of a simple form which describes the growth of the population to a very good degree of accuracy. For example, if you wanted to know the population in 1836, when $t = 46$, you could calculate $3.9 \times 1.03^{46} = 15.2...$, and assert with confidence that in that year the population of the USA was between 15 and $15\frac{1}{2}$ million.

Exercise 32B

1 A rumour spreads exponentially through a college. 100 people have heard it by noon, and 200 by 1 p.m. How many people have heard it

(a) by 3 p.m., (b) by 12.30 p.m., (c) by 1.45 p.m.?

2 A cup of coffee at 85 °C is placed in a freezer at 0 °C. The temperature of the coffee decreases exponentially, so that after 5 minutes it is 30 °C.

(a) What is its temperature after 3 minutes?

(b) Find how long it will take for the temperature to drop to 5 °C.

3 The population of Camford is increasing at a rate of 6% each year. On 1 January 1990 it was 35 200. What was its population on

(a) 1 January 2000,   (b) 1 July 1990,   (c) 1 January 1980?

4 The population of the UK in 1971 was 5.5615×10^7; by 1992 it was estimated to be 5.7384×10^7. Assuming a steady exponential growth estimate the population in

(a) 2003,   (b) 1981.

5 The strength of a radioactive source is said to 'decay exponentially'. Explain briefly what is meant by exponential decay, and illustrate your answer by means of a sketch-graph.

After t years the strength S of a particular radioactive source, in appropriate units, is given by $S = 10\,000 \times 3^{-0.0014t}$. State the value of S when $t = 0$, and find the value of t when the source has decayed to one-half of its initial strength, giving your answer correct to 3 significant figures.

(OCR, adapted)

6 An orchestra tunes to a frequency of 440, which sounds the A which is 9 semitones above middle C. Each octave higher doubles the frequency, and each of the 12 semitones in the octave increases the frequency in the same ratio.

(a) What is this ratio?   (b) Find the frequency of middle C.

(c) How many semitones above the A is a note with a frequency of 600? Where is this on the scale?

7 (a) If $\log_{10} y = 0.4 + 0.6x$, express y in terms of x.

(b) If $\log_{10} y = 12 - 3x$, express y in terms of x.

(c) If $\log_{10} y = 0.7 + 1.7x$, express y in terms of x.

(d) If $\log_{10} y = 0.7 + 2\log_{10} x$, express y in terms of x.

(e) If $\log_{10} y = -0.5 - 5\log_{10} x$, express y in terms of x.

8 Population census data for the USA from 1870 to 1910 were as follows.

Year	1870	1880	1890	1900	1910
Population (millions)	38.6	50.2	63.0	76.0	92.0

Investigate how well these figures can be described by an exponential model.

9 With the data of Example 32.1.3, graph the logarithm of the amount against t, and explain how your graph can be used to show that the amount does not grow exponentially.

10 For the data in Exercise 32A Question 10, use graphs of log(index) for each country to investigate whether the increase or decrease of the index is exponential. Where it is, give an expression for the index in the year $(2000 + t)$ in the form ar^t.

Review exercise 8

1 The diagram shows the curve $y = x^3$. The point P has coordinates $(3, 27)$ and $[PQ]$ is the tangent to the curve at P. Find the area of the region enclosed between the curve, $[PQ]$ and the x-axis.

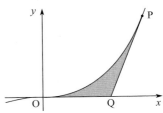

2 Given that $\displaystyle\int_1^p (8x^3 + 6x)\, dx = 39$, find two possible values of p. Use a graph to explain why there are two values.

3 Given that $f(x)$ and $g(x)$ are two functions such that $\displaystyle\int_0^4 f(x)\, dx = 17$ and $\displaystyle\int_0^4 g(x)\, dx = 11$, find, where possible, the value of each of the following.

(a) $\displaystyle\int_0^4 (f(x) - g(x))\, dx$
(b) $\displaystyle\int_0^4 (2f(x) + 3g(x))\, dx$
(c) $\displaystyle\int_0^2 f(x)\, dx$

(d) $\displaystyle\int_0^4 (f(x) + 2x + 3)\, dx$
(e) $\displaystyle\int_0^1 f(x)\, dx + \int_1^4 f(x)\, dx$
(f) $\displaystyle\int_4^0 g(x)\, dx$

4 Evaluate, correct to the nearest whole number,
$$0.99 + 0.99^2 + 0.99^3 + \ldots + 0.99^{99}.$$

5 A post is being driven into the ground by a mechanical hammer. The distance it is driven by the first blow is 8 cm. Subsequently, the distance it is driven by each blow is $\frac{9}{10}$ of the distance it was driven by the previous blow. The post is to be driven a total distance of 70 cm into the ground. Show that at least 20 blows will be needed.

Explain why the post can never be driven a total distance of more than 80 cm into the ground.

6 At the beginning of 1990, an investor decided to invest $6000, believing that the value of the investment should increase, on average, by 6% each year. Show that, if this percentage rate of increase was in fact maintained for 10 years, the value of the investment will be about $10 745.

The investor added a further $6000 at the beginning of each year between 1991 and 1995 inclusive. Assuming that the 6% annual rate of increase continues to apply, show that the total value, in dollars, of the investment at the beginning of the year 2000 may be written as $6000(1.06^5 + 1.06^6 + \ldots + 1.06^{10})$ and evaluate this, correct to the nearest dollar.

7 The sum of the infinite geometric series $1 + r + r^2 + \ldots$ is k times the sum of the series $1 - r + r^2 - \ldots$, where $k > 0$. Express r in terms of k.

8 Prove that $\log\left(\dfrac{p}{q}\right) + \log\left(\dfrac{q}{r}\right) + \log\left(\dfrac{r}{p}\right) = 0.$

9 A savings account is opened with a single payment of $2000. It attracts compound interest at a constant rate of 0.5% per month.

   (a) Find the amount in the account after two complete years.

   (b) Find after how many months the value of the investment will have doubled.

10 A dangerous radioactive substance has a half-life of 90 years. It will be deemed safe when its activity is down to 0.05 of its initial value. How long will it be before it is deemed safe?

11 The membership of a society has grown from 5000 to 7000 over a period of three years. If the growth in membership is exponential, what will it be after a further two years?

12 It is feared that the population of a species of finch on a remote island is endangered. At the beginning of the year 2000 it was estimated that there were 800 breeding pairs. By the beginning of 2005 this number had dropped to 640. If the size of the population is decreasing exponentially, in which year would you expect the number of breeding pairs to drop below 200?

13 (a) Find $\int x(x^2 - 2)\,dx$.

   (b) The diagram shows the graph of $y = x(x^2 - 2)$ for $x \geq 0$. The value of a is such that the two shaded regions have equal areas. Find the value of a.   (OCR)

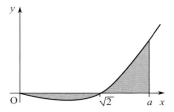

14 The diagram shows a sketch of the graph of $y = x^2$ and the normal to the curve at the point A(1, 1).

   (a) Use differentiation to find the equation of the normal at A. Verify that the point B where the normal cuts the curve again has coordinates $\left(-\frac{3}{2}, \frac{9}{4}\right)$.

   (b) The region which is bounded by the curve and the normal is shaded in the diagram. Calculate its area, giving your answer as an exact fraction.   (OCR)

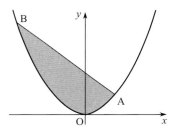

15 The diagram shows the graph of $y = \sqrt[3]{x} - x^2$. Show by integration that the area of the region (shaded in the diagram) between the curve and the x-axis is $\frac{5}{12}$.   (OCR)

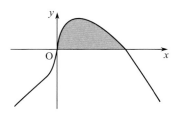

16 Solve each of the following equations to find x in terms of a where $a > 0$ and $a \neq 100$. The logarithms are to base 10.

   (a) $a^x = 10^{2x+1}$ (b) $2\log(2x) = 1 + \log a$ (OCR, adapted)

17 Solve the equation $3^{2x} = 4^{2-x}$, giving your answer to 3 significant figures.   (OCR)

18 Solve the inequality $8^x > 10^{30}$.   (OCR)

Examination questions

1 The figure below shows part of the curve $y = x^3 - 7x^2 + 14x - 7$. The curve crosses the x-axis at the points A, B and C.

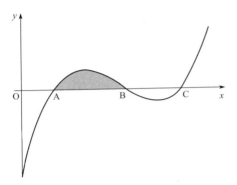

(a) Find the x-coordinate of A.

(b) Find the x-coordinate of B.

(c) Find the area of the shaded region.

(© IBO 2002)

2 The diagram below shows the graph of $y_1 = f(x)$, $0 \le x \le 4$.

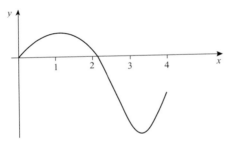

On a copy of the axes below, sketch the graph of $y_2 = \int_0^x f(t)\,dt$, marking clearly the points of inflexion.

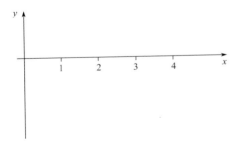

(© IBO 2002)

3 A geometric sequence has all positive terms. The sum of the first two terms is 15 and the sum to infinity is 27. Find the value of

(a) the common ratio,   (b) the first term.

(© IBO 2003)

4 Find the **exact** value of x satisfying the equation $(3^x)(4^{2x+1}) = 6^{x+2}$.

Give your answer in the form $\dfrac{\log a}{\log b}$ where $a, b \in \mathbb{Z}$.   (© IBO 2003)

5 A geometric series has a negative common ratio. The sum of the first two terms is 6. The sum to infinity is 8. Find the common ratio and the first term.   (© IBO 2004)

6 The three terms $a, 1, b$ are in arithmetic progression. The three terms $1, a, b$ are in geometric progression. Find the value of a and of b given that $a \neq b$.   (© IBO 2004)

7 The diagram shows a sector AOB of a circle of radius 1 and centre O, where $A\hat{O}B = \theta$. The lines $(AB_1), (A_1B_2), (A_2B_3)$ are perpendicular to OB. A_1B_1, A_2B_2, A_3B_3 are all arcs of circles with centre O.

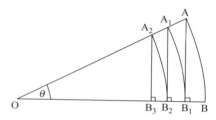

Calculate the sum to infinity of the arc lengths $AB + A_1B_1 + A_2B_2 + A_3B_3 + \ldots$.   (© IBO 2004)

8 Solve the equation $2\log_3 (x - 3) + \log_{\frac{1}{3}} (x + 1) = 2$.   (© IBO 2005)

9 The sum of the first n terms of an arithmetic sequence $\{u_n\}$ is given by the formula $S_n = 4n^2 - 2n$. Three terms of this sequence, u_2, u_m and u_{32}, are consecutive terms in a geometric sequence. Find m.   (© IBO 2005)

10 Find $\displaystyle\sum_{r=1}^{50} \log (2^r)$, giving the answer in the form $a \log 2$, where $a \in \mathbb{Q}$.   (© IBO 2002)

11 A particle moves in a straight line with velocity, in metres per second, at time t seconds, given by $v(t) = 6t^2 - 6t, t \geq 0$.

Calculate the total distance travelled by the particle in the first two seconds of motion.   (© IBO 2002)

12 Solve $\log_{16} \sqrt[3]{100 - x^2} = \frac{1}{2}$.   (© IBO 2003)

13 Solve $2(5^{x+1}) = 1 + \dfrac{3}{5^x}$, giving the answer in the form $a + \log_5 b$, where $a, b \in \mathbb{Z}$.   (© IBO 2003)

14 Find the total area of the two regions enclosed by the curve $y = x^3 - 3x^2 - 9x + 27$ and the line $y = x + 3$.   (© IBO 2004)

15 Find an expression for the sum of the first 35 terms of the series

$$\log x^2 + \log \frac{x^2}{y} + \log \frac{x^2}{y^2} + \log \frac{x^2}{y^3} + \ldots$$

giving your answer in the form $\log \dfrac{x^m}{y^n}$, where $m, n \in \mathbb{N}$.   (© IBO 2004)

16 The first three terms of a geometric sequence are also the first, eleventh and sixteenth term of an arithmetic sequence.

The terms of the geometric sequence are all different.

The sum to infinity of the geometric sequence is 18.

(a) Find the common ratio of the geometric sequence, clearly showing all working.

(b) Find the common difference of the arithmetic sequence.   (© IBO 2005)

33 Discrete probability distributions

This chapter introduces the idea of a random variable. When you have completed it, you should

- understand what a random variable is
- know the properties of a random variable
- be able to construct a probability distribution table for a random variable
- understand and be able to calculate expectation from a probability distribution table
- understand and be able to calculate variance from a probability distribution table.

33.1 Random variables

Most people have played board games at some time. Here is an example.

Game A A turn consists of throwing a dice and then moving a number of squares equal to the score on the dice.

'The number of squares moved in a turn' is a variable because it can take different numerical values, namely 1, 2, 3, 4, 5 and 6. However, the value taken at any one turn cannot be predicted, but depends on chance. For these reasons 'the number of squares moved in a turn' is called a 'random variable'.

> A **random variable** is a quantity whose numerical value depends on chance.

Although you cannot predict the result of the next throw of the dice, you do know that, if the dice is fair, the probability of getting each value is $\frac{1}{6}$. A convenient way of expressing this information is to let X stand for 'the number of squares moved in a turn'. Then, for example, $P(X = 3) = \frac{1}{6}$ means 'the probability that X takes the value 3 is $\frac{1}{6}$'. Generalising, $P(X = x)$ means 'the probability that the variable X takes the value x'.

> Note how the capital letter stands for the variable itself and the small letter stands for the value which the variable takes.

This notation is used in Table 33.1 to give the possible values for the number of squares moved and the probability of each value. This table is called the 'probability distribution' of X.

x	1	2	3	4	5	6	Total
$P(X = x)$	$\frac{1}{6}$	$\frac{1}{6}$	$\frac{1}{6}$	$\frac{1}{6}$	$\frac{1}{6}$	$\frac{1}{6}$	1

Table 33.1

> The **probability distribution** of a random variable is a listing of the possible values x_i of the variable and the corresponding probabilities $P(X = x_i)$.

In some board games, a dice is used in a more complicated way in order to decide how many squares a person should move. Here are two different examples.

Game B A person is allowed a second throw of the dice if a 6 is thrown, and, in this case, moves a number Y of squares equal to the sum of the two scores obtained.

Game C The dice is thrown twice and the number, W, of squares moved is the sum of the two scores.

Figure 33.2 is a tree diagram illustrating Game B.

As Y is the number of squares moved in a turn, it can take the values 1, 2, 3, 4, 5, 7, 8, 9, 10, 11 and 12. The probability of the first five values is $\frac{1}{6}$, as in the previous game. In order to score 7, you have to score 6 followed by 1. Since the two events are independent, the probability of scoring a 6 followed by a 1 is found by multiplying the two probabilities:

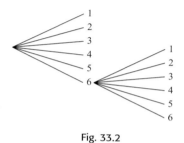

Fig. 33.2

$$P(Y = 7) = P(6 \text{ on first throw}) \times P(1 \text{ on second throw})$$
$$= \tfrac{1}{6} \times \tfrac{1}{6} = \tfrac{1}{36}.$$

The probability that Y takes each of the values 8, 9, 10, 11 and 12 will also be $\frac{1}{36}$. Table 33.3 gives the probability distribution of Y.

y	1	2	3	4	5	7	8	9	10	11	12	Total
$P(Y = y)$	$\frac{1}{6}$	$\frac{1}{6}$	$\frac{1}{6}$	$\frac{1}{6}$	$\frac{1}{6}$	$\frac{1}{36}$	$\frac{1}{36}$	$\frac{1}{36}$	$\frac{1}{36}$	$\frac{1}{36}$	$\frac{1}{36}$	1

Table 33.3

The possible values of W in Game C can be found by constructing a table as shown in Table 33.4.

		Second throw					
		1	2	3	4	5	6
	1	2	3	4	5	6	7
	2	3	4	5	6	7	8
First	3	4	5	6	7	8	9
throw	4	5	6	7	8	9	10
	5	6	7	8	9	10	11
	6	7	8	9	10	11	12

Table 33.4

There are 36 outcomes in the table and they are all equally likely, so, for example, $P(W = 6) = \frac{5}{36}$ and $P(W = 7) = \frac{6}{36}$. Table 33.5 gives the probability distribution of W. The fractions could have been cancelled but in their present forms it is easier to see the shape of the distribution.

w	2	3	4	5	6	7	8	9	10	11	12	Total
$P(W = w)$	$\frac{1}{36}$	$\frac{2}{36}$	$\frac{3}{36}$	$\frac{4}{36}$	$\frac{5}{36}$	$\frac{6}{36}$	$\frac{5}{36}$	$\frac{4}{36}$	$\frac{3}{36}$	$\frac{2}{36}$	$\frac{1}{36}$	1

Table 33.5

Figure 33.6 allows you to compare the probability distributions of X, Y and W.

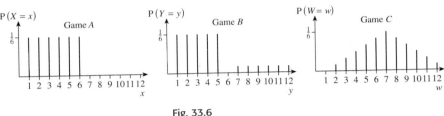

Fig. 33.6

Looking at Fig. 33.6, which method of scoring will take you round the board most quickly and which most slowly? (A method for finding the answer to this question by calculation is given in Example 33.4.1.)

Examples 33.1.1 and 33.1.2 illustrate some other probability distributions.

Example 33.1.1
A bag contains two red and three blue marbles. Two marbles are selected at random without replacement and the number, X, of blue marbles is counted. Find the probability distribution of X.

Figure 33.7 is a tree diagram illustrating this situation.

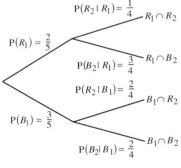

R_1 denotes the event that the first marble is red and R_2 the event that the second marble is red. Similarly B_1 and B_2 stand for the events that the first and second marbles respectively are blue. X can take the values 0, 1 and 2.

Fig. 33.7

$$P(X = 0) = P(R_1 \cap R_2)$$
$$= P(R_1) \times P(R_2 \mid R_1)$$
$$= \tfrac{2}{5} \times \tfrac{1}{4} = \tfrac{2}{20} = \tfrac{1}{10}.$$

$$P(X = 1) = P(B_1 \cap R_2) + P(R_1 \cap B_2)$$
$$= P(B_1) \times P(R_2 \mid B_1) + P(R_1) \times P(B_2 \mid R_1)$$
$$= \tfrac{3}{5} \times \tfrac{2}{4} + \tfrac{2}{5} \times \tfrac{3}{4} = \tfrac{12}{20} = \tfrac{3}{5}.$$

$$P(X = 2) = P(B_1 \cap B_2)$$
$$= P(B_1) \times P(B_2 \mid B_1)$$
$$= \tfrac{3}{5} \times \tfrac{2}{4} = \tfrac{6}{20} = \tfrac{3}{10}.$$

Here is the probability distribution of X.

x	0	1	2	Total
$P(X = x)$	$\frac{1}{10}$	$\frac{3}{5}$	$\frac{3}{10}$	1

Example 33.1.2

A random variable, X, has the probability distribution shown below.

x	1	2	3	4
$P(X = x)$	0.1	0.2	0.3	0.4

Two observations are made of X and the random variable Y is equal to the larger minus the smaller; if the two observations are equal, Y takes the value 0. Find the probability distribution of Y. Which value of Y is most likely?

Table 33.8 gives the values for X and the corresponding value of Y. Since the two observations of X are independent, you find the probability of each pair by multiplying the probabilities for the two X values, as shown in the last column of the table.

First value of X	Second value of X	Y	Probability
1	1	0	$0.1 \times 0.1 = 0.01$
1	2	1	$0.1 \times 0.2 = 0.02$
1	3	2	$0.1 \times 0.3 = 0.03$
1	4	3	$0.1 \times 0.4 = 0.04$
2	1	1	$0.2 \times 0.1 = 0.02$
2	2	0	$0.2 \times 0.2 = 0.04$
2	3	1	$0.2 \times 0.3 = 0.06$
2	4	2	$0.2 \times 0.4 = 0.08$
3	1	2	$0.3 \times 0.1 = 0.03$
3	2	1	$0.3 \times 0.2 = 0.06$
3	3	0	$0.3 \times 0.3 = 0.09$
3	4	1	$0.3 \times 0.4 = 0.12$
4	1	3	$0.4 \times 0.1 = 0.04$
4	2	2	$0.4 \times 0.2 = 0.08$
4	3	1	$0.4 \times 0.3 = 0.12$
4	4	0	$0.4 \times 0.4 = 0.16$

Table 33.8

This table shows that Y takes the values 0, 1, 2 and 3. You can find the total probability for each value of Y by adding the individual probabilities:

$$P(Y = 0) = 0.01 + 0.04 + 0.09 + 0.16 = 0.30,$$
$$P(Y = 1) = 0.02 + 0.02 + 0.06 + 0.06 + 0.12 + 0.12 = 0.40,$$
$$P(Y = 2) = 0.03 + 0.08 + 0.03 + 0.08 = 0.22,$$
$$P(Y = 3) = 0.04 + 0.04 = 0.08.$$

So Y has the probability distribution shown below.

y	0	1	2	3	Total
$P(Y = y)$	0.30	0.40	0.22	0.08	1

The most likely value of Y is 1, because it has the highest probability.

Exercise 33A

1 A fair coin is thrown four times. The random variable X is the number of heads obtained. Tabulate the probability distribution of X.

2 Two fair dice are thrown simultaneously. The random variable D is the difference between the smaller and the larger score, or zero if they are the same. Tabulate the probability distribution of D.

3 A fair dice is thrown once. The random variable X is related to the number N thrown on the dice as follows. If N is even then X is half N; otherwise X is double N. Tabulate the probability distribution of X.

4 Two fair dice are thrown simultaneously. The random variable H is the highest common factor of the two scores. Tabulate the probability distribution of H, combining together all the possible ways of obtaining the same value.

5 When a four-sided dice is thrown, the score is the number on the bottom face. Two fair four-sided dice, each with faces numbered 1 to 4, are thrown simultaneously. The random variable M is the product of the two scores multiplied together. Tabulate the probability distribution of M, combining together all the possible ways of obtaining the same value.

6 A bag contains six red and three green counters. Two counters are drawn from the bag, without replacement. Tabulate the probability distribution of the number of green counters obtained.

7 Tim picks a card at random from an ordinary pack. If the card is an ace, he stops; if not, he continues to pick cards at random, without replacement, until either an ace is picked, or four cards have been drawn. The random variable C is the total number of cards drawn.

Construct a tree diagram to illustrate the possible outcomes of the experiment, and use it to calculate the probability distribution of C.

33.2 An important property of a probability distribution

You have probably noticed that, in all the probability distributions considered so far, the sum of the probabilities is 1. This must always be the case, because one of the outcomes must happen. This is an important property of a probability distribution and a useful check that you have found the probabilities correctly.

For any discrete random variable, X, the sum of the probabilities is 1; that is,

$$\sum P(X = x) = 1.$$

Notice that in this case you are given no upper and lower values for the summation. In this case it is easier to think of it simply as, the sum of the probabilities is 1.

Example 33.2.1

The table below gives the probability distribution of the random variable T.

Find   (a) the value of c,   (b) $P(T \le 3)$,   (c) $P(T > 3)$.

t	1	2	3	4	5
$P(T = t)$	c	$2c$	$2c$	$2c$	c

(a) Since the probabilities must sum to 1,

$$c + 2c + 2c + 2c + c = 1, \quad \text{so} \quad 8c = 1, \quad \text{giving} \quad c = \tfrac{1}{8}.$$

(b) $P(T \le 3) = P(T = 1) + P(T = 2) + P(T = 3)$
$$= c + 2c + 2c$$
$$= 5c = \tfrac{5}{8}.$$

(c) $P(T > 3) = P(T = 4) + P(T = 5)$
$$= 2c + c = 3c = \tfrac{3}{8}.$$

Example 33.2.2

A computer is programmed to give single-digit numbers X between 0 and 9 inclusive in such a way that the probability of getting an odd digit $(1, 3, 5, 7, 9)$ is half the probability of getting an even digit $(0, 2, 4, 6, 8)$. Find the probability distribution of X.

Let the probability of getting an even digit be c. Then the probability of getting an odd digit is $\tfrac{1}{2}c$.

Since the probabilities must sum to 1,

$$\sum P(X = x) = \tfrac{1}{2}c + c + \tfrac{1}{2}c + c + \tfrac{1}{2}c + c + \tfrac{1}{2}c + c + \tfrac{1}{2}c + c = 1$$

which gives $\tfrac{15}{2}c = 1$; that is, $c = \tfrac{2}{15}$.

The probability distribution of X is $P(X = x) = \tfrac{1}{15}$ for $x = 1, 3, 5, 7$ and 9 and $P(X = x) = \tfrac{2}{15}$ for $x = 0, 2, 4, 6$ and 8.

Exercise 33B

1 In the following probability distribution, c is a constant. Find the value of c.

x	0	1	2	3
$P(X = x)$	$\frac{1}{4}$	$\frac{1}{5}$	$\frac{1}{2}$	c

2 In the following probability distribution, d is a constant. Find the value of d.

x	0	1	2	3
$P(X = x)$	d	0.1	0.2	0.4

3 In the following probability distribution, d is a constant. Find the value of d.

x	0	1	2	3	4
$P(X = x)$	d	0.2	0.15	0.2	$2d$

4 The score S on a spinner is a random variable with distribution given by $P(S = s) = k$ ($s = 1, 2, 3, 4, 5, 6, 7, 8$), where k is a constant. Find the value of k.

5 A cubical dice is biased so that the probability of an odd number is three times the probability of an even number. Find the probability distribution of the score.

6 A cubical dice is biased so that the probability of any particular score between 1 and 6 (inclusive) being obtained is proportional to that score. Find the probability of scoring a 1.

7 For a biased cubical dice the probability of any particular score between 1 and 6 (inclusive) being obtained is inversely proportional to that score. Find the probability of scoring a 1.

8 In the following probability distribution, c is a constant. Find the value of c.

x	0	1	2	3
$P(X = x)$	0.6	0.16	c	c^2

33.3   Using a probability distribution as a model

So far, the discussion of probability distributions in this chapter has been very mathematical. At this point it may be helpful to point out the practical application of probability distributions. Probability distributions are useful because they provide models for experiments. Consider again the random variable X, the score on a dice, whose probability distribution was given in Table 33.1. Suppose you actually threw a dice 360 times. Since the values 1, 2, 3, 4, 5 and 6 have equal probabilities, you would expect them to occur with approximately equal frequencies of, in this case, $\frac{1}{6} \times 360 = 60$. It is very unlikely that all the observed frequencies will be exactly equal to 60. However, if the model is a suitable one, the observed frequencies should be close to the expected values.

> What conclusion would you draw about the dice if the observed frequencies were not close to the expected values?

Now look at the random variable Y, whose probability distribution was given in Table 33.3. For this variable the values are not equally likely and so you would not expect to observe approximately equal frequencies. In Section 26.2 you met the idea that

$$\text{probability} \approx \frac{\text{frequency}}{\text{total frequency}}.$$

You can rearrange this equation to give an expression for the frequencies you would expect to observe:

$$\text{frequency} \approx \text{total frequency} \times \text{probability}.$$

For 360 observations of Y, the expected frequencies will be about $360 \times \frac{1}{6} = 60$ for $y = 1, 2, 3, 4, 5$ and $360 \times \frac{1}{36} = 10$ for $y = 7, 8, 9, 10, 11$ and 12.

> What will the expected frequencies be for 360 observations of the random variable W, whose probability distribution is given in Table 33.5?

Exercise 33C

1 A card is chosen at random from a pack and replaced. This experiment is carried out 520 times. State the expected number of times on which the card is

(a) a club,

(b) an ace,

(c) a picture card (K, Q, J)

(d) either an ace or a club or both,

(e) neither an ace nor a club.

2 The biased dice of Exercise 33B, Question 5, is rolled 420 times. State how many times you would expect to obtain

(a) a one,   (b) an even number,   (c) a prime number.

3 The table below gives the cumulative probability distribution for a random variable R. 'Cumulative' means that the probability given is $P(R \le r)$, not $P(R = r)$.

r	0	1	2	3	4	5
$P(R \le r)$	0.116	0.428	0.765	0.946	0.995	1.000

One hundred observations of R are made. Calculate the expected frequencies of each outcome, giving each to the nearest whole number.

4 A random variable G has a probability distribution given by the following formulae:

$$P(G = g) = \begin{cases} 0.3 \times (0.7)^g & (g = 1, 2, 3, 4) \\ k & (g = 5) \\ 0 & \text{(all other values of } g\text{)}. \end{cases}$$

Find the value of k, and find the expected frequency of the result $G = 3$ when 1000 independent observations of G are made.

33.4 Expectation

In a game at a fund-raising event, you can pay to have a turn at spinning a roulette wheel. The wheel is numbered 1, 2, 3, and so on, up to 37. If the ball lands on 10, you win £10; if it lands on a number ending in 5, you win £5; otherwise, you win nothing. The amount, X, that you win is a random variable. If the roulette wheel is fair, X takes the values 10, 5 and 0, with probabilities

$$P(X = 10) = P(\text{ball lands on } 10) = \tfrac{1}{37},$$
$$P(X = 5) = P(\text{ball lands on } 5, \ 15, \ 25, \ 35) = \tfrac{4}{37},$$
$$P(X = 0) = 1 - P(X = 5) - P(X = 10) = 1 - \tfrac{4}{37} - \tfrac{1}{37} = \tfrac{32}{37},$$

and the probability distribution of X is given below.

x	0	5	10
$P(X = x)$	$\tfrac{32}{37}$	$\tfrac{4}{37}$	$\tfrac{1}{37}$

How much should the person running the game charge for a turn? Obviously the idea is to make a profit, so a starting point would be to find the charge if the game is to break even. This involves finding the mean amount won per turn. Consider the situation after 3700 turns at the game. You can calculate the frequencies you would expect using

$$\text{frequency} \approx \text{probability} \times \text{total frequency}$$

(see Section 33.3). You might expect to win nothing about $3700 \times \tfrac{32}{37} = 3200$ times, £5 about $3700 \times \tfrac{4}{37} = 400$ times and £10 about $3700 \times \tfrac{1}{37} = 100$ times. The total amount won in £s in 3700 turns would be about $(0 \times 3200) + (5 \times 400) + (10 \times 100) = 3000$ so the mean amount per turn would be £$\tfrac{3000}{3700} = $ £0.8108... .

If you look at this calculation carefully, you will see that the result obtained is independent of the number of turns. For example, if you had 7400 turns, then the amount won would double but the mean amount would remain the same. This suggests that the person running the stall needs to charge at least 81.08... p, which in practice means 82 p.

The same result can be obtained more directly by multiplying each value by its probability and summing. Using p_i as a shortened form of $P(X = x_i)$, this gives

$$\sum_{i=1}^{n} p_i x_i = \left(\tfrac{32}{37} \times 0\right) + \left(\tfrac{4}{37} \times 5\right) + \left(\tfrac{1}{37} \times 10\right) = \tfrac{30}{37}.$$

The value which has been calculated is a theoretical mean. It is denoted by μ (which you met in Section 6.5). The symbol μ is used in order to distinguish the mean of a probability distribution from $\bar{x}$, the mean of a data set. The mean, μ, of a probability distribution does not represent the amount won at a single turn or even the mean amount won over a finite number of turns. It is the value to which the mean amount won tends as the number of turns gets larger and larger, or, as mathematicians say, 'tends to infinity'. In practice, it is helpful to think of μ as the mean amount you would expect to win in a very long run of turns. For this reason, μ is often called the **expectation** or **expected value** or **mean** of X and is denoted by $E(X)$.

This suggests the following definition.

> The expectation of a random variable X is defined by
> $$E(X) = \mu = \sum p_i x_i, \quad \text{where} \quad p_i = P(X = x_i).$$

> Note that the expected value is not the same as the mode. The mode is the value with the highest probability.

Example 33.4.1
Find the expected value of each of the variables X, Y and W, which have the probability distributions given below. The variables X, Y and W were discussed in Section 33.1 in connection with the number of squares moved in a turn at three different board games.

(a)

x	1	2	3	4	5	6	Total
$P(X = x)$	$\tfrac{1}{6}$	$\tfrac{1}{6}$	$\tfrac{1}{6}$	$\tfrac{1}{6}$	$\tfrac{1}{6}$	$\tfrac{1}{6}$	1

(b)

y	1	2	3	4	5	7	8	9	10	11	12	Total
$P(Y = y)$	$\tfrac{1}{6}$	$\tfrac{1}{6}$	$\tfrac{1}{6}$	$\tfrac{1}{6}$	$\tfrac{1}{6}$	$\tfrac{1}{36}$	$\tfrac{1}{36}$	$\tfrac{1}{36}$	$\tfrac{1}{36}$	$\tfrac{1}{36}$	$\tfrac{1}{36}$	1

(c)

w	2	3	4	5	6	7	8	9	10	11	12	Total
$P(W = w)$	$\tfrac{1}{36}$	$\tfrac{2}{36}$	$\tfrac{3}{36}$	$\tfrac{4}{36}$	$\tfrac{5}{36}$	$\tfrac{6}{36}$	$\tfrac{5}{36}$	$\tfrac{4}{36}$	$\tfrac{3}{36}$	$\tfrac{2}{36}$	$\tfrac{1}{36}$	1

(a) $E(X) = \sum p_i x_i = \left(\tfrac{1}{6} \times 1\right) + \left(\tfrac{1}{6} \times 2\right) + \left(\tfrac{1}{6} \times 3\right) + \left(\tfrac{1}{6} \times 4\right) + \left(\tfrac{1}{6} \times 5\right) + \left(\tfrac{1}{6} \times 6\right) = 3\tfrac{1}{2}.$

You may have spotted that there is a quicker way to find the mean in this example. Since the distribution is symmetrical about $3\tfrac{1}{2}$, the mean must equal $3\tfrac{1}{2}$.

(b) This distribution is not symmetrical and so the mean has to be calculated.

$$\begin{aligned}
E(Y) = \sum p_i y_i &= \left(\tfrac{1}{6} \times 1\right) + \left(\tfrac{1}{6} \times 2\right) + \left(\tfrac{1}{6} \times 3\right) + \left(\tfrac{1}{6} \times 4\right) + \left(\tfrac{1}{6} \times 5\right) + \left(\tfrac{1}{36} \times 7\right) \\
&\quad + \left(\tfrac{1}{36} \times 8\right) + \left(\tfrac{1}{36} \times 9\right) + \left(\tfrac{1}{36} \times 10\right) + \left(\tfrac{1}{36} \times 11\right) + \left(\tfrac{1}{36} \times 12\right) \\
&= \tfrac{1}{6} \times (1 + 2 + 3 + 4 + 5) + \tfrac{1}{36} \times (7 + 8 + 9 + 10 + 11 + 12) \\
&= \tfrac{1}{6} \times 15 + \tfrac{1}{36} \times 57 = 4\tfrac{1}{12}.
\end{aligned}$$

(c) As in part (a), the probability distribution is symmetrical, in this case about 7, so $E(W) = 7$.

This calculation shows that you expect to move round the board fastest in Game C and slowest in Game A. In practice this may not happen in the short term as the actual moves depend on chance and will not necessarily follow the pattern predicted by the model.

Example 33.4.2
A random variable R has the probability distribution shown below.

r	1	2	3	4
$P(R = r)$	0.1	a	0.3	b

Given that $E(R) = 3$, find a and b.

Since $\sum_{r=1}^{4} P(R = r) = 1$,

$$0.1 + a + 0.3 + b = 1, \quad \text{so} \quad a + b = 0.6.$$

Also $E(R) = 3$, so $\sum_{r=1}^{4} P(R = r) \times r = 3$,

$$0.1 \times 1 + a \times 2 + 0.3 \times 3 + b \times 4 = 3, \quad \text{so} \quad 2a + 4b = 2.$$

Solving these two equations simultaneously gives $a = 0.2$ and $b = 0.4$.

33.5 The variance of a random variable

Example 33.4.1 showed that the random variables X, Y and W have different means. If you compare the probability distributions (which are illustrated in Fig. 33.6), you will see that X, Y and W also have different degrees of spread. Just as the spread in a data set can be measured by the standard deviation or variance, so it is possible to define a corresponding measure of spread for a random variable.

Before giving a definition of $\text{Var}(X)$, it is helpful to look at another method of arriving at a suitable formula for the definition of $E(X)$.

Suppose you had a sample of n turns at the roulette wheel game described in Section 33.4 and won nothing with frequency f_1, £5 with frequency f_2 and £10 with frequency f_3. The sample mean $\bar{x}$ for these n turns is given by

$$\bar{x} = \frac{\sum\limits_{i=1}^{n} f_i x_i}{n} = \frac{f_1 \times 0}{n} + \frac{f_2 \times 5}{n} + \frac{f_3 \times 10}{n}.$$

The right side of the expression can be written slightly differently in the form

$$\bar{x} = \frac{f_1}{n} \times 0 + \frac{f_2}{n} \times 5 + \frac{f_3}{n} \times 10 = \sum_{i=1}^{n} \left(\frac{f_i}{n} \times x_i \right).$$

Now consider what happens as n becomes very large: the ratio $\frac{f_i}{n}$, which is the relative frequency, tends to the corresponding theoretical probability, $P(X = x_i)$, or p_i.

This again suggests that

$$E(X) = \sum_{i=1}^{n} p_i x_i \quad \text{where} \quad p_i = P(X = x_i),$$

is a suitable definition for the expectation $E(X)$.

Now consider the formula

$$s_n^2 = \frac{\sum_{i=1}^{n} f_i (x_i - \bar{x})^2}{n} \quad \text{where} \quad n = \sum_{i=1}^{n} f_i$$

given in Section 7.10 for the variance of a data set.

Again consider what happens when n becomes large. The ratio $\frac{f_i}{n}$ tends to p_i, and $\bar{x}$ tends to $E(X)$, making the right side

$$\sum_{i=1}^{n} p_i (x_i - E(X))^2.$$

It is helpful to replace $E(X)$ by μ in this expression, giving

$$\sum_{i=1}^{n} p_i (x_i - \mu)^2.$$

This expression is taken as the definition of the variance, $\text{Var}(X)$, of the distribution.

> The **variance** $\text{Var}(X)$ of a random variable X is defined by
> $$\text{Var}(X) = \sum_{i=1}^{n} p_i (x_i - \mu)^2,$$
> where $p_i = P(X = x_i)$, and $\mu = E(X)$ is the expectation.

Alternatively, starting from the second version of the formula in Section 7.10,

$$s_n^2 = \frac{\sum_{i=1}^{k} f_i x_i^2}{n} - \bar{x}^2 \quad \text{where} \quad n = \sum_{i=1}^{n} f_i$$

for the variance of a data set becomes

$$\frac{\sum_{i=1}^{n} f_i x_i^2}{n} - \bar{x}^2 = \sum_{i=1}^{n} \frac{f_i}{n} \times x_i^2 - \bar{x}^2.$$

When n becomes large, $\dfrac{f_i}{n}$ tends to p_i and $\bar{x}$ tends to $E(X)$, making the right side

$$\dfrac{\sum\limits_{i=1}^{n} f_i x_i^2}{n} - \bar{x}^2 = \sum\limits_{i=1}^{n} p_i x_i^2 - (E(X))^2.$$

Replacing $E(X)$ by μ gives

$$\dfrac{\sum\limits_{i=1}^{n} f_i x_i^2}{n} - \bar{x}^2 = \sum\limits_{i=1}^{n} p_i x_i^2 - \mu^2.$$

As you saw in Chapter 7, the symbol used for the standard deviation of a random variable is σ (a small Greek s, read as 'sigma') and its square, σ^2, the variance of a random variable, is denoted by $Var(X)$. The previous work suggests the following definition.

> The **variance** $Var(X)$ of a random variable X is defined by
>
> $$Var(X) = \sigma^2 = \sum\limits_{i=1}^{n} p_i(x_i - \mu)^2 = \sum\limits_{i=1}^{n} p_i x_i^2 - \mu^2,$$
>
> where $p_i = P(X = x_i)$, and $\mu = E(X)$ is the expectation.
>
> The **standard deviation** σ of a random variable is the square root of $Var(X)$.

Note that $\sum\limits_{i=1}^{n} p_i x_i^2$ is sometimes written as $E(X^2)$.

The second formula for variance then becomes:

> The **variance** $Var(X)$ of a random variable X is given by
>
> $$Var(X) = \sigma^2 = E(X^2) - E(X)^2.$$

In practice it is usually simpler to calculate $Var(X)$ from the second version of the formula rather than the first version.

Example 33.5.1
Calculate the standard deviation of the random variable X in Section 33.1, Game A. The probability distribution of X, reproduced from Table 33.1, is shown below.

x	1	2	3	4	5	6	Total
$P(X = x)$	$\frac{1}{6}$	$\frac{1}{6}$	$\frac{1}{6}$	$\frac{1}{6}$	$\frac{1}{6}$	$\frac{1}{6}$	1

First calculate $\sum\limits_{i=1}^{n} p_i x_i^2$:

$$\sum\limits_{i=1}^{n} p_i x_i^2 = \left(\tfrac{1}{6} \times 1^2\right) + \left(\tfrac{1}{6} \times 2^2\right) + \left(\tfrac{1}{6} \times 3^2\right) + \left(\tfrac{1}{6} \times 4^2\right) + \left(\tfrac{1}{6} \times 5^2\right) + \left(\tfrac{1}{6} \times 6^2\right)$$
$$= \tfrac{1}{6} \times (1^2 + 2^2 + 3^2 + 4^2 + 5^2 + 6^2) = \tfrac{1}{6} \times 91 = 15\tfrac{1}{6}.$$

From Example 33.4.1, $\mu = E(X) = 3\frac{1}{2}$.

Using the second alternative in the blue box,

$$\sigma^2 = \text{Var}(X) = \sum_{i=1}^{n} p_i x_i^2 - \mu^2$$

$$= 15\frac{1}{6} - \left(3\frac{1}{2}\right)^2 = \frac{35}{12}.$$

The standard deviation σ is the square root of the variance, so

$$\text{standard deviation} = \sqrt{\frac{35}{12}} = 1.71 \text{ correct to 3 significant figures.}$$

The standard deviations for the random variables Y and W in Section 33.1, Games B and C, are $\sqrt{\frac{10\,395}{1296}} = 2.83$ and $\sqrt{\frac{35}{6}} = 2.42$ respectively, both given to 3 significant figures. You could check these values. If you look again at Fig. 33.6 you will see how the size of the standard deviation is related to the degree of spread of the distribution. Although Y and W have very similar ranges, W has a smaller standard deviation because the probability distribution rises to a peak at the centre.

Example 33.5.2

In a certain field, each mushroom which is growing gives rise to a number X of mushrooms in the following year. None of the mushrooms present in one year survives until the next year. The random variable X has the probability distribution

x	0	1	2
$P(X = x)$	0.2	0.6	0.2

If there were two mushrooms present in one year, find the probability distribution of Y, the number of mushrooms present in the following year. Hence find the mean and variance of Y.

The possible values of Y are given below.

		First value of X		
		0	1	2
	0	0	1	2
Second value of X	1	1	2	3
	2	2	3	4

The corresponding probabilities are given below.

		First value of X		
		0	1	2
	0	0.2×0.2	0.2×0.6	0.2×0.2
Second value of X	1	0.6×0.2	0.6×0.6	0.6×0.2
	2	0.2×0.2	0.2×0.6	0.2×0.2

Combining these two sets of results gives the probability distribution of Y, from which $E(Y)$ and $Var(Y)$ can be found.

y	$P(Y = y)$	$P(Y = y)y$	$P(Y = y)y^2$
0	0.04	0	0
1	$0.12 + 0.12 = 0.24$	0.24	0.24
2	$0.04 + 0.36 + 0.04 = 0.44$	0.88	1.76
3	$0.12 + 0.12 = 0.24$	0.72	2.16
4	0.04	0.16	0.64
Totals:	$\sum_{i=0}^{4} P(Y = y_i) = 1$	$\sum_{i=0}^{4} P(Y = y_i)y_i = 2$	$\sum_{i=0}^{4} P(Y = y_i)y_i^2 = 4.8$

From the last row of the table $\sum_{i=0}^{4} P(Y = y_i)y_i = 2$, and $\sum_{i=0}^{4} P(Y = y_i)y_i^2 = 4.8$.

Then $\mu = E(Y) = \sum_{i=0}^{4} P(Y = y_i)y_i = 2$, and

$$Var(Y) = \sum_{i=0}^{4} P(Y = y_i)y_i^2 - \mu^2 = 4.8 - 2^2 = 0.8.$$

You could have predicted that $E(Y) = 2$ by symmetry.

Exercise 33D

In this exercise all variables are discrete. Give numerical answers to 4 significant figures when appropriate.

1   Find the mean of the random variables X and Y which have the following probability distributions.

(a)

x	0	1	2	3	4
$P(X = x)$	$\frac{1}{8}$	$\frac{3}{8}$	$\frac{1}{8}$	$\frac{1}{4}$	$\frac{1}{8}$

(b)

y	-2	-1	0	1	2	3
$P(Y = y)$	0.15	0.25	0.3	0.05	0.2	0.05

2   The random variable T has the probability distribution given in the following table.

t	1	2	3	4	5	6	7
$P(T = t)$	0.1	0.2	0.1	0.2	0.1	0.2	0.1

Find $E(T)$ and $Var(T)$.

3 Find the exact expectation and variance of the random variable Y, which has the following probability distribution.

y	3	4	5	6	7
$P(Y = y)$	$\frac{1}{18}$	$\frac{5}{18}$	$\frac{7}{18}$	$\frac{1}{18}$	$\frac{4}{18}$

4 The six faces of a fair cubical dice are numbered 1, 2, 2, 3, 3 and 3. When the dice is thrown once, the score is the number appearing on the top face. This is denoted by X.

(a) Find the mean and standard deviation of X.

(b) The dice is thrown twice and Y denotes the sum of the scores obtained. Tabulate the probability distribution of Y. Hence find $E(Y)$ and $Var(Y)$.

5 A construction company can bid for one of two possible projects and the finance director has been asked to advise on which to choose. She estimates that project A will yield a profit of £150 000 with probability 0.5, a profit of £250 000 with probability 0.2 and a loss of £100 000 with probability 0.3. Project B will yield a profit of £100 000 with probability 0.6, a profit of £200 000 with probability 0.3 and a loss of £50 000 with probability 0.1. Determine which project the finance director should support, by calculating $E(A)$ and $E(B)$.

6 Some of the eggs in a supermarket are sold in boxes of six. The number, X, of broken eggs in a box has the probability distribution given in the following table.

x	0	1	2	3	4	5	6
$P(X = x)$	0.80	0.14	0.03	0.02	0.01	0	0

(a) Find the expectation and variance of X.

(b) Find the expectation and variance of the number of unbroken eggs in a box.

(c) Comment on the relationship between your answers to part (a) and part (b).

7 The random variable X has the probability distribution given in the following table.

x	1	2	3	4	5
$P(X = x)$	a	0.3	0.2	0.1	0.2

Find the values of a, μ and σ for the distribution.

8 The random variable Y has the probability distribution given in the following table.

y	2	3	4	5	6	7
$P(Y = y)$	0.05	0.25	a	b	0.1	0.3

Given that $E(Y) = 4.9$, show that $a = b$, and find the standard deviation of Y.

9 A game is played by throwing a fair dice until either a six is obtained or four throws have been made. Let X denote the number of throws made. Find

(a) the probability distribution of X,   (b) the standard deviation of X.

The number of sixes obtained in the game is denoted by Y. Find $E(Y)$.

If the player throws a six in the course of the game then the player wins 100 points. If a six is not thrown then 150 points are lost. Find the expectation of the number of points received by a player after one game.

10* A committee of 6 men and 4 women appoints two of its members to represent it. Assuming that each member is equally likely to be appointed, obtain the probability distribution of the number of women appointed. Find the expected number of women appointed.

11* The dice of Question 4 is thrown and then an unbiased coin is thrown the number of times indicated by the score on the dice. Let H denote the number of heads obtained.

(a) Show that $P(H = 2) = \frac{13}{48}$.

(b) Tabulate the probability distribution of H.

(c) Show that $E(H) = \frac{1}{2}E(X)$, where X denotes the score on the dice.

(d) Calculate $Var(H)$.

34 The binomial distribution

This chapter introduces you to an important discrete probability distribution called the binomial distribution. When you have completed it, you should

- know the conditions for a random variable to have a binomial distribution
- be able to calculate the probabilities for the binomial distribution
- know the formula for the expectation of a binomial distribution.

34.1 Routes in an American city

Imagine an American city based on a square grid, with the roads running east-west and north-south. The roads are one unit apart and the origin is at the south-west corner of the city. How many different routes of length 6 are there from $(0, 0)$ to $(4, 2)$? And how many routes of length $r + s$ are there to (r, s)?

Figure 34.1 shows part of the city with one of the routes shown.

The first problem is not difficult, but it can be tricky to keep an accurate count of the routes; and you must bear in mind the need to generalise for the second part.

A good way to proceed is to work outwards from the origin. The number of routes from $(0, 0)$ to $(1, 0)$ is 1, and the number from $(0, 0)$ to $(0, 1)$ is 1.

These numbers are shown in Fig. 34.2a where the vertices $(1, 0)$ and $(0, 1)$ are marked with the numbers of different routes from the origin. Similarly, Fig. 34.2b shows the numbers of different routes to $(2, 0)$, $(1, 1)$ and $(0, 2)$. To avoid confusion the labels on the axes have been removed.

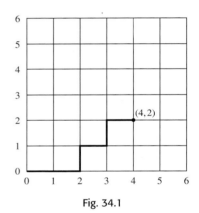

Fig. 34.1

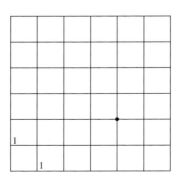

Fig. 34.2a

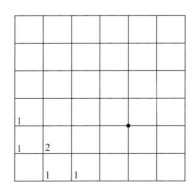

Fig. 34.2b

Moving outwards, Fig. 34.3a shows the numbers of routes of length 5. By this stage you should see that to get to (r, s) you must come from either $(r - 1, s)$ or $(r, s - 1)$: it follows that the number of routes to (r, s) is the sum of the routes to $(r - 1, s)$ and to $(r, s - 1)$. In the diagrams, this means that each number on the axes is 1 and that each number in the body of the grid is the sum of those immediately to the left and below it.

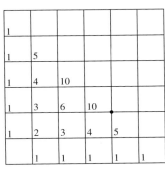

Fig. 34.3a

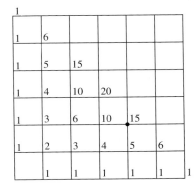

Fig. 34.3b

Figure 34.3b shows that the number of routes to (4, 2) is 15.

This is a pattern you have seen before. If you look at the numbers on the diagonals in the south-east direction, you will see that they are the numbers in Pascal's triangle. And if you refer back to Section 4.3, you will see that the binomial coefficients are given by

$$\binom{r + s}{r} = \binom{r + s}{s} = \frac{(r + s)!}{r! s!}$$

You may wonder what all this has to do with probability. The clue comes from rotating Fig. 34.3b through $45°$ clockwise, and removing some roads, so all the routes of length 6 are shown. This gives Fig. 34.4, which shows the route highlighted in Fig. 34.1.

This is now beginning to look like a tree diagram! In fact, you could denote the routes by writing them as a series of rs and ls according to whether you turn left or right at each junction. So the route highlighted might be written as $r_1 r_2 l_3 r_4 l_5 r_6$, with 4 right turns and 2 left turns to get to (4, 2), and showing exactly what happened at each stage of the route.

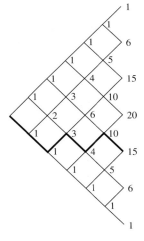

Fig. 34.4

34.2 The binomial distribution

The spinner in Fig. 34.5 is an equilateral triangle. When it is spun it comes to rest on one of its three edges. Two of the edges are white and one is black. In Fig. 34.5 the spinner is resting on the black edge. This will be described as 'showing black'.

Fig. 34.5

The spinner is fair, so the probability that the spinner shows black is $\frac{1}{3}$ and the probability that it shows white is $\frac{2}{3}$.

Suppose now that the spinner is spun on 5 separate occasions. Let the random variable X be the number of times out of 5 that the spinner shows black.

To derive the probability distribution of X, it is helpful to define some terms. The act of spinning the spinner once is called a **trial**. A simple way of describing the result of each trial is to call it a **success** (s) when the spinner shows black, and a **failure** (f) when the spinner shows white. So X could now be defined as the number of successes in the 5 trials.

The event $\{X = 0\}$ would mean that the spinner did not show black on any of its 5 spins. The notation f_1 will be used to mean that the first trial resulted in a failure, f_2 will mean that the second trial resulted in a failure, and so on, giving

$$P(X = 0) = P(\text{there are 5 failures}) = P(f_1 \, f_2 \, f_3 \, f_4 \, f_5).$$

Since the outcomes of the trials are independent,

$$P(f_1 \, f_2 \, f_3 \, f_4 \, f_5) = P(f_1) \times P(f_2) \times P(f_3) \times P(f_4) \times P(f_5)$$
$$= \tfrac{2}{3} \times \tfrac{2}{3} \times \tfrac{2}{3} \times \tfrac{2}{3} \times \tfrac{2}{3} = \tfrac{32}{243}.$$

The probability $P(X = 1)$ is more complicated to calculate. The event $\{X = 1\}$ means that there is one success and also four failures. One possible sequence of a success and four failures is $s_1 \, f_2 \, f_3 \, f_4 \, f_5$ (where s_1 denotes the event that the first trial was a success).

The probability that the first trial is a success and the other four trials are failures is

$$P(s_1 \, f_2 \, f_3 \, f_4 \, f_5) = P(s_1) \times P(f_2) \times P(f_3) \times P(f_4) \times P(f_5)$$
$$= \tfrac{1}{3} \times \tfrac{2}{3} \times \tfrac{2}{3} \times \tfrac{2}{3} \times \tfrac{2}{3}$$
$$= \left(\tfrac{1}{3}\right)\left(\tfrac{2}{3}\right)^4 = \tfrac{16}{243}.$$

However there are four other possible sequences for the event $\{X = 1\}$. They are

$$f_1 s_2 \, f_3 \, f_4 \, f_5 \quad f_1 \, f_2 s_3 \, f_4 \, f_5 \quad f_1 \, f_2 \, f_3 s_4 \, f_5 \quad f_1 \, f_2 \, f_3 \, f_4 s_5.$$

Now

$$P(s_1 \, f_2 \, f_3 \, f_4 \, f_5) = \left(\tfrac{1}{3}\right) \times \left(\tfrac{2}{3}\right)^4.$$
$$P(f_1 s_2 \, f_3 \, f_4 \, f_5) = \left(\tfrac{2}{3}\right) \times \left(\tfrac{1}{3}\right) \times \left(\tfrac{2}{3}\right)^3 = \left(\tfrac{1}{3}\right) \times \left(\tfrac{2}{3}\right)^4.$$
$$P(f_1 \, f_2 s_3 \, f_4 \, f_5) = \left(\tfrac{2}{3}\right)^2 \times \left(\tfrac{1}{3}\right) \times \left(\tfrac{2}{3}\right)^2 = \left(\tfrac{1}{3}\right) \times \left(\tfrac{2}{3}\right)^4.$$
$$P(f_1 \, f_2 \, f_3 s_4 \, f_5) = \left(\tfrac{2}{3}\right)^3 \times \left(\tfrac{1}{3}\right) \times \left(\tfrac{2}{3}\right) = \left(\tfrac{1}{3}\right) \times \left(\tfrac{2}{3}\right)^4.$$
$$P(f_1 \, f_2 \, f_3 \, f_4 s_5) = \left(\tfrac{2}{3}\right)^4 \times \left(\tfrac{1}{3}\right) = \left(\tfrac{1}{3}\right) \times \left(\tfrac{2}{3}\right)^4.$$

Therefore, summing, $P(X = 1) = 5 \times \left(\frac{1}{3}\right) \times \left(\frac{2}{3}\right)^4 = \frac{80}{243}$.

Notice that the probability for each individual sequence is the same as for any other sequence, namely $\left(\frac{1}{3}\right)\left(\frac{2}{3}\right)^4$, and that the 5 in the last line corresponds to the number of different sequences which give $X = 1$. These sequences are just like the routes in the American city to (1, 4): the number of different sequences is $\binom{5}{1}$ (see Section 4.3). Therefore

$$P(X = 1) = \binom{5}{1} \times \left(\frac{1}{3}\right) \times \left(\frac{2}{3}\right)^4.$$

Similarly you could find that for $X = 2$ there are sequences such as $s_1 s_2 f_3 f_4 f_5$ and $f_1 s_2 f_3 s_4 f_5$. To see how many of these sequences there are, it is the same as the number of routes to (2, 3), which is $\binom{5}{2}$. Each of these choices has probability $\left(\frac{1}{3}\right)^2 \times \left(\frac{2}{3}\right)^3$. Using these results

$$P(X = 2) = \binom{5}{2} \times \left(\frac{1}{3}\right)^2 \times \left(\frac{2}{3}\right)^3.$$

Continuing in this way, you can find the distribution of X, given in Table 34.6.

x	$P(X = x)$	
0	$\left(\frac{2}{3}\right)^5$	$= \frac{32}{243}$
1	$\binom{5}{1} \times \left(\frac{1}{3}\right) \times \left(\frac{2}{3}\right)^4$	$= \frac{80}{243}$
2	$\binom{5}{2} \times \left(\frac{1}{3}\right)^2 \times \left(\frac{2}{3}\right)^3$	$= \frac{80}{243}$
3	$\binom{5}{3} \times \left(\frac{1}{3}\right)^3 \times \left(\frac{2}{3}\right)^2$	$= \frac{40}{243}$
4	$\binom{5}{4} \times \left(\frac{1}{3}\right)^4 \times \left(\frac{2}{3}\right)$	$= \frac{10}{243}$
5	$\binom{5}{5} \times \left(\frac{1}{3}\right)^5$	$= \frac{1}{243}$

Table 34.6

Notice that $\sum_{x=0}^{5} P(X = x)$ is 1. This is a useful check for the probabilities in any distribution table.

Notice also that as $\left(\frac{1}{3}\right)^0 = 1$ and $\left(\frac{2}{3}\right)^0 = 1$ you could write $P(X = 0)$ as $\binom{5}{0} \times \left(\frac{1}{3}\right)^0 \times \left(\frac{2}{3}\right)^5$, and $P(X = 5)$ as $\binom{5}{5} \times \left(\frac{1}{3}\right)^5 \times \left(\frac{2}{3}\right)^0$. These results enable you to write $P(X = x)$ as a formula:

$$P(X = x) = \binom{5}{x} \times \left(\frac{1}{3}\right)^x \times \left(\frac{2}{3}\right)^{5-x}.$$

However the formula on its own is not sufficient, because you must also give the values for which the formula is defined. In this case x can take integer values from 0, the minimum value, to 5, the maximum value, inclusive. So a more concise definition of the distribution of X than Table 34.6 would be

$$P(X = x) = \binom{5}{x} \times \left(\frac{1}{3}\right)^x \times \left(\frac{2}{3}\right)^{5-x} \quad \text{for} \quad x = 0, 1, 2, \dots, 5.$$

Although the case of the spinner is not important in itself, it is an example of an important and frequently occurring situation.

- A single trial has just two possible outcomes (often called success, s, and failure, f).
- There is a fixed number of trials, n.
- The outcome of each trial is independent of the outcome of all the other trials.
- The probability of success at each trial, p, is constant.

The random variable X, which represents the number of successes in n trials of this experiment, is said to have a **binomial distribution**.

A consequence of the last condition is that the probability of failure will also be a constant, equal to $1 - p$. This probability is usually denoted by q, which means that $q = 1 - p$.

In a binomial distribution, the random variable X has a probability distribution given by

$$P(X = x) = \binom{n}{x} p^x q^{n-x} \qquad \text{for } x = 0, 1, 2, \dots, n.$$

Provided you are given the values of n and p, you can evaluate all of the probabilities in the distribution table. The values of n and p are therefore the essential pieces of information about the probability distribution. In the example, n was 5 and p was $\frac{1}{3}$. You did not need to be told q, because its value is always $1 - p$, so in the example the value of q was $\frac{2}{3}$.

The values of n and p are called the **parameters** of the binomial distribution. You need to know the parameters of a probability distribution to calculate the probabilities numerically.

To denote that a random variable X has a binomial distribution with parameters n and p, you write $X \sim B(n, p)$. So for the probability distribution in Table 34.6 you write $X \sim B(5, \frac{1}{3})$.

Example 34.2.1
Given that $X \sim B(8, \frac{1}{4})$, find   (a) $P(X = 6)$,   (b) $P(X \le 2)$,   (c) $P(X > 0)$.

(a) Using the binomial probability formula with $n = 8$ and $p = \frac{1}{4}$ you get

$$P(X = 6) = \binom{8}{6} \times \left(\tfrac{1}{4}\right)^6 \times \left(\tfrac{3}{4}\right)^2 = 28 \times \left(\tfrac{1}{4}\right)^6 \times \left(\tfrac{3}{4}\right)^2 = 0.003\,85,$$

correct to 3 significant figures.

(b) $P(X \le 2) = P(X = 0) + P(X = 1) + P(X = 2)$
$$= \binom{8}{0} \left(\tfrac{1}{4}\right)^0 \left(\tfrac{3}{4}\right)^8 + \binom{8}{1} \left(\tfrac{1}{4}\right)^1 \left(\tfrac{3}{4}\right)^7 + \binom{8}{2} \left(\tfrac{1}{4}\right)^2 \left(\tfrac{3}{4}\right)^6$$
$$= 0.1001\dots + 0.2669\dots + 0.3114\dots$$
$$= 0.6785\dots = 0.679, \text{ correct to 3 significant figures.}$$

(c) The easiest way to find $P(X > 0)$ is to use the fact that $P(X > 0)$ is the complement of $P(X = 0)$.

So $P(X > 0) = 1 - P(X = 0)$
$$= 1 - \binom{8}{0} \left(\tfrac{1}{4}\right)^0 \left(\tfrac{3}{4}\right)^8 \qquad \text{(from part (b))}$$
$$= 1 - 0.1001\dots$$
$$= 0.8998\dots = 0.900, \text{ correct to 3 significant figures.}$$

To check that the binomial formula does represent a probability distribution you must show that $\sum_{x=0}^{n} P(X = x) = 1$. Consider the example involving the spinner (Fig. 34.5), but use p and q instead of $\frac{1}{3}$ and $\frac{2}{3}$ respectively. Table 34.7 shows the distribution.

x	$P(X = x)$	
0	q^5	$= q^5$
1	$\binom{5}{1} \times p \times q^4$	$= 5pq^4$
2	$\binom{5}{2} \times p^2 \times q^3$	$= 10p^2q^3$
3	$\binom{5}{3} \times p^3 \times q^2$	$= 10p^3q^2$
4	$\binom{5}{4} \times p^4 \times q$	$= 5p^4q$
5	p^5	$= p^5$

Table 34.7

If you sum the probabilities in the right column you get

$$\sum_{x=0}^{5} P(X = x) = q^5 + 5pq^4 + 10p^2q^3 + 10p^3q^2 + 5p^4q + p^5.$$

The right side of this equation is the binomial expansion of $(q + p)^5$ (see Section 4.3). You could check for yourself by multiplying out $(q + p)(q + p)(q + p)(q + p)(q + p)$, so

$$\sum_{x=0}^{5} P(X = x) = (q + p)^5 = 1^5 = 1.$$

You can use the binomial theorem in Section 4.3 by writing $q = a$ and $p = b$ to show that

$$\sum_{x=0}^{n} P(X = x) = \sum_{x=0}^{n} \left[\binom{n}{x} \times p^x \times q^{n-x} \right]$$
$$= \sum_{x=0}^{n} \left[\binom{n}{x} q^{n-x} p^x \right]$$
$$= \binom{n}{0} q^n + \binom{n}{1} pq^{n-1} + \binom{n}{2} p^2 q^{n-2} + \ldots + \binom{n}{n} p^n$$
$$= (q + p)^n = 1^n = 1.$$

The individual probabilities in the binomial distribution are the terms of the binomial expansion of $(q + p)^n$: these are two similar uses of the word 'binomial'.

Before using the binomial distribution as a model for a situation you need to convince yourself that all the conditions are satisfied. The following example illustrates some of the problems that can occur.

Example 34.2.2

A school car park has 5 parking spaces. At the same time each day, a student observes the number of spaces which are filled. Let X be the number of spaces filled at this time on a randomly chosen day. Is it reasonable to model the distribution of the random variable X with a binomial distribution?

The student looks at each parking space to see whether it is occupied or not. This represents a single trial.

Are there exactly two outcomes for each trial (parking space), and are these mutually exclusive? In other words, is each parking space either occupied by a single car or not? The answer will usually be yes, but sometimes poorly parked vehicles will give the answer no.

Are there a fixed number of trials? The answer is yes. On each day there are 5 parking spaces available so the number of trials is 5 times the number of days on which observations were made.

Are the trials independent? This is not likely. Drivers may be less inclined to park in one of the centre spaces if it is surrounded by cars, because getting out of their own car may be more difficult.

Is the probability p of success (in this case a parking space being filled by a car) constant? Probably not, because, for example, people may be more likely to choose the space closest to the school entrance.

You can see that, when you are proposing to model a practical situation with a binomial distribution, many of the assumptions may be questionable and some may not be valid at all. In this case, however, provided you are aware that the binomial model is far from perfect, you could still use it as a reasonable approximation. You might also have realised that you do not know the value of p in this example, so you would have to estimate it. To do this you would divide the total number of cars observed by the total number of available car parking spaces, which in this case is

$5 \times$ (the number of days for which the survey was carried out).

Example 34.2.3

State whether a binomial distribution could be used in each of the following problems. If the binomial distribution is an acceptable model, define the random variable clearly and state its parameters.

(a) A fair cubical dice is rolled 10 times. Find the probability of getting three fours, four fives and three sixes.

(b) A fair coin is spun until a head occurs. Find the probability that eight spins are necessary, including the one on which the head occurs.

(c) A jar contains 49 balls numbered 1 to 49. Six of the balls are selected at random. Find the probability that four of the six have an even score.

(a) In this case you are interested in three different outcomes: a four, a five and a six. A binomial distribution depends on having only two possible outcomes, success and failure, so it cannot be used here.

You could use the binomial distribution if you just wanted the probability of getting three fours, say. Then there would be only two outcomes: getting three fours and not getting three fours.

(b) The binomial distribution requires a fixed number of trials, n, and this is not the case here, since the number of trials is unknown. In fact, the number of trials is the random variable of interest here.

(c) Whether a binomial model is appropriate or not depends on whether the selection of the balls is done with replacement or without replacement. If the selection is without replacement, then the outcome of each trial will not be independent of all the other trials. If the selection is with replacement, then define the random variable X to be the number of balls with an even score out of six random selections. X will then have a binomial distribution with parameters 6 and $\frac{24}{49}$. You write this as $X \sim B(6, \frac{24}{49})$. You are assuming, of course, that the balls are thoroughly mixed before each selection and that every ball has an equal chance of being selected.

Here is a summary of the binomial distribution:

Binomial distribution
- A single trial has exactly two possible outcomes (success and failure) and these are mutually exclusive.
- A fixed number, n, of trials takes place.
- The outcome of each trial is independent of the outcome of all the other trials.
- The probability of success at each trial is constant.

The random variable X, which represents the number of successes in the n trials of this experiment, has a probability distribution given by

$$P(X = x) = \binom{n}{x} p^x (1 - p)^{n-x} \quad \text{for } x = 0, 1, 2, \dots, n,$$

where p is the probability of success.

When the random variable X satisfies these conditions, $X \sim B(n, p)$.

34.3   Expectation of a binomial distribution

Suppose that you wanted to find the mean of the random variable X, where $X \sim B(3, \frac{1}{4})$. One way would be to write out the probability distribution and calculate $E(X)$ using the equation

$$E(X) = \mu = \sum_{i=0}^{n} p_i x_i.$$

Example 34.3.1

Calculate $E(X)$ for $X \sim B\left(3, \frac{1}{4}\right)$ from the probability distribution.

The probability distribution is found using the binomial probability formula in the blue box,

$$P(X = x) = \binom{n}{x} p^x (1-p)^{n-x}.$$

The distribution is shown in Table 34.8.

x	$P(X = x)$	$x\,P(X = x)$
0	$\binom{3}{0}\left(\frac{1}{4}\right)^0\left(\frac{3}{4}\right)^3 = \frac{27}{64}$	0
1	$\binom{3}{1}\left(\frac{1}{4}\right)^1\left(\frac{3}{4}\right)^2 = \frac{27}{64}$	$\frac{27}{64}$
2	$\binom{3}{2}\left(\frac{1}{4}\right)^2\left(\frac{3}{4}\right)^1 = \frac{9}{64}$	$\frac{18}{64}$
3	$\binom{3}{3}\left(\frac{1}{4}\right)^3\left(\frac{3}{4}\right)^0 = \frac{1}{64}$	$\frac{3}{64}$
Totals:	$\sum_{x=0}^{n} P(X = x) = 1$	$\sum_{x=0}^{n} x P(X = x) = \frac{48}{64}$

Table 34.8

The expectation $E(x)$ is given by

$$E(X) = \mu = \sum_{x=0}^{n} x P(X = x) = \frac{48}{64} = \frac{3}{4}.$$

There is, however, a formula for calculating the mean of a binomial distribution directly from n and p. If you consider the general case $X \sim B(n, p)$, then the mean would be given by

$$\sum_{x=0}^{n} x P(X = x) = \sum_{x=0}^{n} x \binom{n}{x} p^x (1-p)^{n-x}.$$

Each term in this sum depends on the parameters n and p and so it would be reasonable to assume that $E(X)$ also depends on n and p. Although this sum looks very complicated, it can be shown that it simplifies to np.

> The **expectation** or mean of a **binomial distribution** $X \sim B(n, p)$ is given by
>
> $$E(X) = np.$$

> Intuitively you might expect this result, since in n trials
>
> number of successes $\approx$ number of trials $\times$ probability of success at a single trial
> $$= n \times p = np.$$

A proof of the result in the blue box is given in the starred Section 34.5.

Example 34.3.2
Calculate E(X) for $X \sim B(3, \frac{1}{4})$ using the formula $E(X) = \mu = np$.

Using the formula,

$$E(X) = \mu = np = 3 \times \tfrac{1}{4} = \tfrac{3}{4}.$$

You can see that the second method (in Example 34.3.2) is much quicker than the first (in Example 34.3.1). The formula for calculating the mean of a binomial distribution is particularly useful when n is large, as in the following example.

Example 34.3.3
Nails are sold in packets of 100. Occasionally a nail is faulty. The number of faulty nails in a randomly chosen packet is denoted by X. Assuming that faulty nails occur independently and at random, calculate the mean of X, given that the probability of any nail being faulty is 0.04.

Since faulty nails occur independently and at random and with a fixed probability, the distribution of X can be modelled by the binomial distribution with $n = 100$ and $p = 0.04$. Therefore

$$E(X) = \mu = np = 100 \times 0.04 = 4.$$

The mean number of faulty nails in a pack is 4.

To calculate μ using the equation $\mu = E(X) = \sum x_i p_i$ would involve writing out a probability distribution with 101 terms!

34.4 Variance of a binomial distribution

Example 34.4.1
Calculate Var(X) for $X \sim B\left(3, \frac{1}{4}\right)$ from the probability distribution.

Just as for the expectation calculation, the probability distribution is found using the binomial probability formula

$$P(X = x) = \binom{n}{x} p^x (1 - p)^{n-x}$$

with $n = 3$.

The distribution is shown in Table 34.9.

x	$P(X = x)$	$P(X = x)x^2$
0	$\binom{3}{0}\left(\frac{1}{4}\right)^0\left(\frac{3}{4}\right)^3 = \frac{27}{64}$	0
1	$\binom{3}{1}\left(\frac{1}{4}\right)^1\left(\frac{3}{4}\right)^2 = \frac{27}{64}$	$\frac{27}{64}$
2	$\binom{3}{2}\left(\frac{1}{4}\right)^2\left(\frac{3}{4}\right)^1 = \frac{9}{64}$	$\frac{36}{64}$
3	$\binom{3}{3}\left(\frac{1}{4}\right)^3\left(\frac{3}{4}\right)^0 = \frac{1}{64}$	$\frac{9}{64}$
	Totals: $\sum\limits_{i=0}^{3} p_i = 1$	$\sum\limits_{i=0}^{3} p_i x_i^2 = \frac{72}{64}$

Table 34.9

Using the second formula for variance in Section 33.5 and the value of μ found in Example 34.3.2

$$\sigma^2 = \text{Var}(X) = \sum_{i=0}^{n} p_i x_i^2 - \mu^2$$
$$= \tfrac{72}{64} - \left(\tfrac{3}{4}\right)^2$$
$$= \tfrac{9}{8} - \tfrac{9}{16} = \tfrac{9}{16}.$$

It is not easy to predict a general result from this single result, but notice that

$$\tfrac{9}{16} = 3 \times \tfrac{1}{4} \times \tfrac{3}{4},$$

which is $n \times p \times (1 - p)$, or, writing $1 - p$ as q, it becomes $\sigma^2 = \text{Var}(X) = npq$.

> The **variance** of the **binomial distribution** $X \sim B(n, p)$ is given by
>
> $$\text{Var}(X) = \sigma^2 = npq, \text{ where } q = 1 - p.$$

Example 34.4.2
Calculate $\text{Var}(X)$ for $X \sim B\left(3, \tfrac{1}{4}\right)$.

Using the equation $\sigma^2 = \text{Var}(X) = npq$, where $q = 1 - p$,

$$\text{Var}(X) = \sigma^2 = np(1 - p) = 3 \times \tfrac{1}{4} \times \tfrac{3}{4} = \tfrac{9}{16}.$$

Just as for the expectation calculation, you can see that the method using the formula is much quicker.

> Your calculator has in-built routines for calculating binomial probabilities. Make sure you know how to use them.

The following examples give further illustrations of the use of the formulae for expectation and variance.

Example 34.4.3
(a) Given that $X \sim B(10, 0.3)$, find $E(X)$ and $Var(X)$.

(b) For $X \sim B(10, 0.3)$, calculate $P(\mu - \sigma < x < \mu + \sigma)$.

(a) Since $n = 10$ and $p = 0.3$,

$$E(X) = \mu = np = 10 \times 0.3 = 3,$$
$$Var(X) = \sigma^2 = np(1 - p) = 10 \times 0.3 \times 0.7 = 2.1.$$

(b) $P(\mu - \sigma < X < \mu + \sigma) = P(3 - 1.44... < X < 3 + 1.44...)$
$$= P(1.55... < X < 4.44...)$$
$$= P(X = 2) + P(X = 3) + P(X = 4)$$
$$= P(X \le 4) - P(X \le 1)$$
$$= 0.8497 - 0.1493 \text{ (using a calculator)}$$
$$= 0.7004.$$

Thus $P(\mu - \sigma < x < \mu + \sigma) = 0.700$, correct to 3 significant figures.

Example 34.4.4
Suppose that $X \sim B(10, 0.2)$. Find   (a) $P(X = 2)$,   (b) $P(X \le 2)$,   (c) $P(X > 2)$.
(d) Given that $(X \le 2)$, find $P(X = 2)$. Give your answers correct to 4 decimal places.

(a) Using the calculator, $P(X = 2) = 0.3020$.

(b) Using the cumulative probability routine, $P(X \le 2) = 0.6778$.

(c) Using the property that $P(X > 2) = 1 - P(X \le 2)$,

$$P(X > 2) = 1 - P(X \le 2)$$
$$= 1 - 0.6778 = 0.3222.$$

(d) You need to find $P(X = 2 \mid X \le 2)$. Using the definition of conditional probability, Section 27.1,

$$P(X = 2 \mid X \le 2) = \frac{P((X = 2) \cap (X \le 2))}{P(X \le 2)}$$
$$= \frac{P((X = 2) \cap (X = 0, 1, 2))}{P(X \le 2)}$$
$$= \frac{P(X = 2)}{P(X \le 2)}$$
$$= \frac{0.3020}{0.6778} = 0.4456.$$

Example 34.4.5
Given that Y is $B(n, p)$, and $E(Y) = 24$ and $Var(Y) = 8$, find the values of n and p.

Using the formulae in the blue boxes,

$$E(Y) = np = 24 \quad \text{and} \quad Var(Y) = np(1 - p) = 8.$$

Substituting the value of np from the first equation into the second equation gives:

$$24(1-p) = 8, \quad \text{so} \quad 1-p = \tfrac{1}{3} \quad \text{and} \quad p = \tfrac{2}{3}.$$

Using $np = 24$,

$$n = \frac{24}{p} = \frac{24}{\frac{2}{3}} = 24 \times \tfrac{3}{2} = 36.$$

Example 34.4.6

The random variable X is binomially distributed with probability of success 0.6. Find the least number of trials such that $P(X \geq 1) > 0.9$.

Let n be the number of trials, so that $X \sim B(n, 0.6)$.

Then

$$P(X \geq 1) = 1 - P(X = 0)$$
$$= 1 - 0.4^n > 0.9.$$

Thus $0.4^n < 0.1$.

So $n \ln 0.4 < \ln 0.1$,   (remember $\ln 0.4$ is negative, so the inequality changes) giving
$$n > \frac{\ln 0.1}{\ln 0.4} = 2.51... \,.$$

It follows that the smallest possible value of n is 3.

34.5* Proof of the mean and variance formulae for B(n, p)

To establish the formula $\mu = np$ for the binomial distribution B(n, p), you have to go back to the definition of the binomial distribution in which

$$p_i = P(X = x_i) = \binom{n}{x} p^x (1-p)^{n-x},$$

and calculate $\sum_{i=0}^{n} p_i x_i$, using the properties of the binomial theorem in Chapter 4.

In Exercise 4D Question 12(a), you were asked to prove that $x\binom{n}{x} = n\binom{n-1}{x-1}$ when $x \geq 1$. This is the property used to proceed from line 4 to line 5.

$$\mu = E(X)$$

$$= \sum_{i=0}^{n} p_i x_i$$

$$= \sum_{x=0}^{n} \binom{n}{x} p^x (1-p)^{n-x} \times x$$

$$= \binom{n}{0} p^0 (1-p)^{n-0} \times 0 + \sum_{x=1}^{n} \left(x \times \binom{n}{x} \right) p^x (1-p)^{n-x}$$

$$= 0 + \sum_{x=1}^{n} \left(n \times \binom{n-1}{x-1} \right) p^x (1-p)^{n-x}$$

$$= np \sum_{x=1}^{n} \binom{n-1}{x-1} p^{x-1} (1-p)^{n-x}$$

$$= np \sum_{y=0}^{m} \binom{m}{y} p^y (1-p)^{m-y} \qquad \text{(putting } m = n-1 \text{ and } y = x-1)$$

$$= np\,(p + (1-p))^m \qquad \text{(from the binomial expansion of } (p + (1-p))^m)$$

$$= np \times 1^m$$

$$= np.$$

To find the variance of B (n, p), you need to calculate $\sum_{i=0}^{n} p_i x_i^2 - \mu^2$. The result in Exercise 4D Question 12(b) is used to proceed from line 5 to line 6.

Thus, writing $1 - p$ as q,

$$\sigma^2 = \mathrm{Var}(X)$$

$$= \sum_{i=0}^{n} p_i x_i^2 - \mu^2$$

$$= \sum_{x=0}^{n} \binom{n}{x} p^x q^{n-x} \times x^2 - (np)^2$$

$$= \binom{n}{0} p^0 q^n \times 0^2 + \binom{n}{1} p^1 q^{n-1} \times 1^2 + \sum_{x=2}^{n} x^2 \binom{n}{x} p^x q^{n-x} - n^2 p^2$$

$$= npq^{n-1} + \sum_{x=2}^{n} x^2 \binom{n}{x} p^x q^{n-x} - n^2 p^2$$

$$= npq^{n-1} + \sum_{x=2}^{n} \left(n(n-1) \binom{n-2}{x-2} + n \binom{n-1}{x-1} \right) p^x q^{n-x} - n^2 p^2$$

$$= npq^{n-1} + n(n-1) \sum_{x=2}^{n} \binom{n-2}{x-2} p^x q^{n-x} + n \sum_{x=2}^{n} \binom{n-1}{x-1} p^x q^{n-x} - n^2 p^2$$

In the first summation, write $x - 2 = s$ and $n - 2 = S$, and in the second, write $x - 1 = t$ and $n - 1 = T$. Then continuing with the simplification, using the binomial expansions of $(p+q)^S$ and $(p+q)^T$,

$$\sigma^2 = npq^{n-1} + n(n-1)\,p^2 \sum_{s=0}^{S} \binom{S}{s} p^s q^{S-s} + np \sum_{t=0}^{T} \binom{T}{t} p^t q^{T-t} - n\binom{n-1}{0} p^1 q^{n-1} - n^2 p^2$$

$$= npq^{n-1} + n(n-1)\,p^2\,(p+q)^S + np\,(p+q)^T - npq^{n-1} - n^2 p^2$$

$$= n(n-1)\,p^2 \times 1^S + np \times 1^T - n^2 p^2$$

$$= n^2 p^2 - np^2 + np - n^2 p^2$$

$$= np\,(1-p)$$

$$= npq.$$

34.6 Practical activities

1 Penalties or shots

(a) Select a group of students and ask them each to take either 8 penalties at soccer or 8 shots at basketball. For each student record the number of successful penalties or shots.

(b) Does the binomial distribution provide a reasonable model for these results? Is it necessary to use the same goalkeeper for all of the football penalties?

(c) Does the skill level of each person matter if the binomial distribution is to be a reasonable model? Is the basketball example more likely to be fitted by a binomial model than the football example?

Exercise 34

In this exercise use your calculator to give probabilities correct to 4 decimal places.

1 The random variable X has a binomial distribution with $n = 6$ and $p = 0.2$. Calculate

(a) $P(X = 3)$,
(b) $P(X = 4)$,
(c) $P(X = 6)$,
(d) $E(X)$

2 Given that $Y \sim B(7, \frac{2}{3})$, calculate

(a) $P(Y = 4)$,
(b) $P(Y = 6)$,
(c) $P(Y = 0)$,
(d) $E(Y)$

3 Given that $Z \sim B(9, 0.45)$, calculate

(a) $P(Z = 3)$,
(b) $P(Z = 4 \text{ or } 5)$,
(c) $P(Z \geq 7)$,
(d) $E(Z)$.

4 Given that $D \sim B(12, 0.7)$, calculate

(a) $P(D < 4)$,
(b) the smallest value of d such that $P(D > d) < 0.90$.

5 Given that $X \sim B(10, 0.5)$, calculate

(a) $P(2 \leq X \leq 5)$
(b) $P(X \leq 1 \text{ or } X > 5)$

6 Given that $S \sim B(7, \frac{1}{6})$, find the probability that S is

(a) exactly 3,
(b) at least 4.

7 In a certain school, 30% of the students are in the age group 16–19.

(a) Ten students are chosen at random. What is the probability that fewer than four of them are in the 16–19 age group?

(b) If the ten students were chosen by picking ten who were sitting together at lunch, explain why a binomial distribution might no longer have been suitable.

8 A factory makes large quantities of coloured sweets, and it is known that on average 20% of the sweets are coloured green. A packet contains 20 sweets. Assuming that the packet forms a random sample of the sweets made by the factory, calculate the probability that exactly seven of the sweets are green.

If you knew that, in fact, the sweets could have been green, red, orange or brown, would it have invalidated your calculation?

9 Eggs produced at a farm are packaged in boxes of six. Assume that, for any egg, the probability that it is broken when it reaches the retail outlet is 0.1, independent of all other eggs. A box is said to be bad if it contains at least two broken eggs. Calculate the probability that a randomly selected box is bad.

It is known that, in fact, breakages are more likely to occur after the eggs have been packed into boxes, and while they are being transported to the retail outlet. Explain why this fact is likely to invalidate the calculation.

10 On a particular tropical island, the probability that there is a hurricane in any given month can be taken to be 0.08. Use a binomial distribution to calculate the probability that there is a hurricane in more than two months of the year. State two assumptions needed for a binomial distribution to be a good model. Why may one of the assumptions not be valid?

11 It is given that, at a stated time of day, 35% of the adults in the country are wearing jeans.
   (a) At that time, a sample of twelve adults is selected. Use a binomial distribution to calculate the probability that exactly five out of the twelve are wearing jeans.
   (b) If the probability that at least one person is wearing jeans is 0.95, how big should the sample be?

   Explain carefully two assumptions that must be made for your calculation to be valid. (If you say 'sample is random' you must explain what this means in the context of the question.)

12 Explain why a binomial distribution would not be a good model in the following problem. (Do not attempt any calculation.)
   Thirteen cards are chosen at random from an ordinary pack. Find the probability that there are four clubs, four diamonds, three hearts and two spades.

13 Two types of egg, A and B, produced at a farm are packed into boxes of six, all of one type. Egg type A has a probability of $\frac{1}{6}$ of being cracked and egg type B had a probability of $\frac{1}{10}$ of being cracked. A box of type A eggs and a box of type B eggs are selected at random.

   Find the probability that
   (a) exactly one egg in each box is cracked,
   (b) exactly two eggs altogether are cracked.

35 The Poisson distribution

This chapter introduces a discrete probability distribution which is used for modelling random events. When you have completed it, you should

- be able to calculate probabilities for the Poisson distribution both directly and by using cumulative Poisson probabilities on a calculator
- understand the relevance of the Poisson distribution to the distribution of random events
- be able to use the result that the mean and variance of a Poisson distribution are equal.

35.1 The Poisson probability formula

Situations often arise where the variable of interest is the number of occurrences of a particular event in a given interval of space or time. An example is given in Table 35.1. This shows the frequency of 0, 1, 2 etc. phone calls arriving at a switchboard in 100 consecutive time intervals of 5 minutes. In this case the 'event' is the arrival of a phone call and the 'given interval' is a time interval of 5 minutes.

Number of calls	0	1	2	3	4 or more
Frequency	71	23	4	2	0

Table 35.1

Some other examples are

- the number of cars passing a point on a motorway in a time interval of 1 minute,
- the number of misprints on each page of a book,
- the number of radioactive particles emitted by a radioactive source in a time interval of 1 second.

Further examples can be found in the practical activities in Section 35.4.

The probability distribution which is used to model these situations is called the **Poisson distribution** after the French mathematician and physicist Siméon-Denis Poisson (1781–1840). The distribution is defined by the probability formula

$$P(X = x) = e^{-m}\frac{m^x}{x!}, \qquad x = 0,\ 1,\ 2, \ldots .$$

The method by which Poisson arrived at this formula will be outlined in Section 35.2.

This formula involves only one parameter, m. You will see later that m is the mean of the distribution. The notation for indicating that a random variable X has a Poisson distribution with mean m is $X \sim \text{Po}(m)$. Once m is known you can calculate $P(X = 0)$, $P(X = 1)$, etc. Note that there is no upper limit on the value of X.

Example 35.1.1

The number of particles emitted per second by a radioactive source has a Poisson distribution with mean 5. Calculate the probabilities of

(a) 0,   (b) 1,   (c) 2,   (d) 3 or more

emissions in a time interval of 1 second.

(a) Let X be the random variable 'the number of particles emitted in 1 second'. Then $X \sim \text{Po}(5)$. Using the Poisson probability formula $P(X = x) = e^{-m}\dfrac{m^x}{x!}$ with $m = 5$,

$$P(X = 0) = e^{-5}\frac{5^0}{0!} = 0.006\,737... = 0.006\,74, \text{ correct to 3 significant figures.}$$

A reminder: $0! = 1$, (see Section 3.5).

(b) $P(X = 1) = e^{-5}\dfrac{5^1}{1} = 0.033\,68... = 0.0337$, correct to 3 significant figures.

(c) $P(X = 2) = e^{-5}\dfrac{5^2}{2} = 0.084\,22... = 0.0842$, correct to 3 significant figures.

(d) Since there is no upper limit on the value of X the probability of 3 or more emissions must be found by subtraction.

$$P(X \geq 3) = 1 - P(X = 0) - P(X = 1) - P(X = 2)$$
$$= 1 - 0.006\,737... - 0.03368... - 0.084\,22...$$
$$= 0.875, \text{ correct to 3 significant figures.}$$

Example 35.1.2

The number of demands for taxis to a taxi firm is Poisson distributed with, on average, four demands every 30 minutes. Use the Poisson probability distribution formula to find the probabilities of

(a) no demand in 30 minutes

(b) 1 demand in 1 hour

(c) fewer than 2 demands in 15 minutes.

(a) Let X be the random variable 'the number of demands in a 30 minute interval'. Then $X \sim \text{Po}(4)$. Using the Poisson formula with $m = 4$,

$$P(X = 0) = e^{-4}\frac{4^0}{0!} = 0.0183, \text{ correct to 3 significant figures.}$$

(b) Let Y be the random variable 'the number of demands in a 1 hour interval'. As the time interval being considered has changed from 30 minutes to 1 hour, you must change the value of m to equal the mean for this new time interval, that is to 8, giving $Y \sim \text{Po}(8)$. Using the Poisson formula with $m = 8$,

$$P(Y = 1) = e^{-8}\frac{8^1}{1!} = 0.002\,68, \text{ correct to 3 significant figures.}$$

(c) Again the time interval has been altered. Now the appropriate value for m is 2. Let W be the number of demands in 15 minutes. Then $W \sim \mathrm{Po}(2)$.

$$P(W < 2) = P(W = 0) + P(W = 1)$$
$$= e^{-2}\frac{2^0}{0!} + e^{-2}\frac{2^1}{1!}$$
$$= 0.406 \text{ correct to 3 significant figures.}$$

You can simplify the calculation of Poisson probabilities by using your calculator, which probably gives you individual and cumulative Poisson probabilities.

Example 35.1.3

The number of organic particles suspended in a volume V ml of water from a particular pond follows a Poisson distribution with mean $0.2V$. Use your calculator to find the probability that

(a) a volume of 50 ml contains fewer than 8 particles,

(b) a volume of 30 ml contains more than 2 particles,

(c) a volume of 10 ml contains exactly 3 particles.

(a) For $V = 50$, $m = 0.2 \times 50 = 10$. Note first that $P(X < 8) = P(X \le 7)$. Then, using the cumulative Poisson probabilities from your calculator,

$$P(X \le 7) = 0.2202... = 0.220, \text{ correct to 3 significant figures.}$$

(b) For $V = 30$, $m = 0.2 \times 30 = 6$. Note that $P(X > 2) = 1 - P(X \le 2)$. From your calculator,

$$1 - P(X \le 2) = 1 - 0.0619... = 0.938, \text{ correct to 3 significant figures.}$$

(c) For $V = 10$, $m = 0.2 \times 10 = 2$.

So, using the calculator directly,

$$P(X = 3) = 0.1804... = 0.180, \text{ correct to 3 significant figures.}$$

Here is a summary of the results of this section.

The **Poisson distribution** is used as a model for the number, X, of events in a given interval of space or time. It has the probability formula

$$P(X = x) = e^{-m}\frac{m^x}{x!}, \qquad x = 0, 1, 2, ...,$$

where m is equal to the mean number of events in the given interval.

The notation $X \sim \mathrm{Po}(m)$ indicates that X has a Poisson distribution with mean m.

Some books use μ or λ rather than m to denote the parameter of a Poisson distribution.

Exercise 35A

1 The random variable T has a Poisson distribution with mean 3. Calculate

(a) $P(T = 2)$,   (b) $P(T \leq 1)$,   (c) $P(T \geq 3)$.

2 Given that $U \sim \text{Po}(3.25)$, calculate

(a) $P(U = 3)$,   (b) $P(U \leq 2)$,   (c) $P(U \geq 2)$.

3 The random variable W has a Poisson distribution with mean 2.4. Calculate

(a) $P(W \leq 3)$,   (b) $P(W \geq 2)$,   (c) $P(W = 3)$.

4 Accidents on a busy urban motorway occur at a mean rate of 2 per week. Assuming that the number of accidents per week follows a Poisson distribution, calculate the probability that

(a) there will be no accidents in a particular week,

(b) there will be exactly 2 accidents in a particular week,

(c) there will be fewer than 3 accidents in a given two-week period.

5 On average, 15 customers a minute arrive at the check-outs of a busy supermarket. Assuming that a Poisson distribution is appropriate, calculate

(a) the probability that no customers arrive at the check-outs in a given 10-second interval,

(b) the probability that more than 3 customers arrive at the check-outs in a 15-second interval.

6 During April of this year, I received 15 telephone calls. Assuming that the number of telephone calls I receive in April of next year follows a Poisson distribution with the same mean number of calls per day, calculate the probability that

(a) on a given day in April next year I will receive no telephone calls,

(b) in a given 7-day week next April I will receive more than 3 telephone calls.

7 Assume that cars arrive at a motorway service area at a rate of 100 per hour and that a Poisson distribution is appropriate.

(a) What is the probability that during a 3-minute period no cars will arrive at the service area?

(b) What time interval is such that the probability is at least 0.25 that no car will arrive at the service area during that interval?

8* A radioactive source emits particles at an average rate of 1 per second. Assume that the number of emissions follows a Poisson distribution.

(a) Calculate the probability that 0 or 1 particle will be emitted in 4 seconds.

(b) The emission rate changes such that the probability of 0 or 1 emission in 4 seconds becomes 0.8. What is the new emission rate?

35.2   Modelling random events

The examples which you have already met in this chapter have assumed that the variable you are dealing with has a Poisson distribution. How can you decide whether the Poisson distribution is a suitable model if you are not told? The answer to this question can be found by considering the way in which the Poisson distribution is related to the binomial distribution in the situation where the number of trials is very large and the probability of success is very small.

Table 35.2 reproduces Table 35.1 giving the frequency distribution of phone calls in 100 5-minute intervals.

Number of calls	0	1	2	3	4 or more
Frequency	71	23	4	2	0

Table 35.2

If these calls were plotted on a time axis you might see something which looked like Fig. 35.3.

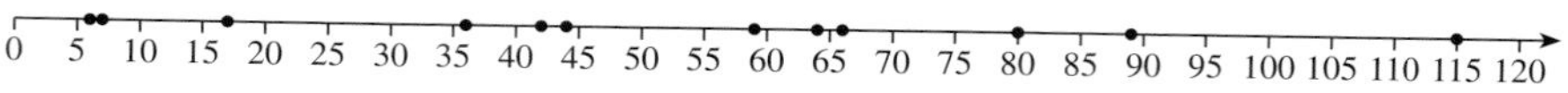

Fig. 35.3

The time axis has been divided into 5-minute intervals (only 24 are shown) and these intervals can contain 0, 1, 2 etc. phone calls. Suppose now that you assume that the phone calls occur *independently* of each other and *randomly* in time. In order to make the terms in italics clearer consider the following. Imagine the time axis is divided up into very small intervals of width δt. These intervals are so small that they never contain more than one call. If the calls are *random* then the probability that one of these intervals contains a call does not depend on which interval is considered; that is, it is constant. If the calls are *independent* then whether or not one interval contains a call has no effect on whether any other interval contains a call.

Looking at each interval of width δt in turn to see whether it contains a call or not gives a series of trials, each with two possible outcomes. This is just the kind of situation which is described by the binomial distribution. These trials also satisfy the conditions for the binomial distribution that they should be independent and have a fixed probability of success.

Suppose that a 5-minute interval contains n intervals of width δt. If there are, on average, m calls every 5 minutes then the proportion of intervals which contain a call will be equal to $\frac{m}{n}$. The probability, p, that one of these intervals contains a call is therefore equal to $\frac{m}{n}$. Since δt is small, n is large and $\frac{m}{n}$ is small. You can verify from Table 35.2 that the mean number of calls in a 5-minute interval is 0.37 so the distribution of X, the number of calls in a 5-minute interval is $B\left(n, \frac{0.37}{n}\right)$.

Finding P($X = 0$)   Using the binomial probability formula $P(X = x) = \binom{n}{x} p^x q^{n-x}$, you can calculate, for example, the probability of zero calls in a 5-minute interval as

$$P(X = 0) = \binom{n}{0} \left(\frac{0.37}{n}\right)^0 \left(1 - \frac{0.37}{n}\right)^n.$$

In order to proceed you need a value for n. Recall that n must be large enough to ensure that the δt-intervals never contain more than one call. Suppose $n = 1000$. This gives

$$P(X = 0) = \binom{1000}{0} \left(\frac{0.37}{1000}\right)^0 \left(1 - \frac{0.37}{1000}\right)^{1000} = 0.690\,68\ldots .$$

However, even with such a large number of intervals there is still a chance that one of the δt-intervals could contain more than one call, so a larger value of n would be better. Try $n = 10\,000$ giving

$$P(X = 0) = \binom{10\,000}{0} \left(\frac{0.37}{10\,000}\right)^0 \left(1 - \frac{0.37}{10\,000}\right)^{10\,000} = 0.690\,72\ldots .$$

Explore for yourself what happens as you increase the value of n still further. You should find that your answers tend towards the value $0.690\,73\ldots$. This is equal to $e^{-0.37}$, which is the value the Poisson probability formula gives for $P(X = 0)$ when $m = 0.37$.

This is an example of the general result that $\left(1 - \frac{x}{n}\right)^n$ tends to the value e^{-x} as n tends to infinity. This result is not proved in this course.

Provided that two events cannot occur simultaneously, allowing n to tend to infinity will ensure that not more than one event can occur in a δt-interval.

Finding P($X = 1$)   In a similar way you can find the probability of one call in a 5-minute interval by starting from the binomial formula and allowing n to increase as follows.

$$P(X = 1) = \binom{n}{1} \left(\frac{0.37}{n}\right)^1 \left(1 - \frac{0.37}{n}\right)^{n-1} = 0.37 \left(1 - \frac{0.37}{n}\right)^{n-1}.$$

Putting $n = 1000$,

$$P(X = 1) = 0.37 \left(1 - \frac{0.37}{1000}\right)^{999} = 0.37 \times 0.690\,94\ldots = 0.255\,64\ldots .$$

Putting $n = 10\,000$,

$$P(X = 1) = 0.37 \left(1 - \frac{0.37}{10\,000}\right)^{9999} = 0.37 \times 0.690\,75\ldots = 0.255\,579\ldots .$$

Again, you should find that as n increases the probability tends towards the value given by the Poisson probability formula,

$$P(X = 1) = 0.37 \times e^{-0.37} = 0.255\,57\ldots .$$

Finding P(X = 2), P(X = 3), etc.   You could verify for yourself that similar results are obtained when the probabilities of $X = 2$, 3 etc. are calculated by a similar method. A spreadsheet program or a programmable calculator would be helpful.

The general result for $P(X = x)$ can be derived as follows. Starting with $X \sim B\left(n, \dfrac{m}{n}\right)$.

$$P(X = x) = \binom{n}{x}\left(\frac{m}{n}\right)^x\left(1 - \frac{m}{n}\right)^{n-x}$$

$$= \frac{n(n-1)(n-2)...(n-x+1)}{x!} \times \frac{m^x}{n^x}\left(1 - \frac{m}{n}\right)^{n-x}$$

$$= \frac{m^x}{x!} \times \frac{n-1}{n} \times \frac{n-2}{n} \times...\times \frac{n-x+1}{n} \times \left(1 - \frac{m}{n}\right)^{n-x}.$$

Now consider what happens as n gets larger. The fractions $\dfrac{n-1}{n}, \dfrac{n-2}{n}$ etc. tend towards 1. The term $\left(1 - \dfrac{m}{n}\right)^{n-x}$ can be approximated by $\left(1 - \dfrac{m}{n}\right)^n$ since x, a constant, is negligible compared with n and, as you have seen previously, this tends towards e^{-m}. Combining these results gives

$$P(X = x) = \frac{m^x}{x!}e^{-m}.$$

The assumptions made in the derivation above give the conditions that a set of events must satisfy for the Poisson distribution to be a suitable model. They are listed below.

The Poisson distribution is a suitable model for events which
- occur randomly in space or time,
- occur singly, that is events cannot occur simultaneously,
- occur independently, and
- occur at a constant rate, that is the mean number of events in a given time interval is proportional to the size of the interval.

Example 35.2.1
For each of the following situations state whether the Poisson distribution would provide a suitable model. Give reasons for your answers.

(a) The number of cars per minute in the outside lane passing under a motorway bridge between 10 a.m. and 11 a.m. when the traffic is flowing freely.

(b) The number of cars per minute entering a city-centre carpark on a busy Saturday between 9 a.m. and 10 a.m.

(c) The number of particles emitted per second by a radioactive source.

(d) The number of currants in currant buns sold at a particular baker's shop on a particular day.

(e) The number of blood cells per ml in a dilute solution of blood which has been left standing for 24 hours.

(f) The number of blood cells per ml in a dilute solution of blood which has been well shaken.

(a) The Poisson distribution should be a good model for this situation as the appropriate conditions should be met: since the traffic is flowing freely the cars should pass independently and at random; it is not possible for cars to pass simultaneously; the average rate of traffic flow is likely to be constant over the time interval given.

(b) The Poisson distribution is unlikely to be a good model: if it is a busy day the cars will be queuing for the carpark and so they will not be moving independently.

(c) The Poisson distribution should be a good model provided that the time period over which the measurements are made is much longer than the lifetime of the source: this will ensure that the average rate at which the particles are emitted is constant. Radioactive particles are emitted independently and at random and, for practical purposes, they can be considered to be emitted singly.

(d) The Poisson distribution should be a good model provided that the following conditions are met: all the buns are prepared from the same mixture so that the average number of currants per bun is constant; the mixture is well stirred so that the currants are distributed at random; the currant buns all have the same volume; the currants do not stick to each other or touch each other so that they are positioned independently.

(e) The Poisson distribution will not be a good model because the blood cells will have tended to sink towards the bottom of the solution. Thus the average number of blood cells per ml will be greater at the bottom than the top.

(f) If the solution has been well shaken the Poisson distribution will be a suitable model. The blood cells will be distributed at random and at a constant average rate. Since the solution is dilute the blood cells will not be touching and so will be positioned independently.

35.3   The variance of a Poisson distribution

In Section 35.2 the Poisson probability formula was deduced from the distribution of $X \sim \mathrm{B}\left(n, \dfrac{m}{n}\right)$ by considering what happens as n tends to infinity. The variance of a Poisson distribution can be obtained by considering what happens to the variance of the distribution of $X \sim \mathrm{B}\left(n, \dfrac{m}{n}\right)$ as n gets very large. In Section 34.4 you met the formula $\mathrm{Var}\,(X) = np(1-p)$ for the variance of a binomial distribution. Substituting for p gives

$$\mathrm{Var}\,(X) = n \times \frac{m}{n}\left(1 - \frac{m}{n}\right) = m\left(1 - \frac{m}{n}\right).$$

As n gets very large the term $\dfrac{m}{n}$ tends to zero. This gives m as the variance of the Poisson distribution. Thus the Poisson distribution has the interesting property that its mean and variance are equal.

For a Poisson distribution $X \sim \text{Po}(m)$

$\quad$ mean $= \mu = \text{E}(X) = m,$

$\quad$ variance $= \sigma^2 = \text{Var}(X) = m.$

The mean and variance of a Poisson distribution are equal.

The equality of the mean and variance of a Poisson distribution gives a simple way of testing whether a variable might be modelled by a Poisson distribution. The mean of the data in Table 35.2 has already been used and is equal to 0.37. You can verify that the variance of these data is 0.4331. These values, which are both 0.4 to 1 decimal place, are sufficiently close to indicate that the Poisson distribution may be a suitable model for the number of phone calls in a 5-minute interval. This is confirmed by Table 35.4 below, which shows that the relative frequencies calculated from Table 35.2 are close to the theoretical probabilities found by assuming that $X \sim \text{Po}(0.37)$. (The values for the probabilities are given to 3 decimal places and the value for $\text{P}(X \geq 4)$ has been found by subtraction.)

Note that if the mean and variance are not approximately equal then the Poisson distribution is not a suitable model. If they are equal then the Poisson distribution may be a suitable model, but is not necessarily so.

x	Frequency	Relative frequency	$\text{P}(X = x)$
0	71	0.71	$e^{-0.37} = 0.691$
1	23	0.23	$e^{-0.37}0.37 = 0.256$
2	4	0.04	$e^{-0.37}\dfrac{0.37^2}{2!} = 0.047$
3	2	0.02	$e^{-0.37}\dfrac{0.37^3}{3!} = 0.006$
≥ 4	0	0	0
Totals	100	1	1

Table 35.4

35.4   Practical activities

1 **Traffic flow**   In order to carry out this activity you will need to make your observations on a road where the traffic flows freely, preferably away from traffic lights, junctions, etc. The best results will be obtained if the rate of flow is one to two cars per minute on average.

(a) Count the number of cars which pass each minute over a period of one hour and assemble your results into a frequency table.

(b) Calculate the mean and variance of the number of cars per minute. Comment on your results.

(c) Compare the relative frequencies with the Poisson probabilities calculated by taking m equal to the mean of your data. Comment on the agreement between the two sets of values.

2 **Random rice**   For this activity you need a chessboard and a few tablespoonfuls of uncooked rice.

(a) Scatter the rice 'at random' on to the chessboard. This can be achieved by holding your hand about 50 cm above the board and moving it around as you drop the rice. Drop sufficient rice to result in two to three grains of rice per square on average.

(b) Count the number of grains of rice in each square and assemble your results into a frequency table.

(c) Calculate the mean and variance of the number of grains per square. If these are reasonably close then go on to part (d). If not, see if you can improve your technique for scattering rice 'at random'!

(d) Compare the relative frequencies with the Poisson probabilities calculated taking m equal to the mean of your data. Comment on the agreement between the two sets of values.

3 **Background radiation**   For this activity you need a Geiger counter with a digital display. When the Geiger counter is switched on it will record the background radiation.

(a) Prepare a table in which you can record the reading on the Geiger counter every 5 seconds for total time of 5 minutes.

(b) Switch the counter on and record the reading every 5 seconds.

(c) Plot a graph of the reading on the counter against time taking values every 30 seconds. Does this graph suggest that the background rate is constant?

(d) The number of counts in each 5 second interval can be found by taking the difference between successive values in the table which you made in parts (a) and (b). Find these values and assemble them into a frequency table.

(e) Calculate the mean and variance of the number of counts per 5 seconds. Comment on your results.

(f) Compare the relative frequencies with the Poisson probabilities calculated by taking m equal to the mean of your data. Comment on the agreement between the two sets of values.

4 **Soccer goals**   For this activity you need details of the results of between 50 and 100 soccer matches in a league for one particular week.

(a) Make a frequency table of the number of goals scored by each team.

(b) Calculate the mean and variance of the number of goals scored.

(c) Compare the relative frequencies with the Poisson probabilities calculated by taking m equal to the mean of your data.

(d) Discuss whether the variable 'number of goals scored by each team' satisfies the conditions required for the Poisson distribution to be a suitable model. Comment on the results you obtained in part (b) and part (c) in the light of your answer.

Exercise 35B

1   For each of the following situations, say whether or not the Poisson distribution might provide a suitable model.

   (a) The number of raindrops that fall into a milk bottle left on a doorstep for collection in a period of 1 minute during a shower.

   (b) The number of occupants of vehicles that pass a given point on a busy road in 1 minute.

   (c) The number of flaws in a given length of material of constant width.

   (d) The number of claims made to an insurance company in a month.

2   Some conservationists recorded the number of hedgehogs found run over by cars on a country lane for 13 weeks. The weekly figures were

   8   9   7   11   5   4   12   10   7   6   11   3   11

   (a) Calculate the mean and variance of these data and comment on whether the Poisson distribution might be a suitable model.

   (b) Use the Poisson distribution with the mean found in part (a) to calculate the probability of 7 or more hedgehogs being found run over in a given week.

   (c) A bypass was built reducing the probability of 7 or more hedgehogs being run over to 0.0244. Use your calculator to find the new mean number of hedgehogs run over per week.

3   The number of telephone calls I received during the month of March is summarised in the table.

Number of telephone calls received per day (x)	0	1	2	3	4
Number of days	9	12	5	4	1

   (a) Calculate the relative frequency for each of $x = 0, 1, 2, 3, 4$.

   (b) Calculate the mean and variance of the distribution. (Give your answers correct to 2 decimal places.) Comment on the suitability of the Poisson distribution as a model for this situation.

   (c) Use the Poisson distribution to calculate $P(X = x)$, for $x = 0, 1, 2, 3$ and 4 using the mean calculated in part (b).

   (d) Compare the theoretical probabilities and the relative frequencies found in part (a). Do these figures support the comment made in part (b)?

4   You are given that $X \sim \text{Po}(m)$ and that $P(X = 1) = 4P(X = 2)$.

   (a) Calculate m.   (b) Calculate $P(X \geq 3)$.   (c) Calculate $P(X \geq 4 \mid X \geq 3)$.

5   The number X of cars passing a given point in 100 10-second intervals around noon on a certain day was observed to satisfy the Poisson distribution $X \sim \text{Po}(0.8)$.

   (a) Calculate the probability that the number passing that point was 3, 4 or 5.

   (b) Given that 3, 4 or 5 cars passed the point, find the probability that the number was exactly 4.

6 The number of telephone calls received by a call centre between 0800 and 0805 follows a Poisson distribution with mean 2.

(a) Calculate the probability that no calls are received between 0800 and 0805 on a given Tuesday, chosen at random.

(b) Calculate the probability that on Tuesday and Wednesday a total of exactly one call was received between those times.

(c) Given that just one call was received between those times on Tuesday and Wednesday, what is the probability that it was received on Tuesday?

1 The number of times a certain factory machine breaks down each working week has been recorded over a long period. From this data, the following probability distribution for the number, X, of weekly breakdowns was produced.

x	0	1	2	3	4	5	6
$P(X = x)$	0.04	0.24	0.28	0.16	0.16	0.08	0.04

(a) Find the mean of X.

(b) What would be the expected total number of breakdowns that will occur over the next 48 working weeks?

2 An absent-minded mathematician is attempting to log on to a computer, which is done by typing the correct password. Unfortunately he can't remember his password. If he types the wrong password he tries again. The computer allows a maximum of four attempts altogether. For each attempt the probability of success is 0.4, independently of all other attempts.

(a) Calculate the probability that he logs on successfully.

(b) The total number of attempts he makes, successful or not, is denoted by X (so that the possible values of X are 1, 2, 3 or 4). Tabulate the probability distribution of X.

3 Three cards are selected at random, without replacement, from a shuffled pack of 52 playing cards. Using a tree diagram, find the probability distribution of the number of honours (A, K, Q, J, 10) obtained.

4 An electronic device produces an output of 0, 1 or 3 volts, each time it is operated, with probabilities $\frac{1}{2}$, $\frac{1}{3}$ and $\frac{1}{6}$ respectively. The random variable X denotes the result of adding the outputs for two such devices which act independently.

(a) Tabulate the possible values of X with their corresponding probabilities.

(b) In 360 independent operations of the device, state on how many occasions you would expect the outcome to be 1 volt. (OCR, adapted)

5 The probability of a novice archer hitting a target with any shot is 0.3. Given that the archer shoots six arrows, find the probability that the target is hit at least twice. (OCR)

6 Joseph and four friends each have an independent probability 0.45 of winning a prize. Find the probability that

(a) exactly two of the five friends win a prize,

(b) Joseph and only one friend win a prize. (OCR)

7 A man rolls ten fair dice. He tells you that one of them is a six. What is the probability that there are at least two sixes?

8 Between the hours of 0800 and 2200, cars arrive at a certain petrol station at an average rate of 0.8 per minute. Assuming that arrival times are random, calculate the probability that at least 2 cars will arrive during a particular minute between 0800 and 2200.   (OCR)

9 The number of night calls to a fire station in a small town can be modelled by a Poisson distribution with mean 4.2 per night. Find the probability that on a particular night there will be 3 or more calls to the fire station.

State what needs to be assumed about the calls to the fire station in order to justify a Poisson model.   (OCR)

10 A shop sells two brands of television sets. The average number of Kubla sets sold per week is 1.8. Sales take place independently at random times.

(a) Find the probability that exactly 2 Kubla sets are sold in a given week.

(b) Find the probability that exactly 4 Kubla sets are sold in a given two-week period.   (OCR, adapted)

11 A householder wishes to sow part of her garden with grass seed. She scatters seed randomly so that the number of seeds falling on any particular region is a random variable having a Poisson distribution, with its mean proportional to the area of the region. The part of the garden that she intends to sow has area $50\,\text{m}^2$ and she estimates that she will sow 10^6 seeds. Calculate the expected number of seeds falling on a region, R, of area $1\,\text{cm}^2$, and show that the probability that no seeds fall on R is 0.135, correct to 3 significant figures.

The number of seeds falling on R is denoted by X. Find the probability that either $X = 0$ or $X > 4$.   (OCR, adapted)

12 A firm investigated the number of employees suffering injuries whilst at work. The results recorded below were obtained for a 52-week period.

Number of employees injured in a week	0	1	2	3	4 or more
Number of weeks	31	17	3	1	0

Give reasons why one might expect this distribution to approximate to a Poisson distribution. Evaluate the mean and variance of the data and explain why this gives further evidence in favour of a Poisson distribution.

Using the calculated value of the mean, find the theoretical frequencies of a Poisson distribution for the number of weeks in which 0, 1, 2, 3, 4 or more employees were injured.   (OCR)

13 Analysis of the scores in football matches in a local league suggests that the total number of goals scored in a randomly chosen match may be modelled by the Poisson distribution with parameter 2.7. The number of goals scored in different matches are independent of one another.

(a) Find the probability that a match will end with no goals scored.

(b) Find the probability that 4 or more goals will be scored in a match.

One Saturday afternoon, 11 matches are played in the league.

(c) State the expected number of matches in which no goals are scored.

(d) Find the probability that there are goals scored in all 11 matches.

(e) State the distribution for the total number of goals scored in the 11 matches. Find the probability that more than 30 goals are scored in total.   (MEI, adapted)

Examination questions

1 Marian shoots ten arrows at a target. Each arrow has probability 0.4 of hitting the target, independently of all other arrows. Let X denote the number of these arrows hitting the target.

(a) Find the mean and standard deviation of X.   (b) Find $P(X \geq 2)$.   (© IBO 2004)

2 A fair six-sided die, with sides numbered 1, 1, 2, 3, 4, 5 is thrown. Find the mean and variance of the score.   (© IBO 2004)

3 When John throws a stone at a target, the probability that he hits the target is 0.4. He throws a stone 6 times.

(a) Find the probability that he hits the target *exactly* 4 times.

(b) Find the probability that he hits the target for the first time on his third throw.

(© IBO 2002)

4 When a boy plays a game at a fair, the probability that he wins a prize is 0.25. He plays the game 10 times. Let X denote the total number of prizes that he wins. Assuming that the games are independent, find

(a) $E(X)$,   (b) $P(X \leq 2)$.   (© IBO 2003)

5 *Give your answer to 4 significant figures.*

A machine produces cloth with some minor faults. The number of faults per metre is a random variable following a Poisson distribution with a mean 3. Calculate the probability that a metre of the cloth contains five or more faults.   (© IBO 2002)

6 Two children, Alan and Belle, each throw two fair cubical dice simultaneously. The score for each child is the sum of the two numbers shown on their respective dice.

(a) (i) Calculate the probability that Alan obtains a score of 9.

(ii) Calculate the probability that Alan and Belle both obtain a score of 9.

(b) (i) Calculate the probability that Alan and Belle obtain the same score.

(ii) Deduce the probability that Alan's score exceeds Belle's score.

(c) Let X denote the largest number shown on the four dice.

(i) Show that $P(X \leq x) = \left(\frac{1}{6}x\right)^4$, for $x = 1, 2, \ldots, 6$.

(ii) Copy and complete the following probability distribution table.

x	1	2	3	4	5	6
$P(X = x)$	$\frac{1}{1296}$	$\frac{15}{1296}$				$\frac{671}{1296}$

(iii) Calculate $E(X)$.   (© IBO 2002)

7 *Give all numerical answers to this question correct to 3 significant figures.*
   Two typists were given a series of tests to complete. On average, Mr Brown made
   2.7 mistakes per test while Mr Smith made 2.5 mistakes per test. Assume that the number
   of mistakes made by any typist follows a Poisson distribution.

   (a) Calculate the probability that, in a particular test,

       (i) Mr Brown made *two* mistakes; (ii) Mr Smith made *three* mistakes;

       (iii) Mr Brown made *two* mistakes and Mr Smith made *three* mistakes.

   (b) In another test, Mr Brown and Mr Smith made a combined total of *five* mistakes.
       Calculate the probability that Mr Brown *made fewer mistakes* than Mr Smith.

                                                (© IBO 2003)

8 Charles knows from past experience that the number of letters per day delivered to his
   house by the postman follows a Poisson distribution with mean 3.

   (a) On a randomly chosen day, find the probability that two letters are delivered.

   (b) On another day, Charles sees the postman approaching his house so he knows that he
       is about to receive a delivery. Calculate the probability that he receives two letters on
       this day.   (© IBO 2004)

9 The random variable X has a Poisson distribution with mean λ. Let p be the probability
   that X takes the value 1 or 2.

   (a) Write down an expression for p.   (b) Sketch the graph of p for $0 \leq \lambda \leq 4$.

   (c) Find the *exact* value of λ for which p is a maximum.   (© IBO 2004)

10 The random variable X is Poisson distributed with mean μ and satisfies

   $$P(X = 3) = P(X = 0) + P(X = 1).$$

   (a) Find the value of μ, correct to four decimal places.

   (b) For this value of μ evaluate $P(2 \leq X \leq 4)$.   (© IBO 2002)

11 On a television channel the news is shown at the same time each day. The probability that
   Alice watches the news on a given day is 0.4. Calculate the probability that on five
   consecutive days, she watches the news on at most three days.   (© IBO 2003)

12 The table below shows the probability distribution of a discrete random variable X.

x	0	1	2	3
$P(X \leq x)$	0.2	a	b	0.25

   (a) Given that $E(X) = 1.55$, find the value of a and of b.

   (b) Calculate Var (X).   (© IBO 2005)

13 The random variable X has a Poisson distribution with mean λ.

   (a) Given that $P(X = 4) = P(X = 2) + P(X = 3)$, find the value of λ.

   (b) Given that $\lambda = 3.2$, find the value of

       (i) $P(X \geq 2)$,   (ii) $P(X \leq 3 \mid X \geq 2)$.   (© IBO 2003)

14 In a game a player pays an entrance fee of $\$n$. He then selects one number from 1, 2, 3, 4, 5, 6 and rolls three standard dice.

If his chosen number appears on all three dice he wins four times his entrance fee.

If his number appears on exactly two of the dice he wins three times the entrance fee.

If his number appears on exactly one dice he wins twice the entrance fee.

If his number does not appear on any of the dice he wins nothing.

(a) Copy and complete the probability table below.

Profit ($)	$-n$	n	$2n$	$3n$
Probability		$\frac{75}{216}$		

(b) Show that the player's expected profit is $\$\left(-\frac{17}{216}n\right)$.

(c) What should the entrance fee be so that the player's expected loss per game is 34 cents?

15 Let X be a random variable with a Poisson distribution, such that $P(X > 2) = 0.404$. Find $P(X < 2)$.

16 The discrete random variable X has the following probability distribution.

$$P(X = x) = \begin{cases} \dfrac{k}{x}, & x = 1, 2, 3, 4, \\ 0, & \text{otherwise.} \end{cases}$$

Calculate

(a) the value of the constant k,   (b) $E(X)$

Answers

1 Numbers

Exercise 1A (page 7)
1 (a) all
    (b) $\mathbb{Q}, \mathbb{R}, \mathbb{Q}^+, \mathbb{R}^+$
    (c) $\mathbb{Q}, \mathbb{R}, \mathbb{Q}^+, \mathbb{R}^+$
    (d) all
    (e) $\mathbb{R}, \mathbb{R}^+$
    (f) $\mathbb{N}, \mathbb{Z}, \mathbb{Q}, \mathbb{R}$
    (g) $\mathbb{R}$
    (h) $\mathbb{Z}, \mathbb{Q}, \mathbb{R}$

2 (a) $\{1, 2, 3\}$
    (b) $\{0, 1, 2, 3, 4\}$
    (c) $\{-2, -1, 0, 1\}$
    (d) $\{0, 1\}$
    (e) $\{1, 2, 3\}$
    (f) $\{0, 1, 2\}$

3 (a) $x > 14$
 (b) $x \le 2.5$
 (c) $x \le -3.2$
    (d) $x \le -4$
 (e) $x \ge -4$
 (f) $x \le 4$
    (g) $x \le 22$
 (h) $x \le 6$
 (i) $x > -2$
    (j) $x \ge -2$
 (k) $x \ge \frac{1}{3}$
 (l) $x < 1$
    (m) $x > 3$
 (n) $x \ge -9$
 (o) $x > 6$
    (p) $x \le \frac{6}{7}$
 (q) $x \ge -1$

Exercise 1B (page 9)
1 (a) 6
    (b) 2
    (c) 28

2 $0 < \dfrac{1}{x^2} < 0.0001$

3 (a) $4.755 \le m \le 4.765$
 (b) $|m - 4.76| \le 0.005$

4 (a) $16.6 \le P \le 17$
    (b) $|P - 16.8| \le 0.2$

5 (a) $16.8625 \le A \le 17.7025$
    (b) $|A - 17.2825| \le 0.42$

6 (a) $2 < x < 4$
    (b) $-2.1 \le x \le -1.9$
    (c) $1.4995 \le x \le 1.5005$
    (d) $-1.25 \le x \le 2.75$

7 (a) $|x - 1.5| \le 0.5$
    (b) $|x - 1| < 2$
    (c) $|x + 3.65| \le 0.15$
    (d) $|x - 2.85| < 0.55$

8 $|x| \in \mathbb{N}$

Exercise 1C (page 12)
1 (a) 3
 (b) 10
 (c) 4
 (d) 8
    (e) 6
 (f) 15
 (g) 30
 (h) 60
    (i) 28
 (j) 27
 (k) 5
 (l) 48

2 (a) $3\sqrt{2}$
 (b) $2\sqrt{5}$
 (c) $2\sqrt{6}$
 (d) $4\sqrt{2}$
    (e) $2\sqrt{10}$
 (f) $3\sqrt{5}$
 (g) $4\sqrt{3}$
 (h) $5\sqrt{2}$

3 (a) $5\sqrt{2}$
    (b) $3\sqrt{3}$
    (c) $\sqrt{5}$
    (d) $2\sqrt{2}$
    (e) 0
    (f) $13\sqrt{5}$

4 (a) 2
 (b) 3
 (c) 2
 (d) 5
    (e) 5
 (f) 3
 (g) $\frac{1}{4}$
 (h) $\frac{1}{2}$

5 (a) 1
 (b) 7
 (c) 4
 (d) 7
    (e) 46
 (f) 5
 (g) 107
 (h) -3

Exercise 1D (page 17)
1 (a) $\frac{1}{3}\sqrt{3}$
 (b) $\frac{1}{5}\sqrt{5}$
 (c) $2\sqrt{2}$
 (d) $\sqrt{6}$
    (e) $\sqrt{11}$
 (f) $\frac{1}{2}\sqrt{2}$
 (g) $4\sqrt{3}$
 (h) $2\sqrt{7}$
    (i) $\sqrt{3}$
 (j) $\frac{1}{3}\sqrt{3}$
 (k) $\sqrt{15}$
 (l) $\frac{4}{5}\sqrt{30}$
    (m) $\frac{7}{6}\sqrt{6}$
 (n) $\frac{2}{3}\sqrt{6}$
 (o) $\frac{3}{2}\sqrt{6}$
 (p) $\frac{1}{9}\sqrt{6}$

2 (a) $7\sqrt{3}$
 (b) $4\sqrt{3}$
 (c) $\sqrt{3}$
 (d) $\sqrt{3}$
    (e) $12\sqrt{3}$
 (f) $-5\sqrt{3}$

3 (a) $20\sqrt{2}$ cm^2
    (b) $3\sqrt{10}$ cm

4 (a) $x = 5\sqrt{2}$
 (b) $y = -4\sqrt{2}$
 (c) $z = 3\sqrt{2}$

5 (a) $2\sqrt[3]{3}$
 (b) $4\sqrt[3]{3}$
 (c) $3\sqrt[3]{3}$
 (d) $5\sqrt[3]{3}$

6 (a) $4\sqrt{13}$ cm
    (b) $5\sqrt{11}$ cm
    (c) $2\sqrt{15}$ cm
    (d) $3\sqrt{5}$ cm

7 (a) $10.198\ 039\ 027\ 2$
 (b) $25.495\ 097\ 568\ 0$
    (c) $2.549\ 509\ 756\ 8$

8 (a) $x = 3\sqrt{5}, y = 4$

9 (a) $\sqrt{2} + 1$
 (b) $\dfrac{3 + \sqrt{3}}{3}$
 (c) $\dfrac{4 + \sqrt{2}}{7}$
    (d) $\dfrac{6 + \sqrt{2}}{17}$
 (e) $3 - 2\sqrt{2}$
 (f) $3 + \sqrt{3}$
    (g) $\dfrac{5 + 3\sqrt{2}}{7}$
 (h) $\dfrac{8 + 9\sqrt{2}}{14}$

10 $\dfrac{27 - 10\sqrt{2}}{23}$

11 $x = \sqrt{5} + 2, y = -\sqrt{5} - 1$

12 (a) $\left(1 - \frac{1}{2}\sqrt{2}\right)$ cm
    (b) $\frac{1}{2}\left(\sqrt{3} - 1\right)$ cm
    (c) $\frac{1}{4}\left(3 - \sqrt{5}\right)$ cm

2 Sequences

Exercise 2A (page 21)
1 (a) $7, 14, 21, 28, 35$
 (b) $13, 8, 3, -2, -7$
    (c) $4, 12, 36, 108, 324$
 (d) $6, 3, 1.5, 0.75, 0.375$
    (e) $2, 7, 22, 67, 202$
 (f) $1, 4, 19, 364, 132\ 499$

2 (a) $u_1 = 2, u_n = u_{n-1} + 2$
    (b) $u_1 = 11, u_n = u_{n-1} - 2$
    (c) $u_1 = 2, u_n = u_{n-1} + 4$
    (d) $u_1 = 2, u_n = 3u_{n-1}$
    (e) $u_1 = \frac{1}{3}, u_n = \frac{1}{3}u_{n-1}$
    (f) $u_1 = \frac{1}{2}a, u_n = \frac{1}{2}u_{n-1}$
    (g) $u_1 = 1, u_n = -u_{n-1}$
    (h) $u_1 = 1, u_n = (1 + x)u_{n-1}$

3 (a) $5, 7, 9, 11, 13; u_1 = 5, u_n = u_{n-1} + 2$
    (b) $1, 4, 9, 16, 25; u_1 = 1, u_n = u_{n-1} + 2n - 1$
    (c) $1, 3, 6, 10, 15; u_1 = 1, u_n = u_{n-1} + n$

(d) $1, 5, 14, 30, 55$; $u_1 = 1, u_n = u_{n-1} + n^2$

(e) $6, 18, 54, 162, 486$; $u_1 = 6, u_n = 3u_{n-1}$

(f) $3, 15, 75, 375, 1875$; $u_1 = 3, u_n = 5u_{n-1}$

4 (a) $u_n = 10 - n$ (b) $u_n = 2 \times 3^n$

(c) $u_n = n^2 + 3$ (d) $u_n = 2n(n+1)$

(e) $u_n = \dfrac{2n-1}{n+3}$ (f) $u_n = \dfrac{n^2+1}{2^n}$

Exercise 2B (page 23)

1 (a) 820   (b) 610   (c) 420   (d) 400

3 (a) n (c) $1^3 = t_1^2 - t_0^2, 2^3 = t_2^2 - t_1^2,$
$3^3 = t_3^2 - t_2^2, \ldots, n^3 = t_n^2 - t_{n-1}^2$

Exercise 2C (page 32)

1 (a), (d), (f), (h); $3, -2, q, x$ respectively

2 (a) $12, 2n$ (b) $32, 14 + 3n$

(c) $-10, 8 - 3n$ (d) $3.3, 0.9 + 0.4n$

(e) $3\frac{1}{2}, \frac{1}{2} + \frac{1}{2}n$ (f) $43, 79 - 6n$

(g) $x + 10, x - 2 + 2n$

(h) $1 + 4x, 1 - 2x + xn$

3 (a) 14   (b) 88   (c) 36   (d) 11

4 (a) 610   (b) 795   (c) -102

(d) $855\frac{1}{2}$ (e) -1025 (f) 998 001

5 (a) $54, 3132$ (b) $20, 920$

(c) $46, 6532$ (d) $28, -910$

(e) $28, 1120$ (f) $125, 42875$

(g) $1000, 5\,005\,000$ (h) $61, -988.2$

6 (a) $a = 3, d = 4$ (b) $a = 2, d = 5$

(c) $a = 1.4, d = 0.3$ (d) $a = 12, d = -2.5$

(e) $a = 25, d = -3$ (f) $a = -7, d = 2$

7 (a) 20   (b) 12   (c) 16

8 (a) 62   (b) 25

9 (a) \$76   (b) \$1272

10 (a) 5050   (b) 15 050   (c) $\frac{1}{2}n(3n+1)$

11 \$1 626 000

Exercise 2D (page 38)

1 (a) $2 + 3$ (b) $2 + 2 + 2$

(c) $1 + \frac{1}{2} + \frac{1}{3} + \frac{1}{4}$ (d) $1 + 4 + 9 + 16$

(e) $5 + 7 + 9 + 11$ (f) $u_0 + u_1 + u_2$

2 (a) $\sum_{i=2}^{4} i$ (b) $\sum_{i=1}^{4} i^2$ (c) $\sum_{i=3}^{7} i^3$

(d) $\sum_{i=1}^{3} \frac{1}{2i}$ (e) $\sum_{i=1}^{4} (2i + 1)$ (f) $\sum_{i=1}^{5} (3i - 1)$

3 (b) $41\,230, 637\,336, 716\,946$

4 (a) True   (b) False   (c) True   (d) False

5 (a) 1   (b) -1 (c) -1 (d) 21

(e) $\frac{17}{60}$ (f) -1

6 (a) $\sum_{i=1}^{101} (-1)^{i+1} i$ (b) $\sum_{i=1}^{25} (-1)^i (2i)^2$

(c) $\sum_{i=1}^{49} (-1)^{i+1} \frac{1}{i}$

7 $\sum_{i=1}^{n} (a + (i-1)d) = \frac{1}{2}n(2a + (n-1)d)$

3   Permutations and combinations

Exercise 3A (page 43)

1 120

2 720

3 40 320

4 120, 24

5 120, 48

6 $3.041\,409\,318 \times 10^{64}$

7 (a) 26

(b) 24 360

8 $\dfrac{20!}{16!}$

9 (a) $n + 1$ (b) $n^3 - n$

Exercise 3B (page 46)

1 720

2 3024, 1680

3 (a) 254 251 200   (b) $\dfrac{50!}{45!}$

4 (a) 46 234   (b) $2\frac{28\,961}{40\,320}$, 2.718

Exercise 3C (page 48)

1 (a) 120   (b) 10 272 278 170

2 22 100

3 126

4 15 504

5 215 760

6 163 800

7 (a) 1024   (b) 210

8 (b) For each subset of r objects, there is a subset of $n - r$ objects left behind.

9 (a) 35, 21, 56   (b) 120, 210, 330
$^nC_{r-1} + {}^n C_r = {}^{n+1} C_r$

10 (a) 16   (b) 32   (c) 64
$\sum_{i=0}^{n} {}^nC_i = 2^n$; the sum is the total number of subsets (including the empty set) that can be formed from a set of n objects.

11 (a) 15   (b) 1800

4 The binomial theorem

Exercise 4A (page 54)

1 (a) $x^3 + 3x^2 + 3x + 1$
   (b) $8x^3 + 12x^2 + 6x + 1$
   (c) $64 + 48p + 12p^2 + p^3$
   (d) $x^3 - 3x^2 + 3x - 1$
   (e) $x^6 + 6x^4 + 12x^2 + 8$
   (f) $8p^3 + 36p^2q + 54pq^2 + 27q^3$
   (g) $1 - 12x + 48x^2 - 64x^3$
   (h) $1 + 2x + \frac{3}{2}x^2 + \frac{1}{2}x^3 + \frac{1}{16}x^4$
   (i) $x^6 + 6x^4 + 12x^2 + 8$
   (j) $1 - 15x^2 + 75x^4 - 125x^6$
   (k) $x^6 + 3x^4y^3 + 3x^2y^6 + y^9$
   (l) $1 - 3x^3 + 3x^6 - x^9$

2 (a) 12   (b) 150

3 (a) 240   (b) 54

4 (a) 270   (b) -1000

5 $m^3 + 12m^2 + 48m + 64$
   $m^4 + 13m^3 + 60m^2 + 112m + 64$

6 $24r^4 + 124r^3 + 234r^2 + 189r + 54$

7 7

8 $a^9 + 9a^8b + 36a^7b^2 + 84a^6b^3 + 126a^5b^4$
   $+ 126a^4b^5 + 84a^3b^6 + 36a^2b^7 + 9ab^8 + b^9$

9 8064

10 $1 - 3x + 9x^2 - 13x^3 + 18x^4 - 12x^5 + 8x^6$

Exercise 4B (page 57)

1 (a) 35   (b) 28   (c) 126   (d) 715
   (e) 15   (f) 45   (g) 11   (h) 1225

2 (a) 10   (b) -56 (c) 165   (d) -560

3 (a) 84   (b) -1512 (c) 4032   (d) $-\frac{99}{4}$

4 (a) 3003   (b) 192 192
   (c) 560 431 872   (d) 48 048

Exercise 4C (page 60)

1 (a) $1 + 13x + 78x^2 + 286x^3$
   (b) $1 - 15x + 105x^2 - 455x^3$
   (c) $1 + 30x + 405x^2 + 3240x^3$
   (d) $128 - 2240x + 16\,800x^2 - 70\,000x^3$

2 (a) $1 + 22x + 231x^2$ (b) $1 - 30x + 435x^2$
   (c) $1 - 72x + 2448x^2$ (d) $1 + 114x + 6156x^2$

3 $1 + 16x + 112x^2; 1.17$

4 $4096 + 122\,880x + 1\,689\,600x^2; 4220.57$

5 $1 + 32x + 480x^2 + 4480x^3; 5920$

6 $1 - 30x + 405x^2; 234$

7 $2 + 56x^2 + 140x^4 + 56x^6 + 2x^8; x = 0.01;$
   $2.005\,601\,400\,056\,000\,2$

9 Each row of Pascal's triangle is symmetrical about its centre.

10 (a) $\frac{3}{4}$ (b) $\frac{7}{4}$

Review exercise 1 (page 62)

1 (a) $4\sqrt{3}$ (b) $\sqrt{7}$
   (c) $111\sqrt{10}$ (d) $3\sqrt[3]{2}$

2 (a) $\frac{3}{2}\sqrt{3}$ (b) $\frac{1}{25}\sqrt{5}$
   (c) $\frac{1}{3}\sqrt{2}$ (d) $\frac{2}{15}\sqrt{30}$

4 (a) 14 cm^2

5 (a) $12\sqrt{3}$ (b) 48

6 $x > \frac{4}{3}$

7 1444

8 $128 - 448x + 672x^2 - 560x^3; 123.59$

9 (a) 1683   (b) 3367

10 $a^{10} + 10a^7 + 40a^4 + 80a + \dfrac{80}{a^2} + \dfrac{32}{a^5}$

11 (a) $2 + \dfrac{2}{3}\sqrt{3}$ (b) $\dfrac{15 - 3\sqrt{5}}{10}$

    (c) $\dfrac{11 - 6\sqrt{2}}{7}$ (d) $\dfrac{11\sqrt{7} - 26}{9}$

12 $2 + \sqrt{3}$

13 $x = 3\sqrt{2} + 4, y = 5\sqrt{2} - 7$

14 $a\left(2 + \sqrt{2}\right);$
    $5\left(2 - \sqrt{2}\right)$ m, $5\left(2 - \sqrt{2}\right)$ m, $10\left(\sqrt{2} - 1\right)$ m

15 (c) They cannot be equal.

16 $1 + 40x + 760x^2;$
    (a) 1.0408   (b) 0.9230

17 B, D

18 (a) 568; 567 and 568   (b) 969 and 970

19 (b) (i) $a = 3, b = 6, c = 8$
        (ii) $a = 6, b = 4, c = 9$

20 3 628 800, 45

21 (a) 40 320   (b) 1152

22 360

23 71 240

24 $n(2n + 3)$

25 168

26 167 167; 111 445

27 (a) 47, 12 years left over   (b) £345 450

28 (b) 22

29 (a) 5   (b) $\frac{1}{2}$

Examination questions (page 65)

1 1080

2 −7

3 2, −3

4 (a) 1, 5, 9   (b) $4n - 3$

5 (a) 4, 8, 16   (b) (i) 2^n

5 Representation of statistical data

Exercise 5A (page 72)

B means 'class boundaries', F means 'frequency'.

1 B: 30   40   50   60   70   80   90
    F: 12   32   56   72   20   8

2 B: 4.5   9.5   14.5   19.5   24.5   29.5
      34.5   39.5
    F: 2   5   8   14   17   11   3

3 (a) 6 cm   (b) 7

4 B: −0.5   9.5   19.5   29.5   39.5   49.5   59.5
    F: 6   21   51   84   82   31

5 Assuming data correct to 1 decimal place
    B: 8.95   9.95   10.95   11.95   12.95   13.95
      14.95   15.95   16.95
    F: 1   4   7   6   9   8   7   3

6 (b) 2.875, 3.875
    (c) B: 2.875   3.875   4.875   5.875   6.875
        7.875   8.875
    F: 3   4   6   7   10   4

7 (a), (b) B: 10   20   30   40   50   60   70   80
        F: 12   40   44   47   32   15   10

Exercise 5B (page 75)

1 Plot at (30, 0), (40, 12), (50, 44), (60, 100),
    (70, 172), (80, 192), (90, 200).

    (a) About 31%   (b) About 52 m.p.h.

2 Plot at (−0.5, 0), (9.5, 6), (19.5, 27), (29.5, 78),
    (39.5, 162), (49.5, 244), (59.5, 275).

    (a) About 26% or 27% (b) About 25

3 (a) Plot at (0, 0), (16, 14.3), (40, 47.4),
        (65, 82.7), (80, 94.6), (100, 100).
    (b) 9.4 million

4 Plot at (0, 0), (2, 15), (3, 42), (4, 106), (5, 178),
    (6, 264), (7, 334), (8, 350), (9, 360).
    About 54 poor days and 14 good days.

5 Plot at (0, 0), (4.5, 12), (9.5, 41), (14.5, 104),
    (19.5, 117), (24.5, 129), (29.5, 132).

    (a) About 8.5 miles   (b) 14 miles

6 Measures of location

Exercise 6A (page 80)

1 5.4 kg; 5.7 kg

2 (a) 27.5 m.p.h.   (b) 1.1 hours

3 13.5

4 £500 approximately

5 (a) B: 0.95, 2.45, 3.95, 5.45, 6.95, 8.45, 9.95,
        11.45, 12.95
        F: 13, 16, 18, 15, 6, 8, 2, 2
    (b) Plot at (0.9, 0), (2.4, 13), (3.9, 29),
        (5.4, 48), (6.9, 62), (8.4, 68), (9.9, 76),
        (11.4, 78), (12.9, 80); 4.8 s
    (c) 5.0 s.
    Data not evenly spread over class 4.0–5.4.

6 34

7 (a) 70.5 inches   (b) 66.0 inches
    On average the men are taller than the
    women.

Exercise 6B (page 86)

1 10.5

2 71.43 inches. Students appear taller, on
    average than the population. This can be
    explained by the large values 75.5, 75.5, 76.5
    and 77.0.

3 (a) 11.3   (b) 105.5

4 0.319

5 3.59 shots

6 24.3

7 59.0 m.p.h.

8 (a) 0–2.5, 2.5–5.5, 5.5–8.5, 8.5–11.5,
        11.5–14.5
    (b) 3.54 minutes.

9 130 cm

10 £12.89; £12.39

11 95 kg

12 117 kg

Exercise 6C (page 91)

1 (a) 0   (b) No mode.   (c) 2–3   (d) Brown

2 (a) Mode   (b) Mean   (c) Median

3 It could be true for mean or mode, not the
    median.

4 (a) Roughly symmetrical
    (b) Skewed
    (c) Skewed
    (d) Roughly symmetrical

5 (a) Mean 4.875, median 5, mode 6: the mean and the median are approximately the same, but the slightly higher mode suggests that the test was reasonably easy.

(b) It has a 'tail' of low values.

7 Measures of spread

Exercise 7A (page 101)

1 (a) 17, 9.5   (b) 9.1, 2.8

2 (a) 2.3   (b) About 5.4

3 Monday: $Q_1 = 110$, $Q_2 = 170$, $Q_3 = 250$
Wednesday: $Q_1 = 240$, $Q_2 = 305$, $Q_3 = 375$
Wednesday has greater audiences in general, with less variation.

4 (a) Negative skew   (b) Positive skew
(c) Roughly symmetrical

5 (a) £38.73, £43.23, £49.24, £54.15, £58.42.
(c) Slight negative skew

6 Box and whisker plots are preferred since they give visual comparison of the shapes of distributions, the quartiles, IQRs and ranges. Histograms will indicate the general shape of the distributions and will give only a rough idea of quartiles and so on. However, means and standard deviations can be estimated from a histogram but not a box and whisker plot.

Exercise 7B (page 107)

1 (a) 4, 2   (b) 5, 4.899

2 (a) 3.489   (b) 4.278

3 50.728 g, 10.076 g^2

4 (a) Anwar is better; his mean of 51.5 is greater than Brian's 47.42 (Anwar scores more runs than Brian).

(b) Brian is more consistent since his standard deviation of 27.16 is less than Anwar's 34.13.

5 149.15 cm, 5.33 cm

6 8.73, 2.45

7 163, 10

Exercise 7C (page 111)

1 0.740, 1.13

3 797.4 min^2, 807.5 min^2

4 250.77(5) g, 3.51 g
Increase the number of classes; weigh more accurately; use more packets.

5 Mid-class values are 18.5, 23.5, 28.5, 33.5, 38.5, 45.5, 55.5, 65.5. Mean 37.35 years, SD 11.68 years. In the second company the general age is lower and with smaller spread.

Review exercise 2 (page 113)

1 (a) F: 17, 11, 10, 9, 3, 4, 2, 2, 1, 1
(b) B: −0.5   9.5   19.5   29.5   39.5   49.5   59.5   69.5   79.5   89.5   99.5
F: 1.7, 1.1, 1.0, 0.9, 0.3, 0.4, 0.2, 0.2, 0.1, 0.1,
(c) Plot at (−0.5, 0), (9.5, 17), (19.5, 28), (29.5, 38), (39.5, 47), (49.5, 50), (59.5, 54), (69.5, 56), (79.5, 58), (89.5, 59), (99.5, 60); 44
(d) It assumes the data are evenly spread over the class 30–39. There are two each of 31, 33 and 39, and one each of 32, 36, 37, so the assumption is not well founded.

2 (a) Both 22.0–23.9
(b) Not supported since modal classes the same. Either mean$_1$ (23.21 °C) is greater than mean$_2$ (22.43 °C) or median$_1$ ($\approx$23 °C) is greater than median$_2$ ($\approx$22 °C).

3 (a) $0.62; $0.717; modes: $0.50, $0.52, $0.59
(b) Median, since it is not affected by extreme values or mean, since it involves all values.
(c) $0.336

4 23.16 cm, 1.32 cm; 22.89 cm, 1.13 cm
House sparrows have smaller variability; little difference in means.

5 (b) 0.060 cm   (c) 1.33 approx.; close to 1.3

6 Mean and standard deviation of the sample are 64.6 kg and 8.36 kg, correct to three significant figures.
The estimates are 64.6 kg and 9.34 kg.

7 (a) 26.9 years, 13.0 years   (b) About 22 years
Median preferred since distribution skewed, more information given by median.

Examination questions (page 114)

1 5, 11

2 1.04 m, 1.05 m

3 (a) 31.3 min   (b) 9.84 min^2

4 6423 euros

5 (a) 154   (b) 44

6 (a) 9.46   (b) 20.81

7 9.3

8 33.18, 3.215

8 Coordinates, points and lines

Exercise 8A (page 123)

1 (a) $13; \left(4\frac{1}{2}, 11\right)$ (b) $5; \left(4, 3\frac{1}{2}\right)$
   (c) $10; (7, 5)$ (d) $5; \left(-1, \frac{1}{2}\right)$
   (e) $5\sqrt{2}; \left(1\frac{1}{2}, -2\frac{1}{2}\right)$ (f) $2\sqrt{13}; (-5, 0)$

3 $(4, -6)$

4 (a) 2   (b) -3 (c) $\frac{1}{2}$ (d) $-\frac{3}{4}$

5 $\frac{1}{2}, \frac{1}{2}$; points lie on a straight line

6 No

7 (a) Gradients PQ and RS both -1,
     QR and SP both $\frac{3}{5}$
   (b) $PQ = RS = 4\sqrt{2}$, $QR = SP = \sqrt{34}$
   (c) Both $\left(3\frac{1}{2}, -1\frac{1}{2}\right)$ (d) Parallelogram

Exercise 8B (page 128)

1 (a) Yes   (b) No

2 (a) $y = 5x - 7$ (b) $y = -3x + 1$
   (c) $2y = x + 8$ (d) $8y = -3x + 2$
   (e) $y = -3x$ (f) $y = 8$
   (g) $4y = -3x - 19$ (h) $2y = x + 3$
   (i) $8y = 3x + 1$ (j) $2y = -x + 11$
   (k) $y = -2x + 3$ (l) $y = 3x + 1$
   (m) $y = 7x - 4$ (n) $y = -x + 2$

3 (a) $y = 3x + 1$ (b) $y = 2x - 3$
   (c) $3y = -2x + 12$ (d) $x = 3$
   (e) $5y = 3x - 45$ (f) $y = -3x + 8$
   (g) $y = -3$ (h) $3y = -x + 2$
   (i) $3y = -5x - 14$ (j) $7y = -2x - 11$
   (k) $x = -3$ (l) $y = -x - 1$
   (m) $y = 3x + 1$ (n) $3y = -5x - 13$
   (o) $y = -\frac{3}{5}x$ (p) $py = qx$

4 (a) $-1, -3, -3$ (b) $3, -4, 12$
   (c) $-2\frac{1}{2}, -\frac{3}{5}, -1\frac{1}{2}$ (d) 0, none, 5
   (e) $1\frac{1}{2}, -1\frac{1}{3}, 2$ (f) Undefined, $1\frac{2}{5}$, none
   (g) $-2, 3\frac{1}{2}, 7$ (h) $\frac{3}{4}, 2\frac{2}{3}, -2$ (i) $-\frac{1}{2}, 7, 3\frac{1}{2}$

5 $y = \frac{1}{2}x + 2$

6 $y = -2x + 6$

Exercise 8C (page 131)

1 (a) $-\frac{1}{2}$ (b) $\frac{1}{3}$ (c) $-1\frac{1}{3}$
   (d) $1\frac{1}{5}$ (e) 1 (f) $-\frac{4}{7}$
   (g) m (h) $-1/m$ (i) $-q/p$
   (j) Undefined (k) $1/m$ (l) $(c - b)/a$

2 (a) $4y = -x + 14$ (b) $y = 2x + 7$
   (c) $5y = x - 27$ (d) $x = 7$
   (e) $2y = 3x + 11$ (f) $3y = -5x + 29$
   (g) $y = -3$ (h) $2y = -x + 6$

3 $2y = -x + 8$

9 Functions and graphs

Exercise 9A (page 136)

1 (a) 11   (b) 5   (c) -3 (d) 0
2 (a) 50   (b) 5   (c) 29   (d) 29
3 (a) 15   (b) $5\frac{1}{4}$ (c) 0   (d) 0
4 (a) 17   (b) 9
5 $\frac{1}{2}$
6 4, 2
7 Semicircle
8 $x = -1, x = 1, y = 1$
9 $-1 \le x \le 3, 0 \le y \le 4$ would do
10 $x = 3, y = -2$

Exercise 9B (page 139)

2 4

3 (a) and (c) are odd; (b) is even.

Exercise 9C (page 142)

1 (a) $x \ge 0$ (b) $x \le 0$ (c) $x \ge 4$ (d) $x \le 4$
   (e) $x \le 0$ and $x \ge 4$ (f) $x \le 0$ and $x \ge 4$
   (g) $x \le -3$ and $x \ge 3$ (h) $x \ge 2$
   (i) All real numbers except 2
   (j) $x > 2$ (k) $x \ge 0$
   (l) All real numbers except 1 and 2

2 (a) $f(x) \ge 4$ (b) $f(x) \ge 10$ (c) $f(x) \ge 6$
   (d) $f(x) \le 7$ (e) $f(x) \ge 2$ (f) $f(x) \ge -1$

3 (a) $0 \le f(x) \le 16$ (b) $-1 \le f(x) \le 7$
   (c) $0 \le f(x) \le 16$ (d) $4 \le f(x) \le 25$

4 (a) $f(x) > 7$ (b) $f(x) < 0$ (c) $f(x) > -1$
   (d) $f(x) > -1$ (e) $f(x) > 2$ (f) $f(x) \ge -\frac{1}{4}$

5 (a) $f(x) \ge 0$ (b) all real numbers
   (c) all real numbers except 0
   (d) $f(x) > 0$ (e) $f(x) \ge 5$
   (f) all real numbers
   (g) $0 \le f(x) \le 2$ (h) $f(x) \ge 0$

6 $0 < w < 12, 0 < A \le 36$

7 $0 < x < 4, 0 < y \le 146$

Exercise 9D (page 146)

3 (a) $\lim_{n \to \infty} u_n = 0$ (b) $\lim_{n \to \infty} s_n = 9$

4 No

5 2

10 Linear and quadratic functions

Exercise 10A (page 148)

4 Changing c moves the graph parallel to the y-axis.

6 The graph stays the same shape, but is moved across and down the graph paper.

10 Changing a makes the graph narrower and steeper.

11 (c)

12 (a)

Exercise 10B (page 152)

1 (a) (i) $(2, 3)$ (ii) $x = 2$
  (b) (i) $(5, -4)$ (ii) $x = 5$
  (c) (i) $(-3, -7)$ (ii) $x = -3$
  (d) (i) $\left(\frac{3}{2}, 1\right)$ (ii) $x = \frac{3}{2}$
  (e) (i) $\left(-\frac{3}{5}, 2\right)$ (ii) $x = -\frac{3}{5}$
  (f) (i) $\left(-\frac{7}{3}, -4\right)$ (ii) $x = -\frac{7}{3}$
  (g) (i) $(3, c)$ (ii) $x = 3$
  (h) (i) (p, q) (ii) $x = p$
  (i) (i) $(-b/a, c)$ (ii) $x = -b/a$

2 (a) (i) -1 (ii) -2 (b) (i) 2 (ii) 1
  (c) (i) 5 (ii) -3 (d) (i) -7 (ii) $-\frac{1}{2}$
  (e) (i) 3 (ii) 4 (f) (i) q (ii) $-p$
  (g) (i) $-q$ (ii) p (h) (i) r (ii) t
  (i) (i) c (ii) $-b/a$

3 (a) (i) $x = 2$ (ii) $2, 5, -1$
    (iii) $y = -x^2 + 4x + 1$
  (b) (i) $x = 2$ (ii) $2, -1, 3$
    (iii) $y = 3x^2 - 12x + 11$

Exercise 10C (page 155)

1 (a) $(x + 1)^2 + 1$ (b) $(x - 4)^2 - 19$
  (c) $\left(x + 1\frac{1}{2}\right)^2 - 9\frac{1}{4}$ (d) $(x - 3)^2 - 4$
  (e) $(x + 7)^2$ (f) $2(x + 3)^2 - 23$
  (g) $3(x - 2)^2 - 9$ (h) $11 - 4(x + 1)^2$
  (i) $2\left(x + 1\frac{1}{4}\right)^2 - 6\frac{1}{8}$

2 (a) 3 when $x = 2$ (b) $2\frac{3}{4}$ when $x = 1\frac{1}{2}$
  (c) 13 when $x = 3$ (d) $-1\frac{1}{8}$ when $x = 1\frac{1}{4}$
  (e) $-4\frac{1}{3}$ when $x = -\frac{1}{3}$ (f) $7\frac{1}{12}$ when $x = -1\frac{1}{6}$

3 (a) (i) $(2, 2)$ (ii) $x = 2$
  (b) (i) $(-3, -11)$ (ii) $x = -3$
  (c) (i) $(-5, 32)$ (ii) $x = -5$
  (d) (i) $\left(-1\frac{1}{2}, -1\frac{1}{4}\right)$ (ii) $x = -1\frac{1}{2}$
  (e) (i) $\left(1\frac{3}{4}, -4\frac{1}{8}\right)$ (ii) $x = 1\frac{3}{4}$
  (f) (i) $(2, -7)$ (ii) $x = 2$

4 (a) $f(x) \geq -28$ (b) $f(x) \leq 5\frac{1}{2}$
  (c) $f(x) \geq -9$ (d) $f(x) > 5$
  (e) $-1\frac{1}{3} \leq f(x) \leq 4$ (f) $5 \leq f(x) \leq 13$

5 (a) $(x + \sqrt{2})^2 - 3$ (b) $2\left(x + \frac{1}{4}\sqrt{3}\right)^2 - \frac{3}{8}$
  (c) $-\sqrt{5}\left(x - \frac{1}{5}\sqrt{5}\right)^2 + \left(1 + \frac{1}{5}\sqrt{5}\right)$

Exercise 10D (page 160)

3 30 m s^{-1}, 45 m

4 (a) Upwards (b) $v = 25 - 10t$
  (c) After 2.5 seconds (d) 31.25 m

5 (a) 2 m s^{-2} (b) $v = 80 - 2t$ (c) 1500 m

6 (a) A straight line from $(0, 5)$ reaching height 7
  (b) 40 s (c) $\frac{1}{20}$ m s^{-2}
  (d) $v = 5 + \frac{1}{20}t$ (e) $5t + \frac{1}{40}t^2$

11 Equations and graphs

Exercise 11A (page 168)

1 (a) $(x + 3)(x + 8)$ (b) $(l - 3)(l - 4)$
  (c) $(q - 5)(q - 7)$ (d) $(x - 2)(x + 3)$
  (e) $(x - 3)(x + 8)$ (f) $(n - 12)(n + 5)$
  (g) $(r - 1)(r - 16)$ (h) $(x - 3)(x - 11)$
  (i) $(x - 3)(x + 7)$

2 (a) $(x - 2)(3x - 2)$ (b) $(2x - 1)(2x - 5)$
  (c) $(3x + 1)(4x - 1)$ (d) $(x - 2)(3x + 2)$
  (e) $(x - 2)(8x + 1)$ (f) $(3x - 2)(2x + 3)$
  (g) $(2x - 5)(2x + 1)$ (h) $3(x - 3)(3x - 1)$
  (i) $2(3x - 4)(2x + 1)$

3 (a) $(x - 1)(x + 1)$ (b) $(2 - 5d)(2 + 5d)$
  (c) $4(5 - z)(5 + z)$ (d) $(1 - x)(1 + 3x)$
  (e) $(x + 1)(3x + 1)$ (f) $(x + 4)(3x - 2)$

4 (a) No factors (b) $(x - 5)(x - 8)$
  (c) No factors (d) No factors
  (e) $x(x + 14)$ (f) $(x - 10)(x + 6)$
  (g) No factors (h) No factors
  (i) $(2x - 1)(x + 3)$

5 (a) $-5, 7$ (b) $-1, 3$ (c) $-9, 3$
  (d) $-\frac{2}{3}, \frac{3}{2}$ (e) $-\frac{2}{3}, \frac{3}{2}$ (f) $-\frac{3}{4}, \frac{2}{3}$

6 (a) $-4, 1$ (b) $-3, 3$ (c) $-\frac{1}{2}, 1$
  (d) $\frac{1}{2}, 2$ (e) 3 (f) $-\frac{1}{3}, \frac{1}{3}$

7 $y = 2x^2 + 4x - 6$; $(-4, 10)$

8 $y = 3x^2 + 12x + 12$

Exercise 11B (page 172)

1 (a) $3 \pm \sqrt{3}$ (b) $0, -4$ (c) $-3 \pm \frac{1}{2}\sqrt{10}$
  (d) $\frac{1}{3}(7 \pm 2\sqrt{2})$ (e) $-p \pm \sqrt{q}$ (f) $-b \pm \sqrt{c/a}$

2 (a) $\frac{1}{2}(-3 \pm \sqrt{29})$ (b) $2 \pm \sqrt{11}$
  (c) -3 (repeated) (d) $\frac{1}{2}(-5 \pm \sqrt{17})$
  (e) No solution (f) $\frac{1}{6}(5 \pm \sqrt{97})$
  (g) -3 and $-\frac{1}{2}$ (h) $\frac{1}{2}(-3 \pm \sqrt{41})$
  (i) $\frac{1}{6}(2 \pm \sqrt{34})$

3 (a) $(x - 7)(x + 5)$ (b) $(x - 22)(x + 8)$
  (c) $(x + 24)(x - 18)$ (d) $(3x + 2)(2x - 3)$
  (e) $(2 + 7x)(7 - 2x)$ (f) $(4x + 3)(3x - 2)$

Exercise 11C (page 174)

1 (a) 2   (b) 1   (c) 0   (d) 0   (e) 2
   (f) 2   (g) 1   (h) 2   (i) 2   (j) 2

2 (a) $-\frac{9}{4}$ (b) $-\frac{25}{32}$ (c) 81
   (d) $\pm 2\sqrt{6}$ (e) $\pm 4\sqrt{6}$ (f) $p^2/4q$

3 (a) $k < \frac{9}{4}$ (b) $k = \frac{49}{4}$ (c) $k > \frac{9}{20}$
   (d) $k > -\frac{25}{12}$ (e) $k = \frac{4}{3}$ (f) $k > \frac{25}{28}$
   (g) $k > 4$ or $k < -4$ (h) $-6 < k < 6$

4 (a) 2   (b) 0   (c) 1   (d) 0   (e) 2
   (f) 2   (g) 0   (h) 0   (i) 1

5 Intersects x-axis twice, faces up.

6 Intersects x-axis twice, faces down.

Exercise 11D (page 175)

1 (a) ± 1, ± 2 (b) ± 1, ± 3 (c) ± 2
   (d) $\pm\sqrt{6}$ (e) $-1, 2$ (f) $\sqrt[3]{3}, -\sqrt[3]{4}$

2 (a) 16   (b) 25, 9   (c) 49
   (d) 25   (e) 9   (f) 16

3 (a) $-2, 5$ (b) $-6, 1$ (c) $-3, \frac{1}{2}$
   (d) $-4, 3$ (e) 36   (f) 9

Exercise 11E (page 179)

1 (a) $(3, 14)$ (b) $(1, 3), (4, 3)$
   (c) $(-4, 8), (2, 8)$ (d) $(-3, -3), (\frac{1}{2}, -3)$

2 (a) $(1, 2), (3, 4)$ (b) $(-4, -5), (3, 9)$
   (c) $(-1\frac{1}{2}, 6\frac{1}{2}), (2, 17)$ (d) $(-2, -7), (2, 9)$

3 (a) $(2, 6)$ (b) $(-3, -1)$

4 (a) $(-4, 14)$ (b) $(-6, 24), (-2, 12)$

5 (a) $(-1, 4), (3, 8)$ (b) $(1, 6)$

6 (a) $(5, 51)$ (b) $(-1, \frac{1}{2}), (1, \frac{1}{2})$
   (c) $(1, 9), (2, 18)$ (d) $(-2, 3)$
   (e) $(-3, 1), (-2, 3)$ (f) $(-1, -5), (2, 19)$

7 (a) 1.586, 4.414   (b) $-2.882, -0.223, 3.105$
   (c) $-3.709, -1.194, 0.903$
   (d) 1.612, 3.821

8 (a) $(4.11, 69.29)$
   (b) $(3.36, 37.77)$ (c) $(1.66, 3.76)$
   (d) $(-4.59, -1.09), (0.25, 19.94), (4.34, 1.15)$

Review exercise 3 (page 180)

2 (a) $3y = 4x - 13$ (b) $(4, 1)$ (c) 5

3 $4y = 3x - 1$

4 9

5 $(-2\frac{1}{2}, -2), (2, 7)$

7 $(0, 108)$

8 $(\sqrt{3}, -5\sqrt{3}), (-\sqrt{3}, 5\sqrt{3})$

11 (a) $f(x) \le 9$ (b) All real values
    (c) $f(x) \ge -69$ (d) $f(x) \ge -36$

12 25; $f(x) \le 25$

13 2.15

14 $|x| > 2$, $x = -2$, $x = 2$, $y = 0$

15 (a) ± 3, ± 9
    (b) ± 16, ± 17, ± 19, ± 23, ± 32, ± 61
    (c),(d) If the quadratics factorise, then the
         discriminants must be squares of
         integers. These expressions are the
         discriminants of the quadratics in (a)
         and (b).

16 $(x - \sqrt{2} - \sqrt{3})(x - \sqrt{2} + \sqrt{3})$

17 $(3, 3)$

18 (a) The equation $0x + 0y = 0$ is satisfied by
        all points (x, y) in the plane, and
        $0x + 0y = c$, where $c \ne 0$, is satisfied by
        no points in the plane. In neither case is
        the graph a line.

19 $3x + 5y = 4$; $\left(\frac{4}{3}, 0\right)$

20 (a) $2\sqrt{3}, 4\sqrt{3}$ (b) $\pm 1.86, \pm 2.63$

21 (a) $(3x + 2)^2 + 3$ (b) $0 < f(x) \le \frac{1}{3}$

22 (a) $4(x - 2)^2 - 8$ (b) $(2, -8)$
    (c) $2 - \sqrt{2}, 2 + \sqrt{2}$

23 (b) 4, 25

Examination questions (page 182)

1 (a) $\frac{1}{2}n(3n + 1)$ (b) 30

2 (a) $-\sqrt{3} < x < \sqrt{3}$ (b) $f(x) \ge \dfrac{1}{\sqrt{3}}$

3 $\left(\frac{2}{3}, -\frac{5}{3}\right), \left(\frac{4}{3}, \frac{11}{3}\right)$

4 $\pm\sqrt{3}$

12 Differentiation

Exercise 12A (page 187)

1 (a) 4   (b) 1.2   (c) -2

2 (a) 5   (b) 9   (c) -3

3 (a) (i) 10   (ii) 24   (iii) -40
   (b) (i) 0.8   (ii) 3   (iii) -2
   (c) (i) 2   (ii) -4 (iii) 8

Exercise 12B (page 189)

1 (a) $20x$ (b) $2x$ (c) $6x - 4$

Exercise 12C (page 193)

1 (a) $2x$ (b) $2x - 1$ (c) $8x$ (d) $6x - 2$
   (e) -3 (f) $1 - 4x$ (g) $4 - 6x$ (h) $\sqrt{2} - 2\sqrt{3}x$

2 (a) 3   (b) $-6x$ (c) 0   (d) $2 + 6x$
  (e) $-2x$ (f) $6 - 6x$ (g) $2 - 4x$ (h) $4x + 1$

3 (a) 6   (b) 3   (c) -3 (d) 8
  (e) -8 (f) -6 (g) 4   (h) -17

4 (a) $\frac{3}{4}$ (b) $\frac{1}{2}$ (c) $-\frac{3}{2}$
  (d) -1 (e) $\frac{3}{2}$ (f) $\frac{1}{2}$

5 (a) 3   (b) 0.75

7 (a) $3x^2 + 4x$ (b) $-6x^2 + 6x$
  (c) $3x^2 - 12x + 11$ (d) $6x^2 - 6x + 1$
  (e) $1 + 3x^2$ (f) $-4x^3$

8 (a) -10 (b) 6   (c) 58
  (d) -1 (e) 8   (f) -8

9 (a) $-2, 2$ (b) $-\frac{4}{3}, 2$ (c) $-5, 7$
  (d) 1   (e) $-1, -\frac{1}{3}$ (f) No values

13 Tangents and normals

Exercise 13 (page 201)

1 (a) $y = -2x - 1$ (b) $y = -x$
  (c) $y = 2x - 1$ (d) $y = 6x + 10$
  (e) $y = 1$ (f) $y = 0$

2 (a) $2y = x - 3$ (b) $4y = -x + 1$
  (c) $8y = -x - 58$ (d) $x = 0$
  (e) $2y = x + 9$ (f) $x = \frac{1}{2}$

3 $4y = 4x - 1$

4 $y = 0$

5 $y = -2x$

6 $12y = 12x - 17$

7 $x = 1$

8 $7y = -x + 64$

9 $y = 4x + 2$

10 $y = x + 2$

12 $y = -2x - 6$

13 (a) $(-1, 1), (2, 4)$
   (b) $y = -2x - 1, y = 4x - 4$ (c) $\left(\frac{1}{2}, -2\right)$

14 Index notation

Exercise 14A (page 205)

1 (a) a^{12} (b) b^8 (c) c^4
  (d) d^9 (e) e^{20} (f) $x^6 y^4$
  (g) $15g^8$ (h) $3h^8$ (i) $72a^8$

2 (a) 2^{26} (b) 2^{12} (c) 2^6
  (d) 2^6 (e) 2^2 (f) 2^1

Exercise 14B (page 209)

1 (a) $\frac{1}{8}$ (b) $\frac{1}{16}$ (c) $\frac{1}{5}$
  (d) $\frac{1}{9}$ (e) $\frac{1}{10000}$ (f) 1

(g) 2   (h) 27   (i) $\frac{2}{5}$
(j) $\frac{1}{128}$ (k) $\frac{1}{216}$ (l) $\frac{27}{64}$

2 (a) $\frac{1}{2}$ (b) $\frac{1}{512}$ (c) $\frac{1}{32}$
  (d) 8   (e) $\frac{1}{8}$ (f) 8

3 (a) $\frac{1}{10}$ (b) $\frac{2}{5}$ (c) $\frac{2}{5}$
  (d) $\frac{1}{10}$ (e) 10   (f) $\frac{2}{5}$

4 (a) a (b) b (c) c^{-6}
  (d) 2   (e) e^{-9} (f) f^{-5}
  (g) $3g^{-1}$ (h) $\frac{1}{9}h^{-4}$ (i) $\frac{1}{9}i^4$
  (j) $8j^6$ (k) $8x^9 y^{-3}$
  (l) $p^{-8}q^{-16}r^{-12}$ (m) $2m$
  (n) $9n^{-9}$ (o) $\frac{1}{64}q^6$

5 (a) $x = -2$ (b) $y = 0$ (c) $z = 4$
  (d) $x = -2$ (e) $y = 120$ (f) $t = 0$

6 (a) 2.7×10^{-5} m^3 (b) 5.4×10^{-3} m^2

7 26.7 km h^{-1} (to 1 decimal place)

8 (a) 1.0×10^{-3} m^3 (to 2 significant figures)
  (b) 101.9 m (to 1 decimal place)
  (c) 5.6×10^{-3} m (to 2 significant figures)

9 (a) 4.375×10^{-4} (b) 4.5×10^{-7}

Exercise 14C (page 215)

1 (a) 5   (b) 2   (c) 6   (d) 2
  (e) 3   (f) $\frac{1}{3}$ (g) $\frac{1}{2}$ (h) $\frac{1}{7}$
  (i) $\frac{1}{10}$ (j) -3 (k) 16   (l) $\frac{1}{625}$

2 (a) 2   (b) $\frac{1}{16}$ (c) 16   (d) $\frac{1}{2}$
  (e) 2   (f) $\frac{1}{2}$ (g) 16   (h) $\frac{1}{2}$

3 (a) 4   (b) 8   (c) $\frac{1}{27}$ (d) 81
  (e) 4   (f) 8   (g) $\frac{1}{32}$ (h) 32
  (i) $\frac{1}{1000}$ (j) 625   (k) $2\frac{1}{4}$ (l) $\frac{2}{3}$

4 (a) a^2 (b) $12b^{-1}$ (c) $12c^{\frac{3}{4}}$
  (d) 1   (e) 2   (f) $5pq^2$

5 (a) 64   (b) 27   (c) 8   (d) 9
  (e) $\frac{1}{4}$ (f) $\frac{1}{27}$ (g) 2   (h) 2

6 (a) 1.9 (to 1 decimal place)
  (b) 2.2 m (to 1 decimal place)

7 6.5 cm (to 1 decimal place)

8 (a) $x = \frac{5}{2}$ (b) $y = -\frac{3}{2}$ (c) $z = \frac{1}{4}$ (d) $x = \frac{3}{2}$
  (e) $y = \frac{4}{3}$ (f) $z = -\frac{7}{3}$ (g) $t = \frac{6}{5}$

9 (a) 1, 4   (b) 9   (c) 1
  (d) 0, 8   (e) 2   (f) 1, -27

10 (a) $x^{-\frac{1}{2}}$ (b) $4x^{\frac{1}{2}}$ (c) $2x^{\frac{1}{2}}$
   (d) $3x^{\frac{5}{2}}$ (e) $x^{-\frac{2}{3}}$ (f) $6x^{-\frac{4}{3}}$

11 (a) $2\sqrt[3]{3}$ (b) $\sqrt[6]{2}$ (c) $\sqrt{6}$

12 (a) (i) 16   (iii) $-\frac{1}{4}$ (iv) 16
   (ii), (v), (vi) No value
   (c) q must be odd

15   Graphs of *n*th power functions

Exercise 15A (page 223)

1 (a) $(2, 4)$

  (b) $(3, \frac{1}{3})$

  (c) $(\sqrt{2}, \sqrt{2}), (-\sqrt{2}, -\sqrt{2})$

  (d) $(\frac{1}{2}, 32), (-\frac{1}{2}, 32)$

  (e) $(\frac{1}{3}, 243), (-\frac{1}{3}, -243)$

  (f) $(2, 4), (-2, 4)$

2 (a) $x > 10$

  (b) $x < -50$ or $x > 50$

  (c) $-\frac{1}{10}\sqrt{10} \le x \le \frac{1}{10}\sqrt{10}, x \ne 0$

  (d) $x < -20$ or $x > 20$

3 (a) RQP   (b) PQR   (c) QPR   (d) QRP

4 (a) $-2x^{-3}, -\dfrac{2}{x^3}$ (b) $-5x^{-6}, -\dfrac{5}{x^6}$

  (c) $-9x^{-4}, -\dfrac{9}{x^4}$ (d) $4x^{-3}, \dfrac{4}{x^3}$

  (e) $-x^{-5}, -\dfrac{1}{x^5}$ (f) $2x^{-7}, \dfrac{2}{x^7}$

5 (a) $-\dfrac{5}{x^2}$ (b) $-\dfrac{1}{4x^2}$

  (c) $-\dfrac{6}{x^3}$ (d) 0

  (e) $-\dfrac{3}{x^2} - \dfrac{1}{x^4}$ (f) $\dfrac{4-x}{x^3}$

6 (a) $y = -4x + 8$ (b) $y = -2x + 3$

  (c) $y = -18x + 9$ (d) $y = 6$

  (e) $y = -x + 1$ (f) $2y = x + 2$

7 (a) $y = x - 1$ (b) $y = \frac{1}{2}x$

  (c) $x = 2$ (d) $4y = x - 3$

Exercise 15B (page 227)

1 (a) $\frac{1}{3}x^{-\frac{2}{3}}$ (b) $\frac{5}{2}x^{\frac{3}{2}}$

  (c) $2x^{-\frac{3}{5}}$ (d) $3x^{-\frac{8}{5}}$

  (e) $-2x^{-\frac{3}{2}}$ (f) $3x^{-\frac{5}{2}}$

2 (a) $\dfrac{3}{4\sqrt[4]{x}}$ (b) $\dfrac{2}{\sqrt[3]{x^2}}$

  (c) $-\dfrac{2}{\sqrt{x^3}}$ (d) $10\sqrt{x^3}$

  (e) $-\dfrac{1}{6\sqrt[3]{x^4}}$ (f) $\dfrac{3x-1}{4\sqrt[4]{x^5}}$

3 (a) (i) $2, 2.008\,298\,8...$ (ii) $0.082\,988...$

    (iii) $\frac{1}{12}$ (iv) $12y = x + 16$

  (b) (i) $4, 4.033\,264\,2...$ (ii) $0.332\,642...$

    (iii) $\frac{1}{3}$ (iv) $3y = x + 4$

  (c) (i) $0.25, 0.247\,938\,1...$ (ii) $-0.020\,618...$

    (iii) $-\frac{1}{48}$ (iv) $48y = -x + 20$

  (d) (i) $0.0625, 0.061\,473\,3...$

    (ii) $-0.010\,266...$

    (iii) $-\frac{1}{96}$

    (iv) $96y = -x + 14$

4 (a) $6y = x + 9$ (b) $8y = -x + 32$

  (c) $y = 3x - 1$ (d) $y = 3$

5 (a) $(8, 4)$ (b) $(-1, -1), (1, 1)$

  (c) $(-8, \frac{3}{4})$ (d) $(1, 4)$

6 $y = 2x + \frac{3}{8}$

7 The line $y = x$ bisects the angle between the axes.

16   Polynomials, factors and remainders

Exercise 16A (page 229)

3 (a) None of the cubics has a vertical axis of symmetry; some but not all of the quartics do.

  (b) All the cubics, but none of the quartics, have a point of symmetry.

5 If n is even: quadrants 1 and 2 if $a > 0$, quadrants 3 and 4 if $a < 0$.
  If n is odd: quadrants 1 and 3 if $a > 0$, quadrants 2 and 4 if $a < 0$.

Exercise 16B (page 232)

1 (a) 3   (b) 1   (c) 4

  (d) 0   (e) 1   (f) 0

2 (a) $4x^2 + 7x + 6$

  (b) $5x^3 + 3x^2 - 6x - 3$

  (c) $8x^4 - 3x^3 + 7x^2 - 3x + 1$

  (d) $2x^5 + 2x^4 - 5x^2 + 3$

  (e) $-x^3 - 2x^2 - 5x + 4$

3 (a) $2x^2 + x - 8$

  (b) $3x^3 + 7x^2 - 8x + 9$

  (c) $-2x^4 - x^3 + 7x^2 + 3x - 3$

  (d) $2x^5 - 2x^4 - 6x^3 + 5x^2 + 1$

  (e) $-x^3 - 6x^2 + 9x + 2$

4 (a) $2x^3 - 3x^2 + 9x - 2$

  (b) $3x^3 - 7x^2 + 16x - 13$

  (c) $x^3 - 4x^2 + 7x - 11$

  (d) $3x^3 - 8x^2 + 17x - 17$

5 (a) $6x^2 - 7x - 3$

  (b) $x^3 + x^2 - 7x + 2$

  (c) $2x^3 + 5x^2 - 3x - 9$

  (d) $12x^3 - 13x^2 + 9x - 2$

  (e) $x^4 + 2x^3 - 2x^2 + 2x - 3$

  (f) $8x^4 - 6x^3 - 15x^2 + 18x - 5$

(g) $x^4 + 5x^3 + 5x^2 + 3x + 18$

(h) $x^5 - 5x^4 + 3x^3 + 10x^2 - 8x + 5$

(i) $6x^3 + 29x^2 - 7x - 10$

(j) $6x^3 + 5x^2 - 13x - 12$

6 (a) (i) 3, 4   (ii) 7   (iii) 8   (iv) −35

(b) (i) 2, 3   (ii) 5   (iii) 6   (iv) 3

(c) (i) 5, 2   (ii) 7   (iii) −3   (iv) 12

(d) (i) 3, 5   (ii) 8   (iii) −35   (iv) 0

7 (a) 0, −1   (b) −11, −1

(c) −3, −9   (d) 25, −8

(e) 20, −21   (f) −16, 13

(g) 106, −81   (h) −5, 11

Exercise 16C (page 236)

1 (a) Yes, $3x - 4$ (b) Yes, $2x + 9$

(c) Yes, $4x + 3$ (d) No

(e) Yes, $3x + 2$ (f) Yes, $2x - 5$

(g) No   (h) Yes, $3x + 8$

2 (a) $x - 3$ (b) $x + 17$

(c) $3x + 11$ (d) $7x - 3$

(e) $x - 3$ (f) $7x - 2$

3 (a) $x - 1, 4x + 5$ (b) $x - 3, 2x + 1$

(c) $x + 1, 4x - 3$ (d) $x + 2, 3x + 4$

(e) $2x + 1, 2x - 5$ (f) $4x - 1, 3x - 4$

(g) $2x + 3, 3x + 2$ (h) $x + 3, 6x - 5$

(i) $2x - 1, 4x + 3$

4 (a) $-14, x + 7$ (b) $9, 2x + 3$

(c) $4, 2x + 1$ (d) $-2, 2x + 1$

(e) $1, x + 1$ or $-2, -2x + 4$

(f) $4, 3x - 2$

Exercise 16D (page 240)

1 (a) Yes, $x^2 - x + 2$

(b) Yes, $4x^2 + 8x + 3 \equiv (2x + 1)(2x + 3)$

(c) No

(d) Yes, $x^2 + 2x - 1 \equiv (x + 1 + \sqrt{2})(x + 1 - \sqrt{2})$

(e) Yes, $x^2 + x + 1$

(f) Yes, $9x^2 + 6x + 1 \equiv (3x + 1)^2$

(g) No

(h) Yes, $x^2 - 4x + 1 \equiv (x - 2 + \sqrt{3})(x - 2 - \sqrt{3})$

2 (a) $x + 1, x - 2, x + 3$

(b) $x - 2, x - 2, x + 5$

(c) $2x - 1, 2x + 1, 3x + 1$

(d) $2x - 1, 2x - 1, 2x - 1$

(e) $x + 3, 3x - 1, 3x + 1$

(f) $x + 2, x - 1 + \sqrt{3}, x - 1 - \sqrt{3}$

(g) $x - 1, x + 1, x + 2, x + 5$

(h) $x - 1, x - 2, x + 3, x + 4$

(i) $x + 1, x - 2$ (repeated), $x + 4$

3 (a) $(x + 1)(x - 3)(x + 4)$ − 4, −1, 3

(b) $(x - 1)(x - 3)(x + 1)$ − 1, 1, 3

(c) $(x - 1)(x - 5)(x + 3)$ − 3, 1, 5

(d) $(x + 1)^2(x - 5)$ − 1, 5

(e) $(x - 2)(x + 2)(x + 3)$ − 3, −2, 2

(f) $(2x + 1)(x - 1)(x + 4)$ − 4, $-\frac{1}{2}$, 1

(g) $(3x - 1)(x - 2)(x + 2)$ − 2, $\frac{1}{3}$, 2

(h) $(x - 1)(x + 2)(x^2 - x + 2)$; −2, 1

(i) $(2x - 1)(2x + 1)(x^2 + x + 1)$; $-\frac{1}{2}, \frac{1}{2}$

4 (a) 6, $(x + 1)(x + 2)(x - 3)$

(b) −13, $(x - 2)(2x + 1)(2x + 3)$

(c) 2, $(2x + 5)(x^2 - 2x + 5)$

(d) 3, $(x + 3)^2(x - 1)$ or

$-6, (x + 3)(x + 1 + \sqrt{13})(x + 1 - \sqrt{13})$

5 (a) $(x - 2)(x^2 + 2x + 4)$

(b) $(x + 2)(x^2 - 2x + 4)$

(c) $(x - a)(x^2 + ax + a^2)$

(d) $(x + a)(x^2 - ax + a^2)$

Exercise 16E (page 244)

1 (a) 1, −5, 22   (b) 1, 8, −11

(c) 3, −4, 0   (d) 3, −1, −4

(e) 4, 1, 4   (f) 7, 1, 8

2 (a) 1, −3, 5, 2   (b) 1, −2, 4, 22

(c) 1, 1, −1, 3   (d) 4, 1, −3, 11

(e) 2, 7, −1, 0   (f) 3, 0, −5, 10

3 (a) $x - 2, -4$

(b) $x + 1, -7$

(c) $2x + 7, 13$

(d) $x + 2, 3$

(e) $2x - 1, -1$

4 (a) $x^2 - 3, 7$

(b) $x^2 + 2x + 15, 71$

(c) $2x^2 - 6x + 22, -71$

(d) $5x^2 + 20x + 77, 315$

(e) $x^2 - x - 1, -6$

(f) $2x^2 + 7x - 1, 3$

5 (a) −5   (b) 13   (c) 50

(d) −355   (e) $\frac{7}{8}$ (f) $7\frac{13}{27}$

(g) 0   (h) 279

6 −1

7 −2

8 −5

9 3

10 1, −1

11 4, −3

12 2, 1

13 5, 3

Exercise 16F (page 247)

1 (a) $x = 3, y = 1$ (b) $x = -1, y = 2$
   (c) $x = 2, y = -3$ (d) $x = \frac{1}{2}, y = \frac{1}{2}$
   (e) $x = -3, y = x - 3$ (f) $x = 1, y = x + 1$
   (g) $x = 2, y = 3x + 5$ (h) $x = -\frac{1}{2}, y = \frac{1}{2}x + \frac{3}{4}$

Review exercise 4 (page 248)

1 $\left(-\frac{1}{3}, -4\frac{17}{27}\right), (2, 13)$

2 1.5×10^{-10} joules

3 $(2, 12)$

4 $\left(-\frac{1}{4}, \frac{1}{16}\right), \left(2\frac{1}{4}, 5\frac{1}{16}\right)$

5 (a) 6   (b) $\frac{1}{16}$ (c) $\frac{1}{2}$ (d) $2\frac{10}{27}$

6 $x = \frac{8}{7}$

7 (b) 1.5×10^{11} m (to 2 significant figures)

8 (a) $S = 2^1 \times 3^1 \times V^{\frac{2}{3}}$
   (b) $V = 2^{-\frac{3}{2}} \times 3^{-\frac{3}{2}} \times S^{\frac{3}{2}}$

9 13

10 (a),(b) $2\sqrt{2}y = x + 3\sqrt{2}$

11 $\left(\frac{11}{20}, \frac{4}{5}\right)$

12 $\left(\frac{67}{32}, \frac{5}{8}\right)$

13 (a) -2 and $\frac{1}{2}$ (b) $mn = -1$

14 $\dfrac{1}{3a^2}$

15 -1 and 8

16 -25

17 (a) $-4x - 7, x^4 - 8x^3 + 13x^2 - 18x - 12$
    (b) $3, -\frac{4}{3}$

18 $48x + 32y + 65 = 0$

19 (b) 1, 16

20 $-1, \frac{1}{2}, -\frac{3}{2}$

21 (a) $y + 5x = 2, (2, -8)$
    (b) $5y - x = -16,$
        $\left(\frac{3}{2} \pm \frac{1}{10}\sqrt{545}, -\frac{29}{10} \pm \frac{1}{50}\sqrt{545}\right)$

22 $A(-\sqrt{3}, 0), B(\sqrt{3}, 0); (x - 2)(x + 1)^2$
    (a) 2   (b) They touch at $(-1, -2)$.

Examination questions (page 250)

1 $x = 1, x = 4, y = 1$

2 $-5x^3 + 12x^2 - 3x + 2$

3 $-21, 14$

4 6

5 4

6 1

7 $-5, 6$

8 $-2, 6$

17 Trigonometry

Exercise 17 (page 259)

1 (a) (i) 0.9063   (ii) 0.4226   (iii) 0.4663
   (b) (i) -0.5736 (ii) 0.8192   (iii) -1.4281
   (c) (i) -0.7071 (ii) -0.7071 (iii) 1
   (d) (i) 0.8192   (ii) -0.5736 (iii) -0.7002
   (e) (i) -0.3420 (ii) 0.9397   (iii) -2.7475
   (f) (i) 0.3843   (ii) 0.9232   (iii) 2.4023
   (g) (i) -0.5721 (ii) 0.8202   (iii) -1.4335
   (h) (i) -0.9703 (ii) -0.2419 (iii) 0.2493

2 (a) Greatest 3 at $x = 90$, least 1 at $x = 270$
   (b) Greatest 11 at $x = 180$, least 3
       at $x = 360$
   (c) Greatest 13 at $x = 180$, least -3
       at $x = 90$
   (d) Greatest 4 at $x = 90$, least 2 at $x = 270$
   (e) Greatest 10 at $x = 27\frac{1}{2}$, least 8
       at $x = 72\frac{1}{2}$
   (f) Greatest 30 at $x = 180$, least 10
       at $x = 360$

3 (a) 160   (b) 320   (c) 240
   (d) 50   (e) 220   (f) 340
   (g) 40, 140   (h) 30, 330   (i) 70, 250
   (j) 80, 100   (k) 160, 200   (l) 100, 280

4 (a) $\frac{1}{2}\sqrt{2}$ (b) $-\frac{1}{2}$ (c) $-\frac{1}{2}$ (d) $\sqrt{3}$
   (e) $-\frac{1}{2}\sqrt{2}$ (f) $\frac{1}{3}\sqrt{3}$ (g) -1 (h) $-\frac{1}{3}\sqrt{3}$
   (i) $-\frac{1}{2}\sqrt{2}$ (j) 0   (k) 1   (l) $\frac{1}{2}\sqrt{2}$
   (m) $-\frac{1}{2}$ (n) -1 (o) $-\frac{1}{2}$ (p) 0

5 (a) 60   (b) 240   (c) 120   (d) 30
   (e) 30   (f) 135   (g) 210   (h) 90
   (i) 120   (j) 60   (k) 270   (l) 180
   (m) 60   (n) 150   (o) 225   (p) 180

7 $A = 5, B = 2.8; 7.42$ m

18 The sine and cosine rules

In this chapter, angles are given correct to
1 decimal place (unless they are exact), and
lengths and areas correct to 3 significant
figures.

Exercise 18A (page 265)

1 (a) 6 cm^2 (b) 11.2 cm^2 (c) 1.93 m^2
  (d) 3.75 cm^2 (e) 5.03 cm^2 (f) 0.311 m^2

2 (a) 5.19 cm   (b) 4 cm   (c) 1.60 m
  (d) 9.53 cm   (e) 43.5 cm   (f) 11.2 m

3 (a) 33.7°   (b) 53.1°   (c) 20.5°
  (d) 56.3°   (e) 11.6°   (f) 10.8°

4 (a) 146.3°   (b) 126.9°   (c) 159.5°
  (d) 123.7°   (e) 168.4°   (f) 169.2°

Exercise 18B (page 269)

1 (a) 6.95 cm   (b) 32.9 cm
  (c) 3.14 cm   (d) 7.65 cm
  (e) 5.81 cm   (f) 8.18 cm

2 (a) $a = 12.4$ cm, $c = 12.5$ cm, 68.9 cm^2
  (b) $p = 8.40$ cm, $r = 7.93$ cm, 29.4 cm^2
  (c) $x = 14.8$ cm, $z = 13.4$ cm, 76.2 cm^2
  (d) $l = 10.4$ cm, $n = 4.17$ cm, 17.7 cm^2

3 (a) $\hat{A} = 64.5°$, $\hat{C} = 24.5°$
  (b) $\hat{Y} = 59.5°$, $\hat{Z} = 49.5°$

4 (a) $\hat{L} = 92.1°$, $\hat{N} = 74.9°$
  (b) $\hat{D} = 28.2°$, $\hat{F} = 111.8°$

5 (a) 119 m   (b) 102 m

6 (a) 80.0°   (b) 90.0°

7 The largest side, a, must be opposite the largest angle, which is therefore $\hat{A}$; but $\hat{B}$ is the largest angle.

8 (a) 5.64 cm   (b) 6.12 cm   (c) 21.5 cm^2

Exercise 18C (page 274)

1 (a) 10.2 cm   (b) 16.3 cm
  (c) 5.91 cm   (d) 28.0 cm

2 (a) 69.5°   (b) 128.0°   (c) 85.6°   (d) 90°

3 (a) 44.0°   (b) 43.8°   (c) 24.1°   (d) 36.9°

4 34.2 cm^2

19 Solving triangles

Exercise 19A (page 278)

1 (a) 58.8°, 100.2° or 121.2°, 38.8°
  (b) 66.8°, 63.2° or 113.2°, 16.8°
  (c) 36.4°, 103.6°

2 (a) 9.37 cm or 14.2 cm
  (b) 7.69 cm or 13.5 cm
  (c) 9.96 cm

Exercise 19B (page 280)

1 $\hat{C} = 70°$, $b = 5.65$ cm, $c = 6.13$ cm

2 $\hat{Y} = 42.4°$, $\hat{Z} = 57.6°$, $y = 4.79$ cm

3 $\hat{P} = 38.2°$, $\hat{Q} = 120°$, $\hat{R} = 21.8°$

4 $\hat{L} = 33.1°$, $\hat{M} = 36.9°$, $n = 17.2$ cm

5 $\hat{E} = 93.6°$, $\hat{F} = 56.4°$, $e = 12.0$ cm or
  $\hat{E} = 26.4°$, $\hat{F} = 123.6°$, $e = 5.34$ cm

20 Radians

Exercise 20 (page 285)

1 (a) $\frac{1}{2}\pi$ (b) $\frac{3}{4}\pi$ (c) $\frac{1}{4}\pi$ (d) $\frac{1}{6}\pi$
  (e) $\frac{2}{5}\pi$ (f) $\frac{1}{10}\pi$ (g) $\frac{2}{3}\pi$ (h) $\frac{1}{8}\pi$
  (i) 4π (j) $\frac{10}{3}\pi$ (k) $\frac{3}{2}\pi$ (l) $\frac{1}{180}\pi$

2 (a) 60°   (b) 9°   (c) 36°   (d) $22\frac{1}{2}°$
  (e) 20°   (f) 120°   (g) $112\frac{1}{2}°$ (h) 108°
  (i) 4°   (j) 1080°   (k) −90°   (l) 50°

3 (a) $s = 8.4$, $A = 29.4$ (b) $s = 7.35$, $A = 12.9$
  (c) $\theta = 1.5$, $A = 48$ (d) $r = 20$, $A = 140$
  (e) $\theta = 2.4$, $s = 12$ (f) $s = 8$
  (g) $r = 8$, $\theta = 2$ (h) $\theta = \frac{5}{3}$

4 (a) 2.26 cm^2 (b) 1.47 cm^2 (c) 830 cm^2
  (d) 9.05 cm^2 (e) 0.556 cm^2

5 6.72 cm^2

6 28.2 cm

7 26.3 cm^2

8 15.5 cm, 14.3 cm^2

9 (a) $\frac{1}{2}\sqrt{3}$ (b) $\frac{1}{2}\sqrt{2}$ (c) $\frac{1}{3}\sqrt{3}$ (d) 0
  (e) $-\frac{1}{2}\sqrt{2}$ (f) $-\frac{1}{2}\sqrt{3}$ (g) $-\sqrt{3}$ (h) $\frac{3}{4}$

21 Three-dimensional problems

Exercise 21 (page 291)

1 68.2°, 60.5°

2 3.68 m

3 35.3°

4 7.78°, 6.50°

5 54.7°

6 56.3°

7 32.3°

8 39.5°

9 (a) 3.47 m   (b) 34.5 m

Review exercise 5 (page 293)

1 (a) 360   (b) 90

2 (0, 1), (±180, 0)

3 (a) 0.1 cm, 0.0009 seconds
  (b) 0.0036 seconds
  (c) 278   (d) 0.002 13 seconds

4 (a) 110 cm and 90 cm   (b) 0.36 seconds
   (c) 0.72 seconds   (d) 0.468

5 6.03 m

6 14.2 cm, 17.4 cm

7 9.45 cm

8 57.4°

9 35.4°, 48.2°, 96.4°, 31.3 cm^2

10 11.3 cm, 47.3°, 57.7°

11 52.2 km

12 (a) 29.0°   (b) 11.6 m^2

13 90°

14 3.6 cm, 10.8 cm^2

15 $\frac{1}{4}$

16 $\sin\gamma° = \sin\alpha° \cos\beta°$

17 22.8°, 309.5°

18 r^2

19 17 cm^2

Examination questions (page 295)

1 93.6°, 26.4

2 2.98 cm^2

3 20.6 cm^2

4 2.75 cm, 5.82 cm

5 0.55

6 13.6 m

22 Inequalities

Exercise 22A (page 300)

1 (a) $-2 < x < 2$ (b) $x < -2$ or $x > 0$
   (c) $-3 \leq x \leq 1$ (d) $-1 < x < 4$
   (e) $x < 2$ or $x > 2$ (f) no solution
   (g) $x > 2$ (h) $x \leq -2$ or $0 \leq x \leq 2$
   (i) $x = 0$ or $x \geq 3$

2 (a) $x \leq -3$ or $x \geq \frac{1}{2}$ (b) $-3 < x < 2$
   (c) $-6 < x < 1$ (d) $x \leq -\sqrt{3}$ or $x \geq \sqrt{3}$
   (e) $x < 2$ or $x \geq 3$ (f) $-\frac{3}{2} < x \leq 0$
   (g) $-3 < x < -1$ or $x > 2$
   (h) $-2 < x \leq 0$ or $x > 2$
   (i) $-2 - \sqrt{3} < x < -2 + \sqrt{3}$

3 (a) $-1.525... < x < 0.258...$ or $x > 1.267...$
   (b) $x > 5.114...$
   (c) $0.596... < x < 9.997...$
   (d) $-4.988... < x < -1.162...$ or $x > 1.037...$

Exercise 22B (page 304)

1 (a) $x < 1$ or $x > 3$ (b) $-\frac{1}{2} \leq x \leq 3$
   (c) $-2 < x < 2$ (d) $x = -1$
   (e) $x < -1$ or $x > \frac{1}{3}$ (f) $2 - \sqrt{2} \leq x \leq 2 + \sqrt{2}$

2 (a) $x < -1.532...$ or $-0.347... < x < 1.879...$
   (b) $x < -1.164...$ or $x > 1.452...$

3 (a) $x \leq -1$ or $0 < x \leq \frac{2}{3}$
   (b) $x < -2$ or $-1 < x < 1$

4 (a) $x \in [-3, 2[$ (b) $x \in]0, 3[$
   (c) $x \in]-2, 3]$ (d) $x \in [0, \infty[$
   (e) $x \in]-\infty, -10[$ (f) $x \in]-\infty, 2[\cup [3, \infty[$

5 (a) $1 < x < 5$ (b) $x \leq 2$
   (c) $-1 < x \leq 4$ (d) $-2 \leq x \leq 2$ or $x > 3$

23 Investigating shapes of graphs

Exercise 23A (page 308)

1 (a) $(-1, -7)$ (b) $(3, 10)$
   (c) $(-3, 27), (1, -5)$ (d) $(-2, 16), (2, -16)$
   (e) $(0, 0), (8, -256)$ (f) $(-1, 8), (1, 0)$
   (g) $(-2, 0), (0, 16), (2, 0)$
   (h) $(-1, 0), \left(-\frac{1}{3}, -\frac{4}{27}\right)$ (i) $(1, 1)$

2 (a) $(1, 4)$ (b) $\left(-\frac{1}{2}, -8\frac{1}{4}\right)$
   (c) $(-2, 9)$ (d) $(2, 0)$
   (e) $(0, 3)$ (f) $(-2, 2), (0, -2)$
   (g) $\left(-\frac{2}{3}, \frac{4}{27}\right), (0, 0)$ (h) $\left(-\frac{3}{4}, -\frac{27}{256}\right), (0, 0)$
   (i) $(-2, -32), (0, 0), (5, -375)$

Exercise 23B (page 313)

1 (a) +, increasing   (b) −, decreasing
   (c) −, decreasing   (d) +, increasing
   (e) +, increasing   (f) +, increasing
   (g) −, decreasing   (h) −, decreasing

2 (a) $2x - 5, x \geq \frac{5}{2}$ (b) $2x + 6, x \geq -3$
   (c) $-3 - 2x, x \leq -\frac{3}{2}$ (d) $6x - 5, x \geq \frac{5}{6}$
   (e) $10x + 3, x \geq -\frac{3}{10}$ (f) $-4 - 6x, x \leq -\frac{2}{3}$

3 (a) $2x + 4, x \leq -2$ (b) $2x - 3, x \leq \frac{3}{2}$
   (c) $-3 + 2x, x \leq \frac{3}{2}$ (d) $4x - 8, x \leq 2$
   (e) $7 - 4x, x \geq \frac{7}{4}$ (f) $-5 - 14x, x \geq -\frac{5}{14}$

4 (a) $3x^2 - 12, x \leq -2$ and $x \geq 2$
   (b) $6x^2 - 18, x \leq -\sqrt{3}$ and $x \geq \sqrt{3}$
   (c) $6x^2 - 18x - 24, x \leq -1$ and $x \geq 4$
   (d) $3x^2 - 6x + 3$, all x
   (e) $4x^3 - 4x, -1 \leq x \leq 0$ and $x \geq 1$
   (f) $4x^3 + 12x^2, x \geq -3$
   (g) $3 - 3x^2, -1 \leq x \leq 1$
   (h) $10x^4 - 20x^3, x \leq 0$ and $x \geq 2$
   (i) $3\left(1 + x^2\right)$, all x

5 (a) $3x^2 - 27$, $-3 \leq x \leq 3$

(b) $4x^3 + 8x$, $x \leq 0$

(c) $3x^2 - 6x + 3$, none

(d) $12 - 6x^2$, $x \leq -\sqrt{2}$ and $x \geq \sqrt{2}$

(e) $6x^2 + 6x - 36$, $-3 \leq x \leq 2$

(f) $12x^3 - 60x^2$, $x \leq 5$

(g) $72x - 8x^3$, $-3 \leq x \leq 0$ and $x \geq 3$

(h) $5x^4 - 5$, $-1 \leq x \leq 1$

(i) $nx^{n-1} - n$; $x \leq 1$ if n is even,
    $-1 \leq x \leq 1$ if n is odd

6 (a) (i) $(4, -12)$ (ii) minimum (iv) $y \geq -12$

(b) (i) $(-2, -7)$ (ii) minimum (iv) $y \geq -7$

(c) (i) $\left(-\frac{3}{5}, \frac{1}{5}\right)$ (ii) minimum (iv) $y \geq \frac{1}{5}$

(d) (i) $(-3, 13)$ (ii) maximum (iv) $y \leq 13$

(e) (i) $(-3, 0)$ (ii) minimum (iv) $y \geq 0$

(f) (i) $\left(-\frac{1}{2}, 2\right)$ (ii) maximum (iv) $y \leq 2$

7 (a) $(-2, 21)$ maximum, $(2, -11)$ minimum

(b) $(-4, -31)$ minimum, $(0, 1)$ maximum

(c) $(-1, 7)$ maximum, $(2, -20)$ minimum

(d) $(1, 2)$ maximum, $\left(1\frac{2}{3}, 1\frac{23}{27}\right)$ minimum

(e) $(-1, 2)$ mimimum, $(0, 3)$ maximum,
    $(1, 2)$ minimum

(f) $(1, 8)$ maximum

8 (a) $(-4, 213)$ maximum, $(3, -130)$ minimum

(b) $(-3, 88)$ maximum, $(5, -168)$ minimum

(c) $(0, 0)$ minimum, $(1, 1)$ neither

(d) $(-2, 65)$ maximum, $(0, 1)$ neither,
    $(2, -63)$ minimum

(e) $\left(-\frac{1}{3}, -\frac{11}{27}\right)$ minimum, $\left(\frac{1}{2}, \frac{3}{4}\right)$ maximum

(f) $(-1, 0)$ neither

Exercise 23C (page 317)

1 $\left(2\frac{1}{2}, -6\frac{1}{4}\right); k > -6\frac{1}{4}$

2 $k > 1\frac{1}{3}$

3 (a) 2   (b) 3   (c) 4   (d) 0

4 (a) 3; one between $-\sqrt{3}$ and -1, one between
    -1 and 0, one greater than $\sqrt{3}$.

(b) 2; 1, and one less than $-\sqrt{3}$ (in fact, -2)

(c) 1; greater than $\sqrt{3}$.

5 If $f(x) = x^3 + 4x$, $f'(x) = 3x^2 + 4 > 0$, so y is
  an increasing function of x for all x.

6 (a) $(-6, 0)$ maximum, $(-2, -32)$ minimum

(c) (i) 2   (ii) 1   (iii) 3   (iv) 1

(d) $-32 < k < 0$; between -8 and -6, between
    -6 and -2, between -2 and 0

7 (a) $\left(-\frac{1}{2}, -\frac{3}{16}\right)$ minimum, $(0, 0)$ maximum,
    $(2, -8)$ minimum

(b) $(1 - \sqrt{3}, 0)$, $(0, 0)$, $(1 + \sqrt{3}, 0)$

(c) (i) 2   (ii) 2   (iii) 1

(d) (i) $k < -8$ (ii) $k = -8$

(iii) $-8 < k < -\frac{3}{16}$ and $k > 0$

(iv) $k = -\frac{3}{16}$ and $k = 0$ (v) $-\frac{3}{16} < k < 0$

(e) Roots lie between $-(\sqrt{3} - 1)$ and $-\frac{1}{2}$,
    between $-\frac{1}{2}$ and 0, between 0 and 2, and
    between 2 and $1 + \sqrt{3}$.

Exercise 23D (page 322)

1 (a) $(-1, -2)$ maximum, $(1, 2)$ minimum

(b) $(2, 3)$ minimum

(c) $(1, 1)$ maximum

(d) $(1, -3)$ minimum

(e) $\left(2, \frac{1}{4}\right)$ maximum

(f) $\left(-\frac{1}{2}, 3\right)$ minimum

(g) $(4, 3)$ minimum

(h) $\left(-3, -\frac{2}{9}\right)$ minimum, $\left(3, \frac{2}{9}\right)$ maximum

(i) $(-8, 16)$ maximum, $(8, -16)$ minimum

2 (a) $x \geq 2$ (b) $x \leq -1$, $x \geq 1$

(c) $x < 0$, $x > 0$

3 (a) $\left(2, -\frac{3}{8}\right)$ minimum

(b) $\left(4, \frac{1}{256}\right)$ maximum

(c) $(-1, 0)$ maximum, $(1, 4)$ minimum

(d) $(-2, 8)$ minimum, $(2, 8)$ minimum

(e) $(0, 0)$ minimum, $(4, 19.0...)$ maximum

(f) $(1, 3)$ maximum

24   Second derivatives

Exercise 24A (page 330)

3 (a) $+, +$ (b) $+, -$ (c) $+, 0$ (d) $-, +$

4 (a) 0   (b) -4 (c) $6x + 10$ (d) $30x^4$

5 (a) $(-1, 0)$, $(0, 0)$, $(1, 0)$ (b) $3x^2 - 1$ (c) $6x$

6 (b) $3x^2 + 1$, $6x$ (c) $x > 0$

7 (a) $(2, -2)$ (b) $\left(-\frac{1}{2}, \frac{5}{8}\right)$, $\left(\frac{1}{2}, \frac{5}{8}\right)$

(c) None   (d) $(1, 7)$, $(2, 16)$

(e) $(5, -31\,250)$ (f) $(1, 4)$

(g) $(1, 0)$ (h) $(10, 0.0004)$

(i) $\left(3, \frac{4}{3}\sqrt{3}\right)$

8 (a) $x > 0$ (b) $x < 2$ (c) $x > -\frac{1}{3}$

(d) $x > 0$ (e) $x < 0$, $x > 0$ (f) $x > 3$

(g) $x < 0$, $x > 2$ (h) $x < 0$, $x > 0$ (i) $x > \frac{1}{4}$

9 $(-3, -47)$, $y = 27x + 34$

10 $y = 15x + 243$

11 0, 4, 6; $(1, 15)$; $y = -32x + 128$, $y = 22x - 7$

Exercise 24B (page 334)

1 (a) $(-1, -2)$ minimum, $(1, 2)$ maximum

(b) $(0, 0)$ maximum, $(2, -4)$ minimum

(c) $(0, 1)$ minimum

(d) $(-1, 11)$ maximum, $(2, -16)$ minimum

(e) $(2, 22)$ neither

2 (a) $(-1, -8)$ minimum, $(0, -3)$ maximum, $(2, -35)$ minimum

(b) None

(c) $\left(-\frac{4}{3}, -14\frac{2}{9}\right)$ minimum, $\left(\frac{4}{3}, 14\frac{2}{9}\right)$ maximum

(d) None   (e) $(0, 1)$ minimum

25 Applications of differentiation

Exercise 25A (page 339)

1 (a) Gradient of road

(b) Rate of increase of crowd inside the stadium

(c) Rate of change of magnetic force with respect to distance

(d) Acceleration of train

(e) Rate of increase of petrol consumption with respect to speed

2 (a) $\dfrac{dp}{dh}$, p in millibars, h in metres

(b) $\dfrac{d\theta}{dt}$, θ in degrees C, t in hours

(c) $\dfrac{dh}{dt}$, h in metres, t in hours

(d) $\dfrac{dW}{dt}$, W in kilograms, t in weeks

3 (a) $6t + 7$ (b) $1 - \dfrac{1}{2\sqrt{x}}$ (c) $1 - \dfrac{6}{y^3}$

(d) $2t - \dfrac{1}{2t\sqrt{t}}$ (e) $2t + 6$ (f) $12s^5 - 6s$

(g) 5 (h) $-\dfrac{2}{r^3} - 1$

4 (a) $\dfrac{dx}{dt} = c$

(b) $\dfrac{dA}{dt} = kA$; A stands for the amount deposited

(c) $\dfrac{dx}{dt} = f(\theta)$; x stands for diameter, θ for air temperature

5 (a) (i) 98 metres per minute

(ii) 22 metres per minute

(b) 60 metres per minute

(c) 25 minutes

6 (a) 25 per km   (b) 15 per km   (c) 20 per km

7 (a) 19 200

(b) (i) 50 per minute   (ii) 102.5 per minute

(c) 90 per minute

8 (a) $2\pi r$ (b) $4\pi r^2$

$\dfrac{dA}{dr}$ is the circumference of the circle,

$\dfrac{dV}{dr}$ is the surface area of the sphere.

9 $-\dfrac{2C}{x^3}$

10 $-\dfrac{1.4k}{V^{2.4}}$

11 (a) $\dfrac{0.1}{\sqrt{l}}$

(b) It will increase by 0.001 26 seconds

Exercise 25B (page 344)

1 (a) Rate of increase of inflation, positive

2 (a) Both positive, sudden change (drop in S), then $\dfrac{dS}{dt}$ is negative changing to positive with $\dfrac{d^2S}{dt^2}$ positive.

(b) Price rose sharply, sudden 'crash', price continued to drop but less quickly and then recovered to give steadier growth.

3 (b) $+, -, -, +$

4 (a) $\dfrac{dN}{dt} = -kN, k > 0$ (c) $+$

5 (a) After 10 hours   (b) After 5 hours

(c) After 15 hours, 22.5 mb per hour

6 (a) \$80 a barrel, \$4.50 a barrel per week

(b) \$100 a barrel   (c) After 20 weeks

7 (a) $42\,\text{m}$, $32\,\text{m s}^{-1}$, $18\,\text{m s}^{-2}$

(b) $1\,\text{m s}^{-1}$, $-1\,\text{m s}^{-2}$ (c) $6\,\text{m s}^{-1}, \frac{3}{4}\,\text{m s}^{-2}$

(d) $5\,\text{s}$; $20\,\text{m}$ (e) $4\,\text{m s}^{-1}$ (f) $22\frac{1}{8}\,\text{m}$, $54\,\text{m s}^{-2}$

8 (a) $18\,\text{m s}^{-1}$ (b) $4\,\text{m s}^{-2}$

9 (a) $120\,\text{s}$, $1380\,\text{m}$ (b) $0.384\,\text{m s}^{-2}$

(c) $1.15\,\text{m s}^{-2}$ (d) $80\,\text{s}$, $20.5\,\text{m s}^{-1}$

10 (b) (A) $120\,\text{cm s}^{-1}$, (B) $160\,\text{cm s}^{-1}$

(B), because $v = 0$ when $t = 3$.

11 (a) $952\,\text{m}$, $62.4\,\text{m s}^{-1}$

(b) $-41.0\,\text{m s}^{-2}$, $-10\,\text{m s}^{-2}$, $-0.328\,\text{m s}^{-2}$

(c) $40\,\text{m s}^{-1}$ (d) $40\,\text{s}$

Exercise 25C (page 353)

1 $80\,\text{km h}^{-1}$

2 20 m

3 36

4 $4\sqrt{5}$

5 Greatest $V = 32\pi$ when $r = 4$, least $V = 0$ when $r = 0$ or $h = 0$.

6 $x = 25$

7 (b) $1800\,\text{m}^2$

8 $0 < x < 20$, 7.36 cm

9 20 cm

10 (b) $38\,400\,\text{cm}^3$ (to 3 significant figures)

11 $2420\,\text{cm}^3$ (to 3 significant figures)

Exercise 25D (page 357)

1 (a) $3x^2 - 10x + 2$, $6x - 10$, 6, 0
  (b) $8x^7$, $56x^6$, $336x^5$, $1680x^4$
  (c) $\dfrac{1}{2\sqrt{x}}$, $-\dfrac{1}{4x\sqrt{x}}$, $\dfrac{3}{8x^2\sqrt{x}}$, $-\dfrac{15}{16x^3\sqrt{x}}$

2 2, 6, 24, 120; $\dfrac{d^n}{dx^n}x^n = n!$

3 (a) $5x^3(4-x)$, $20x^2(3-x)$, $60x(2-x)$,
      $120(1-x)$
  (b) $30\,240x^4(5-x)$

4 $24 \times \dfrac{5-x}{x^6}$

Review exercise 6 (page 358)

1 (a) $(-1, -7)$, $(2, 20)$; $\left(\frac{1}{2}, 6\frac{1}{2}\right)$
  (b) The graph crosses the x-axis 3 times.
  (c) The graph has 3 intersections with the
      line $y = -5$.
  (d) (i) $-7 < k < 20$ (ii) $k < -7$ and $k > 20$

2 $(-1, 5)$, $(0, 10)$, $(2, -22)$
  (a) $5 < k < 10$
  (b) $-22 < k < 5$ and $k > 10$
  $(-0.55, 7.32)$, $(1.22, -8.36)$

3 $+, -, +$

5 $(20 - 4t)$ m s^{-1}, -4 m s^{-2}; for $0 \le t \le 5$

6 50

7 (a) $9\sqrt{2}$ cm   (b) $40\frac{1}{2}$ cm^2

8 Maximum; $\left(1\frac{1}{2}, -\frac{1}{2}\right)$

9 (a) $k < 0$ or $k > 8$
  (b) $-1\frac{1}{2} < k < 1\frac{1}{2}$ provided $k \ne 0$ (if $k = 0$ the
      equation is linear, and has just one root)
  (c) $k < -2$ or $k > 2$

10 $x < -2$ or $x > \frac{2}{3}$

11 $-\frac{1}{2} < x < 0$ or $x > 2$

12 $(-2, 4)$, $(2, -28)$; $-28 \le k \le 4$

13 $\left(\frac{1}{3}, \frac{4}{27}\right)$, $(1, 0)$; $k < -\frac{2}{9}\sqrt{3}$ and $k > \frac{2}{9}\sqrt{3}$

14 (a) $(-1, 0)$, $(2, -27)$
   (b) $x = -1$ maximum, $x = 2$ minimum
   (d) $k < -27$ and $k > 0$

15 (a) $P = 2x + 2r + \frac{1}{2}\pi r$, $A = \frac{1}{4}\pi r^2 + rx$
   (b) $x = \frac{1}{4}r(4 - \pi)$

17 (a) $1100 - 20x$ (b) $\$x(1100 - 20x)$
   (c) $\$(24\,000 - 400x)$
       $\$37.50$

Examination questions (page 360)

1 2, -18, -7

2 $(-0.803, -2.076)$

3 $-\frac{1}{2}\left(\sqrt{13}+1\right) < x < 0$, $1 < x < \frac{1}{2}\left(\sqrt{13}-1\right)$

4 $-4 \le m \le 0$

5 1.33

6 $-3 \le k \le 4\frac{1}{2}$

7 $x < -1$ or $4 < x \le 14$

8 (a) $2\pi r^2 + \dfrac{1000}{r}$ (b) 4.30

9 $8x + 3y - 9 = 0$

10 $x \le \frac{1}{2}$ or $x > 3$

26 Probability

Exercise 26 (page 371)

1 (a) $\frac{1}{2}$ (b) $\frac{2}{3}$ (c) $\frac{1}{2}$ (d) $\frac{1}{2}$
  (e) $\frac{1}{6}$ (f) $\frac{5}{6}$ (g) $\frac{2}{3}$

2 (a) $\frac{1}{2}$ (b) $\frac{3}{13}$ (c) $\frac{5}{13}$ (d) $\frac{5}{26}$ (e) $\frac{9}{13}$

3 (a) $\frac{1}{6}$ (b) $\frac{5}{12}$ (c) $\frac{5}{12}$ (d) $\frac{25}{36}$
  (e) $\frac{11}{36}$ (f) $\frac{5}{18}$ (g) $\frac{1}{6}$ (h) $\frac{1}{2}$

4 $(1, 2)$, $(1, 3)$, $(1, 4)$, $(1, 5)$, $(1, 6)$, $(2, 1)$, $(2, 3)$,
  $(2, 4)$, $(2, 5)$, $(2, 6)$, $(3, 1)$, $(3, 2)$, $(3, 4)$, $(3, 5)$,
  $(3, 6)$, $(4, 1)$, $(4, 2)$, $(4, 3)$, $(4, 5)$, $(4, 6)$, $(5, 1)$,
  $(5, 2)$, $(5, 3)$, $(5, 4)$, $(5, 6)$, $(6, 1)$, $(6, 2)$, $(6, 3)$,
  $(6, 4)$, $(6, 5)$.
  (a) $\frac{1}{5}$ (b) $\frac{2}{5}$ (c) $\frac{1}{3}$ (d) $\frac{1}{2}$

6 (a) $\frac{3}{8}$ (b) $\frac{5}{8}$

7 $\frac{1}{6}$

27 Conditional probability

Exercise 27 (page 383)

1 (a) $\frac{1}{3}$ (b) $\frac{2}{15}$ (c) $\frac{8}{15}$ (d) $\frac{13}{15}$ (e) $\frac{3}{5}$

2 (a) $\frac{11}{221}$ (b) $\frac{10}{17}$ (c) $\frac{7}{17}$ (d) $\frac{77}{102}$

3 (a) 0.27 (b) 0.35 (c) 0.3375

4 (a) $\frac{8}{15}$ (b) $\frac{7}{15}$ (c) $\frac{3}{5}$ (d) $\frac{2}{5}$ (e) $\frac{9}{16}$
  (f) Yes   (g) No

5 (a) 0.24 (b) 0.42 (c) 0.706

6 (a) $\frac{9}{25}$ (b) $\frac{4}{25}$ (c) $\frac{12}{25}$ (d) $\frac{21}{25}$ (e) $\frac{3}{5}$

7 0.75, 0.8

8 (a) $\frac{2}{5}$ (b) $\frac{4}{15}$ (c) $\frac{1}{8}$

9 $\frac{8}{23}$

10 $\frac{2}{3}$

11 (a) $\frac{1}{5}$ (b) $\frac{1}{3}$

Review exercise 7 (page 385)

1 (a) After first draw:

P(A Red) = $\frac{1}{2}$, P(A Black) = $\frac{1}{2}$

After second draw:

P(A 1Red, 1Black) = $\frac{1}{2} + \frac{1}{6} = \frac{2}{3}$

P(A 2Red) = $\frac{1}{3}$

(b) $\frac{2}{3}$

2 (a) 0.58 (b) 0.6

3 (a) $\frac{1}{2}$ (b) $\frac{5}{11}$

4 (a) 20% (b) 10%

5 (a) $\frac{3}{20}$ (b) $\frac{9}{35}$ (c) $\frac{7}{12}$

6 (b) $\frac{9}{26}$

7 (a) (i) $\frac{1}{5}$ (ii) $\frac{5}{13}$ (iii) $\frac{17}{25}$ (iv) $\frac{1}{2}$

(b) $\frac{21}{25}$

8 (a) $\frac{1}{2}$ (b) (i) $5p$ (ii) $4p$ (c) $\frac{1}{40}$

9 $\frac{1}{4}$; (a) 0.0577 (b) 0.1057 (c) 0.6676

10 (a) $\frac{3}{253}$ (b) $\frac{43}{138}$ (c) $\frac{11}{138}$ (d) $\frac{11}{69}$

11 (a) 0.32 (b) 0.56; 8

12 (a) $\frac{1}{8}$ (b) $\frac{3}{8}$ (c) $\frac{8}{9}$

13 (a) 0.030 (b) 0.146 (c) 0 (d) 0.712

14 (a)

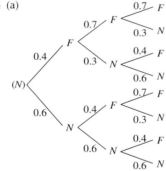

(b) 0.196 (c) 0.288

15 (a) 75% (b) 28%

Examination questions (page 387)

1 (a) $\frac{1}{4}$ (b) $\frac{1}{83}$

2 (a) 0.6 (b) 0.16

3 (a) $\frac{2}{3}$ (b) $\frac{1}{6}$

4 (a) $\frac{183}{250}$ (b) $\frac{44}{183}$

5 $\frac{1}{5}$

6 10 or 15

7 (a) $\frac{37}{56}$ (b) $\frac{16}{37}$

8 $\frac{3}{14}$

28 Integration

Exercise 28A (page 394)

1 (a) $x^4 + k$ (b) $x^6 + k$
(c) $x^2 + k$ (d) $x^3 + x^5 + k$
(e) $x^{10} - x^8 - x + k$ (f) $-x^7 + x^3 + x + k$

2 (a) $3x^3 - 2x^2 - 5x + k$
(b) $4x^3 + 3x^2 + 4x + k$
(c) $7x + k$
(d) $4x^4 - 2x^3 + 5x^2 - 3x + k$
(e) $\frac{1}{2}x^4 + \frac{5}{2}x^2 + k$
(f) $\frac{1}{2}x^2 + \frac{2}{3}x^3 + k$
(g) $\frac{2}{3}x^3 - \frac{3}{2}x^2 - 4x + k$
(h) $x - x^2 - x^3 + k$

3 (a) $y = \frac{1}{5}x^5 + \frac{1}{3}x^3 + x + k$
(b) $y = \frac{7}{2}x^2 - 3x + k$
(c) $y = \frac{2}{3}x^3 + \frac{1}{2}x^2 - 8x + k$
(d) $y = \frac{3}{2}x^4 - \frac{5}{3}x^3 + \frac{3}{2}x^2 + 2x + k$
(e) $y = \frac{1}{6}x^4 + \frac{1}{6}x^3 + \frac{1}{6}x^2 + \frac{1}{6}x + k$
(f) $y = \frac{1}{8}x^4 - \frac{1}{9}x^3 + \frac{1}{2}x^2 - \frac{1}{3}x + k$
(g) $y = \frac{1}{2}x^2 - x^3 + x + k$
(h) $y = \frac{1}{4}x^4 + \frac{1}{3}x^3 + \frac{1}{2}x^2 + x + k$

4 $4x^2 - 5x$

5 $y = 2x^3 - x - 19$

6 $y = \frac{1}{8}x^4 + \frac{1}{8}x^2 + x - 21$

7 $5x^3 - 3x^2 + 4x - 6$

8 (a) No stationary points, no inflexions
(b) No stationary points, no inflexions
(c) Minimum at $x = 0$, no inflexions
(d) Maximum at $x = 3$, no inflexions
(e) Maximum at $x = -1$, minimum at $x = 2$, inflexion at $x = \frac{1}{2}$
(f) Stationary inflexion at $x = \frac{1}{2}$
(g) No stationary points, inflexion at $x = 1$
(h) Stationary inflexion at $x = 0$, maximum at $x = 3$, inflexion at $x = 2$

9 $y = 4x\sqrt{x} - 7$

10 (a) $-\dfrac{1}{x} + k$ (b) $-\dfrac{1}{x^3} + k$
(c) $-\dfrac{3}{x^2} + k$ (d) $2x^2 + \dfrac{3}{x} + k$
(e) $-\dfrac{1}{2x^2} + \dfrac{1}{3x^3} + k$ (f) $-\dfrac{2}{x} - \dfrac{2}{3}x^3 + k$

11 (a) $y = \frac{2}{3}x^{\frac{3}{2}} + k$ (b) $y = 12x^{\frac{1}{3}} + k$
(c) $y = \frac{3}{4}x^{\frac{4}{3}} + k$
(d) $y = \frac{4}{3}x\sqrt{x} - 4\sqrt{x} + k$
(e) $y = \frac{15}{2}\sqrt[3]{x^2} + k$ (f) $y = -6\sqrt[3]{x} + k$

12 $y = -\dfrac{4}{x} + 13$

13 $y = \sqrt{x} - 2$

14 $y = \frac{3}{4}x^{\frac{4}{3}} + 3x^{-2} + \frac{5}{4}$

15 (a) $y = x^3 + 3x^2 + k$

(b) $y = 4x^3 + 2x^2 - 5x + k$

(c) $y = 2x^2 - \dfrac{1}{x} + k$

(d) $y = \frac{2}{3}x\sqrt{x} + 8\sqrt{x} + k$

(e) $y = \frac{1}{2}x^2 + \frac{20}{3}x\sqrt{x} + 25x + k$

(f) $y = x + 10\sqrt{x} + k$

16 (a) $\frac{1}{3}u^3 - \dfrac{1}{u} + k$

(b) $\frac{1}{2}t^6 - \frac{1}{7}t^7 + k$

(c) $p^4 + 4p^3 + 6p^2 + 4p + k$

(d) $-\dfrac{2}{\sqrt{y}} + k$

(e) $\frac{3}{5}z^{\frac{5}{3}} + 2z + 3z^{\frac{1}{3}} + k$

(f) $v^2\left(\frac{1}{2} + \frac{2}{5}\sqrt{v}\right) + k$

17 (a) 118 cm (to 3 s.f.)   (b) 27

18 17 months (to the nearest month)

19 192

Exercise 28B (page 399)

1 (a) $x = t^3 + 8t + 4$; 28 m, 20 m s^{-1}

(b) 2 m, 6 m s^{-1}, 3 m s^{-2}

(c) 20 m   (d) 60 m   (e) -6 m s^{-2}

(f) 22 m   (g) 1.2 m

2 (a) 9 m s^{-1} (b) 8 m s^{-1}, $26\frac{2}{3}$ m

3 (a) 2 s   (b) 8 m   (c) 6 m s^{-2}

29 Calculating areas

Exercise 29A (page 407)

1 (a) 7   (b) 84   (c) 4

(d) 4   (e) $\frac{1}{16}$ (f) 2

2 (a) 22   (b) 22   (c) 36

(d) $7\frac{1}{6}$ (e) 210   (f) 0

3 (a) 72   (b) 15   (c) 195

(d) 80   (e) 80   (f) $10\frac{2}{5}$

4 18

5 16

6 (a) 39   (b) $5\frac{1}{3}$ (c) $10\frac{2}{3}$ (d) 10

7 (a) 144   (b) $1\frac{1}{2}$ (c) 20

(d) $6\frac{3}{4}$ (e) 16   (f) 3

8 (a) $1\frac{3}{4}$ (b) 60   (c) $3\frac{1}{3}$

9 7

10 5

11 (a) $22\frac{2}{3}$ (b) $2\frac{3}{8}$

12 $42\frac{7}{8}$

13 (a) 8 m s^{-1} (b) 27 m s^{-1}; 16.88 m s^{-1}

14 $46\frac{2}{3}$ m

Exercise 29B (page 416)

1 -4; the graph lies below the x-axis for $0 < x < 2$.

2 60

3 21

4 $10\frac{2}{3}$; the negative value of $\displaystyle\int_{-2}^{2} x\,\mathrm{d}y$ indicates that the region is on the left of the x-axis.

5 (a) $10\frac{2}{3}$ (b) 8   (c) $2\frac{1}{4}$ (d) $1\frac{5}{6}$

6 (b) 0 s, 7.2 m s^{-2} (c) 3 s, -1.8 m s^{-2}

(d) 6.75 m, 6.4 m   (f) 7.1 m

7 12

8 $10\frac{2}{3}$

9 32

10 $42\frac{2}{3}$

11 $4\frac{1}{2}$

12 36

13 (a) 500   (b) $5\frac{1}{3}$

14 96

30 Geometric sequences

Exercise 30A (page 422)

1 (a) 2; 24, 48   (b) 4; 128, 512

(c) $\frac{1}{2}$; 4, 2   (d) -3; 162, -486

(e) 1.1; 1.4641, 1.610 51

(f) $\dfrac{1}{x}$; $\dfrac{1}{x}$, $\dfrac{1}{x^2}$

2 (a) $2 \times 3^{n-1}$ (b) $10 \times \left(\frac{1}{2}\right)^{n-1}$

(c) $(-2)^{n-1}$ (d) $81 \times \left(\frac{1}{3}\right)^{n-1}$

(e) x^n (f) $p^{2-n}q^{n+1}$

(b), (d), (e) if $|x| < 1$, (f) if $|q| < |p|$

3 (a) 11   (b) 13   (c) 7

(d) 14   (e) 6   (f) 13

4 (a) 3; $1\frac{1}{3}$ (b) 2; $1\frac{1}{2}$ or -2; $1\frac{1}{2}$

(c) $\frac{1}{3}$; 531 441   (d) $\pm\sqrt{2}$; 4

6 (a) 2   (b) 8th

7 (a) 3   (b) 14th

Exercise 30B (page 427)

1 (a) 59 048   (b) −29 524   (c) 1.9922
   (d) 0.6641   (e) 12 285   (f) 8.9998

2 (a) 2047   (b) 683   (c) 262 143
   (d) $\frac{1023}{512}$ (e) $\frac{14\,762}{19\,683}$ (f) 19.843 75 $\left(= \frac{635}{32}\right)$
   (g) $\frac{341}{1024}$ (h) $2 - \left(\frac{1}{2}\right)^n$

3 (a) 93   (b) −10   (c) $31\frac{7}{8}$ (d) 21 844

4 $2^{64} - 1 \approx 1.84 \times 10^{19}$

5 $2 684 354.55

6 $32 289.76

7 0.979 litres

8 $\left(\frac{3}{4}\right)^{n-1} - \frac{1}{3}$

9 (a) $\dfrac{x(1 - x^n)}{1 - x}$ (b) $\dfrac{x(1 - (-x)^n)}{1 + x}$

Exercise 30C (page 433)

1 (a) 2   (b) $\frac{3}{2}$ (c) $\frac{1}{4}$
   (d) $\frac{1}{9}$ (e) $\frac{3}{4}$ (f) $\frac{1}{6}$
   (g) 3   (h) $\frac{1}{3}$ (i) $\frac{20}{3}$
   (j) 62.5   (k) $\dfrac{x}{1 - x}$ (l) $\dfrac{1}{1 + x^2}$
   (m) $\dfrac{x}{x - 1}$ (n) $\dfrac{x^3}{x + 1}$

2 (a) $\frac{4}{11}$ (b) $\frac{41}{333}$ (c) $\frac{5}{9}$ (d) $\frac{157}{333}$
   (e) $\frac{1}{7}$ (f) $\frac{2}{7}$ (g) $\frac{5}{7}$ (h) $\frac{6}{7}$

3 $\frac{1}{6}$

4 $-\frac{5}{6}$

5 3

6 19.2

7 (a) $\left(\frac{1}{5}\right)^{i-1}$, $\dfrac{2\,441\,406}{1\,953\,125}$, $1\frac{1}{4}$
   (b) 2^i, 2046, not convergent
   (c) 8×2^{-i}, $\dfrac{1023}{128}$, 8
   (d) $\left(-\frac{1}{10}\right)^{i-1}$, $\dfrac{909\,090\,909}{1\,000\,000\,000}$, $\frac{10}{11}$

8 2 m

9 0.375 m east of O, 1.5 m

10 10 seconds

11 19 m

12 (a) Edge of table   (b) 8

31   Exponentials and logarithms

Exercise 31A (page 437)

1 $2^x > 1000$ (a) 10   (b) 20   (c) 40

2 $3^{-x} > 2000$ (a) −7   (b) −14   (c) −15

4 (b) They are reflections of each other in the y-axis.

Exercise 31B (page 439)

1 (a) $8 = 2^3$ (b) $81 = 3^4$
   (c) $0.04 = 5^{-2}$ (d) $x = 7^4$
   (e) $5 = x^t$ (f) $q = p^r$

2 (a) $3 = \log_2 8$ (b) $6 = \log_3 729$
   (c) $-3 = \log_4 \frac{1}{64}$ (d) $8 = \log_a 20$
   (e) $9 = \log_h 8$ (f) $n = \log_m p$

3 (a) 4   (b) 2   (c) −2
   (d) 0   (e) 1   (f) $-\frac{1}{3}$
   (g) $\frac{3}{4}$ (h) $\frac{3}{2}$ (i) 7

4 (a) 7   (b) $\frac{1}{64}$ (c) 5
   (d) $\frac{1}{10}$ (e) $4\sqrt{2}$ (f) 6
   (g) $\frac{1}{256}$ (h) −10   (i) $\frac{1}{3}\sqrt{3}$

Exercise 31C (page 443)

1 (a) $\log_b p + \log_b q + \log_b r$
   (b) $\log_b p + 2\log_b q + 3\log_b r$
   (c) $2 + \log p + 5\log r$
   (d) $\frac{1}{2}(\log_b p - 2\log_b q - \log_b r)$
   (e) $\log_b p + \log_b q - 2\log_b r$
   (f) $-(\log_b p + \log_b q + \log_b r)$
   (g) $\log_b p - \frac{1}{2}\log_b r$
   (h) $\log p + \log q + 7\log r - 1$
   (i) $\frac{1}{2}(1 + 10\log p - \log q + \log r)$

2 (a) 2   (b) −1   (c) $\log 30\,575$ (d) 0
   (e) 3   (f) −3   (g) $\log 8$ (h) 0

3 (a) $r - q$ (b) $2p + q$ (c) $p + \frac{1}{2}r$
   (d) $-q$ (e) $p + 2q + r$
   (f) $p - q + 2r$ (g) $q - p - r$
   (h) $4p + q - 2r$ (i) $p + q - 2r$

5 $c = b^r$, $b = c^s$; $\log_b c \times \log_c b = 1$

6 The hydrogen ion activity of cola is about 1000 times that of beer.

7 $20\log_{10}(5000P)$

   (a) 63.2 microbars
   (b) The man's sound intensity is 6.02 decibels more than the woman's.
   (c) The amplitude is reduced by a factor of 0.316

8 (a) The magnitudes differ by 0.477.
   (b) The ratio of the amplitudes is 3.98 : 1.

Exercise 31D (page 448)

1 (a) 1.46   (b) 1.56   (c) 1.14
   (d) 1.22   (e) 3.58   (f) 1.71
   (g) −2.21   (h) 3   (i) −0.202

2 (a) $x > 1.89$ (b) $x < 1.43$ (c) $x \le -1.68$
   (d) $x > 9.97$ (e) $x > 8.54$ (f) $x < -2$
   (g) $x \ge -2$ (h) $x \le -5.61$ (i) $x \ge 3.77$

3 (a) 27   (b) 16   (c) 31
  (d) 16   (e) 19   (f) 100

4 (a) 74, 1.051×10^3 (b) 149, 1.047×10^{12}
  (c) 33, 5.049×10^3 (d) 45, 1.345×10^7

5 (a) 67, 9.550×10^{-4} (b) 71, 8.228×10^{-7}
  (c) 30, 9.524×10^{-5}

6 37

7 14

8 28

9 7

10 9.56

11 (a) 0.891   (b) 12 days   (c) 19.9 days

12 (a) 1.79   (b) 2.37   (c) 0.486
   (d) −7.97   (e) 1.04   (f) 2.32

13 −0.301, −0.477

32   Exponential growth and decay

Exercise 32A (page 453)
1 5324; 400, 440, 484,

2 2624, 2362

3 $60 000, $72 000, $86 400, $103 680,
  $124 416; $10 000, $12 000, $14 400, $17 280
  $20 736

4 80 000, 64 000, 51 200; 1200, 1440, 1728;
  100, 66.6..., 44.4..., 29.6... ;
  decreases by one-third each decade

5 (a) $\frac{9}{40}$ (b) $\frac{81}{400}, \frac{729}{4000}, \frac{6561}{40\,000}$
  (c) $\frac{3}{4} \times \left(\frac{9}{10}\right)^t$

6 $\$\dfrac{60}{1.06} \times 1.06^i$; yes

7 $\$7500 \times 0.8^i$; yes

8 (a) 17 800   (b) 29 100

9 (a) 85.1 kg   (b) 68.1 kg

10 Armensia, Canadia, Declinia

11 1.11 inches, 1.31 inches

12 0.072; the $\log_{10}$ of the growth factor

Exercise 32B (page 459)
1 (a) 800   (b) 141   (c) 336

2 (a) 45.5 °C   (b) 13.6 minutes

3 (a) 63 000   (b) 36 200   (c) 19 700

4 (a) 5.83×10^7 (b) 5.65×10^7

5 10 000, 451

6 (a) $\sqrt[12]{2} \approx 1.059$ (b) 262
  (c) between 5 and 6; between D and D sharp

7 (a) $y = 2.51 \times 3.98^x$ (b) $y = 10^{12} \times 0.001^x$
  (c) $y = 5.01 \times 50.1^x$ (d) $y = 5.01x^2$
  (e) $y = \dfrac{0.316}{x^5}$

8 $p = 39.7 \times 1.022^x$ gives $p = 39.7, 49.4, 61.3,$
  76.3, 94.8. The exponential model does not
  fit so well in this period.

9 The points do not lie in a straight line

10 Armensia: 185×1.08^t
   Canadia: 100×1.20^t
   Declinia: 180×0.94^t

Review exercise 8 (page 461)

1 $6\frac{3}{4}$

2 ± 2

3 (a) 6   (b) 67   (c) —
  (d) 45   (e) 17   (f) −11

4 62

5 The sum of the infinite series is only 80 cm.

6 $56 007

7 $r = \dfrac{k-1}{k+1}$

9 (a) $2254.32   (b) 139

10 389 years

11 8760

12 2031

13 (a) $\frac{1}{4}x^4 - x^2 + k$ (b) 2

14 (a) $y = -\frac{1}{2}x + \frac{3}{2}$ (b) $2\frac{29}{48}$

16 (a) $\dfrac{1}{\log a - 2}$ (b) $\sqrt{\dfrac{5a}{2}}$

17 0.774

18 $x > 33.2$

Examination questions (page 463)
1 (a) 0.753   (b) 2.445   (c) 1.78

2

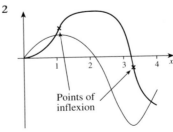

Points of
inflexion

3 (a) $\frac{2}{3}$ (b) 9

4 $\dfrac{\log 9}{\log 8}$

5 $-\frac{1}{2}$, 12

6 $-2, 4$

7 $\dfrac{\theta}{1 - \cos\theta}$

8 15

9 7

10 $1275\log 2$

11 6 m

12 ± 6

13 $-1 + \log_5 3$

14 $101\frac{3}{4}$

15 $\log\dfrac{x^{70}}{y^{595}}$

16 (a) $\frac{1}{2}$ (b) $-\frac{9}{20}$

33 Discrete probability distributions

Exercise 33A (page 469)

1
x	0	1	2	3	4
$P(X = x)$	$\frac{1}{16}$	$\frac{4}{16}$	$\frac{6}{16}$	$\frac{4}{16}$	$\frac{1}{16}$

2
d	0	1	2	3	4	5
$P(D = d)$	$\frac{6}{36}$	$\frac{10}{36}$	$\frac{8}{36}$	$\frac{6}{36}$	$\frac{4}{36}$	$\frac{2}{36}$

3
x	1	2	3	6	10
$P(X = x)$	$\frac{1}{6}$	$\frac{2}{6}$	$\frac{1}{6}$	$\frac{1}{6}$	$\frac{1}{6}$

4
h	1	2	3	4	5	6
$P(H = h)$	$\frac{23}{36}$	$\frac{7}{36}$	$\frac{3}{36}$	$\frac{1}{36}$	$\frac{1}{36}$	$\frac{1}{36}$

5
m	1	2	3	4	6
$P(M = m)$	$\frac{1}{16}$	$\frac{2}{16}$	$\frac{2}{16}$	$\frac{3}{16}$	$\frac{2}{16}$

	8	9	12	16
	$\frac{2}{16}$	$\frac{1}{16}$	$\frac{2}{16}$	$\frac{1}{16}$

6
Number	0	1	2
Probability	$\frac{5}{12}$	$\frac{1}{2}$	$\frac{1}{12}$

7
c	1	2	3	4
$P(C = c)$	$\frac{1}{13}$	$\frac{16}{221}$	$\frac{376}{5525}$	$\frac{4324}{5525}$

Exercise 33B (page 471)

1 $\frac{1}{20}$

2 0.3

3 0.15

4 $\frac{1}{8}$

5
x	1	2	3	4	5	6
$P(X = x)$	$\frac{1}{4}$	$\frac{1}{12}$	$\frac{1}{4}$	$\frac{1}{12}$	$\frac{1}{4}$	$\frac{1}{12}$

6 $\frac{1}{21}$

7 $\frac{20}{49}$

8 0.2

Exercise 33C (page 472)

1 (a) 130   (b) 40   (c) 120
   (d) 160   (e) 360

2 (a) 105   (b) 105   (c) 245

3 12, 31, 34, 18, 5, 0 (0 is better than 1 because it makes the total 100)

4 0.468, 103

Exercise 33D (page 479)

1 (a) $1\frac{7}{8}$ (b) 0.05

2 4, 3.6

3 $5\frac{1}{9}, 1\frac{35}{81}$

4 (a) $\frac{7}{3}, 0.745$

   (b)
y	2	3	4	5	6
$P(Y = y)$	$\frac{1}{36}$	$\frac{1}{9}$	$\frac{5}{18}$	$\frac{1}{3}$	$\frac{1}{4}$

   $\frac{14}{3}, \frac{10}{9}$

5 $E(A) = £95\,000$, $E(B) = £115\,000$; choose B

6 (a) 0.3, 0.51   (b) 5.7, 0.51
   (c) $E(Y) = 6 - E(X)$, $Var(Y) = Var(X)$. The distribution of Y (the number of unbroken eggs) is the reflection of the distribution of X in the line $x = 3$.

7 0.2, 2.8, 1.4

8 $a = b = 0.15$, $\sigma = 1.7$

9 (a)
x	1	2	3	4
$P(X = x)$	$\frac{1}{6}$	$\frac{5}{36}$	$\frac{25}{216}$	$\frac{125}{216}$

   (b) 1.172
   0.5177, -20.56

10
w	0	1	2
$P(W = w)$	$\frac{1}{3}$	$\frac{8}{15}$	$\frac{2}{15}$

   0.8

11 (b)
h	0	1	2	3
$P(H = h)$	$\frac{11}{48}$	$\frac{7}{16}$	$\frac{13}{48}$	$\frac{1}{16}$

   (c) $E(X) = \frac{7}{3}$; $E(H) = \frac{7}{6}$ (d) $\frac{13}{18}$

34 The binomial distribution

Exercise 34 (page 496)

1 (a) 0.0819   (b) 0.0154
  (c) 0.0001   (d) 1.2

2 (a) 0.2561   (b) 0.2048
  (c) 0.0005   (d) $\frac{14}{3}$

3 (a) 0.2119   (b) 0.4728
  (c) 0.0498   (d) 4.05

4 (a) 0.0017   (b) 6

5 (a) 0.6123   (b) 0.3877

6 (a) 0.0781   (b) 0.0176

7 (a) 0.6496
  (b) The students are not chosen independently.

8 0.0545; no (the outcomes are still green and not-green).

9 0.1143; breakages are not independent of each other (if one egg in a box is broken, it is more likely that others will be).

10 0.0652; for example, P(hurricane) is constant for each month, it is clear when there is a hurricane as opposed to a very brisk wind. In practice, hurricanes tend to appear in summer months.

11 (a) 0.2039   (b) 7
  The adults must be independent of each other as to whether they are wearing jeans; the probability that each adult is wearing jeans must be the same. (Do not say there must be only two outcomes; this is automatically implied by the question.)

12 More than one relevant outcome on each trial.

13 (a) 0.1424   (b) 0.2821

35 The Poisson distribution

Exercise 35A (page 501)

1 (a) 0.2240   (b) 0.1991   (c) 0.5768

2 (a) 0.2218   (b) 0.3696   (c) 0.8352

3 (a) 0.7787   (b) 0.6916   (c) 0.2090

4 (a) 0.1353   (b) 0.2707   (c) 0.2381

5 (a) 0.0821   (b) 0.5162

6 (a) 0.6065   (b) 0.4634

7 (a) 0.0067   (b) 49.9 s

8 (a) 0.0916   (b) 0.206 particle s^{-1}

Exercise 35B (page 508)

1 (a) Yes   (b) No   (c) Yes
  (d) Yes, provided claims are not caused by, say, freak weather conditions.

2 (a) 8, 8; yes, as mean = variance
  (b) 0.6866   (c) 2.8

3 (a) 0.29, 0.39, 0.16, 0.13, 0.03
  (b) 1.23, 1.21; Poisson is a suitable model.
  (c) 0.29, 0.36, 0.22, 0.09, 0.03
  (d) Supports comment in part (b).

4 (a) 0.5   (b) 0.0144
  (c) 0.1217

5 (a) 0.0472   (b) 0.162

6 (a) 0.135   (b) 0.0733
  (c) 0.5

Review exercise 9 (page 510)

1 (a) 2.56   (b) 122.9

2 (a) 0.8704

(b)

x	1	2	3	4
$P(X = x)$	0.4	0.24	0.144	0.216

3

Number	0	1	2	3
Probability	$\frac{248}{1105}$	$\frac{496}{1105}$	$\frac{304}{1105}$	$\frac{57}{1105}$

4 (a)

x	0	1	2	3	4	6
$P(X = x)$	$\frac{1}{4}$	$\frac{1}{3}$	$\frac{1}{9}$	$\frac{1}{6}$	$\frac{1}{9}$	$\frac{1}{36}$

(b) 120

5 0.580

6 (a) 0.337   (b) 0.135

7 0.615

8 0.191

9 0.790; the calls occur randomly, independently, singly and at a constant rate.

10 (a) 0.268   (b) 0.191

11 2; 0.188

12 The injuries occur randomly, independently, singly and at a constant rate.
  0.5, 0.481; possibly Poisson since the mean and variance are approximately equal.
  32, 16, 4, 1, 0: note that these frequencies do not add up to 52 because of rounding errors.

13 (a) 0.067   (b) 0.286   (c) 0.739
   (d) 0.465   (e) Po(29.7); 0.430

Examination questions (page 512)

1 (a) 4, 1.549 (b) 0.954

2 $2\frac{2}{3}$, $2\frac{2}{9}$

3 (a) 0.138   (b) 0.144

4 (a) 2.5   (b) 0.526

5 0.1847

6 (a) (i) $\frac{1}{9}$ (ii) $\frac{1}{81}$

  (b) (i) $\frac{11}{24}$ (ii) $\frac{13}{48}$

  (c) (ii) $\frac{65}{1296}$, $\frac{175}{1296}$, $\frac{369}{1296}$ (iii) 5.244

7 (a) (i) 0.245   (ii) 0.214   (iii) 0.0524

  (b) 0.464

8 (a) 0.2240   (b) 0.2358

9 (a) $e^{-\lambda}\left(\lambda + \frac{1}{2}\lambda^2\right)$ (c) $\sqrt{2}$

10 (a) 2.8473   (b) 0.6171

11 0.9130

12 (a) $a = 0.3$, $b = 0.25$ (b) 1.1475

13 (a) 6

  (b) (i) 0.8288

    (ii) 0.5204

14 (a) $\frac{125}{216}$, $\frac{75}{216}$, $\frac{15}{216}$, $\frac{1}{216}$ (c) \$4.32

15 0.3308

16 (a) $\frac{12}{25}$ (b) $\frac{48}{25}$

Index

The page numbers refer to the first mention of each term, or the blue box if there is one.